Transcendentalism

A READER

Joel Myerson

OXFORD
UNIVERSITY PRESS

2000

OXFORD

Oxford   New York

Athens   Auckland   Bangkok   Bogotá   Buenos Aires   Calcutta
Cape Town   Chennai   Dar es Salaam   Delhi   Florence   Hong Kong   Istanbul
Karachi   Kuala Lumpur   Madrid   Melbourne   Mexico City   Mumbai
Nairobi   Paris   São Paulo   Shanghai   Singapore   Taipei   Tokyo   Toronto   Warsaw

and associated companies in
Berlin   Ibadan

Copyright © 2000 by Oxford University Press, Inc.

Published by Oxford University Press, Inc.
198 Madison Avenue, New York, New York 10016

Oxford is a registered trademark of Oxford University Press

Library of Congress Cataloging-in-Publication Data
Transcendentalism : a reader / [edited by] Joel Myerson.
p.   cm.
Includes bibliographical references and index.
ISBN 0-19-512212-7; ISBN 0-19-512213-5 (pbk.)
1. Transcendentalism (New England)—Literary collections.
2. New England—Intellectual life—19th century.
3. American literature—19th century.
4. American literature—New England.   I. Myerson, Joel.
PS541.T73   2000
810.8'0384—dc21   00-021484

1 3 5 7 9 8 6 4 2

Printed in the United States of America
on acid-free paper

Transcendentalism

For Greta
MANY FÊTES

PERMISSIONS

Sermon CXXI (17 July 1831), *The Complete Sermons of Ralph Waldo Emerson*, ed. Albert J. von Frank et al., 4 vols. (Columbia: University of Missouri Press, 1989–1992), vol. 3, ed. Ronald A. Bosco (1991), pp. 189–194; shelf mark Ms.Am1280.215, Houghton Library, Harvard University. Reprinted with permission of the Ralph Waldo Emerson Memorial Association and the Houghton Library, Harvard University.

Sermon CLXII ["The Lord's Supper"], *The Complete Sermons of Ralph Waldo Emerson*, ed. Albert J. von Frank et al., 4 vols. (Columbia: University of Missouri Press, 1989–1992), vol. 4, ed. Wesley T. Mott (1992), pp. 185–194; shelf mark Ms.Am1280.215, Houghton Library, Harvard University. Reprinted with permission of the Ralph Waldo Emerson Memorial Association and the Houghton Library, Harvard University.

"Introductory" lecture (6 December 1837) to Human Culture lecture series, *The Early Lectures of Ralph Waldo Emerson*, ed. Robert E. Spiller, Stephen E. Whicher, and Wallace E. Williams, 3 vols. (Cambridge: Harvard University Press, 1959–1972), 2:213–229. Reprinted by permission of Harvard University Press.

Nancy Craig Simmons, "Margaret Fuller's Boston Conversations: The 1839–1840 Series," *Studies in the American Renaissance 1994*, ed. Joel Myerson (Charlottesville: University Press of Virginia, 1994), pp. 214–219. Reprinted by permission of the editor.

Ralph Waldo Emerson, letter to Ripley, 15 December 1840, *The Letters of Ralph Waldo Emerson*, ed. Ralph L. Rusk and Eleanor M. Tilton, 10 vols. (New York: Columbia University Press, 1939, 1990–1995), 2:368–371. Copyright © 1939 by the Ralph Waldo Emerson Memorial Association. Reprinted by permission of Columbia University Press

Delores Bird Carpenter, "Lidian Emerson's 'Transcendental Bible,'" *Studies in the American Renaissance 1980*, ed. Joel Myerson (Boston: Twayne, 1980), pp. 91–92. Reprinted by permission of the editor.

Jeffrey Steele, "Freeing the 'Prisoned Queen': The Development of Margaret Fuller's Poetry," *Studies in the American Renaissance 1992*, ed. Joel Myerson (Charlottesville: University Press of Virginia, 1992), pp. 140–141, 162–163, 164–165. Reprinted by permission of the editor.

Elizabeth Hall Witherell, "Thoreau's Watershed Season as a Poet: The Hidden Fruits of the Summer and Fall of 1841," *Studies in the American Renaissance 1990*, ed. Joel Myerson (Charlottesville: University Press of Virginia, 1990), pp. 73–75. Reprinted by permission of the editor.

[On fields oer which the reaper's hand has passd], Henry D. Thoreau, *Journal*, ed. Elizabeth Hall Witherell et al., 5 vols. to date (Princeton: Princeton

ACKNOWLEDGMENTS

This book demonstrates the principle that all good scholarship is collaborative. An early version of the contents was vetted and improved by Judith Mattson Bean, Robert Burkholder, Charles Capper, Larry Carlson, Phyllis Cole, Gary Collison, Sterling Delano, Armida Gilbert, Ezra Greenspan, Robert Gross, William Heath, Ronald Wesley Hoag, Robert Hudspeth, Linck Johnson, Jerome Loving, Joseph Moldenhauer, Ralph H. Orth, Larry Reynolds, Robert Sattelmeyer, Merton Sealts, Daniel Shealy, Nancy Craig Simmons, Albert J. von Frank, and Conrad Wright. Helen Deese, Dean Grodzins, and Jeffrey Steele provided additional information about individual selections. I am especially grateful to Ronald Bosco, Lawrence Buell, Philip Gura, Wesley Mott, Barbara Packer, Robert Richardson, and David Robinson for their extended comments on various parts of the manuscript.

T. Susan Chang first suggested I do this anthology and started it into the production process. I am enormously grateful to her for the opportunity to edit this book. Elissa Morris saw this book through production with grace and dispatch. Jessica A. Ryan did an excellent job of producing the book.

I thank Robert Newman, chair of the English department of the University of South Carolina, for his support. Michael McLoughlin and, especially, Chris Nesmith, assisted in the preparation of this book.

As Theodore Parker might say, in a world of transience, Greta is permanent. The dedication to her is, as always, heartfelt and well-deserved.

Edisto Beach, South Carolina
9 September 1999

CHRONOLOGICAL CONTENTS

TOPICAL CONTENTS

Poetry

NOTE ON THE TEXTS

Transcendentalism: A Reader presents unmodernized, fully annotated texts of the writings by this diverse group of people. Inasmuch as possible, I have tried to print the texts that their contemporaries read, usually the first published edition. Also, I have tried to print complete texts, rather then presenting snippets that are more tantalizing than fulfilling. In a few cases, I have printed extracts rather than complete texts. In these cases, the work itself is a seminal one, but the text is too long for inclusion. Partial reprintings are identified as such.

First-edition texts usually represent the author's initial intentions much better than do texts that have been revised later in life, and that show the author's later thoughts on the work or the author's attempt to reposition his or her place in literary history. For example, there are numerous differences between the 1836 first edition of Emerson's *Nature* and the revised one of 1849 that appeared in *Nature; Addresses, and Lectures*. Some of the changes correct errors, but the overwhelming majority represent Emerson's revisions of the text from a decade-later perspective. The 1849 *Nature* is not what the Transcendentalists read, and it is not reprinted here. Obvious errors in the texts reprinted here have been silently corrected. The source for each text is given at the beginning of the annotations to that text. Those texts that were not published in the author's lifetime (such as Emerson's sermons or some of Fuller's poetry) are reprinted from modern scholarly editions.

The Transcendentalists used words and spellings that are not in general use today, and annotations identify these for the reader. The Transcendentalists also employed what today are considered odd punctuation practices. Language and punctuation were in a state of flux in the early nineteenth century, and there were few generally accepted norms of presentation. In the absence of any draconian rulebooks, writers of the time improvised, and I see no reason to create a false sense of consistency in either their spelling or punctuation habits.[1] For example, Emerson distinguished in his writings between using double quotation marks whenever he makes "a *bona fide* quotation from any person," but he uses single quotations "when the question is only rhetorical" or when he quotes himself.[2]

Today's readers will consider these texts overpunctuated. There is a reason for this. In the nineteenth century, authors punctuated according to either rhetorical or grammatical practice. That is, they employed punctuation marks either to affect the meaning conveyed by the sentence (rhetorical) or to follow a set pattern of formal rules (grammatical). Take this section from Fuller's "The Great Lawsuit":

> And, as to men's representing women fairly, at present, while we hear from men who owe to their wives not only all that is comfortable and graceful, but all that is wise in the arrangement of their lives, the frequent remark, "You cannot reason with a woman," when from those of delicacy, nobleness, and poetic culture, the contemptuous phrase, "Women and children," and that in no light sally of the hour, but in works intended to give a permanent statement of the best experiences, when not one man in the million, shall I say, no, not in the hundred million, can rise above the view that woman was made *for man*, when such traits as these are daily forced upon the attention, can we feel that man will always do justice to the interests of woman? (p. 13)

A freshman English instructor would complain not only that this is a run-on sentence but also that there are too many commas. But if we read this aloud, we see that Fuller has inserted commas wherever she wishes to indicate a pause to enhance the impact of her words, a natural way for her to punctuate in an era when reading aloud was quite common. Today's reader must make allowances for these now-idiosyncratic practices, and not allow a schoolmarmish sense of correctness to interfere with directly accessing the Transcendentalists' writings.[3]

Also, a number of words either have stopped being used or have changed their meanings since the early nineteenth century. For example, "reason" and "understanding" convey almost the same sense today, whereas to the Transcendentalists they were polar opposites. Examples such as these are discussed in notes.

Notes

1. Examples of spellings that appear to be incorrect today, but were acceptable by the standards of nineteenth-century dictionaries and usage, are "befal," "Budha," "cotemporaries," "desart," "developement," "forego," "millenium," "Shakspeare," "sphynx," and "wo."
2. *The Letters of Ralph Waldo Emerson*, ed. Ralph L. Rusk and Eleanor M. Tilton, 10 vols. (New York Columbia University Press, 1939, 1990–1995), 8:17.
3. On the other hand, matters of styling (the physical presentation or layout of an author's writing on the printed page) are almost always the result of actions by compositors, not authors, and some styling changes have been made in this edition, most notably setting the first paragraph of each new chapter flush left.

FURTHER READING

This anthology selectively reprints representative major works by the Transcendentalists. A *comprehensive* anthology, on the other hand, would need to contain at least five thick volumes. If you are interested in reading more by the Transcendentalists, try the following:

1. Perry Miller's editions of *The Transcendentalists: An Anthology* and *The American Transcendentalists: Their Prose and Poetry* are still valuable resources. The former is especially good in tracing the religious aspects of Transcendentalism, and even though Miller only reprints one of his selections in full, the volume acts as a type of documentary history of the movement.[1]

2. The letters and journals of the Transcendentalists constitute a continuous interior dialogue over the direction of the movement, and reading the various editions of private writings together provides a fascinating glimpse of the development of Transcendentalism. For example, Phyllis Cole has shown that not only was Waldo Emerson's correspondence with his aunt Mary the source of much of his knowledge about his ancestors and the testing ground for many of his ideas, but that he borrowed from her letters and journal in constructing his own writings.[2]

3. The letters from and reminiscences by the people at Brook Farm constitute a superb informal history of the community, and many of these are available in *The Brook Farm Book: A Collection of First-Hand Accounts of the Community*, edited by Joel Myerson, and *The Autobiography of Brook Farm*, edited by Henry W. Sams.[3] Nathaniel Hawthorne's *The Blithedale Romance* (1852) offers a fictionalized view of the community.

4. *The Poets of Transcendentalism*, edited by George Willis Cooke, and *American Poetry: The Nineteenth Century*, edited by John Hollander, are good starting points to read more poetry by these authors.[4]

5. Because so many of Thoreau's major nature writings appeared after the main Transcendental period, such important books as *Walden* (1854), *The Maine Woods* (1864), and *Cape Cod* (1865), and essays such as "Walking" and "Autumnal Tints" (both 1862), are omitted here. Most of these are now available in affordable reprintings and complement the works in this anthology.

6. The Transcendentalists wrote critical studies of continental literature (especially by French and German authors), art, and music, and many of their writings in these areas are still interesting reading.

7. A number of Transcendentalists were omitted from this book because of reasons of space, but their writings are recommended: Cyrus Augustus Bartol, Charles Timothy Brooks, Samuel Johnson, Sylvester Judd, Charles King Newcomb, and Charles Stearns Wheeler.

8. The second generation of Transcendentalists also produced enduring literary works, and Moncure Daniel Conway, Octavius Brooks Frothingham, Thomas Wentworth Higginson, Franklin Benjamin Sanborn, and John Weiss all are worth reading.

9. The later phases of Transcendentalism are of interest, particularly the reform activities in the 1850s so ably discussed in Albert J. von Frank's *The Trials of Anthony Burns* and the later religious manifestations in such groups as the Free Religious Association outlined in Stow Persons's *Free Religion*.[5]

There is, fortunately, a great deal of bibliographic control over the literature by and about the Transcendentalists, and it is relatively easy to get started in reading their works and about them. *The Transcendentalists: A Review of Research and Criticism*, edited by Joel Myerson, is comprehensive through 1981; after that date the bibliographical essays in the ongoing series *American Literary Scholarship* and various electronic databases (especially the Modern Language Association's *Bibliography*) will bring the reader up to date. There is no good book-length history of Transcendentalism, but reading the following works will provide an excellent basis for further study: Alexander C. Kern, "The Rise of Transcendentalism, 1815–1860"; Lawrence Buell, *Literary Transcendentalism: Style and Vision in the American Renaissance; Critical Essays on American Transcendentalism*, edited by Philip F. Gura and Myerson; Buell, "The Transcendentalists," in the *Columbia Literary History of the United States;* Buell, "The American Transcendentalist Poets," in *The Columbia History of American Poetry;* and especially Barbara Packer, "The Transcendentalists," in *The Cambridge History of American Literature*. The historiography of the movement is discussed in detail in Charles Capper, " 'A Little Beyond: The Problem of the Transcendentalist Movement in History."[6]

Notes

1. *The Transcendentalists: An Anthology*, ed. Perry Miller (Cambridge: Harvard University Press, 1950), and *The American Transcendentalists: Their Prose and Poetry*, ed. Miller (Garden City, N.Y.: Doubleday, 1957).
2. Phyllis Cole, *Mary Moody Emerson and the Origins of Transcendentalism: A Family History* (New York: Oxford University Press, 1998).
3. *The Brook Farm Book: A Collection of First-Hand Accounts of the Community*, ed. Joel Myerson (New York: Garland Publishers, 1987), and *The Auto-*

biography of Brook Farm, ed. Henry W. Sams (Englewood Cliffs, N.J.: Prentice-Hall, 1958).

4. The Poets of Transcendentalism, ed. George Willis Cooke (Boston: Houghton, Mifflin, 1903), and American Poetry: The Nineteenth Century, ed. John Hollander, 2 vols. (New York: Library of America, 1993).

5. Albert J. von Frank, The Trials of Anthony Burns: Freedom and Slavery in Emerson's Boston (Cambridge: Harvard University Press, 1998), and Stow Persons, Free Religion: An American Faith (New Haven: Yale University Press, 1947).

6. The Transcendentalists: A Review of Research and Criticism, ed. Joel Myerson (New York: Modern Language Association, 1984); American Literary Scholarship: An Annual (Durham: Duke University Press, 1965–); Alexander C. Kern, "The Rise of Transcendentalism, 1815–1860," Transitions in American Literary History, ed. Harry Hayden Clark (Durham: Duke University Press, 1954), pp. 247–314; Lawrence Buell, Literary Transcendentalism: Style and Vision in the American Renaissance (Ithaca: Cornell University Press, 1973); Critical Essays on American Transcendentalism, ed. Philip F. Gura and Joel Myerson (Boston: G. K. Hall, 1982); Buell, "The Transcendentalists," Columbia Literary History of the United States, gen. ed. Emory Elliott (New York: Columbia University Press, 1988), pp. 364–378; Buell, "The American Transcendentalist Poets," The Columbia History of American Poetry, ed. Jay Parini (New York: Columbia University Press, 1993), pp. 97–120; Barbara Packer, "The Transcendentalists," The Cambridge History of American Literature, ed. Sacvan Bercovitch, vol. 2, Prose Writing, 1820–1865 (Cambridge: Cambridge University Press, 1995), pp. 329–604; and Charles Capper, " 'A Little Beyond: The Problem of the Transcendentalist Movement in History," Journal of American History, 85 (September 1998): 502–539 (slightly revised and reprinted in Transient and Permanent: The Transcendentalist Movement and Its Contexts, ed. Capper and Conrad Edick Wright [Boston: Northeastern University Press, 1999], pp. 3–45).

INTRODUCTION

Each age, it is found, must write its own books; or rather,
each generation for the next succeeding.
　　　—Ralph Waldo Emerson, "The American Scholar"

Nobody knew what it was, but it was dreamy, mystical,
crazy, and infideleterious to religion.
　　　—Charles Godfrey Leland, *Memoirs*

. . . the age of plain living and high thinking, of pure ideals
and earnest effort, of moral passion and noble experiment.
　　　—Henry James, *The Bostonians*

Defining Transcendentalism is a lot like grasping mercury: both
are fluid and hard to pin down. Emerson's definition of it as
"Idealism as it appears in 1842" provides Transcendentalism with a
philosophical descriptor and a temporal locus, but is far less satisfying
than a declarative and authoritative dictionary definition.[1] Too many
readers suffer a type of hermeneutical paralysis when they are introduced to the Transcendentalists because they expend almost all their
energy in trying to define the movement and have little energy left
to enjoy and understand the literature. To paraphrase Thoreau, "If I
knew for a certainty that a man was coming to my house with the
conscious design of doing me good" by defining Transcendentalism,
"I should run for my life."[2]
　The longer one studies Transcendentalism, the more one realizes
that the looser the definition, the more appropriate it is; even a description of the movement (given to Emerson in 1836) as "A little
beyond" is ultimately more successful than the false security of a
hard-and-fast description that is supposed to fit all the people considered to be Transcendentalists.[3] Even the name Transcendentalists
was not self-imposed, but rather was applied by outsiders in an attempt to easily classify and categorize another group of people, even
though these people did not agree among themselves as to what their
goals were, except in the most general fashion. The Transcendentalists
were essentially syncretic, borrowing from various philosophies, liter-
atures, and religions whatever they felt was appropriate to their developing beliefs, and forging these borrowings into a new system.

While this type of belief formation may be practical, its essential nonlinearity, and inherent potential for internal contradictions among different aspects of disparate intellectual and moral structures, brings to mind Emerson's admonition in "Self-Reliance" that a "foolish consistency is the hobgoblin of little minds," and is a warning to take Transcendentalism on its own terms and not to pin it down by trying too hard to separately define its constituent parts. As recalled by one member of the Transcendental Club, a discussion group in which many Transcendentalists were involved, they were designated "the club of the like-minded" because "no two of us thought alike."[4] Nor should too much attention be paid to those who have parodied or made light of Transcendentalism. Contemporaries were fond of poking fun at such writings as Bronson Alcott's "Orphic Sayings," or such phraseology as that heard from someone at the dinner table at the Brook Farm community who asked "Is the butter within the sphere of your influence?"[5] Rather, we should listen to impartial commentators such as Charles Dickens, who, after visiting America, wrote "if I were a Bostonian, I think I would be a Transcendentalist."[6]

As the epigraph from Emerson reminds us, each generation views anew the ideas and literature of the past. Just as the Transcendentalists looked back to the past only to discover that they would prefer to look forward to the future, so too must we decide whether these people speak to us today, whether their message is still relevant. If we feel that Transcendentalism has become little more than a historical period of American literature and culture, one that we study because it is required by teachers and because it constitutes part of the proverbial well-rounded education, then we are ignoring the visceral impact that the Transcendentalists have had on generations of readers throughout the world. This anthology will introduce a new generation of readers to the Transcendentalists' ideas on religion, philosophy, literature, democracy, and the cultivation of the self.[7]

Perhaps the single most important question raised by the Transcendentalists is: How do we see the world?[8] Visionary imagery infuses their writings, bringing the possibility—and indeed the necessity—of interpretation back to the reader from those who have taken it away, including ministers, whose privileged position was used to keep humankind from a direct relationship with God, and teachers, who created a credentialed and self-perpetuating caste. The basic question of vision (or interpretation, or perception) leads to a discussion of Transcendentalism itself, and this introduction will attempt to describe the major areas in which the Transcendentalists were involved and how their interest was expressed.

Historically, Transcendentalism came about during a major shift in thought and sensibility in American life. The Calvinism of the Puritan past was replaced by less fearful, more humanized religious practices; empirical philosophy was challenged by the role of intuition; classical literature (broadly defined) was under siege by new writers who expressed their beliefs in different literary forms; the function of education was changing from imparting knowledge to bringing out the best in the child; reform movements were sweeping the country; and the proper role of the individual—and the individual's role in a democratic society—was of the greatest concern. There was a sense of "newness" in the air, and the Transcendentalists were often called the "New School."

Many writers have pointed out that Transcendentalism was first and foremost a religious enthusiasm and revolution. Nearly all of the people identified as Transcendentalists were involved with Unitarianism, most of them as ministers. They felt that Unitarianism had not lived up to its pledge to remove theological chains, and that the restrictive structure of Puritanism had been replaced by an equally restrictive (though superficially open) order. To be sure, there was an enormous difference between the predestined universe of the Puritans, in which humankind was corrupted by original sin, lived in a hostile and unknowable world, and whose potential salvation had been determined by chance before birth, as opposed to the Unitarians' ordered universe in which one could progress through good works while living in a benevolent environment, and the quality of the life lived would be taken into consideration on judgment day. Still, once the Unitarians gained the upper hand, they seemed to retreat from their earlier promise that humankind possessed divine attributes, as suggested in William Ellery Channing's sermon "Likeness to God." The result was a remote and arid church, one more interested in maintaining forms than in bringing religion to life. Emerson called it "corpse-cold Unitarianism," and Henry Adams gave an extended description of what it was like to grow up in these intellectual and religious surroundings:

> Nothing quieted doubt so completely as the mental calm of the Unitarian clergy. In uniform excellence of life and character, moral and intellectual, the score of Unitarian clergymen about Boston, who controlled society and Harvard College, were never excelled. . . . For them, difficulties might be ignored; doubts were waste of thought; nothing exacted solution. Boston had solved the universe; or had offered and realized the best solution yet tried. The problem was worked out.[9]

The younger generation was frustrated when it realized that not-yet-asked questions were going to be met with already-prepared answers. And nowhere was this more obvious than in the debate over miracles.

The conservative Unitarians held that the miracles of the New Testament had actually occurred, and that to doubt their existence was to doubt God. These miracles could not be explained by normal means and must be accepted on faith. Conservatives saw miracles as evidence of God's supranatural relationship to the natural world; liberals believed that miracles separated humankind from God by placing a barrier where none should exist. Meanwhile, German biblical scholars had developed a so-called Higher Criticism that argued that the Bible, like all inspired texts, was written by humans, and therefore in its reporting of events it contained illustrative examples more than it did detailed, accurate histories.[10] They supported their ideas by a type of comparative criticism, showing how many themes and examples (such as a world-cleansing flood) are shared by the sacred texts of various cultures. Higher Criticism was seen by the young reformers as a new tool for interpretation, but by the older ministers as an attack on their religion and their scholarship. When dialogue was no longer possible—and after the pages of the established religious journals were closed to them—the Transcendentalists splintered off on their own.

In a sense, the Transcendentalists were merely extending to an obvious conclusion the line of liberal theology that had been started by the Unitarians, when they had countered the triune God (Father, Son, Holy Spirit) of the Puritans, who had created a natural world that was often evil and a source of temptation, with a single God (Jesus was His son sent to humankind) whose benevolent natural order was proof of His existence.[11] The Transcendentalists generally replaced this anthropomorphic God with a nonanthropomorphic force or spirit, one that was present in all things, and one that could be learned about by studying not just God but people and nature as well, since all are emanations from the same source. By combining a frontal attack on theological learning through challenging the existence of miracles with an even deeper and more dangerous perceived belief in pantheism, the Transcendentalists became vulnerable to critics on a number of fronts. But their main point was that all partake of divinity, that there is divinity within humankind and within nature, and that all divinity is perceivable by each person who lives a life in a way that is in harmony with spirit. Moreover, in translating complex theological and philosophical concepts into language and imagery that could be understood by lay people, the Transcendentalists made religion accessible to many who had previously been excluded. By thus democratizing religion, and removing the preacher as a necessary mediator for religious knowledge, the Transcendentalists not only were theologically radical but also challenged the need for a formally credentialed ministerial class. They also set the stage for advocating the doctrine of self-reliance (or to enhance the divinity within one's self) and stressing the importance of observing nature (if nature is divine, then studying nature is a way to examine the expressions and workings of the divine mind). And if all—God, humankind, nature—emanate from the same source, then the natural world and its inhabitants are microcosms of the macrocosmic divinity; that is, an examination of the small—such as, for example, the people and natural world of Walden Pond—encourages learning about the larger pattern of God's designs.[12]

One reason the Transcendentalists placed such emphasis on the individual's interpretation of religious texts was their belief in the importance of intuition. Their parents' generation believed in John Locke's view of the world, one in which all knowledge must be verified by the senses. To Locke, the mind was a blank tablet (*tabula rasa*) or sheet of blank paper on which is inscribed the sum of an individual's experiences. It is as if we are a blank book at birth, and as we proceed through life we write down our experiences, so that our existence ultimately is experientially inscribed in our book of life. The younger generation adapted the ideas of Immanuel Kant to state that there were categories of preexisting knowledge that could be grasped intuitively. To them, the book individuals are handed at birth is not blank, but contains within it certain universally acknowledged truths, and from the start one instinctively reads this book rather than inscribing one's self in it.

To the Transcendentalists, the terms "Understanding" and "Reason" came to be used in their writings to distinguish between, respectively, Lockean empiricism and Kantian intuition. To a great extent, this terminology came to America by way of Samuel Taylor Coleridge, who in his *Aids to Reflection* defined Understanding as "the Faculty judging according to sense" and Reason as "the Power of universal and necessary Convictions, the Source and Substance of Truths above Sense, and having their evidence in themselves."[13] In Emerson's words, "Reason is the highest faculty of the soul—what we mean often by the soul itself; it never *reasons*, never proves, it simply perceives; it is vision. The Understanding toils all the time, compares, contrives, adds, argues, near sighted but strong-sighted, dwelling in the present the expedient the customary."[14] If one were a follower of John Locke, one could not say, as did James Freeman Clarke, "I discovered that I was born a transcendentalist."[15] With this reliance on intuition came the concomitant expression of organicism (form follows function, not just in art but also in life) and choice of genius (originality) over talent (mere replications of inspired originals).

In literature, the Transcendentalists championed continental writings over traditional British ones, and endorsed the British Romantics at a time when their positive reception in America was not at all assured. There was something about the way in which writers like Shelley challenged established assumptions that appealed to the younger generation. Works like Coleridge and Wordsworth's *Lyrical Ballads* (1798), which made daily life the fit subject of poetry, intrigued an audience that was looking to its own surroundings for poetic inspiration and self-definition. In a way, the movement in literature paralleled the movement in art at this time, as more creative artists (in many media) moved away from formal portraits of upper-class or religious subjects toward portraying common people and the natural world (and humankind's place in it).

The Transcendentalists wrote primarily nonfiction prose or poetry. There are no short stories or novels of enduring importance by any of the major participants.[16] Practically, this included writings on religious topics, travel literature, reform literature, and essays that suggestively promoted autodidacticism (or as they are called today, self-help works). Literature was supposed to inspire, and there is a religious quality to their best works, as befits the descendants of Puritans and the contemporaries of the great Unitarian preachers. Almost as if to declare that they were free of "anxiety of influence,"[17] the Transcendentalists did not define their literary craft. Margaret Fuller wrote articles about criticism and critical essays about literature, and Emerson tried to define the role of the poet in generalized orphic or vatic terms as the inspired interpreter of nature, but they left no detailed instructions as, say, Poe did in "The Philosophy of Composition."

They also utilized private writings to a great extent, and much of the best of Transcendentalist literature is in the journals and letters of the period. But "private" is perhaps a misnomer: much of what they wrote for themselves was done with the knowledge that others would see it.[18] Letters were not filed away but shared; they became a way of following the physical and emotional journeys of the writer. Similarly, journals were passed around, and the record of a life contained therein was presented to one's friends as a supplement to conversation.

One reason the Transcendentalists did not try to dictate what was acceptable or proper is that they prized the concept of individuality. This attitude also follows naturally upon the other beliefs they held. If religion is centered in individuals because we are emanations of divinity, and if knowledge is preexistent within us, and if literature is moving toward self-expression rather than merely following externally imposed forms, then of course individualism becomes essential.

The Transcendentalists did not come up with this concept in a vacuum, and there were other contemporary beliefs that they appropriated. Some of their belief in perfectionism came from the writings of Jean-Jacques Rousseau, who argued that humankind was basically good, and, as a result, the evils of society derive from institutions and not from people. The Unitarians contributed the idea of self-culture, that our lives should be spent in self-improvement, as the title of Dr. Channing's *Self-Culture* (1838) proclaims. A new era of democracy was ushered in with the election of the Andrew Jackson as president in 1828, marking the first time a politician west of Appalachia and who had appealed directly to the masses had achieved the office. This period of Jacksonian Democracy is called by one historian the "rise of the common man."[19] The emergence of the middle-class and its prototypical figure, the "self-made man," brought about a social class that was not hereditary: no longer were the only choices the fortunate one of being born into the aristocracy and being well-off for life, versus the unfortunate one of being born into the lower class from which escape was impossible. Middle-classness was achievable through hard work and by a reliance upon the self, rather than the result of a predestined social order; here social mobility and religious salvation merged, just as the pre-ordained Puritan world in which one never knew whether one was to be saved or damned until the afterlife had been replaced by the Unitarian version of religious progress in which salvation was knowable and measured by one's good works on earth.

The rise of the middle class also paralleled the continued change in America from a subsistence to a market economy. For example, a farmer who once raised cattle for food and hides now sold his cattle in town and used the money to purchase steaks and shoelaces. Whereas earlier generations had grown or made what was necessary for survival, and bartered for anything else that was needed, now they engaged in transactions based upon currency. As money (an arbitrary value system imposed upon an object by the supply and demand of the marketplace) replaced personal craftsmanship (the value of an object as measured by the time and individuality inherent in it), people became disengaged from their surroundings, and instead of computing the amount of time necessary to make something, they started to think about how much time was required to work in order to earn the money necessary to purchase that object. Thoreau makes this point in *Walden*, where he contrasts someone putting in hard day labor in order to buy a ticket for a short journey on the railroad train to Fitchburg with his own leisurely pace on foot toward the same destination, and his ability to observe and interact with the people and scenery on the way; and he also makes the point that he would probably arrive before his friend. Or, as Thoreau sums up his own economic theory for the modern age, "the cost of a thing is the amount of what I will call life which is required to be exchanged for it, immediately or in the long run."[20]

The resulting loss of economic individuality or selfhood came about at the same time as the industrial revolution (and its mass-produced objects created in factories by a faceless and interchangeable workforce) was making serious inroads in New England, and the Transcendentalists found themselves responding to this loss by proposing a solution to the anomie of their contemporaries. Moreover, money came to take on an almost totemic value: the importance of possessing it, and the power and status which it represented, was in a sense just as crucial as obtaining possessions with it. To the Transcendentalists, this meant that money was becoming a more widespread and important standard of personal worth than was individual moral conduct, resulting in people's souls being weighed on a banker's balance and not on a higher scale.[21]

When they opposed viewing the world in a Lockean, empirical, pecuniary, materialistic way with their own angle of vision, one that takes the Kantian, intuitive, moral, idealistic path, the Transcendentalists demonstrated the interconnectedness of their moral and intellectual outlook. Not surprisingly, their desire to bring about a different manner of viewing the world often took concrete shape in a number of reform projects, perhaps the most important of which was education, which some might argue is the main goal of all reform, and which all would agree is the initial step toward and venue for self-culture.

The emphasis on education is something in which all the Transcendentalists—clerics, former clerics, and lay people—could participate. Preaching is, after all, one way of educating people about themselves and their relationship to God. Lecturing is nothing more than educating audiences on days other than Sunday. School teaching is talking to a younger, rather than an older, audience. All the Transcendentalists either were the product of the so-called best of the day's educational system or had been schoolteachers themselves; some, like Emerson, had been on both sides of the desk, attending college and teaching schools for young people as well. They all knew about the educational system first-hand, and did not like what they saw. In the early nineteenth century, teaching was characterized by rote memorization intended to impose upon students a bounded world of knowledge; according to this method, a successful student was one who could best memorize the material. Original, creative, and synthetic thinking were less important than imitation and repetition—indeed, in distinguishing between genius and talent, traditionalists strongly discouraged wandering from the accepted path. In addition, schoolrooms were drab and unhealthy affairs, with little concern shown for interior decoration or ventilation, and, as one scholar has written, they appealed "only to nostalgic adults or penurious taxpayers."[22] Teachers like Alcott and Peabody replaced poorly lit, unventilated, drably furnished classrooms in which discipline was imposed by force with teaching areas that were well-lighted, had open windows, contained comfortable seats, surrounded the students with books and works of art, and in which discipline was enforced by students' peers. They applied their concept of Kantian intuition by using a Socratic question-and-answer technique and student journals to draw out children and let them discover and deduce concepts instead of having answers spoon-fed to them.

Nor was education limited to the young. A number of Transcendentalists became lecturers, most notably Emerson, who gave some fifteen hundred lectures over four decades. Alcott, Fuller, and Peabody all gave "Conversations," or classes for adults (what would today be called "continuing education") on topics ranging from mythology to self-improvement to reminiscences of the Transcendental period. The rhetoric of much Transcendentalist writing carries with it a sense of drawing out the reader by prompting or provoking rather than by didactically instructing.[23] In the often irregular rhythms and development of Emerson's prose, for instance, we can see parallels to the way our own minds work in thinking through a problem.

Transcendentalist education was aimed at creating a new generation who would be free of the restraints and conventions of the older and the present generations; and to reach those groups, reform movements were necessary. As so often happened during transitional periods in American history, social and political changes in the culture at large inspired other, more focused reform movements to come forward. The antebellum period was, of course, dominated by antislavery or abolitionism as the most significant reform movement, but many others existed as well. Social reform was centered in movements to create new types of social structures, the most noticeable at this time being communitarianism, and the Transcendentalist-related communities at Brook Farm (1841–1847) and Fruitlands (1843–1844) are examples. But other Transcendentalists felt that the individual needed to be reformed before there could be any hope for a new social order, and they stayed away from communal efforts and chose instead to concentrate on self-improvement. In a sense, they felt that the reformation of the individual was a macrocosmic reform that would, once accomplished, bring about changes in the more specialized, microcosmic movements.

This was also a great era of health reform. When Thoreau writes in *Walden* that bathing in the pond is "a religious exercise" (p. 88), he gets to the heart of nineteenth-century health reform: our bodies are temples, and good health is a form of worship. The general tenor of health reform is that we are living in ways that harm our bodies and we need to act out our lives in a different, more natural fashion. This was the time of the water-cure, whose proponents argued that cold baths and wrappings of wet sheets were more effective in drawing out bodily impurities than were medicines ingested internally. Dietary reform was also a major force, and both Brook Farm and Fruitlands stressed revising dietary habits. Temperance organizations flourished, as did movements away from using commercially processed foods toward ones that were more naturally prepared. The Transcendentalists avoided such fads as phrenology, a pseudo-science holding that character is reflected in the bumps on one's head, which can be "read" by charting their relative sizes and positions, or such plans for environmental engineering as sending ships to the poles to bring back icebergs in the summer to cool down the temperature.

Reform was a natural outgrowth and end product of the Transcendentalist view of the world. If we live in a religious environment in which we can perceive God directly by cultivating our innate divinity, if we act on the basis of intuition rather than sensory experience, if we believe in self-culture and self-reliance (which is, after all, godreliance), and if we wish to eliminate those who try to deny us all these things by insisting that only a credentialed intermediate body can interpret them for us, then, naturally, the result is religious, philosophic, literary, and social change. And, in a way, reform is merely a democratic process that allows us to see the world through a different angle of vision; after all, if we look at the world in the same way in each generation, if we depend on the past for guidance rather than our selves, why would change or reform be necessary at all? Transcendentalism is not a concept that operates in isolation from the rest of its world; it is not navel gazing. There is a strong sense of social commitment in Transcendentalism, be it Emerson provoking thought, or Thoreau arguing for nonviolent passive disobedience, or Fuller leading classes to enable women to gain in self-confidence, or the Ripleys trying to change society through Brook Farm. As Emerson describes the ultimate goal of enabling one to be self-reliant, "A man is fed, not that he may be fed, but that he may work."[24]

Is Transcendentalism relevant today? Millions of readers must think so. The writings of Emerson and Thoreau have never gone out of print, and *Walden* is arguably the American book translated into the most languages. The issues the Transcendentalists raised and examined have never gone out of fashion; and while discussion of some of these issues turn on specific and sometimes arcane points (such as the miracles debate), the larger questions raised by the small individual issues (who is able to interpret the Bible and is a fundamentalist interpretation of it valid?) are still being debated. Indeed, what was raised at the beginning as the basic question put to us by the Transcendentalists— How do we see the world?—is also a question about interpretation, about who has the right to interpret and how it can be accomplished. If we define "text" in a loose fashion, as did the Transcendentalists, then we can see that they are asking fundamental questions about how we "read" not only printed texts (ranging from the most recent bestseller to the Bible) but also such other texts as nature, and even the *tabula rasa* of our own lives. It is only proper, then, that this anthology present the Transcendentalists in their own words so that new generations of readers can judge for themselves whether these writings are, to use Theodore Parker's terms, transient or permanent.[25]

Notes

1. Emerson, "The Transcendentalist," first paragraph.
2. *Walden*, ed. J. Lyndon Shanley (Princeton: Princeton University Press, 1971), p. 74.
3. Almira Barlow, quoted in *The Journals and Miscellaneous Notebooks of Ralph Waldo Emerson*, ed. William H. Gilman, Ralph H. Orth, et al., 16 vols. (Cambridge: Harvard University Press, 1960–1982), 5:218.
4. James Freeman Clarke, quoted in James Elliot Cabot, *A Memoir of Ralph Waldo Emerson*, 2 vols. (Boston: Houghton, Mifflin, 1887), 1:249.
5. Lindsay Swift, *Brook Farm: Its Members, Scholars, and Visitors* (New York: Macmillan, 1900), p. 57. Another story of Brook Farm tells of a visitor arriving and having this as his first sight of the community: "Outside the door was painted in flaming colors a yellow sun, at the center of whose blazing rays was the motto 'Universal Unity,' while beneath it hung another inscription in black and white letters, 'Please wipe your feet' " (Thomas Wentworth Higginson, *Margaret Fuller Ossoli* [Boston: Houghton, Mifflin, 1884], p. 177).
6. Dickens, *American Notes for General Circulation*, 2 vols. (London: Chapman and Hall, 1842), 1:134.
7. This anthology concentrates on Transcendentalism's major phase, from 1836 (with the publication of Emerson's *Nature* and works by others of importance) through 1844 (when the last issue of the *Dial* appeared).
8. Both Emerson and Thoreau argue that the angle at which we view things can make an enormous difference, and both use the earthy example of inverting one's head between one's legs to see how the world looks from a different perspective (see *Nature*, "Idealism," and *Walden*, p. 186).

9. Emerson's "corpse-cold Unitarianism" is in *Journals and Miscellaneous Notebooks*, 9:381; *The Education of Henry Adams* (Boston: Houghton Mifflin, 1973 [1907]), p. 34.

10. See Jerry Wayne Brown, *The Rise of Biblical Criticism in America, 1800–1870: The New England Scholars* (Middletown, Conn.: Wesleyan University Press, 1969).

11. As Theodore Parker describes the difference as he experienced it, "In my early childhood, after a severe but silent struggle, I made away with the ghastly doctrine of Eternal Damnation and a Wrathful God. . . . From my seventh year I have had no *Fear* of God, only an ever-greatening LOVE and TRUST" (*Theodore Parker's Experience as a Minister* [Boston: Rufus Leighton, Jr., 1859], p. 35).

12. Whitman extends this analogy by studying *Leaves of Grass* in order to generalize about the world at large.

13. Quoted from the text that most of the Transcendentalists were familiar with, *Aids to Reflection*, ed. James Marsh (Burlington, Vt.: Chauncey Goodrich, 1829), p. 137. Coleridge goes on to say that the Understanding is "discursive" while the Reason is "fixed"; that the "Understanding in all its judgments refers to some other Faculty as its ultimate Authority" while "Reason in all its decisions appeals to itself, as the ground and *substance* of their truth"; and that "Understanding is the Faculty of *Reflection*" while Reason is the one of "Contemplation" (p. 142).

14. *The Letters of Ralph Waldo Emerson*, ed. Ralph L. Rusk and Eleanor M. Tilton, 10 vols. (New York Columbia University Press, 1939, 1990–1995), 1:412–413.

15. Clarke, *Autobiography, Diary, and Correspondence*, ed. Edward Everett Hale (Boston: Houghton, Mifflin, 1891), p. 39.

16. Sylvester Judd's *Margaret* (1845) is considered the only Transcendental novel, but Judd was on the periphery of the movement; both Fuller and William Henry Channing tried writing short fiction; and Christopher Pearse Cranch later became a successful writer of stories and books for children.

17. For Harold Bloom's idea that poets write against the influence of the past and other writers, see his *The Anxiety of Influence: A Theory of Poetry* (New York: Oxford University Press, 1973).

18. See Lawrence Rosenwald, *Emerson and the Art of the Diary* (New York: Oxford University Press, 1988), and William Merrill Decker, *Epistolary Practices: Letter Writing in America Before Telecommunications* (Chapel Hill: University of North Carolina Press, 1998).

19. Carl Russell Fish, *The Rise of the Common Man 1830–1850* (New York: Macmillan, 1927). A more recent study of this phenomenon is Stuart M. Blumin, *The Emergence of the Middle Class: Social Experience in the American City, 1760–1900* (New York: Cambridge University Press, 1989).

20. *Walden*, pp. 53, 31.

21. Unfortunately, the self-reliant aspects of Transcendentalism (and particularly Emerson's writings) were recast and appropriated as a type of social

Darwinism by the late nineteenth-century robber barons as a means of justifying their actions. A good example of this is discussed in Howard Horwitz, "The Standard Oil Trust as Emersonian Hero," *Raritan*, 6, n.s. 4 (Spring 1987): 97–119.

22. Bruce A. Ronda, *Elizabeth Palmer Peabody: A Reformer on Her Own Terms* (Cambridge: Harvard University Press, 1999), p. 84.

23. As Emerson writes in the Divinity School Address, "it is not instruction, but provocation, that I can receive from another soul."

24. Emerson, *Nature*, "Commodity."

25. Both the Further Reading at the front of this anthology and Bibliographies at the end are good starting places for learning more about the Transcendentalists.

Transcendentalism

William Ellery Channing

"Likeness to God"

(1828)

WILLIAM ELLERY CHANNING (1780–1842) was the most famous Unitarian
preacher of the day, and one of the major spokespersons for denominational
matters and public polity. In 1819, his sermon "Unitarian Christianity"
helped name the movement. His *Self-Culture* (1838) was one of the documents
used by the Transcendentalists in the formation of their concept of self-
realization, and *Slavery* (1835) was one of the earliest attacks on that institution by the church establishment. "Likeness to God" distinguished between
the Deist and Calvinist Gods that were so remote from humankind, and the
potential for godliness that existed for the new generation. In a sense, the
Transcendentalists were merely extending Channing's ideas when they called
for human perfectibility; and the backlash from their seniors was all the more
puzzling for that reason.

Be ye therefore followers of god, as dear children.

—Ephesians, V: 1.

To promote true religion is the purpose of the christian ministry.
For this it was ordained. On the present occasion, therefore, when
a new teacher is to be given to the church, a discourse on the character
of true religion will not be inappropriate. I do not mean, that I shall
attempt, in the limits to which I am now confined, to set before you
all its properties, signs, and operations; for in so doing I should burden
your memories with divisions and vague generalities, as uninteresting
as they would be unprofitable. My purpose is, to select one view of
the subject, which seems to me of primary dignity and importance;
and I select this, because it is greatly neglected, and because I attribute
to this neglect much of the inefficacy, and many of the corruptions of
religion.

The text calls us to follow or imitate God, to seek accordance with
or likeness to him; and to do this, not fearfully and faintly, but with
the spirit and hope of beloved children. The doctrine, which I propose
to illustrate, is derived immediately from these words, and is incorporated with the whole New Testament. I affirm, and would maintain,

that true religion consists in proposing as our great end, a growing likeness to the Supreme Being. Its noblest influence consists, in making us more and more partakers of the Divinity. For this it is to be preached. Religious instruction should aim chiefly to turn men's aspirations and efforts to that perfection of the soul, which constitutes it a bright image of God. Such is the topic now to be discussed; and I implore Him, whose glory I seek, to aid me in unfolding and enforcing it with simplicity and clearness, with a calm and pure zeal, and with unfeigned charity.

I begin with observing, what all indeed will understand, that the likeness to God, of which I propose to speak, belongs to man's higher or spiritual nature. It has its foundation in the original and essential capacities of the mind. In proportion as these are unfolded by right and vigorous exertion, it is extended and brightened. In proportion as these lie dormant, it is obscured. In proportion as they are perverted and overpowered by the appetites and passions, it is blotted out. In truth, moral evil, if unresisted and habitual, may so blight and lay waste these capacities, that the image of God in man may seem to be wholly destroyed.

The importance of this assimilation to our Creator, is a topic, which needs no labored discussion. All men, of whatever name, or sect, or opinion, will meet me on this ground. All, I presume, will allow, that no good in the compass of the universe, or within the gift of omnipotence, can be compared to a resemblance of God, or to a participation of his attributes. I fear no contradiction here. Likeness to God is the supreme gift. He can communicate nothing so precious, glorious, blessed as himself. To hold intellectual and moral affinity with the Supreme Being, to partake his spirit, to be his children by derivations of kindred excellence, to bear a growing conformity to the perfection which we adore, this is a felicity which obscures and annihilates all other good.

It is only in proportion to this likeness that we can enjoy either God, or the universe. That God can be known and enjoyed only through sympathy or kindred attributes, is a doctrine which even Gentile philosophy discerned. That the pure in heart can alone see and commune with the pure Divinity, was the sublime instruction of ancient sages as well as of inspired prophets. It is indeed the lesson of daily experience. To understand a great and good being, we must have the seeds of the same excellence. How quickly, by what an instinct, do accordant minds recognise one another! No attraction is so powerful as that which subsists between the truly wise, and good; whilst the brightest excellence is lost on those who have nothing congenial in their own breasts. God becomes a real being to us, in proportion as his own nature is unfolded within us. To a man who is growing in the likeness of God, faith begins even here to change into vision. He carries within himself a proof of a Deity, which can only be understood by experience. He more than believes, he feels the divine presence; and gradually rises to an intercourse with his Maker, to which it is not irreverent to apply the name of friendship and intimacy. The apostle John intended to express this truth, when he tells us that he, in whom a principle of divine charity or benevolence has become a habit and life, 'dwells in God and God in him.'

It is plain, too, that likeness to God is the true and only preparation for the enjoyment of the universe. In proportion as we approach and resemble the mind of God, we are brought into harmony with the creation; for, in that proportion we possess the principles from which the universe sprung; we carry within ourselves the perfections of which, its beauty, magnificence, order, benevolent adaptations, and boundless purposes, are the results and manifestations. God unfolds himself in his works to a kindred mind. It is possible, that the brevity of these hints may expose to the charge of mysticism, what seems to me the calmest and clearest truth. I think, however, that every reflecting man will feel, that likeness to God must be a principle of sympathy or accordance with his creation; for the creation is a birth and shining forth of the Divine Mind, a work through which his spirit breathes. In proportion as we receive this spirit, we possess within ourselves the explanation of what we see. We discern more and more of God in everything, from the frail flower to the everlasting stars. Even in evil, that dark cloud which hangs over the creation, we discern rays of light and hope, and gradually come to see in suffering and temptation, proofs and instruments of the sublimest purposes of Wisdom and Love.

I have offered these very imperfect views, that I may show the great importance of the doctrine which I am solicitous to enforce. I would teach, that likeness to God is a good so unutterably surpassing all other good, that whoever admits it as attainable, must acknowledge it to be the chief aim of life. I would show that the highest and happiest office of religion, is to bring the mind into growing accordance with God, and that by the tendency of religious systems to this end their truth and worth are to be chiefly tried.

I am aware that it may be said, that the scriptures, in speaking of man as made in the image of God, and in calling us to imitate him, use bold and figurative language. It may be said, that there is danger from too literal an interpretation; that God is an unapproachable being; that I am not warranted in ascribing to man a like nature to the

Divine; that we and all things illustrate the Creator by contrast, not by resemblance; that religion manifests itself chiefly in convictions and acknowledgments of utter worthlessness; and that to talk of the greatness and divinity of the human soul, is to inflate that pride through which Satan fell, and through which man involves himself in that fallen spirit's ruin.

I answer, that, to me, scripture and reason hold a different language. In Christianity particularly, I meet perpetual testimonies to the divinity of human nature. This whole religion expresses an infinite concern of God for the human soul, and teaches that he deems no methods too expensive for its recovery and exaltation. Christianity, with one voice, calls me to turn my regards and care to the spirit within me, as of more worth than the whole outward world. It calls us to 'be perfect as our Father in heaven is perfect;' and everywhere, in the sublimity of its precepts, it implies and recognises the sublime capacities of the being to whom they are addressed. It assures us that human virtue is 'in the sight of God of great price,' and speaks of the return of a human being to virtue as an event which increases the joy of heaven. In the New Testament, Jesus Christ, the Son of God, the brightness of his glory, the express and unsullied image of the Divinity, is seen mingling with men as a friend and brother, offering himself as their example, and promising to his true followers a share in all his splendors and joys. In the New Testament, God is said to communicate his own spirit, and all his fulness to the human soul. In the New Testament man is exhorted to aspire after 'honor, glory, and immortality;' and Heaven, a word expressing the nearest approach to God, and a divine happiness, is everywhere proposed as the end of his being. In truth, the very essence of christian faith is, that we trust in God's mercy, as revealed in Jesus Christ, for a state of celestial purity, in which we shall grow forever in the likeness, and knowledge, and enjoyment of the Infinite Father. Lofty views of the nature of man are bound up and interwoven with the whole christian system. Say not, that these are at war with humility; for who was ever humbler than Jesus, and yet who ever possessed such a consciousness of greatness and divinity? Say not that man's business is to think of his sin, and not of his dignity; for great sin implies a great capacity; it is the abuse of a noble nature; and no man can be deeply and rationally contrite, but he who feels, that in wrong doing he has resisted a divine voice, and warred against a divine principle, in his own soul.—I need not, I trust, pursue the argument from revelation. There is an argument from nature and reason, which seems to me so convincing, and is at the same time so fitted to explain what I mean by man's possession of a like nature to God, that I shall pass at once to its exposition.

That man has a kindred nature with God, and may bear most important and ennobling relations to him, seems to me to be established by a striking proof. This proof you will understand, by considering, for a moment, how we obtain our ideas of God. Whence come the conceptions which we include under that august name? Whence do we derive our knowledge of the attributes and perfections which constitute the Supreme Being? I answer, we derive them from our own souls. The divine attributes are first developed in ourselves, and thence transferred to our Creator. The idea of God, sublime and awful as it is, is the idea of our own spiritual nature, purified and enlarged to infinity. In ourselves are the elements of the Divinity. God then does not sustain a figurative resemblance to man. It is the resemblance of a parent to a child, the likeness of a kindred nature.

We call God a Mind. He has revealed himself as a spirit. But what do we know of mind, but through the unfolding of this principle in our own breasts? That unbounded spiritual energy which we call God, is conceived by us only through consciousness, through the knowledge of ourselves.—We ascribe thought or intelligence to the Deity as one of his most glorious attributes. And what means this language? These terms we have framed to express operations or faculties of our own souls. The Infinite Light would be forever hidden from us, did not kindred rays dawn and brighten within us. God is another name for human intelligence, raised above all error and imperfection, and extended to all possible truth.

The same is true of God's goodness. How do we understand this but by the principle of love implanted in the human breast? Whence is it, that this divine attribute is so faintly comprehended, but from the feeble developement of it in the multitude of men? Who can understand the strength, purity, fulness, and extent of divine philanthropy, but he in whom selfishness has been swallowed up in love?

The same is true of all the moral perfections of the Deity. These are comprehended by us, only through our own moral nature. It is conscience within us, which, by its approving and condemning voice, interprets to us God's love of virtue and hatred of sin; and without conscience these glorious conceptions would never have opened on the mind. It is the lawgiver in our own breasts, which gives us the idea of divine authority and binds us to obey it. The soul, by its sense of right, or its perception of moral distinctions, is clothed with sovereignty over itself, and through this alone, it understands and recognises the Sovereign of the Universe. Men, as by a natural inspiration, have agreed to speak of conscience as the voice of God, as the Divinity within us. This principle, reverently obeyed, makes us more and more partakers of the moral perfection of the Supreme Being, of that very excellence, which constitutes the rightfulness of his sceptre, and enthrones him over the universe. Without this inward law, we should be as incapable of receiving a law from Heaven, as the brute. Without this, the thunders of Sinai might startle the outward ear, but would have no meaning, no authority to the mind. I have expressed here a great truth. Nothing teaches so encouragingly our relation and resemblance to God; for the glory of the Supreme Being, is eminently moral. We blind ourselves to his chief splendor, if we think only or mainly of his power, and overlook those attributes of rectitude and goodness, to which he subjects his omnipotence, and which are the foundations and very substance of his universal and immutable Law. And are these attributes revealed to us through the principles and convictions of our own souls? Do we understand through sympathy God's perception of the right, the good, the holy, the just? Then with what propriety is it said, that in his own image he made man!

I am aware, that it may be objected to these views, that we receive our idea of God from the universe, from his works, and not so exclusively from our own souls. The universe, I know, is full of God. The heavens and earth declare his glory. In other words, the effects and signs of power, wisdom, and goodness, are apparent through the whole creation. But apparent to what? Not to the outward eye; not to the acutest organs of sense; but to a kindred mind, which interprets the universe by itself. It is only through that energy of thought, by which we adapt various and complicated means to distant ends, and give harmony and a common bearing to multiplied exertions, that we understand the creative intelligence which has established the order, dependencies and harmony of nature. We see God around us, because he dwells within us. It is by a kindred wisdom, that we discern his wisdom in his works. The brute, with an eye as piercing as ours, looks on the universe; and the page, which to us is radiant with characters of greatness and goodness, is to him a blank. In truth, the beauty and glory of God's works are revealed to the mind by a light beaming from itself. We discern the impress of God's attributes in the universe by accordance of nature, and enjoy them through sympathy.—I hardly need observe, that these remarks in relation to the universe apply with equal, if not greater force, to revelation.

I shall now be met by another objection which to many may seem strong. It will be said, that these various attributes of which I have spoken, exist in God in Infinite Perfection, and that this destroys all affinity between the human and the divine mind. To this I have two replies. In the first place, an attribute, by becoming perfect, does not part with its essence. Love, wisdom, power, and purity, do not change their nature by enlargement. If they did, we should lose the Supreme

Being through his very infinity. Our ideas of him would fade away into mere sounds. For example, if wisdom in God, because unbounded, have no affinity with that attribute in man, why apply to him that term? It must signify nothing. Let me ask what we mean, when we say that we discern the marks of intelligence in the universe? We mean, that we meet there the proofs of a mind like our own. We certainly discern proofs of no other; so that to deny this doctrine, would be to deny the evidences of a God, and utterly to subvert the foundations of religious belief. What man can examine the structure of a plant or an animal, and see the adaptation of its parts to each other and to common ends, and not feel, that it is the work of an intelligence akin to his own, and that he traces these marks of design by the same spiritual energy in which they had their origin?

But I would offer another answer to this objection, that God's infinity places him beyond the resemblance and approach of man. I affirm, and I trust that I do not speak too strongly, that there are traces of infinity in the human mind, and that in this very respect, it bears a likeness to God. The very conception of infinity is the mark of a nature, to which no limit can be prescribed. This thought indeed comes to us not so much from abroad as from our own souls. We ascribe this attribute to God, because we possess capacities and wants, which only an unbounded being can fill, and because we are conscious of a tendency in spiritual faculties to unlimited expansion. We believe in the divine infinity through something congenial with it in our own breasts. I hope I speak clearly, and if not, I would ask those to whom I am obscure, to pause before they condemn. To me it seems that the soul, in all its higher actions, in original thought, in the creations of genius, in the soarings of imagination, in its love of beauty and grandeur, in its aspirations after a pure and unknown joy, and especially in disinterestedness, in the spirit of selfsacrifice, and in enlightened devotion, has a character of infinity. There is often a depth in human love which may be strictly called unfathomable. There is sometimes a lofty strength in moral principle, which all the power of the outward universe cannot overcome. There seems a might within which can more than balance all might without. There is, too, a piety, which swells into a transport too vast for utterance, and into an immeasurable joy. I am speaking indeed of what is uncommon, but still of realities. We see however the tendency of the soul to the infinite in more familiar and ordinary forms. Take for example the delight which we find in the vast scenes of nature, in prospects which spread around us without limits, in the immensity of the heavens and the ocean, and especially in the rush and roar of mighty winds, waves, and torrents, when, amidst our deep awe, a power within seems to respond to the omnipotence around us. The same principle is seen in the delight ministered to us by works of fiction or of imaginative art, in which our own nature is set before us in more than human beauty and power. In truth the soul is always bursting its limits. It thirsts continually for wider knowledge. It rushes forward to untried happiness. It has a deep want which nothing limited can appease. Its true element and end is an unbounded good. Thus God's infinity has its image in the soul, and through the soul much more than through the universe, we arrive at this conception of the Deity.

In these remarks I have spoken strongly. But I have no fear of expressing too strongly the connexion between the divine and the human mind. My only fear is, that I shall dishonor the great subject. The danger to which we are most exposed, is that of severing the Creator from his creatures. The propensity of human sovereigns to cut off communication between themselves and their subjects, and to disclaim a common nature with their inferiors, has led the multitude of men, who think of God chiefly under the character of a king, to conceive of him as a being, who places his glory in multiplying distinctions between himself and all other beings. The truth is, that the union between the Creator and the creature surpasses all other bonds in strength and intimacy. He penetrates all things and delights to irradiate all with his glory. Nature, in its lowest and inanimate forms, is pervaded by his power; and when quickened by the mysterious property of life, how wonderfully does it show forth the perfections of its Author! How much of God may be seen in the structure of a single leaf, which, though so frail as to tremble in every wind, yet holds connexions and living communications with the earth, the air, the clouds, and the distant sun; and, through these sympathies with the universe, is itself a revelation of an omnipotent mind. God delights to diffuse himself everywhere. Through his energy, unconscious matter clothes itself with proportions, powers, and beauties which reflect his wisdom and love. How much more must he delight to frame conscious and happy recipients of his perfections, in whom his wisdom and love may substantially dwell, with whom he may form spiritual ties, and to whom he may be an everlasting spring of moral energy and happiness. How far the Supreme Being may communicate his attributes to his intelligent offspring, I stop not to inquire. But that his almighty goodness will impart to them powers and glories, of which the material universe is but a faint emblem, I cannot doubt. That the soul, if true to itself and its Maker, will be filled with God, and will manifest him, more than that sun, I cannot doubt. Who can doubt it, that believes and understands the doctrine of human immortality?

The views which I have given in this discourse respecting man's participation of the divine nature, seem to me to receive strong confirmation, from the title or relation most frequently applied to God in the New Testament; and I have reserved this as the last corroboration of this doctrine, because to my own mind it is singularly affecting. In the New Testament God is made known to us as a Father, and a brighter feature of that book cannot be named. Our worship is to be directed to him as our Father. Our whole religion is to take its character from this view of the Divinity. In this he is to rise always to our minds. And what is it to be a Father? It is to communicate one's own nature, to give life to kindred beings; and the highest function of a Father is to educate the mind of the child, and to impart to it what is noblest and happiest in his own mind. God is our Father, not merely because he created us, or because he gives us enjoyment; for he created the flower and the insect, yet we call him not their Father. This bond is a spiritual one. This name belongs to God, because he frames spirits like himself, and delights to give them what is most glorious and blessed in his own nature. Accordingly Christianity is said with special propriety, to reveal God as the Father, because it reveals him as sending his Son, to cleanse the mind from every stain, and to replenish it forever with the spirit and moral attributes of its Author. Separate from God this idea of his creating and training up beings after his own likeness, and you rob him of the paternal character. This relation vanishes, and with it, vanish the glory of the gospel, and the dearest hopes of the human soul.

The great use which I would make of the principles laid down in this discourse, is to derive from them just and clear views of the nature of religion. What then is religion? I answer; it is not the adoration of a God, with whom we have no common properties; of a distinct, foreign, separate being; but of an all-communicating Parent. It recognises and adores God as a being, whom we know through our own souls, who has made man in his own image, who is the perfection of our own spiritual nature, who has sympathies with us as kindred beings, who is near us, not in place only like this all surrounding atmosphere, but by spiritual influence and love, who looks on us with parental interest, and whose great design it is to communicate to us forever, and in freer and fuller streams, his own power, goodness, and joy. The conviction of this near and ennobling relation of God to the soul, and of his great purposes towards it, belongs to the very essence of true religion; and true religion manifests itself chiefly and most conspicuously in desires, hopes, and efforts corresponding to this truth. It desires and seeks supremely the assimilation of the mind to God, or the perpetual unfolding and enlargement of those powers and virtues by which it is constituted his glorious image. The mind, in proportion as it is enlightened and penetrated by true religion, thirsts and labors for a godlike elevation. What else indeed can it seek, if this good be placed within its reach? If I am capable of receiving and reflecting the intellectual and moral glory of my Creator, what else in comparison shall I desire? Shall I deem a property in the outward universe as the highest good, when I may become partaker of the very mind from which it springs, of the prompting love, the disposing wisdom, the quickening power, through which its order, beauty, and beneficent influences subsist? True religion is known by these high aspirations, hopes, and efforts. And this is the religion which most truly honors God. To honor him, is not to tremble before him as an unapproachable sovereign, nor to utter barren praise which leaves us as it found us. It is to become what we praise. It is to approach God as an inexhaustible Fountain of light, power, and purity. It is to feel the quickening and transforming energy of his perfections. It is to thirst for the growth and invigoration of the divine principle within us. It is to seek the very spirit of God. It is to trust in, to bless, to thank him for that rich grace, mercy, love, which was revealed and proffered by Jesus Christ, and which proposes as its great end the perfection of the human soul.

I regard this view of religion as infinitely important. It does more than all things to make our connexion with our Creator ennobling and happy; and in proportion as we want it, there is danger that the thought of God may itself become the instrument of our degradation. That religion has been so dispensed as to depress the human mind, I need not tell you; and it is a truth, which ought to be known, that the greatness of the Deity, when separated in our thoughts from his parental character, especially tends to crush human energy and hope. To a frail dependent creature, an omnipotent Creator easily becomes a terror, and his worship easily degenerates into servility, flattery, self-contempt, and selfish calculation. Religion only ennobles us, in as far as it reveals to us the tender and intimate connexion of God with his creatures, and teaches us to see in the very greatness which might give alarm, the source of great and glorious communications to the human soul. You cannot, my hearers, think too highly of the majesty of God. But let not this majesty sever him from you. Remember, that his greatness is the infinity of attributes which yourselves possess. Adore his infinite wisdom; but remember that this wisdom rejoices to diffuse itself, and let an exhilarating hope spring up, at the thought of the immeasurable intelligence which such a Father must communicate to his children. In like manner adore his power. Let the boundless creation fill you with awe and admiration of the energy which sustains it. But remember that God has a nobler work than the outward creation, even the spirit within yourselves; and that it is his purpose to replenish this with his own energy, and to crown it with growing power and triumphs over the material universe. Above all, adore his unutterable goodness. But remember, that this attribute is particularly proposed to you as your model; that God calls you, both by nature and revelation, to a fellowship in his philanthropy; that he has placed you in social relations for the very end of rendering you ministers and representatives of his benevolence; that he even summons you to espouse and to advance the sublimest purpose of his goodness, the redemption of the human race, by extending the knowledge and power of christian truth. It is through such views, that religion raises up the soul, and binds man by ennobling bonds to his Maker.

To complete my views of this topic, I beg to add an important caution. I have said that the great work of religion is to conform ourselves to God, or to unfold the divine likeness within us. Let none infer from this language, that I place religion in unnatural effort, in straining after excitements which do not belong to the present state, or in anything separate from the clear and simple duties of life. I exhort you to no extravagance. I reverence human nature too much to do it violence. I see too much divinity in its ordinary operations, to urge on it a forced and vehement virtue. To grow in the likeness of God, we need not cease to be men. This likeness does not consist in extraordinary or marvellous gifts, in supernatural additions to the soul, or in anything foreign to our original constitution; but in our essential faculties, unfolded by vigorous and conscientious exertion in the ordinary circumstances assigned by God. To resemble our Creator, we need not fly from society, and entrance ourselves in lonely contemplation and prayer. Such processes might give a feverish strength to one class of emotions, but would result in disproportion, distortion, and sickliness of mind. Our proper work is to approach God by the free and natural unfolding of our highest powers, of understanding, conscience, love, and the moral will.

Shall I be told that by such language, I ascribe to nature the effects which can only be wrought in the soul by the Holy Spirit? I anticipate this objection, and wish to meet it by a simple exposition of my views. I would on no account disparage the gracious aids and influences which God imparts to the human soul. The promise of the Holy Spirit is among the most precious in the sacred volume. Worlds could not tempt me to part with the doctrine of God's intimate connexion with the mind, and of his free and full communications to it. But these views are in no respect at variance with what I have taught of the method, by which we are to grow in the likeness of God. Scripture and experience concur in teaching, that by the Holy Spirit, we are to understand a divine assistance adapted to our moral freedom, and accordant with the fundamental truth, that virtue is the mind's own work. By the Holy Spirit, I understand an aid, which must be gained and made effectual by our own activity; an aid, which no more interferes with our faculties, than the assistance which we receive from our fellow beings; an aid, which silently mingles and conspires with all other helps and means of goodness; an aid by which we unfold our natural powers in a natural order, and by which we are strengthened to understand and apply the resources derived from our munificent Creator. This aid we cannot pursue too much, or pray for too earnestly. But wherein, let me ask, does it war with the doctrine, that God is to be approached by the exercise and unfolding of our highest powers and affections, in the ordinary circumstances of human life?

I repeat it, to resemble our Maker we need not quarrel with nature or our lot. Our present state, made up, as it is, of aids and trials, is worthy of God, and may be used throughout to assimilate us to him. For example, our domestic ties, the relations of neighbourhood and country, the daily interchanges of thoughts and feelings, the daily occasions of kindness, the daily claims of want and suffering, these and the other circumstances of our social state, form the best sphere and school for that benevolence, which is God's brightest attribute; and we should make a sad exchange, by substituting for these natural aids, any self-invented artificial means of sanctity. Christianity, our great guide to God, never leads us away from the path of nature, and never wars with the unsophisticated dictates of conscience. We approach our Creator by every right exertion of the powers he gives us. Whenever we invigorate the understanding by honestly and resolutely seeking truth, and by withstanding whatever might warp the judgment; whenever we invigorate the conscience by following it in opposition to the passions; whenever we receive a blessing gratefully, bear a trial patiently, or encounter peril or scorn with moral courage; whenever we perform a disinterested deed; whenever we lift up the heart in true adoration to God; whenever we war against a habit or desire which is strengthening itself against our higher principles; whenever we think, speak, or act, with moral energy, and resolute devotion to duty, be the occasion ever so humble, obscure, familiar, then the divinity is growing within us, and we are ascending towards our Author. True religion thus blends itself with common life. We are thus to draw nigh to God, without forsaking men. We are thus, without parting with our human nature, to clothe ourselves with the divine.

My views on the great subject of this discourse have now been given. I shall close with a brief consideration of a few objections, in the course of which I shall offer some views of the christian ministry, which this occasion and the state of the world, seem to me to demand.—I anticipate from some an objection to this discourse, drawn as they will say from experience. I may be told, that I have talked of the godlike capacities of human nature, and have spoken of man as a divinity; and where, it will be asked, are the warrants of this high estimate of our race? I may be told that I dream, and that I have peopled the world with the creatures of my lonely imagination. What! Is it only in dreams, that beauty and loveliness have beamed on me from the human countenance, that I have heard tones of kindness, which have thrilled through my heart, that I have found sympathy in suffering, and a sacred joy in friendship? Are all the great and good men of past ages only dreams? Are such names as Moses, Socrates, Paul, Alfred, Milton, only the fictions of my disturbed slumbers?[1] Are the great deeds of history, the discoveries of philosophy, the creations of genius, only visions? Oh! no. I do not dream when I speak of the divine capacities of human nature. It was a real page in which I read of patriots and martyrs, of Fenelon and Howard, of Hampden and Washington.[2] And tell me not that these were prodigies, miracles, immeasurably separated from their race; for their very reverence, which has treasured up and hallowed their memories, the very sentiments of admiration and love with which their names are now heard, show that the principles of their greatness are diffused through all your breasts. The germs of sublime virtue are scattered liberally on our earth. How often have I seen in the obscurity of domestic life, a strength of love, of endurance, of pious trust, of virtuous resolution, which in a public sphere would have attracted public homage. I cannot but pity the man, who recognises nothing godlike in his own nature. I see the marks of God in the heavens and the earth; but how much more in a liberal intellect, in magnanimity, in unconquerable rectitude, in a philanthropy which forgives every error, and which, never despairs of the cause of Christ and human virtue. I do and I must reverence human nature. Neither the sneers of a worldly scepticism, nor the groans of a gloomy theology, disturb my faith in its godlike powers and tendencies. I know how it is despised, how it has been oppressed, how civil and religious establishments have for ages conspired to crush it. I know its history. I shut my eyes on none of its weaknesses and crimes. I understand the proofs, by which despotism demonstrates, that man is a wild beast, in want of a master, and only safe in chains. But injured, trampled on, and scorned as our nature is, I still turn to it with intense sympathy and strong hope. The signatures of its origin and its end are impressed too deeply to be ever wholly effaced. I bless it for its kind affections, for its strong and tender love. I honor it for its struggles against oppression, for its growth and progress under the weight of so many chains and prejudices, for its achievements in science and art, and still more for its examples of heroic and saintly virtue. These are marks of a divine origin and the pledges of a celestial inheritance; and I thank God that my own lot is bound up with that of the human race.

But another objection starts up. It may be said, 'Allow these views to be true; are they fitted for the pulpit? fitted to act on common minds? They may be prized by men of cultivated intellect and taste; but can the multitude understand them? Will the multitude feel them? On whom has a minister to act? On men immersed in business, and buried in the flesh; on men, whose whole power of thought has been spent on pleasure or gain; on men, chained by habit, and wedded to sin. Sooner may adamant be riven by a child's touch, than the human heart be pierced by refined and elevated sentiment. Gross instruments will alone act on gross minds. Men sleep, and nothing but thunder, nothing but flashes from the everlasting fire of hell, will thoroughly wake them.'

I have all along felt that such objections would be made to the views I have urged. But they do not move me. I answer, that I think these views singularly adapted to the pulpit, and I think them full of power. The objection is that they are *refined*. But I see God accomplishing his noblest purposes by what may be called refined means. All the great agents of nature, attraction, heat, and the principle of life, are refined, spiritual, invisible, acting gently, silently, imperceptibly; and yet brute matter feels their power, and is transformed by them into surpassing beauty. The electric fluid, unseen, unfelt, and everywhere diffused, is infinitely more efficient, and ministers to infinitely nobler productions, than when it breaks forth in thunder. Much less can I believe, that in the moral world, noise, menace, and violent appeals to gross passions, to fear and selfishness, are God's chosen means of calling forth spiritual life, beauty, and greatness. It is seldom that human nature throws off all susceptibility of grateful and generous impressions, all sympathy with superior virtue; and here are springs and principles to which a generous teaching, if simple, sincere, and fresh from the soul, may confidently appeal.

It is said, men cannot *understand* the views which seem to me so precious. This objection I am anxious to repel, for the common intellect has been grievously kept down and wronged through the belief of its incapacity. The pulpit would do more good, were not the mass of men looked upon and treated as children. Happily for the race, the time is passing away, in which intellect was thought the monopoly of a few, and the majority were given over to helpless ignorance. Science is leaving her solitudes to enlighten the multitude. How much more may religious teachers take courage to speak to men on subjects, which are nearer to them than the properties and laws of matter, I mean their own souls. The multitude, you say, want capacity to receive the great truths relating to their spiritual nature. But what, let me ask you, is the christian religion? A spiritual system, intended to turn men's minds upon themselves, to frame them to watchfulness over thought, imagination, and passion, to establish them in an intimacy with their own souls. What are all the christian virtues, which men are exhorted to love and seek? I answer, pure and high motions or determinations of the mind. That refinement of thought, which, I am told, transcends the common intellect, belongs to the very essence of Christianity. In confirmation of these views, the human mind seems to me to be turning itself more and more inward, and to be growing more alive to its own worth, and its capacities of progress. The spirit of education shows this, and so does the spirit of freedom. There is a spreading conviction that man was made for a higher purpose than to be a beast of burden, or a creature of sense. The divinity is stirring within the human breast, and demanding a culture and a liberty worthy of the child of God. Let religious teaching correspond to this advancement of the mind. Let it rise above the technical, obscure, and frigid theology which has come down to us from times of ignorance, superstition, and slavery. Let it penetrate the human soul, and reveal it to itself. No preaching, I believe, is so intelligible, as that which is true to human nature, and helps men to read their own spirits.

But the objection which I have stated not only represents men as incapable of understanding, but still more of being moved, quickened, sanctified, and saved, by such views as I have given. If by this objection nothing more is meant, than that these views are not alone or of themselves sufficient, I shall not dispute it; for true and glorious as they are, they do not constitute the whole truth, and I do not expect great moral effects from narrow and partial views of our nature. I have spoken of the godlike capacities of the soul. But other and very different elements enter into the human being. Man has animal propensities as well as intellectual and moral powers. He has a body as well as mind. He has passions to war with reason, and self-love with conscience. He is a free being and a tempted being, and, thus constituted he may and does sin, and often sins grievously. To such a being, religion, or virtue, is a conflict, requiring great spiritual effort, put forth in habitual watchfulness and prayer; and all the motives are needed, by which force and constancy may be communicated to the will. I exhort not the preacher, to talk perpetually of man as 'made but a little lower than the angels.' I would not narrow him to any class of topics. Let him adapt himself to our whole and various nature. Let him summon to his aid all the powers of this world, and the world to come. Let him bring to bear on the conscience and the heart, God's milder and more awful attributes, the promises and threatenings of the divine word, the lessons of history, the warnings of experience. Let the wages of sin here and hereafter be taught clearly and earnestly. But amidst the various motives to spiritual effort, which belong to the minister, none are more quickening than those drawn from the soul itself, and from God's desire and purpose to exalt it, by every aid consistent with its freedom. These views I conceive are to mix with all others, and without them all others fail to promote a generous virtue. Is it said, that the minister's proper work is, to preach Christ and not the dignity of human nature? I answer, that Christ's greatness is manifested in the greatness of the nature which he was sent to redeem; and that his chief glory consists in this, that he came to restore God's image where it was obscured or effaced, and to give an everlasting impulse and life to what is divine within us. Is it said, that the malignity of sin is to be the minister's great theme? I answer, that this malignity can only be understood and felt, when sin is viewed as the ruin of God's noblest work, as darkening a light brighter than the sun, as carrying discord, bondage, disease, and death into a mind framed for perpetual progress towards its Author. Is it said, that terror is the chief instrument of saving the soul? I answer, that if by terror, be meant a rational and moral fear, a conviction and dread of the unutterable evil incurred by a mind which wrongs, betrays, and destroys itself, then I am the last to deny its importance. But a fear like this, which regards the debasement of the soul as the greatest of evils, is plainly founded upon and proportioned to our conceptions of the greatness of our nature. The more common terror, excited by vivid images of torture and bodily pain, is a very questionable means of virtue. When strongly awakened, it generally injures the character, breaks men into cowards and slaves, brings the intellect to cringe before human authority, makes man abject before his Maker, and, by a natural reaction of the mind, often terminates in a presumptuous confidence, altogether distinct from virtuous self-respect, and singularly hostile to the unassuming, charitable spirit of Christianity. The preacher should rather strive to fortify the soul against physical pains, than to bow it to their mastery, teaching it to dread nothing in comparison with sin, and to dread sin as the ruin of a noble nature.

Men, I repeat it, are to be quickened and raised by appeals to their highest principles. Even the convicts of a prison may be touched by kindness, generosity, and especially by a tone, look, and address, expressing hope and respect for their nature. I know, that the doctrine of ages has been, that terror, restraint, and bondage are the chief safeguards of human virtue and peace. But we have begun to learn that affection, confidence, respect, and freedom are mightier as well as nobler agents. Men *can* be wrought upon by generous influences. I would that this truth were better understood by religious teachers. From the pulpit generous influences too seldom proceed. In the church men too seldom hear a voice to quicken and exalt them. Religion, speaking through her public organs, seems often to forget her natural tone of elevation. The character of God, the principles of his government, his relations to the human family, the purposes for which he brought us into being, the nature which he has given us, and the condition in which he has placed us, these and the like topics, though the sublimest which can enter the mind, are not unfrequently so set forth as to narrow and degrade the hearers, disheartening and oppressing with gloom the timid and sensitive, and infecting coarser minds with the unhallowed spirit of intolerance, presumption, and exclusive pretension to the favor of God. I know, and rejoice to know, that preaching in its worst forms does good; for so bright and piercing is the light of Christianity, that it penetrates in a measure the thickest clouds in which men contrive to involve it. But that evil mixes with the good, I also know; and I should be unfaithful to my deep convictions, did I not say, that human nature requires for its elevation, more generous treatment from the teachers of religion.

I conclude with saying, let the minister cherish a reverence for his own nature. Let him never despise it even in its most forbidding forms. Let him delight in its beautiful and lofty manifestations. Let him hold fast as one of the great qualifications for his office, a faith in the greatness of the human soul, that faith, which looks beneath the perishing body, beneath the sweat of the laborer, beneath the rags and ignorance of the poor, beneath the vices of the sensual and selfish, and discerns in the depths of the soul a divine principle, a ray of the Infinite Light, which may yet break forth and 'shine as the sun' in the kingdom of God. Let him strive to awaken in men a consciousness of the heavenly treasure within them, a consciousness of possessing what is of more worth than the outward universe. Let hope give life to all his labors. Let him speak to men, as to beings liberally gifted, and made for God. Let him always look round on a congregation with the encouraging trust, that he has hearers prepared to respond to the simple, unaffected utterance of great truths, and to the noblest workings of his own mind. Let him feel deeply for those, in whom the divine nature is overwhelmed by the passions. Let him sympathize tenderly with those, in whom it begins to struggle, to mourn for sin, to thirst for a new life. Let him guide and animate to higher and diviner virtue those, in whom it has gained strength. Let him strive to infuse courage, enterprise, devout trust, and an inflexible will, into men's labors for their own perfection. In one word, let him cherish an unfaltering and growing faith in God as the Father and quickener of the human mind, and in Christ as its triumphant and immortal friend. That by such preaching he is to work miracles, I do not say. That he will rival in sudden and outward effects what is wrought by the preachers of a low and terrifying theology, I do not expect or desire. That all will be made better, I am far from believing. His office is to act on free beings, who after all must determine themselves; who have power to withstand all foreign agency; who are to be saved, not by mere preaching, but by their own prayers and toil. Still I believe, that such a minister will be a benefactor beyond all praise to the human soul. I believe, and know, that on those, who will admit his influence, he will work deeply, powerfully, gloriously. His function is the sublimest under heaven; and his reward will be, a growing power of spreading truth, virtue, moral strength, love, and happiness, without limit, and without end.

Source: William Ellery Channing, *A Discourse Delivered at the Ordination of the Rev. Frederick A. Farley, as Pastor of the Westminster Congregational Society in Providence, Rhode Island, September 10, 1828* (Boston: Bowles and Dearborn, 1828); titled "Likeness to God" in later editions of Channing's works.

Notes

1. Socrates (ca. 470–399 B.C.), one of the most famous Greek philosophers, known for his dialogic method of teaching, which gained many adherents; Alfred the Great (849–899), King of England from 871 to his death; John Milton (1608–1674), English poet and political writer.
2. François de Salignac de La Motte-Fénelon (1651–1715), French archbishop and man of letters; John Howard (1726–1790), English prison reformer and philanthropist; John Hampden (1594–1643), English statesman who supported Parliament against the attempts of King Charles I to abolish it.

Sampson Reed

"Genius"

(1821)

SAMPSON REED (1800–1880) was an unlikely figure to command the interest and respect of the Transcendentalists, becoming, after he was graduated from Harvard in 1821, both a druggist and a follower of Emanuel Swedenborg. Nevertheless, his "Oration on Genius," delivered at his graduation, so impressed young Waldo Emerson, who was in the audience, that he asked to read a copy in manuscript, which he then partially copied himself and circulated among friends. Emerson quoted Reed's works into the 1870s. Reed's anti-Lockean belief in the innate ability of people would feed into the romantic debate about genius versus talent, and his work was finally published in 1849 in the sole issue of Elizabeth Palmer Peabody's *Aesthetic Papers*.

The world was always busy; the human heart has always had love of some kind; there has always been fire on the earth. There is something in the inmost principles of an individual, when he begins to exist, which argues him onward; there is something in the centre of the character of a nation, to which the people aspire; there is something which gives activity to the mind in all ages, countries, and worlds. This principle of activity is love: it may be the love of good or of evil; it may manifest itself in saving life or in killing; but it is love.

The difference in the strength and direction of the affections creates the distinctions in society. Every man has a form of mind peculiar to himself. The mind of the infant contains within itself the first rudiments of all that will be hereafter, and needs nothing but expansion; as the leaves and branches and fruit of a tree are said to exist in the seed from which it springs. He is bent in a particular direction; and, as some objects are of more value than others, distinctions must exist. What it is that makes a man great depends upon the state of society: with the savage, it is physical strength; with the civilized, the arts and sciences; in heaven, the perception that love and wisdom are from the Divine.

There prevails an idea in the world, that its great men are more like God than others. This sentiment carries in its bosom sufficient evil to bar the gates of heaven. So far as a person possesses it, either with respect to himself or others, he has no connection with his Maker, no love for his neighbor, no truth in his understanding. This was at the root of heathen idolatry: it was this that made men worship saints and images. It contains within itself the seeds of atheism, and will ultimately make every man insane by whom it is cherished. The life which circulates in the body is found to commence in the head; but, unless it be traced through the soul up to God, it is merely corporeal, like that of the brutes.

Man has often ascribed to his own power the effects of the secret operations of divine truth. When the world is immersed in darkness, this is a judgment of the Most High; but the light is the effect of the innate strength of the human intellect.

When the powers of man begin to decay, and approach an apparent dissolution, who cannot see the Divinity? But what foreign aid wants the man who is full of his own strength? God sends the lightning that blasts the tree; but what credulity would ascribe to him the sap that feeds its branches? The sight of idiotism leads to a train of religious reflections; but the face that is marked with lines of intelligence is admired for its own inherent beauty. The hand of the Almighty is visible to all in the stroke of death; but few see his face in the smiles of the new-born babe.

The intellectual eye of man is formed to see the light, not to make it; and it is time that, when the causes that cloud the spiritual world are removed, man should rejoice in the truth itself, and not that *he* has found it. More than once, when nothing was required but for a person to stand on this world with his eyes open, has the truth been seized upon as a thing of his own making. When the power of divine truth begins to dispel the darkness, the objects that are first disclosed to our view—whether men of strong understanding, or of exquisite taste, or of deep learning—are called geniuses. Luther, Shakespeare, Milton, Newton, stand with the bright side towards us.[1]

There is something which is called genius, that carries in itself the seeds of its own destruction. There is an ambition which hurries a man after truth, and takes away the power of attaining it. There is a desire which is null, a lust which is impotence. There is no understanding so powerful, that ambition may not in time bereave it of its last truth, even that two and two are four. Know, then, that genius is divine, not when the man thinks that he is God, but when he acknowledges that his powers are from God. Here is the link of the finite with the infinite, of the divine with the human: this is the humility which exalts.

The arts have been taken from nature by human invention; and, as the mind returns to its God, they are in a measure swallowed up in the source from which they came. We see, as they vanish, the standard to which we should refer them. They are not arbitrary, having no foundation except in taste: they are only modified by taste, which varies according to the state of the human mind. Had we a history of music, from the war-song of the savage to the song of angels, it would be a history of the affections that have held dominion over the human heart. Had we a history of architecture, from the first building erected by man to the house not made with hands, we might trace the variations of the beautiful and the grand, alloyed by human contrivance, to where they are lost in beauty and grandeur. Had we a history of poetry, from the first rude effusions to where words make one with things, and language is lost in nature, we should see the state of man in the language of licentious passion, in the songs of chivalry, in the descriptions of heroic valor, in the mysterious wildness of Ossian;[2] till the beauties of nature fall on the heart, as softly as the clouds on the summer's water. The mind, as it wanders from heaven, moulds the arts into its own form, and covers its nakedness. Feelings of all kinds will discover themselves in music, in painting, in poetry; but it is only when the heart is purified from every selfish and worldly passion, that they are created in real beauty; for in their origin they are divine.

Science is more fixed. It consists of the laws according to which natural things exist; and these must be either true or false. It is the natural world in the abstract, not in the concrete. But the laws according to which things exist, are from the things themselves, not the opposite. Matter has solidity; solidity makes no part of matter. If, then, the natural world is from God, the abstract properties, as dissected and combined, are from him also. If, then, science be from Him who gave the ten commandments, must not a life according to the latter facilitate the acquirement of the former? Can *he* love the works of God who does not love his commandments? It is only necessary that the heart be purified, to have science like poetry its spontaneous growth. Self-love has given rise to many false theories, because a selfish man is disposed to make things differently from what God has made them. Because God is love, nature exists; because God is love, the Bible is poetry. If, then, the love of God creates the scenery of nature, must not he whose mind is most open to this love be most sensible of natural beauties? But in nature both the sciences and the arts exist embodied.

Science may be learned from ambition; but it must be by the sweat of the brow. The filthy and polluted mind *may* carve beauties from nature, with which it has no allegiance: the rose is blasted in the gathering. The olive and the vine had rather live with God, than crown the head of him whose love for them is a lust for glory. The man is cursed who would rob nature of her graces, that he may use them to allure the innocent virgin to destruction.

Men say there is an inspiration in genius. The genius of the ancients was the good or evil spirit that attended the man. The moderns speak of the magic touch of the pencil, and of the inspiration of poetry. But this inspiration has been esteemed so unlike religion, that the existence of the one almost supposes the absence of the other. The spirit of God is thought to be a very different thing when poetry is written, from what it is when the heart is sanctified. What has the inspiration of genius in common with that of the cloister? The one courts the zephyrs; the other flies them. The one is cheerful; the other, sad. The one dies; the other writes the epitaph. Would the Muses take the veil?[3] Would they exchange Parnassus for a nunnery?[4] Yet there has been learning, and even poetry, under ground. The yew loves the graveyard; but other trees have grown there.

It needs no uncommon eye to see, that the finger of death has rested on the church. Religion and death have in the human mind been connected with the same train of associations. The churchyard is the graveyard. The bell which calls men to worship is to toll at their funerals, and the garments of the priests are of the color of the hearse and the coffin. Whether we view her in the strange melancholy that sits on her face, in her mad reasonings about truth, or in the occasional convulsions that agitate her limbs, there are symptoms, not of life, but of disease and death. It is not strange, then, that genius, such as could exist on the earth, should take its flight to the mountains. It may be said, that great men are good men. But what I mean is, that, in the human mind, greatness is one thing, and goodness another; that philosophy is divorced from religion; that truth is separated from its source; that that which is called goodness is sad, and that which is called genius is proud.

Since things are so, let men take care that the life which is received be genuine. Let the glow on the cheek spring from the warmth of the heart, and the brightness of the eyes beam from the light of heaven. Let ambition and the love of the world be plucked up by their roots. How can he love his neighbor, who desires to be above him? He may love him for a slave; but that is all. Let not the shrouds of death be removed, till the living principle has entered. It was not till Lazarus was raised from the dead, and had received the breath of life, that the Lord said, "Loose him, and let him go."

When the heart is purified from all selfish and worldly affections, then may genius find its seat in the church. As the human mind is cleansed of its lusts, truth will permit and invoke its approach, as the coyness of the virgin subsides into the tender love of the wife. The arts will spring in full-grown beauty from Him who is the source of beauty. The harps which have hung on the willows will sound as sweetly as the first breath of heaven that moved the leaves in the garden of Eden. Cannot a man paint better when he knows that the picture ought not to be worshipped?

Here is no sickly aspiring after fame,—no filthy lust after philosophy, whose very origin is an eternal barrier to the truth. But sentiments will flow from the heart warm as its blood, and speak eloquently; for eloquence is the language of love. There is a unison of spirit and nature. The genius of the mind will descend, and unite with the genius of the rivers, the lakes, and the woods. Thoughts fall to the earth with power, and make a language out of nature.

Adam and Eve knew no language but their garden. They had nothing to communicate by words; for they had not the power of concealment. The sun of the spiritual world shone bright on their hearts, and their senses were open with delight to natural objects. In the eye were the beauties of paradise; in the ear was the music of birds; in the nose was the fragrance of the freshness of nature; in the taste was the fruit of the garden; in the touch, the seal of their eternal union. What had they to *say?*

The people of the golden age have left us no monuments of genius, no splendid columns, no paintings, no poetry. They possessed nothing which evil passions might not obliterate; and, when their "heavens were rolled together as a scroll," the curtain dropped between the world and their existence.

Science will be full of life, as nature is full of God. She will wring from her locks the dew which was gathered in the wilderness. By science, I mean natural science. The science of the human mind must change with its subject. Locke's mind will not always be the standard of metaphysics. Had we a description of it in its present state, it would make a very different book from "Locke on the Human Understanding."[5]

The time is not far distant. The cock has crowed. I hear the distant lowing of the cattle which are grazing on the mountains. "Watchman, what of the night? Watchman, what of the night?" The watchman saith, "The morning cometh."

Source: Sampson Reed, "Genius" (1821), *Aesthetic Papers*, 1 (1849): 58–64. For Emerson's later use of Reed, see Ronald A. Bosco, "His Lectures Were Poetry, His Teaching the Music of the Spheres: Annie Adams Fields and Francis Greenwood Peabody on Emerson's 'Natural History of the Intellect' University Lectures at Harvard in 1870," *Harvard Library Bulletin*, n.s. 8 (Summer 1997): 14*n*22, 19, 27*n*60, 31*n*97.

1. Martin Luther (1483–1546), famous German prelate who began the Reformation; Sir Isaac Newton (1642–1727), English mathematician and natural philosopher known for his work on gravity.
2. Ossian, the supposed third-century Gaelic author of the verses "translated" between 1760 and 1763 by James Macpherson (1736–1796), proved to be a fraud, to the disappointment of his many admirers.
3. Muses, the nine goddesses who presided over the arts and sciences.
4. Mount Parnassus, in ancient Greece, was considered sacred to Apollo, the Roman god of sun and music, and thus became the seat of the arts.
5. John Locke (1632–1704), English founder of the sensationalist school of philosophy, believed that all our knowledge comes through the experience of the senses. He published his *Essay Concerning Human Understanding* in 1690.

Sampson Reed

Observations on the Growth of the Mind

(1826)

REED's book would go through numerous editions, the last in 1889, making it one of the most valuable statements of Swedenborgianism for the period. It contains ideas about the correspondences between the heavenly and the physical worlds (the invisible and the visible), the ability of the mind to create and fix reality, education as an unfolding of innate abilities rather than being the sum of learned knowledge, the role of the poet, and biblical interpretation. It also shows how the world grows through organic means (form follows function), how language begins and is used, and how spiritualism differs from materialism. Although much of this pamphlet can be seen as a template for many of the Transcendentalist ideas that followed, Reed disassociated himself from the movement in his preface to the 1838 edition of *Observations*, calling it "the product of man's own brain; and when the human mind has been compelled to relax its grip on sensualism, and the philosophy based on the senses, it may first be expected to take refuge here."

\\\///,

So build we up the Being that we are;
Thus deeply drinking-in the Soul of Things
We shall be wise perforce; and while inspired

By choice, and conscious that the will is free,
Unswerving shall we move, as if impell'd
By strict necessity, along the path
Of order and of good.

         —Wordsworth, *The Excursion*

Nothing is a more common subject of remark than the changed condition of the world. There is a more extensive intercourse of thought, and a more powerful action of mind upon mind than formerly. The good and the wise of all nations are brought nearer together, and begin to exert a power, which though yet feeble as infancy, is felt throughout the globe. Public opinion, that helm which directs the progress of events by which the world is guided to its ultimate destination, has received a new direction. The mind has attained an upward and onward look, and is shaking off the errors and prejudices of the past. The gothic structure of the feudal ages, the ornament of the desert, has been exposed to the light of heaven; and continues to be gazed at for its ugliness, as it ceases to be admired for its antiquity. The world is deriving vigour, not from that which is gone by, but from that which is coming; not from the unhealthy moisture of the evening, but from the nameless influences of the morning. The loud call on the past to instruct us, as it falls on the rock of ages, comes back in echo from the future. Both mankind, and the laws and principles by which they are governed, seem about to be redeemed from slavery. The moral and intellectual character of man has undergone, and is undergoing a change; and as this is effected it must change the aspect of all things, as when the position-point is altered from which a landscape is viewed. We appear to be approaching an age which will be the silent pause of merely physical force before the powers of the mind; the timid, subdued, awed condition of the brute, gazing on the erect and godlike form of man.

These remarks with respect to the present era are believed to be just, when it is viewed on the bright side. They are not made by one who is insensible to its evils. Least of all are they intended to countenance that feeling of self-admiration, which carries with it the seeds of premature disease and deformity; for to be proud of the truth is to cease to possess it. Since the fall of man, nothing has been more difficult for him than to know his real condition, since every departure from divine order is attended with a loss of the knowledge of what it is. When our first parents left the garden of Eden, they took with them no means by which they might measure the depths of degradation to which they fell; no chart by which they might determine their moral longitude. Most of our knowledge implies relation and comparison. It is not difficult for one age, or one individual, to be compared with another; but this determines only their relative condition. The actual condition of man, can be seen only from the relation in which he stands to his immutable creator; and this relation is discovered from the light of revelation, so far as by conforming to the precepts of revelation, it is permitted to exist according to the laws of divine order. It is not sufficient that the letter of the Bible is in the world. This may be, and still mankind continue in ignorance of themselves. It must be obeyed from the heart to the hand. The book must he eat, and constitute the living flesh. When only the relative condition of the world is regarded, we are apt to exult over other ages and other men, as if we ourselves were a different order of beings, till at length we are enveloped in the very mists from which we are proud of being cleared. But when the relative state of the world is justly viewed from the real state of the individual, the scene is lighted from the point of the beholder with the chaste light of humility which never deceives; it is not forgotten that the way lies forward; the cries of exultation cease to be heard in the march of progression, and the mind, in whatever it learns of the past and the present, finds food for improvement, and not for vain-glory.

As all the changes which are taking place in the world originate in the mind, it might be naturally expected that nothing would change more than the mind itself, and whatever is connected with a description of it. While men have been speculating concerning their own powers, the sure but secret influence of revelation has been gradually changing the moral and intellectual character of the world, and the ground on which they were standing has passed from under them, almost while their words were in their mouths. The powers of the mind are most intimately connected with the subjects by which they are occupied. We cannot think of the will without feeling, of the understanding without thought, or of the imagination without something like poetry. The mind is visible when it is active; and as the subjects on which it is engaged are changed, the powers themselves present a different aspect. New classifications arise, and new names are given. What was considered simple is thought to consist of distinct parts, till at length the philosopher hardly knows whether the African be of the same or a different species; and though the soul is thought to continue after death, angels are universally considered a distinct class of intellectual beings. Thus it is that there is nothing fixed in the philosophy of the mind; it is said to be a science which is not demonstrative; and though now thought to be brought to a state of great perfection, another century under the providence of God, and nothing will be found in the structure which has cost so much labour, but the voice "he is not here, but is risen."

Is then every thing that relates to the immortal part of man fleeting and evanescent, while the laws of physical nature remain unaltered? Do things become changeable as we approach the immutable and the eternal? Far otherwise. The laws of the mind are in themselves as fixed and perfect as the laws of matter; but they are laws from which we have wandered. There is a philosophy of the mind, founded not on the aspect it presents in any part or in any period of the world, but on its immutable relations to its first cause; a philosophy equally applicable to man, before or after he has passed the valley of the shadow of death; not dependent on time or place, but immortal as its subject. The light of this philosophy has begun to beam faintly on the world, and mankind will yet see their own moral and intellectual nature by the light of revelation, as it shines through the moral and intellectual character it shall have itself created. It may be remarked also that the changes in the sciences and the arts are entirely the effect of revelation. To revelation it is to be ascribed, that the genius which has taught the laws of the heavenly bodies and analyzed the material world, did not spend itself in drawing the bow or in throwing the lance, in the chase or in war; and that the vast powers of Handel did not burst forth in the wild notes of the war-song.[1] It is the tendency of revelation to give a right direction to every power of every mind; and when this is effected, inventions and discoveries will follow of course, all things assume a different aspect, and the world itself again become a paradise.

It is the object of the following pages not to be influenced by views of a temporal or local nature, but to look at the mind as far as possible in its essential revealed character, and beginning with its powers of acquiring and retaining truth, to trace summarily that development which is required, in order to render it truly useful and happy. It is believed that they will not be found at variance with the state of the public mind on the subject of education, whether of the child or the man.

It was said, *the powers of acquiring and retaining truth*, because truth is not retained without some continued exertion of the same powers by which it is acquired. There is the most intimate connexion of the memory with the affections. This connexion is obvious from many familiar expressions; such as remember me to any one, by which is signified a desire to be borne in his or her affections—do not forget me, by which is meant do not cease to love me—get by heart, which means commit to memory. It is also obvious from observation of our own minds; from the constant recurrence of those subjects which we most love, and the extreme difficulty of detaching our own minds or the minds of others from a favourite pursuit. It is obvious from the power of attention on which the memory principally depends, which if the subject have a place in our affections requires no effort; if it have not, the effort consists principally in giving it a real or an artificial hold of our feelings, as it is possible if we do not love a subject, to attend to it because it may add to our fame or our wealth. It is obvious from the never fading freshness retained by the scenes of childhood, when the feelings are strong and vivid, through the later periods of life. As the old man looks back on the road of his pilgrimage, many years of active life lie unseen in the valley, as his eye rests on the rising ground of his younger days; presenting a beautiful illustration of the manner in which the human mind when revelation shall have accomplished its work, shall no longer regard the scene of sin and misery behind, but having completed the circle, shall rest as next to the present moment on the golden age, the infancy of the world. The connexion of the memory with the affections is also obvious from the association of ideas; since the train of thoughts suggested by any scene or event in any individual, depends on his own peculiar and prevailing feelings; as whatever enters into the animal system whenever it may arise, seems first to be recognized as a part of the man, when it has found its way to the heart, and received from that its impulse. It is but a few years, (how strange to tell,) since man discovered that the blood circulated through the human body. We have perhaps, hardly learned the true nature of that intellectual circulation, which gives life and health to the human mind. The affections are to the soul, what the heart is to the body. They send forth their treasures with a vigour not less powerful, though not material, throughout the intellectual man, strengthening and nourishing; and again receive those treasures to themselves, enlarged by the effect of their own operation.

Memory is the *effect* of learning, through whatever avenue it may have entered the mind. It is said the *effect*; because the man who has read a volume and can perhaps tell you nothing of its contents, but simply express his own views on the same subject with more clearness and precision, may as truly be said to have remembered, as he that can repeat the very words. In the one case, the powers of the mind have received a new tone; in the other, they are encumbered with a useless burthen—in the one, they are made stronger; in the other they are more oppressed with weight—in the one, the food is absorbed and becomes a part of the man; in the other it lies on the stomach in a state of crude indigestion.

There is no power more various in different individuals, than the memory. This may be ascribed to two reasons. First, this partakes of every power of the mind, since every mental exertion is a subject of memory, and may therefore be said to indicate all the difference that actually exists. Secondly, this power varies in its character as it has more or less to do with time. Simple divine truth has nothing to do with time. It is the same yesterday, to-day and to-morrow. The memory of this is simply the development of the mind. But we are so surrounded by facts of a local and temporal nature; the place where, and the time when, make so great a part of what is presented to our consideration; that the attribute is mistaken for the subject, and this power sometimes appears to have exclusive reference to time, though strictly speaking it has no relation to it. There is a power of growth in the spiritual man, and if in his progress we be able to mark as in the grain of the oak the number of the years, this is only a circumstance; and all that is gained would be as real if no such lines existed. The mind ought not to be limited by the short period of its own duration in the body, with a beginning and end comprising a few years; it should be poised on its own immortality, and what is learned, should be learned with a view to that real adaptation of knowledge to the mind which results from the harmony of creation, and whenever or wherever we exist, it will be useful to us. The memory has in reality, nothing to do with time, any more than the eye has with space. As the latter learns by experience to measure the distance of objects, so the consciousness of the present existence of states of mind, is referred to particular periods of the past. But when the soul has entered on its *eternal* state, there is reason to believe that the past and the future will be swallowed up in the present; that memory and anticipation will be lost in consciousness; that every thing of the past will be comprehended in the present, without any reference to time, and every thing of the future will exist in the divine effort of progression.

What is time? There is perhaps no question that would suggest such a variety of answers. It is represented to us from our infancy as producing such important changes, both in destroying some, and in healing the wounds it has inflicted on others, that people generally imagine, if not an actual person, it is at least a real existence. We begin with time in the primer, and end with reasoning about the foreknowledge of God. What is time? The difficulty of answering the question, (and there are few questions more difficult,) arises principally from our having ascribed so many important effects to that which has no real existence. It is true that all things in the natural world are subject to change. But however these changes may be connected in our minds with time, it requires but a moment's reflection to see that time has no agency in them. They are the effects of chemical, or more properly perhaps, of natural decompositions and reorganizations. Time, or rather our idea of it, so far from having produced any thing, is itself the effect of changes. There are certain operations in nature, which depending on fixed laws, are in themselves perfectly regular; if all things were equally so, the question how long? might never be asked. We should never speak of a late season, or of premature old age; but every thing passing on in an invariable order, all the idea of time that would remain with respect to any object, would be a sort of instinctive sense of its condition, its progress or decay. But most of the phenomena in the natural world are exceedingly irregular; for though the same combination of causes would invariably produce the same effect, the same combination very rarely occurs. Hence in almost every change, and we are conversant with nothing but changes, we are assisted in ascertaining its nature and extent, by referring it to something in itself perfectly regular. We find this regularity in the apparent motions of the sun and moon. It is difficult to tell how much our idea of time is the effect of artificial means of keeping it, and what would be our feelings on the subject, if left to the simple operations of nature—but they would probably be little else than a reference of all natural phenomena to that on which they principally depend, the relative situation of the sun and earth; and the idea of an actual succession of moments, would be in a measure resolved into that of cause and effect.

Eternity is to the mind what time is to nature. We attain a perception of it, by regarding all the operations in the world within us, as they exist in relation to their first cause; for in doing this, they are seen to partake somewhat of the nature of that Being on whom they depend. We make no approaches to a conception of it, by heaping day upon day or year upon year. This is merely an accumulation of time; and we might as well attempt to convey an idea of mental greatness by that of actual space, as to communicate a conception of eternity by years or thousands of years. Mind and matter are not more distinct from each other than their properties; and by an attempt to embrace all time we are actually farther from an approach to eternity than when we confine ourselves to a single instant—because we merely collect the largest possible amount of natural changes, whereas that which is eternal approaches that which is immutable. This resembles the attempt to ascend to heaven by means of the tower of Babel, in which they were removed by their pride from that which they would have approached, precisely in proportion to their apparent progress. It is impossible to conceive of either time or space without matter. The reason is, they are the effect of matter; and as it is by creating matter that they are produced, so it is by thinking of it that they are conceived of. It need not be said how exceedingly improper it is to apply the usual ideas of time and space to the Divine Being; making him subject to that which he creates.

Still our conceptions of time, of hours, days or years, are among the most vivid we possess, and we neither wish nor find it easy to call them in question. We are satisfied with the fact; that time is indicated on the face of the watch; without seeking for it among the wheels and machinery. But what is the idea of a year? Every natural change that comes under our observation, leaves a corresponding impression on the mind; and the sum of the changes which come under a single revolution of the earth round the sun, conveys the impression of a year. Accordingly, we find that our idea of a year is continually changing, as the mind becomes conversant with different objects, and is susceptible of different impressions; and the days of the old man as they draw near their close, seem to gather rapidity from their approach to the other world. We have all experienced the effect of pleasure and pain in accelerating and retarding the passing moments; and since our feelings are constantly changing, we have no reason to doubt, that they constantly produce a similar effect, though it may not be often noticed. The divisions of time then, however real they may seem to be, and however well they may serve the common purposes of conversation, cannot be supposed to convey the same impression to any two minds, nor to any one mind in different periods of its existence. Indeed, unless this were the fact, all artificial modes of keeping it, would be unnecessary. Time then, is nothing real so far as it exists in our own minds.

Nor do we find a nearer approach to reality, by any analysis of nature. Every thing as was said, is subject to change, and one change prepares the way for another; by which there is growth and decay. There are also motions of bodies both in nature and art, which in their operation observe fixed laws, and here we end. The more we enter into an analysis of things, the farther are we from finding any thing that answers to the distinctness and reality which are usually attached to a conception of time; and there is reason to believe that when this distinctness and reality are most deeply rooted, (whatever may be the theory) they are uniformly attended with a practical belief of the actual motion of the sun, and are indeed the effect of it. Let us then continue to talk of time, as we talk of the rising and setting of the sun; but let us think rather of those changes in their origin and effect, from which a sense of time is produced. This will carry us one degree nearer the actual condition of things; it will admit us one step further into the temple of creation—no longer a temple created six thousand years ago, and deserted by him who formed it; but a temple with the hand of the builder resting upon it, perpetually renewing, perpetually creating—

and as we bow ourselves to worship the "I am," "Him who liveth forever and ever, who created heaven and the things that are therein, and the earth and the things that are therein, and the sea and the things that are therein," we may hear in accents of divine love the voice that proclaims "that there shall be time no longer."

It is not the living productions of nature, by which the strongest impression of time is produced. The oak over which may have passed a hundred years, seems to drive from our minds the impression of time, by the same power by which it supports its own life, and resists every tendency to decay. It is that which is decayed, though it may have been the offspring of an hour—it is the ruined castle mouldering into dust, still more, if the contrast be strengthened by its being covered with the living productions of nature—it is the half consumed remains of some animal, once strong and vigorous, the discoveries of the undertaker, or the filthy relics of the catacomb, by which the strongest impression of time is conveyed. So it is with the possessions of the mind. It is that which is not used, which seems farthest in the memory, and which is held by the most doubtful tenure; that which is suffered to waste and decay because it wants the life of our own affections; that which we are about to lose because it does not properly belong to us—whereas that truth, which is applied to the use and service of mankind, acquires a higher polish the more it is thus employed, like the angels of heaven, who forever approximate to a state of perfect youth, beauty and innocence. It is not a useless task then, to remove from our minds the usual ideas of time, and cultivate a memory of things. It is to leave the mind in the healthy, vigorous and active possession of all its attainments, and exercise all its powers—it is to remove from it, that only which contains the seeds of decay and putrefaction; to separate the living from the dead; to take from it the veil by which it would avoid the direct presence of Jehovah, and preserve its own possessions without using them.

Truth, all truth is practical. It is impossible from its nature and origin, that it should be otherwise. Whether its effect be directly to change the conduct, or it simply leave an impression on the heart, it is in the strictest sense practical. It should rather be our desire to use what we learn, than to remember it. If we desire to use it, we shall remember it of course; if we wish merely to remember, it is possible we may never use it. It is the tendency of all truth to effect some object. If we look at this object, it will form a distinct and permanent image on the mind; if we look merely at the truth it will vanish away, like rays of light falling into vacancy.

Keeping in view what has been said on the subject of time then, the mind is presented to us, as not merely active in the acquirement of truth, but active in its possession. The memory is the fire of the vestal virgins, sending forth perpetual light; not the grave, which preserves simply because annihilation is impossible. The reservoir of knowledge should be seated in the affections, sending forth its influence throughout the mind and terminating in word and deed, if I may be allowed the expression, merely because its channels and outlets are situated below the watermark. There prevails a most erroneous sentiment, that the mind is originally vacant, and requires only to be filled up; and there is reason to believe, that this opinion is most intimately connected with false conceptions of time. The mind is originally a most delicate germ, whose husk is the body; planted in this world, that the light and heat of heaven may fall upon it with a gentle radiance, and call forth its energies. The process of learning is not by synthesis, or analysis. It is the most perfect illustration of both. As subjects are presented to the operation of the mind, they are decomposed and reorganized in a manner peculiar to itself, and not easily explained.

Another object of the preceding remarks upon time, is that we may be impressed with the immediate presence and agency of God, without which a correct understanding of mind or matter can never be attained; that we may be able to read on every power of the mind, and on every particle of matter the language of our Lord, "My Father worketh hitherto, and I work." We usually put the Divine Being to an immense distance, by supposing that the world was created many years ago, and subjected to certain laws, by which it has since been governed. We find ourselves capable of constructing machines, which move on without our assistance, and imagine that the world was constructed in the same way. We forget that the motions of our machines depend on the uniform operation of what we call the laws of nature; and that there can be nothing beyond, on which these depend, unless it be the agency of that Being from whom they exist. The pendulum of the clock continues to move from the uniform operation of gravitation. It is no explanation, to say that it is a law of our machinery that the pendulum should move. We simply place things in a situation to be acted upon by an all-pervading power—but what all-pervading power is there by which gravitation is itself produced, unless it be the power of God?

The tendency of bodies to the earth, is something with which from our childhood we have been so familiar; something which we have regarded so much as a cause, since in a certain sense it is the cause of all the motions with which we are acquainted; that it is not agreeable to our habits of thinking, to look at it as an effect. Even the motions of the heavenly bodies seem completely accounted for, by simply extending to these phenomena the feelings with which we have been accustomed to regard the tendency of bodies to the earth; whereas if the two things were communicated at the same period of life, they would appear equally wonderful. An event appears to be explained, when it is brought within the pale of those youthful feelings and associations, which in their simplicity do not ask the reason of things. There is formed in the mind of the child, from his most familiar observations, however imperfect they may be, as it were a little nucleus, which serves as the basis of his future progress. This usually comprises a large proportion of those natural appearances, which the philosopher in later periods of life, finds it most difficult to explain. The child grows up in his Father's house, and collects and arranges the most familiar operations and events. Into this collection, he afterwards receives whatever history or science may communicate, and still feels at home; a feeling with which wonder is never associated.

This is not altogether as it should be. It is natural for the mature mind to ask the cause of things. It is unsatisfied when it does not find one, and can hardly exclude the thought of that Being, from whom all things exist. When therefore we have gone beyond the circle of youthful knowledge, and found a phenomenon in nature, which in its insulated state fills us with the admiration of God; let us beware how we quench this feeling. Let us rather transfer something of this admiration to those phenomena of the same class, which have not hitherto directed our minds beyond the fact of their actual existence. As the mind extends the boundaries of its knowledge, let a holy reference to God descend into its youthful treasures. That light which in the distance seemed to be a miraculous blaze, as it falls on our own native hills may still seem divine, but will not surprise us; and a sense of the constant presence of God will be happily blended with the most perfect freedom.

Till the time of Newton, the motion of the heavenly bodies was in the strictest sense a miracle. It was an event which stood alone, and was probably regarded with peculiar reference to the Divine Being. The feeling of worship with which they had previously been regarded, had subsided into a feeling of wonder; till at length they were received into the family of our most familiar associations. There is one step further. It is to regard gravitation wherever it may be found, as an effect of the constant agency of the Divine Being, and from a consciousness of his presence and co-operation in every step we take, literally "to walk humbly with our God." It is agreeable to the laws of moral and intellectual progression, that all phenomena, whether of matter or mind, should become gradually classified; till at length all things, wherever they are found; all events, whether of history or experience, of mind or matter; shall at once conspire to form one stupendous miracle, and cease to be such. They will form a miracle, in that they are seen to depend constantly and equally on the power of the Lord; and they will cease to be a miracle, in that the power which pervades them, is so constant, so uniform and so mild in its operation, that it produces nothing of fear, nothing of surprise. From whatever point we contemplate the scene, we feel that we are still in our Father's house; go where we will, the paternal roof, the broad canopy of heaven is extended over us.

It is agreeable to our nature, that the mind should be particularly determined to one object. The eye appears to be the point, at which the united rays of the sun within and the sun without, converge to an expression of unity; and accordingly the understanding can be conscious of but one idea or image at a time. Still there is another and a different kind of consciousness which pervades the mind, which is coextensive with every thing it actually possesses. There is but one object in nature on which the *eye* looks directly, but the whole body is pervaded with nerves which convey perpetual information of the existence and condition of every part. So it is with the possessions of the mind; and when an object ceases to be the subject of this kind of consciousness, it ceases to be remembered. The memory therefore, as was said, is not a dormant, but an active power. It is rather the possession than the retention of truth. It is a consciousness of the will; a consciousness of character; a consciousness which is produced by the mind's preserving in effort, whatever it actually possesses. It is the power which the mind has of preserving truth, without actually making it the subject of thought; bearing a relation to thought, analagous to what this bears to the actual perception of the senses, or to language. Thus we remember a distant object without actually thinking of it, in the same way that we think of it, without actually seeing it.

The memory is not limited, because to the affections viewed simply as such, number is not applicable. They become distinct and are classified, when connected with truths, or from being developed are applied to their proper objects. Love may be increased, but not multiplied. A man may feel intensely, and the quantity and quality of his feeling may affect the character of his thought, but still it preserves its unity. The most ardent love is not attended with more than one idea, but on the contrary has a tendency to confine the mind to a single object. Every one must have remarked, that a peculiar state of feeling belongs to every exercise of the understanding; unless somewhat of this feeling remained after the thought had passed away, there would be nothing whereby the latter could be recalled. The impression thus left exists continually in the mind; though as different objects engage the attention, it may become less vivid. These impressions go to comprise the character of an individual; especially when they have acquired a reality and fixedness, in consequence of the feelings in which they originated, having resulted in the actions to which they tend. They enter into every subject about which we are thinking, and the particular modification they receive from that subject gives them the appearance of individuality; while they leave on the subject itself, the image of that character which they constitute. When a man has become acquainted with any science, that state of the affections which properly belongs to this science, (whatever direction his mind may take afterwards) still maintains a certain influence; and this influence is the creative power by which his knowledge on the subject is reproduced. Such impressions are to the mind, what logarithms are in numbers; preserving our knowledge in its fulness indeed, but before it has expanded into an infinite variety of thoughts. Brown remarks, "we will the existence of certain ideas, it is said, and they arise in consequence of our volition; though assuredly to will any idea is to know that we will, and therefore to be conscious of that very idea, which we surely need not desire to know when we already know it so well as to will its actual existence."[2] The author does not discriminate between looking at an object and thence desiring it, and simply that condition of feeling between which and certain thoughts there is an established relation, so that the former cannot exist to any considerable degree without producing the latter. Of this exertion of the will, every one must have been conscious in his efforts of recollection. Of this exertion of the will the priest must be conscious, when (if he be sincere) by the simple prostration of his heart before his maker, his mind is crowded with the thoughts and language of prayer. Of this exertion of the will, the post must be conscious, when he makes bare his bosom for the reception of nature, and presents her breathing with his own life and soul. But it is needless to illustrate that of which every one must be sensible.

It follows from these views of the subject, that the true way to store the memory is to develop the affections. The mind must grow, not from external accretion, but from an internal principle. Much may be done by others in aid of its development; but in all that is done, it should not be forgotten, that even from its earliest infancy, it possesses a character and a principle of freedom, which *should be* respected, and *cannot* be destroyed. Its peculiar propensities may be discerned, and proper nutriment and culture supplied—but the infant plant, not less than the aged tree, must be permitted, with its own organs of absorption, to separate that which is peculiarly adapted to itself; otherwise it will be cast off as a foreign substance, or produce nothing but rottenness and deformity.

The science of the mind itself will be the effect of its own development. This is merely an attendant consciousness, which the mind possesses of the growth of its own powers; and therefore it would seem, need not be made a distinct object of study. Thus the power of reason may be imperceptibly developed by the study of the demonstrative sciences. As it is developed, the pupil becomes conscious of its existence and its use. This is enough. He can in fact learn nothing more on the subject. If he learns to use his reason what more is desired? Surely it were useless, and worse than useless, to shut up the door of the senses, and live in indolent and laborious contemplation of one's own powers; when if any thing is learned truly, it must be what these powers are, and therefore that they ought not to be thus employed. The best affections we possess will find their home in the objects around us, and, as it were, enter into and animate the whole rational, animal and vegetable world. If the eye were turned inward to a direct contemplation of these affections, it would find them bereft of all their loveliness; for when they are active, it is not of them we are thinking, but of the objects on which they rest. The science of the mind then, will be the effect of all the other sciences. Can the child grow up in active usefulness, and not be conscious of the possession and use of his own limbs? The body and the mind should grow together, and form the sound and perfect man, whose understanding may be almost measured by his stature. The mind will see itself in what it loves and is able to accomplish. Its own works will be its mirror; and when it is present in the natural world, feeling the same spirit which gives life to every object by which it is surrounded, in its very union with nature it will catch a glimpse of itself, like that of pristine beauty united with innocence, at her own native fountain.

What then is that development which the nature of the human mind requires? What is that education which has heaven for its object, and such a heaven as will be the effect of the orderly growth of the spiritual man?

As all minds possess that in common which makes them human, they require to a certain extent the same general development, by which will be brought to view the same powers however distinct and varied they may be found in different individuals; and as every mind possesses something peculiar, to which it owes its character and its effect, it requires a particular development by which may be produced a full, sincere and humble expression of its natural features, and the most vigorous and efficient exertion of its natural powers. These make one, so far as regards the individual.

Those sciences which exist embodied in the natural world, appear to have been designed to occupy the first place in the development of all minds, or in that which might be called the general development of the mind. These comprise the laws of the animal, vegetable, and mineral kingdoms. The human mind, being as it were planted in nature by its heavenly Father, was designed to enter into matter, and detect knowledge for its own purposes of growth and nutrition. This gives us a true idea of memory, or rather of what memory should be. We no longer think of a truth as being laid up in a mind for which it has no affinity, and by which it is perhaps never to be used; but the latent affections as they expand under proper culture, absolutely require the truth to receive them, and its first use is the very nutriment it affords. It is not more difficult for the tree to return to the seed from which it sprung, than for the man who has learned thus, to cease to remember. The natural sciences are the basis of all useful knowledge, alike important to man in whatever time, place or condition he is found. They are coeval with our race, and must continue so long as the sun, moon and stars endure. Before there were facts for the pen of history to record, or vices for the arm of law to restrain, or nations for the exhibition of institutions for the government of themselves, and intercourse with each other; at the very creation, these were pronounced good in the general benediction—and when history shall have finished her tale of sin and wo, and law shall have punished her millions of offenders, and civil society shall have assumed every possible form, they will remain the same as when presented in living characters to the first parents of the human race. Natural philosophy seems almost essential to an enlightened independence of thought and action. A man may lean upon others, and be so well supported by an equal pressure in all directions, as to be apparently dependent on no one; but his independence is apt to degenerate into obstinacy, or betray itself in weakness, unless his mind is fixed on this unchanging basis. A knowledge of the world may give currency to his sentiments and plausibility to his manners; but it is more frequently a knowledge of *the world* that gives light to the path and stability to the purposes. By the one he may learn what coin is current, by the other what possesses intrinsic value. The natural world was precisely and perfectly adapted to invigorate and strengthen the intellectual and moral man. Its first and highest use was not to support the vegetables which adorn, or the animals which cover its surface; nor yet to give sustenance to the human body—it has a higher and holier object, in the attainment of which these are only means. It was intended to draw forth and mature the latent energies of the soul; to impart to them its own verdure and freshness; to initiate them into its own mysteries; and by its silent and humble dependence on its creator, to leave on them when it is withdrawn by death, the full impression of his likeness.

It was the design of Providence, that the infant mind should possess the germ of every science. If it were not so, they could hardly be learned. The care of God provides for the flower of the field, a place wherein it may grow, regale with its fragrance, and delight with its beauty. Is his providence less active over those, to whom this flower offers its incense? No. The soil which produces the vine in its most healthy luxuriance, is not better adapted to the end, than the world we inhabit to draw forth the latent energies of the soul, and fill them with life and vigour. As well might the eye see without light, or the ear hear without sound; as the human mind be healthy and athletic, without descending into the natural world, and breathing the mountain air. Is there aught in eloquence, which warms the heart? She draws her fire from natural imagery. Is there aught in poetry to enliven the imagination? There is the secret of all her power. Is there aught in science to add strength and dignity to the human mind? The natural world is only the body, of which she is the soul. In books science is presented to the eye of the pupil, as it were in a dried and preserved state; the time may come when the instructer will take him by the hand, and lead him by the running streams, and teach him all the principles of science as she comes from her maker, as he would smell the fragrance of the rose without gathering it.

This love of nature, this adaptation of man to the place assigned him by his heavenly Father, this fulness of the mind as it descends into the works of God, is something which has been felt by every one, though to an imperfect degree; and therefore needs no explanation. It is the part of science, that this be no longer a blind affection, but that the mind be opened to a just perception of what it is, which it loves. The affection, which the lover first feels for his future wife, may be attended only by a general sense of her external beauty; but his mind gradually opens to a perception of the peculiar features of the soul, of which the external appearance is only an image. So it is with nature. Do we love to gaze on the sun, the moon, the stars and the planets? This affection contains in its bosom the whole science of astronomy, as the seed contains the future tree. It is the office of the instructer, to give it an existence and a name, by making known the laws which govern the motions of the heavenly bodies, the relation of these bodies to each other, and their uses. Have we felt delight in beholding the animal creation, in watching their pastimes and their labours? It is the office of the instructer to give birth to this affection, by teaching the different classes of animals with their peculiar characteristics, which inhabit the earth, air, and sea. Have we known the inexpressible pleasure of beholding the beauties of the vegetable world? This affection can only expand in the science of botany. Thus it is that the love of nature in the mass, may become the love of all the sciences; and the mind will grow and bring forth fruit from its own inherent power of development. Thus it is that memory refers to the growth and expansion of the mind; and what is thus, as it were incorporated into its substance, can be forgotten only by a change in the direction of the affections, or the course of conduct of the individual analogous to that in his physical man, by which his very flesh and bones are exchanged for those of a different texture; nor does he then entirely cease to remember, inasmuch as he preserves a sense of his own identity.

It is in this way the continual endeavour of Providence, that the natural sciences should be the spontaneous production of the human mind. To these should certainly be added, poetry and music; for when we study the works of God as we should, we cannot disregard that inherent beauty and harmony in which these arts originate. These occasion in the mind its first glow of delight, like the taste of food as it is offered to the mouth; and the pleasure they afford, is a pledge of the strength and manhood afterwards imparted by the sciences.

By poetry is meant all those illustrations of truth by natural imagery, which spring from the fact that this world is the mirror of him who made it. Strictly speaking, nothing has less to do with fiction, than poetry. The day will come, and it may not be far distant, when this art will have another test of merit than mere versification, or the invention of strange stories; when the laws by which poetry is tested, will be as fixed and immutable as the laws of science; when a change will be introduced into taste corresponding to that which Bacon introduced into philosophy, by which both will be confined within the limits of things as they actually exist.[3] It would seem that genius would be cramped; that the powers of invention would be destroyed; by confining the human mind, as it were, at home, within the bounds which nature has assigned. But what wider scope need it have? It reaches the throne of God; it rests on his footstool. All things spiritual and natural are before it. There is as much that is true as false; and truth presented in natural imagery, is only dressed in the garments which God has given it.

The imagination was permitted for ages to involve the world in darkness, by putting theory in the place of fact; till at length the greatest man revealed the simplest truth, that our researches must be governed by actual observation. God is the source of all truth. Creation, (and what truth does not result from creation?) is the effect of the Divine Love and Wisdom. Simply to will and to think with the Divine Being, result in creating; in actually producing those realities, which form the ground-work of the thoughts and affections of man. But for the philosopher to desire a thing, and to think that it existed, produced nothing but his own theory. Hence it was necessary that he should bring his mind into coincidence with things as they exist, or in other words with the truth.

Fiction in poetry must fall with theory in science, for they depend equally on the works of creation. The word fiction however is not intended to be used in its most literal sense; but to embrace whatever is not in exact agreement with the creative spirit of God. It belongs to the true poet to feel this spirit, and to be governed by it; to be raised above the senses; to live and breathe in the inward efforts of things; to feel the power of creation, even before he sees the effect; to witness the innocence and smiles of nature's infancy, not by extending the imagination back to chaos, but by raising the soul to nature's origin. The true poetic spirit, so far from misleading any, is the strongest bulwark against deception. It is the soul of science. Without it, the latter is a cheerless, heartless study, distrusting even the presence and power of Him to whom it owes its existence. Of all the poetry which exists, that only possesses the seal of immortality, which presents the image of God which is stamped on nature. Could the poetry which now prevails, be viewed from the future, when all partialities and antipathies shall have passed away, and things are left to rest on their own foundations; when good works shall have dwindled into insignificance from the mass of useless matter that may have fallen from them, and bad ones shall have ceased to allure with false beauty; we might catch a glimpse of the rudiments of this divine art, amid the weight of extraneous matter by which it is now protected, and which it is destined to throw off. The imagination will be refined into a chaste and sober view of unveiled nature. It will be confined within the bounds of reality. It will no longer lead the way to insanity and madness by transcending the works of creation, and as it were, wandering where God has no power to protect it; but finding a resting-place in every created object, it will enter into it and explore its hidden treasures, the relation in which it stands to mind, and reveal the love it bears to its Creator.

The state of poetry has always indicated the state of science and religion. The Gods are hardly missed more, when removed from the temples of the ancients, than they are when taken from their poetry; or than theory is when taken from their philosophy. Fiction ceases to be pleasing when it ceases to gain credence; and what they admired in itself, commands much of its admiration now, as a relic of antiquity. The painting which in a darkened room only impressed us with the reality, as the sun rises upon it discovers the marks of the pencil; and that shade of the mind can never again return, which gave to ancient poetry its vividness and its power. Of this we may be sensible, by only considering how entirely powerless it would be, if poetry in all respects similar were produced at the present day. A man's religious sentiments, and his knowledge of the sciences, are so entirely interwoven with all his associations; they shed such light throughout every region of the mind; that nothing can please which is directly opposed to them— and though the forms which poetry may offer, may sometimes be presented, where this light begins to sink into obscurity; they should serve, like the sky and the clouds, as a relief to the eye, and not like some unnatural body protruding on the horizon, disturb the quiet they are intended to produce. When there shall be a religion which shall see God in every thing, and at all times; and the natural sciences not less than nature itself, shall be regarded in connexion with Him—the fire of poetry will begin to be kindled in its immortal part, and will burn without consuming. The inspiration so often feigned, will become real; and the mind of the poet will feel the spark which passes from God to nature. The veil will be withdrawn, and beauty and innocence displayed to the eye; for which the lasciviousness of the imagination and the wantonness of desire may seek in vain.

There is a language, not of words but of things. When this language shall have been made apparent, that which is human will have answered its end, and being as it were resolved into its original elements, will lose itself in nature. The use of language is the expression of our feelings and desires; the manifestation of the mind. But every thing which is, whether animal or vegetable, is full of the expression of that use for which it is designed, as of its own existence. If we did but understand its language, what could our words add to its meaning? It is because we are unwilling to hear, that we find it necessary to say so much; and we drown the voice of nature, with the discordant jargon of ten thousand dialects. Let a man's language be confined to the expression of that which actually belongs to his own mind; and let him respect the smallest blade which grows and permit it to speak for itself. Then may there be poetry which may not be written perhaps, but which may be felt as a part of our being. Every thing which surrounds us, is full of the utterance of one word, completely expressive of its nature. This word is its name; for God, even now could we but see it, is creating all things, and giving a name to every work of his love, in its perfect adaptation to that for which it is designed. But man has abused his power, and has become insensible to the real character of the brute creation, still more so, to that of inanimate nature, because in his selfishness, he is disposed to reduce them to slavery. Therefore he is deaf. We find the animal world, either in a state of savage wildness, or enslaved submission. It is possible that as the character of man is changed, they may attain a midway condition equally removed from both. As the mind of man acknowledges its dependence on the Divine Mind, brutes may add to their instinct submission to human reason; preserving an unbroken chain from our Father in Heaven, to the most inanimate parts of creation. Such may be supposed to have been the condition of the animal, on which the King of Zion rode into Jerusalem; at once free and subject to the will of the rider. Every thing will seem to be conscious of its use; and man will become conscious of the use of every thing.

It may be peculiar, and is said with deference to the opinions of others, but to my ear, rhymes add nothing to poetry, but rather detract from its beauty. They possess too strongly the marks of art, and produce a sameness which tires, and sometimes disgusts. We seek for them in vain in nature, and may therefore reasonably presume that they spring out of the peculiar state of the public taste, without possessing any real foundation in the mind itself; that they are rather the fashion of the dress, than any essential part. In the natural world we find nothing which answers to them, or feels like them—but a happy assemblage of living objects springing up, not in straight lines and at a fixed distance, but in God's own order, which by its apparent want of design, conveys the impression of perfect innocence and humility. It is not for that which is human to be completely divested of the marks of art; but every approach towards this end, must be an approach towards perfection. The poet should be free and unshackled as the eagle; whose wings, as he soars in the air, seem merely to serve the office of a helm, while he moves on simply by the agency of the will.

By music is meant not merely that which exists in the rational world, whether in the song of angels or men; not merely the singing of birds and the lowing of cattle, by which the animal world express their affections and their wants—but that harmony which pervades also all orders of creation; the music of the harp of universal nature, which is touched by the rays of the sun, and whose song is the morning, the evening and the seasons. Music is the voice of God, and poetry his language, both in his word and works. The one is to the ear, what the other is to the eye. Every child of nature must feel their influence. There was a time, when the human mind was in more perfect harmony with the Divine Mind, than the lower orders of creation; and the tale of the harp of Orpheus, to which the brutes, the vegetables and the rocks listened, is not altogether unfounded in reality—but when the selfish and worldly passions usurped the place of love to our God and our neighbour, the mind of man began to be mute in its praise.[4] The original order was reversed. The very stones cry out, and we do well to listen to them.

There is a most intimate and almost inseparable connexion between poetry and music. This is indicated by the fact that they are always united. Nothing is sung which has not some pretensions to poetry; and nothing has any pretensions to poetry, in which there is not something of music. A good ear is essential to rhythm; and rhythm is essential to verse. It is the perfection of poetry, that it addresses two senses at once, the ear and the eye; that it prepares the affections for the object before it is presented; that it sends light through the understanding, by forming a communication between the heart of man, and the works of God. The character of music must have always harmonized with that of poetry. It is essential to the former that it should be in agreement with our feelings; for it is from this circumstance, that it derives its power. That music which is in unison with the Divine Mind, alone deserves the name. So various is it found in the different conditions of man, that it is hardly recognized as the same thing. There is music in the war-song of the savage, and in the sound for battle. Alas! how unlike that music which proclaimed peace on earth and good will towards men. Poetry and music like virtuous females in disguise, have followed our race into the darkest scenes to which the fall has brought them. We find them in the haunts of dissipation and vice; in the song of revelry and lewdness. We meet them again kindling the fire of devotion at the altar of God; and find them more and more perfect, as we approach their divine origin.

There prevail at present two kinds of music, as diverse as their origins; profane and religious. The one is the result of the free, unrestrained expression of natural feelings; the other, of a kind which indicates that these feelings are placed under restraint. In the one, there is often something of sensuality; in the other of sadness. There is a point in moral improvement, in which the sensual will be subdued, and the sorrowful disappear; which will combine the pleasure of the one, with the sanctity of the other. When a sense of the presence of God shall be coextensive with the thoughts of the mind, and religion shall consecrate every word and action of our lives; the song of Zion will be no longer sung in a strange land. The Divine Love, the soul and essence of music, will descend, not in the thunders of Sinai, but will seem to acquire volume, as it tunes the heart in unison with itself, and the tongue in unison with the heart. The changes in the character of our music, which may be the effect of the gradual regeneration of the world, are hardly within the reach of conjecture.

Enough has been said to illustrate generally, the influence of the natural world in the development of the mind. The actual condition of society operates to produce the same effect, with hardly less power. In this, are comprised the religious and civil institutions of one's own country; that peculiar character in which they originate; and a knowledge of the past, as by disclosing the origin and progress of things, it throws light on the prospect actually before us. As the philosophy connected with the natural world, is that in which the mind may take root, by which it may possess an independence worthy a being whose eternal destiny is in his own hands—so the moral and civil institutions, the actual condition of society, is the atmosphere which surrounds and protects it; in which it sends forth its branches, and bears fruit. The spiritual part of man is as really a substance, as the material; and is as capable of acting upon spirit, as matter is upon matter. It is not from words of instruction and advice, that the mind of the infant derives its first impetus; it gathers strength from the warmth of those affections which overshadow it, and is nourished by a mother's love, even before it has attained the power of thought. It is the natural tendency of things, that an individual should be brought into a situation, in which the external condition of the place, and the circle of society in which he is, are particularly adapted to bring forth to view his hereditary character. The actual condition of the human mind, is as it were the solid substance, in which the laws of moral and intellectual philosophy and political economy, (whatever may be their quality) exist embodied, as the natural sciences do in the material world. A knowledge of those laws, such as they exist, is the natural consequence of the development of the affections, by which a child is connected with those that surround him. The connexion of mind is not less powerful or universal than that of matter. All minds, whatever may be their condition, are not unconnected with God; and consequently not unconnected with each other. All nations, under whatever system of government, and in whatever state of civilization, are under the Divine Providence, surely but almost imperceptibly advancing to a moral and political order, such as the world has not yet seen. They are guided by the same hand, and with a view to the same destiny. Much remains to be done, and more to be suffered; but the end is certain. The humblest individual may, nay *must* aid in the accomplishment of this consummation. It is not for time or space to set limits to the effects of the life of a single man. Let then the child be so initiated into a knowledge of the condition of mankind, that the love at first indulged in the circle of his father's family, shall gradually subside into a chaste and sober love of his country; and of his country, not as opposed to other countries, but as aiding them in the same great object. Let the young mind be warmed and cherished by whatever is chaste and generous in the mind of the public; and be borne on to a knowledge of our institutions, by the rich current of the disposition to preserve them.

Thus it is that the child is no sooner brought into this world, than the actual condition both of the world itself, and of society, acts powerfully to draw forth the energies of his mind. If mankind had retained that order in which they were created, this influence in co-operation with the Divine, would have been sufficient, as it was designed to have been, for all the purposes of God. Nature, the very image of divine loveliness, and the purest affections of the heart, which approach still nearer the same origin, acting together on the infant mind; it would seem as if the effect would be almost as certain, as any process of growth which is witnessed among the productions of the natural world. But man is fallen—and the operation of this influence in different conditions of society, may produce different results; but in none is sufficient to capacitate him for that life of usefulness and happiness, for which he was designed. The influence of society cannot be sufficient, since this cannot raise a man above its own level; and the society of earth is no longer the society of heaven. This influence may bring forward all the warlike energies of the young savage, and direct them in their utmost vigour to the destruction of his enemies and of the beasts of the forest; and he may look onward with rapture to the happy hunting grounds beyond the grave. What disappointment awaits him in the other world, all of us may easily imagine. This influence may bring forth and gratify the unchaste and beastly passions of the Turk; and he may look forward, with his Koran in his hand, to a heaven of sensuality and crime. It need not be said how widely different will be found the reality. Christians generally are standing in expectation of a happiness as boundless in extent, as it is undefined in its nature; and with an infinite variety of passions in whose gratification alone they have experienced delight, are expecting a heaven in which simple useless enjoyment will rise like a flood and immerse the mind. The result must of necessity be as various, as the condition of the individuals by whom it is anticipated. Still there is a society yet in its coming, unseen though not unseeing, shrouded from the rest of the world by the very brilliancy of its own light, which would resist the impulse of every evil affection, and look for heaven simply in the delight of that which is chaste, pure and holy; which by removing that which renders duty undelightful, would draw nigh to the only source of real enjoyment; which would find its happiness and its God, in the very commandments which have been the terrour of the world; to which the effect is no longer doubtful, since it is made acquainted with the cause, and which as it anticipates no reward, will meet with no disappointment. When this society shall be fully established on the earth, the voice of the Lord will be no longer obstructed as it descends from above the heavens;—*"Suffer little children to come unto me and forbid them not, for of such is the kingdom of God."*

The influence of the natural world, however beneficial it may prove, is not such as it was designed to have been. Man has ever sought a condition in nature, which should correspond with the state of his own mind. The savage would pine and droop, if too suddenly removed to scenes of civilization, like grass which had grown in rank luxuriance under the shade of the oak, if the branches were cleft and it was at once exposed to the power of the sun. The character of all the lower orders of creation has suffered a change in consequence of that in the condition of man, the extent of which cannot be measured. That the sun was darkened at the crucifixion of our Lord, was no miracle. It was as much the natural consequence of that event, as its present lustre is of His glory. It is not then for these the objects of nature, to restore to us that moral order, the want of which has wrought such changes on themselves.

There is then another power which is necessary to the orderly development of the mind; the power of the Word of God. This indeed has been implied in all the preceding remarks. No possessions and no efforts of the mind are unconnected with it, whatever may be the appearance. Revelation so mingles with every thing which meets us, that it is not easy for us to measure the degree to which our condition is affected by it. Its effects appear miraculous at first, but after they have become established, the mind as in the ordinary operations of nature, is apt to become unconscious of the power by which they are produced. All growth or development is effected from within, outward. It is so with animals; it is so with vegetables; it is so with the body; it is so with the mind. Were it not for a power within the soul, as the soul is within the body, it could have no possibility of subsistence. That the growth of the material part depends on the presence of that which is spiritual, is obvious from the fact, that at death the former falls to decay. If it were possible for God to be detached from our spiritual part, this would decay likewise. The doctrine then of the immortality of the soul is simply, "I in my Father, and ye in me and I in you." It is the union of the Divine, with the human—of that from which all things are, and on which they depend the Divine Will, with man through the connecting medium of Divine Truth. It is the tendency of the Bible to effect this union, and of course to restore a consciousness of it. It is a union which God desires with all, therefore even the wicked who reject it, partake of his immortality, though not of his happiness. When in the process of regeneration, this union is accomplished, the fear of dissolution will be as impossible in this world as in the other; and before this is effected, the fear of dissolution may exist there, as well as here. It is not the place where a person is, but the condition of mind which is to be regarded; and there is no antidote against the fear of death, but the consciousness of being united with the fountain of life. But it is asked, how can the fear of death exist after it has actually taken place? The separation of the spiritual and material part so far as the nature of their connexion is understood, can produce no fear. Were it not for evil in ourselves, it would rather wear the appearance of a state of uncommon quiet. There is upon no subject a more powerful tendency to instinctive knowledge, than upon that of death. The darkness with which it is veiled, presents but a lamentable picture of our present condition. It is its own dissolution of which the mind is afraid; and that want of conjunction with God which renders this fear possible here, may render it possible any where. It is the sole object of the Bible to conjoin the soul with God; and as this is effected it may be understood in what way the Holy Spirit operates interiously to produce its development. It is not a mere metaphor, it is a plain and simple fact, that the Spirit of God is as necessary to the development of the mind, as the power of the natural sun to the growth of vegetables and in the same way. But let us remember, that as in nature the heat and light may be converted into the most noxious poison; so the Spirit of God in itself perfectly pure and holy, may be converted into passions the most opposite to its nature. It is left to us to open our hearts to its influence, by obeying its commandments. "If ye love me, keep my commandments; and I will pray the Father, and he shall give you another comforter that he may abide with you forever." "He that believeth in the Son *hath* everlasting life;" and he will become conscious of living and growing from God.

It is not consistent with the nature of things, that the full practical effect of a subject should be at once revealed to the mind. The child is led on to a knowledge of his letters, by a thousand little enticements, and by the tender coercion of parental authority, while he is yet ignorant of the treasures mysteriously concealed in their combinations. The arts have been courted merely for the transient gratification they afford. Their connexion with religion and with the sciences is beginning to be discovered; and they are yet to yield a powerful influence in imparting to the mind, its moral harmony and proportions. The sciences themselves have been studied principally as subjects of speculation and amusement. They have been sought for the gratification they afford, and for the artificial standing they give in society, by the line of distinction which is drawn between the learned and the vulgar. The discovery of their connexion with the actual condition of man, is of later origin; and though their application to use is yet in its infancy, they are beginning to throw a light on almost every department of labour, hitherto unexampled in the annals of the world. Religion too has been a subject of speculation, something evanescent, a theory, a prayer, a hope. It remains for this also to become practical, by the actual accomplishment of that which it promises. It remains for the promise of reward to be swallowed up in the work of salvation. It remains for the soul to be restored to its union with God—to heaven. Christianity is the tree of life again planted in the world; and by its own vital power it has been, year after year, casting off the opinions of men, like the external bark which partakes not of its life. It remains for the human mind to become conformed to its spirit, that its principles may possess the durability of their origin.

Such are the effects to be anticipated from the Bible in the development of the mind. It has begun the work, and will perfect it in each individual, so far as by a life according to the commandments he becomes willing that it should. There is within it a secret power, which exerts an influence on the moral and intellectual world, like that of the sun on the physical; and however long and successfully it may be resisted by some, not the less certain in its effect on the ultimate condition of society. I am aware that in these remarks, I am ascribing to the spirit of God, to the spirit of the Word, a power which some may be unwilling to allow to it. The Bible is thought to resemble other books, and to be subject to the same laws of criticism; and we may be sometimes in danger of becoming insensible to its internal power, from the very mass of human learning, with which it is encumbered. "Is not this the carpenter's son?"

There is one law of criticism, the most important to the thorough understanding of any work, which seems not to have been brought sufficiently into view in the study of the Bible. It is that by which we should be led by a continued exercise of those powers which are most clearly demonstrated in an author; by continued habits of mind and action; to approximate to that intellectual and moral condition, in which the work originated. If it were desired to make a child thoroughly acquainted with the work of a genuine poet, I would not put the poem and lexicon in his hand and bid him study and learn—I would rather make him familiar with whatever was calculated to call forth the power of poetry in himself, since it requires the exercise of the same powers to understand, that it does to produce. I would point him to that source from which the author himself had caught his inspiration, and as I led him to the baptismal fount of nature, I would consecrate his powers to that Being from whom nature exists. I would cultivate a sense of the constant presence and agency of God, and direct him inward to the presence chamber of the Most High, that his mind might become imbued with His spirit. I would endeavour by the whole course of his education to make him a living poem, that when he read the poetry of others, it might be effulgent with the light of his own mind. The poet stands on the mountain with the face of nature before him, calm and placid. If we would enter into his views, we must go where he is. We must catch the direction of his eye, and yield ourselves up to the instinctive guidance of his will, that we may have a secret foretaste of his meaning—that we may be conscious of the image in its first conception—that we may perceive its beginnings and gradual growth, till at length it becomes distinctly depicted on the retina of the mind. Without this, we may take the dictionary in our hands and settle the definition of every word, and still know as little of the lofty conceptions of the author, as the weary traveller who passes round in the farthest verge which is visible from the mountain, knows of the scenery which is seen from its summit. It has been truly said that Johnson was incapable of conceiving the beauties of Milton.[5] Yet Johnson was himself a living dictionary of Milton's language. The true poet, when his mind is full, fills his language to overflowing; and it is left to the reader to preserve what the words cannot contain. It is that part which cannot be defined; that which is too delicate to endure the unrestrained gaze; that which shrinks instinctively from the approach of any thing less chaste than itself, and though present, like the inhabitants of the other world, is unperceived by flesh and blood, which is worth all the rest. This acknowledges no dwelling-place but the mind. Stamp the living light on the extended face of nature, beyond the power of darkness at the setting of the sun, and you may preserve such light as this, when the mind rises not to meet it in its coming.

If it were desired to make an individual acquainted with a work in one of the abstract sciences, this might be best effected by leading him gradually to whatever conduced to the growth of those powers on which a knowledge of these sciences depend; by cultivating a principle of dependence on the Divine Being, a purity and chastity of the affections, which will produce a tranquil condition, of all things the most favourable to clear perceptions; by leading him to an habitual observation of the relations of things, and to such continued exertion of the understanding, as calling into use its full powers without inducing fatigue, may impart the strength of the labourer, without the degradation of the slave; in a word, by forming a penetrating, mathematical mind, rather than by communicating mathematical information. The whole character and complexion of the mind will be gradually changed; till at length it will become (chemically speaking) in its very nature an active solvent of these subjects. They fall to pieces as soon as they come in contact with it, and assume an arrangement agreeable to that of the mind itself, with all the precision of crystallization. They are then understood—for the most perfect understanding of a subject is simply a perception of harmony existing between the subject and the mind itself. Indeed the understanding which any individual possesses of a subject might be mathematically defined $\frac{\text{the subject proposed,}}{\text{the actual character of his mind}}$; and there is a constant struggle for the numerator and denominator to become the same by a change in the one or the other, that the result may be unity, and the understanding perfect.

There is an analogy, (such as may exist between things human and things divine) between that discipline which is required in order to understand a production of taste or science, and that which is necessary to a clear perception of the truths of the Bible. As it is requisite to a full sense of the beauties of poetry, that the individual should be himself a poet, and to a thorough knowledge of a work of science that he should not merely have scientific information, but a scientific mind; so it is necessary to a knowledge of the Bible, that the mind should be formed in the image and likeness of God. An understanding of the Word is the effect of a life according to its precepts. It requires, not the obedience of the rich man who went away sorrowful, but the obedience of him who holds every other possession, whether it consist in the acquirements of the mind or in earthly property, in subjection to the Holy Spirit within him. "If ye will do the will of God, ye shall know of the doctrines" is a law of exegesis, before which false sentiments will melt away like frost before the rising sun. There is within the mind the golden vein of duty, which if followed aright will lead to an increasing brightness, before which the proudest monuments of human criticism will present an appearance like that of the dark disk of this world, as the eye of the dying man opens on the scenes of the other.

The world is beginning to be changed from what it was. Physical power instead of boasting of its deeds of prowess, and pointing with the tomahawk or the lance to the bloody testimonies of its strength, is beginning to leave its image on the rugged face of nature, and to feel the living evidence of its achievements, in the happy circle of domestic life. It remains for intellectual strength to lose the consciousness of its existence in the passions subdued, and to reap the reward of its labours, not in the spoils of an enemy, but in the fruits of honest industry. It remains for us to become more thoroughly acquainted with the laws of moral mechanism. Instead of making unnecessary and ineffectual exertions in the direct attainment of truth, it remains for us to make equal efforts to cleanse our own minds and to do good to others; and what was before unattainable will become easy, as the rock which untutored strength cannot move, may be raised by a touch of the finger.

The Bible differs from other books as our Lord differed from men. He was born of a woman, but His Spirit was the everlasting Father. It is humble in its appearance, as nature is when compared to art; and some parts which Providence has permitted to remain within the same cover, have often attracted more attention than that which is really divine. From the very nature of perfect innocence its presence is unnoticed, save by him by whom it is loved. Divine Love, in its perfect thoughtlessness of itself, enters the atheistical heart, unperceived. Such an one thinks meanly of those who think humbly of themselves, and with perfect humility the last vestige of reality disappears. To him, both nature and the Word are like a deserted building, through which as he passes, he is conscious of nothing but the sound of his own footsteps; but to him whose heart opens to the Divine Influence, this building appears to assume from the internal cause of its creation, the symmetry of perfect proportions, till at length as he becomes more and more conscious of the presence with which it is filled, he sees no temple, "for the Lord God Almighty, and the Lamb are the temple." The Word resembles the hebrew language in which much of it is written. To him who knows not its spirit, it is an empty form without sound or vowel; but to him who is alive to the Divine Influence it is filled with the living voice of God.

The Bible can never be fully understood, either by making it subservient to natural reason, or by blindly adopting what reason would reject; but by that illumination of the understanding and enlargement of the reason, which will result from a gradual conformity to its precepts. Reason now, is something very different from what it was a few centuries past. We are in the habit of thinking that the mode of reasoning has changed; but this appears to be merely an indication of a change which has taken place in the character of the mind itself. Syllogistic reasoning is passing away. It has left no permanent demonstration, but that of its own worthlessness. It amounts to nothing but the discernment and expression of the particulars which go to comprise something more general; and as the human mind permits things to assume a proper arrangement from their own inherent power of attraction, it is no longer necessary to bind them together with syllogisms. Few minds can now endure the tediousness of being led blindfold to a conclusion, and of being satisfied with the result merely from the recollection of having been satisfied on the way to it. The mind requires to view the parts of a subject, not only separately but together; and the understanding in the exercise of those powers of arrangement by which a subject is presented in its just relations to other things, takes the name of reason. We appear to be approaching that condition which requires the union of reason and eloquence, and will be satisfied with neither without the other. We neither wish to see an anatomical plate of bare muscles, nor the gaudy daubings of finery; but a happy mixture of strength and beauty. We desire language neither extravagant nor cold; but blood-warm. Reason is beginning to learn the necessity of simply tracing the relations which exist between created things, and of not even touching what it examines lest it disturb the arrangement in the cabinet of creation—and as in the progress of moral improvement, the imagination (which is called the creative power of man) shall coincide with the actively creative will of God, reason will be clothed with eloquence as nature is with verdure.

Reason is said to be a power given to man for his protection and safety. Let us not be deceived by words. If this were the particular design, it should be found in equal perfection in every condition of the mind; for all are in equal need of such a power. It is the office of the eye to discern the objects of nature, and it may protect the body from any impending injury; and the understanding may be useful in a similar way to the spiritual man. Reason is partly a natural and partly an acquired power. The understanding is the eye with simply the power of discerning the light; but reason is the eye whose powers have been enlarged by exercise and experience, which measures the distance of objects, compares their magnitudes, discerns their colours and selects and arranges them according to the relation they bear to each other. In the progress of moral improvement no power of the mind, or rather no mode of exercising the understanding, undergoes a more thorough and decisive change than this. It is like the change from chaos to creation; since it requires a similar exercise of the understanding in man to comprehend creation, to what it does in God to produce it; and every approach to Him by bringing us nearer the origin of things, enables us to discover analogies in what was before chaotic. This is a change which it is the grand design of revelation to accomplish; reason should therefore come to revelation in the spirit of prayer, and not in that of judgment. Nothing can be more intimately, and necessarily connected with the moral character of an individual, than his rational powers, since it is his moral character which is the grand cause of that peculiar classification and arrangement which characterizes his mind; hence revelation in changing the former, must change the latter also.

The insufficiency of reason to judge of the Bible, is obvious on the very face of revelation from its miracles. The laws of Divine Operation are perfectly uniform and harmonious; and a miracle is a particular instance of Divine Power, which for a want of a more interiour and extended knowledge of the ways of God, appearing to stand alone, and to have been the result of an unusual exertion of the Divine Will, creates in the minds of men, what its name implies, a sensation of wonder. That there are miracles in the Bible, proves that there are laws of the Divine Operation and of the Divine Government, which are not embraced within the utmost limits of that classification and arrangement, which is the result of natural reason. While therefore human reason professes to be convinced of the reality of revelation from its miracles, let it humble itself before them. Let it bow itself to the earth, that it may be exalted to a more intimate acquaintance with these heavenly strangers. Let it follow the Lord in the regeneration, till the wonderful disappear in the paternal. Miracles are like angels who have sometimes been visible to men—who would much more willingly have introduced them to an acquaintance with the laws and society of heaven, than have filled them with fear and consternation. They are insulated examples of laws as boundless as the universe, and by the manner in which we are affected by them, prove how much we have to learn, and how utterly incompetent we are to judge of the ways of God, from that reason, which is founded on our own limited and fallacious observation. The resurrection of our Lord must have been a very different miracle to the angels at the sepulchre, from what it was to Mary. They saw it from the other side of the grave, with a knowledge of the nature of that death which they had themselves experienced; she saw an insulated fact not at all coincident with her views on the subject of which it was an illustration. They saw the use and design of that which had been accomplished; she saw the sepulchre and the linen clothes lying. As they gazed intensely at the same subject, the veil of heaven was withdrawn, and they beheld each other, face to face. She was filled with fear; they with love and compassion. If Mary were to persist in judging of this subject from her own reason; from a knowledge of those laws with which she was previously acquainted; how could her views ever become angelic? How could the dark cloud of admiration be ever filled with the rich light of the rising sun?

Man alone of all created things, appears on his own account to want the full measure of his happiness; because he alone has left the order of his creation. He stands even at the present period half-convinced of the reality of the future state. It is the design of revelation to restore to him that moral condition, in which he will possess as necessarily the consciousness of immortality, as the brute does that of existence—

for a consciousness of existence united with that of union with God, is a consciousness of eternal life. Let us come to the Bible then, with no hopes of arbitrary reward, and no fears of arbitrary punishment; but let us come to it, as to that which if followed aright, will produce a condition of mind of which happiness will be the natural and necessary consequence.

It is often said that the Bible has nothing to do with metaphysics or the sciences. An individual, whatever be his condition, always retains to a certain extent, a consciousness of his moral and intellectual character, and the more this character is exalted, the more minute and discriminating will be this consciousness. Who is it that formed the human mind, and who is here endeavouring to restore it to its true order? The Bible has the mind for its subject, that condition of mind which is heaven for its object, and the Father of mind for its author. Has it nothing to do with metaphysics? It has indeed nothing to do with that metaphysics which we shall leave with our bodies in the graves; but of that, which will shine with more and more brilliancy, as the passage is opened, not through distant regions of space, but through the secret part of our own souls to the presence of God, it is the very life and being. Can omniscience contemplate the happiness of the mind, without regard to its nature? Were we disposed to improve the condition of the savage, what course should we pursue? Should we not endeavour to change his habits of mind and body, by teaching him the arts of civilization; instructing him in the sciences; and gradually introducing him to that portion of social order which is here attained? And are not all these most intimately connected with our own condition of mind? Are they not merely the expression of its countenance? In the same way is it the endeavour of the Divine Mind in the Bible, to restore all to his own image and likeness—and to say that the Bible has nothing to do with metaphysics, is to say that the present condition of the mind has nothing to do with what it should be, and that present metaphysics have nothing to do with religion. It is said that the Bible has nothing to do with the sciences. It is true that it does not teach them directly, but it is gradually unfolding a condition of mind, out of which the sciences will spring as naturally, as the leaves and blossoms from the tree that bears them. It is the same power which acts simultaneously to develop the soul itself, and to develop nature—to form the mind and the mould which is destined to receive it. As we behold the external face of the world, our souls will hold communion with its spirit; and we shall seem to extend our consciousness beyond the narrow limits of our own bodies, to the living objects that surround us. The mind will enter into nature by the secret path of him who forms her; and can be no longer ignorant of her laws, when it is a witness of her creation.

I have endeavoured to illustrate generally, in what way the natural sciences, the actual condition of society, and the Word of God are necessary to the development of all minds, in a manner analogous to that in which the earth, the atmosphere and the sun combine to bring forth the productions of nature. I shall say but a few words with respect to that particular development, which is requisite to the full manifestation of the peculiar powers possessed by any individual.

It is well known that at a certain period of life, the character of a man begins to be more distinctly marked. He appears to become separated from that which surrounds him—to stand in a measure aloof from his associates—to raise his head above the shadow of any earthly object into the light of heaven, and to walk with a more determined step on the earth beneath. This is the manifestation of a character which has always existed, and which has, as it were been accumulating by little and little, till at length it has attained its full stature.

When a man has become his own master, it is left to himself to complete his own education. "He has one Father, God." For the formation of his character thus far, he is not in the strictest sense accountable; that is, his character is not as yet so fixed, but that it is yielding and pliable. It is left to himself to decide, how far it shall remain in its present form. This is indeed a period of deep responsibility. He has taken the guidance of a human being, and is not the less accountable, that this being is himself. The ligament is now cut asunder by which his mind was bound to its earthly guardian, and he is placed on his own feet, exposed to the bleak winds and refreshing breezes, the clouds and the sunshine of this world, fully accountable to God and man for his conduct. Let him not be made dizzy from a sense of his own liberty, nor faint under his own weight; but let him remember that the eye of God is now fixed full, it might almost be said anxiously upon him.

It is with the human mind, as with the human body. All our race have those limbs and features, and that general aspect, from which they are denominated men. But on a nearer view we find them divided into nations possessed of peculiar appearance and habits, and these subdivided into families and individuals, in all of which there is something peculiarly their own. The human mind (speaking in the most general sense) requires to be instructed in the same sciences and needs the same general development, and is destined to make one common and universal effort for its own emancipation. But the several nations of the earth also, will at a future period, stand forth with a distinctness of character which cannot now be conceived of. The part which each is to perform in the regeneration of the world, will become more and more distinctly marked and universally acknowledged; and every nation will be found to possess resources in its own moral and intellectual character, and its own natural productions, which will render it essential to the well-being and happiness of the whole. Every government must find that the real good of its own people precisely harmonizes with that of others; and standing armies must be converted into willing labourers for the promotion of the same object. Then will the nations of the earth resemble the well organized parts of the same body, and no longer convert that light which is given them for the benefit of their brethren, into an instrument by which they are degraded and enslaved.

But we stop not here. Every individual also possesses peculiar powers, which should be brought to bear on society in the duties best fitted to receive them. The highest degree of cultivation of which the mind of any one is capable, consists in the most perfect development of that peculiar organization, which as really exists in infancy, as in maturer years. The seed which is planted, is said to possess in miniature the trunk, branches, leaves and fruit of the future tree. So it is with the mind; and the most that can possibly be done, is to afford facilities by which its development may be effected with the same order. In the process of the formation of our minds, there exists the spirit of prophecy; and no advancement can create surprise, because we have always been conscious of that from which it is produced. We must not seek to make one hair white or black. It is in vain for us to attempt to add one cubit to our stature. All adventitious or assumed importance should be cast off, as a filthy garment. We should seek an employment for the mind, in which all its energies may be warmed into existence; which, (if I may be allowed the expression) may bring every muscle into action. There is something which every one can do better than any one else; and it is the tendency and must be the end of human events, to assign to each his true calling. Kings will be hurled from their thrones and peasants exalted to the highest stations, by this irresistible tendency of mind to its true level. These effects may not be fully disclosed in the short period of this life, but even the most incredulous must be ultimately convinced that the truth is no respecter of persons, by learning the simple fact that a man cannot be other than what he is. Not that endless progression in moral goodness and in wisdom are not within the reach of any one; but that the state will never arrive, when he may not look back to the first rudiments—the original stamina of his own mind; and he almost able to say, I possessed all at the time of my birth. The more a person lives in singleness of heart, in simplicity and sincerity, the more will this be apparent.

It becomes us then to seek and to cherish this *peculium* of our own minds,[6] as the patrimony which is left us by our Father in heaven— as that by which the branch is united to the vine—as the forming power within us, which gives to our persons that by which they are distinguished from others—and by a life entirely governed by the commandments of God, to leave on the duties we are called to perform, the full impress of our real characters. Let a man's ambition to be great, disappear in a willingness to be what he is; then may he fill a high place without pride, or a low one without dejection. As our desires become more and more concentrated to those objects which correspond to the peculiar organization of our minds, we shall have a foretaste of that which is coming, in those internal tendencies of which we are conscious. As we perform with alacrity whatever duty presents itself before us, we shall perceive in our own hearts; a kind of preparation for every external event or occurrence of our lives, even the most trivial, springing from the all-pervading tendency of the Providence of God to present the opportunity of being useful wherever there is the disposition.

Living in a country whose peculiar characteristic is said to be a love of equal liberty, let it be written on our hearts, that the end of all education is a life of active usefulness. We want no education which shall raise a man out of the reach of the understanding or the sympathies of any of his species. We are disgusted with that kind of dignity which the possessor is himself obliged to guard; but venerate that which, having its origin in the actual character of the man, can receive no increase from the countenance of power, and suffer no diminution from the approach of weakness—that dignity in which the individual appears to live rather in the consciousness of the light which shines from above, than in that of his own shadow beneath. There is a spiritual atmosphere about such an one, which is at once its own protection, and the protection of him with whom it is connected— which while it is free as air alike to the most powerful and the most humble, conveys a tacit warning that too near an approach is not permitted. We acknowledge the invisible chain which binds together all classes of society, and would apply to it the electric spark of knowledge with the hand of tenderness and caution. We acknowledge the healthy union of mental and bodily exercise, and would rather see all men industrious and enlightened, than to see one half of mankind slaves to the other, and these slaves to their passions. We acknowledge that the natural world is one vast mine of wisdom, and for this reason it is the scene of the labours of man; and that in seeing this wisdom, there is philosophy, and in loving it, there is religion. Most sensibly do we feel that, as the true end of instruction is to prepare a man for some particular sphere of usefulness; that when he has found this sphere, his education has then truly commenced, and the finger of God is pointing to the very page of the book of his oracles, from which he may draw the profoundest wisdom. It was the design of Providence that there should be enough of science connected with the calling of each, for the highest and holiest purposes of heaven. It is the natural world from which the philosopher draws his knowledge; it is the natural world in which the slave toils for his bread. Alas! when will they be one? When we are willing to practise what we learn, and religion makes our duty our delight. The mass of mankind must always labour; hence it is supposed that they must be always ignorant. Thus has the pride of man converted that discipline into an occasion of darkness and misery, which was intended only to give reality to knowledge, and to make happiness eternal. Truth is the way in which we should act; and then only is a man truly wise, when the body performs what the mind perceives. In this way, flesh and blood are made to partake of the wisdom of the spiritual man; and the palms of our hands will become the book of our life, on which is inscribed all the love and all the wisdom we possess. It is the light which directs a man to his duty; it is by doing his duty that he is enlightened— thus does he become identified with his own acts of usefulness, and his own vocation is the silken chord which directs to his heart, the knowledge and the blessings of all mankind.

Source: Sampson Reed, *Observations on the Growth of the Mind* (Boston: Cummings, Hilliard, 1826). The quotation is from the 1838 third edition (Boston: Otis Clapp), p. vi. The epigraph is from *The Excursion*, Book 4, ll. 1264–1270, by William Wordsworth (1770–1850), British poet and, with Samuel Taylor Coleridge (1772–1834), founder of the Romantic movement.

Notes

1. George Frideric Handel (1685–1759), German-born composer.
2. Thomas Brown (1778–1820), Scottish common sense philosopher.
3. Francis Bacon (1561–1626), English essayist, statesman, and philosopher.
4. Orpheus, Greek legendary hero who played the lyre.
5. Samuel Johnson (1709–1784), English editor, lexicographer, and critic.
6. *peculium*: "private property" or "savings."

Ralph Waldo Emerson

Sermon CXXI

(17 July 1831)

THIS SERMON BY Ralph Waldo Emerson (1803–1882) is a good example of how he found himself moving away from the doctrinal strictures of Unitarianism toward what would become his Transcendental beliefs. Picking up on Channing's sense of "Likeness to God," Emerson extends it outwards into all visible and invisible nature, using one of his favorite metaphors, vision (here called "spiritual discernment").

> The natural man receiveth not the things of the spirit of God: for they are foolishness unto him; neither can he know them because they are spiritually discerned.
>
> —I Corinthians 2:14

I invite your attention to some considerations upon the nature of spiritual discernment, and to notice some of the mistakes into which men are prone to fall upon religious subjects, from an inattention to the truth declared by St. Paul in the text.

A man is wonderfully placed in the possession of two worlds. By his body, he is joined to the earth. By his spirit, to the spiritual world. This is his natural condition, but by his own choice he becomes more united to one or to the other. Here are some persons who say—'he is all earth; there is no other world. How do you know there is heaven? how do you know there is hell? It is all delusion.'

Here are others,—here is St. Paul who says, 'There is a spirit in the Universe, that is, God, and we are made by Him and of Him, but spiritual truths are spiritually discerned.' And this seems to me the true account, and consistent with what I see. I observe that a good man has uniformly a strong conviction of God's being. I observe that a bad man loses the evidence of God's being, and doubts and denies that there is any such being. What is this but a devotion in one to the body, and in the other to the soul,—so that to one, the material world becomes all in all,—and to the other, the spiritual. A sensual man neglects his soul and attends to the gratification of his bodily appetites. He spends all his time in the pursuit of these pleasures, and, of course, all his thoughts. His attention is thus gradually withdrawn from spiritual objects, and imbedded in the senses. Is it strange that what he has ceased to see, he should cease to believe? that as he now knows nothing of God but the name, he should believe that it is only a name? And, since the objects of sense are more real and dear to him, every day, by the growth of his habits, he may be said to *worship* them, he thinks they always were, and death, which, he sees, takes him from them, seems to him total annihilation.

On the other hand, here is a person who has preferred the law of his mind to the temptations of the flesh, and has resisted these temptations. He feels the pleasing peace and greatness which that victory gives, and repeats and increases his efforts. It becomes *easier* to subdue his body. He does not care so much for his meats and drinks, for his dress, his amusements, or the amount of his property as he did before. He holds these consideration at their true value; for example, the improvement of his estate second to the improvement of his character. By thinking much, his thoughts become more to him.

By keeping the commandments he learns them better. By drawing nigh to God, God draws nigh to him. The pleasures of virtue are heightened. New and exalted sentiments begin to inhabit his mind. He begins to find he has some pleasures which common misfortunes cannot take away. The outward man perishes but the inward man is strengthened day by day. Spiritual things begin to show more real than material things. The belief in God grows strong, whilst the whole world seems to him only an apparition—a temporary creation from the everlasting Wisdom. Having his eye fixed upon divine things he becomes more firmly convinced every day of the existence of an ever present parental Power that governs and guides and rewards him and all; and to whom it is his duty and his joy to commit his whole being. He finds these thoughts lend each other support, and one truth paves the way for another; he believes he shall always live by the same laws. Thus he becomes fit to receive all declarations of the scriptures—a believer in all the doctrines of a spiritual world.

This observation of these two sorts of men and their tastes may lead us at once into an insight into the manner of spiritual discernment. The whole secret is in one word, *Likeness*. The way to see a body is to draw near it with the eye. The way to perceive a spirit is to *become like it*. What is unlike us, we cannot perceive. We cannot perceive the spirit of purity without being pure; of justice, without being just; of wisdom, without being wise. The only way to understand what love means, is to love; and what envy and hatred mean, is to covet and to hate.

If this fact is borne in mind it will serve to explain many things which puzzle the unreflecting.

I. And first it will show the *certainty* of Faith; that the legitimate objects of faith are not deficient in evidence, but are their own evidence. It seems sometimes to be thought that there is something of the imagination in faith, as if men converted their wishes into belief. On the contrary, I suppose what we are taught by faith, to be the most real and certain part of knowledge. Faith in the gospel sense, is, the perception of spiritual things. It is itself fulfilment. It is not hope, it is sight. As a man thinketh so he is. A man who leads a devout life *knows without any shadow of doubt*, that the principle of purity is better for him, gives him more happiness than impurity would give. He knows without doubt, that forgiveness of injuries is better for him, gives him more happiness than retaliation would give, that industry is happier than sloth. When he has given up his will to God and said, 'Thou art wiser than I; let me be obscure and unhappy so that thy purposes are accomplished. I am wholly thine and I find my good in the happiness of the whole,'—he is assured with a perfect assurance, from the calmness and greatness of his own feelings, that this sentiment is true.

This is the meaning of that memorable language of our Lord, If they believe not Moses and the prophets neither will they believe, though one rose from the dead. That is to say; if the commandments that they should not worship false gods; that they should not steal; nor kill; nor bear false witness; nor commit adultery; are not now plainly felt to be their duty,—if the dead should come back, they could not make it plain.

And the reason is clear. They do not see the force of these laws because they have by their vices so depraved their understandings that they cannot see what is true. And they must change their conduct, before their spiritual discernment can be opened.

II. In the next place, the knowledge that spiritual discernment is likeness will show why a bad man is skeptical and why a good man, (as we call good men) never attains at any time a more distinct knowledge of God. I suppose it will be admitted readily and with great sorrow by the most religious persons, that, whilst the name of God, and some form of worship, and some imperfect ideas of him, are found in all nations, yet nothing is more rare than consistent, distinct, steadfast views of his character and providence. Our communion with Him is not face to face, as a man with his friend. But that very dimness with which we conceive of him, is the necessary result of our sinfulness. We are not good enough to know him better. We are not enough like God, to see God. He is the source of our life, the Father of our spirits, the Perfection of those faculties which are rude and impure in us. He will become present to us as these faculties become more pure and perfect. When we are filled with benevolence, we shall see that it is his character. When we have exterminated every impure desire we shall feel that we have approached him. In short all the cultivation of our moral and intellectual powers is teaching us to say, 'Thy will be done'; that our will as far as it is separate from the will of God is evil and pernicious, and as the soul comes to breathe that sentiment, the presence and the perfection of God is felt.

III. But besides this very imperfect faith in God, there are many specific errors widely prevalent among such as lead decent and in some respects religious lives, who believe in God and honour his word. And the reason why gross errors prevail in what we think the broad daylight of Christianity upon religious questions, is still the same, that is, for want of more religion. It marks a very sensual state of the Church, when things are understood sensually, or by pictures addressed to the senses, and not spiritually.

For example, we all know in what a number of minds the idea of Heaven and of Hell is still wholly a picture from the senses. I have heard a Christian who esteemed his views very elevated, describe the happiness of heaven in language wholly got from the eye. The saints are really to be arrayed in crowns and palms. There is to be a heaven of great pomp, of immense numbers, of vast space. All peoples, generations, worlds shall meet—We shall all praise and glorify God forever—with all the redeemed, with all happy spirits around his throne. The imagination is strained to present some adequate conception, and it gives no more pleasing or true result for the employment of human minds than that they are to utter commendations and anthems to a great king. Now this is a false picture—magnify it as much as you will.

Let the multitudes with which the prolific world has teemed now for sixty centuries, be a handful to the hosts of harmonious angels that should there be met. Let the throne be brightness before which the sun shall be black. Let the floor of this temple of eternal worship be "sanded with suns."[1] Carry out these thoughts to what visions of grandeur you will—it is all poor and mean at the last, it is all merely an image addressed to the eye and the ear, and what is addressed to the natural man can never satisfy one moment the desires of the spiritual man. God and man are alike dishonoured by these representations. To utter with the lips ascriptions—is a poor and unsuitable homage to glorify Him. The Source of all Being is not indigent and needy of our praise. The fault is, it is *unlike*; it is comparing spiritual things with sensual. The wants are spiritual, and so must the objects be.

The true heaven is, in the raising of this poor sinful soul to His love, knowledge, and likeness; to purity, to humility,—to kindness, to truth, to trust; to the possession of the treasures of unbounded truth; the fellowship and cooperation with all good minds in all works of love; and the enlargement of this soul to the great and increasing capacity for virtue. This is heaven.

The same attention to spiritual things corrects our false opinions respecting the manner in which the Judgment is passed and executed upon every mind. We take the parable for a literal description of facts. Men in general suppose that the separation of good and evil spirits is performed by a physical force; is really made in the way of a shepherd dividing his sheep and goats,—these are forced into one place, those are forced into another; instead of interpreting this Scripture by their own observation of what is done in the world every day and by their spiritual eye. They would then find the real power of that solemn moral law, by which, every where in the universe, the good seek the good, and the evil seek the evil. They would find, that God does not need to appoint tormenting whips and flames for the sinner,—for, *of their own accord*, they go down to death;—they invite to them their own lusts; they indulge their own love of falsehood, of anger, of evil speaking, of pride, of covetousness, of hatred, of blasphemy; they seek, whilst in this mind, companions who love the same things. They shun the society of good men precisely as the lustful, the glutton, the miser, the robber, the murderer here shuns the society of wise and pious men. It would not only be felt as insupportably tedious, but as a perpetual accusation of their life.

And it is not as plain, that the good there, the pure, the lowly, the benefactor, the martyr, the patriot, would seek the society of each other with the same strong desire which here draws them together? It is a law of spirits, wholly independent of time and place, that *like shall be joined with like*, and it holds of the good, as of the evil.

Another of the errors which an attention to spiritual things might correct, is the ungrounded expectation that when this world has failed to make us happy, another will make us happy. How gross are the errors of men on this topic may be every where noticed in conversation.

In this spirit men express weariness, disgust, hatred of life. I speak not of that insanity which appears in suicide, but of the disgust of life expressed by men esteemed sane and wise. One of the eminent writers and statesmen of the last century says, "The best of life is but just tolerable 'tis the most we can make of it."[2] And there are multitudes who, some in faith and some in infidelity, call the grave a refuge, and look with gloomy satisfaction to the prospect of release from the evils of life. Yet what shall be the bitter disappointment of such a mind to wake up again after death the same wretched being he was—existence the same intolerable burden,—with the added conviction that the future has now no further resource from that hatred of life which made his head reel and his heart sick. I say he finds himself the same, for what can a departure from the body and from bodily circumstances do to heal and cheer a diseased *soul?* It is the soul that is sick and gives the appearance of evil to external condition. The true cause of the vexation we regret, is not in our peculiar circumstances, but in a querulous mind, which is not humble, or diligent, or kind enough to be at peace. And, as these are not disorders of the body, dying, i.e., passing out of the body, will not cure them, and the same things will remain to be done, that now ought to be done, namely, to become pure and humble and industrious and kind.

My friends, no man can take the principles of the New Testament for his guide, without becoming alive to numberless errors that prevail in the life and conversation of men around us. He will become alive to his own errors of opinion and faults of practice. He will find that men do not listen to the secret instructions of their own inward Teacher. He will find that they are looking for heaven and for hell in an *outward condition*, instead of receiving that word of our Lord, 'the kingdom of God is within you.' We sit still and hope that our salvation will be wrought out for us, instead of working out our own. We imagine that whilst we are under good influences, we are insensibly growing better, and *passively* too, instead of perceiving that our own effort is indispensable. The time will come, if in humble trust we will keep the commandments—the time will come when we shall see as we are seen, we shall know as we are known, and shall become wise unto eternal life.

Source: Sermon CXXI (17 July 1831), from *The Complete Sermons of Ralph Waldo Emerson*, ed. Albert J. von Frank et al., 4 vols. (Columbia: University of Missouri Press, 1989–1992), vol. 3, ed. Ronald A. Bosco (1991), pp. 189–194.

Notes

1. *Night Thoughts* (1742–1745), "Night IX," l. 2312, by Edward Young (1683–1765), English poet, critic, and dramatist.
2. Quoted from Jonathan Swift (1667–1745), Irish satirist famous for *Gulliver's Travels* (1726).

Ralph Waldo Emerson

Sermon CLXII ["The Lord's Supper"]

(9 September 1832)

EMERSON'S SERMON resigning his ministry was preached only once, four years to the day before the publication of *Nature*. In it he gives his reasons for refusing to administer the sacrament of the Lord's Supper, and why, even though his congregation was willing to give him some flexibility on the issue, he nevertheless felt "It is my desire, in the office of a Christian minister, to do nothing which I cannot do with my whole heart."

> The kingdom of God is not meat and drink; but right-
> eousness and peace and joy in the holy ghost.
> —Romans 14:17

In the history of the Church no subject has been more fruitful of controversy than the Lord's Supper.[1] There never has been any unanimity in the understanding of its nature nor any uniformity in the mode of celebrating it. Without considering the frivolous questions which have been hotly debated as to the posture in which men should partake or whether mixed or unmixed wine should be served, whether leavened or unleavened bread should be broken, the questions have been settled differently in every church, who should be admitted to partake, and how often it should be prepared. In the Catholic Church once infants were permitted and then forbidden to partake. Since the ninth Century, bread only is given to the laity and the cup is reserved to the priesthood. So as to the time. In the fourth Lateran Council it was decreed that every believer should communicate once in a year at Easter. Afterwards three times—But more important have been the controversies respecting its nature. The great question of the Real Presence was the main controversy between the Church of England and the Church of Rome. The doctrine of the Consubstantiation maintained by Luther was denied by Calvin.[2] In the Church of England Archbishops Laud and Wake maintained that it was a Eucharist or sacrifice of thanksgiving to God, Cudworth and Warburton that it was not a sacrifice but a feast after a sacrifice, and Bishop Hoadly that it was a simple commemoration.[3]

If there seem to you an agreement in this last opinion among our churches it is only but of yesterday and within narrow limits.

And finally it is now near 200 years since the society of Quakers denied the authority of the supper altogether and gave good reasons for discussing it.[4]

I allude to these facts only to show that so far from the Supper being a tradition in which all are fully agreed, there has always been the widest room for difference of opinion upon this particular.

Having recently paid particular attention to this subject, I was led to the conclusion that Jesus did not intend to establish an institution for perpetual observance when he ate the passover with his disciples; and further to the opinion that it is not expedient to celebrate it as we do. I shall now endeavour to state distinctly my reasons for these two opinions.

An account of the last Supper of Christ with his disciples is given by the four Evangelists, Matthew, Mark, Luke and John.

In St. Matthew's Gospel (26:26) are recorded the words of Jesus in giving bread and wine on that occasion to his disciples but no expression occurs intimating that this feast was hereafter to be commemorated.

In St. Mark the same words are recorded and still with no intimation that the occasion was to be remembered (14:22).

St. Luke, after relating the breaking of the bread, has these words: 'This do in remembrance of me' (22:15).

In St. John, although other occurrences of the same evening are related, this whole transaction is passed over without notice.

Now observe the facts. Two of the evangelists (namely, Matthew and John) were of the twelve disciples and were present on that occasion. Neither of them drops the slightest intimation of any intention on the part of Jesus to set up any thing permanent. John especially, the beloved disciple, who has recorded with minuteness the conversation and the transactions of that memorable evening, has quite omitted such a notice.

Neither did it come to the knowledge of St. Mark, who relates the other facts. It is found in Luke alone, who was not present. There is no reason, however, that we know for rejecting the account of Luke. I doubt not that the expression was used by Jesus. I shall presently consider its meaning. I have only brought these accounts together that you may judge whether it is likely that a solemn institution to be continued to the end of time, by all mankind, as they should come, nation after nation, within the influence of the Christian religion, was to be established in this slight manner, in a manner so slight that the intention of remembering it should not have caught the ear or dwelt in the mind of the only two among the twelve, who wrote down what happened!

Still we must suppose that this expression—This do in remembrance of me—had come to the ear of Luke from some disciple present. What did it really signify? It is a prophetic and an affectionate expression. Jesus is a Jew sitting with his countrymen celebrating their national feast. He thinks of his own impending death and wishes the minds of his disciples to be prepared for it and says to them, "When hereafter you shall keep the passover it will have an altered aspect in your eyes. It is now a historical covenant of God with the Jewish nation. Hereafter it will remind you of a new covenant sealed with my blood. In years to come, as long as your people shall come up to Jerusalem to keep this feast (forty years) the connexion which has subsisted between us will give a new meaning in your eyes to the national festival as the anniversary of my death."—I see natural feeling and beauty in the use of such language from Jesus, a friend to his friends. I can readily imagine that he was willing and desirous that when his disciples met, his memory should hallow their intercourse, but I cannot bring myself to believe that he looked beyond the living generation, beyond the abolition of the festival he was celebrating and the scattering of the nation, and meant to impose a memorial feast upon the whole world.

But though the words *Do this in remembrance*, to which so much meaning has been given, do not occur in Matthew, Mark, or John, yet many persons are apt to imagine that the very striking and formal manner in which this eating and drinking is described intimates a striking and formal purpose to found a festival. This opinion would easily occur to any one reading only the New Testament, but the impression is removed by reading any narrative of the mode in which the ancient or the modern Jews kept the passover. It is then perceived at once that the leading circumstances in the gospel are only a faithful account of that ceremony. Jesus did not celebrate the passover and afterwards the supper, but the supper *was* the passover. He did with his disciples exactly what every master of a family in Jerusalem was doing at the same hour with his household. It appears that the Jews ate the lamb and the unleavened bread and drank wine after a prescribed manner. It was the custom for the Lord or master of the feast to break the bread and to bless it, using this formula, which the Talmudists have preserved to us, 'Blessed be thou O Lord who givest us the fruits of the earth,' and to give it to every one at the table. It was the custom for the master of the family to take the cup which contained the wine and to bless it saying, 'Blessed be thou O Lord who givest us the fruit of the vine,' and then to give the cup to all. Among the modern Jews, a hymn is sung after this ceremony, specifying the twelve great works done by God for the deliverance of their fathers out of Egypt. And Jesus did the same thing.

But why did he use expressions so extraordinary and emphatic as these: This is my body which is broken for you. Take, Eat. This is my blood which is shed for you. Drink it. They are not extraordinary expressions from him. They were familiar in his mouth. He always taught by parables and symbols. It was the national way of teaching and was largely used by him. Remember the readiness which he always showed to spiritualize every occurrence. He stooped and wrote on the sand. He admonished his disciples respecting the leaven of the Pharisees.[5] He instructed the woman of Samaria respecting living water. He permitted himself to be anointed, declaring it was for interment. He washed the feet of his disciples. These are admitted to be symbolical actions and expressions. Here in like manner he calls the bread his body and bids the disciples eat. He had used the same expression repeatedly before. The reason why St. John does not repeat the words here, seems to be that he had narrated a similar discourse of Jesus to the people of Capernaum more at length already (John 6:27). He there tells the Jews—'Except ye eat the flesh of the Son of Man and drink his blood ye have no life in you.'

And when the Jews on that occasion complained that they did not comprehend what he meant, he added for their better understanding, and as if for our understanding, that we might not think that his body was to be actually eaten, that he only meant we should live by his commandment. He closed his discourse with these explanatory expressions: "The flesh profiteth nothing;—the *words* that I speak to you, they are spirit and they are life."

Whilst I am upon this topic I cannot help remarking that it is very singular we should have preserved this rite and insisted upon perpetuating one symbolical act of Christ whilst we have totally neglected others, particularly one other which had at least an equal claim to our observance. Jesus washed the feet of his disciples and told them that 'As he had washed their feet, they ought to wash one another's feet, for he had given them an example that they should do as he had done to them.' I ask any person who believes the Supper to have been designed by Jesus to be commemorated forever, to go and read the account of it in the other gospels, and then compare with it the account of this transaction in St. John and tell me if it is not much more explicitly authorized than the supper. It only differs in this, that we have found the Supper used in New England and the washing of the feet not. If we had found this rite established, it would be much more difficult to show its defective authority. That rite is used by the

Church of Rome and the Sandemanians.[6] It has been very properly dropped by other Christians. Why? 1. Because it was a local custom and unsuitable in western countries, and 2. because it was typical and all understand that humility is the thing signified. But the passover was local too and does not concern us; and its bread and wine were typical and do not help us to understand the love which they signified.

These views of the original account of the Lord's Supper lead me to esteem it an occasion full of solemn and prophetic interest but never intended by Jesus to be the foundation of a perpetual institution.

It appears however from Paul's Epistle to the Corinthians that the disciples had very early taken advantage of these impressive words of Christ to hold religious meetings where they broke bread and drank wine as symbols.

I look upon this fact as very natural in the circumstances of the Church. The disciples lived together; they threw all their property into a common stock; they were bound together by the memory of Christ and nothing could be more natural than that this eventful evening should be affectionately remembered by them; that they, Jews like Jesus, should adopt his expression and his type, and furthermore that what was done with peculiar propriety by them, by his personal friends, should come to be extended to their companions also. In this way religious feasts grew up among the early Christians. They were readily adopted by the Jewish converts who were familiar with religious feasts, and also by the Pagan converts whose idolatrous worship had been made up of sacred festivals and who very readily abused these to gross riot as appears from the censures of St. Paul. Many persons consider this fact, the observance of such a memorial feast by the early disciples, decisive of the question whether it ought to be observed by us. For my part I see nothing to wonder at in its originating there; all that is surprizing is that it should exist amongst us. It had great propriety for his personal friends to remember their friend and repeat his words. It was but too probable that among the half-converted Pagans and Jews any rite, any form would be cherished whilst yet unable to comprehend the spiritual character of Christianity.

The circumstance however that St. Paul favors these views has seemed to many persons conclusive in favor of the institution. I am of opinion that it is wholly on this passage and not upon the gospels that the ordinance stands. A careful examination of that passage will not I think make that evidence so weighty as it seems. That passage, the eleventh chapter I Corinthians, appears to be a reproof to the Corinthian converts of certain gross abuses that had grown up among them, offending against decency not less than against Christianity: accusing their contentiousness; the fanaticism of certain of their women; and the intemperance into which they had fallen at the Lord's supper. The end he has in view, in that Chapter, and this is observable, is not to enjoin upon them to observe the supper, but to censure their abuse of it. We quote the passage nowadays as if it enjoined attendance on the supper, but he wrote it merely to chide them for drunkenness. To make their enormity plainer he goes back to the origin of this religious feast to show what that feast was out of which this their riot came and so relates the transactions of the Lord's supper. *I have received of the Lord*, he says. By this expression it is often thought that a miraculous communication is implied, but certainly without good reason if it is remembered that St. Paul was living in the lifetime of all the apostles who could give him an account of the transaction, and it is contrary to all experience to suppose that God should work a miracle to convey information that might be so easily got by natural means. So that the import of the expression is that he had got the account of the Evangelists, which we also possess.

But the material circumstance which diminishes our confidence in the correctness of the apostle's view is the observation that his mind had not escaped the prevalent error of the primitive Church, the belief namely that the second coming of Christ would shortly occur, until which time, he tells them, this feast was to be kept. At that time the world would be burnt with fire, and a new government established in which the Saints would sit on thrones; so slow were the disciples during the life and after the ascension of Christ to receive the idea which we receive that his Second Coming was a spiritual kingdom, the dominion of his religion in the hearts of men to be extended gradually over the whole world.

In this manner I think we may see clearly enough how this ancient ordinance got its footing among the early Christians and this single expectation of a speedy reappearance of a temporal messiah upon earth, which kept its influence even over so spiritual a man as St. Paul, would naturally tend to preserve the use of the rite when once established.

We arrive then at this conclusion: 1. That it does not appear from a careful examination of the account of the Last Supper in the Evangelists that it was designed by Jesus to be perpetual. 2. It does not appear that the opinion of St. Paul, all things considered, ought to alter our opinion derived from the Evangelists.

I have not attempted to ascertain precisely the purpose in the mind of Jesus. But you will see that many opinions may be entertained of his intention all consistent with the opinion that he did not design the ordinance to be perpetual. He may have foreseen that his disciples would meet together to remember him and seen good in it. It may have crossed his mind that this would be easily continued a hundred or a thousand years, as men more easily transmit a form than a virtue, and yet have been altogether out of his purpose to fasten it upon men in all times and all countries.

Admitting that the disciples kept it and admitting Paul's feeling of its perpetuity, that does not settle the question for us. I think it was good for them. I think it is not suited to this day. We do not take them for guides in other things. They were, as we know, obstinately attached to their Jewish prejudices. All the intercourse with the most persuasive of teachers seems to have done very little to enlarge their views. On every subject we have learned to think differently, and why shall not we form a judgment upon this, more in accordance with the spirit of Christianity than was the practice of the early ages?

But it is said, Admit that the rite was not designed to be perpetual. What harm doth it? Here it stands generally accepted under some form by the Christian world, the undoubted occasion of much good; is it not better it should remain? This is the question of Expediency.

I proceed to notice a few objections that in my judgment lie against its use in its present form.

1. If the view which I have taken of the history of the institution to be correct, then the claim of authority should be dropped in administering it. You say, every time you celebrate the rite, that Jesus enjoined it, and the whole language you use conveys that impression. But if you read the New Testament as I do, you do not believe he did.

2. It has seemed to me (yet I make the objection with diffidence) that the use of this ordinance tends to produce confusion in our views of the relation of the soul to God. It is the old objection to the doctrine of the Trinity that the true worship was transferred from God to Christ or that such confusion was introduced into the soul that an undivided worship was given nowhere. Is not that the effect of the Lord's Supper? I appeal now to the convictions of communicants and ask such persons whether they have not been occasionally conscious of a painful confusion of thought between the worship due to God and the commemoration due to Christ. For the service does not stand upon the basis of a voluntary act, but is imposed by authority. It is an expression of gratitude to him enjoined by him. There is an endeavour to keep Jesus in mind whilst yet the prayers are addressed to God. I fear it is the effect of this ordinance to clothe Jesus with an authority which he never claimed and which distracts the mind of the worshipper. I know our opinions differ much respecting the nature and offices of Christ and the degree of veneration to which he is entitled. I am so much a Unitarian as this, that I believe the human mind cannot admit but one God, and that every effort to pay religious homage to more than

one being goes to take away all right ideas. I appeal, brethren, to your individual experience. In the moment when you make the least petition to God, though it be but a silent wish that he may approve you, or add one moment to your life—do you not—in the very act—necessarily exclude all other beings from your thought? In that act the soul stands alone with God, and Jesus is no more present to the mind than your brother or your child.

But is not Jesus called in Scripture the Mediator? He is the Mediator in that only sense in which possibly any being can mediate between God and man, that is an Instructer of man. He teaches us how to become like God. And a true disciple of Jesus will receive the light he gives most thankfully, but the thanks he offers and which an exalted being will accept are not compliments, commemorations—but the use of that instruction.

3. To pass by other objections, I come to this: that the *use of the elements*, however suitable to the people and the modes of thought in the East where it originated, is foreign and unsuited to affect us. Whatever long usage and strong association may have done in some individuals to deaden this repulsion I apprehend that their use is rather tolerated than loved by any of us. We are not accustomed to express our thoughts or emotions by symbolical actions. Most men find the bread and wine no aid to devotion and to some persons it is an impediment. To eat bread is one thing; to love the precepts of Christ and resolve to obey them is quite another. It is of the greatest importance that whatever forms we use should be animated by our feelings; that our religion through all its acts should be living and operative.

The statement of this objection leads me to say that I think this difficulty, wherever it is felt, to be entitled to the greatest weight. It is alone a sufficient objection to the ordinance. It is my own objection. This mode of commemorating Christ is not suitable to me. That is reason enough why I should abandon it. If I believed that it was enjoined by Jesus on his disciples, and that he even contemplated to make permanent this mode of commemoration every way agreeable to an Eastern mind, and yet on trial it was disagreeable to my own feelings, I should not adopt it. I should choose other ways which he would approve more. For what could he wish to be commemorated for? Only that men might be filled with his spirit. I find that other modes comport with my education and habits of thought. For I chuse that my remembrances of him should be pleasing, affecting, religious. I will love him as a glorified friend after the free way of friendship and not pay him a stiff sign of respect as men do to those whom they fear. A passage read from his discourses, the provoking each other to works like his, any act or meeting which tends to awaken a pure thought, a glow of love, an original design of virtue I call a worthy, a true commemoration.

4. In the last place the importance ascribed to this particular ordinance is not consistent with the spirit of Christianity. The general object and effect of this ordinance is unexceptionable. It has been and is, I doubt not, the occasion of indefinite good, but an importance is given by the friends of the rite to it which never can belong to any form. My friends, the kingdom of God is not meat and drink. Forms are as essential as bodies. It would be foolish to declaim against them, but to adhere to one form a moment after it is outgrown is foolish. That form only is good and Christian which answers its end. Jesus came to take the load of ceremonies from the shoulders of men and substitute principles. If I understand the distinction of Christianity, the reason why it is to be preferred over all other systems and is divine is this, that it is a moral system; that it presents men with truths which are their own reason, and enjoins practices that are their own justification; that if miracles may be said to have been its evidence to the first Christians they are not its evidence to us, but the doctrines themselves; that every practice is Christian which praises itself and every practice unchristian which condemns itself. I am not engaged to Christianity by decent forms; it is not saving ordinances, it is not usage, it is not what I do not understand that engages me to it—let these be the sandy foundation of falsehoods. What I revere and obey in it is its reality, its boundless charity, its deep interior life, the rest it gives to my mind, the echo it returns to my thoughts, the perfect accord it makes with my reason, the persuasion and courage that come out of it to lead me upward and onward.

Freedom is the essence of Christianity. It has for its object simply to make men good and wise. Its institutions should be as flexible as the wants of men. That form out of which the life and suitableness have departed should be as worthless in its eyes as the dead leaves that are falling around us.

And therefore, though for the satisfaction of others I have labored to show by the history that it was not intended to be perpetual, though I have gone back to weigh the expressions of Paul, I feel that here is the true way of viewing it. In the midst of considerations as to what Paul thought and why he so thought, I cannot help feeling that it is labor misspent to argue to or from his convictions or those of Luke or John respecting any form. I seem to lose the substance in seeking the shadow. That for which Paul lived and died so gloriously; that for which Jesus was crucified; the end that animated the thousand martyrs and heroes that have followed him, was to redeem us from a formal religion, and teach us to seek our wellbeing in the reformation of the soul. The whole world was full of idols and ordinances. The Jewish was a religion of forms; the Pagan was a religion of forms; it was all body, it had no life,—and the Almighty God was pleased to qualify and send forth a man to teach men that they must serve him with the heart; that only that life was religious which was thoroughly good, that sacrifice was smoke and forms were shadows, and this man lived and died true to this purpose, and now, with his blessed words and life before us, Christians must contend that it is a matter of vital importance, really a duty, to commemorate him by a certain form, whether that form be agreeable to their understanding or not.

Is not this to make vain the gift of God? Is not this to turn back the hand on the dial? Is not this to make men, to make ourselves, forget that not forms but duties, not names but righteousness and love are enjoined and that in the eye of God there is no other measure of the value of any one form than the measure of its use?

There remain some practical objections to the ordinance which I need not state. There is one on which I had intended to say a few words, the unfavorable relation in which it puts those persons who abstain from it merely from disinclination to that rite.

Influenced by these considerations, I have proposed to the brethren of the church to drop the use of the elements and the claim of authority in the administration of this ordinance, and have suggested a mode in which a meeting for the same purpose might be held, free of objection.

They have considered my views with patience and candor, and have recommended unanimously an adherence to the present form. I have therefore been compelled to consider whether it becomes me to administer it. I am clearly of opinion that I ought not. This discourse has already been so far extended that I can only say that the reason of my determination is shortly this—It is my desire, in the office of a Christian minister, to do nothing which I cannot do with my whole heart. Having said this, I have said all. I have no hostility to this institution. I am only stating my want of sympathy with it. Neither should I ever have obtruded this opinion upon other people, had I not been called by my office to administer it. That is the end of my opposition, that I am not interested in it. I am content that it stand to the end of the world if it please men and please heaven, and shall rejoice in all the good it produces.

As it is the prevailing opinion and feeling in our religious community that it is an indispensable part of the pastoral office to administer this ordinance, I am about to resign into your hands that office which you have confided to me. It has many duties for which I am feebly qualified. It has some which it will always be my delight to discharge according to my ability wherever I exist. And whilst the thought of its claims oppresses me with a sense of my unworthiness, I am consoled by the hope that no time and no change can deprive me of the satisfaction of pursuing and exercising its highest functions.

Source: Sermon CLXII ["The Lord's Supper"], from *The Complete Sermons of Ralph Waldo Emerson*, ed. Albert J. von Frank et al., 4 vols. (Columbia: University of Missouri Press, 1989–1992), vol. 4, ed. Wesley T. Mott (1992), pp. 185–194.

Notes

1. As Emerson makes clear in his sermon, he believes that the symbolic import of the Last Supper has formalized and pushed aside its true religious meaning.
2. John Calvin (1509–1564), Protestant theologian and reformer. The argument is about the heretical doctrine of consubstantiation, which held that the substance of Christ's Body exists together with the substance of bread, and the substance of His Blood together with the substance of wine, as opposed to the orthodox interpretation of transubstantiation, where the bread and wine in the Mass is converted into the body and blood of Christ.
3. The English theologians and clerics are William Laud (1573–1645), archbishop of Canterbury; William Wake (1657–1737), bishop of Lincoln and archbishop of Canterbury; Ralph Cudworth (1617–1688), ethical philosopher and Platonist; William Warburton (1698–1779), English bishop of Gloucester and critic; and Benjamin Hoadley (1676–1761), bishop of Winchester. The Eucharist is the sacrament of the Lord's Supper.
4. The Quakers or Society of Friends, English sect founded in the seventeenth century known for its pacifism and belief in a inner spiritual voice.
5. Pharisees, an ancient Jewish sect that strictly observed religious and secular laws.
6. Sandemanians, an eighteenth-century Scots religious sect that attempted to return to the teachings and practices of early Christianity.

Frederic Henry Hedge

"Coleridge's Literary Character"

(March 1833)

FREDERIC HENRY HEDGE (1805–1890) was the Transcendentalist most conversant with German literature. He would be one of the founders of the Transcendental Club, which often met when he traveled to Boston from his pastorate in Bangor, Maine. Although he disappointed many of his contemporaries by taking conservative religious positions (he later became president of the American Unitarian Association), at this time he was an enthusiastic proponent of German and continental learning and ideas. As Perry Miller aptly describes it, Hedge's essay "marks the point at which Transcendentalism went over to the offensive." While conceding some problems with Coleridge's abilities as a poet and critic, Hedge nevertheless fails to concede an inch to those who have dismissed Coleridge out of hand; indeed, he dismisses *them* with "To those only is [Coleridge] obscure who have no depths within themselves corresponding to his depths."

There is no writer of our times whose literary rank appears so ill-defined as that of Mr. Coleridge. Perhaps there is no one whose true standing in the literary world it is so difficult to determine. For ourselves we know not a more doubtful problem in criticism than this author and his works present. If it were lawful to judge men by what they are, rather than by what they have done, by the evidence they give of what they might accomplish, rather than by the value of that which they have accomplished, few would stand higher than Mr. Coleridge. His talents and acquirements, the original powers, and the exceeding rich cultivation of his mind, place him among the foremost of this generation. But this method of estimating a man's merit will hardly be thought righteous judgment in an age which is peculiarly prone to try every man by his works. Tried by his works, Mr. Coleridge, we fear, must ultimately fall, not only below the rank which nature and education had fitted him to maintain, but even below that which he now actually holds in the estimation of literary men.

As a prose-writer he has never been popular, though skilled beyond most men in the use of language, and writing on subjects of the deepest interest. As a poet, though gifted in no common degree with the essentials of the poetic character, he has not been successful. As a philosopher, though at once both subtile and profound, and deeply versed in all the mysteries of the inner man, he has gained little else than smiles of compassion and ominous shaking of heads by his metaphysical speculations. For a reconciliation of these several antitheses we must have recourse to the history of the man. In the "Biographia Literaria," by far the most entertaining, and in our opinion the most instructive of his works, we have that history in part; the influences which operated most powerfully on our author's youth, and the elements both of thought and feeling which entered most largely into the formation of his literary character, are there set before us with great clearness and precision; and from the data which this book furnishes we are enabled to account for much that would otherwise be unintelligible in the doings and not-doings of this remarkable man. Nature, it would seem, had endowed Mr. Coleridge with a singularly fertile and creative mind,—a mind which, if left to itself with no other training than opportunity might supply, would have enriched the world with manifold and pleasing productions. The marks of this creative tendency are still visible in some of his poetical productions; we would mention in particular the "Ancient Mariner," and the tragedies.

But at an early period of his education, our author's mind acquired a bias which proved injurious to its productive faculty, and which, by changing the tendency of his intellect from the creative to the reflective, in process of time seduced him from the open highway of literary fame, into more devious and darksome paths. We refer to the discipline which he received at the grammar school at Christ's-Hospital, as described in his life.[1] Such a discipline, though admirably adapted to invigorate the understanding, and to strengthen the judgment, was ill-suited to unfold a poet's talent, or to nourish creative genius of any kind. It was precisely the training to make a critic; and although we are unwilling to ascribe any irresistible influence to education alone, we cannot help believing that the strong tendency to criticism which has ever marked Mr. Coleridge's literary pursuits, is in part the effect of early discipline. We do not mean that Mr. Coleridge has at any period of his life been a writer of critiques, as that business is generally understood, but that he has ever inclined to comment upon the sayings and doings of others, rather than to say and do himself. This propensity, however, has not been exercised on literary subjects alone; it has found a wider scope and a freer field in deep and comprehensive speculations on topics of national and universal interest, particularly those which agitated Europe at the commencement of the present century. It has been employed on knotty questions in politics, philosophy, and religion, it has canvassed the rights and duties of civil government, criticized the movements of nations, and passed judgment on the tendencies and characteristics of the age. The results of these speculations were first given to the world in "The Morning Post," and afterwards in "The Friend," a collection of original essays, which for depth of thought, clearness of judgment, sound reasoning, and forcible expression, have few rivals in the English language. For the American edition of this work, as also for the republication of the "Aids to Reflection," and "The Statesman's Manual," we take this opportunity of expressing our obligations to President Marsh.[2] Next to the writer of a good book, he most deserves our gratitude, who in any way helps to increase its circulation. This praise is due, in an eminent degree, to Mr. Marsh; nor does this comprise the whole of his claims to our regard and good wishes; in the valuable dissertation which accompanies the "Aids to Reflection," he has done much to illustrate Mr. Coleridge's philosophical opinions, and has evinced a philosophical talent of his own, which we cannot but hope will some day be employed in more extensive undertakings.

To return to our author. After finding him engaged in the desultory and patch-work business of journal composition and essay writing, we are no longer surprised that he should have produced nothing of a more lofty and epic character. Whether the habit of small writing (under which name we include essays, reviews, and critiques of all kinds) be cause or effect, we shall not undertake to say; but certain we are, that this habit is always connected with an indisposition for more dignified and sustained efforts. From a skilful essayist we might expect excellence in small matters,—a spirited ode or a pointed epigram,—but never should we expect from such a one a well sustained epic poem, or perfect drama, a complete history, or system of philosophy. That species of talent which leads to fragmentary composition, will generally be found to be the offspring of a mind which loves rather to dwell on particulars than to contemplate universals, and is more accustomed to consider things in their special relations and minutest bearings, than to expatiate in large and comprehensive views. In such minds the centrifugal force is out of all proportion to the centripetal; they are ever losing themselves in endless diffusion, without the ability to recover themselves in systematic results, or to concentrate their powers into regular and definite forms. Such a habit of mind is decidedly anti-creative, and therefore fatal to success in the higher departments of literary production. In proportion as the mind accustoms itself to dwell on particulars, it loses sight of unity and totality, and becomes incapable of contemplating or producing a whole. And herein, we conceive, lies the secret of Mr. Coleridge's failures. Here we have the answer to the oft repeated question, why a mind of such copious resources, so filled and overflowing with various and rich material, should have produced so little, and that little so loose and desultory.

Something more than abundance of material is wanted to constitute a perfect literary production. In every intellectual, as well as in every material creation, there are two essential elements, substance and form. Of substance Mr. Coleridge has enough, but in respect to form he is strikingly deficient, and being deficient in this, he wants that which constitutes the perfection of genius.

The characteristics of genius have been variously defined. To us it has always seemed, that, as there are two degrees of this mental quality, so there are also two characteristics, the one common to both degrees, the other peculiar to, and, indeed, constituting the highest. The first characteristic is originality. By this we mean not merely a disposition to think and act differently from the rest of mankind, but the power of imparting novelty, and a sense of freshness to common thoughts and familiar objects. In poetry this faculty constitutes what is called the poetical feeling; it is that which distinguishes genuine poetry, whether metrical or unmetrical, from mere eloquence. In this quality Mr. Coleridge is by no means deficient. The following quotation may serve to illustrate our meaning; it is from the story of an orphan girl, contained in "The Friend."

> Maria followed Harlin, for that was the name of her guardian angel, to her home hard by. The moment she entered the door she sank down and lay at her full length, as if only to be motionless in a place of rest had been the fulness of delight. *As when a withered leaf that has long been whirled about by the gusts of autumn is blown into a cave or the hollow of a tree, it stops suddenly, and all at once looks the very image of quiet.* Such might this poor orphan girl appear to the eye of a meditative imagination.

In the words which are here marked with Italics we have a plain but accurate description of an incident familiar to all of us. Nothing can be simpler,—perhaps some will think nothing could be less indicative of genius than the mention of such a circumstance. And yet it is this faculty of seizing upon a natural incident, of presenting it exactly as it is, without embellishment or emotion, yet at the same time making it impressive by gently emphasizing its most distinctive feature, and by diffusing over the whole a kind of ideality,—it is this faculty which gives life to poetry; it is this which gives to the poetry of the ancients in particular, its strange and peculiar charm. Who has not seen a leaf whirled about by the wind, and then lodged in the hollow of a tree? but who except a poet would have recalled the circumstance? who but a poet would have found in it an analogy to any thing in the moral world? This is to look upon nature with a poet's eye, and to interpret nature with a poet's sense. This is to clothe with new beauty, and as it were to sanctify, a common sight, so that it can never more seem common, nor pass unnoticed again. An incident thus selected from the daily spectacle of nature, and associated with a particular state of moral being, becomes thenceforward and for ever a poetical image; by the poet's magic synthesis a natural object has become inseparably linked with a human feeling, so that the one must thenceforth always suggest the other. We feel assured that after reading this passage we shall never again behold the thing there described without a new sensation. We shall add a few extracts from Mr. Coleridge's poetry for the purpose of further illustrating what we mean by the *poetical feeling*.

The first is a description of nocturnal silence from the "Frost at Midnight."

> 'T is calm indeed, so calm that it disturbs
> And vexes meditation with its strange
> And extreme silentness.
>   Sea, hill, and wood,
> With all the numberless goings-on of life
> Inaudible as dreams,
> Only that film which fluttered on the grate
> Still flutters there, the sole unquiet thing.
> Methinks its motion in this hush of nature
> Gives it dim sympathies with me, who live
> Making it a companionable form.

The following is from the same piece:

> Therefore all seasons shall be sweet to thee,
> Whether the summer clothe the general earth
> With greenness, or the redbreast sit and sing
> Betwixt the tufts of snow on the bare branch
> Of mossy apple-tree, while the nigh-thatch
> Smokes in the sun-thaw. Whether the eave-drops fall
> Heard only in the trances of the blast,
> Or if the secret ministry of frost
> Shall hang them up in silent icicles,
> Quietly shining to the quiet moon.

How aptly is a well known state of mind described in the following passage from the ode, entitled "Dejection."

> A grief without a pang, void, dark, and drear,
> A stifled, drowsy, unimpassioned grief,
> Which finds no natural outlet, no relief
> In word or sigh or tear.

"The Ancient Mariner" is so full of beauties that we find it difficult to make a selection. The description of a vessel becalmed near the equator is probably familiar to many of our readers.

> All in a hot and copper sky
> The bloody sun at noon

Right up above the mast did stand
No bigger than the moon.
Day after day, day after day
We stuck, nor breath nor motion,
As idle as a painted ship
Upon a painted ocean.

The effects of a sudden breeze are set forth with the same nervous and graphic power.

But in a minute she 'gan stir
With a short uneasy motion,
Backwards and forwards half her length
With a short uneasy motion:
Then, like a pawing horse let go,
She made a sudden bound.

The influence of superstitious fears is portrayed with great truth.

Like one who on a lonesome road
Doth walk in fear and dread,
And having once turned round, walks on
And turns no more his head,
Because he knows a frightful fiend
Doth close behind him tread.

Sometimes the poetical merit consists solely in a happy choice of epithets.

The moonlight *steeped* in *silentness*
The *steady* weathercock.

In the following passage from "Christabel," the poetical feeling is equally diffused over the whole.

There is not wind enough to twirl
The one red leaf, the last of its clan
That dances as often as dance it can,
Hanging so light and hanging so high
On the topmost twig that looks up at the sky.

The second characteristic of genius, that which distinguishes its highest degree, relates to form. It may be termed completeness, or the power of producing a well-proportioned whole. By a well-proportioned whole, we mean a work of art in which one central idea pervades, connects, and determines all the parts; where the greatest diversity of matter is nicely balanced by unity of purpose; where the same leading thought shines visibly through every variety of attitude and scene;—a work which, originating in a happy conception, and grounded upon a rational plan, has all its parts proportioned to that plan, pursues a consistent course, has beginning, middle, and end, moulds itself, as it were, by the self-determining power of its subject, into a compact and pleasing form, and produces, when finished, a simple and undivided impression. Thus a good literary composition may be known by the same test by which we judge of an architectural work, unity of design and totality of effect. Some of Shakspeare's plays, "Othello," for example, or "Romeo and Juliet," will illustrate our meaning. Indeed, the greatest literary productions of ancient and modern times, whether dramatic, epic, or didactic, whether they be histories, orations, or systems of philosophy, all are marked with this characteristic. And not only literary productions, but all that is great in every department of intellectual exertion, a good painting, a masterpiece of sculpture, or in active life a masterpiece of policy, or in mechanics a useful invention, a well-contrived machine, any and every creation of the human mind, so far as it conforms to this standard,—unity and completeness,—is a work of genius. Genius then, in its most perfect state, is known by its *"perfect work."* A writer in whom this quality is wanting, betrays the defect in the loose and disjointed character of his composition. The difference between such a writer and one who possesses the quality we have described, is like the contrast we may suppose between the *coup d'œil*[3] of an eagle who surveys whole landscapes from his perch amid the clouds, and the vision of an insect to whose microscopic eye the minutest object divides itself into numberless fragments. The difference in the productions of these men resembles that which distinguishes the growth of an organic from that of a mineral product;—the one developes itself into determinate forms by the evolution of a single germinal principle, the other irregularly swells its bulk by heterogeneous accretions. Mr. Coleridge is one of those in whom this quality of completeness, the power of producing a whole, is entirely wanting. We have never met with a writer whose works are so patched and ill made up. There does not occur to us at this moment a single production of his, which has the least pretensions to shape.

As to the charge of obscurity, so often and obstinately urged against Mr. Coleridge's prose writings, we cannot admit it in any thing like the extent in which it has been applied. So far as there is *any* ground for this complaint, it is owing to the author's excessive anxiety to make himself intelligible, an anxiety which leads him to present a subject in so many points of view, that we are sometimes in danger of losing the main topic amid the variety of collateral and illustrative matter which he gathers round it. We are inclined, however, to suspect that the greater part of this alleged obscurity exists in the mind of the reader, and not in the author. In an age when all classes read, and when a consequent demand for popular works has rendered every thing superficial that could be made superficial, and excluded almost every thing that could not, when the best books in the language are the least read, when such works as Butler's Analogy and others of the same stamp are confined within the narrow circle of professional reading,[4]— while at the same time complaints are heard that we have no good books to put into the hands of infidels,—when in religion and philosophy superficial treatises and books of amusement have almost supplanted scientific inquiry,—when, even in the department of taste, novels and tales supersede Shakspeare and Milton;—in such an age, we are not surprised to hear the charge of obscurity preferred against books whose only fault is that they deserve, and therefore require, a little more study than we are compelled to bestow upon a novel or a tract. It is to be feared that the men of this generation have been spoiled by the indulgence shown to their natural indolence, and made tender by the excessive pains which have been taken to render every thing easy and smooth. Our intellects are dwarfed and stunted by the constant stimulus of amusement which is mixed up with all our literary food. There is no taste for hardy application, no capacity for vigorous and manly efforts of the understanding. Whatever taxes the mind, instead of exciting it, is deemed a burthen. A hard word scares us; a proposition, which does not explain itself at first glance, troubles us; whatever is *supersensual* and cannot be made plain by images addressed to the senses, is denounced as obscure, or beckoned away as mystical and extravagant. Whatever lies beyond the limits of ordinary and outward experience, is regarded as the ancient geographers regarded the greater portion of the globe,—as a land of shadows and chimæras. In a treatise on mechanics or astronomy, many things would be unintelligible to one who is ignorant of mathematics; but would it be fair in such a one to charge the author with a difficulty which arises from his own ignorance? Some writers are clear because they are shallow. If it be complained that Mr. Coleridge is not one of these, we shall not deny a charge which is applicable also, and in a much greater degree to much wiser men. He is certainly not a shallow writer, but, as we think, a very profound one, and his style is for the most part as clear as the nature of his thoughts will admit. To those only is he obscure who have no depths within themselves corresponding to his depths, and such will do well to consider, as Bishop Butler has said in reference to his own work,—"that the question is not whether a more intelligible book might have been written, but whether the subjects which he handles will admit of greater perspicuity in the treatment of them."

In a review of Mr. Coleridge's literary life, we must not omit to notice that marked fondness for metaphysics, and particularly for German metaphysics, which has exercised so decisive an influence over all his writings. Had it been given to him to interpret German metaphysics to his countrymen, as Mr. Cousin has interpreted them to the French nation, or had it been possible for him to have constructed a system of his own, we should not have regretted his indulgence of a passion which we must now condemn as a source of morbid dissatisfaction with received opinions, unjustified by any serious attempt to introduce others and better.[5] From his vigorous understanding, his acute dialectic powers, his complete knowledge of the subject, his historical research, and power of expression, something more might have been expected than the meagre sketch contained in his autobiography.[6] That Mr. Coleridge has done so little in the way of original production in this department, we ascribe to the same mental defect which has already been remarked upon, namely, the preponderance of the reflective over the creative faculty, and the consequent inability to collect, and embody in systematic forms, the results of his inquiries. But though so ill-qualified for the work of production, one would think the translator of Wallenstein might have interpreted for us all that is most valuable in the speculations of Kant and his followers.[7] It has been said that these works are untranslatable, but without sufficient grounds. That they are not translatable by one who has not an intimate acquaintance with the transcendental philosophy, is abundantly evident from the recent attempt which has been made in England to translate Tennemann.[8] But in this respect, and indeed in every respect, Mr. Coleridge is eminently fitted for such a task; and it is the more to be regretted that he has not undertaken it, as the number of those who are thus fitted is exceedingly small, while the demand for information on this subject is constantly increasing. We are well aware that a mere translation, however perfect, would be inadequate to convey a definite notion of transcendentalism to one who has not the metaphysical talent necessary to conceive and reproduce in himself a system whose only value to us must depend upon our power to construct it for ourselves from the materials of our own consciousness, and which in fact exists to us only on this condition.

While we are on this ground, we beg leave to offer a few explanatory remarks respecting German metaphysics,[9] which seem to us to be called for by the present state of feeling among literary men in relation to this subject. We believe it impossible to understand fully the design of Kant and his followers, without being endowed to a certain extent with the same powers of abstraction and synthetic generalization which they possess in so eminent a degree. In order to become fully master of their meaning, one must be able to find it in himself. Not all are born to be philosophers, or are capable of becoming philosophers, any more than all are capable of becoming poets or musicians. The works of the transcendental philosophers may be translated word for word, but still it will be impossible to get a clear idea of their philosophy, unless we raise ourselves at once to a transcendental point of view. Unless we take our station with the philosopher and proceed from his ground as our starting-point, the whole system will appear to us an inextricable puzzle. As in astronomy the motions of the heavenly bodies seem confused to the geocentric observer, and are intelligible only when referred to their heliocentric place, so there is only one point from which we can clearly understand and decide upon the speculations of Kant and his followers; that point is the interior consciousness, distinguished from the common consciousness, by its being an active and not a passive state. In the language of the school, it is a free intuition, and can only be attained by a vigorous effort of the will. It is from an ignorance of this primary condition, that the writings of these men have been denounced as vague and mystical. Viewing them from the distance we do, their discussions seem to us like objects half enveloped in mist; the little we can distinguish seems most portentously magnified and distorted by the unnatural refraction through which we behold it, and the point where they touch the earth is altogether lost. The effect of such writing upon the uninitiated, is like being in the company of one who has inhaled an exhilarating gas. We witness the inspiration, and are astounded at the effects, but we can form no conception of the feeling until we ourselves have experienced it. To those who are without the veil, then, any *exposé* of transcendental views must needs be unsatisfactory. Now if any one chooses to deny the point which these writers assume, if any one chooses to call in question the metaphysical existence of this interior consciousness, and to pronounce the whole system a mere fabrication, or a gross self-delusion,—to such a one the disciples of this school have nothing further to say; for him their system was not conceived. Let him content himself, if he can, with "that compendious philosophy which talking of mind, but thinking of brick and mortar, or other images equally abstracted from body, contrives a theory of spirit, by nicknaming matter, and in a few hours can qualify the dullest of its disciples to explain the *omne scibile*[10] by reducing all things to impressions, ideas, and sensations." The disciples of Kant wrote for minds of quite another stamp, they wrote for minds that seek with faith and hope a solution of questions which that philosophy meddles not with,—questions which relate to spirit and form, substance and life, free will and fate, God and eternity. Let those who feel no interest in these questions, or who believe not in the possibility of our approaching any nearer to a solution of them, abstain for ever from a department of inquiry for which they have neither talent nor call. There are certain periods in the history of society, when, passing from a state of spontaneous production to a state of reflection, mankind are particularly disposed to inquire concerning themselves and their destination, the nature of their being, the evidence of their knowledge, and the grounds of their faith. Such a tendency is one of the characteristics of the present age, and the German philosophy is the strongest expression of that tendency; it is a striving after information on subjects which have been usually considered as beyond the reach of human intelligence, an attempt to penetrate into the most hidden mysteries of our being. In every philosophy there are three things to be considered, the object, the method, and the result. In the transcendental system, the *object* is to discover in every form of finite existence, an infinite and unconditioned as the ground of its existence, or rather as the ground of our knowledge of its existence, to refer all phenomena to certain *noumena*,[11] or laws of cognition. It is not a *ratio essendi*, but a *ratio cognoscendi*;[12] it seeks not to explain the existence of God and creation, objectively considered, but to explain our knowledge of their existence. It is not a skeptical philosophy;[13] it seeks not to overthrow, but to build up; it wars not with the common opinions and general experience of mankind, but aims to place these on a scientific basis, and to verify them by scientific demonstrations.

The method is synthetical, proceeding from a given point, the lowest that can be found in our consciousness, and deducing from that point "the whole world of intelligences, with the whole system of their representations." The correctness or philosophical propriety of the construction which is to be based upon this given point, this absolute thesis, must be assumed for a while, until proved by the successful completion of the system which it is designed to establish. The test by which we are to know that the system is complete, and the method correct, is the same as that by which we judge of the correct construction of the material arch,—continuity and self-dependence. The last step in the process, the keystone of the fabric, is the deduction of time, space, and variety, or, in other words, (as time, space, and variety include the elements of all empiric knowledge) the establishing of a coincidence between the facts of ordinary experience and those which we have discovered within ourselves, and scientifically derived from our first fundamental position. When this step is accomplished, the system is complete, the hypothetical frame-work may then fall, and the structure will support itself.[14]

We have called the method synthetical; we should rather say that it is an alternation of synthesis and antithesis. Every synthesis, according to Fichte in the "Wissenschaftslehre,"[15] presupposes an antithesis; every antithesis, by limitation of the terms opposed, must be reconciled into a synthesis; in every new synthesis thus obtained, new antitheses are found; these again must be reconciled, and so on, till we come to a stand. The first proposition in the "Wissenschaftslehre" is stated thus, $A = A$. In this proposition the first term is a something, A unconditionally proposed; the second term is the same A reflected upon. I propose A, and then, reflecting upon it, find that it is A. This identity arises not from any quality in the thing proposed; it exists solely in my own consciousness. $A = A$, because I, the being who proposed it, am the same with I, the being who reflects upon it. Consequently the proposition, $A = A$, is equivalent to the proposition, $I = I$. Again, I propose $-A = -A$, or A unconditionally denied not equal to A unconditionally proposed; consequently not equal to A, the object of reflection in the former proposition. Now the possibility of my denying A presupposes and depends upon my power of proposing or affirming A. $-A$ is relative, and can exist only so far as A exists in my consciousness. Consequently, I, the being who now denies A, must be the same with I, the being who first proposed or affirmed A, otherwise $-A$ might be equal to A. This is what is meant by identity of consciousness. I find then in consciousness, two opposites apparently incompatible with each other, absolute affirmation, and absolute negation. Here then is the first antithesis. Now how can these two things exist together? Why does not the one exclude the other? They can be reconciled only by the introduction of a new term.[16] This new term is the idea of divisibility or limitation. It is then no longer absolute, but partial affirmation and negation. What was first unconditionally affirmed to exist, and if allowed unconditional existence must of course exclude its opposite, is now allowed to exist only so far as its opposite does not exist, and the opposite exists only so far as this does not exist, i.e., they coexist by mutual limitation; they define and determine each other. The *I* proposes itself as divisible or limitable, and determined by the *not-I*, and it proposes the *not-I* as divisible and determined by the *I*, and here we have the first synthesis. In this synthesis we find new antithesis, which, by further qualification must be reconciled as the first was reconciled into new syntheses, and so on till we arrive at absolute unity, or absolute contradiction.

This mode of proceeding is peculiar to Fichte, but it is a form of the method used to a greater or less extent by all the philosophers of that school. Defining it by that which is common to all its forms, we may call it the method of synthetic conclusions from opposite terms. Kant first suggested this method in his treatise entitled "The use of Negative Quantities in Metaphysics." To *him*, the father of the critical philosophy, we are indebted for the successful cultivation of the preparatory, or, to use his own expression, the "propaideutic" branches of the science. He did not himself create a system, but he furnished the hints and materials from which all the system of his followers have been framed. In his preface to the second edition of the "Critique of pure Reason," he makes us acquainted with the train of reasoning which led to the course he has adopted in his metaphysical inquiries. "He had been struck with the fact, that, while other departments of knowledge, availing themselves of scientific method, were constantly and regularly advancing, intellectual philosophy alone, although the most ancient of all sciences, and the one which would remain, though all the rest should be swallowed up in the vortex of an all-ingulphing barbarism,—intellectual philosophy alone, appears to be still groping in the dark, sometimes advancing and sometimes receding, but making on the whole little actual progress. How are we to account for this fact? Is a science of metaphysics impossible? Why then has nature implanted within us this ardent longing after certain and progressive knowledge on subjects of all others the most interesting to the human soul; or how can we place any confidence in our reason, when it fails us in the investigation of such topics as these? But perhaps the fault lies with us. May not our want of success be owing to a wrong method? The science of geometry was probably for some time in the same condition that metaphysical inquiry is now; but ever since the demonstration of the equilateral triangle commonly ascribed to Thales, it has advanced in regular and rapid progression. Physical science has done the same since Bacon.[17] It is evident that both these branches of knowledge are indebted for the success with which they have been cultivated, to the fortunate discovery of a right method. May not the want of such a method constitute the sole obstacle to the progress of metaphysical science? Hitherto philosophers have assumed that our cognitions are determined by the objects they represent. On this assumption it is evident that every attempt to establish any thing *a priori* concerning them (the objects) must be vain. Let us therefore try whether, in metaphysical problems, we may not succeed better by assuming that the objects without us are determined by our cognitions. Copernicus, when he found that he could not explain the motions of the heavenly bodies on the supposition that the starry host revolves around the observer, changed his theory and made the observer revolve, and the stars stand still.[18] Reversing this process, let us, since the supposition that our intuitions depend on the nature of the world without, will not answer, assume that the world without depends on the nature of our intuitions. Thus perhaps we shall be enabled to realize that great desideratum—*a priori* knowledge."

We have here the key to the whole critical philosophy, the very essence of which consists in proposing an absolute self as unconditionally existing, incapable of being determined by any thing higher than itself, but determining all things through itself. On this fundamental position, Fichte, in his "Wissenschaftslehre," endeavoured to found a system of consequential deductions, explanatory of the grounds of all human belief; a system which should serve as a foundation-science for all other sciences. With whatever success this attempt was attended in the author's own estimation, it has never been generally satisfactory to others. The system is altogether too subjective. The possibility of any knowledge of the absolute or self-existing, is denied; we can know only concerning our knowledge; man's personal freedom is the basis of all reality; with many other assertions of like character.

Next to Fichte in the order of time, but differing widely from him as it respects the tendency of their respective systems, appears Schelling, the projector of the "natural philosophy" so called; a branch of transcendentalism which was afterwards more fully developed, and reduced to a system by Oken.[19] If Fichte confined himself too exclusively to the subjective, Schelling on the other hand treats principally of the object, and endeavours to show that the outward world is of the same essence with the thinking mind, both being different manifestations of the same divine principle. He is the ontologist of the Kantian school. All knowledge, according to him,[20] consists in an agreement between an object and a subject. In all science, therefore, there are these two elements or poles, subject and object, or nature and intelligence; and corresponding to these two poles there are two fundamental sciences, the one beginning with nature and proceeding upward to intelligence, the other beginning with intelligence and ending in nature. The first is natural philosophy, the second transcendental philosophy. Of all the Germans who have trod the path of metaphysical inquiry under the guidance of Kant, Schelling is the most satisfactory. In him intellectual philosophy is more ripe, more substantial, more promising, and, if we may apply such a term to such speculations, more practical than in any of the others. Though in one sense a follower of Kant, he begins a new period, and may be considered as the founder of a new school. Of the other successors of Kant, Hegel, Oken, Fries, Reinhold, Krug, Platner and others, our information would not enable us to say much, and our limits forbid us to say any thing.[21]

The three whom we have particularized are the only ones who appear to us to possess much individuality, or to have exercised much influence in the philosophical world. In designating these, we have done all that this brief sketch requires. We need only add, that the best histories of philosophy, and, with the exception of Cousin's, the only good ones we have, are productions of German philosophers.

If now it be asked, as probably it will be asked, whether any definite and substantial good has resulted from the labors of Kant and his followers, we answer, Much. More than metaphysics ever before accomplished, these men have done for the advancement of the human intellect. It is true the immediate, and if we may so speak, the calculable results of their speculations are not so numerous nor so evident as might have been expected: these are chiefly comprised under the head of method. Yet even here we have enough to make us rejoice that such men have been, and that they have lived and spoken in our day. We need mention only the sharp and rightly dividing lines that have been drawn within and around the kingdom of human knowledge; the strongly marked distinctions of subject and object, reason and understanding, phenomena and noumena;—the categories established by Kant; the moral liberty proclaimed by him as it had never been proclaimed by any before; the authority and evidence of law and duty set forth by Fichte; the universal harmony illustrated by Schelling. But in mentioning these things, which are the direct results of the critical philosophy, we have by no means exhausted all that that philosophy has done for liberty and truth. The preeminence of Germany among the nations of our day in respect of intellectual culture, is universally acknowledged; and we do fully believe that whatever excellence that nation has attained in science, in history, or poetry is mainly owing to the influence of her philosophy, to the faculty which that philosophy has imparted of seizing on the spirit of every question, and determining at once the point of view from which each subject should be regarded,—in one word, to the transcendental method. In theology this influence has been most conspicuous. We are indebted to it for that dauntless spirit of inquiry which has investigated, and for that amazing erudition which has illustrated, every corner of biblical lore. Twice it has saved the religion of Germany,—once from the extreme of fanatic extravagance, and again, from the verge of speculative infidelity. But, though most conspicuous in theology, this influence has been visible in every department of intellectual exertion to which the Germans have applied themselves for the last thirty years. It has characterized each science and each art, and all bear witness to its quickening power. A philosophy which has given such an impulse to mental culture and scientific research, which has done so much to establish and to extend the spiritual in man, and the ideal in nature, needs no apology; it commends itself by its fruits, it lives in its fruits, and must ever live, though the name of its founder be forgotten, and not one of its doctrines survive.

We have wandered far from the subject of our critique. It is time we should return and take our final leave. It was not our intention in this brief review of Mr. Coleridge's literary merits to criticize in particular any one of the works whose titles stand at the head of this article. But the "Aids to Reflection," as containing an account of the author's religious views, demand a passing notice in a work like this. In his biography, Mr. Coleridge describes the state of his mind, with respect to religion, previous to his leaving England, by saying that his head was with Spinoza, and his heart with Paul and John;[22] which means, we presume, that he found it impossible to reconcile his religion with his philosophy. In another passage, he tells us that he was at this time a Unitarian, "or more accurately a *Psilanthropist*," which term he chooses to consider as synonymous with the former. We understand it very differently. Psilanthropism, according to our definition, means Humanitarianism,—a doctrine which has no more necessary connexion with the Unitarian faith than with the Roman Catholic. In the "Aids to Reflection," our author would have us believe that he has accomplished at last the wished for reconciliation between his head and his heart. To us the breach seems as wide as ever. In this work he appears as a zealous Trinitarian, and a warm defender of the doctrines of the English church. We have no doubt of his sincerity; but unless we err greatly, he has either misunderstood his own views, or grossly misinterpreted the doctrines of his church. His view of the Trinity, as far as we can understand it, is as consistent with Unitarianism, to say the least, as his former psilanthropic scheme. His opinion of the atonement is far from Orthodox; the idea of vicarious suffering he rejects with disdain. The strong expressions used by St. Paul in reference to this subject, he tells us are not intended to designate the *act* of redemption, but are only figurative expressions descriptive of its effects. The *act* of redemption he calls a "mystery," which term, as it may mean any thing, means, in reality, nothing. The other doctrines fare in the same way. Every thing is first mystified into a sort of imposing indistinctness, and then pronounced to be genuine Orthodoxy. The truth is, Mr. Coleridge, though a great scholar, was not qualified in point of biblical learning for an undertaking like this. Many of his assertions, we are persuaded, would not have been hazarded, had he not taken his understanding of the New Testament for granted, but studied that book with the same diligence and perseverance which he appears to have bestowed upon other works. With these exceptions, however, we consider the "Aids to Reflection" as a very valuable work. The distinctions between prudence and morality, and between natural and spiritual religion, are sound and important.

On the whole, in summing up Mr. Coleridge's merits, we cannot but regard him as endowed with an intellect of the highest order, as a profound thinker, and a powerful writer, though not a successful poet or an amiable critic. As a translator, he has no equal in English literature. His prejudices are strong,[23] his tastes confined, his pedantry often oppressive, his egotism unbounded. Yet we can never read a chapter in any one of his prose works, without feeling ourselves intellectually exalted and refined. Never can we sufficiently admire the depth and richness of his thoughts, the beauty of his illustrations, the exceeding fitness and force of all his works. If he is too minute in details to shine in the higher walks of literature, too anxious in the elaboration of single parts, to succeed in the total effect, it must be allowed that few compositions will bear so close an inspection, and still maintain their color and their gloss so well as his. If he divides nature and life and human art into too many particulars, it cannot be denied that his divisions, like those of the prism, give to each particular an individuality and a glory, which it did not possess while merged and lost in the whole to which it belonged. If he has produced far less than might have been expected from a mind so ready and so rich, we will nevertheless cheerfully accord to him the credit which he claims in his own appeal against a similar charge. "Would that the criterion of a scholar's utility were the number and moral value of the truths which he has been the means of throwing into the general circulation, or the number and value of the minds whom by his conversation or letters he has excited into activity, and supplied with the germs of their after-growth. A distinguished rank might not even then be awarded to my exertions, but I should dare look forward with confidence to an honorable acquittal."[24]

Source: Frederic Henry Hedge, "Coleridge's Literary Character," *Christian Examiner*, 14 (March 1833): 109–129. This reviews *Biographia Literaria* (1817), *The Poetical Works of S. T. Coleridge* (1829), *Aids to Reflection*, ed. James Marsh (1829), and *The Friend* (1809–1810). The quote is from *The Transcendentalists*, ed. Perry Miller (Cambridge: Harvard University Press, 1950), p. 67.

Notes

1. See Biographia Literaria, Chapter 1. [Hedge's note]
2. *The Statesman's Manual* (1816); James Marsh (1794–1842), minister and philosopher, was president of the University of Vermont when he prepared

the first American edition of Coleridge's *Aids to Reflection* with a lengthy introduction.

3. *coup d'œil*: a glance (literally, stroke of the eye).
4. *The Analogy of Religion, Natural and Revealed, to the Constitution and Course of Nature* (1736), by Joseph Butler (1692–1752), bishop of Bristol and of Durham.
5. Victor Cousin (1792–1867), French transcendental philosopher.
6. See Biographia Literaria, Chapter 12. [Hedge's note]
7. Coleridge had translated *Wallenstein*, by the German romantic philosopher Johann Christoph Friedrich von Schiller (1759–1805), in 1800; Immanuel Kant (1724–1804), German philosopher who proposed the importance of innate ideas.
8. Wilhelm Gottlieb Tennemann (1761–1819), German philosopher.
9. When we speak of *German* metaphysics we wish to be understood as referring to the systems of intellectual philosophy which have prevailed in Germany since Kant. Our remarks do not apply to Leibnitz, Wolf, or any of Kant's predecessors. [Hedge's note] Gottfried Wilhelm von Leibnitz (1646–1716), German philosopher and mathematician; Friedrich August Wolf (1759–1824), classicist and philologist.
10. *omne scibile*: the whole of.
11. Kant, Kritik der renen Vernunft. [Hedge's note to *Critique of Pure Reason* (1781)] This is part of Kant's paired distinction between things as they appear to us (phenomena) and things as they are in themselves (noumena).
12. *ratio essendi*: reason for being; *ratio cognoscendi*: reason for thinking.
13. Perhaps the writings of Fichte may be considered as an exception to this statement. [Hedge's note] Johann Gottlieb Fichte (1762–1814), German metaphysician.
14. We give the *ideal* of the method proposed; we are by no means prepared to say that this idea has been realized, or that it can be realized. [Hedge's note]
15. Coleridge translates this word, "lore of ultimate science"; it means the science of knowing. [Hedge's note]
16. It was found necessary to abridge the process so much, that perhaps the conclusions may not appear strictly consequential. Let it be understood, then, that affirmation and negation stand for existence and non-existence—the *I* and *not I*—which of course, when absolute must eventually exclude each other. [Hedge's note]
17. Thales (ca. 640–ca. 546 B.C.), Greek geometrician and astronomer; Roger Bacon (ca. 1214–1294), English scientist and philosopher.
18. Nicolaus Copernicus (1473–1543), Polish astronomer credited with founding the science of modern astronomy, believed that the planets revolved around the sun.
19. Friedrich Wilhelm Joseph von Schelling (1775–1854), German philosopher; Lorenz Oken (1779–1851), German naturalist and philosopher.
20. Schelling, Transcendentalem Idealismus. [Hedge's note to *System des transzendentalem Idealismus* (1800)]

21. The German philosophers Georg Wilhelm Friedrich Hegel (1770–1831), Jakob Friedrich Fries (1773–1843), Karl Leonhard Reinhold (1757–1823), Wilhelm Traugott Krug (1770–1842), and Ernst Platner (1744–1818).
22. Baruch Spinoza (1632–1677), Dutch philosopher and pantheist.
23. Mr. Coleridge's prejudices against the French nation, and all that belongs to them, are unreasonable and absurd in the extreme. He is said, upon one occasion, during the delivery of a public lecture, in the presence of a numerous assembly, to have thanked God in the most serious manner, for so ordering events, "that he was entirely ignorant of a single word of that frightful jargon, the French language." [Hedge's note]
24. Biographia Literaria, Chapter 10. [Hedge's note]

Elizabeth Palmer Peabody

from "Explanatory Preface" to Record of a School: Exemplifying the General Principles of Spiritual Culture

(1836)

ELIZABETH PALMER PEABODY (1804–1894) published the first edition of the *Record*, her edited account of Bronson Alcott's Temple School, in 1835. In it, she recorded her descriptions of how Alcott taught such typical subjects as geography, writing, math, art, religion, and languages, and such atypical topics as "Conversations on the Human Body and Its Culture." Alcott's Socratic method of questioning (rather than instructing by rote drills, as was the general practice) presupposed the innate goodness of his students, and he felt his role was to bring out their abilities, rather than his following tradition and seeing them as empty vessels to be filled with knowledge. His unusual methods (and his—for the time—frank discussions of sexuality and religion) would eventually bring down the wrath of the Boston public when he published his two-volume *Conversations with Children on the Gospels* (1836–1837). Here, Peabody has a sense of what is going to be the public reaction to Alcott, and her preface (which was also published as a pamphlet) is as much an attempt to clarify his methods to the general public as it is an attempt to distance herself from him and the gathering storm.

A fascinating figure in the Transcendentalist movement, Peabody championed reform causes her entire life, beginning with her service as Channing's amanuensis and ending with her octogenarian support for Native Americans. Her West Street bookstore carried one of the finest selections of continental literature in New England, and was the site in the 1840s for Margaret Fuller's Conversations. She published the *Dial* (in 1842–1843) and her own journal,

Aesthetic Papers (1849), which lasted for one issue. Her main interest was in educational reform, and she is considered one of the founders of the American kindergarten movement. Her preface to the *Record* also puts forth many of her own theories of teaching, either on their own or in contrast to Alcott's.

T he work now put to the press, for the second time, has, in several particulars, been misunderstood. And I am told that I must ascribe this to my own want of perspicacity,—especially in the last chapter, in which I undertook to sum up the general principles of Spiritual Culture, deduced from a view of the soul, that some persons say is unintelligible. On this account, I here attempt another explanation of the psychology, which is made the basis of Mr. Alcott's School, with the principles and methods, which are evolved from it; intending to alter that chapter considerably, although there is nothing in it, which I wish to take back, or by which I did not mean something important.

To contemplate Spirit in the Infinite Being, has ever been acknowledged to be the only ground of true Religion. To contemplate Spirit in External nature, is universally allowed to be the only true Science. To contemplate Spirit in ourselves, and in our fellow men, is obviously the only means of understanding social duty, and quickening within ourselves a wise Humanity.—In general terms,—Contemplation of Spirit is the first principle of Human Culture; the foundation of Self-education.

This principle, Mr. Alcott begins with applying to the education of the youngest children. Considering early education as a leading of the young mind to self-education, he would have it proceed on the same principles. And few will disagree with him, in drawing this inference from the premises.

But it is not pretended, that it is peculiar to the system of education, developed in the following pages, to aim at the contemplation of Spirit, at least in theory. But perhaps it will be admitted that Mr. Alcott is somewhat peculiar in the faith which he puts in this principle, in his fearless and persevering application of it; and especially, in his not setting the child to look for Spirit, *first*, in the vast and varied field of external nature; as seems to be the sole aim of common education. For, in common education as is well known, the attention is primarily and principally directed to the part of language which consists of the names of outward things; as well as to books which scientifically class and explain them; or, which narrate events in a matter-of-fact manner.

One would think that there has been proof enough, that this common plan is a bad one, in the universally acknowledged difficulty, of making children study those things to which they are first put, without artificial stimulus;—also, in the absolute determination, with which so many fine minds turn aside, from word-knowledge and dry science, to play and fun, and to whatever interests the imagination or heart;—and, finally, in the very small amount of acquisition, which after all the pains taken, is generally laid up, from school days. Besides, is it not *a priori* absurd? Is not external nature altogether too vast a field for the eye of childhood to command? And is it not impossible for the mind to discover the Spirit in unity, unless the field is, as it were, commanded? The result of the attempt, has generally been that no spiritual culture has taken place at school. In most cases, the attention has been bewildered, discouraged, or dissipated by a variety of objects and in the best cases, the mind has become onesided and narrow, by being confined to some particular department. Naturalists are generally full of oddities.

Instead, therefore, of making it his aim to make children investigate External nature, after Spirit, Mr. Alcott leads them in the first place, to the contemplation of Spirit as it unveils itself within themselves. He thinks there is no intrinsic difficulty in doing this, inasmuch as a child can as easily perceive and name pleasure, pain, love, anger, hate and any other exercises of soul, to which himself is subjected, as he can see the objects before his eyes, and thus a living knowledge of that part of language, which expresses intellectual and moral ideas, and involves the study of his own consciousness of feelings and moral law, may be gained, External nature being only made use of, as imagery, to express the inward life which he experiences. Connected with this self contemplation, and constantly checking any narrowing effect of egotism, or self complacency, which it may be supposed to engender, is the contemplation of God, that can so easily be associated with it. For as the word finite gives meaning to the word infinite, so the finite virtue always calls up in the mind, an Idea which is henceforth named, and becomes an attribute to the Eternal Spirit. Thus a child, having felt what a just action is, either in himself or another, henceforth has an Idea of Justice, which is pure and perfect, in the same ratio, as he is unsophisticated; and is more and more comprehensive of particular applications, as his Reason unfolds. How severe and pure it often is, in a child, thousands have felt!

So when a cause is named,—the First Cause becomes the immediate object of inquiry. Who taught the hen to lay its eggs, said a little boy to his mother. The hen's mother, was the reply. Who taught the hen's mother? That mother had a mother. But who taught the first hen that ever laid an egg in the world?—he exclaimed impatiently. This child had never heard of a God. What mother or nurse, will not recognize that this is the way children talk? It is proverbial, that children ask questions so deep, that they cannot be answered. The perception of the finite, seems with them, to be followed immediately, by a plunge into the infinite. A wise observer will see this, even through the broken language of infancy, and often through its voiceless silence. And a deep reasoner on such facts, will see, that a plan of education, founded on the idea of studying Spirit in their own consciousness, and in God,—is one that will meet children just where they are,—much more than will the common plan of pursuing the laws of nature, as exhibited in movements of the external world.

But some say, that the philosophy of the Spirit is a disputed philosophy;—that the questions,—what are its earliest manifestations upon earth? and what are the means and laws of its growth?—are unsettled; and therefore it is not a subject for dogmatic teaching.

Mr. Alcott replies to this objection, that his teaching is not dogmatic; that nothing more is assumed by him, than that Spirit exists, bearing a relation to the body in which it is manifested, analogous to the relation which God bears to the external creation. And it is only those persons who are spiritualists, so far as to admit this, whom he expects to place children under his care.

At this point, his dogmatic teaching ends; and here he takes up the Socratic mode. He begins with asking questions upon the meanings of the words, which the children use in speaking, and which they find in their spelling lessons, requiring illustrations of them, in sentences composed or remembered. This involves the study of Spirit. He one day began with the youngest of thirty scholars, to ask illustrations of the word brute; and there were but three literal answers. A brute, was a man who killed another; a drunken man; a man who beat his wife; a man without any love; but it was always a man. In one instance, it was a boy beating a dog. Which is the brute, said Mr. Alcott, the boy or the dog? The boy; said the little girl, with the gravest face. This case indicates a general tendency of childhood, and is an opening therefore, for speaking of the outward as the sign of the inward, and for making all the reading and spelling lessons, exercises for defining and illustrating words.—The lessons on language, given in the Record, have generally been admitted to be most valuable. Most persons seem to be struck with the advantages, necessarily to be derived from the habit of inquiring into the history of words from their material origin, and throughout the spiritual applications of them, which the Imagination makes.

It is true, that one person, in leading such an exercise, may sometimes give a cast to the whole inquiry, through the influence of his own idiosyncracies and favorite doctrines; and Mr. Alcott's definitions may not be defensible in every instance. I am not myself prepared to say, that I entirely trust his associations. But he is so successful, in arousing the activity of the children's own minds, and he gives such free scope to their associations, that his personal peculiarities are likely to have much less influence than those of most instructors. Not by any means, so much objection could be made to his school, on this account, as can be made to Johnson's Dictionary; for the manner in which the words are studied and talked about in school, is such, that the children must be perpetually reminded, that nothing connected with spiritual subjects can be finally settled into any irreversible formula of doctrine, by finite and unperfected minds;—excepting, perhaps the two moral laws, on which hang the law and the prophets.

Some objections have been made, however, to the questionings upon consciousness, of which specimens are given in the lessons on Self-Analysis.—It is said, that their general tendency must be to produce egotism.—This might be, if, in self-analysis, a perfect standard was not always kept before the mind, by constant reference to Jesus Christ, as the "truth of our nature;" and by means of that generalizing tendency, which I have noticed before; which always makes children go from finite virtue, to the Idea of the Perfect. We have found the general influence of the lessons on Self-Analysis, to be humbling to the self-conceited and vain,—though they have also encouraged and raised up the depressed and timid, in one or two instances. The objection seems to me, to have arisen from taking the word *self* in a too limited signification. The spirit within, is what is meant by *self* considered as an object of philosophical investigation. I think myself, that the lessons would more appropriately have been styled, analysis of human nature, than self-analysis; for excepting the first one, they were of a very general character, and constantly became more so, in their progress. Yet the impression of that first lesson is very probably the strongest on the mind of many readers. It consisted of a series of questions, calculated to bring out the strongest and most delicate sentiments of the individual soul. Testing questions were asked, which placed the child in the painful alternative of claiming the spirit of martyrdom, or denying her sincere affections for beloved friends. I believe there was no untruth told, and no selfexaltation felt, and consequently no harm done, in the particular instance; but I will admit that it was too much an analysis of the individual, and should certainly agree with those who think that the effect of such a course, might ultimately be to dwarf or dissipate, by forcing an expression of sentiments strictly personal, and perhaps to corrupt them. If there is one object more than another, to which may be applied Wordsworth's beautiful lines:—

> —Our meddling intellect,
> Misshapes the beauteous forms of things,
> We murder to dissect—[1]

it is to the personalities of the soul.

The instinctive delicacy with which children veil their deepest thoughts of love and tenderness for relatives, and their reasonable self gratulations, should not be violated I think, in order to gain knowledge, or for any imagined benefit to others. Indeed no knowledge can be gained, in this way. It would be as wise to tear the rosebud open, or invade the solitude of the chrysalis, with the hope of obtaining insight into the process of bloom or metamorphosis, as to expect to gain any knowledge of the soul, by drawing forth, by the personal power which an instructor may possess over the heart, conscience, or imagination, that confidence, which it is the precious prerogative of an individual to bestow spontaneously, when old enough to choose its depository. And Mr. Alcott, I believe, agrees with me in this, notwithstanding that he practically goes sometimes upon the very verge of the rights of reserve, as in the instance referred to. He doubted, immediately, whether that first lesson was wise, and materially changed the character of his questioning afterwards, and an attentive reader will observe, that questions of the same kind were not repeated after the first day. But I felt bound in conscience to put into the Record, every thing that transpired during that winter, and to present even the exercises that were afterwards modified; because I had called my book the Record of the actual School. I expected, however, that it would be read in the liberal spirit, a work on such a plan required; and that the general character of the exercises would be regarded, rather than the peculiarities of any one lesson, and especially of an introductory one, on entirely new ground.

But what I have said of the rights of reserve, does not respect all that is in the soul. There are relations and sentiments which regard objects of common interest to all souls; such as God, Jesus Christ, the human race as such, and duties in the abstract. These are fair subjects of questioning, with the affections appertaining to them, and there is a great good, which may arise from the consciousness of these sentiments in each individual being analysed and discriminated, and the relations themselves being discussed in a large company, all of whom share them, and the duties which spring from them. For so all narrowness and peculiar associations have a chance to be exchanged for something more enlarged, and the clearer Reason of some may aid the dimmer apprehension of others, less favored by nature or education. And, in this case, there is no fear, as has sometimes been suggested, of the mind's being dwarfed. It may and will take narrow views comparatively of Truth itself, but the danger is less, if this subject is first apprehended in childhood, than if it is approached for the first time at a later age; for in childhood the sense of Justice, and the sentiment of the Good and Beautiful, have not yet lost the holiness and divine balance of Innocence, or the glow and impulse first received from the Divine Being, who projected the individual soul into time and space, there to clothe itself with garments, by which it may see itself, and be seen by its fellow beings.

This view of childhood's comprehension, is confirmed by all, who have had much to do with cultivating the minds of children. Madame Neckar de Saussure, in her work on Progressive Education, says,—that the younger children are, the more exclusively they are moral beings, a position which she defends with much fine remark, replete with her usual practical good sense.[2] The phrenologists remark that conscientiousness is, generally speaking, larger in proportion in children, than in adults,[3]—(what a satire is this fact, if it be a fact, on our modes of education!)—and lastly, Jesus Christ always spoke of childhood as having peculiar moral sympathies;—being of the kingdom of heaven, &c.

There is however, one way, in which there is some danger of dwarfing the minds of children on these subjects. It is this. As it is sometimes necessary to imagine or refer to practical applications of principles, and to outward occasions of sentiments, in order to identify them, we are liable to present cases which are not entirely comprehensible by children who can perfectly realize the principle or sentiment, either in their own consciousness, or in application to a case whose terms they do understand. And Mr. Alcott may sometimes err in selecting his instances of application. But I think it is very rarely that he does. In the first edition of the Record, I noticed an instance, where I thought he had erred in this way. But after the book was printed, I found I had misrepresented his opinion. He told me he did not decidedly believe, as I there stated, that government had not the right of capital punishment. Still less did he mean to dogmatise on that point with his scholars. I thought at the time, it was a singular departure from the spirit of his method, to bring the children to a decision, on a disputed point of legislation,—that most extensive and complicated of all applications of principle to practice, and necessarily entirely out of the comprehension of children. And the only excuse I can give for making this misrepresentation, is, that on that day for the only time, I left the record in the hands of another, and left the room, and then made my inferences from it as it stood. Mr. Alcott says, that had I been there I should probably have heard nothing to which even I should have objected, notwithstanding my own opinion is, that society, in its collective capacity, has a right to inflict capital punishment on individuals, in defence of its members.

The contemplation of Spirit in God, is necessarily wrapt up in a study of language, leading to the study of the Soul, whose existence, sentiments, reason and strength of will, are God's gifts of spirit. But Mr. Alcott did not intend to confine himself to such allusions to Jesus Christ as are found in the Record. Having arranged the four gospels into a continuous story, to illustrate the career of Spirit on earth, he began the second year of his school, by reading these with conversations, and he expects to prove that this mode of studying Spirit, is peculiarly within the reach of childhood, and particularly congenial to its holy Instincts, strong sympathies, ready Imagination, and unsophisticated Reason. In this, as in all his other questionings, his plan is a perfectly liberal one. Having read the lesson for the day, he asks for their own associations with words, their impressions of events, the action of their Imagination, and the conclusions of their Reason upon them. All sides of every subject are presented by the various children, and dwelt upon, at least until they are fully expressed; and there the subject is left, Mr. Alcott making no further decision upon what is said, than can be derived from the paraphrase, with which he generally closes, and which he makes, on the impulse of the moment. He does not wish the children to think, that the meaning of Scripture is a matter of authority; and this is the chief reason why he does not decide in favor of particular views, dogmatically. He thinks it is enough to start the mind on some subjects, to "wake the echo that will not sleep again," and lays out to guard them from error, rather by the general influences of his moral and intellectual discipline, than by giving them the formulas of his own creed. So successful has he proved to be, in avoiding controverted points, and keeping free from the technology of sect, that one day, when two ladies,—one a Trinitarian, and the other a Humanitarian,—were present at a lesson, on the first chapter of John, each left the room, saying to Mr. Alcott, "I perceive that my views are taught here."

Before dismissing this part of the subject, however, let me notice one thing, which is very extensively said, namely, that Mr. Alcott goes further, in his dogmatics, than to teach the existence of Spirit, in that relation to the body which the Deity holds to the Creation; for that he teaches the oriental doctrine of preexistence and emanation.

But this is not the case. Mr. Alcott indeed believes, that the body of an individual is a consequence, and was the first consequence of the existence of the individual spirit, that the first act of the soul, when breathed from the Divine Spirit, is an arrangement of particles around itself, as a means of expressing its individuality. In other words, he believes that birth is a Spiritual act and fact prior to embodiment. And does not every one believe this, who does not think the soul of an individual the temperament of a body, the effect of matter? For my own part, I believe, that this is the only way of conceiving the unity of a spirit; and that it is all the preexistence that is meant in Wordsworth's ode on Immortality, or that Plato himself meant to teach;[4] and that it certainly is the doctrine of Christianity, taught by Jesus Christ. But even this doctrine, Mr. Alcott has never taught dogmatically. It has come out spontaneously from the children themselves; and almost invariably, as soon as they come to see the divine nature of the conscience and the sentiments, and the relations of the human with the divine Being. It is entirely against the spirit of Mr. Alcott's plan to dogmatise even on what he believes. Some of the children have expressed a materialist theory, and I would venture to say, that they have never thought, with which party Mr. Alcott agrees, so entirely is he out of the habit of expressing his own views; and so entirely Socratic is his method of instruction. Indeed it is almost impossible for one who has not been in the school, to understand, how truly the opinion of others, even that of Mr. Alcott, becomes a secondary object of attention, after the mind has been opened into the region of Ideas through consciousness, by the key of well understood words. There is real intellectual activity, in these little minds; and a pursuit of truth on the true principles. This is the case, before it is evidenced by ready answers. It often happens that a child is some weeks and even months or a year, at school, without saying many things; but perfectly absorbed and attentive, and giving a silent vote, on all questions so decided: at last he begins to speak, and almost astonishes us, by his thoughts and expressions. The journals which the children begin to keep, as soon as they can join letters, also, often give indications of attention and interest, before there is much said. Mr. Alcott requires from all, undivided attention; excepting from a small class, consisting of those who do not read at all. These do not join in the general exercises, but sit at a side desk, and write, draw, and look at pictures, while he attends to the large class.

It will be granted that the general influence of studying language, consciousness, and the life of Jesus Christ, for the manifestations of Spirit, must be favorable to moral culture, unless there is something very forced about it; and the Record of a School will probably convince any impartial reader, that it can be done very easily and naturally, by such an instructor as Mr. Alcott. Speculating and talking about the moral nature, has, of itself, a tendency to place it uppermost in the mind; since there is an inward feeling, which raises the moral part of our nature above the intellectual and instinctive, whenever they are all brought into comparison. But this is not enough; especially where there is no dogmatic teaching. Thought should ever be accompanied with appropriate action. Mr. Alcott rests his chief dependence for the moral culture of his pupils, upon the moral discipline to which he subjects them. He makes every day's duties, the means of illustrating every day's speculations;—and vice versa. This will appear in the sequel.

But some of his methods of discipline have been questioned. Before I had had an opportunity of observing their operation with my own eyes, I was very much inclined to question some of them myself; and perhaps it will be the best means of doing both him and myself justice, to relate my own views upon this subject, and the modifications they have undergone, since I have been a spectator of his School.

I will begin with saying, that I have no doubt at all, that as far as regards this particular school, the methods have been in every respect salutary, and the best possible for the members of it. General intelligence, order, self-control, and goodwill, have been produced to a degree that is marvellous to see; especially, when we consider that his scholars' ages range from three years to twelve, and none are older, and most of them only eight or nine years old. I can indeed conceive of something quite equal, if not superior, in moral beauty, that may be gained on a different plan, supposing the school is composed of older scholars; and the education is a more private one, from the beginning. I do not know, however, but that my differing methods are applicable, more especially and exclusively, to girls.

The point from which I diverge from Mr. Alcott, in theory, is this: I think that a private conscience in the young will naturally be the highest. Mr. Alcott thinks a common conscience is to be cultivated in a school, and that this will be higher in all, than any one conscience would be, if it were private.

Pursuing my own idea in my own school, my method has, in theory, been this. I have begun with every individual, by taking it for granted, in the first place, that there is a predominating sense of duty. This is not artificial on my part; for the germ of the principle of duty, lies in every mind, I know; and generally, it is accompanied by a wish, at least, to follow duty. With this I would sympathise, and let my sympathy be felt, by showing my scholars that I can find the wish out, even when enveloped in many shadows. All derelictions from duty, I would meet with surprise, as accidental mistakes or indisputable misfortunes, according as the fact might be, and offer my advice, endeavoring to win a confidential exposure of the individual's own moral condition, as it appears to themselves, in order that I might wisely and tenderly give suitable advice. Thus would I establish a separate understanding with each particular scholar, and act the part of a religious friend, with each; while in general assembly, no reference should be made to any moral wrong-doing of any one; but it be courteously and charitably taken for granted, that all mean to act conscientiously and religiously.

This plan is of very fine influence, in many respects. Its tendency is to break up that odious combat which seems to go on in many schools, where there is a struggle, as it were, for power;—the children trying how far they can do wrong with impunity, and the teachers constantly feeling obliged to keep on a watch, in order to preserve their prerogative. Instead of this, it introduces a sentiment of discipleship, in which the contest is, who shall be beforehand,—the pupils in yielding a willing obedience; or the teachers in giving those parental tokens, which ensure this willing obedience.

Another tendency, no less salutary, is, to produce a tender and respectful courtesy, in the pupils, towards each other. Conscious of being engaged in the same moral course, of being assisted and inspired by the mind of the same respected friend, who only brings them to think of each other, on those points of the character of each, where there may be sympathy and understanding, they are not obliged to know any thing of one another, which is not a ground of respect, or at least of moral interest.

This method also tends to preserve all the delicate individualities of character, and to give appropriate and differing atmosphere and scope, to those flowers of delicacy and of sensibility, which, like the violets of the landscape are sunbeams in the shady places of private life. In this connection I would also observe that nothing will so effectually preserve the soul from habits of secresy, and undue reserve, as culture of the individual, as such; for nothing is so favorable to frank, open, unsuspicious, transparency of soul, expressed in look and manner,—as never to have been wounded, or ridiculed, or unjustly regarded, during that impressible season of life, when self-estimation is first forming. The human being was made, like every thing in the creation of God, for Expression. To be cherished, and helped forward, by the respectful tenderness, and generous liberality of mind, of the guardians and companions of its infancy, involves no danger of producing that folding up of the soul within itself, which is too often the disease of those, who have within them, what it would be a delight and a benefit for all their race to know. This disease, we shall find, is most frequent in those who have been put for education into some common mill, whence nothing can come out without bearing some particular stamp and superscription, and where of course all individualities, all that springs from the wonderful depths of personality, is rigorously worn off, or driven in. A delicate nature, in such a situation, is another form of a fact, I have seen in some work on natural history; where it is said, that the plants, which grow so large and beautiful in the tropical regions, and come out from the beginning in a bud consisting merely of a naked fold, do, when transplanted to a cold climate, become dwarfed, many leaflets being arrested in their growth, and forced to degenerate into scales, in order to protect from the atmosphere, the growth of the interior leaves, that the whole may not perish. So, in the ungenial atmosphere of unsympathising guardianship or companionship, a part of the mental powers, intended to spread forth in beauty and fragrance, are forced to degenerate into mere self-defences, that all may not be lost. A fastidious reserve, where it is not affectation, is always the effect of want of sympathy and intelligent appreciation or of a forced intercourse with the rude; and it never comes from the respectfulness of the method of education, which I am defending,—but is prevented by it; provided this method is pursued with good sense on the part of the instructor.

The last good influence which I shall mention, of my favorite mode of procedure, is its tendency to break up that constant reference to general opinion, which is so apt to degenerate into subserviency to it. The mind that is accustomed to commune in silence with its own ideal, and with God,—is apt to forget the low views which govern the world; and by this forgetfulness to be withdrawn from the world's dethroning influences. The soul, also, feeling how far off it is from its own standard, even in its best estate, may be entirely unconscious of how beautiful and how elevated it appears to those around it, and thus becomes more and more humble, has more and more of the "beauty of contrition" about it, as it advances. And what expression is there on earth, of the unseen and unknown heaven of character, to which we all aspire, that is so powerful, as the unconsciousness and humility of the holiest virtue?

But while I bear testimony to having found that the method of individual culture, can be pursued in a school, and with all the above fine influences, I must be ingenuous, and also state its peculiar difficulties.

It requires, in the first place, that the school be small in numbers; for no instructor can take time to study out the individualities of every pupil, and feed each with appropriate food, without a greater tax upon thought and feeling, than any individual can bear, for many successive years. It requires, also, that the instructor should be free for the school, so as to make it the first object; and free also for general culture, and for such degree of general intercourse as there is felt a need for. It is not every well disposed, or well taught person, that is capable of the attitude of friend and guardian to a company of young minds. It requires, even more than much learning, a spirit of philosophic liberality, a mind of ready and various resource, and a heart of all-comprehending sympathies.

But supposing the instructor is found, and the school is numerically within compass, it will often take years to get entire possession of some individuals, who may come into it; the general influences of whose life and companionship, out of school, may not be in harmony with the influence exerted by the instructor. Where so much is aimed at, relative success alone must be expected; and an instructor must not be surprised if every degree of want of success makes a great noise in the world, and there be little appreciation of the success actually obtained, except by the pupils themselves, who will inevitably feel and acknowledge it, as they grow older.

When I went into Mr. Alcott's school, full of the above views, and rather inclined to believe that the method I had endeavoured to pursue, was the only one that was not absolutely wrong,—my mind was forcibly turned to consider other modes.

Here was a school of thirty children, mostly boys under ten years of age, who were creatures of instinct more than any thing else, with undeveloped consciences and minds, but well-disposed, good-natured, overflowing with animal spirits, and all but intoxicated with play. It was plain enough that my plan could get no foothold in a school of such materials; at least until some other one had prepared the way. And I soon found that Mr. Alcott had quite a different way. A common conscience was the first object towards which he aimed. And this he defended on the ground that the general conscience of a school would be the highest; for which also, he had some very excellent arguments. He said that the soul, when nearest infancy, was the purest and most moral; that the artlessness of children made them express their strongest convictions, even when it made against themselves; and that though the very young were very apt to do wrong things, they did not defend wrong in the abstract, ever. From all this, it was to be inferred, that the moral judgements of the majority would be higher than their conduct; while those few, whose conduct was more in proportion to their moral judgement, would still keep their high place, and occasionally throw their finer elements, into the general conscience, which might be called the treasury of the school.—I admitted the reasonableness of all this, and felt, that the plan would work for the benefit of the worst scholars, certainly, and might work for the benefit of the best; and I am bound to say, that no evil effects to the better portion, have transpired under my observation, quickened though it has been by my doubts; and that the majority of the school have made moral progress, which, considering their age, and the time that has transpired, is beyond all parallel in my observation—I say *moral* progress, and I wish to be understood, in the largest sense of that word, in which is included religious ideas, the sense of accountability, and the habit of virtuous effort.—I, therefore, must acknowledge myself vanquished, as far as my skepticism regarded such a school as Mr. Alcott's, though I reserve my own opinion, respecting one of a very limited number of girls, of an age extending from the time they can read to the time when girls generally leave school. As it is the ideal of a girl's education to be educated by an accomplished mother, in the sacred retreat of home,—the nearest approach to these circumstances, is the ideal of a girl's school.

The methods of discipline, which I mentioned, as having been questioned, all arise out of this principle of having a common conscience, and these objections I will now briefly consider.

Mr. A. has an office of superintendent of conduct, including attitude, appearances of inattention, &c. This is delegated to scholars, selected for the day, whom sometimes he chooses himself, and sometimes the scholars choose, and to whom the whole always agree, promising to submit without complaint to any punishments Mr. Alcott may found on their judgements, experience having proved to them, that this office generally creates that sense of responsibility, which makes the marks strictly just; especially as they know that Mr. Alcott always reserves a right of judgement, over and above that of the superintendents. Of this office, I was very jealous at first. I predicted various evils. But the result has proved that Mr. Alcott was right in expecting from it excellent effects. The worst boys, when put into that office, become scrupulously just, and get an idea of superintending themselves, which nothing else can give them.

General discussion of the conduct of individual scholars, is also another method of discipline, arising out of the principle of forming a common conscience. The objections to this course are obvious. And I have felt some; though not those usually urged. And, with respect to the objections I made, I cannot say that any positive evil has been done, while I must admit that positive good does certainly arise. A degree of honesty, simplicity, self-surrender, and general acknowledgement of a standard of action beyond the control of any individual, are produced, such as no other school in the land, I will venture to say, can show; while all false pretensions, vanity, and self-exaltation, are completely taken down. Some persons have thought vanity was cherished in the school. But I think there can be no greater mistake. The first display of a new scholar, is that of all his vanity, and this is so uniformly the case, that the development is quite amusing to a constant spectator. But this blossom is indeed short-lived. It soon falls, and the infant fruit of a sober estimate of himself appears. In short, there can be no doubt, at all, that the immediate effect of this part of Mr. Alcott's plan, is favorable to self-knowledge and humility, when the scholars compare themselves with one another.—It has been said, that the children are vain of the school, and think it is the only place where the right method is pursued, and that they are the only persons, in the world, who have the right standard, &c. A sort of party spirit about a school, is not uncommon with children, especially when there is any thing peculiar in the school. And if this is stronger than usual in this instance, it must be said, in defence of the children, that they constantly hear the most absurd misrepresentations of it, and of Mr. Alcott, from people who judge without knowing the truth; and the most wild criticisms and enquiries concerning it, from those who are inclined to take marvellous views of it. They often tell Mr. Alcott, that people do not understand him or his school. And this is perfectly true. However, let the case be as it may, if the children overrate the school while they are in it, they are so much more liable to receive all its advantages; and they will soon be undeceived, after they have left it.

Having spoken thus elaborately of the school, with respect to the principles and methods of moral culture, I will proceed to speak of it, with respect to its intellectual effects; and here, I, for one, have never had any doubts, in any particular. I think it can be proved *a priori*, and *a posteriori*, that the intellectual influences are, in all respects, salutary.

In the first place, the cultivation of attention as a moral duty, with the constant exposition of all which interferes with it in instinctive habits, is of the first importance to the intellectual life. The mode in which this state of mind is cultivated, is not merely that of stating it as a duty, but stating it as a duty, after having used all the resources of his own and others' genius to attract and reward their attention. When a child has been led to enjoy his intellectual life, in any way, and then is made to observe whence his enjoyment has arisen,—he can feel and understand the argument of duty which may be urged in favor of attention. Those who commonly instruct children would be astonished, to witness the degree of attention which Mr. Alcott succeeds in obtaining from his scholars constantly. Indeed, the majority of adults might envy them. It is, generally speaking, complete, profound, and as continuous as any would wish the attention of children to be.

The first object of investigation is also in the highest degree fruitful for the intellect. Spirit, as it appears within themselves, whether in the form of feeling, law, or thought, is universally interesting. No subject interests children so much as self-analysis. To give name to inward movements of heart and mind, whether in themselves or others, is an employment of their faculties which will enchain the attention of the most volatile. There is no one class of objects in external nature, which interests all children; for children are very differently gifted with respect to their sympathies with nature. But all are conscious of something within themselves which moves, thinks, and feels; and as a mere subject of curiosity, and of investigation, for the sake of knowledge, it may take place of all others. In order to investigate it, a great many things must be done, which are in themselves very agreeable. Mr. Alcott reads, and tells stories, calculated to excite various moral emotions. On these stories, he asks questions, in order to bring out from each, in words, the feelings which have been called forth. These feelings receive their name, and history, and place in the moral scale. Then books, and passages from books are read, calculated to exercise various intellectual faculties, such as Perception, Imagination, Judgement, Reason (both in apprehension and comprehension); and these various exercises of mind are discriminated and named. There can be no intellectual action more excellent than this, whether we consider the real exercise given to the mind, or its intrinsic interest to the children, and consequently the naturalness of the exercise. And its good influence with respect to preparing for the study of Science is literally incalculable. There is not a single thing that cannot be studied with comparative ease, by a child, who can be taught what faculties he must use, and how they are to be brought to bear on the subject, and what influence on those faculties the subject will have, after it is mastered.

But Mr. Alcott would not sequestrate children from Nature, even while this preparatory study of spirit is going on. He would be very thankful to throw all the precious influences of a country life, its rural employments, its healthful recreations, its beautiful scenery, around his scholars' minds. He thinks that the forms of nature, as furniture for the imagination, and an address to the sentiments of wonder and beauty and also as a delight to the eye, and as models for the pencil, cannot be too early presented, or too lovingly dwelt upon. In lieu of these circumstances, which of course cannot be procured in Boston, he reads to them of all in nature which is calculated to delight the imagination and heart. He surrounds them, also, with statuary and pictures in his school-room; and he has drawing taught to all his scholars, by a gentleman[5] who probably possesses the spirit of Art more completely than any instructor who has ever taught in this country.

And in the lessons on words, in the spelling, reading, and grammatical exercises, on which the intellectual benefits of Mr. Alcott's school are mainly based, if the spiritual part of language is dwelt on so much, both as a means and as an effect of the study of the Spirit within; yet the names of external objects as external, and the technical terms of art, are not necessarily excluded. A great deal of knowledge of things is conveyed in this way, and attention is more and more directed to this part of language, as scholars continue at the school, and need less and less exclusive conversation on the subjects appertaining to moral discipline.

The more scientific study of nature, also, Mr. Alcott thinks has its place in education, nor is he sure that he shall always exclude it from his school, although the age of his scholars, together with his views as to what ought to be taught first, throw natural science out of his course, excepting what is included in the study of Language, Geography, and Arithmetic, on the plans mentioned in the Record. Is it however, peculiar to his school, that attainments in the natural sciences are not made at the age of twelve? Will not most persons admit that, however difficult soul-analysis may be, it is still more difficult for children to seize Science, which is "nature without the matter;" that the Laws of the Eternal Spirit displayed in external nature, are far more abstracted from their own consciousness, than are those emotions and moral laws, to which Mr. Alcott so often directs their attention? There is not a little illusion on this subject of science. If children learn the names of the stars; if they gather flowers into herbariums; and stones and minerals and shells and insects into cabinets; and witness some experiments in chemistry, it is supposed that they have studied the sciences. But all this is child's play; or, at best, only useful for the healthful bodily exercise, which is sometimes involved in making herbariums and cabinets. Astronomy does not consist of the heavenly bodies, but of their laws of motion, and relations to each other; nor chemistry of the earthly substances of which it treats, but of their laws of combination and means of analysis. In short, nothing need be said to prove that it is absurd to attempt to teach the sciences to children under twelve years old. They should be led to nature for the picturesque and for poetry, not for the purpose of scientific analysis and deduction. They should look upon its synthesis as sacred. The time will come when they may explore it, as God's means for aiding and completing the building up of their own Intellect; and it is a positive moral injury to them to study it while they are too young to understand this object. My readers may smile, and yet it is true, that in teaching Geometry I have been in the habit of so presenting it to the minds of my pupils, that fretting and passion when occasioned by the difficulty of mastering a demonstration of those laws by which the Creator constituted the universe, could easily be checked by a single word reminding them that it was the Creator's mind we were studying. Nothing can be more blessed than the influence of this view, when connected, as it should be, with benignant views of the Deity, as the all-cherishing, and all-animating Father of our Spirits. Mr. Alcott says,—Let children sketch from Nature, cultivate flowers, cherish animals, keep shells, and pretty stones, but not study natural Philosophy, Botany, Zoology, Conchology, Mineralogy, &c. &c. till after they have learnt those principles of arrangement, which are to be found within the soul and which are nearer and more easily apprehended than any natural science: and is not this rational?

Also, if Mr. Alcott does not pretend to teach the natural sciences, he does what will ultimately prove of the highest service to Scientific Education, in giving his scholars the habit of weighing the meaning, and considering the comparative force of words. A long preparation of this kind for the study of the Sciences, is fully made up by the ease with which any science is mastered, through a previous knowledge of words. Time is wasted to an incalculable extent, in common education, and even in self-education, on account of our want of precision in the ideas we attach to words, which are too familiar to our ear, for us to realise that we do not clearly understand them. A great effort is made to remember lessons, and then they are forgotten. Perhaps those are the soonest forgotten, which it is the greatest effort to remember. But if the study is chosen with reference to the state of the mind, and the words of the lesson are perfectly understood, there need be no effort of mere memory. A clear and vivid conception, together with actual growth of mind, is remembered, involuntarily. Nothing is more common than to confound intellectual labour with fagging.[6] Yet nothing can be more different than these. Bodily accomplishments, sleight of hand, &c. are attained by mere repetition, but intellectual accomplishment and acuteness are not attained by mere repetition of impression, though this is very commonly thought, but by a perfectly clear and vivid conception in the first place, dwelt upon so long that its most important relations may be developed, and not long enough to harass or weary the mind. Indeed, it is well known, that repetition of the same mental impressions, may destroy the memory altogether. The laws of bodily and mental discipline, are precisely the reverse of each other. I could deduce a thousand facts under my own observation, to confirm this view with respect to the true culture of memory. But

I will merely state, in this place, that I have tested the advantage of a nice logical preparation for the study of the sciences, in my own school. Convinced that children were not benefitted, by committing to memory text-books of natural science, or even by witnessing experiments, until they had previously looked upon the creation with the poetical and religious eye which regards every fact as an exponent of Spiritual truth, I steadily opposed their studying them, making the sole exception of Geometry, which is not so much a science of external nature, as a contemplation of the Intellect. I found their knowledge of the intellectual habit of abstraction made the theory of geometry easy to them, while their understanding of words enabled them to master the particular demonstrations, rapidly and completely. It was a favorite study with a whole school of thirty-five scholars, minds never subjected to the slightest artificial stimulus, not even what might arise from my keeping a weekly record, or changing their places in a class. All became expert in geometrical reasoning. Even the slowest of all, a child formed intellectually, as well as bodily, for the early death she met; and whom I never could carry farther in grammar, than to separate the names of sensible objects from other words, nor deeper in natural history than to remember the facts that addressed her social affections; did go through the plane Geometry with pleasure, and do all the problems with success, though not without long and faithful labour. When, at about thirteen years of age, these children were set to the study of natural philosophy; even without the advantage of an apparatus for experiments, and with no means of verification but geometrical demonstration; they made a progress which more than answered my own expectations, and has astonished every experienced person who has heard the details. It would be perfectly safe, and perhaps even better, were language taught as it should be, that the natural sciences, together with history, should not come among school studies, but be deferred to the period of life immediately succeeding the school period. Drawing, language, arithmetic, geography and geometry, indeed whatever can be more easily acquired by the assistance of others, should be school studies. These would train the mind to a maturity, which makes books of natural science, and of political history, easily understood, and acquired. It is very easy for a prepared mind to learn, or at least to reason without an instructor, upon facts, which no mere industry could apprehend in relation to each other. And it is to form this prepared mind that Mr. Alcott aims.

For it is not for moral education only, that self-analysis and the study of the "truth of our nature" in Jesus Christ is desirable. It is no less beneficial to the intellectual education. The soul itself, when looked on as an object, becomes a subject of scientific classification, in its faculties and operations; and the consideration of the true principles and conduct of life, is most favorable to the development of right judgement, especially when parallel lives, shewing approximations to the Ideal, or even wanderings from it, are given in connexion with the study of the life of Jesus, affording variety of illustration. Indeed, there is something peculiarly appropriate to the young, in the study of Biography. But there is very little biography written, which gives an insight into the life of the mind, and especially into its formation. It is only occasionally that we find a philosopher who can read other men's experience, and to whom the incidents of a life are transparent. But for the purposes of education, there should be biographies of the childhood of genius and virtue, on the plan of Carlyle's life of Schiller, and his articles on Burns and others.[7]

To supply the want of biography, Mr. Alcott relies a great deal upon Journal writing, which is autobiography, while it hardly seems so to the writer.[8] To learn to use words, teaches us to appreciate their force. And, while Mr. Alcott presents this exercise as a means of self-inspection and self-knowledge, enabling the writers to give unity to their own being, by bringing all outward facts into some relation with their individuality, and gathering up fragments which would otherwise be lost; he knows he is also assisting them in the art of composition, in a way that the rules of Rhetoric would never do. Every one knows that a technical memory of words and of rules of composition, gives very little command of language; while a rich consciousness, a quick imagination, and force of feeling, seem to unlock the treasury: and even so vulgar a passion as anger produces eloquence, and quickens perception to the slightest inuendo.

Self-analysis, biography, and journal writing, therefore, since they bear upon the skilful use of language, are as truly the initiation of intellectual as of moral education. And language has always professedly, stood in the forefront of children's studies. The Ancient languages, although they took their place in that early stage of education which they now occupy, when they were living languages, and necessary for the purpose of any reading whatever, have retained the same position, notwithstanding many disadvantages which the study of them, at that period, has involved, mainly because of the good effect which has been experienced from the concentration of attention upon the vernacular words by which the Latin and Greek words are translated; and from the acquisition of the spirit of one's native tongue, by the recognition of its idioms in contradistinction to those of other languages. For no thorough method of studying English, independently, has been practised; and it may be freely admitted, that to study another language is better than to study none at all. And it would have a much more creative influence upon the faculties of the young, besides saving much time and distress, if the study of English, on Mr. Alcott's plan, should come first; and that of the ancient languages be delayed a few years. Boys, generally speaking, would be better fitted for college at fourteen or fifteen, even in Latin and Greek, if they did not begin to learn them till they were twelve years old; always providing, however, that they thoroughly study English by means of self-analysis, poetry, and religious revelation up to that time.

Mr. Alcott, it is true, has Latin taught in his school, with reference to fitting boys for the other schools; and it does not interfere with the prosecution of his own plans, since his assistant has long been in the habit of teaching it, with reference to such results as he secures by his exercises on English words.

These observations on the intellectual bearings of the study of language, will explain much that is peculiar in Mr. Alcott's school. And it will show that the intellectual results are never separated from the moral, and consequently never neglected. Gradually, self-knowledge becomes psychology; knowledge of language, grammar; and the practice of composition, leads to the true principles of rhetoric. Even if, by removal from the school, these results are not attained under his immediate observation, he cannot doubt that they will surely come out, from the principles which he sets into operation.

But I am frequently asked,—will children ever be willing to study from books, who have been educated by Mr. Alcott? I have always answered to this question, and I will here repeat it, they will study from books more intelligently, thoroughly and profoundly, just in proportion as they imbibe the spirit of his instructions; for they will have an object whenever they open a book, and the beautiful things, Mr. Alcott constantly reads to them, have a tendency to make them feel what treasures are locked up in books.—Yet they may not be book-worms. They learn that there are other sources of knowledge, and especially, that thought is the chief source of wisdom. There is much illusion concerning children's reading; the book-devouring, which is frequently seen, nowadays, in children, is of no advantage to them. There is a great deal, in the spirit of that maxim of Aquinas, "Read one book to be learned."[9] Mr. Alcott's scholars may show less interest, than some other children, in the miserable juvenile literature, which cheats so many poor little things, into the idea that they know the sciences, history, biography, and the creations of the imagination, and if it be so, it is a blessing to their minds. But many of the parents of the children, have told me, that they read over and over again, at home, the books of classical literature, which he reads to them in school. And what can be finer than this effect?

Nor is the study of Books excluded from the school. This is so common a mistake, with respect to Mr. Alcott's plan, that perhaps I could not do better than to enter into some details, respecting the precise manner in which the studying from books, in its various departments, is carried on.

. . . .

The objections made against the intellectual influences of Mr. Alcott's school, by those who do not know much about it, are chiefly of the negative character, which the foregoing pages have attempted to answer. There is one however, of a positive character, on which I wish to make some observations, and then I shall close this protracted essay.

It is said that Mr. Alcott cultivates the Imagination of his scholars, inordinately, by leading them to the works of the poets, and to the prose creations of such writers as Krummacher, Bunyan, Carové, &c.[10]—It is thought, that by exercising the minds of the children in following authors of this class; requiring them to picture out all the imagery of their language; and leading them to consider, also, the inward life which this imagery is intended to symbolize, the energy of the Imagination is increased. But I apprehend that all this is but guiding the Imagination, freeing it from the dominion of the senses and passions, and placing it under its true lawgiver—the Idea of Beauty; and that it does not increase its natural energy, which is always a gift of nature. The decision does not lie with us, whether there shall be Imagination or not; or what degree of it there shall be. It exists equally energetic, whether cultivated or not. It presides over the sports of childhood just in the same ratio as that of the spirit to the body of the child. It acts in every walk of the most prosaic business. The victims of uncultivated Imagination are all around us,—in the wild speculators of commercial life; in the insane pursuers of outward goods, to the destruction of all inward peace; in the fanatics of all sects of religion, and all parties of politics, and all associations for general objects. Nothing is to be gained by neglecting to use this faculty, or by omitting to give name to its movements, or by checking the soul's natural tendency to gratify it. Could we succeed in doing so, yet events would wake it up from its slumber, and might do so at any time, and it will be all the more liable to deem itself some god or demon from the hidden world, because it does not understand itself. To cultivate the Imagination, is rather to disarm its energy than to increase it; but in lieu of mere energy, cultivation gives beauty, safety, and elevating influences to all its movements.

But Mr. Alcott has no intention of cultivating one faculty, more than another. His plan is to follow the natural order of the mind. He begins with analysing the speech the children use. In doing this, they are led immediately, to consider the action of the Imagination, since it is this faculty which has formed language. We find that language clothes thoughts and emotions with the forms of nature,—its staple being the imagery of outward nature, as truly as that the staple of sculptures and paintings is the material of outward nature, and all are Psyche's drapery.[11] Mr. Alcott asks a child questions, in order to turn his attention upon what passes within his own mind, and what the child says, when making this inward survey, will determine what faculties are most active in his nature, for the time being. Or, if his words must be taken with caution, and it is true that they sometimes must, since some children learn words by rote so easily,—his inward state can be determined, by taking a wide range of reading, and constantly observing what character of books interests him most strongly. He will like those books best, which exercise the faculties and feelings that are already in agreeable activity, and these should be cherished and nurtured, in a full confidence, that they will wake up in due time the other faculties of the soul. Mr. Alcott, by pursuing this course faithfully, has found that the Imagination is the first faculty which comes forth, leading all the others in its train. He has therefore not failed to meet it, and give it food. If he were to give it other than the healthy food, supplied by Nature, Providence, and that true Genius which embodies Nature and Providence, in its creations; or if he were to allow it to degenerate into fancy, or phantasy, or stray from the Principle of Beauty, which is the Law of the Imagination, I should be the last to defend it. But wisely fed and governed, the Imagination need not be feared. It is the concentration of Profound Feeling, Reason, and the Perception of outward nature, into one act of the mind; and prepares the soul for vigorous effort, in all the various departments of its activity.

Source: Elizabeth Palmer Peabody, from "Explanatory Preface," *Record of a School: Exemplifying the General Principles of Spiritual Culture*, 2d ed. (Boston: Russell, Shattuck; New York: Leavitt, Lord, 1836), pp. iii–xxviii, xl–xlii.

Notes

1. "The Tables Turned" (1798), ll. 26–28, by William Wordsworth.
2. Albertine-Adrienne Necker de Saussure (1766–1841), Swiss woman of letters and educator, published *Progressive Education* between 1828 and 1838, which was first translated into English (in part) in 1835.
3. Phrenology, a popular pseudo-science holding that a person's character could be "read" by examining the bumps on the head, which corresponded to areas of "influence" in the brain. The Unitarians and the Transcenden-

talists were concerned by this because it suggested parallels to the determinism of Calvinism.

4. "Ode. Intimations of Immortality from Recollections of Early Childhood" (1807), by Wordsworth; Plato (ca. 428–ca. 348 B.C.), the most famous of the Greek philosophers.

5. Mr. Francis Graeter, who has in contemplation to publish a work developing the whole art of drawing, especially from nature, in the same way as he has often done orally to such pupils as have received the most benefit from him; and more completely than he could do in a course of desultory lessons;—more completely than has ever been done in a book for learners. We trust no discouragement from publishers and booksellers will prevent or delay this great desideratum to *all* lovers of the pencil. [Peabody's note]

6. Fagging, laborious drudgery.

7. *The Life of Friedrich Schiller* (1825) and "Burns" (*Edinburgh Review*, 1828), by Thomas Carlyle (1795–1881), prolific Scottish writer who was Emerson's lifelong friend and correspondent.

8. For examples of journals kept by students at Alcott's school, see Alfred G. Litton and Joel Myerson, "The Temple School Journals of George and Martha Kuhn," *Studies in the American Renaissance 1993*, ed. Myerson (Charlottesville: University Press of Virginia, 1993), pp. 55–145.

9. St. Thomas Aquinas (1224/25–1274), Italian theologian and poet.

10. Friedrich Adolph Krummacher (1767–1845), German theologian and writer of parables; John Bunyan (1628–1688), English cleric and author of *The Pilgrim's Progress* (1678), in which the title character runs from a fair of the vanities; Freidrich Wilhelm Carové (1789–1852), German Hegelian philosopher.

11. Psyche, princess in classical mythology whose exceptional beauty aroused Venus' jealousy and Cupid's love.

1836

PERRY MILLER CALLS THIS the "Annus Mirabilis" of Transcendentalism, and it was indeed quite a year, with the publication of the second edition of *Record of a School*, a newspaper exchange between Andrews Norton and George Ripley over theology, William Henry Furness's *Remarks on the Four Gospels*, Orestes A. Brownson's *New Views of Christianity, Society, and the Church*, Ralph Waldo Emerson's *Nature*, and the first volume of Bronson Alcott's *Conversations with Children on the Gospels* (not to mention the first meeting of the Transcendental Club).

William Henry Furness (1802–1896) went to Boston Latin School with Emerson, with whom he formed a lifelong friendship, and served for many years as the Unitarian minister in Philadelphia. His book is an attempt to find a human, rather than a theological, response to the gospels. Furness admits that to be "duly appreciated," the arguments for the "truth of the great facts recorded in the New Testament" require "a degree of intellectual cultivation and an amount of learning entirely out of the reach of the great body of readers." As Theodore Parker and Emerson would later argue, Furness suggests that the perduring value of Christianity resides in the teachings of Christ rather than his supposed deeds; but he is not willing to venture as far as do Parker and Emerson in questioning the very existence of miracles. He does state that "The existence of the merest atom, when we duly consider it, is an unspeakable miracle. The universe—all being—is miraculous," but he goes on to discuss "another" type of miracle, "represented as departures from the natural order of things." These latter miracles must be taken on faith, because not to do so suggests that "the whole order of nature is known to us, that the limits of our knowledge are commensurate with all the laws and modes of existence"; and, thus, "With our very limited knowledge of Nature, how, I ask again, shall we pronounce an alleged fact a violation of its order." To Furness, we cannot disprove the existence of miracles because of our limited knowledge of the natural world, and we must believe in their truthfulness because of a higher faith: "it is in the perfect correspondence of the miracles of Jesus, both in spirit and in form or manner, with the simplicity, originality and dignity of his character, that I discern an overwhelming evidence of their reality." He does "admit that there are errors and mistakes in the Gospels," but these are the result of the writers being distracted by the "exciting" events that they were reporting. The heart of Furness' argument—and this is why he stands perched between the literalness of an Andrews Norton and the liberality of a Parker or an Emerson—is that if we look beyond miracles, we can see that the ultimate strength of the Christian religion is internalized:

> again it may be intimated that it was the miracles he wrought, that operated so powerfully in convincing and urging onward his followers.

It is true his works of power did much; they filled an important and indispensable place in producing that state of feeling in his disciples, requisite to qualify them to carry on what he had begun. But then the main power of his miracles lies not in their mere power, but in their relation to his character, which they help far more strikingly than anything else to glorify. . . . It was by the force of his character that the apostles were swayed.[1]

The importance of the personality of Jesus held Furness's interest: in 1838 he turned *Remarks on the Fours Gospels* into *Jesus and His Biographers: or, the Remarks on the Four Gospels, Revised with Copious Additions*, and over the years he continued to preach and publish on this topic, in such works as a nearly three-hundred-page *History of Jesus* (1850), *Jesus, the Heart of Christianity* (1882), and *Jesus and Christianity* (1889).

If Furness was interested in stressing the humanity of Christianity in religious terms, then Orestes Augustus Brownson (1803–1876) wanted to apply Christianity to humanity in social terms. In *New Views* (published by the same firm that would also publish Emerson's *Nature*), he put forth one of the most developed concepts of the interrelatedness of church and society of the day. His search for answers in this book reflects his own personal quest: raised a Congregationalist, he went on to embrace Presbyterianism, Universalism, agnosticism, Unitarianism, and, finally, Roman Catholicism. A prolific writer, Brownson both defended and criticized the Transcendentalists in the *Christian Examiner* and in his own *Boston Quarterly Review* (1838–1842), and while he attended some meetings of the Transcendental Club and offered the Transcendentalists a place in his *Review*, he never fully sympathized with them, often feeling they were too aristocratic for his tastes (he opposed, for example, Emerson's belief that a few great leaders from the educated or privileged classes set the tenor of the time with his own faith in leaders who came from the masses and expressed the desires of the masses).

Like Furness, Brownson argues for the importance of religion, but, unlike Furness, he argues that religious institutions have perverted the original sense of Christian goodness: "But it is only religion, as distinguished from religious institutions, that is natural to man. The religious sentiment is universal, permanent, and indestructible; religious institutions depend on transient causes, and vary in different countries and epochs." And he also sees humankind as a developing organism coexisting with a stagnant church and an entrenched social order: "We are creatures of growth; it is, therefore, impossible that all our institutions should not be mutable and transitory." Where Furness saw the apostles as swept up by the spirit of Jesus, Brownson sees them distorting his message and setting the stage for a binary division of humankind that has lasted for millennia:

Christianity, as it existed in the mind of Jesus, was the type of the most perfect religious institution to which the human race will, probably, ever attain. It was the point where the sentiment and the institution, the idea and the symbol, the conception and its realization appear to meet and become one. But the contemporaries of Jesus were not equal to this profound thought. They could not comprehend the God-Man, the deep meaning of his assertion, "I and my Father are one." . . .

Two systems then disputed the Empire of the World; Spiritualism represented by the Eastern world, the old world of Asia, and Materialism represented by Greece and Rome. Spiritualism regards purity or holiness as predictable of Spirit alone, and Matter as essentially impure, possessing and capable of receiving nothing of the Holy,—the prison house of the soul, its only hindrance to a union with God, or absorption into his essence, the cause of all uncleanliness, sin, and evil, consequently to be contemned, degraded, and as far as possible annihilated. Materialism takes the other extreme, does not recognize the claims of Spirit, disregards the soul, counts the body everything, earth all, heaven nothing, and condenses itself into the advice, "Eat and drink, for tomorrow we die."

One effect of the division between Spiritualism and Materialism was that theologians denied that "Jesus came in the flesh," for "if he had a material body, [he] must have been unholy." As a result, they "separated the humanity of Jesus by its very origin from common humanity." Brownson traces these two streams of civilization forward into the present day, as they appear in the church (as opposed to Christianity) and in society. As Materialism claimed the ascendancy, "Men labor six days for this world and at most but one for the world to come. The great strife is for temporal goods, fame or pleasure. God, the Soul, Heaven, and Eternity, are thrown into the back ground, and almost entirely disappear in the distance."

In the present day, Brownson sees Spiritualism returning, a major reason being the rise of an educated populace. Materialism could triumph earlier, Brownson argues, because the collection of knowledge was in the hands of the clergy and the nobility, who used their power for personal, ecclesiastical, or class purposes. This is becoming harder to do as an educated class arises out of the lower and middle classes, making the present the time to "reconcile spirit and matter." One way to do this is to share power, particularly religious power. If Furness believed that the Miracles reflected Jesus' personality, then Brownson goes one step further and states that they represent our own ability to interpret them as well as the clerics can:

how distinguish a real revelation from a pretended one? By miracles? But how determine that what are alleged to be miracles, really are miracles? or the more difficult question still, that the miracles, admitting them to be genuine, do necessarily involve the truth of the doctrines they are wrought to prove? Shall we be told that we must believe the revelation is a true one, because made by an authorized teacher? Where is the warrant of his authority? What shall assure us that the warrant is not a forgery? Have we any thing but our own nature with which to answer these and a hundred more questions like them and equally important?[2]

And thus Brownson sets the stage for the major players. Furness's radicalism, while attacked by some of his conservative contemporaries, is still worked out well within the traditional confines of Unitarianism, and Brownson's proto-Marxist belief in giving power to the people, expressed in such verbal detail over so many articles and pamphlets that it is hard to stay focused on his main theme, is well outside the social norms. It was now up to the people positioned well within Boston society to come forth and engage the controversies.

Notes

1. William Henry Furness, *Remarks on the Four Gospels* (Philadelphia: Carey, Lea, and Blanchard, 1836), pp. 17, 146, 151, 153, 205–206, 321–322, 226.
2. Orestes A. Brownson, *New Views of Christianity, Society, and the Church* (Boston: James Munroe, 1836), pp. 1, 3, 7, 11–12, 19, 46, 64, 70.

Ralph Waldo Emerson

Nature

(1836)

EMERSON'S BOOK WAS published at exactly the right time. The British Romantic poets—especially Wordsworth—had been publishing works in which they had changed the natural world from something to be observed at a distance to a force in which the poet (as representative of the reader) was a participant observer. Nature, in other words, was less a spectacle to be seen than it was a text to be read, and the ideal reader was one whose emotions were fully in sympathy with the natural world. Also, as the miracles controversy began to heat up, Emerson's view of nature as something that was explainable and also useful as a guide became a welcome contrast to the conservative Unitarian view of inexplicable natural occurrences that could only be interpreted by credentialed ministers for the less informed and privileged masses. And, unlike Furness, whose book is based upon religious texts and arguments, and Brownson, whose positions are all undergirded by a revolutionary philosophy that needs to be constantly explained and detailed, Emerson addresses complex issues in a straightforward manner, in only ninety-five uncluttered pages, using such literary devices as metaphors to present his compelling answer to the question "to what end is nature?" Even the structure of the book owes more to literature than it does to theology: *Nature*, which stresses the need for organicism in art, begins with the lowest use of nature (commodity) and moves toward the highest (spirit), so that form (structure) follows function (the upward development of ideas). In short, those people who would later be known as the Transcendentalists, who were reading in various philosophical and theological works the many bits and pieces of interesting concepts that they hoped would coalesce into a new mode of interpretation and living, found in Emerson's book a cohesiveness that brought it all together. *Nature* was a common text for all interested in the "Newness" because it provided a locus for their discussions; no longer would it be necessary to refer to Coleridge for something, Wordsworth for something else, Kant for yet another concept, for it was all brought together in a palatable— and understandable—fashion by Emerson.

> Nature is but an image or imitation of wisdom, the last thing of the soul; nature being a thing which doth only do, but not know.
>
> —Plotinus

Introduction

Our age is retrospective.[1] It builds the sepulchres of the fathers. It writes biographies, histories, and criticism. The foregoing generations beheld God and nature face to face; we, through their eyes. Why should not we also enjoy an original relation to the universe? Why should not we have a poetry and philosophy of insight and not of tradition, and a religion by revelation to us, and not the history of theirs? Embosomed for a season in nature, whose floods of life stream around and through us, and invite us by the powers they supply, to action proportioned to nature, why should we grope among the dry bones of the past, or put the living generation into masquerade out of its faded wardrobe? The sun shines to-day also. There is more wool and flax in the fields. There are new lands, new men, new thoughts. Let us demand our own works and laws and worship.

Undoubtedly we have no questions to ask which are unanswerable. We must trust the perfection of the creation so far, as to believe that whatever curiosity the order of things has awakened in our minds, the order of things can satisfy. Every man's condition is a solution in hieroglyphic to those inquiries he would put. He acts it as life, before he apprehends it as truth. In like manner, nature is already, in its forms and tendencies, describing its own design. Let us interrogate the great apparition, that shines so peacefully around us. Let us inquire, to what end is nature?

All science has one aim, namely, to find a theory of nature. We have theories of races and of functions, but scarcely yet a remote approximation to an idea of creation. We are now so far from the road to truth, that religious teachers dispute and hate each other, and speculative men are esteemed unsound and frivolous. But to a sound judgment, the most abstract truth is the most practical. Whenever a true theory appears, it will be its own evidence. Its test is, that it will explain all phenomena. Now many are thought not only unexplained but inexplicable; as language, sleep, dreams, beasts, sex.

Philosophically considered, the universe is composed of Nature and the Soul. Strictly speaking, therefore, all that is separate from us, all which Philosophy distinguishes as the NOT ME, that is, both nature and art, all other men and my own body, must be ranked under this name, NATURE. In enumerating the values of nature and casting up their sum, I shall use the word in both senses;—in its common and in its philosophical import. In inquiries so general as our present one, the inaccuracy is not material; no confusion of thought will occur. *Nature*, in the common sense, refers to essences unchanged by man; space, the air, the river, the leaf. *Art* is applied to the mixture of his will with the same things, as in a house, a canal, a statue, a picture. But his operations taken together are so insignificant, a little chipping, baking, patching, and washing, that in an impression so grand as that of the world on the human mind, they do not vary the result.

Nature

To go into solitude, a man needs to retire as much from his chamber as from society. I am not solitary whilst I read and write, though nobody is with me. But if a man would be alone, let him look at the stars. The rays that come from those heavenly worlds, will separate between him and vulgar things. One might think the atmosphere was made transparent with this design, to give man, in the heavenly bodies, the perpetual presence of the sublime. Seen in the streets of cities, how great they are! If the stars should appear one night in a thousand years, how would men believe and adore; and preserve for many generations the remembrance of the city of God which had been shown![2] But every night come out these preachers of beauty, and light the universe with their admonishing smile.

The stars awaken a certain reverence, because though always present, they are always inaccessible; but all natural objects make a kindred impression, when the mind is open to their influence. Nature never wears a mean appearance. Neither does the wisest man extort all her secret, and lose his curiosity by finding out all her perfection. Nature never became a toy to a wise spirit. The flowers, the animals, the mountains, reflected all the wisdom of his best hour, as much as they had delighted the simplicity of his childhood.

When we speak of nature in this manner, we have a distinct but most poetical sense in the mind. We mean the integrity of impression made by manifold natural objects. It is this which distinguishes the stick of timber of the wood-cutter, from the tree of the poet. The charming landscape which I saw this morning, is indubitably made up of some twenty or thirty farms. Miller owns this field, Locke that, and Manning the woodland beyond. But none of them owns the land-scape. There is a property in the horizon which no man has but he whose eye can integrate all the parts, that is, the poet. This is the best part of these men's farms, yet to this their land-deeds give them no title.

To speak truly, few adult persons can see nature. Most persons do not see the sun. At least they have a very superficial seeing. The sun illuminates only the eye of the man, but shines into the eye and the heart of the child. The lover of nature is he whose inward and outward senses are still truly adjusted to each other; who has retained the spirit of infancy even into the era of manhood. His intercourse with heaven and earth, becomes part of his daily food. In the presence of nature, a wild delight runs through the man, in spite of real sorrows. Nature says,—he is my creature, and maugre all his impertinent griefs, he shall be glad with me. Not the sun or the summer alone, but every hour and season yields its tribute of delight; for every hour and change corresponds to and authorizes a different state of the mind, from breathless noon to grimmest midnight. Nature is a setting that fits equally well a comic or a mourning piece. In good health, the air is a cordial of incredible virtue. Crossing a bare common, in snow pud-dles, at twilight, under a clouded sky, without having in my thoughts any occurrence of special good fortune, I have enjoyed a perfect ex-hilaration. Almost I fear to think how glad I am. In the woods too, a man casts off his years, as the snake his slough, and at what period soever of life, is always a child. In the woods, is perpetual youth. Within these plantations of God, a decorum and sanctity reign, a perennial festival is dressed, and the guest sees not how he should tire of them in a thousand years. In the woods, we return to reason and faith. There I feel that nothing can befal me in life,—no disgrace, no calamity, (leaving me my eyes,) which nature cannot repair. Standing on the bare ground,—my head bathed by the blithe air, and uplifted into infinite space,—all mean egotism vanishes. I become a transparent eye-ball. I am nothing. I see all. The currents of the Universal Being circulate through me; I am part or particle of God. The name of the nearest friend sounds then foreign and accidental. To be brothers, to be acquaintances,—master or servant, is then a trifle and a disturbance. I am the lover of uncontained and immortal beauty. In the wilderness, I find something more dear and connate than in streets or villages. In the tranquil landscape, and especially in the distant line of the horizon, man beholds somewhat as beautiful as his own nature.

The greatest delight which the fields and woods minister, is the suggestion of an occult relation between man and the vegetable. I am not alone and unacknowledged. They nod to me and I to them. The waving of the boughs in the storm, is new to me and old. It takes me by surprise, and yet is not unknown. Its effect is like that of a higher thought or a better emotion coming over me, when I deemed I was thinking justly or doing right.

Yet it is certain that the power to produce this delight, does not reside in nature, but in man, or in a harmony of both. It is necessary to use these pleasures with great temperance. For, nature is not always tricked in holiday attire, but the same scene which yesterday breathed perfume and glittered as for the frolic of the nymphs, is overspread with melancholy today. Nature always wears the colors of the spirit. To a man laboring under calamity, the heat of his own fire hath sadness in it. Then, there is a kind of contempt of the landscape felt by him who has just lost by death a dear friend. The sky is less grand as it shuts down over less worth in the population.

Commodity

Whoever considers the final cause of the world, will discern a multitude of uses that enter as parts into that result. They all admit of being thrown into one of the following classes; Commodity; Beauty; Language; and Discipline.

Under the general name of Commodity, I rank all those advantages which our senses owe to nature. This, of course, is a benefit which is temporary and mediate, not ultimate, like its service to the soul. Yet although low, it is perfect in its kind, and is the only use of nature which all men apprehend. The misery of man appears like childish petulance, when we explore the steady and prodigal provision that has been made for his support and delight on this green ball which floats him through the heavens. What angels invented these splendid ornaments, these rich conveniences, this ocean of air above, this ocean of water beneath, this firmament of earth between? This zodiac of lights, this tent of dropping clouds, this striped coat of climates, this fourfold year? Beasts, fire, water, stones, and corn serve him. The field is at once his floor, his work-yard, his play-ground, his garden, and his bed.

> More servants wait on man
> Than he'll take notice of.———[3]

Nature, in its ministry to man, is not only the material, but is also the process and the result. All the parts incessantly work into each other's hands for the profit of man. The wind sows the seed; the sun evaporates the sea; the wind blows the vapor to the field; the ice, on the other side of the planet, condenses rain on this; the rain feeds the plant; the plant feeds the animal; and thus the endless circulations of the divine charity nourish man.

The useful arts are but reproductions or new combinations by the wit of man, of the same natural benefactors. He no longer waits for favoring gales, but by means of steam, he realizes the fable of Æolus's bag, and carries the two and thirty winds in the boiler of his boat.[4] To diminish friction, he paves the road with iron bars, and, mounting a coach with a ship-load of men, animals, and merchandise behind him, he darts through the country, from town to town, like an eagle or a swallow through the air. By the aggregate of these aids, how is the face of the world changed, from the era of Noah to that of Napoleon![5] The private poor man hath cities, ships, canals, bridges, built for him. He goes to the post-office, and the human race run on his errands; to the book-shop, and the human race read and write of all that happens, for him; to the court-house, and nations repair his wrongs. He sets his house upon the road, and the human race go forth every morning, and shovel out the snow, and cut a path for him.

But there is no need of specifying particulars in this class of uses. The catalogue is endless, and the examples so obvious, that I shall leave them to the reader's reflection, with the general remark, that this mercenary benefit is one which has respect to a farther good. A man is fed, not that he may be fed, but that he may work.

Beauty

A nobler want of man is served by nature, namely, the love of Beauty.

The ancient Greeks called the world κόσμος, beauty.[6] Such is the constitution of all things, or such the plastic power of the human eye, that the primary forms, as the sky, the mountain, the tree, the animal, give us a delight in *and for themselves*; a pleasure arising from outline, color, motion, and grouping. This seems partly owing to the eye itself.

The eye is the best of artists. By the mutual action of its structure and of the laws of light, perspective is produced, which integrates every mass of objects, of what character soever, into a well colored and shaded globe, so that where the particular objects are mean and unaffecting, the landscape which they compose, is round and symmetrical. And as the eye is the best composer, so light is the first of painters. There is no object so foul that intense light will not make beautiful. And the stimulus it affords to the sense, and a sort of infinitude which it hath, like space and time, make all matter gay. Even the corpse hath its own beauty. But beside this general grace diffused over nature, almost all the individual forms are agreeable to the eye, as is proved by our endless imitations of some of them, as the acorn, the grape, the pine-cone, the wheat-ear, the egg, the wings and forms of most birds, the lion's claw, the serpent, the butterfly, sea-shells, flames, clouds, buds, leaves, and the forms of many trees, as the palm.

For better consideration, we may distribute the aspects of Beauty in a threefold manner.

1. First, the simple perception of natural forms is a delight. The influence of the forms and actions in nature, is so needful to man, that, in its lowest functions, it seems to lie on the confines of commodity and beauty. To the body and mind which have been cramped by noxious work or company, nature is medicinal and restores their tone. The tradesman, the attorney comes out of the din and craft of the street, and sees the sky and the woods, and is a man again. In their eternal calm, he finds himself. The health of the eye seems to demand a horizon. We are never tired, so long as we can see far enough.[7]

But in other hours, Nature satisfies the soul purely by its loveliness, and without any mixture of corporeal benefit. I have seen the spectacle of morning from the hill-top over against my house, from day-break to sun-rise, with emotions which an angel might share. The long slender bars of cloud float like fishes in the sea of crimson light. From the earth, as a shore, I look out into that silent sea. I seem to partake its rapid transformations: the active enchantment reaches my dust, and I dilate and conspire with the morning wind. How does Nature deify us with a few and cheap elements! Give me health and a day, and I will make the pomp of emperors ridiculous. The dawn is my Assyria; the sun-set and moon-rise my Paphos, and unimaginable realms of faerie;[8] broad noon shall be my England of the senses and the understanding; the night shall be my Germany of mystic philosophy and dreams.

Not less excellent, except for our less susceptibility in the afternoon, was the charm, last evening, of a January sunset. The western clouds divided and subdivided themselves into pink flakes modulated with tints of unspeakable softness; and the air had so much life and sweetness, that it was a pain to come within doors. What was it that nature would say? Was there no meaning in the live repose of the valley behind the mill, and which Homer or Shakspeare could not re-form for me in words? The leafless trees become spires of flame in the sunset, with the blue east for their background, and the stars of the dead calices of flowers, and every withered stem and stubble rimed with frost, contribute something to the mute music.

The inhabitants of cities suppose that the country landscape is pleasant only half the year. I please myself with observing the graces of the winter scenery, and believe that we are as much touched by it as by the genial influences of summer. To the attentive eye, each moment of the year has its own beauty, and in the same field, it beholds, every hour, a picture which was never seen before, and which shall never be seen again. The heavens change every moment, and reflect their glory or gloom on the plains beneath. The state of the crop in the surrounding farms alters the expression of the earth from week to week. The succession of native plants in the pastures and road-sides, which make the silent clock by which time tells the summer hours, will make even the divisions of the day sensible to a keen observer. The tribes of birds and insects, like the plants punctual to their time, follow each other, and the year has room for all. By water-courses, the variety is greater. In July, the blue pontederia or pickerel-weed blooms in large beds in the shallow parts of our pleasant river, and swarms with yellow butterflies in continual motion. Art cannot rival this pomp of purple and gold. Indeed the river is a perpetual gala, and boasts each month a new ornament.

But this beauty of Nature which is seen and felt as beauty, is the least part. The shows of day, the dewy morning, the rainbow, mountains, orchards in blossom, stars, moonlight, shadows in still water, and the like, if too eagerly hunted, become shows merely, and mock us with their unreality. Go out of the house to see the moon, and 't is mere tinsel; it will not please as when its light shines upon your necessary journey. The beauty that shimmers in the yellow afternoons of October, who ever could clutch it? Go forth to find it, and it is gone: 't is only a mirage as you look from the windows of diligence.

2. The presence of a higher, namely, of the spiritual element is essential to its perfection. The high and divine beauty which can be loved without effeminacy, is that which is found in combination with the human will, and never separate. Beauty is the mark God sets upon virtue.[9] Every natural action is graceful. Every heroic act is also decent, and causes the place and the bystanders to shine. We are taught by

great actions that the universe is the property of every individual in it. Every rational creature has all nature for his dowry and estate. It is his, if he will. He may divest himself of it; he may creep into a corner, and abdicate his kingdom, as most men do, but he is entitled to the world by his constitution. In proportion to the energy of his thought and will, he takes up the world into himself. "All those things for which men plough, build, or sail, obey virtue;" said an ancient historian.[10] "The winds and waves," said Gibbon, "are always on the side of the ablest navigators."[11] So are the sun and moon and all the stars of heaven. When a noble act is done,—perchance in a scene of great natural beauty; when Leonidas and his three hundred martyrs consume one day in dying, and the sun and moon come each and look at them once in the steep defile of Thermopylæ when Arnold Winkelried, in the high Alps, under the shadow of the avalanche, gathers in his side a sheaf of Austrian spears to break the line for his comrades;[12] are not these heroes entitled to add the beauty of the scene to the beauty of the deed? When the bark of Columbus nears the shore of America;—before it, the beach lined with savages, fleeing out of all their huts of cane; the sea behind; and the purple mountains of the Indian Archipelago around, can we separate the man from the living picture? Does not the New World clothe his form with her palm-groves and savannahs as fit drapery? Ever does natural beauty steal in like air, and envelope great actions. When Sir Harry Vane was dragged up the Tower-hill, sitting on a sled, to suffer death, as the champion of the English laws, one of the multitude cried out to him, "You never sate on so glorious a seat."[13] Charles II., to intimidate the citizens of London, caused the patriot Lord Russell to be drawn in an open coach, through the principal streets of the city, on his way to the scaffold. "But," to use the simple narrative of his biographer, "the multitude imagined they saw liberty and virtue sitting by his side."[14] In private places, among sordid objects, an act of truth or heroism seems at once to draw to itself the sky as its temple, the sun as its candle. Nature stretcheth out her arms to embrace man, only let his thoughts be of equal greatness. Willingly does she follow his steps with the rose and the violet, and bend her lines of grandeur and grace to the decoration of her darling child. Only let his thoughts be of equal scope, and the frame will suit the picture. A virtuous man, is in unison with her works, and makes the central figure of the visible sphere. Homer, Pindar, Socrates, Phocion, associate themselves fitly in our memory with the whole geography and climate of Greece.[15] The visible heavens and earth sympathize with Jesus. And in common life, whosoever has seen a person of powerful character and happy genius, will have remarked how easily he took all things along with him,—the persons, the opinions, and the day, and nature became ancillary to a man.

3. There is still another aspect under which the beauty of the world may be viewed, namely, as it becomes an object of the intellect. Beside the relation of things to virtue, they have a relation to thought. The intellect searches out the absolute order of things as they stand in the mind of God, and without the colors of affection. The intellectual and the active powers seem to succeed each other in man, and the exclusive activity of the one, generates the exclusive activity of the other. There is something unfriendly in each of the other, but they are like the alternate periods of feeding and working in animals; each prepares and certainly will be followed by the other. Therefore does beauty, which, in relation to actions, as we have seen comes unsought, and comes because it is unsought, remain for the apprehension and pursuit of the intellect; and then again, in its turn, of the active power. Nothing divine dies. All good is eternally reproductive. The beauty of nature reforms itself in the mind, and not for barren contemplation, but for new creation.

All men are in some degree impressed by the face of the world. Some men even to delight. This love of beauty is Taste. Others have the same love in such excess, that, not content with admiring, they seek to embody it in new forms. The creation of beauty is Art.

The production of a work of art throws a light upon the mystery of humanity. A work of art is an abstract or epitome of the world. It is the result or expression of nature, in miniature. For although the works of nature are innumerable and all different, the result or the expression of them all is similar and single. Nature is a sea of forms radically alike and even unique. A leaf, a sun-beam, a landscape, the ocean, make an analogous impression on the mind. What is common to them all,—that perfectness and harmony, is beauty. Therefore the standard of beauty, is the entire circuit of natural forms,—the totality of nature; which the Italians expressed by defining beauty "il piu nell' uno."[16] Nothing is quite beautiful alone: nothing but is beautiful in the whole. A single object is only so far beautiful as it suggests this universal grace. The poet, the painter, the sculptor, the musician, the architect seek each to concentrate this radiance of the world on one point, and each in his several work to satisfy the love of beauty which stimulates him to produce. Thus is Art, a nature passed through the alembic of man. Thus in art, does nature work through the will of a man filled with the beauty of her first works.

The world thus exists to the soul to satisfy the desire of beauty. Extend this element to the uttermost, and I call it an ultimate end.

No reason can be asked or given why the soul seeks beauty. Beauty, in its largest and profoundest sense, is one expression for the universe. God is the all-fair. Truth, and goodness, and beauty, are but different faces of the same All. But beauty in nature is not ultimate. It is the herald of inward and eternal beauty, and is not alone a solid and satisfactory good. It must therefore stand as a part and not as yet the last or highest expression of the final cause of Nature.

Language

A third use which Nature subserves to man is that of Language. Nature is the vehicle of thought, and in a simple, double, and threefold degree.

    1. Words are signs of natural facts.

    2. Particular natural facts are symbols of particular spiritual facts.

    3. Nature is the symbol of spirit.

    1. Words are signs of natural facts. The use of natural history is to give us aid in supernatural history. The use of the outer creation is to give us language for the beings and changes of the inward creation. Every word which is used to express a moral or intellectual fact, if traced to its root, is found to be borrowed from some material appearance. *Right* originally means *straight; wrong* means *twisted. Spirit* primarily means *wind; transgression*, the crossing of a *line; supercilious*, the *raising of the eye-brow*. We say the *heart* to express emotion, the *head* to denote thought; and *thought* and *emotion* are, in their turn, words borrowed from sensible things, and now appropriated to spiritual nature. Most of the process by which this transformation is made, is hidden from us in the remote time when language was framed; but the same tendency may be daily observed in children. Children and savages use only nouns or names of things, which they continually convert into verbs, and apply to analogous mental acts.

    2. But this origin of all words that convey a spiritual import,—so conspicuous a fact in the history of language,—is our least debt to nature. It is not words only that are emblematic; it is things which are emblematic. Every natural fact is a symbol of some spiritual fact. Every appearance in nature corresponds to some state of the mind, and that state of the mind can only be described by presenting that natural appearance as its picture. An enraged man is a lion, a cunning man is a fox, a firm man is a rock, a learned man is a torch. A lamb is innocence; a snake is subtle spite; flowers express to us the delicate affections. Light and darkness are our familiar expression for knowledge and ignorance; and heat for love. Visible distance behind and before us, is respectively our image of memory and hope.

Who looks upon a river in a meditative hour, and is not reminded of the flux of all things? Throw a stone into the stream, and the circles that propagate themselves are the beautiful type of all influence. Man is conscious of a universal soul within or behind his individual life, wherein, as in a firmament, the natures of Justice, Truth, Love, Freedom, arise and shine. This universal soul, he calls Reason: it is not mine or thine or his, but we are its; we are its property and men. And the blue sky in which the private earth is buried, the sky with its eternal calm, and full of everlasting orbs, is the type of Reason. That which, intellectually considered, we call Reason, considered in relation to nature, we call Spirit. Spirit is the Creator. Spirit hath life in itself. And man in all age and countries, embodies it in his language, as the FATHER.

It is easily seen that there is nothing lucky or capricious in these analogies, but that they are constant, and pervade nature. These are not the dreams of a few poets, here and there, but man is an analogist, and studies relations in all objects. He is placed in the centre of beings, and a ray of relation passes from every other being to him. And neither can man be understood without these objects, nor these objects without man. All the facts in natural history taken by themselves, have no value, but are barren like a single sex. But marry it to human history, and it is full of life. Whole Floras, all Linnæus' and Buffon's volumes, are but dry catalogues of facts;[17] but the most trivial of these facts, the habit of a plant, the organs, or work, or noise of an insect, applied to the illustration of a fact in intellectual philosophy, or, in any way associated to human nature, affects us in the most lively and agreeable manner. The seed of a plant,—to what affecting analogies in the nature of man, is that little fruit made use of, in all discourse, up to the voice of Paul, who calls the human corpse a seed,—"It is sown a natural body; it is raised a spiritual body."[18] The motion of the earth round its axis, and round the sun, makes the day, and the year. These are certain amounts of brute light and heat. But is there no intent of an analogy between man's life and the seasons? And do the seasons gain no grandeur or pathos from that analogy? The instincts of the ant are very unimportant considered as the ant's; but the moment a ray of relation is seen to extend from it to man, and the little drudge is seen to be a monitor, a little body with a mighty heart, then all its habits, even that said to be recently observed, that it never sleeps, become sublime.

Because of this radical correspondence between visible things and human thoughts, savages, who have only what is necessary, converse in figures. As we go back in history, language becomes more picturesque, until its infancy, when it is all poetry; or, all spiritual facts are represented by natural symbols. The same symbols are found to make the original elements of all languages. It has moreover been observed, that the idioms of all languages approach each other in passages of the greatest eloquence and power. And as this is the first language, so is it the last. This immediate dependence of language upon nature, this conversion of an outward phenomenon into a type of somewhat in human life, never loses its power to affect us. It is this which gives that piquancy to the conversation of a strong-natured farmer or back-woodsman, which all men relish.

Thus is nature an interpreter, by whose means man converses with his fellow men. A man's power to connect his thought with its proper symbol, and so utter it, depends on the simplicity of his character, that is, upon his love of truth and his desire to communicate it without loss. The corruption of man is followed by the corruption of language. When simplicity of character and the sovereignty of ideas is broken up by the prevalence of secondary desires, the desire of riches, the desire of pleasure, the desire of power, the desire of praise,—and duplicity and falsehood take place of simplicity and truth, the power over nature as an interpreter of the will, is in a degree lost; new imagery ceases to be created, and old words are perverted to stand for things which are not; a paper currency is employed when there is no bullion in the vaults. In due time, the fraud is manifest, and words lose all power to stimulate the understanding or the affections. Hundreds of writers may be found in every long-civilized nation, who for a short time believe, and make others believe, that they see and utter truths, who do not of themselves clothe one thought in its natural garment, but who feed unconsciously upon the language created by the primary writers of the country, those, namely, who hold primarily on nature.

But wise men pierce this rotten diction and fasten words again to visible things; so that picturesque language is at once a commanding certificate that he who employs it, is a man in alliance with truth and God. The moment our discourse rises above the ground line of familiar facts, and is inflamed with passion or exalted by thought, it clothes itself in images. A man conversing in earnest, if he watch his intellectual processes, will find that always a material image, more or less luminous, arises in his mind, cotemporaneous with every thought, which furnishes the vestment of the thought. Hence, good writing and brilliant discourse are perpetual allegories. This imagery is spontaneous. It is the blending of experience with the present action of the mind. It is proper creation. It is the working of the Original Cause through the instruments he has already made.

These facts may suggest the advantage which the country-life possesses for a powerful mind, over the artificial and curtailed life of cities. We know more from nature than we can at will communicate. Its light flows into the mind evermore, and we forget its presence. The poet, the orator, bred in the woods, whose senses have been nourished by their fair and appeasing changes, year after year, without design and without heed,—shall not lose their lesson altogether, in the roar of cities or the broil of politics. Long hereafter, amidst agitation and terror in national councils,—in the hour of revolution,—these solemn images shall reappear in their morning lustre, as fit symbols and words of the thoughts which the passing events shall awaken. At the call of a noble sentiment, again the woods wave, the pines murmur, the river rolls and shines, and the cattle low upon the mountains, as he saw and heard them in his infancy. And with these forms, the spells of persuasion, the keys of power are put into his hands.

3. We are thus assisted by natural objects in the expression of particular meanings. But how great a language to convey such peppercorn informations! Did it need such noble races of creatures, this profusion of forms, this host of orbs in heaven, to furnish man with the dictionary and grammar of his municipal speech? Whilst we use this grand cipher to expedite the affairs of our pot and kettle, we feel that we have not yet put it to its use, neither are able. We are like travellers using the cinders of a volcano to roast their eggs. Whilst we see that it always stands ready to clothe what we would say, we cannot avoid the question, whether the characters are not significant of themselves. Have mountains, and waves, and skies, no significance but what we consciously give them, when we employ them as emblems of our thoughts? The world is emblematic. Parts of speech are metaphors because the whole of nature is a metaphor of the human mind. The laws of moral nature answer to those of matter as face to face in a glass. "The visible world and the relation of its parts, is the dial plate of the invisible."[19] The axioms of physics translate the laws of ethics.[20] Thus, "the whole is greater than its part;" "reaction is equal to action;" "the smallest weight may be made to lift the greatest, the difference of weight being compensated by time;" and many the like propositions, which have an ethical as well as physical sense. These propositions have a much more extensive and universal sense when applied to human life, than when confined to technical use.

In like manner, the memorable words of history, and the proverbs of nations, consist usually of a natural fact, selected as a picture or parable of a moral truth. Thus; A rolling stone gathers no moss; A bird in the hand is worth two in the bush; A cripple in the right way, will beat a racer in the wrong; Make hay whilst the sun shines; 'T is hard to carry a full cup even; Vinegar is the son of wine; The last ounce broke the camel's back; Long-lived trees make roots first;—and the like. In their primary sense these are trivial facts, but we repeat them for the value of their analogical import. What is true of proverbs, is true of all fables, parables, and allegories.

This relation between the mind and matter is not fancied by some poet, but stands in the will of God, and so is free to be known by all men. It appears to men, or it does not appear.[21] When in fortunate hours we ponder this miracle, the wise man doubts, if, at all other times, he is not blind and deaf;

> ———— Can these things be,
> And overcome us like a summer's cloud,
> Without our special wonder?[22]

for the universe becomes transparent, and the light of higher laws than its own, shines through it. It is the standing problem which has exercised the wonder and the study of every fine genius since the world began; from the era of the Egyptians and the Brahmins, to that of Pythagoras, of Plato, of Bacon, of Leibnitz, of Swedenborg.[23] There sits the Sphinx at the road-side, and from age to age, as each prophet comes by, he tries his fortune at reading her riddle.[24] There seems to be a necessity in spirit to manifest itself in material forms; and day and night, river and storm, beast and bird, acid and alkali, preëxist in necessary Ideas in the mind of God, and are what they are by virtue of preceding affections, in the world of spirit. A Fact is the end or last issue of spirit. The visible creation is the terminus or the circumference of the invisible world. "Material objects," said a French philosopher, "are necessarily kinds of *scoriæ* of the substantial thoughts of the Creator, which must always preserve an exact relation to their first origin; in other words, visible nature must have a spiritual and moral side."[25]

This doctrine is abstruse, and though the images of "garment," "scoriæ," "mirror," &c., may stimulate the fancy, we must summon the aid of subtler and more vital expositors to make it plain. "Every scripture is to be interpreted by the same spirit which gave it forth,"— is the fundamental law of criticism.[26] A life in harmony with nature, the love of truth and of virtue, will purge the eyes to understand her text. By degrees we may come to know the primitive sense of the permanent objects of nature, so that the world shall be to us an open book, and every form significant of its hidden life and final cause.

A new interest surprises us, whilst, under the view now suggested, we contemplate the fearful extent and multitude of objects; since "every object rightly seen, unlocks a new faculty of the soul."[27] That which was unconscious truth, becomes, when interpreted and defined in an object, a part of the domain of knowledge,—a new amount to the magazine of power.

Discipline

In view of this significance of nature, we arrive at once at a new fact, that nature is a discipline.[28] This use of the world includes the preceding uses, as parts of itself.

Space, time, society, labor, climate, food, locomotion, the animals, the mechanical forces, give us sincerest lessons, day by day, whose meaning is unlimited. They educate both the Understanding and the Reason. Every property of matter is a school for the understanding,— its solidity or resistance, its inertia, its extension, its figure, its divisibility. The understanding adds, divides, combines, measures, and finds everlasting nutriment and room for its activity in this worthy scene. Meantime, Reason transfers all these lessons into its own world of thought, by perceiving the analogy that marries Matter and Mind.

1. Nature is a discipline of the understanding in intellectual truths. Our dealing with sensible objects is a constant exercise in the necessary lessons of difference, of likeness, of order, of being and seeming, of progressive arrangement; of ascent from particular to general; of combination to one end of manifold forces. Proportioned to the importance of the organ to be formed, is the extreme care with which its tuition is provided,—a care pretermitted in no single case. What tedious training, day after day, year after year, never ending, to form the common sense; what continual reproduction of annoyances, inconveniences, dilemmas; what rejoicing over us of little men; what disputing of prices, what reckonings of interest,—and all to form the Hand of the mind;—to instruct us that "good thoughts are no better than good dreams, unless they be executed!"[29]

The same good office is performed by Property and its filial systems of debt and credit. Debt, grinding debt, whose iron face the widow, the orphan, and the sons of genius fear and hate;—debt, which consumes so much time, which so cripples and disheartens a great spirit with cares that seem so base, is a preceptor whose lessons cannot be foregone, and is needed most by those who suffer from it most. Moreover, property, which has been well compared to snow,—"if it fall level to-day, it will be blown into drifts to-morrow,"—is merely the surface action of internal machinery, like the index on the face of a clock. Whilst now it is the gymnastics of the understanding, it is hiving in the foresight of the spirit, experience in profounder laws.

The whole character and fortune of the individual is affected by the least inequalities in the culture of the understanding; for example, in the perception of differences. Therefore is Space, and therefore Time, that man may know that things are not huddled and lumped, but sundered and individual. A bell and a plough have each their use, and neither can do the office of the other. Water is good to drink, coal to burn, wool to wear; but wool cannot be drunk, nor water spun, nor coal eaten. The wise man shows his wisdom in separation, in gradation, and his scale of creatures and of merits, is as wide as nature. The foolish have no range in their scale, but suppose every man is as every other man. What is not good they call the worst, and what is not hateful, they call the best.

In like manner, what good heed, nature forms in us! She pardons no mistakes. Her yea is yea, and her nay, nay.

The first steps in Agriculture, Astronomy, Zoölogy, (those first steps which the farmer, the hunter, and the sailor take,) teach that nature's dice are always loaded; that in her heaps and rubbish are concealed sure and useful results.

How calmly and genially the mind apprehends one after another the laws of physics! What noble emotions dilate the mortal as he enters into the counsels of the creation, and feels by knowledge the privilege to BE! His insight refines him. The beauty of nature shines in his own breast. Man is greater that he can see this, and the universe less, because Time and Space relations vanish as laws are known.

Here again we are impressed and even daunted by the immense Universe to be explored. 'What we know, is a point to what we do not know.'[30] Open any recent journal of science, and weigh the problems suggested concerning Light, Heat, Electricity, Magnetism, Physiology, Geology, and judge whether the interest of natural science is likely to be soon exhausted.

Passing by many particulars of the discipline of nature we must not omit to specify two.

The exercise of the Will or the lesson of power is taught in every event. From the child's successive possession of his several senses up to the hour when he saith, "thy will be done!" he is learning the secret, that he can reduce under his will, not only particular events, but great classes, nay the whole series of events, and so conform all facts to his character. Nature is thoroughly mediate. It is made to serve. It receives the dominion of man as meekly as the ass on which the Saviour rode. It offers all its kingdoms to man as the raw material which he may mould into what is useful. Man is never weary of working it up. He forges the subtile and delicate air into wise and melodious words, and gives them wing as angles of persuasion and command. More and more, with every thought, does his kingdom stretch over things, until the world becomes, at last, only a realized will,— the double of the man.

2. Sensible objects conform to the premonitions of Reason and reflect the conscience. All things are moral; and in their boundless changes have an unceasing reference to spiritual nature. Therefore is nature glorious with form, color, and motion, that every globe in the remotest heaven; every chemical change from the rudest crystal up to the laws of life; every change of vegetation from the first principle of growth in the eye of a leaf, to the tropical forest and antediluvian coalmine; every animal function from the sponge up to Hercules, shall hint or thunder to man the laws of right and wrong, and echo the Ten Commandments.[31] Therefore is nature always the ally of Religion: lends all her pomp and riches to the religious sentiment. Prophet and priest, David, Isaiah, Jesus, have drawn deeply from this source.

This ethical character so penetrates the bone and marrow of nature, as to seem the end for which it was made. Whatever private purpose is answered by any member or part, this is its public and universal function, and is never omitted. Nothing in nature is exhausted in its first use. When a thing has served an end to the uttermost, it is wholly new for an ulterior service. In God, every end is converted into a new means. Thus the use of Commodity, regarded by itself, is mean and squalid. But it is to the mind an education in the great doctrine of Use, namely, that a thing is good only so far as it serves; that a conspiring of parts and efforts to the production of an end, is essential to any being. The first and gross manifestation of this truth, is our inevitable and hated training in values and wants, in corn and meat.

It has already been illustrated, in treating of the significance of material things, that every natural process is but a version of a moral sentence. The moral law lies at the centre of nature and radiates to the circumference. It is the pith and marrow of every substance, every relation, and every process. All things with which we deal, preach to us. What is a farm but a mute gospel? The chaff and the wheat, weeds and plants, blight, rain, insects, sun,—it is a sacred emblem from the first furrow of spring to the last stack which the snow of winter overtakes in the fields. But the sailor, the shepherd, the miner, the merchant, in their several resorts, have each an experience precisely parallel and leading to the same conclusions. Because all organizations are radically alike. Nor can it be doubted that this moral sentiment which thus scents the air, and grows in the grain, and impregnates the waters of the world, is caught by man and sinks into his soul. The moral influence of nature upon every individual is that amount of truth which it illustrates to him. Who can estimate this? Who can guess how much firmness the sea-beaten rock has taught the fisherman? how much tranquillity has been reflected to man from the azure sky, over whose unspotted deeps the winds forevermore drive flocks of stormy clouds, and leave no wrinkle or stain? how much industry and providence and affection we have caught from the pantomime of brutes? What a searching preacher of self-command is the varying phenomenon of Health!

Herein is especially apprehended the Unity of Nature,—the Unity in Variety,—which meets us everywhere. All the endless variety of things make a unique, an identical impression. Xenophanes complained in his old age, that, look where he would, all things hastened back to Unity.[32] He was weary of seeing the same entity in the tedious variety of forms. The fable of Proteus has a cordial truth.[33] Every particular in nature, a leaf, a drop, a crystal, a moment of time is related to the whole, and partakes of the perfection of the whole. Each particle is a microcosm, and faithfully renders the likeness of the world.

Not only resemblances exist in things whose analogy is obvious, as when we detect the type of the human hand in the flipper of the fossil saurus, but also in objects wherein there is great superficial unlikeness. Thus architecture is called 'frozen music,' by De Stael and Goethe.[34] 'A Gothic church,' said Coleridge, 'is a petrified religion.' Michael Angelo maintained, that, to an architect, a knowledge of anatomy is essential.[35] In Haydn's oratorios, the notes present to the imagination not only motions, as, of the snake, the stag, and the elephant, but colors also; as the green grass.[36] The granite is differenced in its laws only by the more or less of heat, from the river that wears it away. The river, as it flows, resembles the air that flows over it; the air resembles the light which traverses it with more subtile currents; the light resembles the heat which rides with it through Space. Each creature is only a modification of the other; the likeness in them is more than the difference, and their radical law is one and the same. Hence it is, that a rule of one art, or a law of one organization, holds true throughout nature. So intimate is this Unity, that, it is easily seen, it lies under the undermost garment of nature, and betrays its source in universal Spirit. For, it pervades Thought also. Every universal truth which we express in words, implies or supposes every other truth. *Omne verum vero consonat*.[37] It is like a great circle on a sphere, comprising all possible circles; which, however, may be drawn, and comprise it, in like manner. Every such truth is the absolute Ens seen from one side.[38] But it has innumerable sides.

The same central Unity is still more conspicous in actions. Words are finite organs of the infinite mind. They cannot cover the dimensions of what is in truth, They break, chop, and impoverish it. An action is the perfection and publication of thought. A right action seems to fill the eye, and to be related to all nature. "The wise man, in doing one thing, does all; or, in the one thing he does rightly, he sees the likeness of all which is done rightly."[39]

Words and actions are not the attributes of mute and brute nature. They introduce us to that singular form which predominates over all other forms. This is the human. All other organizations appear to be degradations of the human form. When this organization appears among so many that surround it, the spirit prefers it to all others. It says, 'From such as this, have I drawn joy and knowledge. In such as this, have I found and beheld myself. I will speak to it. It can speak again. It can yield me thought already formed and alive.' In fact, the eye,—the mind,—is always accompanied by these forms, male and female; and these are incomparably the richest informations of the power and order that lie at the heart of things. Unfortunately, every one of them bears the marks as of some injury; is marred and superficially defective. Nevertheless, far different from the deaf and dumb nature around them, these all rest like fountain-pipes on the unfathomed sea of thought and virtue whereto they alone, of all organizations, are the entrances.

It were a pleasant inquiry to follow into detail their ministry to our education, but where would it stop? We are associated in adolescent and adult life with some friends, who, like skies and waters, are co-extensive with our idea; who, answering each to a certain affection of the soul, satisfy our desire on that side; whom we lack power to put at such focal distance from us, that we can mend or even analyze them. We cannot chuse but love them. When much intercourse with a friend has supplied us with a standard of excellence, and has increased our respect for the resources of God who thus sends a real person to outgo our ideal; when he has, moreover, become an object of thought, and, whilst his character retains all its unconscious effect, is converted in the mind into solid and sweet wisdom,—it is a sign to us that his office is closing, and he is commonly withdrawn from our sight in a short time.

Idealism

Thus is the unspeakable but intelligible and practicable meaning of the world conveyed to man, the immortal pupil, in every object of sense. To this one end of Discipline, all parts of nature conspire.

A noble doubt perpetually suggests itself, whether this end be not the Final Cause of the Universe; and whether nature outwardly exists.

It is a sufficient account of that Appearance we call the World, that God will teach a human mind, and so makes it the receiver of a certain number of congruent sensations, which we call sun and moon, man and woman, house and trade. In my utter impotence to test the authenticity of the report of my senses, to know whether the impressions they make on me correspond with outlying objects, what difference does it make, whether Orion is up there in heaven, or some god paints the image in the firmament of the soul?[40] The relations of parts and the end of the whole remaining the same, what is the difference, whether land and sea interact, and worlds revolve and intermingle without number or end,—deep yawning under deep, and galaxy balancing galaxy, throughout absolute space, or, whether, without relations of time and space, the same appearances are inscribed in the constant faith of man. Whether nature enjoy a substantial existence without, or is only in the apocalypse of the mind, it is alike useful and alike venerable to me. Be it what it may, it is ideal to me, so long as I cannot try the accuracy of my senses.

The frivolous make themselves merry with the Ideal theory, as if its consequences were burlesque; as if it affected the stability of nature. It surely does not. God never jests with us, and will not compromise the end of nature, by permitting any inconsequence in its procession. Any distrust of the permanence of laws, would paralyze the faculties of man. Their permanence is sacredly respected, and his faith therein is perfect. The wheels and springs of man are all set to the hypothesis of the permanence of nature. We are not built like a ship to be tossed, but like a house to stand. It is a natural consequence of this structure, that, so long as the active powers predominate over the reflective, we resist with indignation any hint that nature is more short-lived or mutable than spirit. The broker, the wheelwright, the carpenter, the toll-man, are much displeased at the intimation.

But whilst we acquiesce entirely in the permanence of natural laws, the question of the absolute existence of nature, still remains open. It is the uniform effect of culture on the human mind, not to shake our faith in the stability of particular phenomena, as of heat, water, azote;[41] but to lead us to regard nature as a phenomenon, not a substance; to attribute necessary existence to spirit; to esteem nature as an accident and an effect.

To the senses and the unrenewed understanding, belongs a sort of instinctive belief in the absolute existence of nature. In their view, man and nature are indissolubly joined. Things are ultimates, and they never look beyond their sphere. The presence of Reason mars this faith. The first effort of thought tends to relax this despotism of the senses, which binds us to nature as if we were a part of it, and shows us

nature aloof, and, as it were, afloat. Until this higher agency inter-
vened, the animal eye sees, with wonderful accuracy, sharp outlines
and colored surfaces. When the eye of Reason opens, to outline and
surface are at once added, grace and expression. These proceed from
imagination and affection, and abate somewhat of the angular distinctness of objects. If the Reason be stimulated to more earnest vision,
outlines and surfaces become transparent, and are no longer seen;
causes and spirits are seen through them. The best, the happiest moments of life, are these delicious awakenings of the higher powers, and
the reverential withdrawing of nature before its God.

Let us proceed to indicate the effects of culture. 1. Our first institution in the Ideal philosophy is a hint from nature herself.

Nature is made to conspire with spirit to emancipate us. Certain
mechanical changes, a small alteration in our local position apprizes
us of a dualism. We are strangely affected by seeing the shore from a
moving ship, from a balloon, or through the tints of an unusual sky.
The least change in our point of view, gives the whole world a pictorial
air. A man who seldom rides, needs only to get into a coach and
traverse his own town, to turn the street into a puppet-show. The
men, the women,—talking, running, bartering, fighting,—the earnest
mechanic, the lounger, the beggar, the boys, the dogs, are unrealized
at once, or, at least, wholly detached from all relation to the observer,
and seen as apparent, not substantial beings. What new thoughts are
suggested by seeing a face of country quite familiar, in the rapid movement of the rail-road car! Nay, the most wonted objects, (make a very
slight change in the point of vision,) please us most. In a camera
obscura,[42] the butcher's cart, and the figure of one of our own family
amuse us. So a portrait of a well-known face gratifies us. Turn the eyes
upside down, by looking at the landscape through your legs, and how
agreeable is the picture, though you have seen it any time these twenty
years!

In these cases, by mechanical means, is suggested the difference
between the observer and the spectacle,—between man and nature.
Hence arises a pleasure mixed with awe; I may say, a low degree of
the sublime is felt from the fact, probably, that man is hereby apprized,
that, whilst the world is a spectacle, something in himself is stable.

2. In a higher manner, the poet communicates the same pleasure.
By a few strokes he delineates, as on air, the sun, the mountain, the
camp, the city, the hero, the maiden, not different from what we know
them, but only lifted from the ground and afloat before the eye. He
unfixes the land and the sea, makes them revolve around the axis of
his primary thought, and disposes them anew. Possessed himself by a
heroic passion, he uses matter as symbols of it. The sensual man con-

forms thoughts to things; the poet conforms things to his thoughts. The one esteems nature as rooted and fast; the other, as fluid, and impresses his being thereon. To him, the refractory world is ductile and flexible; he invests dust and stones with humanity, and makes them the words of the Reason. The imagination may be defined to be, the use which the Reason makes of the material world. Shakespeare possesses the power of subordinating nature for the purposes of expression, beyond all poets. His imperial muse tosses the creation like a bubble from hand to hand, to embody any capricious shade of thought that is uppermost in his mind. The remotest spaces of nature are visited, and the farthest sundered things are brought together, by a subtile spiritual connexion. We are made aware that magnitude of material things is merely relative, and all objects shrink and expand to serve the passion of the poet. Thus, in his sonnets, the lays of birds, the scents and dyes of flowers, he finds to be the *shadow* of his beloved; time, which keeps her from him, is his *chest*; the suspicion she has awakened, is her *ornament*;

> The ornament of beauty is Suspect,
> A crow which flies in heaven's sweetest air.[43]

His passion is not the fruit of chance; it swells, as he speaks, to a city, or a state.

> No, it was builded far from accident;
> It suffers not in smiling pomp, nor falls
> Under the brow of thralling discontent;
> It fears not policy, that heretic,
> That works on leases of short numbered hours,
> But all alone stands hugely politic.[44]

In the strength of his constancy, the Pyramids seem to him recent and transitory. And the freshness of youth and love dazzles him with its resemblance to morning.

> Take those lips away
> Which so sweetly were forsworn;
> And those eyes,—the break of day,
> Lights that do mislead the morn.[45]

The wild beauty of this hyperbole, I may say, in passing, it would not be easy to match in literature.

This transfiguration which all material objects undergo through the passion of the poet,—this power which he exerts, at any moment, to magnify the small, to micrify the great,—might be illustrated by a thousand examples from his Plays. I have before me the Tempest, and will cite only these few lines.

> ARIEL. The strong based promontory
> Have I made shake, and by the spurs plucked up
> The pine and cedar.

Prospero calls for music to sooth the frantic Alonzo, and his companions;

> A solemn air, and the best comforter
> To an unsettled fancy, cure thy brains
> Now useless, boiled within thy skull.

Again;

> The charm dissolves space
> And, as the morning steals upon the night,
> Melting the darkness, so their rising senses
> Begin to chase the ignorant fumes that mantle
> Their clearer reason.

> Their understanding
> Begins to swell: and the approaching tide
> Will shortly fill the reasonable shores
> That now lie foul and muddy.[46]

The perception of real affinities between events, (that is to say, of *ideal* affinities, for those only are real,) enables the poet thus to make free with the most imposing forms and phenomena of the world, and to assert the predominance of the soul.

3. Whilst thus the poet delights us by animating nature like a creator, with his own thoughts, he differs from the philosopher only herein, that the one proposes Beauty as his main end; the other Truth. But, the philosopher, not less than the poet, postpones the apparent order and relations of things to the empire of thought. "The problem of philosophy," according to Plato, "is, for all that exists conditionally, to find a ground unconditioned and absolute."[47] It proceeds on the faith that a law determines all phenomena, which being known, the phenomena can be predicted. That law, when in the mind, is an idea. Its beauty is infinite. The true philosopher and the true poet are one, and a beauty, which is truth, and a truth, which is beauty, is the aim of both. Is not the charm of one of Plato's or Aristotle's definitions, strictly like that of the Antigone of Sophocles?[48] It is, in both cases, that a spiritual life has been imparted to nature; that the solid seeming block of matter has been pervaded and dissolved by a thought; that

this feeble human being has penetrated the vast masses of nature with an informing soul, and recognised itself in their harmony, that is, seized their law. In physics, when this is attained, the memory disburthens itself of its cumbrous catalogues of particulars, and carries centuries of observation in a single formula.

Thus even in physics, the material is ever degraded before the spiritual. The astronomer, the geometer, rely on their irrefragable analysis, and disdain the results of observation. The sublime remark of Euler on his law of arches, "This will be found contrary to all experience, yet is true;"[49] had already transferred nature into the mind, and left matter like an outcast corpse.

4. Intellectual science has been observed to beget invariably a doubt of the existence of matter. Turgot said, "He that has never doubted the existence of matter, may be assured he has no aptitude for metaphysical inquiries."[50] It fastens the attention upon immortal necessary uncreated natures, that is, upon Ideas; and in their beautiful and majestic presence, we feel that our outward being is a dream and a shade. Whilst we wait in this Olympus of gods, we think of nature as an appendix to the soul.[51] We ascend into their region, and know that these are the thoughts of the Supreme Being. "These are they who were set up from everlasting, from the beginning, or ever the earth was. When he prepared the heavens, they were there; when he established the clouds above, when he strengthened the fountains of the deep. Then they were by him, as one brought up with him. Of them took he counsel."[52]

Their influence is proportionate. As objects of science, they are accessible to few men. Yet all men are capable of being raised by piety or by passion, into their region. And no man touches these divine natures, without becoming, in some degree, himself divine. Like a new soul, they renew the body. We become physically nimble and lightsome; we tread on air; life is no longer irksome, and we think it will never be so. No man fears age or misfortune or death, in their serene company, for he is transported out of the district of change. Whilst we behold unveiled the nature of Justice and Truth, we learn the difference between the absolute and the conditional or relative. We apprehend the absolute. As it were, for the first time, *we exist*. We become immortal, for we learn that time and space are relations of matter; that, with a perception of truth, or a virtuous will, they have no affinity.

5. Finally, religion and ethics, which may be fitly called,—the practice of ideas, or the introduction of ideas into life,—have an analogous effect with all lower culture, in degrading nature and suggesting its dependence on spirit. Ethics and religion differ herein; that the one is

the system of human duties commencing from man; the other, from God. Religion includes the personality of God; Ethics does not. They are one to our present design. They both put nature under foot. The first and last lesson of religion is, "The things that are seen, are temporal; the things that are unseen are eternal."[53] It puts an affront upon nature. It does that for the unschooled, which philosophy does for Berkeley and Viasa.[54] The uniform language that may be heard in the churches of the most ignorant sects, is,—'Contemn the unsubstantial shows of the world; they are vanities, dreams, shadows, unrealities; seek the realities of religion.' The devotee flouts nature. Some theosophists have arrived at a certain hostility and indignation towards matter, as the Manichean and Plotinus.[55] They distrusted in themselves any looking back to these flesh-pots of Egypt. Plotinus was ashamed of his body. In short, they might all better say of matter, what Michael Angelo said of external beauty, "it is the frail and weary weed, in which God dresses the soul, which he has called into time."[56]

It appears that motion, poetry, physical and intellectual science, and religion, all tend to affect our convictions of the reality of the external world. But I own there is something ungrateful in expanding too curiously the particulars of the general proposition, that all culture tends to imbue us with idealism. I have no hostility to nature, but a child's love to it. I expand and live in the warm day like corn and melons. Let us speak her fair. I do not wish to fling stones at my beautiful mother, nor soil my gentle nest. I only wish to indicate the true position of nature in regard to man, wherein to establish man, all right education tends; as the ground which to attain is the object of human life, that is, of man's connexion with nature. Culture inverts the vulgar views of nature, and brings the mind to call that apparent, which it uses to call real, and that real, which it uses to call visionary. Children, it is true, believe in the external world. The belief that it appears only, is an afterthought, but with culture, this faith will as surely arise on the mind as did the first.

The advantage of the ideal theory over the popular faith, is this, that it presents the world in precisely that view which is most desirable to the mind. It is, in fact, the view which Reason, both speculative and practical, that is, philosophy and virtue, take. For, seen in the light of thought, the world always is phenomenal; and virtue subordinates it to the mind. Idealism sees the world in God. It beholds the whole circle of persons and things, of actions and events, of country and religion, not as painfully accumulated, atom after atom, act after act, in an aged creeping Past, but as one vast picture, which God paints on the instant eternity, for the contemplation of the soul. Therefore the soul holds itself off from a too trivial and microscopic study of the universal tablet. It respects the end too much, to immerse itself in the means. It sees something more important in Christianity, than the scandals of ecclesiastical history or the niceties of criticism; and, very incurious concerning persons or miracles, and not at all disturbed by chasms of historical evidence, it accepts from God the phenomenon, as it finds it, as the pure and awful form of religion in the world. It is not hot and passionate at the appearance of what it calls its own good or bad fortune, at the union or opposition of other persons. No man is its enemy. It accepts whatsoever befals, as part of its lesson. It is a watcher more than a doer, and it is a doer, only that it may the better watch.

Spirit

It is essential to a true theory of nature and of man, that it should contain somewhat progressive. Uses that are exhausted or that may be, and facts that end in the statement, cannot be all that is true of this brave lodging wherein man is harbored, and wherein all his faculties find appropriate and endless exercise. And all the uses of nature admit of being summed in one, which yields the activity of man an infinite scope. Through all its kingdoms, to the suburbs and outskirts of things, it is faithful to the cause whence it had its origin. It always speaks of Spirit. It suggests the absolute. It is a perpetual effect. It is a great shadow pointing always to the sun behind us.

The aspect of nature is devout. Like the figure of Jesus, she stands with bended head, and hands folded upon the breast. The happiest man is he who learns from nature the lesson of worship.

Of that ineffable essence which we call Spirit, he that thinks most, will say least. We can foresee God in the coarse and, as it were, distant phenomena of matter; but when we try to define and describe himself, both language and thought desert us, and we are as helpless as fools and savages. That essence refuses to be recorded in propositions, but when man has worshipped him intellectually, the noblest ministry of nature is to stand as the apparition of God. It is the great organ through which the universal spirit speaks to the individual, and strives to lead back the individual to it.

When we consider Spirit, we see that the views already presented do not include the whole circumference of man. We must add some related thoughts.

Three problems are put by nature to the mind; What is matter? Whence is it? and Whereto? The first of these questions only, the ideal theory answers. Idealism saith: matter is a phenomenon, not a substance. Idealism acquaints us with the total disparity between the evidence of our own being, and the evidence of the world's being. The one is perfect; the other, incapable of any assurance; the mind is a part of the nature of things; the world is a divine dream, from which we may presently awake to the glories and certainties of day. Idealism is a hypothesis to account for nature by other principles than those of carpentry and chemistry. Yet, if it only deny the existence of matter, it does not satisfy the demands of the spirit. It leaves God out of me. It leaves me in the splendid labyrinth of my perceptions, to wander without end. Then the heart resists it, because it baulks the affections in denying substantive being to men and women. Nature is so pervaded with human life, that there is something of humanity in all, and in every particular. But this theory makes nature foreign to me, and does not account for that consanguinity which we acknowledge to it.

Let it stand then, in the present state of our knowledge, merely as a useful introductory hypothesis, serving to apprize us of the eternal distinction between the soul and the world.

But when, following the invisible steps of thought, we come to inquire, Whence is matter? and Whereto? many truths arise to us out of the recesses of consciousness. We learn that the highest is present to the soul of man, that the dread universal essence, which is not wisdom, or love, or beauty, or power, but all in one, and each entirely, is that for which all things exist, and that by which they are; that spirit creates; that behind nature, throughout nature, spirit is present; that spirit is one and not compound; that spirit does not act upon us from without, that is, in space and time, but spiritually, or through ourselves. Therefore, that spirit, that is, the Supreme Being, does not build up nature around us, but puts it forth through us, as the life of the tree puts forth new branches and leaves through the pores of the old. As a plant upon the earth, so a man rests upon the bosom of God; he is nourished by unfailing fountains, and draws, at his need, inexhaustible power. Who can set bounds to the possibilities of man? Once inspire the infinite, by being admitted to behold the absolute natures of justice and truth, and we learn that man has access to the entire mind of the Creator, is himself the creator in the finite. This view, which admonishes me where the sources of wisdom and power lie, and points to virtue as to

> The golden key
> Which opes the palace of eternity,[57]

carries upon its face the highest certificate of truth, because it animates me to create my own world through the purification of my soul.

The world proceeds from the same spirit as the body of man. It is a remoter and inferior incarnation of God, a projection of God in the unconscious. But it differs from the body in one important respect. It is not, like that, now subjected to the human will. Its serene order is inviolable by us. It is therefore, to us, the present expositor of the divine mind. It is a fixed point whereby we may measure our departure. As we degenerate, the contrast between us and our house is more evident. We are as much strangers in nature, as we are aliens from God. We do not understand the notes of birds. The fox and the deer run away from us; the bear and tiger rend us. We do not know the uses of more than a few plants, as corn and the apple, the potato and the vine. Is not the landscape, every glimpse of which hath a grandeur, a face of him? Yet this may show us what discord is between man and nature, for you cannot freely admire a noble landscape, if laborers are digging in the field hard by. The poet finds something ridiculous in his delight, until he is out of the sight of men.

Prospects

In inquiries respecting the laws of the world and the frame of things, the highest reason is always the truest. That which seems faintly possible—it is so refined, is often faint and dim because it is deepest seated in the mind among the eternal verities. Empirical science is apt to cloud the sight, and, by the very knowledge of functions and processes, to bereave the student of the manly contemplation of the whole. The savant becomes unpoetic. But the best read naturalist who lends an entire and devout attention to truth, will see that there remains much to learn of his relation to the world, and that it is not to be learned by any addition or subtraction or other comparison of known quantities, but is arrived at by untaught sallies of the spirit, by a continual self-recovery, and by entire humility. He will perceive that there are far more excellent qualities in the student than preciseness and infallibility; that a guess is often more fruitful than an indisputable affirmation, and that a dream may let us deeper into the secret of nature than a hundred concerted experiments.

For, the problems to be solved are precisely those which the physiologist and the naturalist omit to state. It is not so pertinent to man to know all the individuals of the animal kingdom, as it is to know whence and whereto is this tyrannizing unity in his constitution, which evermore separates and classifies things, endeavouring to reduce the most diverse to one form. When I behold a rich landscape, it is less to my purpose to recite correctly the order and superposition of the strata, than to know why all thought of multitude is lost in a tranquil sense of unity. I cannot greatly honor minuteness in details, so long as there is no hint to explain the relation between things and thoughts; no ray upon the *metaphysics* of conchology, of botany, of the arts, to show the relation of the forms of flowers, shells, animals, architecture, to the mind, and build science upon ideas. In a cabinet of natural history, we become sensible of a certain occult recognition and sympathy in regard to the most bizarre forms of beast, fish, and insect. The American who has been confined, in his own country, to the sight of buildings designed after foreign models, is surprised on entering York Minster or St. Peter's at Rome, by the feeling that these structures are imitations also,—faint copies of an invisible archetype.[58] Nor has science sufficient humanity, so long as the naturalist overlooks that wonderful congruity which subsists between man and the world; of which he is lord, not because he is the most subtile inhabitant, but because he is its head and heart, and finds something of himself in every great and small thing, in every mountain stratum, in every new law of color, fact of astronomy, or atmospheric influence which observation or analysis lay open. A perception of this mystery inspires the muse of George Herbert, the beautiful psalmist of the seventeenth century. The following lines are part of his little poem on Man.

> Man is all symmetry,
> Full of proportions, one limb to another,
> And to all the world besides.
> Each part may call the farthest, brother;
> For head with foot hath private amity,
> And both with moons and tides.
>
> Nothing hath got so far
> But man hath caught and kept it as his prey;
> His eyes dismount the highest star;
> He is in little all the sphere.
> Herbs gladly cure our flesh, because that they
> Find their acquaintance there.
>
> For us, the winds do blow,
> The earth doth rest, heaven move, and fountains flow;
> Nothing we see, but means our good,
> As our delight, or as our treasure;
> The whole is either our cupboard of food,
> Or cabinet of pleasure.
>
> The stars have us to bed:
> Night draws the curtain; which the sun withdraws.
> Music and light attend our head.
> All things unto our flesh are hind,

In their descent and being; to our mind,
    In their ascent and cause.

    More servants wait on man
Than he'll take notice of. In every path,
    He treads down that which doth befriend him
    When sickness makes him pale and wan.
Oh mighty love! Man is one world, and hath
    Another to attend him.[59]

The perception of this class of truths makes the eternal attraction which draws men to science, but the end is lost sight of in attention to the means. In view of this half-sight of science, we accept the sentence of Plato, that, "poetry comes nearer to vital truth than history." Every surmise and vaticination[60] of the mind is entitled to a certain respect, and we learn to prefer imperfect theories, and sentences, which contain glimpses of truth, to digested systems which have no one valuable suggestion. A wise writer will feel that the ends of study and composition are best answered by announcing undiscovered regions of thought, and so communicating, through hope, new activity to the torpid spirit.

I shall therefore conclude this essay with some traditions of man and nature, which a certain poet sang to me;[61] and which, as they have always been in the world, and perhaps reappear to every bard, may be both history and prophecy.

The foundations of man are not in matter, but in spirit. But the element of spirit is eternity. To it, therefore, the longest series of events, the oldest chronologies are young and recent. In the cycle of the universal man, from whom the known individuals proceed, centuries are points, and all history is but the epoch of one degradation.

'We distrust and deny inwardly our sympathy with nature. We own and disown our relation to it, by turns. We are, like Nebuchadnezzar, dethroned, bereft of reason, and eating grass like an ox.[62] But who can set limits to the remedial force of spirit?

'A man is a god in ruins. When men are innocent, life shall be longer, and shall pass into the immortal, as gently as we awake from dreams. Now, the world would be insane and rabid, if these disorganizations should last for hundreds of years. It is kept in check by death and infancy. Infancy is the perpetual Messiah, which comes into the arms of fallen men, and pleads with them to return to paradise.

'Man is the dwarf of himself. Once he was permeated and dissolved by spirit. He filled nature with his overflowing currents. Out from him sprang the sun and moon; from man, the sun; from woman, the moon. The laws of his mind, the periods of his actions externized themselves into day and night, into the year and the seasons. But, having made for himself this huge shell, his waters retired; he no longer fills the veins and veinlets; he is shrunk to a drop. He sees, that the structure still fits him, but fits him colossally. Say, rather, once it fitted him, now it corresponds to him from far and on high. He adores timidly his own work. Now is man the follower of the sun, and woman the follower of the moon. Yet sometimes he starts in his slumber, and wonders at himself and his house, and muses strangely at the resemblance betwixt him and it. He perceives that if his law is still paramount, if still he have elemental power, "if his word is sterling yet in nature," it is not conscious power, it is not inferior but superior to his will.[63] It is Instinct.' Thus my Orphic poet sang.

At present, man applies to nature but half his force. He works on the world with his understanding alone. He lives in it, and masters it by a penny-wisdom; and he that works most in it, is but a half-man, and whilst his arms are strong and his digestion good, his mind is imbruted and he is a selfish savage. His relation to nature, his power over it, is through the understanding; as by manure; the economic use of fire, wind, water, and the mariner's needle; steam, coal, chemical agriculture; the repairs of the human body by the dentist and the surgeon. This is such a resumption of power, as if a banished king should buy his territories inch by inch, instead of vaulting at once into his throne. Meantime, in the thick darkness, there are not wanting gleams of a better light,—occasional examples of the action of man upon nature with his entire force,—with reason as well as understanding. Such examples are; the traditions of miracles in the earliest antiquity of all nations; the history of Jesus Christ; the achievements of a principle, as in religious and political revolutions, and in the abolition of the Slave-trade; the miracles of enthusiasm, as those reported of Swedenborg, Hohenlohe, and the Shakers; many obscure and yet contested facts, now arranged under the name of Animal Magnetism; prayer; eloquence; self-healing; and the wisdom of children.[64] These are examples of Reason's momentary grasp of the sceptre; the exertions of a power which exists not in time or space, but an instantaneous instreaming causing power. The difference between the actual and the ideal force of man is happily figured by the schoolmen, in saying, that the knowledge of man is an evening knowledge, *vespertina cognitie*, but that of God is a morning knowledge, *matutina cognitie*.[65]

The problem of restoring to the world original and eternal beauty, is solved by the redemption of the soul. The ruin or the blank, that we see when we look at nature, is in our own eye. The axis of vision is not coincident with the axis of things, and so they appear not transparent but opake. The reason why the world lacks unity, and lies broken and in heaps, is, because man is disunited with himself. He cannot be a naturalist, until he satisfies all the demands of the spirit. Love is as much its demand, as perception. Indeed, neither can be perfect without the other. In the uttermost meaning of the words, thought is devout, and devotion is thought. Deep calls unto deep. But in actual life, the marriage is not celebrated. There are innocent men who worship God after the tradition of their fathers, but their sense of duty has not yet extended to the use of all their faculties. And there are patient naturalists, but they freeze their subject under the wintry light of the understanding. Is not prayer also a study of truth,—a sally of the soul into the unfound infinite? No man ever prayed heartily, without learning something. But when a faithful thinker, resolute to detach every object from personal relations, and see it in the light of thought, shall, at the same time, kindle science with the fire of the holiest affections, then will God go forth anew into the creation.

It will not need, when the mind is prepared for study, to search for objects. The invariable mark of wisdom is to see the miraculous in the common. What is a day? What is a year? What is summer? What is woman? What is a child? What is sleep. To our blindness, these things seem unaffecting. We make fables to hide the baldness of the fact and conform it, as we say, to the higher law of the mind. But when the fact is seen under the light of an idea, the gaudy fable fades and shrivels. We behold the real higher law. To the wise, therefore, a fact is true poetry; and the most beautiful of fables. These wonders are brought to our own door. You also are a man. Man and woman, and their social life, poverty, labor, sleep, fear, fortune, are known to you. Learn that none of these things is superficial, but that each phenomenon hath its roots in the faculties and affections of the mind. Whilst the abstract question occupies your intellect, nature brings it in the concrete to be solved by your hands. It were a wise inquiry for the closet, to compare, point by point, especially at remarkable crises in life, our daily history, with the rise and progress of ideas in the mind.

So shall we come to look at the world with new eyes. It shall answer the endless inquiry of the intellect,—What is truth? and of the affections,—What is good? by yielding itself passive to the educated Will. Then shall come to pass what my poet[66] said; 'Nature is not fixed but fluid. Spirit alters, moulds, makes it. The immobility or bruteness of nature, is the absence of spirit; to pure spirit, it is fluid, it is volatile, it is obedient. Every spirit builds itself a house; and beyond its house, a world; and beyond its world, a heaven. Know then, that the world exists for you. For you is the phenomenon perfect. What we are, that only can we see. All that Adam had, all that Cæsar could, you have and can do.[67] Adam called his house, heaven and earth; Cæsar called his house, Rome; you perhaps call yours, a cobler's trade; a hundred acres of ploughed land; or a scholar's garret. Yet line for line and point for point, your dominion is as great as theirs, though without fine names. Build, therefore, your own world. As fast as you conform your life to the pure idea in your mind, that will unfold its great proportions. A correspondent revolution in things will attend the influx of the spirit. So fast will disagreeable appearances, swine, spiders, snakes, pests, mad-houses, prisons, enemies, vanish; they are temporary and shall be no more seen. The sordor and filths of nature, the sun shall dry up, and the wind exhale. As when the summer comes from the south, the snow-banks melt, and the face of the earth becomes green before it, so shall the advancing spirit create its ornaments along its path, and carry with it the beauty it visits, and the song which enchants it; it shall draw beautiful faces, and warm hearts, and wise discourse, and heroic acts, around its way, until evil is no more seen. The kingdom of man over nature, which cometh not with observation,—a dominion such as now is beyond his dream of God,—he shall enter without more wonder than the blind man feels who is gradually restored to perfect sight.'

Source: Ralph Waldo Emerson, *Nature* (Boston: James Munroe, 1836).

Notes

1. The epigraph is a quote from Plotinus (ca. 204–ca. 270), Greek philosopher who set out the basic tenets of Neo-Platonism. In the 1849 edition of *Nature*, Emerson replaced this motto with lines from his poem "Nature": "A subtle chain of countless rings/The next unto the farthest brings;/The eye reads omens where it goes,/And speaks all languages the rose;/And, striving to be man, the worm/Mounts through all the spires of form" (*Complete Works*, 9:281).

2. "If the stars should appear one night in a thousand years, how would men believe and adore, and preserve for many generations the remembrance of the city of God?" is adapted as the epigraph to the famous science-fiction story "Nightfall" (1941) by Isaac Asimov (1920–1992).

3. "Man" (1633), ll. 43–44, by George Herbert (1593–1633), English metaphysical poet.

4. Aeolus, in Homer's *Odyssey,* gave Odysseus a good wind and tied up the unfavorable winds in a bag; to the Greeks, the name became synonymous with the god of the winds.

5. Napoleon Bonaparte (1769–1821), French general and ruler.

6. κόσμος: cosmos or order.

7. Quoted from Emerson's brother, Charles Chancy Emerson (1808–1836).

8. Assyria, a kingdom in northern Mesopotamia; Paphos, a Greek city on Cyprus where a famous temple of the goddess of beauty, Aphrodite, was located, and where, according to legend, she had been born from the sea foam.

9. "Of Love" by Plutarch (b. ca. 16), Greek historian best known for his series of lives of famous Greek and Roman figures.

10. Emerson attributes this to Sallust (ca. 86–ca. 35 B.C.), Roman historian, in the 1849 edition of *Nature*, but it actually appears in *Apology for Smectymnuus* (1641), by John Milton.

11. *History of the Decline and Fall of the Roman Empire* (1776–1788), by Edward Gibbon (1737–1794), English scholar and historian.

12. Leonidas (d. 480 B.C.), Spartan king whose troops held off a Persian army at the pass of Thermopylae, fighting to the last man; Arnold Winkelried, according to legend, helped the Swiss win the Battle of Sempach (1386) over the Austrians by absorbing into his own body the lances from the advancing Austrians.

13. Sir Henry Vane the Younger (1613–1662), English Parliamentarian, was executed for his past political activities by King Charles II.

14. Charles II (1630–1685), restored the monarchy to England after the Commonwealth was overthrown; William Russell, Lord Russell (1639–1683), English politician executed for plotting to murder Charles II and his brother.

15. Pindar (ca. 522–443 B.C.), the greatest of the Greek lyric poets; Phocion (ca. 402–317 B.C.), Athenian general and statesman.

16. *il piu nell' uno*: "multitude in unity" in Emerson's source, *Specimens of the Table Talk of the Late Samuel Taylor Coleridge* (1835 edition).

17. Carolus Linnaeus (1707–1778), Swedish botanist, is considered one of the founders of modern systematic botany; Georges-Louis Leclerc, Count de Buffon (1707–1788), French naturalist.

18. I Corinthians 15:44.

19. Quoted from Emanuel Swedenborg (1688–1772), Swedish scientist, theologian, and mystic.

20. Paraphrased from *Germany* (1810), by Madame de Staël (1766–1817), French novelist and social critic.

21. *Enneads*, 5.5, by Plotinus.

22. *Macbeth*, act 3, scene 4, ll. 110–112.

23. Brahmins, worshipers of Brahma, were of the priestly class and thus in the highest social order in Hinduism; Pythagoras (d. 497 B.C.), Greek philosopher who raised mathematics to a science.

24. In "The Sphinx" (1841), Emerson answers the riddle, after which the Sphinx says "Who telleth one of my meanings/Is Master of all I am."

25. *scoriæ*: the dross of metals; quoted from *The True Messiah; or the Old and New Testaments, Examined According to the Principles of the Language of Nature*, trans. E. P. Peabody (1842), by Guillaume Oegger (ca. 1790–ca. 1853), French cleric, linguist, and Swedenborgian.

26. Quoted from George Fox (1624–1691), founder of the Society of Friends (Quakers).
27. Quoted from *Aids to Reflection*, by Coleridge.
28. Emerson is using this term in the sense of education or instruction.
29. Paraphrased from "Of Great Place" (1612), by Francis Bacon.
30. Attributed to Joseph Butler (1692–1752), English bishop and philosopher, in the novel *Tremaine* (1825), by Robert Plumer Ward.
31. Hercules, Greek god of strength.
32. Xenophanes (ca. 560–ca. 478 B.C.), Greek poet and philosopher who stressed the unity of all things.
33. Proteus, in Greek mythology, knew all things but disliked sharing his knowledge. He could only be forced to divulge his secrets when caught, and even then he had to be held because he shifted shapes while attempting to escape.
34. Johann Wolfgang von Goethe (1749–1832), Germany's most famous writer and a great favorite of Emerson's.
35. Michelangelo Buonarroti (1475–1564), Italian painter, sculptor, and poet.
36. Joseph Haydn (1732–1809), Austrian composer.
37. *Omne verum vero consonat*: all truth accords with the truth.
38. Ens, an entity or being.
39. Quoted from Goethe's *Wilhelm Meister's Travels* (1821, 1829) as translated by Carlyle.
40. Orion, Greek mythological hunter whose name is used for a constellation.
41. Azote, a type of gas that is fatal when breathed.
42. Camera obscura, a device that allows images to be reflected through a lens or mirror onto paper so that they may be traced.
43. "Sonnet LXX," ll. 3–4, by Shakespeare.
44. "Sonnet CXXIV," ll. 5–11, by Shakespeare.
45. *Measure for Measure*, act 4, scene 1, ll. 1–4.
46. From *The Tempest*, act 5, scene i, ll. 46–68.
47. Plato, quoted from *The Friend*, by Coleridge.
48. Aristotle (384–322 B.C.), Greek philosopher and scientist; *Antigone*, a play by Sophocles (ca. 496–406 B.C.), Greek dramatist.
49. Quoted from Leonhard Euler (1707–1783), Swiss mathematician, in *Aids to Reflection*, by Coleridge.
50. Anne Robert Jacques Turgot (1727–1781), French economist.
51. Olympus, the home of the gods in Greek and Roman mythology.
52. Paraphrased from Proverbs 8:23, 27, 28, 30.
53. Paraphrased from 2 Corinthians 4:18.
54. George Berkeley (1685–1753), Anglo-Irish bishop, scientist, and philosopher known for his belief that everything except for the spiritual exists only insofar as we perceive matter through the senses; Viasa or Vyāsā, compiler of the *Mahābhārata*, a major Indian epic.

55. Manicheans, followers of the Iranian cleric Mani (216–ca. 274), who believed in a dualistic universe in which good and evil are always present, and in which knowledge is the way to salvation.

56. "Sonnet LI," ll. 9–11, by Michelangelo.

57. *Comus* (1637), ll. 13–14, by Milton.

58. York Minster cathedral in York, England, was built between the thirteenth and fifteenth centuries; St. Peter's Basilica (1506–1615) in Rome is the mother church of Roman Catholicism.

59. "Man" (1633), by George Herbert.

60. Vaticination, a prediction or prophecy.

61. Many scholars consider this "orphic poet" to be based on Amos Bronson Alcott (1799–1888), Emerson's longtime friend and Concord neighbor.

62. Nebuchadnezzar II (ca. 630–ca. 561 B.C.), king of Babylon, captured Jerusalem and, according to the Book of David, went mad for seven years near the end of his life.

63. Paraphrased from *King Richard II*, act 4, scene 1, l. 264.

64. Prince Alexander Leopold of Hohenlohe-Waldenberg-Schillingsfürst (1794–1849), German bishop and author; Shakers, English communal order whose leaders came to America in 1774, known for its pacificism and furniture making; animal magnetism, a type of hypnosis.

65. The distinctions are drawn from *An Essay Towards the Theory of the Ideal of Intellectual World* (1701–1704), by John Norris (1657–1711), English cleric and Platonist philosopher.

66. Again, this may be a reference to Alcott.

67. Gaius Julius Caesar (100–44 B.C.), Roman general and statesman.

Andrews Norton

[Letter to the Editor]

5 November 1836

ANDREWS NORTON (1786–1853), professor at the Harvard Divinity School, was so influential that he was often called the "Unitarian Pope." He devoted his life to a Lockean examination of biblical texts, attempting to prove the truthfulness of the Bible through historical research, retiring from teaching in 1830 to apply himself to completing a three-volume study of *Evidences of the Genuineness of the Gospels* (1837–1844). The Higher Criticism of Germany was anathema to him because it demoted the Bible from divine text to mere literature. And when his former student George Ripley published a favorable review of the Englishman James Martineau's *The Rationale of Religious Inquiry* in the November 1836 *Christian Examiner*, Norton was upset that an essay favoring more liberal approaches to religious study (and complaining about how "the heart is pulverized" under "our prevailing systems of theology") had been allowed to appear in the flagship journal of New England Unitarianism. And he took the unusual step of writing to a local newspaper about his objections.

To the Editor of the Boston Daily Advertiser:

SIR—As the Editor of the Christian Register, from personal considerations to which I fully assent, is reluctant to publish the following communication, will you give it a place in your paper, and oblige

Yours, &c.

ANDREWS NORTON.

Cambridge, 4th Nov. 1836.

I have seen with great surprise and sorrow in the last number of the Christian Examiner, the conclusion of an article on "Martineau's Rationale of Religious Enquiry," (pp 248–254). I should not think it necessary to express these feelings in so public a manner; but every individual, however little conspicuous, has a certain degree of influence which it is his duty not to suffer to be perverted; and my name has been connected with that work since its commencement, and lately announced among those of its supporters. I, therefore, feel bound to the performance of a duty, which, on many accounts, is of the most unpleasant nature; to declare that I wholly dissent from the main opinions (for there seems to me much inconsistency) in the passage referred to; that I consider them as vitally injurious to the cause of religion, because tending to destroy faith in the only evidence on which the truth of Christianity *as a revelation* must ultimately rest; and that I regard the publication of them in the work in which they have appeared as directly and indirectly disastrous to the progress of religious truth. I speak only of the opinions; for I am well aware that almost any form of faith or scepticism may be held in connexion with many amiable and respectable qualities. Nor is it here the place to enter into any discussion of them. My present purpose is personal; arising from a wish to have it understood by all who may feel any interest in the subject, that I am in no degree responsible for their publication, and that I shall not continue one of the supporters of a work in which such opinions are maintained.

It is but doing justice to many other gentlemen who have heretofore been contributors to the work to say that I am persuaded they agree with me in the sentiments I have expressed.

To preclude all occasion of mistake I wish distinctly to present to view the sole ground of this communication. It is, that, the article in question having appeared in the Christian Examiner, others beside the writer seem responsible for the publication of opinions from which they entirely dissent. I have no wish to interfere with the rights of free discussion; but these rights, I may add, are sometimes misunderstood. Without intending any particular or unkind application to the case before us, of which I am not qualified to judge, it may be laid down as general principle, that he who controverts doctrines, which many, who have thought most concerning them, think of the highest importance to the happiness of man, should thoroughly settle his own belief, that he should satisfy himself that he has ability to discuss the subject and has viewed it, as far as possible, in all bearings, and that he should further be convinced, after very serious consideration, that the promulgation of his views will serve the interests of truth and goodness. Let him then publish them in such a form, as far as may be, that they will first go into the hands only of those who are capable of judging of their correctness.

Source: Andrews Norton, [Letter to the Editor], *Boston Daily Advertiser*, 5 November 1836, p. 2. Ripley is quoted from his "Martineau's Rationale of Religious Inquiry," *Christian Examiner*, 21 (November 1836): 225–253.

George Ripley

from [Letter to the Editor]

9 November 1836

GEORGE RIPLEY (1802–1880) would later serve briefly as business manager of the *Dial* and become known as the founder, along with his wife Sophia, of the Brook Farm community. When Brook Farm collapsed, he paid the debts himself and moved to New York to work on the *Tribune*. As one of the Transcendentalists interested in continental philosophy, he began publishing in 1838 *Specimens of Foreign Standard Literature*, which would eventually run to fourteen volumes of edited and translated works before it ceased in 1842. By calling the foreign literature "standard," he was, like Hedge in his review of Coleridge, making the point that the latest British and continental writers and philosophers had been accepted by European audiences; now was the time for American audiences to treat them seriously and not as foreign fads or un-American (and therefore unacceptable) ideas. His reply to Norton sets the stage for the miracles controversy of 1838, as Ripley asks how we interpret texts and who has the ultimate authority to do so.

To the Editor of the Daily Advertiser,

Sir—I do not like to burden your columns with so great a novelty as a theological discussion; but as I have been somewhat unceremoniously brought before the public therein, I must beg permission to add a few words of my own. I assure you, that if anything further needs to be said, I shall select a more appropriate medium for my remarks than a secular paper.

Respectfully, yours, G. R.

Boston, 7th Nov. 1836.

To Mr. Andrews Norton, of Cambridge.

Dear Sir—I was glad to perceive that the views presented by me in the last number of the Christian Examiner were of sufficient importance to attract your attention. I was still more glad to find that you thought them worthy of so much notice, as to require you to disavow in a public print, under your own name, all responsibility for their publication. Nothing seems to me more desirable than a frank expression of opinion on all subjects, which involve important interests, whether of science or of conduct; and I rejoice that you have set the example of an open disclaimer of certain views which I have defended in the article alluded to. It will create a fresh interest in the subject, and lead to a more thorough examination of my opinions, than I could have ventured to hope, from the imperfect manner in which they are set forth.

With regard to the mode in which you declare your want of agreement with my article, and the step you purpose to take in consequence thereof, I have nothing to say; it is a question of individual taste with which no one has a right to interfere. There is, indeed, a tone in your remarks, slightly suppressed, which a stranger to both of us might think betrayed more of the *odium theologicum*[1] than of personal friendship; but presuming that this is not the case, I shall reply to them in the spirit of candor and charity, by which I will not doubt that they were suggested. I must forget the benefits I have received from the severity of your taste and the minuteness of your learning in a former pupilage, before I can persuade myself to discuss any subject with you in a manner incompatible with your superiority in years and attainments to myself.

I will add, at the same time, that if you find heresies in my Review, I also find them in your comments upon it; but we are both too deeply laden with offences of that kind, to make the spectacle of our flinging stones at each other any thing but ludicrous.

On this account, my personal feelings would lead me to pass over your notice, in silence. I should much prefer to leave it to act, as it may, upon the good sense of our community. They who do not know you, would hardly deem it worth while to attach much value to your avowal of disagreement, unsupported as it is, by any reasonings or new exhibitions of facts. They would wonder that you should feel called upon to disclaim the responsibility of an article, addressed to scientific readers, appearing under the signature of its author, in a work of which you are not the Editor; and would ask, in their perplexity, if the writer were not of age to assume his own responsibilities and bear his own burdens.

But those who are aware of your position in society, your eminence among learned theologians, your freedom of speculation, and the exceeding deference, which for many reasons, we have all been wont to pay to your opinions, will perceive the necessity under which I labor, of doing what I can to turn aside the sharp edge of your denunciation. You have presented me, without the usual formalities of prosecution, before the jury of my fellow citizens, as a dangerous man. You have declared, with singular indefiniteness, that I have uttered views "vitally injurious to the cause of religion," "tending to destroy faith in the only evidence of Christianity—as a revelation;" and you also intimate, that I have done this rashly and unadvisedly, without a wise regard "to the interests of truth and goodness."

A certain sense of decorum, then, towards that portion of the public, whose servant I am, towards my neighbors and friends, with whom I live in relations of mutual trust, forces me to give them a distinct opportunity of judging between you and myself. If you are right, I am unworthy of the confidence they are pleased to repose in me: if you are wrong, it is due to them that they should be made to know it.

I should have been better able to meet you on fair ground, had you been more explicit in stating the propositions, from which you dissent and the inconsistencies of which you complain. You oblige me, in some sense, both to discover your "dream" and to point out the "interpretation thereof." As you thus loosely refer to the passage contained on pp. 248–254, I will confine myself to the main position which is there defended.

It may be shortly summed up in these words. The evidence of miracles depends on a previous belief in Christianity, rather than the evidence of Christianity on a previous belief in miracles. In presenting the argument for our faith to an unbeliever, I would begin with establishing its coincidence with the divine testimony of our spiritual nature; and having done that I would proceed to shew the probability of miracles. This, Sir, I suppose is the view for which you are unwilling to be responsible. I am not now required to defend it in its scientific form. A sketch of the argument on which it rests is contained in the article in question, and I leave it with perfect freedom,—to stand or fall according to its merits,—to the consideration of our theologians by profession, as well as of our intelligent laymen, to whose verdict on such points, I attach more importance, than you think it deserves. I am only called upon here to shew that this view is not likely to be so disastrous to our community as you seem to imagine. It will be sufficient for my defence, in this regard, to demonstrate that it is no theological novelty of my own, but one which has had the sanction of devout and thinking minds in every age of the Church. In proof of this, I shall appeal to the Scriptures, to the Fathers, to the Reformers and early Protestants, and to theologians of the present day. I must be brief now and more full hereafter, if occasion be presented.[2]

....

I have thus presented some proofs which may shew that I did not utter my opinion without thought or from a vain love of novelty. I am as firmly persuaded of the truth and importance of my views as you are of your own. Perhaps I am not less deeply or practically interested in the progress of religious truth, the cause of human happiness than yourself. At all events, I would lay no restriction upon the free discussion of the former, or upon any honest efforts for the promotion of the latter. We live in an age of skepticism and vague thought on many of the most important subjects of belief; but for myself I am certain that no cold reserve, no coward fear, no spiritual despotism can remove or mitigate the evil. We want scientific inquiry and discussion, in which the love of truth shall be blended with a heartfelt trust in its power. I see most clearly the work that is to be done for this age, before a return to deep religious convictions is possible. Would that you and others to whom the gift is granted might engage in this work with such wisdom and energy as to prevent so obscure a pen as mine from being called before the public.

There is one thing, Sir, in your article which I confess struck me with much surprise. I allude to the appeals you have made to the fears of the uninstructed. You have not shewn me wherein I have erred. You have made no attempt to set me right. You merely say that my opinions are dangerous, without giving a hint as to the means of their correction. I had thought that we lived at too late a day for this. I had thought that we had breathed the air of freedom too long, to substitute an appeal to popular prejudice in the place of reason and argument. The same course, Sir, that you have taken, has been pursued before against the innovator on traditional ideas. A similar charge was brought against our Saviour by the Pharisees and against the Apostle Paul by the Ephesians. It was uttered by Athanasius against Arius and by Augustine against Pelagius.[3] It has been uttered by monks and inquisitors in all ages, against those who united a free spirit with a frank and fearless zeal. I have found from the whole current of Christian history, that it has seldom been successful to attempt the destruction of an opinion in this mode. The truth has usually survived though the advocate thereof has perished. I would be far, Sir, from impairing your legitimate influence in our theological circles, but when you so far forget the principles of our Protestant fathers, as to wish to place shackles upon the press and to drown the voice of discussion by the cry of alarm, I must take leave to say, that I regret to see you manifesting the spirit of a class of men, who are too well known in the annals of the Church, and with whom I would gladly hope that few among us have any thing in common.

I will add in conclusion, that I have no hope, in these remarks of gaining your assent to the doctrine which I believe. Our differences of opinion arise from a radical difference in our philosophical views. You are a disciple of the school which was founded by Locke—the successor of Hobbes and the precursor of Condillac and Voltaire.[4] For that philosophy I have no respect. I believe it to be superficial, irreligious and false in its primary elements. The evils it has brought upon humanity, by denying to the mind the power of perceiving spiritual truth, are great and lamentable. They have crept over Theology, Literature, Art, and Society. This age has no higher mission than to labor for their cure. I wish to go back to the philosophy of the most enlightened Fathers, to that of the giants of English Theology in the days of their unshorn strength, to that lofty spiritual faith which is now held by the most eminent philosophers of the continent of Europe. With the prevalence of this philosophy, a true reform of theology may be predicted; and the living and practical faith of the heart take the place of bondage to a dead letter.

If you should see fit, Sir, to continue this controversy, which I am as far from shrinking from as I am from courting, I trust it will be with a desire to elicit truth by discussion rather than to silence it by authority. Let there be "the wisdom of love as well as the love of wisdom,"[5] and you will find no one more ready to listen to your arguments and to be convinced by your instructions than

Your Friend and Servant,
The Reviewer of Martineau's Letters,
in the Christian Examiner.

Source: George Ripley, from [Letter to the Editor], *Boston Daily Advertiser*, 9 November 1836, p. 2.

Notes

1. *odium theologicum*: theological loathing.
2. Ripley's citations of sources and texts to support his points are omitted here.
3. St. Paul's letter to the Ephesians attacked their dualistic religious philosophy and argued that all are saved through Christ; Saint Athanasius (ca. 293–373), Egyptian theologian and ecclesiastic writer, believed that God had entered human form through Jesus; Arius (ca. 250–336), Libyan-born Egyptian cleric whose followers (Arians) believed that Christ was not co-equal with God; St. Augustine (354–430), early Christian church father and philosopher, attacked the views of Pelagius (ca. 354–ca. 418), an English-born clergyman who argued that humankind's nature was basically good and that the church had moved away from allowing individuals any agency in their own salvation.
4. Thomas Hobbes (1588–1679), English philosopher; Étienne Bonnot de Condillac (1715–1780), French philosopher of sensationalism; François Marie Arouet Voltaire (1694–1778), French author and intellectual.
5. Quoted from *Biographia Literaria*, Chapter IX, by Coleridge.

A. Bronson Alcott

The Doctrine and Discipline
of Human Culture

(1836)

AMOS BRONSON ALCOTT (1799–1888) was an educator, philosopher, lecturer, reformer, conversationalist, poet, essayist, and—this would secure his fame—the father of Louisa May Alcott. He was also a member of the Transcendental Club, contributor to the *Dial*, founder of the Concord School of Philosophy, and chronicler of the movement from his home in Concord, just up the street from Emerson's house. A self-taught Connecticut farmer's son, Alcott was the only male Transcendentalist not formally educated or with a Harvard connection. He proposed educational reforms that we are startled to learn were then considered controversial, such as light and airy classrooms, comfortable furnishings, Socratic question-and-answer discussions, allowing students to come to knowledge on their own rather than having it spoon-fed to them, and keeping journals. On the other hand, he spoke—for the time—rather freely about sexuality and religion, and he put more emphasis on the moral and spiritual growth of his charges than he did on their obtaining practical book knowledge. (Elizabeth Peabody joined the Temple School primarily to supply the students with instruction in the more traditional branches of learning.) This work, which sets out Alcott's educational philosophy as practiced in the Temple School, appeared both as a pamphlet and as the introduction to *Conversations with Children on the Gospels*.

Idea of Man

Man is the noblest of the Creator's works. He is the most richly gifted of all his creatures. His sphere of action is the broadest; his influence the widest; and to him is given Nature and Life for his heritage and his possession. He holds dominion over the Outward. He is the rightful Sovereign of the Earth, fitted to subdue all things to himself, and to know of no superior, save God. And yet he enters upon the scene of his labors, a feeble and wailing Babe, at first unconscious of the place assigned him, and needs years of tutelage and discipline to fit him for the high and austere duties that await him.

Idea of Education

The Art, which fits such a being to fulfil his high destiny, is the first and noblest of arts. Human Culture is the art of revealing to a man the true Idea of his Being—his endowments—his possessions—and of fitting him to use these for the growth, renewal, and perfection of his Spirit. It is the art of completing a man. It includes all those influences, and disciplines, by which his faculties are unfolded and perfected. It is that agency which takes the helpless and pleading Infant from the hands of its Creator; and, apprehending its entire nature, tempts it forth—now by austere, and now by kindly influences and disciplines—and thus moulds it at last into the Image of a Perfect Man; armed at all points, to use the Body, Nature, and Life, for its growth and renewal, and to hold dominion over the fluctuating things of the Outward. It seeks to realize in the Soul the Image of the Creator.—Its end is a perfect man. Its aim, through every stage of influence and discipline, is self-renewal. The body, nature, and life are its instruments and materials. Jesus is its worthiest Ideal. Christianity its purest Organ. The Gospels its fullest Text-Book. Genius its Inspiration. Holiness its Law. Temperance its Discipline. Immortality its Reward.

History and Type of this Idea

This divine Art, including all others, or subordinating them to its Idea, was never apprehended, in all its breadth and depth of significance, till the era of Jesus of Nazareth. He it was that first revealed it. Over his Divine Intellect first flitted the Idea of man's endowments and destiny. He set no limits to the growth of our nature. "Be Ye Perfect even as my Father in Heaven is Perfect," was the high aim which he placed before his disciples; and in this he was true to our nature, for the sentiment lives in every faculty and function of our being. It is the ever-sounding Trump of Duty, urging us to the perpetual work of self-renewal. It is the deep instinct of the spirit. And his Life gives us the promise of its realization. In his attributes and endowments he is a Type of our common nature. His achievements are a glimpse of the Apotheosis of Humanity. They are a glorious unfolding of the Godlike in man. They disclose the Idea of Spirit. And if he was not, in himself, the complete fulfilment of Spirit, he apprehended its law, and set forth its conditions. He bequeathed to us the phenomena of its manifestation; for in the Gospels we have the history of Spirit accomplishing its mission on the earth. We behold the Incarnate One, dealing with flesh and blood—tempted, and suffering—yet baffling and overcoming the ministries of Evil and of Pain.

Idea and Type Misapprehended

Still this Idea, so clearly announced, and so fully demonstrated in the being and life of Jesus, has made but little advance in the minds of men. Men have not subdued it to themselves. It has not become the ground and law of human consciousness. They have not married their nature to it by a living Faith. Nearly two millenniums have elapsed since its announcement, and yet, so slow of apprehension have been the successors of this Divine Genius, that even at this day, the deep and universal significance of his Idea has not been fully taken in. It has been restricted to himself alone. He stands in the minds of this generation, as a Phenomenon, which God, in the inscrutable designs of his Providence, saw fit to present, to the gaze and wonder of mankind, yet as a being of unsettled rank in the universe, whom men may venture to imitate, but dare not approach. In him, the Human Nature is feebly apprehended, while the Divine is lifted out of sight, and lost in the ineffable light of the Godhead. Men do not deem him as the harmonious unfolding of Spirit into the Image of a Perfect Man—as a worthy Symbol of the Divinity, wherein Human Nature is revealed in its Fulness. Yet, as if by an inward and irresistible Instinct, all men have been drawn to him; and, while diverse in their opinions; explaining his Idea in different types, they have given him the full and unreserved homage of their hearts. They have gathered around the altars, inscribed with his perfections, and, through his name, delighted to address the God and Father of Spirits. Disowning him in their minds, unable to grasp his Idea, they have deified him in their hearts. They have worshipped the Holiness which they could not define.

Era of its Revival

It is the mission of this Age, to revive his Idea, give it currency, and reinstate it in the faith of men. By its quickening agency, it is to fructify our common nature, and reproduce its like. It is to unfold our being into the same divine likeness. It is to reproduce Perfect Men. The faded Image of Humanity is to be restored, and man reappear in his original brightness. It is to mould anew our Institutions, our Manners, our Men. It is to restore Nature to its rightful use; purify Life; hallow the functions of the Human Body, and regenerate Philosophy, Literature, Art, Society. The Divine Idea of a Man is to be formed in the common consciousness of this age, and genius mould all its products in accordance with it.

Means of its Revival

The means for reinstating this Idea in the common mind, in order to conduce to these results, are many. Yet all are simple. And the most direct and effectual are by apprehending the Genius of this Divine Man, from the study of those Records wherein his career is delineated with so much fidelity, simplicity, and truth. Therein have we a manifestation of Spirit, while undergoing the temptations of this corporeal life; yet faithful to the laws of its renovation and its end. The Divine Idea of Humanity gleams forth through every circumstance of his terrestrial career. The fearful agencies of the Spirit assert their power. In him Nature and Life are subordinated to the spiritual force. The Son of God appears on Earth, enrobed in Flesh, and looks forth serenely upon Man. We feel the significance of the Incarnation; the grandeur of our nature. We associate Jesus with our holiest aspirations, our deepest affections; and thus does he become a fit Mediator between the last age and the new era, of which he was the herald and the pledge. He is to us the Prophet of two millenniums. He is the brightest Symbol of a Man that history affords, and points us to yet fuller manifestations of the Godhead.

Ideal of a Teacher

And the Gospels are not only a fit Text-Book for the study of Spirit, in its corporeal relations, but they are a specimen also of the true method of imparting instruction. They give us the practice of Jesus himself. They unfold the means of addressing human nature. Jesus was a Teacher; he sought to renovate Humanity. His method commends itself to us. It is a beautiful exhibition of his Genius, bearing the stamp of naturalness, force, and directness. It is popular. Instead of seeking formal and austere means, he rested his influence chiefly on the living word, rising spontaneously in the soul, and clothing itself at once, in the simplest, yet most commanding forms. He was a finished extemporaneous speaker. His manner and style are models. In these, his Ideas became like the beautiful, yet majestic Nature, whose images he wove so skilfully into his diction. He was an Artist of the highest order. More perfect specimens of address do not elsewhere exist. View him in his conversation with his disciples. Hear him in his simple colloquies with the people. Listen to him when seated at the well-side discoursing with the Samaritan woman, on the IDEA OF WORSHIP; and at night with Nicodemus, on SPIRITUAL RENEWAL.[1] From facts and objects the most familiar, he slid easily and simply into the highest and holiest themes, and, in this unimposing guise, disclosed the great Doctrines, and stated the Divine Ideas, that it was his mission to bequeath to his race. Conversation was the form of utterance that he sought. Of formal discourse but one specimen is given, in his Sermon on the Mount; yet in this the inspiration bursts all forms, and he rises to the highest efforts of genius, at its close.

Organ of Instruction

This preference of Jesus for Conversation, as the fittest organ of utterance, is a striking proof of his comprehensive Idea of Education. He knew what was in man, and the means of perfecting his being. He saw the superiority of this exercise over others for quickening the Spirit. For, in this all the instincts and faculties of our being are touched. They find full and fair scope. It tempts forth all the powers. Man faces his fellow man. He holds a living intercourse. He feels the quickening life and light. The social affections are addressed; and these bring all the faculties in train. Speech comes unbidden. Nature lends her images. Imagination sends abroad her winged words. We see thought as it springs from the soul, and in the very process of growth and utterance. Reason plays under the mellow light of fancy. The Genius of the Soul is waked, and eloquence sits on her tuneful lip. Wisdom finds an organ worthy her serene, yet imposing products. Ideas stand in beauty and majesty before the Soul.

Organ of Genius

And Genius has ever sought this organ of utterance. It has given us full testimony in its favor. Socrates—a name that Christians can see coupled with that of their Divine Sage—descanted thus on the profound themes in which he delighted. The market-place; the workshop; the public streets were his favorite haunts of instruction. And the divine Plato has added his testimony, also, in those enduring works, wherein he sought to embalm for posterity, both the wisdom of his master and the genius that was his own. Rich text-books these for the study of philosophic genius. They rank next in finish and beauty, to the specimens of Jesus as recorded by his own beloved John.

Genius alone Renews

It is by such organs that Human Nature is to be unfolded into the Idea of its fulness. Yet to do this, teachers must be men in possession of their Idea. They must be men of their kind; men inspired with great and living Ideas, as was Jesus. Such alone are worthy. They alone can pierce the customs and conventions that hide the Soul from itself. They alone can release it from the slavery of the corporeal life, and give it back to itself. And such are ever sent at the call of Humanity. Some God, instinct with the Idea that is to regenerate his era, is ever vouchsafed. As a flaming Herald he appears in his time, and sends abroad the Idea which it is the mission of the age to organize in institutions, and quicken into manners. Such mould the Genius of the time. They revive in Humanity the lost idea of its destiny, and reveal its fearful endowments. They vindicate the divinity of man's nature, and foreshadow on the coming Time the conquests that await it. An Age preëxists in them; and History is but the manifestation and issue of their Wisdom and Will. They are the Prophets of the Future.

Genius Misapprehended

At this day, men need some revelation of Genius, to arouse them to a sense of their nature; for the Divine Idea of a Man seems to have died out of our consciousness. Encumbered by the gluts of the appetites, sunk in the corporeal senses, men know not the divine life that stirs within them, yet hidden and enchained. They revere not their own nature. And when the phenomenon of Genius appears, they marvel at its advent. They cannot own it. Laden with the gifts of the Divinity it touches their orb. At intervals of a century it appears. Some Nature, struggling with vicissitude, tempts forth the Idea of Spirit from within, and unlooses the Promethean God to roam free over the earth. He possesses his Idea and brings it as a blessed gift to his race. With awe-struck visage, the tribes of semi-unfolded beings survey it from below, deeming it a partial or preternatural gift of the Divinity, into whose life and being they are forbidden, by a decree of the Eternal, from entering; whose law they must obey, yet cannot apprehend. They dream not, that this phenomenon is but the complement of their common nature; and that in this admiration and obedience, which they proffer, is both the promise and the pledge of the same powers in themselves; that this is but their fellow-creature in the flesh. And thus the mystery remains sealed, till at last it is revealed, that this is but the unfolding of human nature in its fulness; working free of every incumbrance, by possessing itself.

Idea of Genius

For Genius is but the free and harmonious play of all the faculties of a human being. It is a Man possessing his Idea and working with it. It is the Whole Man—the central Will—working worthily, subordinating all else to itself; and reaching its end by the simplest and readiest means. It is human nature rising superior to things and events, and transfiguring these into the image of its own Spiritual Ideal. It is the Spirit working in its own way, through its own organs and instruments, and on its own materials. It is the Inspiration of all the faculties of a Man by a life conformed to his Idea. It is not indebted to others for its manifestation. It draws its life from within. It is self-subsistent. It feeds on Holiness; lives in the open vision of Truth; enrobes itself in the light of Beauty; and bathes its powers in the fount of Temperance. It aspires after the Perfect. It loves Freedom. It dwells in Unity. All men have it, yet it does not appear in all men. It is obscured by ignorance; quenched by evil; discipline does not reach it; nor opportunity cherish it. Yet there it is—an original, indestructible element of every spirit; and sooner or later, in this corporeal, or in the spiritual era—at some period of the Soul's development—it shall be tempted forth, and assert its claims in the life of the Spirit. It is the province of education to wake it, and discipline it into the perfection which is its end, and for which it ever thirsts. Yet Genius alone can wake it. Genius alone inspire it. It comes not at the incantation of mere talent. It respects itself. It is strange to all save its kind. It shrinks from vulgar gaze, and lives in its own world. None but the eye of Genius can discern it, and it obeys the call of none else.

Wane of Genius

Yet among us Genius is at its wane. Human Nature appears shorn of her beams. We estimate man too low to hope for bright manifestations. And our views create the imperfection that mocks us. We have neither great men, nor good institutions. Genius visits us but seldom. The results of our culture are slender. Thirsting for life and light, Genius is blessed with neither. It cannot free itself from the incumbrance that it inherits. The Idea of a Man does not shine upon it from any external Image. Such Corporeal Types it seeks in vain. It cries for instruction, and none satisfies its wants. There is little genius in our schoolrooms. Those who enter yearly upon the stage of life, bearing the impress of our choicest culture, and most watchful discipline, are often unworthy specimens of our nature. Holiness attends not their steps. Genius adorns not their brow. Many a parent among us—having lavished upon his child his best affections, and spared no pains which money and solicitude could supply, to command the best influences within his reach—sees him return, destitute of that high principle, and those simple aims, that alone ennoble human nature, and satisfy the parental heart. Or, should the child return with his young simplicity and truth, yet how unarmed is his intellect with the quiver of genius, to achieve a worthy name, and bless his race. The Soul is spilt out in lust; buried in appetite; or wasted in vulgar toils; and retreats, at last, ignobly from the scene of life's temptations; despoiled of its innocence; bereft of its hopes, and sets in the dark night of disquietude, lost to the race.

Cause of Declension

Yet not all depravity nor ignorance is to be laid at the door of our Institutions. The evil has two faces. It is deeper in its origin. It springs from our low estimate of human nature, and consequent want of reverence and regard for it. It is to be divided between parents and institutions. The young but too often enter our institutions of learning, despoiled of their virtue, and are of course disabled from running an honorable intellectual career. Our systems of nursery discipline are built on shallow or false principles; the young repeat the vices and reproduce the opinions of parents; and parents have little cause to complain. They cannot expect fruits of institutions, for which they have taken so little pains to sow the seeds. They reap as they sow. Aiming at little they attain but little. They cast their own horoscope, and determine by their aim the fate of the coming generation. They are the organized Opportunity of their era.

Faith of Genius

To work worthily, man must aspire worthily. His theory of human attainment must be lofty. It must ever be lifting him above the low plain of custom and convention, in which the senses confine him, into the high mount of vision, and of renovating ideas. To a divine nature, the sun ever rises over the mountains of hope, and brings promises on its wings; nor does he linger around the dark and depressing valley of distrust and of fear. The magnificent bow of promise ever gilds his purpose, and he pursues his way steadily, and in faith to the end. For Faith is the soul of all improvement. It is the Will of an Idea. It is an Idea seeking to embody and reproduce itself. It is the All-Proceeding Word going forth, as in the beginning of things, to incarnate itself, and become flesh and blood to the senses. Without this faith an Idea works no good. It is this which animates and quickens it into life. And this must come from living men.

Genius alone Inspires

And such Faith is the possession of all who apprehend Ideas. Such faith had Jesus, and this it was that empowered him to do the mighty works of which we read. It was this which inspired his genius. And Genius alone can inspire others. To nurse the young spirit as it puts forth its pinions in the fair and hopeful morning of life, it must be placed under the kindly and sympathising agency of Genius—heaven-inspired and hallowed—or there is no certainty that its aspirations will not die away in the routine of formal tuition, or spend themselves in the animal propensities that coexist with it. Teachers must be men of genius. They must be men inspired. The Divine Idea of a Man must have been unfolded from their being, and be a living presence. Philosophers, and Sages, and Seers,—the only real men—must come as of old, to the holy vocation of unfolding human nature. Socrates, and Plato, and the Diviner Jesus, must be raised up to us, to breathe their wisdom and will into the genius of our era, to recast our institutions, remould our manners, and regenerate our men. Philosophy and Religion, descending from the regions of cloudy speculation, must thus become denizens of our common earth, known among us as friends, and uttering their saving truths through the mouths of our little ones. Thus shall our being be unfolded. Thus the Idea of a man be reinstated in our consciousness. Thus Jesus be honored among us. And thus shall Man grow up, as the tree of the primeval woods, luxuriant, vigorous—armed at all points, to brave the winds and the storms of the finite and the mutable—bearing his Fruit in due season.

Idea of Inspiration

To fulfil its end, Instruction must be an Inspiration. The true Teacher, like Jesus, must inspire in order to unfold. He must know that instruction is something more than mere impression on the understanding. He must feel it to be a kindling influence; that, in himself alone, is the quickening, informing energy; that the life and growth of his charge preëxist in him. He is to hallow and refine as he tempts forth the soul. He is to inform the understanding, by chastening the appetites, allaying the passions, softening the affections, vivifying the imagination, illuminating the reason, giving pliancy and force to the will; for a true understanding is the issue of these powers, working freely and in harmony with the Genius of the soul, conformed to the law of Duty. He is to put all the springs of Being in motion. And to do this, he must be the personation and exampler of what he would unfold in his charge. Wisdom, Truth, Holiness, must have preëxistence in him, or they will not appear in his pupils. These influence alone in the concrete. They must be made flesh and blood in him, to reappear to the senses, and reproduce their like.—And thus shall his Genius subordinate all to its own force. Thus shall all be constrained to yield to its influence; and this too, without violating any Law, spiritual, intellectual, corporeal—but in obedience to the highest Agency, co-working with God. Under the melting force of his Genius, thus employed, Mind shall become fluid, and he shall mould it into Types of Heavenly Beauty. His agency is that of mind leaping to meet mind; not of force acting on opposing force. The Soul is touched by the live coal of his lips. A kindling influence goes forth to inspire; making the mind think; the heart feel; the pulse throb with his own. He arouses every faculty. He awakens the Godlike. He images the fair and full features of a Man. And thus doth he drive at will the drowsy Brute, that the Eternal hath yoked to the chariot of Life, to urge man across the Finite!

Hallowed Genius

To work worthily in the ministry of Instruction, requires not only the highest Gifts, but that these should be refined by Holiness. This is the condition of spiritual and intellectual clearness. This alone unfolds Genius, and puts Nature and Life to their fit uses. "If any man will know of the Doctrine, let him do the will of my Father," said Jesus; and he, who does not yield this obedience, shall never shine forth in the true and full glory of his nature.

Quenching of Genius

Yet this truth seems to have been lost sight of in our measures of Human Culture. We incumber the body by the gluts of the appetites; dim the senses by self-indulgence; abuse nature and life in all manner of ways, and yet dream of unfolding Genius amidst all these diverse agencies and influences. We train Children amidst all these evils. We surround them by temptations, which stagger their feeble virtue, and they fall too easily into the snare which we have spread. Concupiscence defiles their functions; blunts the edge of their faculties; obstructs the passages of the soul to the outward, and blocks it up. The human body, the soul's implement for acting on Nature, in the ministry of life, is thus depraved; and the soul falls an easy prey to the Tempter. Self-Indulgence too soon rings the knell of the spiritual life, as the omen of its interment in the flesh. It wastes the corporeal functions; mars the Divine Image in the human form; estranges the affections; paralyzes the will; clouds the intellect; dims the fire of genius; seals conscience, and corrupts the whole being. Lusts entrench themselves in the Soul; unclean spirits and demons nestle therein. Self-subjection, self-sacrifice, self-renewal are not made its habitual exercises, and it becomes the vassal of the Body. The Idea of Spirit dies out of the Consciousness; and Man is shorn of his glories. Nature grows over him. He mistakes Images for Ideas, and thus becomes an Idolater. He deserts the Sanctuary of the Indwelling Spirit, and worships at the throne of the Outward.

Means of Reform

Our plans of influence, to be successful, must become more practical. We must be more faithful. We must deal less in abstractions; depend less on precepts and rules. We must fit the soul for duty by the practice of duty. We must watch and enforce. Like unsleeping Providence, we must accompany the young into the scenes of temptation and trial, and aid them in the needful hour. Duty must sally forth an attending Presence into the work-day world, and organize to itself a living body. It must learn the art of uses. It must incorporate itself with Nature. To its sentiments we must give a Heart. Its Ideas we must arm with Hands. For it ever longs to become flesh and blood. The Son of God delights to take the Son of Man as a co-mate, and to bring flesh and blood even to the very gates of the Spiritual Kingdom. It would make the word Flesh, that it shall be seen and handled and felt.

Spiritual Culture

The Culture, that is alone worthy of Man, and which unfolds his Being into the Image of its fulness, casts its agencies over all things. It uses Nature and Life as means for the Soul's growth and renewal. It never deserts its charge, but follows it into all the relations of Duty; at the table it seats itself, and fills the cup for the Soul; caters for it; decides when it has enough; and heeds not the clamor of appetite and desire. It lifts the body from the drowsy couch; opens the eyes upon the rising sun; tempts it forth to breathe the invigorating air; plunges it into the purifying bath; and thus whets all its functions for the duties of the coming day. And when toil and amusement have brought weariness over it, and the drowsed senses claim rest and renewal, it remands it to the restoring couch again, to feed it on dreams. Nor does it desert the Soul in seasons of labor, of amusement, of study. To the place of occupation it attends it, guides the corporeal members with skill and faithfulness; prompts the mind to diligence; the heart to gentleness and love; directs to the virtuous associate; the pure place of recreation; the innocent pastime. It protects the eye from the foul image; the vicious act; the ear from the vulgar or profane word; the hand from theft; the tongue from guile;—urges to cheerfulness and purity; to forbearance and meekness; to self-subjection and self-sacrifice; order and decorum; and points, amid all the relations of duty, to the Law of Temperance, of Genius, of Holiness, which God hath established in the depths of the Spirit, and guarded by the unsleeping sentinel of Conscience, from violation and defilement. It renews the Soul day by day.

Self-Apprehension

Man's mission is to subdue Nature; to hold dominion over his own Body; and use both these, and the ministries of Life, for the growth, renewal, and perfection of his Being. As did Jesus, he must overcome the World, by passing through its temptations, and vanquishing the Tempter. But before he shall attain this mastery he must apprehend himself. In his Nature is wrapt up the problem of all Power reduced to a simple unity. The knowledge of his own being includes, in its endless circuit, the Alphabet of all else. It is a Universe, wherein all else is imaged. God—Nature—are the extremes, of which he is the middle term, and through his Being flow these mighty Forces, if, perchance, he shall stay them as they pass over his Consciousness, apprehend their significance—their use—and then conforming his being to the one; he shall again conform the other to himself.

Childhood a Type of the Godhead

Yet, dimmed as is the Divine Image in Man, it reflects not the full and fair Image of the Godhead. We seek it alone in Jesus in its fulness; yet sigh to behold it with our corporeal senses. And this privilege God ever vouchsafes to the pure and undefiled in heart; for he ever sends it upon the earth in the form of the Child. Herein have we a Type of the Divinity. Herein is our Nature yet despoiled of none of its glory. In flesh and blood he reveals his Presence to our senses, and pleads with us to worship and revere.

Misapprehension of Childhood

Yet few there are who apprehend the significance of the Divine Type. Childhood is yet a problem that we have scarce studied. It has been and still is a mystery to us. Its pure and simple nature; its faith and its hope, are all unknown to us. It stands friendless and alone, pleading in vain for sympathy and aid. And, though wronged and slighted, it still retains its trustingness; still does it cling to the Adult for renovation and light.—But thus shall it not be always. It shall be apprehended. It shall not be a mystery and made to offend. "Light is springing up, and the day-spring from on high is again visiting us." And, as in times sacred to our associations, the Star led the Wise Men to the Infant Jesus, to present their reverent gifts, and was, at once, both the herald and the pledge of the advent of the Son of God on the earth; even so is the hour approaching, and it lingers not on its errand, when the Wise and the Gifted, shall again surround the cradles of the New Born Babe, and there proffer, as did the Magi,[2] their gifts of reverence and of love to the Holiness that hath visited the earth, and shines forth with a celestial glory around their heads;—and these, pondering well, as did Mary, the Divine Significance, shall steal from it the Art—so long lost in our Consciousness—of unfolding its powers into the fulness of the God.

Renovation of Nature

And thus Man, repossessing his Idea, shall conform Nature to himself. Institutions shall bear the fruits of his regenerate being. They shall flourish in vigor and beauty. They shall circulate his Genius through Nature and Life, and repeat the story of his renewal.

Human Renewal

Say not that this Era is distant. Verily, it is near. Even at this moment, the heralds of the time are announcing its approach. Omens of Good hover over us. A deeper and holier Faith is quickening the Genius of our Time. Humanity awaits the hour of its renewal. The renovating Fiat has gone forth, to revive our Institutions, and remould our Men. Faith is lifting her voice, and, like Jesus near the Tomb of Lazarus, is uttering the living words, "I am the Resurrection and the Life, and he that Believeth, though dead in doubts and sins, shall be reassured of his Immortality, and shall flourish in unfading Youth! I will mould Nature and Man according to my Will. I will transfigure all things into the Image of my Ideal."[3]—And by such Faith, and such Vision, shall Education work its mission on the Earth. Apprehending the Divine Significance of Jesus—yet filled with the assurance of coming Messiahs to meet the growing nature of Man—shall inspired Genius go forth to renovate his Era; casting out the unclean spirits and the demons that yet afflict the Soul. And then shall Humanity, leaving her infirmities, her wrongs, her sufferings, and her sins, in the corrupting grave, reappear in the consciousness of Physical Purity; Inspired Genius; and Spotless Holiness. Men shall be one with God, as was the Man of Nazareth.

Source: A. Bronson Alcott, *The Doctrine and Discipline of Human Culture* (Boston: James Munroe, 1836); also included in his *Conversations with Children on the Gospels,* 2 vols. (Boston: James Munroe, 1836–1837), 1:xxix–liii.

Notes

1. Jesus' encounter with the Samarian woman and his explaining to her about "living water" and "eternal life" is in John 4:14, and his discussion

with Nicodemus about the kingdom of God and rebirth is in John 3:1–
21.
2. Magi, the three wise men from the east who brought gifts of gold, frank-
incense, and myrrh to Mary right after Jesus' birth.
3. A paraphrase of John 11:25–26.

A. Bronson Alcott

from Conversations with Children on the Gospels

(1836–1837)

ALCOTT WAS HOPEFUL THAT *Conversations* would go beyond the *Record* in
helping set forth his educational goals and practices but, instead, its publication resulted in abuse being heaped upon him and parents withdrew their
students from the Temple School (and even more did so after he admitted an
African-American student). Elizabeth Peabody tried to warn him that much
of what he was discussing with the students could be controversial—indeed
there are footnotes to the book that she asked to be added so that her role
in recording the conversations could be clarified—but Alcott's response was
to shift the potentially damaging material from the main text to a single
series of notes at the end where they could be found and studied—and upset
people—with ease. An even more selective use of the offending sentences was
made when newspapers cited them in their reviews; Andrews Norton was
quoted (without his name being mentioned) as saying of the book that one-
third was absurd, one-third blasphemous, and one-third obscene. Emerson
was so disturbed by the tarring of Alcott by selective quotation that he wrote
to the *Boston Daily Courier* to argue "Let it be read," noting that any "reasonable man will perceive that fragments out of a new theory of Christian
instruction, are not quite in the best place for examination, betwixt the price
current and the shipping list."

CONVERSATION VIII
NATIVITY OF SPIRIT
FAMILY RELATION

Birth and Naming of John the Baptist, from the Sacred Text.—Ideas
of Birth-place and Birth.—Birth.—Sacredness of Birth.—Travail of
Body with Spirit.—Emblems of Birth.—Naming of Spirit incarnate.—Influence of Nature on Imagination.—Analysis of Zacharias'
Prophecy.—Emblems of John and Jesus.—Prejudice.—Subject.

Review

Mr. Alcott began by asking, What was our conversation upon the last time?

Charles and Others. The journey of Mary. The visit to her cousin Elisabeth. Their conversation.
  Mr. Alcott then read.[1]

Idea of Birthplace and Birth

Now what came into your minds while I was reading?

Josiah. The deserts seemed to me a great space covered with sand, like that in the hour-glass. The sun was shining on it, and making it sparkle. There were no trees. John was there alone.

Edward J. I thought the deserts meant woods, with paths here and there.

Lucy. I thought of a space covered with grass and some wild flowers, and John walking about.

Charles. I thought of a prairie.

Alexander. I thought of a rocky country.

Augustine. I thought of a few trees scattered over the country, with bees in the trunks.

George K. I thought of a place without houses, excepting John's; and flowers, trees, and bee-hives.

Birth

Mr. Alcott. I should like to hear all your pictures, but as I have not time, you may tell me now what interested you most?[2]

Charles. The prophecy of Zacharias.

Lucia. Elisabeth's saying the child's name must be John.

Lucy. Zacharias finding his speech again.

Andrew. The birth of the child.

Mr. Alcott. How was it?

Andrew. I thought, one night, as Elizabeth was sleeping, an angel brought her a child, and made her dream she had one, and she awoke and it was lying at her side.

William B. I think he was born like other children except that Elisabeth had visions.[3]

George K. I thought God sent an angel to give her a child. It cried as soon as it came and waked up its mother to give it something to eat.

Lucia. When John was first born, his mother did not know it, for he was born in the night; but she found it by her side in the morning.

Charles. Elisabeth must have had some vision as well as Zacharias, or how could she know the child was theirs? Zacharias could not speak.

Nathan. I don't see why John came in the night. All other children come in the day.

Sacredness of Birth

Mr. Alcott. No; more frequently in the night. God draws a veil over these sacred events, and they ought never to be thought of except with reverence. The coming of a spirit is a great event. It is greater than death. It should free us from all wrong thoughts.[4]

Mr. Alcott. Yes, the deliverance of the spirit is the first thing. And I am glad to find, that you have so strong an impression of that. The physiological facts, sometimes referred to, are only a sign of the spiritual birth. You have seen the rose opening from the seed with the assistance of the atmosphere; this is the birth of the rose. It typifies the bringing forth of the spirit, by pain, and labor, and patience.[5]

Travail of Body with Spirit

What is meant by "delivered"?

William B. She delivered her child to Zacharias.

Others. No; God delivered the child to Elisabeth.

Charles. Elisabeth's thoughts made the child's soul, and when it was fairly born she was delivered from the anxiety of the thought.

Emblems of Birth

Mr. Alcott. You may give me some emblems of birth.

Alexander. Birth is like the rain. It comes from heaven.

Lucia. I think it is like a small stream coming from a great sea; and it runs back every night, and so becomes larger and larger every day, till at last it is large enough to send out other streams.

Lemuel. Lives streamed from the ocean first; now smaller streams from the larger ones, and so on.

Samuel R. Birth is like the rising light of the sun; the setting is death.

Andrew. God's wind came upon the ocean of life, and washed up the waters a little into a channel, and that is birth. They run up farther, and that is living.

Mr. Alcott. I should like to have all your emblems but have not time. There is no adequate sign of birth in the outward world, except the physiological facts that attend it, with which you are not acquainted.

Naming of Spirit Incarnate

Why did they call the child John?

Several. Because the angel told them to.

Recorder. The Hebrew word *John* means gift of God. They felt he was so kindly given that they called him Gift.[6]

Mr. Alcott. Why did the people marvel?

Franklin and others. Because it was the custom to name children from relations.

Joseph. And the people did not know that the angel had told them to name him John.

Mr. Alcott. What loosed Zacharias' tongue?

Edward J. The power of God.

Another. His faith.

Lucia. The child was born, and it was said that he should speak then.

Charles. It was promised that he should speak.

Frank. Because God did not want to make the angel tell a lie.

Franklin. It was a reward of his obedience.

William B. He gave up a natural desire to name him from himself.

Influence of Nature on Imagination

Mr. Alcott. Why was it "noised abroad"?

Several. It was a great event to have a child born from such old parents.

Mr. Alcott. And in the country, especially a hilly country, the people being imaginative, seem quite disposed to look beyond external things. They are apt to think singular events typify, or are a sign of, something supernatural.[7] They wondered what kind of child this would be.

Analysis of the Prophecy of Zacharias

How had the Lord "visited his people"?[8]

Lemuel. He had visited their spirits.

Franklin. By sending John to tell that Jesus was coming.

Mr. Alcott. What is it to redeem a people?

Lucia. To make them good.

Edward B. To save them from sin.

Mr. Alcott. A man who loves to eat and drink, an intemperate man, a passionate man, is a slave to the body; and when his spirit is released from his body, by renewing thoughts, that withdraw his attention from his body, he is redeemed, just as a prisoner taken out of a dungeon is said to be redeemed from captivity.[9] What is meant by "horn of salvation"?

Charles. A great deal of mercy.

Mr. Alcott. What is meant by "house of David"?

Franklin. Jesus was a descendant of David.

Mr. Alcott. What enemies are mentioned here?

Charles. Spiritual enemies.

Mr. Alcott. What fathers are meant here?

Charles. All good people who went before.

Mr. Alcott. What is "holy covenant"?

(No answer.)

It is a promise, on condition of holiness, of giving blessings. And the oath?

(Here it was found necessary to discriminate between profane swearing and judicial oaths, which they had confounded.[10])

Is there any such promise to us, as was made by that covenant?

Charles. It is made to all good people.

Mr. Alcott. What is meant by "prophet of the highest"?

Charles. Announcer of Jesus Christ.

Mr. Alcott. What is it to "give knowledge of salvation"?

Charles. To tell us how to be good, and forgive our sins that are repented of.

Mr. Alcott. What is "day-spring"?

Charles. Righteousness, wisdom.

Mr. Alcott. What is it to "sit in darkness"?[11]

Charles. To be wicked.

Emblems of John and Jesus

Mr. Alcott. If John was the day-spring, who was the risen sun?

All. Jesus.

Mr. Alcott. What is it to "wax strong in spirit"?

Charles. To stand fast by God.

Franklin. To grow better and better.

Mr. Alcott reads. "And he was in the deserts."

Charles. In the country; at his father's house.

Prejudice

Edward B. Why are Jews held in such contempt, when Jesus was born a Jew?

Franklin. Because they killed Jesus, and said, "his blood be on us and our children."

Edward B. And Jews are mean, avaricious.

(Mr. Alcott explained the last characteristics by the oppressions they had suffered.)

Mr. Alcott. Who think it is a wicked prejudice?

Welles. It is a right prejudice.

All. There are no right prejudices.

Subject

Mr. Alcott. What has been the subject of this conversation?

Nathan. Putting spirits into bodies.

Mr. Alcott. And the nativity, or birth of spirit in the flesh.

CONVERSATION XXIV
SPIRITUAL REFINEMENT
CHASTITY

Marriage Festival at Cana, from the Sacred Text.—Affability.—Human
Supremacy.—Views of Phenomena.—Idea and Emblem of Purity.—

Views of Phenomena.—Intermission.—Origin and Cause of Miracles in Spirit.—Types of Miraculous Agency.—Apprehension of Phenomena.—Type of Marriage and Chastity.—Recorder's Remark.

Review

Mr. Alcott. Where did we leave Jesus?

Several. In Galilee, with John, and Andrew, and Peter.

Mr. Alcott. Do you remember the last words?

George K. "Hereafter ye shall see heaven open, and the angels of God ascending and descending upon the Son of man."

Frederic. And we said, that meant good thoughts entering in and proceeding from the Spirit of man.

Mr. Alcott then read and asked the usual question.[12]

Human Supremacy

Josiah. The changing of the water into wine interested me most. If we had faith, and were as good as Jesus, we could change water into wine.

Mr. Alcott. Do all think so?

(Most held up hands.)

Views of Phenomena

Nathan. I liked the water changing into wine. He had more spirit than we have, but I don't see how he did it.

Edward J. I liked his mother telling him there was no wine.

Martha. I was most interested in his answer. I thought it meant that his time to do the miracle would come. I was rather surprised that his mother told him they had no wine. It seemed as if she believed he could make some, and yet he had worked no miracles before.

George K. I thought, when he said, "My hour is not yet come," that he meant his hour to die was not yet come, so he would do this miracle.

Andrew. I cannot express my thoughts about his turning water into wine.

John B. And I cannot express my thought about his saying, "Woman, what have I to do with thee?" and yet I think I know what it means.

Mr. Alcott. Do you often have thoughts which you cannot express?

John and Andrew. Yes.

Augustine. I had some thoughts I could not express about the angels of God ascending and descending upon the Son of man.

Franklin. I thought in this place, that Mary had faith that Jesus would do the miracle, and his answer meant that he would, bye and bye. It is plain she expected it, from what she said to the servants.

Frederic. I think as George said.

(He repeated it.)

Lemuel. I thought "mine hour is not yet come," meant the hour to do the miracle.

George B. I saw the stone watering pots in the court.

Alexander. I do not think we could turn water into wine, even if we were as good as Jesus.

Samuel R. I think his answer meant, that there was no need of making the wine quite yet.

Mr. Alcott. Was it such wine as we have in our decanters?

Samuel R. No; it tasted like wine, but it was like water. It would not intoxicate.

George K. I think it was a mysterious medicinal wine.

Lemuel. I think they were made to think it was wine.

Mr. Alcott. Was the miracle worked in their minds or upon the water?

(Half thought one way, half the other.)

Emma. I think his mother telling him there was no wine, shows her faith in him.

Lucia. I have nothing to say, but I was interested.

Mr. Alcott. I like to have you say freely, that you have nothing to say, when you have nothing.

But now can you tell me what is the significance of this?

(None answered.)

Idea and Emblem of Purity

What does marriage mean?

George K. Deep love.

Charles. Union of Spirit.

Mr. Alcott. What did Jesus mean to teach by this miracle?

Hales. What he could do.

Emma. His faith and power.

Nathan. For us to believe in God as he did.

Charles. It was to teach temperance.

Frederic. Faith in God.

(The rest said they did not know.)

Mr. Alcott. Do you think that you see all the meaning of this miracle?

(All.)

When you were talking of the Temptation, you were somewhat puzzled, as you are now, for you were thinking altogether of outward things. The mountain, the pinnacle of the temple, troubled you. Can you not turn your thoughts inward, as you did then, and ask yourselves, what these things may be emblems of?

Charles. Water is an emblem of purity.

Mr. Alcott. And wine?

(There was no answer.)

And the change?

Lemuel. Of growing better; making good better.

One. The bride was purity.

Mr. Alcott. Charles said marriage was spiritual union. Can you work up these emblems into something?

Nathan. The water meant purity, the wine goodness.

Mr. Alcott. And did Christ's presence sanctify the union?

View of Phenomena

Augustine. There must have been real wine made, for the governor of the feast tasted it.

Mr. Alcott. Do you think that to view it all as an outward fact, would be more interesting and wonderful, than to view it as emblematic?

Augustine. No; not more wonderful; but that is the way it really was.

Mr. Alcott. Did he do this to gratify their appetites?

Augustine. No; but to supply their wants.

Mr. Alcott. Do you think that the whole matter was simply that there was a wedding, and there was not wine enough, and Jesus being there, kindly made them some wine?

Augustine and Others. Yes.

Mr. Alcott. Do any of you think that it means more?

(Some rose.)

Now all who think Jesus turned water into wine, literally and actually, may rise.

(All rose.)

And as an emblem of a beautiful truth?

(They still stood up.)

Intermission

(Here there was an intermission, and when they assembled again, Mr. Alcott again read the passage, paraphrasing the fourth verse, — "Woman, my thoughts are not like yours; you are thinking of making wine; I am thinking what wine signifies.")

Mr. Alcott. What does this whole story signify?

(No answer.)

Which do you think was the greatest miracle, to change water into wine, or to open the minds of men into the real meaning of marriage?

(No answer.)

Origin and Cause of Miracles in Spirit

Where do miracles begin?

(No answer.)

Do they begin in the Spirit, and flow out into things, or begin in things?

Several. In the Spirit.

Mr. Alcott. Where is the cause of miracles?

Several. In the Spirit.

Mr. Alcott. Where is the Life that causes a seed to spring out and seek the light?

Lucia. In God.

Mr. Alcott. Where is God?

Lucia. In the seed.

Mr. Alcott. How is spiritual "glory" shown forth?

Lucia. By being good.

Types of Miraculous Agency

Mr. Alcott. Give me some fact of Nature, by which spiritual glory is shown forth.

Augustine. In the oak coming out of the acorn.

Andrew. In the rose coming out of the bud, for there is power.

Franklin. Dr. Channing shows forth spiritual glory in his thoughts and feelings, when he preaches and tries to make people good.

Emma. God shows forth glory in Nature, and in the Soul of man.

Samuel T. A little baby shows forth spiritual glory.

Martha. A dove shows forth God's glory.

Alexander. An elephant shows forth patience and nobleness.

George K. A lion shows forth the power of God.

Others. The sun. The moon. The stars, &c.

Mr. Alcott. The glory is not of things themselves; but things shadow forth the glory of God.

Does any outward thing show it forth completely? Lions, flowers, stars?

(They signified dissent while he remained in the Outward creation; but when he said,)

In Human Nature?

All. Yes; in Jesus Christ.

Mr. Alcott. Do you think that Jesus showed forth all the glory of God; that nothing at all was withheld?

(Some said yes, some no.)

Apprehension of Phenomena

Now tell me, do you think the change of water into wine was actually made in the outward world?

(All held up hands but Francis and Franklin.)

Was that all the miracle?

(All said no, but Alexander and Augustine.)

Augustine. I think he had no other meaning than to show that he was willing to supply their needs.

Mr. Alcott. Had Jesus never performed any other miracle, should you have regarded this as something very great?

(Most held up hands.)

Welles. If he had not done any other miracle, I should have thought that Jesus brought the wine himself.

Type of Marriage and Chastity

Franklin. I think the miracle was emblematic.

Mr. Alcott. Do others think so? and of what?

John B. It was emblematic of power.

Franklin. I think it was emblematic of purity, united to greater purity—to faith and love.

Emma. And that is marriage.

Mr. Alcott. Is marriage an emblem?

Emma. Yes; it is an emblem of two spirits united in purity and love.

Samuel R. I think the whole story is an emblem of changing good into better.

George K. I think water was pure, and wine was purer, and it signified that they must purify their spirits.

Martha. The wine was purer than the water.

Augustine. Wine is not so pure as water—water represents truth.

Andrew. I think the wine was the Spirit of Jesus.

Welles. Water represents purity, but wine means more things, love, faith, &c.

Mr. Alcott. Did you ever hear the word Chastity? That word represents something more than purity, for it implies self-restraint. This story may represent deep love, as one of you said at the beginning of the Conversation, and when deep love is restrained by principles, it is chastity.

Recorder's Remark

Recorder.[13] I think you have led the children into an allegorical interpretation of this passage, when their own minds did not tend towards it. In no conversation has it been so difficult to keep them to the subject, nor have you suggested so much. I cannot help being gratified at this, myself; because I do not believe the Evangelist had any idea of setting forth any thing but the kind sanction of Jesus to the innocent festivities which celebrate marriage.

Mr. Alcott. It is remarkable, that this is the only instance in which I have premeditated one of these Conversations. I studied this passage beforehand, and in no instance have we succeeded so ill. It is better to give the subject up to the children, and let them lead us where they will. The course pursued in this, is in violation of the plan proposed at the beginning of the Conversations, and confirms the naturalness of that plan, by the want of success which has attended this effort, I think this worthy of remark.

Source: A. Bronson Alcott, from *Conversations with Children on the Gospels*, 2 vols. (Boston: James Munroe, 1836–1837), 1:61–66, 2:10–18. Each volume also has a separate title page reading *Record of Conversations on the Gospels, Held in Mr. Alcott's School; Unfolding the Doctrine and Discipline of Human Culture.* Emerson is quoted from *Letters*, 7:277–279.

Notes

1. Omitted here is Alcott's reading from Luke 1:57–80.
2. *(Here Charles changed his picture, and supposed John dressed in a camel's hairy hide, with his tail for a belt.)*

   Mr. Alcott. You make him quite a savage. Who was John the Baptist like?

   Charles. Dr. Graham. [Note in original]
   Sylvester Graham (1794–1851), clergyman and dietary reformer responsible for the graham cracker.
3. *Mr. Alcott.* Do any of you think your mothers had visions of you?
   (Several.) [Note in original]
4. *Mr. Alcott.* And now I don't want you to speak; but to hold up your hands, if you have ever heard any disagreeable or vulgar things about birth. *(None raised hands.)*
   Men have been brought before Courts of Justice for saying vulgar things about the birth of Christ; and all birth is sacred as Jesus Christ's. And I have heard of children saying very profane things about it; and have heard fathers and mothers do so. I hope that none of us will ever violate the sacredness of this subject. [Note in original, identified as *"Restored by the Editor,"* or Alcott himself]
5. *Mr. Alcott.* Edward B., it seems, had some profane notions of birth, connected with some physiological facts; but they were corrected here. Did you every hear this line,
   "The throe of suffering is the birth of bliss?"

   George K. Yes; it means that Love and Joy, and Faith, lead you to have suffering, which makes more happiness for you.

   Mr. Alcott. Yes; you have the thought. And a mother suffers when she has a child. When she is going to have a child, she gives up her body to God, and he works upon it, in a mysterious way, and with her aid, brings forth the Child's Spirit in a little Body of its own, and when it has come, she is blissful. But I have known some mothers who are so timid that they are not willing to bear the pain; they fight against God, and suffer much more.

   Charles. I should think it ought to be the father, he is so much stronger.

Mr. Alcott. He suffers because it is his part to see the suffering in order to relieve it. But it is thought, and with good reason, that if there were no wrong doing there would be no suffering attending this mysterious act. When Adam and Eve did wrong, it was said that Adam should earn bread by the sweat of his brow, and Eve have pain in bringing her children into the world. We never hear of trees groaning to put forth their leaves.

Charles. They have no power to do wrong.

Mr. Alcott. True; God only gives them power to put forth, and they do it without pain. [Note in original, identified as *"Restored by the Editor,"* or Alcott himself]

6. *(Here Mr. Alcott asked if every child was not a gift of God. They assented, and then there was some conversation upon names, and their own names were traced.)* [Note in original]

7. *Charles.* Why in a hill country more than any where else?

George K. Because they see more and have more imagination.

Nathan. One can't have imagination in a city.

Charles. Some country fellows are very stupid.

Mr. Alcott. That is true; but still the country affords advantages which the city does not. Should you not like to have more mountains and valleys and streams about Boston?

Andrew. Yes; a great many more.

(Mr. Alcott spoke of the effect of the Ocean on himself, seen first, when he was twelve years old.) [Note in original]

8. *Mr. Alcott.* Does the Lord visit his people now?

Charles. Yes; in little babies.

Mr. Alcott. Every one is a visiter on the Earth from the Lord. I hope you will all be pleasant visiters. Some visiters are very unpleasant; they do not like what is given them to eat and drink; they do not like the beds they lie on. Do you think a drunkard is a pleasant visiter? Is he doing what he is sent to?

(They all laughed.)

Emma. I am not a very pleasant visiter, but I have a very pleasant visit. [Note in original]

9. *Mr. Alcott.* How many of you are redeemed?

Nathan. I am not quite, but almost. [Note in original]

10. *(Here Mr. Alcott repeated that to speak of God without having a holy feeling was profanity; but an oath in a Court of Justice was sacred. It was speaking of God seriously, with a holy feeling.)* [Note in original]

11. *Mr. Alcott.* Tell me what the shadow of death means.
Would there be any shadow without light?
What was made first, light or darkness?

Charles. Darkness. It seems to me that there was darkness first; I can't think otherwise.

Mr. Alcott. Is darkness real, positive? I thought darkness was the shadow of light. What if the sun should be put out?

Andrew. Then there would be darkness.

Nathan. When there is darkness we would not know it if light had not been first.

Mr. Alcott. Which of you think light came first? If light made the darkness, then if there had been no light there would have been no darkness. When the light goes out of this room does any thing come in?

Charles. Yes; darkness comes in.

Mr. Alcott. Nothing comes in; and I cannot conceive of there not being light. Darkness is the absence of light to our external senses. [Note in original]

12. Omitted here is Alcott's reading from John 2:1–12.
13. The "Recorder" is Peabody.

Ralph Waldo Emerson

"The American Scholar"

(1837)

EMERSON'S SEVENTY-FIVE-MINUTE address was called by Oliver Wendell Holmes America's "intellectual Declaration of Independence." Under the guise of delivering a traditional commencement address, Emerson enters what was to many the finest university in the land, in the greatest city in the land, and says to the best members of the graduating class that they should have spent their time more wisely. He warns about such dangers as industrialization (the "iron lids" covering the eyes of "the sluggard intellect"), "our long apprenticeship to the learning of other lands," and the misuse of books ("Books are for the scholar's idle times"). To combat these, he proposes the "AMERICAN SCHOLAR," or *Man Thinking*," who will not be encumbered by what has gone before, who will be guided by "self-trust," and who will rely upon Nature as an influence. Rather than complimenting Harvard for educating these young men, Emerson looks elsewhere for "signs of the coming days": the rise of British Romanticism, as seen in the new interest in "the near, the low, the common"; Emanuel Swedenborg's philosophy; and "the new importance given to the single person." To Emerson, "We have listened too long to the courtly muses of Europe. The spirit of the American freeman is already suspected to be timid, imitative, tame. . . . The scholar is decent, indolent, complaisant." And one can almost visualize Emerson as he raises his eyes from his manuscript to focus on his audience as he speaks the next sentence: "See already the tragic consequence." The answer: "if the single man plant himself indomitably on his instincts, and there abide, the huge world will come round to him."

MR. PRESIDENT, AND GENTLEMEN,

I greet you on the re-commencement of our literary year. Our anniversary is one of hope, and, perhaps, not enough of labor. We do not meet for games of strength or skill, for the recitation of histories, tragedies and odes, like the ancient Greeks; for parliaments of love and poesy, like the Troubadours; nor for the advancement of science, like our cotemporaries in the British and European capitals. Thus far, our holiday has been simply a friendly sign of the survival of the love of letters amongst a people too busy to give to letters any more. As such, it is precious as the sign of an indestructible instinct. Perhaps the time is already come, when it ought to be, and will be something else; when the sluggard intellect of this continent will look from under its iron lids and fill the postponed expectation of the world with something better than the exertions of mechanical skill. Our day of dependence, our long apprenticeship to the learning of other lands, draws to a close. The millions that around us are rushing into life, cannot always be fed on the sere remains of foreign harvests. Events, actions arise, that must be sung, that will sing themselves. Who can doubt that poetry will revive and lead in a new age, as the star in the constellation Harp which now flames in our zenith, astronomers announce, shall one day be the pole-star for a thousand years.[1]

In the light of this hope, I accept the topic which not only usage, but the nature of our association, seem to prescribe to this day,—the AMERICAN SCHOLAR. Year by year, we come up hither to read one more chapter of his biography. Let us inquire what new lights, new events and more days have thrown on his character, his duties and his hopes.

It is one of those fables, which out of an unknown antiquity, convey an unlooked for wisdom, that the gods, in the beginning, divided Man into men, that he might be more helpful to himself; just as the hand was divided into fingers, the better to answer its end.

The old fable covers a doctrine ever new and sublime; that there is One Man,—present to all particular men only partially, or through one faculty; and that you must take the whole society to find the whole man. Man is not a farmer, or a professor, or an engineer, but he is all. Man is priest, and scholar, and statesman, and producer, and soldier.

In the *divided* or social state, these functions are parcelled out to individuals, each of whom aims to do his stint of the joint work, whilst each other performs his. The fable implies that the individual to possess himself, must sometimes return from his own labor to embrace all the other laborers. But unfortunately, this original unit, this fountain of power, has been so distributed to multitudes, has been so minutely subdivided and peddled out, that it is spilled into drops, and cannot be gathered. The state of society is one in which the members have suffered amputation from the trunk, and strut about so many walking monsters,—a good finger, a neck, a stomach, an elbow, but never a man.

Man is thus metamorphosed into a thing, into many things. The planter, who is Man sent out into the field to gather food, is seldom cheered by any idea of the true dignity of his ministry. He sees his bushel and his cart, and nothing beyond, and sinks into the farmer, instead of Man on the farm. The tradesman scarcely ever gives an ideal worth to his work, but is ridden by the routine of his craft, and the soul is subject to dollars. The priest becomes a form; the attorney, a statute-book; the mechanic, a machine; the sailor, a rope of a ship.

In this distribution of functions, the scholar is the delegated intellect. In the right state, he is, *Man Thinking*. In the degenerate state, when the victim of society, he tends to become a mere thinker, or, still worse, the parrot of other men's thinking.

In this view of him, as Man Thinking, the whole theory of his office is contained. Him nature solicits, with all her placid, all her monitory pictures. Him the past instructs. Him the future invites. Is not, indeed, every man a student, and do not all things exist for the student's behoof? And, finally, is not the true scholar the only true master? But, as the old oracle said, "All things have two handles. Beware of the wrong one."[2] In life, too often, the scholar errs with mankind and forfeits his privilege. Let us see him in his school, and consider him in reference to the main influences he receives.

I. The first in time and the first in importance of the influences upon the mind is that of nature. Every day, the sun; and, after sunset, night and her stars. Ever the winds blow; ever the grass grows. Every day, men and women, conversing, beholding and beholden. The scholar must needs stand wistful and admiring before this great spectacle. He must settle its value in his mind. What is nature to him? There is never a beginning, there is never an end to the inexplicable continuity of this web of God, but always circular power returning into itself. Therein it resembles his own spirit, whose beginning, whose ending he never can find—so entire, so boundless. Far, too, as her splendors shine, system on system shooting like rays, upward, downward, without centre, without circumference,—in the mass and in the particle nature hastens to render account of herself to the mind. Classification begins. To the young mind, every thing is individual, stands by itself. By and by, it finds how to join two things, and see in them one nature; then three, then three thousand; and so, tyrannized over by its own unifying instinct, it goes on tying things together, diminishing anomalies, discovering roots running under ground, whereby contrary and remote things cohere, and flower out from one stem. It presently learns, that, since the dawn of history, there has been a constant accumulation and classifying of facts. But what is classification but the perceiving that these objects are not chaotic, and are not foreign, but have a law which is also a law of the human mind? The astronomer discovers that geometry, a pure abstraction of the human mind, is the measure of planetary motion. The chemist finds proportions and intelligible method throughout matter: and science is nothing but the finding of analogy, identity in the most remote parts. The ambitious soul sits down before each refractory fact; one after another, reduces all strange constitutions, all new powers, to their class and their law, and goes on forever to animate the last fibre of organization, the outskirts of nature, by insight.

Thus to him, to this school-boy under the bending dome of day, is suggested, that he and it proceed from one root; one is leaf and one is flower; relation, sympathy, stirring in every vein. And what is that Root? Is not that the soul of his soul?—A thought too bold—a dream too wild. Yet when this spiritual light shall have revealed the law of more earthly natures,—when he has learned to worship the soul, and to see that the natural philosophy that now is, is only the first gropings of its gigantic hand, he shall look forward to an ever expanding knowledge as to a becoming creator. He shall see that nature is the opposite of the soul, answering to it part for part. One is seal, and one is print. Its beauty is the beauty of his own mind. Its laws are the laws of his own mind. Nature then becomes to him the measure of his attainments. So much of nature as he is ignorant of, so much of his own mind does he not yet possess. And, in fine, the ancient precept, "Know thyself," and the modern precept, "Study nature," become at last one maxim.[3]

II. The next great influence into the spirit of the scholar, is, the mind of the Past,—in whatever form, whether of literature, of art, of institutions, that mind is inscribed. Books are the best type of the influence of the past, and perhaps we shall get at the truth—learn the amount of this influence more conveniently—by considering their value alone.

The theory of books is noble. The scholar of the first age received into him the world around; brooded thereon; gave it the new arrangement of his own mind, and uttered it again. It came into him— life; it went out from him—truth. It came to him—short-lived actions; it went out from him—immortal thoughts. It came to him— busness; it went from him—poetry. It was—dead fact; now, it is quick thought. It can stand, and it can go. It now endures, it now flies, it now inspires. Precisely in proportion to the depth of mind from which it issued, so high does it soar, so long does it sing.

Or, I might say, it depends on how far the process had gone, of transmuting life into truth. In proportion to the completeness of the distillation, so will the purity and imperishableness of the product be. But none is quite perfect. As no air-pump can by any means make a perfect vacuum, so neither can any artist entirely exclude the conventional, the local, the perishable from his book, or write a book of pure thought that shall be as efficient, in all respects, to a remote posterity, as to cotemporaries, or rather to the second age. Each age, it is found, must write its own books; or rather, each generation for the next succeeding. The books of an older period will not fit this.

Yet hence arises a grave mischief. The sacredness which attaches to the act of creation,—the act of thought,—is instantly transferred to the record. The poet chanting, was felt to be a divine man. Henceforth the chant is divine also. The writer was a just and wise spirit. Henceforward it is settled, the book is perfect; as love of the hero corrupts into worship of his statue. Instantly, the book becomes noxious. The guide is a tyrant. We sought a brother, and lo, a governor. The sluggish and perverted mind of the multitude, always slow to open to the incursions of Reason, having once so opened, having once received this book, stands upon it, and makes an outcry, if it is disparaged. Colleges are built on it. Books are written on it by thinkers, not by Man Thinking; by men of talent, that is, who start wrong, who set out from accepted dogmas, not from their own sight of principles. Meek young men grow up in libraries, believing it their duty to accept the views which Cicero, which Locke, which Bacon have given, forgetful that Cicero, Locke and Bacon were only young men in libraries when they wrote these books.[4]

Hence, instead of Man Thinking, we have the bookworm. Hence, the book-learned class, who value books, as such; not as related to nature and the human constitution, but as making a sort of Third Estate with the world and the soul. Hence, the restorers of readings, the emendators, the bibliomaniacs of all degrees.

This is bad; this is worse than it seems. Books are the best of things, well used; abused, among the worst. What is the right use? What is the one end which all means go to effect? They are for nothing but to inspire. I had better never see a book than to be warped by its attraction clean out of my own orbit, and made a satellite instead of a system. The one thing in the world of value, is, the active soul,— the soul, free, sovereign, active. This every man is entitled to; this every man contains within him, although in almost all men, obstructed, and as yet unborn. The soul active sees absolute truth; and utters truth, or creates. In this action, it is genius; not the privilege of here and there a favorite, but the sound estate of every man. In its essence, it is progressive. The book, the college, the school of art, the institution of any kind, stop with some past utterance of genius. This is good, say they,—let us hold by this. They pin me down. They look backward and not forward. But genius always looks forward. The eyes of man are set in his forehead, not in his hindhead. Man hopes. Genius creates. To create,—to create,—is the proof of a divine presence. Whatever talents may be, if the man create not, the pure efflux of the Deity is not his:—cinders and smoke, there may be, but not yet flame. There are creative manners, there are creative actions, and creative words; manners, actions, words, that is, indicative of no custom or authority, but springing spontaneous from the mind's own sense of good and fair.

On the other part, instead of being its own seer, let it receive always from another mind its truth, though it were in torrents of light, without periods of solitude, inquest and self-recovery, and a fatal disservice is done. Genius is always sufficiently the enemy of genius by over-influence. The literature of every nation bear me witness. The English dramatic poets have Shakspearized now for two hundred years.

Undoubtedly there is a right way of reading,—so it be sternly subordinated. Man Thinking must not be subdued by his instruments. Books are for the scholar's idle times. When he can read God directly, the hour is too precious to be wasted in other men's transcripts of their readings. But when the intervals of darkness come, as come they must,—when the soul seeth not, when the sun is hid, and the stars withdraw their shining,—we repair to the lamps which were kindled by their ray to guide our steps to the East again, where the dawn is. We hear that we may speak. The Arabian proverb says, "A fig tree looking on a fig tree, becometh fruitful."

It is remarkable, the character of the pleasure we derive from the best books. They impress us ever with the conviction that one nature wrote and the same reads. We read the verses of one of the great English poets, of Chaucer, of Marvell, of Dryden, with the most modern joy,—with a pleasure, I mean, which is in great part caused by the abstraction of all *time* from their verses.[5] There is some awe mixed with the joy of our surprise, when this poet, who lived in some past world, two or three hundred years ago, says that which lies close to my own soul, that which I also had well nigh thought and said. But for the evidence thence afforded to the philosophical doctrine of the identity of all minds, we should suppose some pre-established harmony, some foresight of souls that were to be, and some preparation of stores for their future wants, like the fact observed in insects, who lay up food before death for the young grub they shall never see.

I would not be hurried by any love of system, by any exaggeration of instincts, to underrate the Book. We all know, that as the human body can be nourished on any food, though it were boiled grass and the broth of shoes, so the human mind can be fed by any knowledge. And great and heroic men have existed, who had almost no other information than by the printed page. I only would say, that it needs a strong head to bear that diet. One must be an inventor to read well. As the proverb says, "He that would bring home the wealth of the Indies, must carry out the wealth of the Indies."[6] There is then creative reading, as well as creative writing. When the mind is braced by labor and invention, the page of whatever book we read becomes luminous with manifold allusion. Every sentence is doubly significant, and the sense of our author is as broad as the world. We then see, what is always true, that as the seer's hour of vision is short and rare among heavy days and months, so is its record, perchance, the least part of his volume. The discerning will read in his Plato or Shakspeare, only that least part,—only the authentic utterances of the oracle,—and all the rest he rejects, were it never so many times Plato's and Shakspeare's.

Of course, there is a portion of reading quite indispensable to a wise man. History and exact science he must learn by laborious reading. Colleges, in like manner, have their indispensable office,—to teach elements. But they can only highly serve us, when they aim not to drill, but to create; when they gather from far every ray of various genius to their hospitable halls, and, by the concentrated fires, set the hearts of their youth on flame. Thought and knowledge are natures in which apparatus and pretension avail nothing. Gowns, and pecuniary foundations, though of towns of gold, can never countervail the least sentence or syllable of wit. Forget this, and our American colleges will recede in their public importance whilst they grow richer every year.

III. There goes in the world a notion that the scholar should be a recluse, a valetudinarian,[7]—as unfit for any handiwork or public labor, as a penknife for an axe. The so called "practical men" sneer at speculative men, as if, because they speculate or *see*, they could do nothing. I have heard it said that the clergy,—who are always more universally than any other class, the scholars of their day,—are addressed as women: that the rough, spontaneous conversation of men they do not hear, but only a mincing and diluted speech. They are often virtually disfranchised; and, indeed, there are advocates for their celibacy. As far as this is true of the studious classes, it is not just and wise. Action is with the scholar subordinate, but it is essential. Without it, he is not yet man. Without it, thought can never ripen into truth. Whilst the world hangs before the eye as a cloud of beauty, we cannot even see its beauty. Inaction is cowardice, but there can be no scholar without the heroic mind. The preamble of thought, the transition through which it passes from the unconscious to the conscious, is action. Only so much do I know, as I have lived. Instantly we know whose words are loaded with life, and whose not.

The world,—this shadow of the soul, or *other me*, lies wide around. Its attractions are the keys which unlock my thoughts and make me acquainted with myself. I launch eagerly into this resounding tumult. I grasp the hands of those next me, and take my place in the ring to suffer and to work, taught by an instinct that so shall the dumb abyss be vocal with speech. I pierce its order; I dissipate its fear; I dispose of it within the circuit of my expanding life. So much only of life as I know by experience, so much of the wilderness have I vanquished and planted, or so far have I extended my being, my dominion. I do not see how any man can afford, for the sake of his nerves and his nap, to spare any action in which he can partake. It is pearls and rubies to his discourse. Drudgery, calamity, exasperation, want, are instructers in eloquence and wisdom. The true scholar grudges every opportunity of action past by, as a loss of power.

It is the raw material out of which the intellect moulds her splendid products. A strange process too, this, by which experience is converted into thought, as a mulberry leaf is converted into satin. The manufacture goes forward at all hours.

The actions and events of our childhood and youth are now matters of calmest observation. They lie like fair pictures in the air. Not so with our recent actions,—with the business which we now have in hand. On this we are quite unable to speculate. Our affections as yet circulate through it. We no more feel or know it, than we feel the feet, or the hand, or the brain of our body. The new deed is yet a part of life,—remains for a time immersed in our unconscious life. In some contemplative hour, it detaches itself from the life like a ripe fruit, to become a thought of the mind. Instantly, it is raised, transfigured; the corruptible has put on incorruption. Always now it is an object of beauty, however base its origin and neighborhood. Observe, too, the impossibility of antedating this act. In its grub state, it cannot fly, it cannot shine,—it is a dull grub. But suddenly, without observation, the selfsame thing unfurls beautiful wings, and is an angel of wisdom. So is there no fact, no event, in our private history, which shall not, sooner or later, lose its adhesive inert form, and astonish us by soaring from our body into the empyrean.[8] Cradle and infancy, school and playground, the fear of boys, and dogs, and ferules,[9] the love of little maids and berries, and many another fact that once filled the whole sky, are gone already; friend and relative, profession and party, town and country, nation and world, must also soar and sing.

Of course, he who has put forth his total strength in fit actions, has the richest return of wisdom. I will not shut myself out of this globe of action and transplant an oak into a flower pot, there to hunger and pine; nor trust the revenue of some single faculty, and exhaust one vein of thought, much like those Savoyards, who, getting their livelihood by carving shepherds, shepherdesses, and smoking Dutchmen, for all Europe, went out one day to the mountain to find stock, and discovered that they had whittled up the last of their pine trees.[10] Authors we have in numbers, who have written out their vein, and who, moved by a commendable prudence, sail for Greece or Palestine, follow the trapper into the prairie, or ramble round Algiers to replenish their merchantable stock.

If it were only for a vocabulary the scholar would be covetous of action. Life is our dictionary. Years are well spent in country labors; in town—in the insight into trades and manufactures; in frank intercourse with many men and women; in science; in art; to the one end of mastering in all their facts a language, by which to illustrate and embody our perceptions. I learn immediately from any speaker how much he has already lived, through the poverty or the splendor of his speech. Life lies behind us as the quarry from whence we get tiles and copestones for the masonry of to-day. This is the way to learn grammar. Colleges and books only copy the language which the field and the work-yard made.

But the final value of action, like that of books, and better than books, is, that it is a resource. That great principle of Undulation in nature, that shows itself in the inspiring and expiring of the breath; in desire and satiety; in the ebb and flow of the sea, in day and night, in heat and cold, and as yet more deeply ingrained in every atom and every fluid is known to us under the name of Polarity,—these "fits of easy transmission and reflection," as Newton called them, are the law of nature because they are the law of spirit.

The mind now thinks; now acts; and each fit reproduces the other. When the artist has exhausted his materials, when the fancy no longer paints, when thoughts are no longer apprehended, and books are a weariness,—he has always the resource *to live*. Character is higher than intellect. Thinking is the function. Living is the functionary. The stream retreats to its source. A great soul will be strong to live, as well as strong to think. Does he lack organ or medium to impart his truths? He can still fall back on this elemental force of living them. This is a total act. Thinking is a partial act. Let the grandeur of justice shine in his affairs. Let the beauty of affection cheer his lowly roof. Those "far from fame" who dwell and act with him, will feel the force of his constitution in the doings and passages of the day better than it can be measured by any public and designed display. Time shall teach him that the scholar loses no hour which the man lives. Herein he unfolds the sacred germ of his instinct, screened from influence. What is lost in seemliness is gained in strength. Not out of those on whom systems of education have exhausted their culture, comes the helpful giant to destroy the old or to build the new, but out of un-handselled savage nature, out of terrible Druids and Berserkirs, come at last Alfred and Shakspeare.[11]

I hear therefore with joy whatever is beginning to be said of the dignity and necessity of labor to every citizen. There is virtue yet in the hoe and the spade, for learned as well as for unlearned hands. And labor is every where welcome; always we are invited to work; only be this limitation observed, that a man shall not for the sake of wider activity sacrifice any opinion to the popular judgments and modes of action.

I have now spoken of the education of the scholar by nature, by books, and by action. It remains to say somewhat of his duties.

They are such as become Man Thinking. They may all be comprised in self-trust. The office of the scholar is to cheer, to raise, and to guide men by showing them facts amidst appearances. He plies the slow, unhonored, and unpaid task of observation. Flamsteed and Herschel, in their glazed observatory, may catalogue the stars with the praise of all men, and, the results being splendid and useful, honor is sure.[12] But he, in his private observatory, cataloguing obscure and nebulous stars of the human mind, which as yet no man has thought of as such,—watching days and months, sometimes, for a few facts; correcting still his old records;—must relinquish display and immediate fame. In the long period of his preparation, he must betray often an ignorance and shiftlessness in popular arts, incurring the disdain of the able who shoulder him aside. Long he must stammer in his speech; often forego the living for the dead. Worse yet, he must accept—how often! poverty and solitude. For the ease and pleasure of treading the old road, accepting the fashions, the education, the religion of society, he takes the cross of making his own, and, of course, the self-accusation, the faint heart, the frequent uncertainty and loss of time which are the nettles and tangling vines in the way of the self-relying and self-directed; and the state of virtual hostility in which he seems to stand to society, and especially to educated society. For all this loss and scorn, what offset? He is to find consolation in exercising the highest functions of human nature. He is one who raises himself from private considerations, and breathes and lives on public and illustrious thoughts. He is the world's eye. He is the world's heart. He is to resist the vulgar prosperity that retrogrades ever to barbarism, by preserving and communicating heroic sentiments, noble biographies, melodious verse, and the conclusions of history. Whatsoever oracles the human heart in all emergencies, in all solemn hours has uttered as its commentary on the world of actions,—these he shall receive and impart. And whatsoever new verdict Reason from her inviolable seat pronounces on the passing men and events of to-day,—this he shall hear and promulgate.

These being his functions, it becomes him to feel all confidence in himself, and to defer never to the popular cry. He and he only knows the world. The world of any moment is the merest appearance. Some great decorum, some fetish of a government, some ephemeral trade, or war, or man, is cried up by half mankind and cried down by the other half, as if all depended on this particular up or down. The odds are that the whole question is not worth the poorest thought which the scholar has lost in listening to the controversy. Let him not quit his belief that a popgun is a popgun, though the ancient and honorable of the earth affirm it to be the crack of doom. In silence, in steadiness, in severe abstraction, let him hold by himself; add observation to observation; patient of neglect, patient of reproach, and bide his own time,—happy enough if he can satisfy himself alone that this day he has seen something truly. Success treads on every right step. For the instinct is sure that prompts him to tell his brother what he thinks. He then learns that in going down into the secrets of his own mind, he has descended into the secrets of all minds. He learns that he who has mastered any law in his private thoughts, is master to that extent of all men whose language he speaks, and of all into whose language his own can be translated. The poet in utter solitude remembering his spontaneous thoughts and recording them, is found to have recorded that which men in "cities vast" find true for them also. The orator distrusts at first the fitness of his frank confessions,—his want of knowledge of the persons he addresses,—until he finds that he is the complement of his hearers;—that they drink his words because he fulfils for them their own nature; the deeper he dives into his privatest secretest presentiment,—to his wonder he finds, this is the most acceptable, most public, and universally true. The people delight in it; the better part of every man feels, This is my music: this is myself.

In self-trust, all the virtues are comprehended. Free should the scholar be,—free and brave. Free even to the definition of freedom, "without any hindrance that does not arise out of his own constitution."[13] Brave; for fear is a thing which a scholar by his very function puts behind him. Fear always springs from ignorance. It is a shame to him if his tranquillity, amid dangerous times, arise from the presumption that like children and women, his is a protected class; or if he seek a temporary peace by the diversion of his thoughts from politics or vexed questions, hiding his head like an ostrich in the flowering bushes, peeping into microscopes, and turning rhymes, as a boy whistles to keep his courage up. So is the danger a danger still: so is the fear worse. Manlike let him turn and face it. Let him look into its eye and search its nature, inspect its origin,—see the whelping of this lion,—which lies no great way back; he will then find in himself a perfect comprehension of its nature and extent; he will have made his hands meet on the other side, and can henceforth defy it, and pass on superior. The world is his who can see through its pretension. What deafness, what stone-blind custom, what overgrown error you behold, is there only by sufferance,—by your sufferance. See it to be a lie, and you have already dealt it its mortal blow.

Yes, we are the cowed,—we the trustless. It is a mischievous notion that we are come late into nature; that the world was finished a long time ago. As the world was plastic and fluid in the hands of God, so it is ever to so much of his attributes as we bring to it. To ignorance and sin, it is flint. They adapt themselves to it as they may; but in proportion as a man has anything in him divine, the firmament flows before him, and takes his signet and form. Not he is great who can alter matter, but he who can alter my state of mind. They are the kings of the world who give the color of their present thought to all nature and all art, and persuade men by the cheerful serenity of their carrying the matter, that this thing which they do, is the apple which the ages have desired to pluck, now at last ripe, and inviting nations to the harvest. The great man makes the great thing. Wherever Macdonald sits, there is the head of the table.[14] Linnæus makes botany the most alluring of studies and wins it from the farmer and the herbwoman. Davy, chemistry: and Cuvier, fossils.[15] The day is always his, who works in it with serenity and great aims. The unstable estimates of men crowd to him whose mind is filled with a truth, as the heaped waves of the Atlantic follow the moon.

For this self-trust, the reason is deeper than can be fathomed,—darker than can be enlightened. I might not carry with me the feeling of my audience in stating my own belief. But I have already shown the ground of my hope, in adverting to the doctrine that man is one. I believe man has been wronged: he has wronged himself. He has almost lost the light that can lead him back to his prerogatives. Men are become of no account. Men in history, men in the world of to-day are bugs, are spawn, and are called "the mass" and "the herd." In a century, in a millenium, one or two men; that is to say—one or two approximations to the right state of every man. All the rest behold in the hero or the poet their own green and crude being—ripened; yes, and are content to be less, so *that* may attain to its full stature. What a testimony—full of grandeur, full of pity, is borne to the demands of his own nature, by the poor clansman, the poor partisan, who rejoices in the glory of his chief. The poor and the low find some amends to their immense moral capacity, for their acquiescence in a political and social inferiority. They are content to be brushed like flies from the path of a great person, so that justice shall be done by him to that common nature which it is the dearest desire of all to see enlarged and glorified. They sun themselves in the great man's light, and feel it to be their own element. They cast the dignity of man from their downtrod selves upon the shoulders of a hero, and will perish to add one drop of blood to make that great heart beat, those giant sinews combat and conquer. He lives for us, and we live in him.

Men such as they are, very naturally seek money or power; and power because it is as good as money,—the "spoils," so called, "of office." And why not? for they aspire to the highest, and this, in their sleep-walking, they dream is highest. Wake them, and they shall quit the false good and leap to the true, and leave governments to clerks and desks. This revolution is to be wrought by the gradual domestication of the idea of Culture. The main enterprise of the world for splendor, for extent, is the upbuilding of a man. Here are the materials strown along the ground. The private life of one man shall be a more illustrious monarchy,—more formidable to its enemy, more sweet and serene in its influence to its friend, than any kingdom in history. For a man, rightly viewed, comprehendeth the particular natures of all men. Each philosopher, each bard, each actor, has only done for me, as by a delegate, what one day I can do for myself. The books which once we valued more than the apple of the eye, we have quite exhausted. What is that but saying that we have come up with the point of view which the universal mind took through the eyes of that one scribe; we have been that man, and have passed on. First, one; then, another; we drain all cisterns, and waxing greater by all these supplies, we crave a better and more abundant food. The man has never lived that can feed us ever. The human mind cannot be enshrined in a person who shall set a barrier on any one side to this unbounded, unboundable empire. It is one central fire which flaming now out of the lips of Etna, lightens the capes of Sicily; and now out of the throat of Vesuvius, illuminates the towers and vineyards of Naples.[16] It is one light which beams out of a thousand stars. It is one soul which animates all men.

But I have dwelt perhaps tediously upon this abstraction of the Scholar. I ought not to delay longer to add what I have to say, of nearer reference to the time and to this country.

Historically, there is thought to be a difference in the ideas which predominate over successive epochs, and there are data for making the genius of the Classic, of the Romantic, and now of the Reflective or Philosophical age. With the views I have intimated of the oneness or the identity of the mind through all individuals, I do not much dwell on these differences. In fact, I believe each individual passes through all three. The boy is a Greek; the youth, romantic; the adult, reflective. I deny not, however, that a revolution in the leading idea may be distinctly enough traced.

Our age is bewailed as the age of Introversion. Must that needs be evil? We, it seems, are critical. We are embarrassed with second thoughts. We cannot enjoy any thing for hankering to know whereof the pleasure consists. We are lined with eyes. We see with our feet. The time is infected with Hamlet's unhappiness,—

"Sicklied o'er with the pale cast of thought."[17]

Is it so bad then? Sight is the last thing to be pitied. Would we be blind? Do we fear lest we should outsee nature and God, and drink truth dry? I look upon the discontent of the literary class as a mere announcement of the fact that they find themselves not in the state of mind of their fathers, and regret the coming state as untried; as a boy dreads the water before he has learned that he can swim. If there is any period one would desire to be born in,—is it not the age of Revolution; when the old and the new stand side by side, and admit of being compared; when the energies of all men are searched by fear and by hope; when the historic glories of the old, can be compensated by the rich possibilities of the new era? This time, like all times, is a very good one, if we but know what to do with it.

I read with joy some of the auspicious signs of the coming days as they glimmer already through poetry and art, through philosophy and science, through church and state.

One of these signs is the fact that the same movement which effected the elevation of what was called the lowest class in the state, assumed in literature a very marked and as benign an aspect. Instead of the sublime and beautiful, the near, the low, the common, was explored and poetised. That which had been negligently trodden under foot by those who were harnessing and provisioning themselves for long journies into far countries, is suddenly found to be richer than all foreign parts. The literature of the poor, the feelings of the child, the philosophy of the street, the meaning of household life, and the topics of the time. It is a great stride. It is a sign—is it not? of new vigor, when the extremities are made active, when currents of warm life run into the hands and the feet. I ask not for the great, the remote, the romantic; what is doing in Italy or Arabia; what is Greek art, or Provencal Minstrelsy; I embrace the common, I explore and sit at the feet of the familiar, the low. Give me insight into to-day, and you may have the antique and future worlds. What would we really know the meaning of? The meal in the firkin;[18] the milk in the pan; the ballad in the street; the news of the boat; the glance of the eye; the form and the gait of the body;—show me the ultimate reason of these matters;—show me the sublime presence of the highest spiritual cause lurking, as always it does lurk, in these suburbs and extremities of nature; let me see every trifle bristling with the polarity that ranges it instantly on an eternal law; and the shop, the plough, and the ledger, referred to the like cause by which light undulates and poets sing;— and the world lies no longer a dull miscellany and lumber room,[19] but has form and order; there is no trifle; there is no puzzle; but one design unites and animates the farthest pinnacle and the lowest trench.

This idea has inspired the genius of Goldsmith, Burns, Cowper, and, in a newer time, of Goethe, Wordsworth, and Carlyle.[20] This idea they have differently followed and with various success. In contrast with their writing, the style of Pope, of Johnson, of Gibbon, looks cold and pedantic.[21] This writing is blood-warm. Man is surprised to find that things near are not less beautiful and wondrous than things remote. The near explains the far. The drop is a small ocean. A man is related to all nature. This perception of the worth of the vulgar, is fruitful in discoveries. Goethe, in this very thing the most modern of the moderns, has shown us, as none ever did, the genius of the ancients.

There is one man of genius who has done much for this philosophy of life, whose literary value has never yet been rightly estimated;—I mean Emanuel Swedenborg. The most imaginative of men, yet writing with the precision of a mathematician, he endeavored to engraft a purely philosophical Ethics on the popular Christianity of his time. Such an attempt, of course, must have difficulty which no genius could surmount. But he saw and showed the connexion between nature and the affections of the soul. He pierced the emblematic or spiritual character of the visible, audible, tangible world. Especially did his shade-loving muse hover over and interpret the lower parts of nature; he showed the mysterious bond that allies moral evil to the foul material forms, and has given in epical parables a theory of insanity, of beasts, of unclean and fearful things.

Another sign of our times, also marked by an analogous political movement is, the new importance given to the single person. Every thing that tends to insulate the individual,—to surround him with barriers of natural respect, so that each man shall feel the world is his, and man shall treat with man as a sovereign state with a sovereign state;—tends to true union as well as greatness. "I learned," said the melancholy Pestalozzi, "that no man in God's wide earth is either willing or able to help any other man."[22] Help must come from the bosom alone. The scholar is that man who must take up into himself all the ability of the time, all the contributions of the past, all the hopes of the future. He must be an university of knowledges. If there be one lesson more than another which should pierce his ear, it is, The world is nothing, the man is all; in yourself is the law of all nature, and you know not yet how a globule of sap ascends; in yourself slumbers the whole of Reason; it is for you to know all, it is for you to dare all. Mr. President and Gentlemen, this confidence in the unsearched might of man, belongs by all motives, by all prophecy, by all preparation, to the American Scholar. We have listened too long to the courtly muses of Europe. The spirit of the American freeman is already suspected to be timid, imitative, tame. Public and private avarice make the air we breathe thick and fat. The scholar is decent, indolent, complaisant. See already the tragic consequence. The mind of this country taught to aim at low objects, eats upon itself. There is no work for any but the decorous and the complaisant. Young men of the fairest promise, who begin life upon our shores, inflated by the mountain winds, shined upon by all the stars of God, find the earth below not in unison with these,—but are hindered from action by the disgust which the principles on which business is managed inspire, and turn drudges, or die of disgust,—some of them suicides. What is the remedy? They did not yet see, and thousands of young men as hopeful now crowding to the barriers for the career, do not yet see, that if the single man plant himself indomitably on his instincts, and there abide, the huge world will come round to him. Patience—patience;—with the shades of all the good and great for company; and for solace, the perspective of your own infinite life; and for work, the study and the communication of principles, the making those instincts prevalent, the conversion of the world. Is it not the chief disgrace in the world, not to be an unit;—not to be reckoned one character;—not to yield that peculiar fruit which each man was created to bear, but to be reckoned in the gross, in the hundred, or the thousand, of the party, the section, to which we belong; and our opinion predicted geographically, as the north, or the south. Not so, brothers and friends,—please God, ours shall not be so. We will walk on our own feet; we will work with our own hands; we will speak our own minds. Then shall man be no longer a name for pity, for doubt, and for sensual indulgence. The dread of man and the love of man shall be a wall of defence and a wreath of love around all. A nation of men will for the first time exist, because each believes himself inspired by the Divine Soul which also inspires all men.

Source: Ralph Waldo Emerson, "The American Scholar," *An Oration, Delivered before the Phi Beta Kappa Society, at Cambridge, August 31, 1837* (Boston: James Munroe, 1837). It was first published as a pamphlet in England in 1843 as *Man Thinking*; and was first called "The American Scholar" when included in Emerson's *Nature; Addresses, and Lectures* (1849). Holmes is quoted from Bliss Perry, "Emerson's Most Famous Speech," in his *The Praise of Folly and Other Papers* (Boston: Houghton Mifflin, 1923), p. 95.

Notes

1. Harp is probably the constellation Lyra, which in Greek mythology was formed from the lyre of Arion.
2. Quoted from Epictetus, second-century Greek Stoic philosopher.
3. "Know thyself" is attributed to Solon (ca. 630–ca. 560 B.C.), Athenian statesman and lawgiver.
4. Marcus Tullius Cicero (106–43 B.C.), Roman orator, philosopher, and statesman.
5. Geoffrey Chaucer (ca. 1342–1400), English poet best known for his *Canterbury Tales*; Andrew Marvell (1621–1678), English poet and satirist; John Dryden (1631–1700), English metaphysical poet and dramatist.
6. Quoted from *Life of Samuel Johnson* (1791), by James Boswell (1740–1795), Scottish biographer and friend of Samuel Johnson.
7. Valetudinarian, someone who is weak, sickly, or infirm.
8. Empyrean, the highest heaven, where pure fire supposedly exists.
9. Ferule, a piece of wood used to strike unruly children on the palm of the hand.

10. Savoyards, natives of Savoy, a mountainous region in eastern France.

11. Druids, the learned class among the ancient Celts, often the priests; Berserkers, in Norse mythology, a member of a warrior group who worshiped the supreme deity Odin and formed the bodyguards for nobility.

12. John Flamsteed (1646–1719) and Sir John Frederick William Herschel (1792–1871), English astronomers.

13. Emerson is undoubtedly paraphrasing a dictionary definition here, probably from *Webster's*.

14. Actually attributed to Rob Roy Macgregor (ca. 1671–1734), Scottish highwayman, in the novel *Rob Roy* (1818) by Sir Walter Scott (1771–1832), prolific Scottish novelist.

15. Sir Humphry Davy (1778–1829), English chemist; Georges Léopold Chrétien Cuvier (1769–1832), French naturalist and comparative anatomist.

16. Mount Etna, in Sicily, and Mount Vesuvius, overlooking the Bay of Naples, both active volcanos.

17. *Hamlet*, act 3, scene 1, ll. 85–87.

18. Firkin, a small cask or vessel.

19. Lumber room, colloquially, a place where useless things are stored.

20. Oliver Goldsmith (1728–1774), multifaceted English writer; Robert Burns (1759–1796), Scotland's most famous poet; William Cowper (1731–1806), English poet and satirist.

21. Alexander Pope (1688–1744), poet who championed the heroic couplet.

22. Johann Heinrich Pestalozzi (1746–1827), Swiss educational reformer, whose emphasis on bringing out the best in students in order to strengthen their own abilities was championed by Alcott and Peabody.

Ralph Waldo Emerson

"Introductory" lecture to Human Culture lecture series

(6 December 1837)

EMERSON, IN *Nature*, promises that the main goal of life is the "upbuilding of a man," so it is not surprising that his first successful lecture series partakes of his lifelong interest in how we may best and most profitably live our lives (as his last major work, *The Conduct of Life* [1860], also attests). This lecture helps to explain the individualism that infuses *Nature* and the great addresses of the late 1830s and early 1840s, as well as many of his essays.

There is a historical progress of man. The ideas which predominate at one period are accepted without effort by the next age, which is absorbed in the endeavor to express its own. An attentive observer will easily see, by comparing the character of the institutions and books of the present day, with those of any former period—say of ancient Judaea, or the Greek, or the Italian era, or the Reformation, or the Elizabethan age of England,—that the tone and aims are entirely changed. The former men acted and spoke under the thought that a shining social prosperity was the aim of men, and compromised ever the individuals to the nation. The modern mind teaches (in extremes) that the nation exists for the individual; for the guardianship and education of every man. The Reformation contained the new thought. The English Revolution is its expansion. The American Declaration of Independence is a formal announcement of it by a nation to nations, though a very limited expression. The Church of Calvin and of the Friends have preached it ever. The Missions announce it, which have girdled the globe with their stations "to preach the gospel to every creature." The charity which is thought to distinguish Christendom over ancient paganism, is another expression of the same thought. The Vote,—universal suffrage—is another; the downfall of war, the attack upon slavery, are others. The furious democracy which in this country from the beginning of its history, has shown a wish, as the royal governors complained, to leave out men of mark and send illiterate and low persons as deputies,—a practice not unknown at this day—is only a perverse or as yet obstructed operation of the same instinct,—a stammering and stuttering out of impatience to articulate the awful words I *am*. The servile statesman who once cried, "Prerogative!" now on every stump and in every caucus has learned to snuffle, "The Poor! the Poor!" Then science has been adopted at last by nations. War is turned out of the throne, and wit is coming in. Instead of piratical voyages sent out by the English crown to hunt the Spanish Manilla galleon, the same crown visits Australasia with gifts, and sends its best blood—keen draughtsmen, post captains, and naturalists, beyond the terminal snowbanks,—the farthest step to which mortal Esquimaux or wolverine dared approach the deadly solitude of the Pole. War subsides into engineering. The desperadoes go a-whaling or vent their superabundant activity on the bear and catamount-hunt[1] of the frontier. Men say, if there is any interest that is oppressed in large assemblies, it is that of the rich: and lastly, the word is forming, is formed, and is already articulated by legislatures,—*Education*.

Thus, in gross, the growth of the new Idea may be observed as it inscribes itself on modern history. Of course, in the mind of the philosopher it has far more precision, and is already attaining a depth and splendor which eclipse all other claims. In the eye of the philosopher, the Individual has ceased to be regarded as a part, and has come to be regarded as a whole. He is the world. Man who has been—in how many tedious ages—esteemed an appendage to a fortune, to a trade, to an army, to a law, to a state, now discovers that property, trade, war, government, geography, nay, the great globe itself and all that it inherits, are but counterparts of mighty faculties which dwell peacefully in his mind, and that it is a state of disease which makes him seem the servant of his auxiliaries and effects. He exists and the world exists to him in a new relation of subject and object, neither of which is valid alone, but only in their marriage have a creative life.

The new view which now tends to remould metaphysics, theology, science, law, trades and professions, and which, in its earnest creation, must modify or destroy the old, has as yet attained no clearer name than *Culture*.

His own Culture,—the unfolding of his nature, is the chief end of man. A divine impulse at the core of his being, impels him to this. The only motive at all commensurate with his force, is the ambition to discover *by exercising* his latent power, and to this, the trades and occupations men follow, the connexions they form, their fortunes in the world, and their particular actions are quite subordinate and auxiliary. The true culture is a discipline so universal as to demonstrate that no part of a man was made in vain. We see men who can do nothing but cipher—dot and carry one;—others, who can only fetch and carry; others who can only write or speak; how many who hardly seem to have a right of possession to their legs, their shoulders, and who get the least service out of their eyes. So concentrated to some focal point is their vitality, that the limbs and constitution appear supernumerary. Scholars are noted to be unskilful and aukward. Montaigne says, that, "men of supercelestial opinions have subterranean manners."[2] Much oftener, we see men whose emotive, whose intellectual, whose moral faculties, lie dormant.

The philosopher laments the inaction of the higher faculties.

He laments to see men poor who are able to labor.

He laments to see men blind to a beauty that is beaming on every side of them.

He laments to see men offending against laws and paying the penalty, and calling it a visitation of Providence.

He regrets the disproportion so manifest in the minds of men. Cannot a man know the mathematics, and love Shakspear also? Cannot he unite an eye for beauty, with the ardours of devotion? Can he not join the elegant accomplishments of the gentleman, to the adoration of justice?

He laments the foreign holdings of every man, his dependence for his faith, for his political and religious estimates and opinions, on other men, and on former times.

And from all these oppressions is a wise culture to redeem the soul.

Is it not possible to clear and disencumber a man of a thousand causes of unhappiness; to show him that he has but one interest in the world, that in his own character. Why should he sit groaning there at mischiefs he cannot help? Why should he be a dependant? Why should he be a pretender? Why should he seem and shuffle and apologize any longer, when there is nothing good, nothing lovely, nothing noble and sweet, that is not his own; when he himself is a commander; when with him he has reality; he only is rich; and when the universe is one choral invitation to him to put forth his thousand hands? Culture in the high sense does not consist in polishing and varnishing, but in so presenting the attractions of nature that the slumbering attributes of man may burst their sleep and rush into day. The effect of Culture on the man will not be like the trimming and turfing of gardens, but the educating the eye to the true harmony of the unshorn landscape, with horrid thickets, wide morasses, bald mountains, and the balance of the land and sea.

And what is the foundation on which so vast an ambition rests? How dare we in the face of the miserable world; in the face of all history, which records nothing but savage and semi-savage life; in the face of the sensual nations, among whom no man puts entire confidence in the virtue of another, scarcely in the virtue of the pure and select souls; and where the heights of self-denial and benevolence are reached always by mixed motives and a winding stair—how can any observer hope so highly of man and reconcile his views with the faces and speech of the mob of men that you shall see pass, if you stand at the corner of a street; with the market and the jail?

I answer the basis of Culture is that part of human nature which in philosophy is called the Ideal. A human being always compares any action or object with somewhat he calls the Perfect: that is to say, not with any action or object now existing in nature, but with a certain Better existing in the mind. That Better we call the Ideal. Ideal is not opposed to Real, but to Actual. The Ideal is the Real. The Actual is but the apparent and the Temporary. Ideal justice is justice, and not that imperfect, halting compensation which we can attain by courts and juries. The mathematicians say there is no perfect circle in nature and their reasonings are not true of any actual circle but only of the Ideal circle.

The universal presence of this vision of the Better in all parts of life is the characteristic of human nature. The lover enraptured with the new consent of a maiden's affection with his own is instantly sobered by observing that her living form detaches itself from the beautiful image in his mind. They never, never will unite and always in seeing her he must remark deficiency.

The patriot worshipping in his thoughts the pure Republic wherein every citizen should be free, just, and contented, strives evermore to realize his idea upon the green earth, upheaves the foundations of the state to build his own commonwealth. Instantly younger men see faults as gross in the new as he in the old and Reform is only a step to Reform.

The pious heart bewails the deadness of religion. Luther, Huss, Cobham, Knox, moved by this painful contrast of the actual with the ideal worship, shake down the churches of a thousand years;[3] and already the youthful saint following the same eternal instinct sees the shortcomings of their reformation.

The great works of art are unable to check our criticism. They create a want they do not gratify. They instantly point us to somewhat better than themselves.

In Nature it is no otherwise. No particular form of man or horse or oak entirely satisfies the mind. The physiologist sees ever floating over the individuals the idea which nature never quite successfully executes in any one form.

In human actions the man compares incessantly his deed with what he calls his duty; with the perfect action; and to the best action there is still in the mind a Better.

In human condition the Ideal suggests ever the pictures of Heaven.

In character the mind is constrained ever to refer to a moral Ideal which we call God.

The fruit of this constitutional aspiration is labor. This aspiration is the centrifugal force in moral nature, the principle of expansion resisting the tendency to consolidation and rest. The first consequence of a new possession is a new want. The first fruit of a new knowledge is a new curiosity. Much will have more. We cannot go fast enough on our own legs, and so we tame the horse. The horse can no more equal the ideal speed, and so we forge and build the locomotive. The ideal still craves a speed like a cannon ball, a speed like a wish, and the inventive and practical faculties will never cease to toil for this end.

Now what is the disclosure of the mind in regard to the state of society? There is no part of society which conforms to its laws but rather, yawning chasms between. Man, upright, reasoning, royal man, the master of the lower world, cannot be found, but instead—a deformed society which confessedly does not aim at an ideal integrity, no longer believes it possible, and only aims by the aid of falsehoods at keeping down universal uproar, at keeping men from each other's throats. The great endeavors of men are paralysed. Men do not imagine that they are anything more than fringes and tassels to the institutions into which they are born. They take the law from things; they serve their property; their trade or profession; books; other men; some religious dogma; some political party or school of opinion that has been palmed upon them; and bow the neck and the knee and the soul to their own creation. I need not specify with accusing finger the unsound parts of our social life. A universal principle of compromise has crept into use. A Routine which no man made and for whose abuses no man holds himself accountable tyrannizes over the spontaneous will and character of all the individuals. A very nice sense of honor would be a very great inconvenience in a career of political, of professional, of commercial activity. A devotion to absolute truth would be unacceptable in the Academy also. An asceticism built on the study and worship of Nature would be rude and harsh to the men of refinement.

The loss of faith is the greatest mischief. We are overpowered by this great Actual which by the numbers, by the extent, by the antiquity lost in darkness of its arrangements daunts our resolution and though condemned by the mind yet we look elsewhere in vain for a realized reform and we say, This is the way of the world, this is necessary, and we accept the yoke and accommodate our feet to the treadmill.

And what temerity is it that refuses this yoke, cries Society always to the aspirant? Art thou better than our father Jacob who gave us this well?[4] Alleviation is all we can expect, not health. "The best of life is just tolerable, it is the most we can make of it." What folly, "says Richard to Robin" and "says Every one,"[5] that one man should make himself wiser than the public, than the whole world.

We reply that all the worth that resides in the existing men and institutions was the fruit of successive efforts of this absolute truth to embody itself, and moreover that this is the instinct of the Ideal, its antagonism to numbers, to custom, and the precise mode of its activity.

There is a celebrated property of fluids which is called by natural philosophers the hydrostatic paradox, by reason of which a column of water of the diameter of a needle, is able to balance the ocean. This fact is a symbol of the relation between one man and all men.

A man may see that his conviction is the natural counterbalance of the opposite persuasion of any number of men or of all men. An appeal to his own Reason is good against the practice of all mankind. Numbers weigh nothing. The ideal of Right in our mind we know is not less peremptory authority though not an individual on the face of the earth obeyed its injunctions. Before the steady gaze of the soul, the whole life of man, the societies, laws, property, and pursuits of men, and the long procession of history do blench and quail. Before this indomitable soul ever fresh and immortal the aged world owns its master. There is not among the most frivolous or sordid a man who is not capable of having his attention so fastened upon the image of higher life in his mind that the whole past and the present state of society shall seem to him a mere circumstance—somewhat defective and ephemeral in comparison with the Law which they violate. And the clear perception of a single soul that somewhat universally allowed in society is wrong and rotten, is a prophecy as certain that sooner or later that thing will fall as if all creatures arose and cried out, It shall end.

This Ideal is the shining side of man. This is the bosom of discovery. This is the seed of revolutions. This is the Foresight that never slumbers or sleeps. This is the Morrow, ever dawning, forgetting all the yesterdays that ever shone.

We say that the allegiance of all the faculties is the birthright of this; that the denial of its oracles is the death of hope, is the treason of human nature; that it has been made shamefully subservient to the Actual, which is as if the head should serve the feet. We say the great Reform is to do it justice, to restore it to the sovereignty. We say that all which is great and venerable in character is measured by the degree in which this instinct predominates; that there is always sublimity about every the least leaning to its suggestions. It breathes a fragrancy and grace over the whole manners and form. Finally we say that it is the property of the Ideal in man to make him at home everywhere and forever. It belongs to the inactive mind to honor only the Old or the Remote. He who can open his mind to the disclosures of the Reason will see that glory without cloud belongs to the *present hour*; for the Ideal is the presence of the universal mind to the particular.

And what are the Means of Culture? The means of Culture is the related nature of man. He is so strangely related to every thing that he can go nowhere without meeting objects which solicit his senses, and yield him new meanings. The world treats him ever with a series of symbolical paintings whose moral he gradually finds out. He cannot do the most trivial act but a secret sense is smiling through it which philosophers and poets repeat. The light that shines on his shoes came from the sun and the entire laws of nature and the soul unite their energies in every moment and every place. There is no trifle in nature. No partiality in her laws. A grain of unregarded dust nature loves with her heart and soul. Out of it goes an attraction which leaps to the planets and from star to star. On it play light, heat, electricity, Gravity, Chemistry, Cohesion, Motion, Rest, so that the history of physical nature might be read from that grain.

So is it with the life of man. It is made up of little parts, but small details are dignified by this pervading relation which connects every point to the brain and the heart. Our culture comes not alone from the grand and beautiful but also from the trivial and sordid. We wash and purify every day for sixty years this temple of the human body. We buy wood and tend our fires and deal with the baker and fisherman and grocer and take a world of pains which nothing but concealed moral and intellectual ends of great worth can exalt to an ideal level.

Natural objects address him. If he look at a flower it awakes in him a pleasing emotion. He cannot see a stone, but his fancy and his understanding are attracted to the varieties of its texture and law of its crystallization, until he finds even this rude body is no stranger to him, and though it cannot speak, yet it is the history of the earth down to the period of written history. He cannot see a star, but instantly this marriage begins of object and subject, of Nature and man, whose offspring is power. In short, it is because of this universally cognate essence of man, that science is possible. The obscure attractions which natural objects have for him are only indications of the truth which appears at last, that the laws of nature preexisted in his mind.

But his relation is not only intellectual to surrounding things. He is active also. He can hew the tree and hammer the stone and sow the barren ground. That is to say, he is so related to the elements that they are his stock, flexible in his hands; he takes the obedient mountain and puts his own will into it and it becomes a city, temples, and towers. His power is straitly hooped in by a necessity which by constant experiments he touches on every side until at length he learns its arc, which is learning his own nature. An hourly instruction proceeds out of his employment, his disasters, his friends, his antagonists. His life is a series of experiments upon the external world, by every one of which a new power is awaked in his mind. A countryman bred in the woods, cannot go into a crowded city, see its spectacles, and the manners of its inhabitants, and trade in its market and go back to his cabin the same man he left it. A man cannot enter the army and see service and bring home the mind and manners of a boy. He cannot follow the seas without a sea change. He cannot see a mob or hear music or be vexed or frightened; he cannot behold a cataract, a volcano, a meteor, without a new feeling, a new thought. He is as changeable as the face of a looking glass carried through the street, a new creature as he stands in the presence of new objects. Go into a botanical garden; is not that a place of some delight? Go to a muster-field where four or five regiments are marching with flags, music, and artillery; is not that a moving spectacle? Go to a dance, and watch the forms and movement of the youths and maidens; have they nothing of you in keeping? Go to a church where gray old men and matrons stand or sit with the young in serious silence. A new frame of mind. Climb the White Hills;—enter the Vatican; descend to the unburied Pompeii;—go hearken to the enraged eloquence of Faneuil Hall;—each of these shall make a new impression, shall enlarge the scope of the beholder's knowledge and power.[6]

It will be seen at once that in the philosophic view of Human Culture, we look at all things in a new point of view from the popular one, viz. we consider mainly not the things but their effect on the beholder. And this habit of respecting things for their relation to the soul—for their intrinsic and universal effects, it is a part of Culture to form.

It is the office of Culture to domesticate man in his regal place in nature.

A great step is made before the soul can feel itself not a charity boy, not a bastard or an orphan, not an interloper in the world which exists for it. To most men, a palace, a statue, or a costly book, have an alien and forbidding air, much like a gay equipage, and seem to say like that, who are you, sir? A man is to know that they all are his; suing his notice, petitioners to his faculties that they will come out and take possession; born thralls to his sovereignty; conundrums he alone can guess; chaos until he come like a creator and give them light and order. My position in the world is wholly changed as soon as I see that a picture waits for my verdict and is not to command me but I am to settle its claims to praise. The arts are appeals to my taste. The laws to my Understanding. Religion to my Reason. Indeed it is a changed position. Now I come meek but well assured as a youth who comes to the College to be taught, not like an interloper who skulks whilst he gazes at the magnificent ornaments he has broken in to see. That popular fable of the sot who was picked up dead drunk in the street, carried to the duke's house, washed and dressed and put in the duke's bed, and then on his waking treated with all obsequious cere-mony like the duke and assured that he had been insane, owes its popularity to the fact that it symbolizes so well the state of man, who is in the actual world a sort of sot and vagabond, but now and then wakes up, exercises his reason, and finds himself a true Prince.

This is the discipline of man in the degrees of Property. He learns that above the merely external rights to the picture, to the park, to the equipage, rights which the law protects,—is a spiritual property which is Insight. The kingdom of the Soul transcendeth all the walls and muniments[7] of possession and taketh higher rights not only in the possession but in the possessor, and with this royal reservation, can very well afford to leave the so-called proprietor undisturbed as its keeper or trustee.

Therefore the wise soul cares little to whom belongs the legal ownership of the grand Monadnoc, of the cataract of Niagara, or of the Belvedere Apollo, or whatever else it prizes.[8] It soon finds that no cabinet, though extended along miles of marble colonnade, would suffice to hold the beautiful wonders it has made its own. It has found beauty and wonder progressive, incessant, universal. At last it discovers that the whole world is a museum and that things are more glorious in their order and home than when a few are carried away to glitter alone.

In viewing the relations of objects to the mind we are entitled to disregard entirely those considerations which are of great importance in viewing the relation of things to each other. For example, magnitude, number, nearness of place and time are things of no importance; the spiritual effect is all that concerns us. What moves the mind we are entitled to say was designed to move it, however far off in the apparent chain of cause and effect. Our being floats on the whole culture of the past, on the whole hope of the future. Men dead and buried now for some thousands of years affect my mode of being much more than some of my contemporaries. As things lie in my thought, as they recur to speech and to action—such is their value, and not according to time or to place. How can any thing die to the mind? To this end they all are alive.

To what end existed those gods of Olympus or the tradition so irresistibly embodied in sculpture, architecture, and a perdurable literature that the old names, Jupiter, Apollo, Venus, still haunt us in this cold, Christian, Saxon America and will not be shaken off?[9] To what end the ethical revelation which we call Christianity, with all its history, its corruption, its Reformation;[10] the Revivals of Letters; the press; the planting of America; the conversion of the powers of nature to the domestic service of man, so that the ocean is but a waterwheel and the solar system but a clock? To what end are we distributed into electoral nations; half subject still to England through the dominion of British intellect and in common with England having not yet mastered or comprehended the astonishing infusions of the Hebrew soul in the morning of the world?

Why is never a local political arrangement made by a Saxon lawgiver for the getting justice in a market or keeping the peace in a village but it drafts a jury today in my county or levies a tax on my house?

Why is never a pencil moved in the hand of Rembrandt or Raphael and never a pen in that of Moses or Shakspear but it communicates emotion and thought to one of us at the end of an age and across the breadth of half a globe?[11] Thus is the prolific power of nature to yield spiritual aliment over a period of 3 or 4000 years epitomized and brought to a focus on the stripling now at school. These things and all things are there for me, and in relation to me. It may not be strictly philosophical—it may be a little beyond strictness of speech to say these all were designed to teach us as they have, but we may affirm that this effect and this action meet as accurately as the splendid lights of morning and evening meet the configuration of the human eye and within that, the more subtle eye of taste.

Once begin to count the problems which invite our research, which answer each to somewhat in the unknown soul, and you find that they are coextensive with the limits of being. Boldly, gladly, the soul plunges into this broad element, not fearing but cheered by the measureless main. Nothing is so old, nothing so mean, nothing so far but it has something for me. The progress of science is to bring the remote near. The kelp which grew neglected on the roaring seabeach of the Orkneys now comes to the shops; the seal, the otter, the ermine, that no man saw but the Indian in the Rocky Mountains, they must come to Long Wharf.[12] The seashells, strombus, turbo, and pearl, that hid a hundred fathoms down in the warm waters of the Gulf, they must take the bait and leave their silent houses and come to Long Wharf also: even the ducks of Labrador that laid their eggs for ages on the rocks, must send their green eggs now to Long Wharf.

So I think it will be the effect of insight to show nearer relations than are yet known between remote periods of history and the present hour. The Assyrian, the Persian, the Egyptian era now fading fast into twilight must reappear and, as a varnish brings out the original colors of an antique picture, so a better understanding of our own time and our own life, will be a sunbeam to search the faintest traces of human character in the first plantation of man. When we consider how much nearer in our own time Egypt, Greece, Homer, and Rome have come to us through Wolf, Niebuhr, Müller, Winckelmann, and Champollion we may believe that Olympus and Memphis, Zoroaster and Tubal Cain have not yet spoken to us their last word.[13]

Having spoken of the aim; the basis; the apparatus; and the scope; I proceed to speak of the scale of Culture. What is the rule that is to introduce a just harmony in the universal school in which it seems we study? Where every being in nature addresses me shall I not be bewildered and without compass or chart?

Proportion certainly is a great end of culture. A man should ask God morning and evening with the philosopher that he might be instructed to give to every being in the universe its just measure of importance. And it may be thought an obvious objection to views which set so high the hopes and powers of the individual that they foster the prejudices of a private soul which Bacon pointed out as one of the sources of error under the name of the idols of the Cave.[14]

But let it not be said that the only way to break up the idols of the cave is conversation with many men and a knowledge of the world. This is also distorting. State Street or the Boulevards of Paris are no truer pictures of the world than is a cloister or a laboratory.[15] The brokers and attorneys are quite as wide of the mark on one side as monks and academicians on the other.

There are two ways of cultivating proportion of character.

1. The habit of attending to all sensations and putting ourselves in a way to receive a variety, as by attending spectacles, visiting theatres, prisons, senates, churches, factories, museums, barracks, ships, hells, a thing impossible to many and except in merest superficiality impossible to any, for a man is not in the place to which he goes unless his mind is there.

But suppose a man goes to all such places as I have named and many more, will he have seen all? What does he know about the miners of Cornwall, or the lumberers of Maine?[16] Is he sure to allow all that is due to the Thugs of the Desert?[17] Does he appreciate insanity? or know the military life of Russia? or that of the Italian lazzaroni?[18] or the aspirations and tendencies of the Sacs and Foxes?[19] The shortness of life and the limited walks in which most men pass it forbid any hope of multiplying particular observations.

2. The other mode of cultivating gradation and forming a just scale is to compare the depth of thought to which different objects appeal. Nature and the course of life furnish every man the most recluse with a sufficient variety of objects to supply him with the elements and divisions of a scale. Looking back upon any portion of his life he will see that things have entirely lost the relative proportions which they wore to the eye at the moment when they transpired. The once dearest aims of his ambition have sunk our of sight and some transient shade of thought looms up out of forgotten years.

Proportion is not the effect of circumstances but a habit of mind. The truth is the mind is a perfect measure of all things and the only measure. I acknowledge that the mind is also a distorting medium so long as its aims are not pure. But the moment the individual declares his independence, takes his life into his own hand, and sets forth in quest of Culture, the love of truth is a sufficient guage. It is very clear that he can have no other. What external standard, what authority can teach the paramount rank of truth and justice but the mind's own unvarying instinct? Who shall tell it the claim of other things but Affection and Need and the incessant oracles of the overhanging Ideal? I confess my toleration does not increase to those who do not reverence their own mind. He is not a skeptic who denies a miracle, who denies both angel and resurrection, who does not believe in the existence of such a city as Thebes or Rome; but he is a skeptic who does not think it always an absolute duty to speak the truth, who pretends not to know how to discriminate between a duty and an inclination, and who thinks the mind itself is not a measure of things.

With such views of the aim, of the reason, of the apparatus, of Human Culture I have thought its transcendant claims should be laid before you. I think it the enterprize which out of the urn of God has fallen the lot of the present age. I think the time has come to ask the question, Why are there no heroes? Why is not every man venerable? Why should any be vulgar and vile? I wish that Education should not be trusted to the feeble hand of Societies but we should speak to the individual that which he ought to hear, the voice of faith and of truth. I wish him to perceive that his imitation, his fear, his dependency are child's clothes it is now time to cast off and assume his own vows. I wish him, instead of following with a mendicant admiration the great names that are inscribed on the walls of memory, let him know that they are only marks and memoranda for his guidance, with which his own experience should come up. Let him know that the stars shone as benignantly on the hour of his advent as on any Milton or Washington or Howard.[20] There is no combination of powers that comes into the world in a child that is not new and that is not needed. No sign indicates beforehand that a great man—that is, that a true man, has been born. No faculty is marked with a broad arrow beforehand but every gift of noble origin is breathed upon by Hope's perpetual breath. Whoever is alive, may be good and wise. I wish him to adopt this end with a great heart and lay himself generously open to the influences of Heaven and earth. Let him survey in succession his instincts and faculties. Let him examine his senses and his use of them. Is a man's body to be regarded as a philosophic apparatus, a school of science, a generator of power, or is it designed only for the taste of sugar, salt, and wine and for agreeable sensations? Then let him contemplate the Intellect and ask if justice has been done it, if its great instincts have been observed. Let him explore the Active powers, and see if he is the able, self-helping, man-helping laborer or an afternoon man and a nuisance. Let him enter the enchanted ground of the Affections and know if he have appropriated their sweetness and health; let him explore the laws of Prudence. Let him learn the higher discipline of the heroic; and ascend to the study and practice of the Holy.

Into these depths I wish to drop my sounding line. Into the several districts of human nature I wish to cast the inquiring glances of one observer. I do not underestimate the difficulties of the task. I see the utter incompetency of a single mind to draw the chart of human nature. I have as much doubt as any one of the value of general rules. There are heights of character to which a man must ascend alone— not to be foreshown,—that can only exist by the arrival of the man and the crisis. It is very far from being my belief that teaching can make a hero or that Virtue can be analysed in the lecture room and her deepest secret shown. I rely too much on the inexhaustible Ideal, whose resources always astonish. But I think and I feel that confidence may be inspired in the powers of the Will and in the aspirations of the Better by the voice and the faith of a believing man. I wish to inspire hope and shall esteem it the highest success if any ingenuous mind shall own that his scope has been extended; his conscience fortified and that more has been suggested than said.

Source: "Introductory" lecture (6 December 1837) to Human Culture lecture series, from *The Early Lectures of Ralph Waldo Emerson*, ed. Robert E. Spiller, Stephen E. Whicher, and Wallace E. Williams, 3 vols. (Cambridge: Harvard University Press, 1959–1972), 2:213–229.

Notes

1. Catamount, a wild cat, living in the mountains.
2. "Of Experience" by Michel Eyquem Montaigné (1533–1592), French essayist and philosopher, usually identified with skepticism.
3. John Huss (ca. 1369–1415), Czech religious reformer burned at the stake for heresy; Sir John Oldcastle, Lord Cobham (ca. 1378–1417), English soldier and Protestant reformer; John Knox (ca. 1514–1572), Scottish architect of the Reformation.
4. John 4:12.
5. The child's "folk-chant" is documented in *The Oxford Dictionary of Nursery Rhymes*, ed. Iona and Peter Opie (Oxford: Clarendon Press, 1951), pp. 367–370.
6. White Hills, Emerson's reference to the White Mountains in New Hampshire; Pompeii, near Naples in Italy, was buried by an eruption of Mount Vesuvius in A.D. 79; Faneuil Hall in Boston, first built in 1742, served as the city's town hall.
7. Muniments, written evidences.
8. Monadnoc, a mountain in New Hampshire; the statue of Apollo in the Belvedere Gallery of the Vatican is considered one of the finest of antiquity.

9. Jupiter, the supreme Roman god; Venus, Roman goddess of love.

10. Reformation, sixteenth-century religious revolution that resulted in the formation of Protestantism.

11. Rembrandt van Rijn (1606–1669), Dutch etcher and painter; Raphael (1483–1520), Italian painter whose works adorn the Vatican.

12. Orkneys, islands off the Scottish mainland; Long Wharf, in Boston.

13. Barthold Georg Niebuhr (1776–1831), German historian and critic; Johannes von Müller (1752–1809), Swiss public official and historian; Johann Joachim Winckelmann (1717–1868), German antiquities expert; Jean-François Champollion (1790–1832), French historian and linguist instrumental in deciphering the Egyptian hieroglyphics on the Rosetta stone; Memphis, city near Cairo that was the capital of ancient Egypt; Zoroaster (ca. 628–ca. 551 B.C.), Iranian religious reformer and founder of Zoroastrianism (also known as Zarathustra); Tubal-Cain, in the Bible, the great-great-great-great-great-grandson of Cain.

14. In his *Novum Organum* (1620), Francis Bacon wrote about how, in Emerson's paraphrase, each individual has "his own dark cavern or den into which the light is imperfectly admitted and to some error there lurking truth is sacrificed" (*Early Lectures*, 1:331).

15. State Street, the main commercial center of Boston.

16. Cornwall, a mining district in England.

17. Thugs, professional gangs of assassins and robbers in India.

18. Italian lazzaroni, the homeless people in Naples.

19. Sacs (or Sauks) and Foxes, Indians in Wisconsin.

20. Charles Howard, Earl of Nottingham (1536–1624), commander of the successful British fleet against the Spanish Armada.

Ralph Waldo Emerson

[Letter to Martin Van Buren]

(23 April 1838)

EMERSON DISLIKED PUBLIC confrontations, but the government's removal of the Cherokee Indians from their lands in Georgia to Mississippi lit a spark in him. He appeared at a public meeting in Concord, though his wife noted that he "very unwillingly takes part in public movements like that of yesterday preferring individual action." Emerson himself described such scenes as being "like dead cats around one's neck," calling the letter "hated of me." Yet in a letter to a friend, he explained his reasons for involving himself in public affairs that were uncongenial to him: "I hate myself when I go out of my sphere, but a man must have bowels sometimes & there was a moment when to my ignorance of what was doing, our people seemed dead asleep upon this black proceeding." Emerson's Transcendentalism did indeed have a political, as well as an individualistic, side.

Concord, Massachusetts, April 23, 1838

Sir: The seat you fill places you in a relation of credit and dearness to every citizen. By right and natural position, every citizen is your friend. Before any acts, contrary to his own judgment or interest, have repelled the affections of any man, each may look with trust and loving anticipations to your government. Each has the highest right to call your attention to such subjects as are of a public nature, and properly belong to the Chief Magistrate; and the good Magistrate will feel a joy in meeting such confidence. In this belief, and at the instance of a few of my friends and neighbors, I crave of your patience, through the medium of the press, a short hearing for their sentiments and my own; and the circumstance that my name will be utterly unknown to you will only give the fairer chance to your equitable construction of what I have to say.

Sir, my communication respects the sinister rumors that fill this part of the country concerning the Cherokee people. The interest always felt in the aboriginal population—an interest naturally growing as that decays—has been heightened in regard to this tribe. Even to our distant State, some good rumor of their worth and civility has arrived. We have learned with joy their improvement in social arts. We have read their newspapers. We have seen some of them in our schools and colleges. In common with the great body of the American People, we have witnessed with sympathy the painful endeavors of these red men to redeem their own race from the doom of eternal inferiority, and to borrow and domesticate in the tribe the inventions and customs of the Caucasian race.[1] And notwithstanding the unaccountable apathy with which, of late years, the Indians have been sometimes abandoned to their enemies, it is not to be doubted that it is the good pleasure and the understanding of all humane persons in the Republic, of the men and the matrons sitting in thriving independent families all over the land, that they shall be duly cared for, that they shall taste justice and love from all to whom we have delegated the office of dealing with them.

The newspapers now inform us that in December, 1835, a treaty, contracting for the exchange of the entire Cherokee territory, was pretended to be made by an agent on the part of the United States with some persons appearing on the part of the Cherokees; that the fact afterwards[2] transpired that these individual Indians did by no means represent the will of the nation; and that, out of eighteen thousand souls composing the nation, fifteen thousand six hundred and sixty-eight have protested against the so-called treaty. It now appears that the Government of the United States choose to hold the Cherokees to this sham treaty, and the proceeding to execute the same. Almost the entire Cherokee nation stand up and say, "This is not our act. Behold us! Here are we. Do not mistake that handful of deserters for us." And the President and his Cabinet, the Senate and the House of Representatives, neither hear these men nor see them, and are contracting to put this nation into carts and boats, and to drag them over mountains and rivers to a wilderness at a vast distance beyond the Mississippi. And a paper, purporting to be an army order, fixes a month from this day as the hour for this doleful removal.

In the name of God, sir, we ask you if this is so? Do the newspapers rightly inform us? Men and women, with pale and perplexed faces, meet one another in streets and churches here, and ask if this be so? We have inquired if this be a gross misrepresentation from the party opposed to the Government and anxious to blacken it with the People. We have looked into newspapers of different parties, and find a horrid confirmation of the tale. We are slow to believe it. We hoped the Indians were misinformed, and their remonstrance was premature, and would turn out to be a needless act of terror. The piety, the principle, that is left in these United States—if only its coarsest form, a regard to the speech of men—forbid us to entertain it as a fact. Such a dereliction of all faith and virtue, such a denial of justice, and such deafness to screams for mercy, were never heard of in times of peace, and in the dealing of a nation with its own allies and wards, since the earth was made. Sir, does the Government think that the People of the United States are become savage and mad? From their minds are the sentiments of love and of a good nature wiped clean out? The soul of man, the justice, the mercy, that is the heart's heart in all men, from Maine to Georgia, does abhor this business.

In speaking thus the sentiments of my neighbors and my own, perhaps I overstep the bounds of decorum. But would it not be a higher indecorum coldly to argue a matter like this? We only state the fact, that a crime is projected that confounds our understandings by its magnitude—a crime that really deprives us as well as the Cherokees of a country; for how could we call the conspiracy that should crush these poor Indians our Government, or the land that was cursed by their parting and dying imprecations our country, any more? You, sir, will bring down that renowned chair in which you sit into infamy if your seal is set to this instrument of perfidy; and the name of this nation, hitherto the sweet omen of religion and liberty, will stink to the world.

You will not do us the injustice of connecting this remonstrance with any sectional or party feeling. It is in our hearts the simplest commandment of brotherly love. We will not have this great and solemn claim upon national and human justice huddled aside under the flimsy plea of its being a party act. Sir, to us the questions upon which the Government and the People have been agitated during the past year, touching the prostration of the currency and of trade, seem motes in the comparison. The hard times, it is true, have brought this discussion home to every farmhouse and poor man's table in this town, but it is the chirping of grasshoppers, beside the immortal question whether justice shall be done by the race of civilized to the race of savage man; whether all the attributes of reason, of civility, of justice, and even of mercy, shall be put off by the American People, and so vast an outrage upon the Cherokee nation, and upon human nature, shall be consummated.

One circumstance lessens the reluctance with which I intrude on your attention: my conviction that the Government ought to be admonished of a new historical fact, which the discussion of this question has disclosed, namely, that there exists in a great part of the Northern People a gloomy diffidence of the *moral* character of the Government. On the broaching of this question, a general expression of despondency, of disbelief that any good will accrue from a remonstrance on an act of fraud and robbery, appeared in those men to whom we naturally turn for aid and counsel. Will the American Government steal? will it lie? will it kill? We asked triumphantly. Our wise men shake their heads dubiously. Our counsellors and old statesmen here say that, ten years ago, they would have staked their life on the affirmation that the proposed Indian measures could not be executed; that the unanimous country would put them down. And now the steps of this crime follow each other so fast, at such fatally quick time, that the millions of virtuous citizens whose agents the Government are, have no space to interpose, and must shut their eyes until the last howl and wailing of these poor tormented villages and tribes shall afflict the ear of the world.

I will not hide from you as an indication of this alarming distrust, that a letter addressed as mine is, and suggesting to the mind of the Executive the plain obligations of man, has a burlesque character in the apprehension of some of my friends. I, sir, will not beforehand treat you with the contumely of this distrust. I will at least state to you this fact, and show you how plain and humane people whose love would be honor regard the policy of the Government and what injurious inferences they draw as to the mind of the governors. A man with your experience in affairs must have seen cause to appreciate the futility of opposition to the moral sentiment. However feeble the sufferer, and however great the oppressor, it is in the nature of things that the blood should recoil on the aggressor. For, God is in the sentiment, and it cannot be withstood. The potentate and the People perish before it; but with it and as its executors, they are omnipotent.

I write thus, sir, to inform you of the state of mind these Indian tidings have awakened here, and to pray with one voice more, that you, whose hands are strong with the delegated power of fifteen millions of men, will avert, with that might, the terrific injury which threatens the Cherokee tribe.

With great respect, sir, I am, your fellow-citizen,
Ralph Waldo Emerson.

Source: Ralph Waldo Emerson, [Letter to Martin Van Buren], *Daily National Intelligencer* [Washington], 14 May 1838, p. 2. The quotations are from *The Selected Letters of Lidian Jackson Emerson*, ed. Delores Bird Carpenter (Columbia: University of Missouri Press, 1987), pp. 74–75; *Journals and Miscellaneous Notebooks*, 5:477, 479; *Letters*, 7:309.

Notes

1. The Cherokees had adopted an alphabet by which to express their mainly oral language, published a newspaper, established a representative type of government, and formed a public school system.
2. *Note by a friend of the writer.*—The fact that few Cherokees who made the treaty were not authorized to make it was known to the Executive at the time, not afterwards discovered, as supposed by Mr. Emerson. [Note in the *Daily National Intelligencer*]

Ralph Waldo Emerson

Divinity School Address

(15 July 1838)

EMERSON TOLD HIS audience at the Phi Beta Kappa Society a year earlier that Harvard College had not taught them well; now he makes the same accusation against the teachers of the graduates of the Divinity School. He speaks forcefully about how "one mind is everywhere" (or "unity in variety"), how evil is not an active force in the world ("Good is positive. Evil is merely privative, not absolute. It is like cold, which is the privation of heat"), and how religion can be received intuitively. He complains of the "historical Christianity" that has made a "demigod" of Christ by exaggerating His person and not paying attention to His teachings, and has ignored humankind's "Moral Nature," and he urges his audience to "rekindle the smouldering, nigh quenched fire on the altar" by using the Sabbath more wisely and to reinvigorate the art of preaching by making it less dependent on the memory and more about the preacher imparting his soul.

In this refulgent summer it has been a luxury to draw the breath of life. The grass grows, the buds burst, the meadow is spotted with fire and gold in the tint of flowers. The air is full of birds, and sweet with the breath of the pine, the balm-of-Gilead, and the new hay. Night brings no gloom to the heart with its welcome shade. Through the transparent darkness pour the stars their almost spiritual rays. Man under them seems a young child, and his huge globe a toy. The cool night bathes the world as with a river, and prepares his eyes again for the crimson dawn. The mystery of nature was never displayed more happily. The corn and the wine have been freely dealt to all creatures, and the never-broken silence with which the old bounty goes forward, has not yielded yet one word of explanation. One is constrained to respect the perfection of this world, in which our senses converse. How wide; how rich; what invitation from every property it gives to every faculty of man! In its fruitful soils; in its navigable sea; in its mountains of metal and stone; in its forests of all woods; in its animals; in its chemical ingredients; in the powers and path of light, heat, attraction, and life, is it well worth the pith and heart of great men to subdue and enjoy it. The planters, the mechanics, the inventors, the astronomers, the builders of cities, and the captains, history delights to honor.

But the moment the mind opens, and reveals the laws which traverse the universe, and make things what they are, then shrinks the great world at once into a mere illustration and fable of this mind. What am I? and What is? asks the human spirit with a curiosity new-kindled, but never to be quenched. Behold these outrunning laws, which our imperfect apprehension can see tend this way and that, but not come full circle. Behold these infinite relations, so like, so unlike; many, yet one. I would study, I would know, I would admire forever. These works of thought have been the entertainments of the human spirit in all ages.

A more secret, sweet, and overpowering beauty appears to man when his heart and mind open to the sentiment of virtue. Then instantly he is instructed in what is above him. He learns that his being is without bound; that, to the good, to the perfect, he is born, low as he now lies in evil and weakness. That which he venerates is still his own, though he has not realized it yet. *He ought.* He knows the sense of that grand word, though his analysis fails entirely to render account of it. When in innocency, or when by intellectual perception, he attains to say,—'I love the Right; Truth is beautiful within and without, forevermore. Virtue, I am thine: save me: use me: thee will I serve, day and night, in great, in small, that I may be not virtuous, but virtue;'—then is the end of the creation answered, and God is well pleased.

The sentiment of virtue is a reverence and delight in the presence of certain divine laws. It perceives that this homely game of life we play, covers, under what seem foolish details, principles that astonish. The child amidst his baubles, is learning the action of light, motion, gravity, muscular force; and in the game of human life, love, fear, justice, appetite, man, and God, interact. These laws refuse to be adequately stated. They will not by us or for us be written out on paper, or spoken by the tongue. They elude, evade our persevering thought, and yet we read them hourly in each other's faces, in each other's actions, in our own remorse. The moral traits which are all globed into every virtuous act and thought,—in speech, we must sever, and describe or suggest by painful enumeration of many particulars. Yet, as this sentiment is the essence of all religion, let me guide your eye to the precise objects of the sentiment, by an enumeration of some of those classes of facts in which this element is conspicuous.

The intuition of the moral sentiment is an insight of the perfection of the laws of the soul. These laws execute themselves. They are out of time, out of space, and not subject to circumstance. Thus; in the soul of man there is a justice whose retributions are instant and entire. He who does a good deed, is instantly ennobled himself. He who does a mean deed, is by the action itself contracted. He who puts off impurity, thereby puts on purity. If a man is at heart just, then in so far is he God; the safety of God, the immortality of God, the majesty of God do enter into that man with justice. If a man dissemble, deceive, he deceives himself, and goes out of acquaintance with his own being. A man in the view of absolute goodness, adores, with total humility. Every step so downward, is a step upward. The man who renounces himself, comes to himself by so doing.

See how this rapid intrinsic energy worketh everywhere, righting wrongs, correcting appearances, and bringing up facts to a harmony with thoughts. Its operation in life, though slow to the senses, is, at last, as sure as in the soul. By it, a man is made the Providence to himself, dispensing good to his goodness, and evil to his sin. Character is always known. Thefts never enrich; alms never impoverish; murder will speak out of stone walls. The least admixture of a lie,—for example, the smallest mixture of vanity, the least attempt to make a good impression, a favorable appearance,—will instantly vitiate the effect. But speak the truth, and all nature and all spirits help you with unexpected furtherance. Speak the truth, and all things alive or brute are vouchers, and the very roots of the grass underground there, do seem to stir and move to bear you witness. See again the perfection of the Law as it applies itself to the affections, and becomes the law of society. As we are, so we associate. The good, by affinity, seek the good; the vile, by affinity, the vile. Thus of their own volition, souls proceed into heaven, into hell.

These facts have always suggested to man the sublime creed, that the world is not the product of manifold power, but of one will, of one mind; and that one mind is everywhere, in each ray of the star, in each wavelet of the pool, active; and whatever opposes that will, is everywhere baulked and baffled, because things are made so, and not otherwise. Good is positive. Evil is merely privative, not absolute. It is like cold, which is the privation of heat. All evil is so much death or nonentity. Benevolence is absolute and real. So much benevolence as a man hath, so much life hath he. For all things proceed out of this same spirit, which is differently named love, justice, temperance, in its different applications, just as the ocean receives different names on the several shores which it washes. All things proceed out of the same spirit, and all things conspire with it. Whilst a man seeks good ends, he is strong by the whole strength of nature. In so far as he roves from these ends, he bereaves himself of power, of auxiliaries; his being shrinks out of all remote channels, he becomes less and less, a mote, a point, until absolute badness is absolute death.

The perception of this law of laws always awakens in the mind a sentiment which we call the religious sentiment, and which makes our highest happiness. Wonderful is its power to charm and to command. It is a mountain air. It is the embalmer of the world. It is myrrh and storax, and chlorine and rosemary. It makes the sky and the hills sublime, and the silent song of the stars is it. By it, is the universe made safe and habitable, not by science or power. Thought may work cold and intransitive in things, and find no end or unity. But the dawn of the sentiment of virtue on the heart, gives and is the assurance that Law is sovereign over all natures; and the worlds, time, space, eternity, do seem to break out into joy.

This sentiment is divine and deifying. It is the beatitude of man. It makes him illimitable. Through it, the soul first knows itself. It corrects the capital mistake of the infant man, who seeks to be great by following the great, and hopes to derive advantages *from another*,— by showing the fountain of all good to be in himself, and that he, equally with every man, is a door into the deeps of Reason. When he says, "I ought;" when love warms him; when he chooses, warned from on high, the good and great deed; then, deep melodies wander through his soul from Supreme Wisdom. Then he can worship, and be enlarged by his worship; for he can never go behind this sentiment. In the sublimest flights of the soul, rectitude is never surmounted, love is never outgrown.

This sentiment lies at the foundation of society, and successively creates all forms of worship. The principle of veneration never dies out. Man fallen into superstition, into sensuality, is never wholly without the visions of the moral sentiment. In like manner, all the expressions of this sentiment are sacred and permanent in proportion to their purity. The expressions of this sentiment affect us deeper, greatlier, than all other compositions. The sentences of the oldest time, which ejaculate this piety, are still fresh and fragrant. This thought dwelled always deepest in the minds of men in the devout and contemplative East; not alone in Palestine, where it reached its purest expression, but in Egypt, in Persia, in India, in China. Europe has always owed to oriental genius, its divine impulses. What these holy bards said, all sane men found agreeable and true. And the unique impression of Jesus upon mankind, whose name is not so much written as ploughed into the history of this world, is proof of the subtle virtue of this infusion.

Meantime, whilst the doors of the temple stand open, night and day, before every man, and the oracles of this truth cease never, it is guarded by one stern condition; this, namely; It is an intuition. It cannot be received at second hand. Truly speaking, it is not instruction, but provocation, that I can receive from another soul. What he announces, I must find true in me, or wholly reject; and on his word, or as his second, be he who he may, I can accept nothing. On the contrary, the absence of this primary faith is the presence of degradation. As is the flood so is the ebb. Let this faith depart, and the very words it spake, and the things it made, become false and hurtful. Then falls the church, the state, art, letters, life. The doctrine of the divine nature being forgotten, a sickness infects and dwarfs the constitution. Once man was all; now he is an appendage, a nuisance. And because the indwelling Supreme Spirit cannot wholly be got rid of, the doctrine of it suffers this perversion, that the divine nature is attributed to one or two persons, and denied to all the rest, and denied with fury. The doctrine of inspiration is lost; the base doctrine of the majority of voices, usurps the place of the doctrine of the soul. Miracles, prophecy, poetry, the ideal life, the holy life, exist as ancient history merely; they are not in the belief, nor in the aspiration of society; but, when suggested, seem ridiculous. Life is comic or pitiful, as soon as the high ends of being fade out of sight, and man becomes near-sighted, and can only attend to what addresses the senses.

These general views, which, whilst they are general, none will contest, find abundant illustration in the history of religion, and especially in the history of the Christian church. In that, all of us have had our birth and nurture. The truth contained in that, you, my young friends, are now setting forth to teach. As the Cultus, or established worship of the civilized world, it has great historical interest for us. Of its blessed words, which have been the consolation of humanity, you need not that I should speak. I shall endeavor to discharge my duty to you, on this occasion, by pointing out two errors in its administration, which daily appear more gross from the point of view we have just now taken.

Jesus Christ belonged to the true race of prophets. He saw with open eye the mystery of the soul. Drawn by its severe harmony, ravished with its beauty, he lived in it, and had his being there. Alone in all history, he estimated the greatness of man. One man was true to what is in you and me. He saw that God incarnates himself in man, and evermore goes forth anew to take possession of his world. He said, in this jubilee of sublime emotion, 'I am divine. Through me, God acts; through me, speaks. Would you see God, see me; or, see thee, when thou also thinkest as I now think.' But what a distortion did his doctrine and memory suffer in the same, in the next, and the following ages! There is no doctrine of the Reason which will bear to be taught by the Understanding. The understanding caught this high chant from the poet's lips, and said, in the next age, 'This was Jehovah come down out of heaven. I will kill you, if you say he was a man.' The idioms of his language, and the figures of his rhetoric, have usurped the place of his truth; and churches are not built on his principles, but on his tropes. Christianity became a Mythus, as the poetic teaching of Greece and of Egypt, before. He spoke of miracles; for he felt that man's life was a miracle, and all that man doth, and he knew that this daily miracle shines, as the man is diviner. But the very word Miracle, as pronounced by Christian churches, gives a false impression; it is Monster. It is not one with the blowing clover and the falling rain.

He felt respect for Moses and the prophets; but no unfit tenderness at postponing their initial revelations, to the hour and the man that now is; to the eternal revelation in the heart. Thus was he a true man. Having seen that the law in us is commanding, he would not suffer it to be commanded. Boldly, with hand, and heart, and life, he declared it was God. Thus was he a true man. Thus is he, as I think, the only soul in history who has appreciated the worth of a man.

1. In thus contemplating Jesus, we become very sensible of the first defect of historical Christianity. Historical Christianity has fallen into the error that corrupts all attempts to communicate religion. As it appears to us, and as it has appeared for ages, it is not the doctrine of the soul, but an exaggeration of the personal, the positive, the ritual. It has dwelt, it dwells, with noxious exaggeration about the *person* of Jesus. The soul knows no persons. It invites every man to expand to the full circle of the universe, and will have no preferences but those of spontaneous love. But by this eastern monarchy of a Christianity, which indolence and fear have built, the friend of man is made the injurer of man. The manner in which his name is surrounded with expressions, which were once sallies of admiration and love, but are now petrified into official titles, kills all generous sympathy and liking. All who hear me, feel, that the language that describes Christ to Europe and America, is not the style of friendship and enthusiasm to a good and noble heart, but is appropriated and formal,—paints a demigod, as the Orientals or the Greeks would describe Osiris or Apollo.[1] Accept the injurious impositions of our early catechetical instruction, and even honesty and self-denial were but splendid sins, if they did not wear the Christian name. One would rather be

'A pagan suckled in a creed outworn,'[2]

than to be defrauded of his manly right in coming into nature, and finding not names and places, not land and professions, but even virtue and truth foreclosed and monopolized. You shall not be a man even. You shall not own the world; you shall not dare, and live after the infinite Law that is in you, and in company with the infinite Beauty which heaven and earth reflect to you in all lovely forms; but you must subordinate your nature to Christ's nature; you must accept our interpretations; and take his portrait as the vulgar draw it.

That is always best which gives me to myself. The sublime is excited in me by the great stoical doctrine, Obey thyself. That which shows God in me, fortifies me. That which shows God out of me, makes me a wart and a wen. There is no longer a necessary reason for my being.

Already the long shadows of untimely oblivion creep over me, and I shall decease forever.

The divine bards are the friends of my virtue, of my intellect, of my strength. They admonish me, that the gleams which flash across my mind, are not mine, but God's; that they had the like, and were not disobedient to the heavenly vision.[3] So I love them. Noble provocations go out from them, inviting me also to emancipate myself; to resist evil; to subdue the world; and to Be. And thus by his holy thoughts, Jesus serves us, and thus only. To aim to convert a man by miracles, is a profanation of the soul. A true conversion, a true Christ, is now, as always, to be made, by the reception of beautiful sentiments. It is true that a great and rich soul, like his, falling among the simple, does so preponderate, that, as his did, it names the world. The world seems to them to exist for him, and they have not yet drunk so deeply of his sense, as to see that only by coming again to themselves, or to God in themselves, can they grow forevermore. It is a low benefit to give me something; it is a high benefit to enable me to do somewhat of myself. The time is coming when all men will see, that the gift of God to the soul is not a vaunting, overpowering, excluding sanctity, but a sweet, natural goodness, a goodness like thine and mine, and that so invites thine and mine to be and to grow.

The injustice of the vulgar tone of preaching is not less flagrant to Jesus, than it is to the souls which it profanes. The preachers do not see that they make his gospel not glad, and shear him of the locks of beauty and the attributes of heaven. When I see a majestic Epaminondas, or Washington;[4] when I see among my contemporaries, a true orator, an upright judge, a dear friend; when I vibrate to the melody and fancy of a poem; I see beauty that is to be desired. And so lovely, and with yet more entire consent of my human being, sounds in my ear the severe music of the bards that have sung of the true God in all ages. Now do not degrade the life and dialogues of Christ out of the circle of this charm, by insulation and peculiarity. Let them lie as they befel, alive and warm, part of human life, and of the landscape, and of the cheerful day.

2. The second defect of the traditionary and limited way of using the mind of Christ is a consequence of the first; this, namely; that the Moral Nature, that Law of laws, whose revelations introduce greatness,—yea, God himself, into the open soul, is not explored as the fountain of the established teaching in society. Men have come to speak of the revelation as somewhat long ago given and done, as if God were dead. The injury to faith throttles the preacher; and the goodliest of institutions becomes an uncertain and inarticulate voice.

It is very certain that it is the effect of conversation with the beauty of the soul, to beget a desire and need to impart to others the same knowledge and love. If utterance is denied, the thought lies like a burden on the man. Always the seer is a sayer. Somehow his dream is told. Somehow he publishes it with solemn joy. Sometimes with pencil on canvas; sometimes with chisel on stone; sometimes in towers and aisles of granite, his soul's worship is builded; sometimes in anthems of indefinite music; but clearest and most permanent, in words.

The man enamored of this excellency, becomes its priest or poet. The office is coeval with the world. But observe the condition, the spiritual limitation of the office. The spirit only can teach. Not any profane man, not any sensual, not any liar, not any slave can teach, but only he can give, who has; he only can create, who is. The man on whom the soul descends, through whom the soul speaks, alone can teach. Courage, piety, love, wisdom, can teach; and every man can open his door to these angels, and they shall bring him the gift of tongues. But the man who aims to speak as books enable, as synods use, as the fashion guides, and as interest commands, babbles. Let him hush.

To this holy office, you propose to devote yourselves. I wish you may feel your call in throbs of desire and hope. The office is the first in the world. It is of that reality, that it cannot suffer the deduction of any falsehood. And it is my duty to say to you, that the need was never greater of new revelation than now. From the views I have already expressed, you will infer the sad conviction, which I share, I believe, with numbers, of the universal decay and now almost death of faith in society. The soul is not preached. The Church seems to totter to its fall, almost all life extinct. On this occasion, any complaisance, would be criminal, which told you, whose hope and commission it is to preach the faith of Christ, that the faith of Christ is preached.

It is time that this ill-suppressed murmur of all thoughtful men against the famine of our churches; this moaning of the heart because it is bereaved of the consolation, the hope, the grandeur, that come alone out of the culture of the moral nature; should be heard through the sleep of indolence, and over the din of routine. This great and perpetual office of the preacher is not discharged. Preaching is the expression of the moral sentiment in application to the duties of life. In how many churches, by how many prophets, tell me, is man made sensible that he is an infinite Soul; that the earth and heavens are passing into his mind; that he is drinking forever the soul of God? Where now sounds the persuasion, that by its very melody imparadises my heart, and so affirms its own origin in heaven? Where shall I hear words such as in elder ages drew men to leave all and follow,—father and mother, house and land, wife and child? Where shall I hear these august laws of moral being so pronounced, as to fill my ear, and I feel ennobled by the offer of my uttermost action and passion? The test of the true faith, certainly, should be its power to charm and command the soul, as the laws of nature control the activity of the hands,—so commanding that we find pleasure and honor in obeying. The faith should blend with the light of rising and of setting suns, with the flying cloud, the singing bird, and the breath of flowers. But now the priest's Sabbath has lost the splendor of nature; it is unlovely; we are glad when it is done; we can make, we do make, even sitting in our pews, a far better, holier, sweeter, for ourselves.

Whenever the pulpit is usurped by a formalist, then is the worshipper defrauded and disconsolate. We shrink as soon as the prayers begin, which do not uplift, but smite and offend us. We are fain to wrap our cloaks about us, and secure, as best we can, a solitude that hears not. I once heard a preacher who sorely tempted me to say, I would go to church no more. Men go, thought I, where they are wont to go, else had no soul entered the temple in the afternoon. A snowstorm was falling around us. The snowstorm was real; the preacher merely spectral; and the eye felt the sad contrast in looking at him, and then out of the window behind him, into the beautiful meteor of the snow. He had lived in vain. He had no one word intimating that he had laughed or wept, was married or in love, had been commended, or cheated, or chagrined. If he had ever lived and acted, we were none the wiser for it. The capital secret of his profession, namely, to convert life into truth, he had not learned. Not one fact in all his experience, had he yet imported into his doctrine. This man had ploughed, and planted, and talked, and bought, and sold; he had read books; he had eaten and drunken; his head aches; his heart throbs; he smiles and suffers; yet was there not a surmise, a hint, in all the discourse, that he had ever lived at all. Not a line did he draw out of real history.[5] The true preacher can always be known by this, that he deals out to the people his life,—life passed through the fire of thought. But of the bad preacher, it could not be told from his sermon, what age of the world he fell in; whether he had a father or a child; whether he was a freeholder or a pauper; whether he was a citizen or a countryman; or any other fact of his biography.

It seemed strange that the people should come to church. It seemed as if their houses were very unentertaining, that they should prefer this thoughtless clamor. It shows that there is a commanding attraction in the moral sentiment, that can lend a faint tint of light to dulness and ignorance, coming in its name and place. The good hearer is sure he has been touched sometimes; is sure there is somewhat to be reached, and some word that can reach it. When he listens to these vain words, he comforts himself by their relation to his remembrance of better hours, and so they clatter and echo unchallenged.

I am not ignorant that when we preach unworthily, it is not always quite in vain. There is a good ear, in some men, that draws supplies to virtue out of very indifferent nutriment. There is poetic truth concealed in all the common-places of prayer and of sermons, and though foolishly spoken, they may be wisely heard; for, each is some select expression that broke out in a moment of piety from some stricken or jubilant soul, and its excellency made it remembered. The prayers and even the dogmas of our church, are like the zodiac of Denderah,[6] and the astronomical monuments of the Hindoos, wholly insulated from anything now extant in the life and business of the people. They mark the height to which the waters once rose. But this docility is a check upon the mischief from the good and devout. In a large portion of the community, the religious service gives rise to quite other thoughts and emotions. We need not chide the negligent servant. We are struck with pity, rather, at the swift retribution of his sloth. Alas for the unhappy man that is called to stand in the pulpit, and *not* give bread of life. Everything that befals, accuses him. Would he ask contributions for the missions, foreign or domestic? Instantly his face is suffused with shame, to propose to his parish, that they should send money a hundred or a thousand miles, to furnish such poor fare as they have at home, and would do well to go the hundred or the thousand miles, to escape. Would he urge people to a godly way of living;—and can he ask a fellow creature to come to Sabbath meetings, when he and they all know what is the poor uttermost they can hope for therein? Will he invite them privately to the Lord's Supper? He dares not. If no heart warm this rite, the hollow, dry, creaking formality is too plain, than that he can face a man of wit and energy, and put the invitation without terror. In the street, what has he to say to the bold village blasphemer? The village blasphemer sees fear in the face, form, and gait of the minister.

Let me not taint the sincerity of this plea by any oversight of the claims of good men. I know and honor the purity and strict conscience of numbers of the clergy. What life the public worship retains, it owes to the scattered company of pious men, who minister here and there in the churches, and who, sometimes accepting with too great tenderness the tenet of the elders, have not accepted from others, but from their own heart, the genuine impulses of virtue, and so still command our love and awe, to the sanctity of character. Moreover, the exceptions are not so much to be found in a few eminent preachers, as in the better hours, the truer inspirations of all,—nay, in the sincere moments of every man. But with whatever exception, it is still true, that tradition characterizes the preaching of this country; that it comes out of the memory, and not out of the soul; that it aims at what is usual, and not at what is necessary and eternal; that thus, historical Christianity destroys the power of preaching, by withdrawing it from the exploration of the moral nature of man, where the sublime is, where are the resources of astonishment and power. What a cruel injustice it is to that Law, the joy of the whole earth, which alone can make thought dear and rich; that Law whose fatal sureness the astronomical orbits poorly emulate, that it is travestied and depreciated, that it is behooted and behowled, and not a trait, not a word of it articulated. The pulpit in losing sight of this Law, loses all its inspiration, and gropes after it knows not what. And for want of this culture, the soul of the community is sick and faithless. It wants nothing so much as a stern, high, stoical, Christian discipline, to make it know itself and the divinity that speaks through it. Now man is ashamed of himself; he skulks and sneaks through the world, to be tolerated, to be pitied, and scarcely in a thousand years does any man dare to be wise and good, and so draw after him the tears and blessings of his kind.

Certainly there have been periods when, from the inactivity of the intellect on certain truths, a greater faith was possible in names and persons. The Puritans in England and America, found in the Christ of the Catholic Church, and in the dogmas inherited from Rome, scope for their austere piety, and their longings for civil freedom.[7] But their creed is passing away, and none arises in its room. I think no man can go with his thoughts about him, into one of our churches, without feeling that what hold the public worship had on men, is gone or going. It has lost its grasp on the affection of the good, and the fear of the bad. In the country,—neighborhoods, half parishes are *signing off*,—to use the local term. It is already beginning to indicate character and religion to withdraw from the religious meetings. I have heard a devout person, who prized the Sabbath, say in bitterness of heart, "On Sundays, it seems wicked to go to church."[8] And the motive, that holds the best there, is now only a hope and a waiting. What was once a mere circumstance, that the best and the worst men in the parish, the poor and the rich, the learned and the ignorant, young and old, should meet one day as fellows in one house, in sign of an equal right in the soul,—has come to be a paramount motive for going thither.

My friends, in these two errors, I think, I find the causes of that calamity of a decaying church and a wasting unbelief, which are casting malignant influences around us, and making the hearts of good men sad. And what greater calamity can fall upon a nation, than the loss of worship? Then all things go to decay. Genius leaves the temple, to haunt the senate, or the market. Literature becomes frivolous. Science is cold. The eye of youth is not lighted by the hope of other worlds, and age is without honor. Society lives to trifles, and when men die, we do not mention them.

And now, my brothers, you will ask, What in these desponding days can be done by us? The remedy is already declared in the ground of our complaint of the Church. We have contrasted the Church with the Soul. In the soul, then, let the redemption be sought. In one soul, in your soul, there are resources for the world. Wherever a man comes, there comes revolution. The old is for slaves. When a man comes, all books are legible, all things transparent, all religions are forms. He is religious. Man is the wonderworker. He is seen amid miracles. All men bless and curse. He saith yea and nay, only. The stationariness of religion; the assumption that the age of inspiration is past, that the Bible is closed; the fear of degrading the character of Jesus by representing him as a man; indicate with sufficient clearness the falsehood of our theology. It is the office of a true teacher to show us that God is, not was; that He speaketh, not spake. The true Christianity,—a faith like Christ's in the infinitude of man,—is lost. None believeth in the soul of man, but only in some man or person old and departed. Ah me! no man goeth alone. All men go in flocks to this saint or that poet, avoiding the God who seeth in secret. They cannot see in secret; they love to be blind in public. They think society wiser than their soul; and know not that one soul, and their soul, is wiser than the whole world. See how nations and races flit by on the sea of time, and leave no ripple to tell where they floated or sunk, and one good soul shall make the name of Moses, or of Zeno, or of Zoroaster, reverend forever.[9] None assayeth the stern ambition to be the Self of the nation, and of nature, but each would be an easy secondary to some Christian scheme, or sectarian connexion, or some eminent man. Once leave your own knowledge of God, your own sentiment, and take secondary knowledge, as St. Paul's, or George Fox's, or Swedenborg's, and you get wide from God with every year this secondary form lasts, and if, as now, for centuries,—the chasm yawns to that breadth, that men can scarcely be convinced there is in them anything divine.

Let me admonish you, first of all, to go alone; to refuse the good models, even those most sacred in the imagination of men, and dare to love God without mediator or veil. Friends enough you shall find who will hold up to your emulation Wesleys and Oberlins, Saints and Prophets.[10] Thank God for these good men, but say, 'I also am a man.'

Imitation cannot go above its model. The imitator dooms himself to hopeless mediocrity. The inventor did it, because it was natural to him, and so in him it has a charm. In the imitator, something else is natural, and he bereaves himself of his own beauty, to come short of another man's.

Yourself a newborn bard of the Holy Ghost,—cast behind you all conformity, and acquaint men at first hand with Deity. Be to them a man. Look to it first and only, that you are such; that fashion, custom, authority, pleasure, and money are nothing to you,—are not bandages over your eyes, that you cannot see,—but live with the privilege of the immeasurable mind. Not too anxious to visit periodically all families and each family in your parish connexion,—when you meet one of these men or women, be to them a divine man; be to them thought and virtue; let their timid aspirations find in you a friend; let their trampled instincts be genially tempted out in your atmosphere; let their doubts know that you have doubted, and their wonder feel that you have wondered. By trusting your own soul, you shall gain a greater confidence in other men. For all our penny-wisdom, for all our soul-destroying slavery to habit, it is not to be doubted, that all men have sublime thoughts; that all men do value the few real hours of life; they love to be heard; they love to be caught up into the vision of principles. We mark with light in the memory the few interviews, we have had in the dreary years of routine and of sin, with souls that made our souls wiser; that spoke what we thought; that told us what we knew; that gave us leave to be what we inly were. Discharge to men the priestly office, and, present or absent, you shall be followed with their love as by an angel.

And, to this end, let us not aim at common degrees of merit. Can we not leave, to such as love it, the virtue that glitters for the commendation of society, and ourselves pierce the deep solitudes of absolute ability and worth? We easily come up to the standard of goodness in society. Society's praise can be cheaply secured, and almost all men are content with those easy merits; but the instant effect of conversing with God, will be, to put them away. There are sublime merits; persons who are not actors, not speakers, but influences; persons too great for fame, for display; who disdain eloquence; to whom all we call art and artist, seems too nearly allied to show and by-ends, to the exaggeration of the finite and selfish, and loss of the universal. The orators, the poets, the commanders encroach on us only as fair women do, by our allowance and homage. Slight them by preoccupation of mind, slight them, as you can well afford to do, by high and universal aims, and they instantly feel that you have right, and that it is in lower places that they must shine. They also feel your right; for they with you are open to the influx of the all-knowing Spirit, which annihilates before its broad noon the little shades and gradations of intelligence in the compositions we call wiser and wisest.

In such high communion, let us study the grand strokes of rectitude: a bold benevolence, an independence of friends, so that not the unjust wishes of those who love us, shall impair our freedom, but we shall resist for truth's sake the freest flow of kindness, and appeal to sympathies far in advance; and,—what is the highest form in which we know this beautiful element,—a certain solidity of merit, that has nothing to do with opinion, and which is so essentially and manifestly virtue, that it is taken for granted, that the right, the brave, the generous step will be taken by it, and nobody thinks of commending it. You would compliment a coxcomb doing a good act, but you would not praise an angel. The silence that accepts merit as the most natural thing in the world, is the highest applause. Such souls, when they appear, are the Imperial Guard of Virtue, the perpetual reserve, the dictators of fortune. One needs not praise their courage,—they are the heart and soul of nature. O my friends, there are resources in us on which we have not drawn. There are men who rise refreshed on hearing a threat; men to whom a crisis which intimidates and paralyzes the majority—demanding not the faculties of prudence and thrift, but comprehension, immovableness, the readiness of sacrifice,—comes graceful and beloved as a bride. Napoleon said of Massena, that he was not himself until the battle began to go against him; then, when the dead began to fall in ranks around him, awoke his powers of combination, and he put on terror and victory as a robe.[11] So it is in rugged crises, in unweariable endurance, and in aims which put sympathy out of question, that the angel is shown. But these are heights that we can scarce remember and look up to, without contrition and shame. Let us thank God that such things exist.

And now let us do what we can to rekindle the smouldering, nigh quenched fire on the altar. The evils of that church that now is, are manifest. The question returns, What shall we do? I confess, all attempts to project and establish a Cultus with new rites and forms, seem to me vain. Faith makes us, and not we it, and faith makes its own forms. All attempts to contrive a system, are as cold as the new worship introduced by the French to the goddess of Reason,—to-day, pasteboard and fillagree, and ending to-morrow in madness and murder. Rather let the breath of new life be breathed by you through the forms already existing. For, if once you are alive, you shall find they shall become plastic and new. The remedy to their deformity is, first, soul, and second, soul, and evermore, soul. A whole popedom of forms, one pulsation of virtue can uplift and vivify. Two inestimable advantages Christianity has given us; first; the Sabbath, the jubilee of the whole world; whose light dawns welcome alike into the closet of the philosopher, into the garret of toil, and into prison cells, and everywhere suggests, even to the vile, a thought of the dignity of spiritual being. Let it stand forevermore, a temple, which new love, new faith, new sight shall restore to more than its first splendor to mankind. And secondly, the institution of preaching,—the speech of man to men,—essentially the most flexible of all organs, of all forms. What hinders that now, everywhere, in pulpits, in lecture-rooms, in houses, in fields, wherever the invitation of men or your own occasions lead you, you speak the very truth, as your life and conscience teach it, and cheer the waiting, fainting hearts of men with new hope and new revelation.

I look for the hour when that supreme Beauty, which ravished the souls of those Eastern men, and chiefly of those Hebrews, and through their lips spoke oracles to all time, shall speak in the West also. The Hebrew and Greek Scriptures contain immortal sentences, that have been bread of life to millions. But they have no epical integrity; are fragmentary; are not shown in their order to the intellect. I look for the new Teacher, that shall follow so far those shining laws, that he shall see them come full circle; shall see their rounding complete grace; shall see the world to be the mirror of the soul; shall see the identity of the law of gravitation with purity of heart; and shall show that the Ought, that Duty, is one thing with Science, with Beauty, and with Joy.

Source: Ralph Waldo Emerson [Divinity School Address], *An Address Delivered before the Senior Class in Divinity College, Cambridge, Sunday Evening, 15 July, 1838* (Boston: James Munroe, 1838).

Notes

1. Osiris, Egyptian god of fertility.
2. "The world is too much with us" (1806), l. 10, by William Wordsworth.
3. See Acts 26:19.
4. Epaminondas (ca. 410–362 B.C.), statesman and military leader of Thebes.
5. The minister here is Emerson's minister in Concord, the appropriately named Barzillai Frost (1804–1858).
6. The carving of the heavens in the Egyptian temple of Denderah (or Dendera) was cut out by the French and brought to Paris.
7. Puritans, late sixteenth- and early seventeenth-century English reformers noted for their religious and moral earnestness, a number of whom helped settle America.
8. Said by Emerson's wife, Lidian.

9. Zeno (ca. 335–ca. 263 B.C.), Greek founder of the Stoic school of philosophy.
10. John Wesley (1703–1791), one of the founders of Methodism; Johann Friedrich Oberlin (1740–1826), French Lutheran pastor and worker with the poor.
11. André Massena (ca. 1758–1817), French marshal who defended Genoa in 1800.

Andrews Norton

"The New School in Literature and Religion"

(27 August 1838)

NORTON'S RESPONSE to Emerson's address was immediate and furious. Just as he had earlier with Ripley, Norton took the unusual step of writing to a daily newspaper to register his complaints. In addition to associating the "New School" with all sorts of errors and evils, Norton complains that Emerson was allowed to create this fuss at Harvard itself, thus discrediting the institution. Indeed, Emerson was not to be asked back by the university in an official capacity for nearly three decades—and the Divinity students lost the right to invite the speaker for their commencement.

There is a strange state of things existing about us in the literary and religious world, of which none of our larger periodicals has yet taken notice. It is the result of this restless craving for notoriety and excitement, which, in one way or another, is keeping our community in a perpetual stir. It has shown itself, we think, particularly since that foolish woman, Miss Martineau, was among us, and stimulated the vanity of her flatterers by loading them in return with the copper coin of her praise, which they easily believed was as good as gold.[1] She was accustomed to talk about her mission, as if she were a special dispensation of Providence, and they too thought that they must all have their missions, and began to "vaticinate," as one of their number has expressed it. But though her genial warmth may have caused the new school to bud and bloom, it was not planted by her.— It owes its origin in part to ill-understood notions, obtained by blundering through the crabbed and disgusting obscurity of some of the worst German speculatists, which notions, however, have been received by most of its disciples at second hand, through an interpreter. The atheist Shelley has been quoted and commended in a professedly religious work, called the Western Messenger, but he is not, we conceive, to be reckoned among the patriarchs of the sect.[2] But this honor is due to that hasher up of German metaphysics, the Frenchman, Cousin; and, of late, that hyper-Germanized Englishman, Carlyle, has been the great object of admiration and model of style. Cousin and Carlyle indeed seem to have been transformed into idols to be publicly worshipped; the former for his philosophy, and the latter both for his philosophy and his fine writing; while the veiled image of the German pantheist, Schleiermacher, is kept in the sanctuary.[3]

The characteristics of this school are the most extraordinary assumption, united with great ignorance, and incapacity for reasoning. There is indeed a general tendency among its disciples to disavow learning and reasoning as sources of their higher knowledge.—The mind must be its own unassisted teacher. It discerns transcendental truths by immediate vision, and these truths can no more be communicated to another by addressing his understanding, than the power of *clairvoyance* can be given to one not magnetized. They announce themselves as the prophets and priests of a new future, in which all is to be changed, all old opinions done away, and all present forms of society abolished. But by what process this joyful revolution is to be effected as are not told; nor how human happiness and virtue is to be saved from the universal wreck, and regenerated in their Medea's caldron.[4] There are great truths with which they are laboring, but they are unutterable in words to be understood by common minds. To such minds they seem nonsense, oracles as obscure as those of Delphi.[5]

The rejection of reasoning is accompanied with an equal contempt for good taste. All modesty is laid aside. The writer of an article for an obscure periodical, or a religious newspaper, assumes a tone as if he were one of the chosen enlighteners of a dark age.—He continually obtrudes himself upon his reader, and announces his own convictions, as if from their having that character, they were necessarily indisputable.—He floats about magnificently on bladders, which he would have it believed are swelling with ideas.—Common thoughts, sometimes true, oftener false, and "Neutral nonsense, neither false nor true," are exaggerated, and twisted out of shape, and forced into strange connexions, to make them look like some grand and new conception. To produce a more striking effect, our common language is abused; antic tricks are played with it; inversions, exclamations, anomalous combinations of words, unmeaning, but coarse and violent, metaphors abound, and withal a strong infusion of German barbarians. Such is the style of Carlyle, a writer of some talent; for his great deficiency is not in this respect, it is in good sense, good taste and soundness of principle; but a writer, who, through his talents, such as they are, through that sort of buffoonery and affectation of manner which throws the reader off his guard, through the indisputable novelty of his way of writing, and through a somewhat too prevalent taste among us for an over-excited and *convulsionary* style, which we mistake for eloquence, has obtained a degree of fame in this country, very disproportioned to what he enjoys at home, out of the Westminister Review. Carlyle, however, as an original, might be tolerated, if one could forget his admirers and imitators.

The state of things described might seem a matter of no great concern, a mere insurrection of folly, a sort of Jack Cade rebellion;[6] which in the nature of things must soon be put down, if those engaged in it were not gathering confidence from neglect, and had not proceeded to attack principles which are the foundation of human society and human happiness. "Silly women," it has been said, and silly young men, it is to be feared, have been drawn away from their christian faith, if not divorced from all that can properly be called religion. The evil is becoming, for the time, disastrous and alarming; and of this fact there could hardly be a more extraordinary and ill boding evidence, than is afforded by a publication, which has just appeared, entitled an "Address, delivered before the Senior class in Divinity College, Cambridge," upon the occasion of that class taking leave of the Institution, "By Ralph Waldo Emerson."

It is not necessary to remark particularly on this composition. It will be sufficient to state generally, that the author professes to reject all belief in Christianity as a revelation, that he makes a general attack upon the Clergy, on the ground that they preach what he calls "Historical Christianity," and that if he believe in God in the proper sense of the term, which one passage might have led his hearers to suppose, his language elsewhere is very ill-judged and indecorous. But what *his* opinions may be is a matter of minor concern; the main question is how it has happened, that religion has been insulted by the delivery of these opinions in the Chapel of the Divinity College at Cambridge, as the last instruction which those were to receive, who were going forth from it, bearing the name of christian preachers. This is a question in which the community is deeply interested. No one can doubt for a moment of the disgust and strong disapprobation with which it must have been heard by the highly respectable officers of that Institution. They must have felt it not only as an insult to religion, but as personal insult to themselves. But this renders the fact of its having been so delivered only the more remarkable. We can proceed but a step in accounting for it. The preacher was invited to occupy the place he did, not by the officers of the Divinity College, but by the members of the graduating class. These gentlemen, therefore, have become accessories, perhaps innocent accessories, to the commission of a great offence; and the public must be desirous of learning what exculpation or excuse they can offer.

It is difficult to believe that they thought this incoherent rhapsody a specimen of fine writing, that they listened with admiration, for instance, when they were told that the religious sentiment "is myrrh, and storax and chlorine and rosemary;" or that they wondered at the profound views of their present Teacher, when he announced to them that "the new Teacher," for whom he is looking, would "see the identity of the law of gravitation with purity of heart;" or that they had not some suspicion of inconsistency, when a new Teacher was talked of, after it had been declared to them, that religious truth "is an intuition," and "cannot be received at second hand."

But the subject is to be viewed under a far more serious aspect. The words God, Religion, Christianity, have a definite meaning, well understood. They express conceptions and truths of unutterable moment to the present and future happiness of man. We well know how shamefully they have been abused in modern times by infidels and pantheists; but their meaning remains the same; the truths which they express are unchanged and unchangeable. The community know what they require when they ask for a Christian Teacher; and should any one approving the doctrines of this discourse assume that character, he would deceive his hearers; he would be guilty of a practical falsehood for the most paltry of temptations; he would consent to live, a lie, for the sake of being maintained by those whom he had cheated. It is not, however, to be supposed that his vanity would suffer him long to keep his philosophy wholly to himself. This would break out in obscure intimations, ambiguous words, and false and mischievous speculations. But should such preachers abound, and grow confident in their folly, we can hardly overestimate the disastrous effects upon the religious and moral state of the community.

Source: Andrews Norton, "The New School in Literature and Religion," *Boston Daily Advertiser,* 27 August 1838, p. 2.

Notes

1. Harriet Martineau (1802–1876), English novelist and religious and economic writer, had chronicled her trip to the United States (1834–1836) in *Society in America* (1837) and *Retrospect of Western Travel* (1838).
2. Percy Bysshe Shelley (1792–1822), English Romantic poet. Norton refers to "Shelley and Pollok" in the February 1837 *Western Messenger* (3:474–478), a journal espousing Transcendental views in the Ohio Valley, and

edited by William Henry Channing, James Freeman Clarke, and Christopher Pearse Cranch, among others.

3. Friedrich Schleiermacher (1768–1834), German cleric and Protestant theologian.

4. Medea, Greek sorceress who gained immortality for refusing the advances of the god Zeus.

5. Delphi, in Greek mythology, a city with a famous oracle who could predict the future.

6. John (Jack) Cade (d. 1450), leader of a rebellion against the crown and character in Shakespeare's *Henry VI, Part 2*.

Henry Ware, Jr.

The Personality of the Deity

(1838)

HENRY WARE, JR. (1794–1843) was Emerson's predecessor at the Second Church in Boston, and his sermon shortly after Emerson's Divinity School Address is far more measured—and typical—than is Norton's response (which has, unfortunately, been used to characterize the general Unitarian reaction). The day of Emerson's address, Ware wrote him to praise "the lofty ideas and beautiful images of spiritual life" Emerson had presented, although other ideas "appear to me more than doubtful, and . . . would tend to overthrow the authority and influence of Christianity." Emerson's response was typical of the man: while confessing to feeling "pain in saying some things in that place and presence, which I supposed might meet dissent," he "would rather say" to those dissenters, "These things look thus to me; to you otherwise. Let us say out our uttermost word, and be the all-pervading truth, as surely it will, judge between us." And in October, in a letter to Emerson accompanying a copy of his pamphlet, Ware states the reasons for his writing it. While he realizes that others regard it as "controverting some positions taken by you at various times, and was indeed, written partly with a view to them," Ware confesses that "I am not perfectly aware of the precise nature of your opinions on the subject of the discourse," and so he gives his "own views of an important subject, and of the evils which seem to be attendant on a rejection of the established opinions." And in response, Emerson calls himself " 'a chartered libertine,' free to worship and free to rail," and concludes that "you should say your thought, whilst I say mine." This evenhanded intellectual debate would not, alas, extend to the dialogue between Ripley, Norton, and Theodore Parker.

He is the living God and an everlasting king.

—Jeremiah x. 10.

In treating the doctrine respecting God, the mind is deeply impressed with a sense of its importance in its bearing on human duty and happiness. It is the doctrine of a Creator, the Governor and Father of man. The discussion relates not merely to the laws of the universe and the principles by which its affairs are directed, but to the character and dispositions of the Being, who presides over those laws, and by whose will those affairs are determined. It teaches, not only that there is a wise and holy order to which it is for every man's interest to conform; but that that order is ordained and upheld by an active, overruling Intelligence; and that hence virtue is not merely conformity to a rule, but allegiance to a rightful Lawgiver; and happiness not the result merely of obedience to a command, but of affectionate subjection to a Parent.

The importance of this consideration to a true and happy virtue cannot be overestimated. The difference between conformity to a statute and obedience to a father is a difference not to be measured in words, but to be realized in the experience of the soul. It is slightly represented in the difference between the condition of a little child that lives in the presence of a judicious and devoted mother, an object of perpetual affection, and of another that is placed under the charge of a public institution, which knows nothing but a set of rules. Each is alike provided for and governed; but the one enjoys the satisfactions of a trusting and loving heart, while the other, deprived of the natural objects of affection, knows nothing but a life of order and restraint. Take away the Father of the universe, and, though every ordinance remain unchanged, mankind becomes but a company of children in an orphan asylum; clothed, fed, governed, but objects of pity rather than congratulation, because deprived of those resting-places for the affections, without which the soul is not happy.

Our representations of the being and perfections of God are therefore incomplete, until we have taken into consideration the additional view now suggested. The idea of personality must be added to that of natural and moral perfection, in order to obtain the full definition of the Deity. Without this he is but a set of principles or a code of laws. Yet by some philosophers at various times it has been speculatively denied, and by too many in common life it is practically lost sight of. It may be well, then, in connexion with our preceding discussion, to consider a little particularly the doctrine of the Divine Personality; to state what it is; to show the grounds on which it is established; and to survey the evils which must result from a denial of it.

I begin with stating what is meant by the Personality of the Deity.

A *person* is an intelligent, conscious agent; one who thinks, perceives, understands, wills, and acts. What we assert is, that God is such. It is not implied, that any distinct form or shape is necessary to personality. In the case of man, the bodily form is not the person. That form remains after death; but we no longer call it a person, because consciousness and the power of will and of action are gone. The personality resided in them. So also in the case of the Deity; consciousness, and the power of will and of action constitute him a person. Shape, form, or place make no part of the idea.

The evidence of this fact is found in the works of design with which the universe is filled. They imply forethought, plan, wisdom, a designing mind; in other words, an Intelligent Being who devised and executed them. If we suppose, that there is no conscious, intelligent person, we say that there is no plan, no purpose, no design; there is nothing but a set of abstract and unconscious principles. And, strange as it may seem to Christian ears, which have been accustomed to far other expressions of the Divinity, there have been those who maintain this idea; who hold, that the principles which govern the universe constitute the Deity; that power, wisdom, veracity, justice, benevolence, are God; that gravitation, light, electricity, are God. Speculative men have been sometimes fond of this assertion, and in various forms have set up this opposition to the universal sentiment; sometimes with the design of removing the associations of reverence and worship, which make men religious; sometimes under the supposition, that they thereby elevate the mind to a conception of the truth more worthy of its exalted subject. But it will be evident upon a little inquiry, that, in either case, the speculation is inconsistent with just and wholesome doctrine.

1. For, in the first place, one of the most observable and least questionable principles, drawn from our observation of man and nature, is, that the person, the conscious being, is the chief thing, for the sake of which all else is, and subservient to which all principles operate. The person, the conscious, intelligent, active, enjoying, suffering being, is foremost in importance and honor; principles and laws operate for its support, guidance, and well-being; and therefore are secondary. Some of these principles and laws have their origin in the relations which exist amongst intelligent, moral agents; most of them come into action in consequence of the previous existence of those relations. If there were no such agents, there either would be no such principles, or they would have no operation. Thus, for example, veracity, justice, love, are sentiments or obligations which spring up from the relations subsisting between different beings, and can exist only where there

are persons. We may say, indeed, that they exist abstractly, in the nature of things; but, if there be no beings to recognise them, no agents to conform to or violate them, they would be as if they were not. They are qualities of being; and like all qualities have no actual existence independent of the substances in which they inhere. They have relation to acts,—voluntary acts of truth, justice, goodness; and acts belong to persons. If there existed no persons in the universe, but only things, there could be neither the act nor the sentiment of justice, goodness, truth; these are qualities of persons, not of things; of actions, not of substances. Suppose the Deity to exist alone in the universe which he has made. Then, from the conscious enjoyment of his own perfections and the exercise of his power in the physical creation, He must dwell in bliss; but, as he has no relations to other conscious existences, he cannot exercise justice, or truth, or love; they lie in the infinite bosom as if they were not; they have only a contingent existence. But the instant he should *create* various tribes, they spring into actual existence; they no longer may be, they are; they rise out of the new relations which are created, and are the expression of sentiments and duties which had not before been possible.

Or make another supposition. Upon the newly created earth one man is placed alone. He knows no other conscious existence but himself. What are truth, justice, charity, to him? They are nothing to him. He cannot have ideas of them. They are sentiments that belong to certain relations between beings, which relations he does not stand in, and knows nothing of. To him, therefore, they do not exist. Now send him companions, and the relations begin, which give those sentiments birth and make their expression possible. He is in society; and those principles, which make the strength and order of society, immediately come into action. The necessities of conscious being call them forth.

Thus what is chiefest in the universe, is conscious, active mind; abstract principles are but the laws of its various relations.

This may be illustrated, if necessary, from the analogies of the physical universe. Which is chief, the law of gravitation, or the universe which it sustains? The one is but means, the other is end; and the end is always greater than the means. If you say, "No, gravitation is the superior, because it is the universal power of God;" then I reply, "You thereby assent to the superiority of the person over the principle; for, as his power, it is his servant; he controls and directs it." But if you take the other ground, and speak of gravitation as a power independent of any being, then you cannot deny that it exists and is active for the sake of the systems and their inhabitants; operating for their sake, it is their servant and inferior; without them it would be inert and non-existent. Thus the analogy of the physical universe corroborates the position. If there were no material masses, there could be no gravitation; if there were no persons, there could be no truth, or justice, or love.

There is another way of considering this point. What is it, that in the whole history and progress of man has proved most interesting to man? What has been the favorite study, the chief subject of contemplation and care? Has it not been men, persons? Have not their character, fortunes, words, deeds, been the chief themes of thought, of conversation, of letters, of arts? Is it not the interest which the soul takes in persons, that is the foundation of society, of its activity, its inventions, its advancement in civilization, its institutions, its laws? And what is the happiness of human life?—from the moment that the conscious infant opens its eyes to the mother's smile and comes to the perception of her care and love, through all the years of filial and fraternal satisfaction, the confidence of friendship, the delights of love, the endearments of home, and the honors and toils of manhood, until the death-bed of weary age is brightened by the kindness of faithful affection,—what, through the whole, is the happiness of life, but this connexion with kindred beings? Where has the heart rested through all, but on the bosom of those whose personal interests were one with its own? We cannot cast this slightest glance upon life, without perceiving the place which belongs to personality; for, take it away, and the whole of that beautiful scene vanishes; sympathy, friendship, love, all social enjoyment, all social life, are annihilated.

Thus the doctrine, which denies personality to God, is in opposition to the general economy of nature, which, as we have seen, sets peculiar honor on persons. In all the other relations of its being, the soul is concerned with nothing so much. Why should it be less so in its highest relation?

2. It also, in the next place, amounts to a virtual denial of God. Indeed, this is the only sense in which it seems possible to make that denial. No one thinks of denying the existence of principles and laws. Gravitation, order, cause and effect, truth, benevolence,—no one denies that these exist; and, if these constitute the Deity, he has not been, and cannot be, denied. The only denial possible is by this exclusion of a personal existence. There can be no atheism but this; and this is atheism. If the material universe rests on the laws of attraction, affinity, heat, motion, still all of them together are no Deity; if the moral universe is founded on the principles of righteousness, truth, love, neither are these the Deity. There must be some Being to put in action these principles, to exercise these attributes. To call the principles and the attributes *God*, is to violate the established use of language, and confound the common apprehensions of mankind. It is in

vain to hope by so doing to escape the charge of atheism; there is no other atheism conceivable. There is a personal God, or there is none.

We reason in this case, as in that of a man. Man was made in the image of God. But when we have described so much power, wisdom, goodness, so much beauty, justice, truth, love, we have not described a man; the very essential element is wanting; without adding personality, we may speak of these qualities for ever, and they will not make a man. So, too, we may enlarge them infinitely, but unless we add personality, they will never make up the idea of God.

3. Further; to exclude personality from the idea of God, is, in effect, to destroy the object of worship, and thus to annihilate that essential duty of religion. The sentiment of reverence may, undoubtedly, be felt for a principle, for a code of laws, for an institution of government. But worship, which is the expression of that sentiment, is applicable only to a conscious being; as all the language and customs of men signify. It is praise, thanks, honor, and petition, addressed to one who can hear and reply. If there be no such one,—if the government of the world be at the disposal of unconscious power and self-executing law,—then there can be no such thing as worship.

Let this be seriously considered. What a desolation is wrought in society and in the soul, when the foundation of worship is thus taken away. It is the suppression of a chief instinct; it is the overthrow of a system which has always made an inseparable part of the social order, and in which human character and happiness are intimately concerned. The relation of man, in his weakness and wants, to a kindred spirit infinitely ready to aid him, of the insufficient child of earth to a watchful Father in heaven, is destroyed. There remains no mind higher than my own, which is knowing to my desires; there is no Parent above, to whom my affections can rise and find peace. I am left to myself, and to men as weak as myself. If, following the impulses of my heart and the example of good men, I call on One who cares for me and will bless,—I am driven back, and my heart is chilled by the reply, "The power that is over all sustains and guides, but, having no personality, it cannot appreciate affection, nor give it back in return; be satisfied to reverence and submit." And so the filial spirit is mocked;— as if the little child, with its full heart, longing for the embrace of its absent mother, should be told, "That mother is but an idea, not a person; you may think of her, but you can have no intercourse with her; be satisfied with this." And this poor substitute for the dearest of the heart's inestimable privileges, is what philosophy would impose on man in the place of a sympathizing Father!

We must not consent to the injustice which is thus done to the affections. What an instinct is in them, and how they yearn for something to love and trust, is taught us in all the religious history of the race. From this cause men so multiplied their divinities, that, from amid that great diversity, every variety of human soul might find its want of sympathy supplied. Hence, too, in the Catholic church, the worship of the Virgin; because, in the love for that beautiful and spotless person, was found a gratification that the heart is always seeking. And yet, in the face of this great instinct of humanity, everywhere manifested, Philosophy steps forth, and insists that the soul is to be satisfied with abstractions. As if human nature were any thing, without its affections! as if a man were a man, without his heart! as if to deny and baffle them, were not to pour bitterness into the very fountain of the soul's peace! And this is done, whenever man is made to believe, that the altar at which he kneels is consecrated to a set of principles, and not to a "Living God."

4. In the next place, this notion removes the sense of responsibility, and so puts in jeopardy the virtue of man, as we have just seen that it trifles with his happiness. The idea of responsibility implies some one, to whom we are responsible, and who has a right to treat us according to our fidelity. We indeed sometimes use the word with a little different application; we say that a man is responsible to his country, to posterity, to the cause of truth; but this is plainly employing the word in a secondary sense; it is not the original, literal signification. We hear it said, also, that a man is responsible to his own conscience; and this is sometimes spoken of as the most solemn responsibility. In one point of view, justly; since it is responsibility to that person, whose disapprobation is nearest to us, and whose awards are of the highest consequence to our peace. We are not, therefore, to speak lightly of the tribunal within the breast. But why is it terrible? Because it is thought to represent and foreshadow the decisions of the higher tribunal of God. Let a man believe that it is ultimate, and he can learn to brave it; and how many accordingly have hardened themselves against it, and persevered in sin, as if it were not! Or let him think that the retributions of guilt are simply the accomplishment of natural laws, which go on mechanically to execute themselves, unattended by any sentiment of approbation or disapprobation, and he can, without great difficulty, defy them. They do not address his moral sensibility. This is the case with the improvident, the miserly, the intemperate; they are perfectly aware that grievous ill consequences will pursue their folly, yet they are not restrained thereby; if they have a mind to risk them, whose concern is it? they will judge for themselves what makes their happiness. But, if they had been made sensible to the disapprobation of a Living Father, if they had realized that

the sentence against their iniquities was to be executed by Him to whom they owe every thing, then they would have paused in their bad career.

And this is agreeable to what takes place under our daily observation. What could not be effected by all the experience of evils following in the natural train of events, has, in thousands of instances, been at once brought about by the powerful thought of the Divine Being, who observes and judges. Many a man, long familiar with crime, who had been only exasperated and hardened by the natural consequences which plagued him in his pursuit, has been touched, alarmed, subdued, converted, by coming to the knowledge of that Gracious Sovereign, who holds all destiny in his hands, and who sent his Son to bring his wayward children home. It is idle to talk to men in general of responsibility, without directing them to the Being to whom the account is to be rendered. It is the thought of the Living Lawgiver and Judge, which affects them,—of one whose displeasure they can dread, whose good opinion they can value, whose favor they perceive to be life. And herein is perceived the wisdom of the gospel of Christ, herein is found its efficacy,—that, casting aside all such abstractions, it appeals wholly to the relations of conscious beings, and subdues, and reforms, and blesses, by drawing the human soul to the soul of its Saviour and its God.

5. If now we pass to the declarations of the divine word, we find that the doctrine we are opposing stands in direct contradiction to the whole language and teaching of the Old and the New Testaments. Those volumes speak of God, uniformly and distinctly, as possessed of personal attributes. They so describe his perfections and his government, they so recite his words and his acts, they so assign to him the relations and titles of the Creator, King, Lawgiver, Father,—that no reader could so much as dream that his name is used simply to express the principles and laws of the universe. To fancy it, is to make Scripture unintelligible, and set at naught its express authority. Until language changes its meaning, and all description is falsified, the doctrine of the Divine Impersonality is a direct contradiction of the doctrine of revelation.

6. Further still, it destroys the possibility of a revelation, in any intelligible sense of the word. A revelation is a message, or a direct communication, from the Infinite mind to the human mind. But in order to do this, there is required a conscious and individual action on the part of the communicator; and this implies personality. So that this doctrine virtually accuses the Scriptures of imposture, since they purport to contain a revelation from God, which in the nature of

things is impossible. Nay, let us see the worst of it;—it accuses the apostles of Christ, and the blessed Saviour himself, of deliberate fraud and imposition; since they and he declared, with the most solemn asseverations, that he was directly sent by God, the Father of mankind, when, if there be no such Being, but only certain principles and laws, he could not have been sent by him. Their language in that case is altogether deceptive. It seems to mean one thing, when it really means something quite the reverse. When Jesus declares again and again, that he came from the Father and speaks his word, he does not intend what the words assert, but only what is equally true, in a degree, of all men. He was merely giving utterance to thoughts poured into his mind by the everlasting stream which flows into all minds. There was nothing special in his case, excepting, that, as he was purer and better than other men, his thoughts were higher and purer. They were from God in the same sense in which any man's thoughts are from God,—Plato's, Mahomet's, Luther's; they have the same authority; that is, no authority beyond what lies in their own evident truth; the doctrine of Plato or Mahomet, of Luther or Confucius, is just as divine, and just as authoritative, if it but recommend itself as strongly to my mind; and a holy thought of Fenelon or Swedenborg is as truly a divine revelation, as the gospel of Christ. This is the result at which the doctrine arrives. It destroys the possibility of a revelation in any sense which makes it peculiar and valuable, by making all truth a revelation, and all men revealers. It takes away all special divinity and authority from the Gospel, reduces it to a level with any other wisdom, and thus robs it of its power over the earth. Its pure and holy author becomes a pretender; for he professed to be sent from God, and to bring his message; he worshipped him, and spake of holding continual personal intercourse with him; and by such means he gained a hearing and an influence among men,—gained them, however, only by deceiving the world, if there be, after all, no personal God.

By thus tracking this doctrine through its various bearings and observing its tendencies, we come to a clear discernment of its falseness and mischievousness. We see, that it opposes what is taught in nature by all the marks of design which cover the works of creation;—it sets aside the fundamental fact, that conscious, intelligent being, in its various relations, is the chief interest of the universe, for the sake of which every thing else is;—it is a virtual denial of God, and a consequent overthrow of worship and devotion;—it injures happiness by taking from the affections their highest object, and virtue by enfeebling the sense of responsibility;—it contradicts the express lessons of the Bible, excludes the possibility of a revelation in any proper sense of the word, and denies to the Gospel its right to authority and power.

Of course, it will not happen, that all these disastrous consequences will follow from this doctrine in the case of every individual who may receive it. To the pure all things are pure; and some men will dwell for ever in the midst of abstraction and falsehood without being injuriously affected. Express infidelity is not vice, and may exist together with great integrity and purity of life. Atheism is not immorality, and may consist with an unblemished character. But, however it may be with individuals, living in the midst of a believing and worshipping community, it is not to be doubted that a community, unbelieving and godless, would rush to evil unmitigated and hopeless. A philosopher here and there, by his science and skill, might perhaps live without the sun; but, strike it out from the path of all men, and despair and death ensue.

On this subject, then, we are first to look for the truth, and then at the consequences of denying it. And those consequences, we are to remember, may flow as certainly from a practical disregard of it, as from a speculative rejection. It is possible by the mouth to profess God, and in works to deny him. The number of those, who can be misled by the ingenuity of an imaginative mind, is comparatively small; but the world is crowded with those who become aliens from God through the hardening influences of a worldly career, while they fancy themselves to know and acknowledge him as he is. On this account, the views of the present discourse ask the serious regard of all men. For who can doubt, that, among the causes which produce in society so much moral and religious deadness, this is one;—that men satisfy themselves with referring to the laws and principles of nature, and stop short of that Being in whom they reside? How much is this a habit amongst us! We talk of the "laws of our being," and of living by them, and of the consequences of violating them, as we should talk of a machine or of fate. We thus throw out of view the agency and love of the Living God, whose children we are, and claim relationship to inanimate abstractions. According to the common phrase, we stop at second causes. And in so doing, we not only wrong the truth, which is thus denied, but defraud ourselves of that exercise and enjoyment of the thinking, affectionate spirit, in which our highest action and bliss are to be found. This ought not so to be. And, until men come more to realize the presence and the authority of the Living Father, who governs them now, and who will judge them in the end, it is vain to hope for any wider prevalence of elevated piety or of happy devotion to duty.

Source: Henry Ware, Jr., *The Personality of the Deity. A Sermon, Preached in the Chapel of Harvard University, September 23, 1838* (Boston: James Munroe, 1838). The Ware-Emerson correspondence is quoted from John Ware, *Memoir of the Life of Henry Ware, Jr.* (Boston: James Munroe, 1846), pp. 394–399.

"Levi Blodgett" [*Theodore Parker*]

The Previous Question between Mr. Andrews Norton and His Alumni Moved and Handled, in a Letter to All Those Gentlemen

(1840)

IF EMERSON AND WARE engaged in civilized dialogue about their philosophical and ecclesiastical differences, then two old adversaries, Norton and Ripley, did not. As had happened with their differences over Martineau's book in 1836, they now engaged each other over issues of authority, interpretation, and philosophy in a series of five pamphlets containing over five hundred pages of densely argued (and annotated) theological matters. Norton fired the opening salvo with his response to Emerson's Divinity School Address, delivered, appropriately, on the same occasion as Emerson had spoken, though this time the speaker was not invited by the students, as his title makes clear: *A Discourse on the Latest Form of Infidelity, Delivered at the Request of the Association of the Alumni of the Cambridge Theological School, on the 19th of July, 1839* (1839). Norton's argument was simple: "Nothing is left that can be called Christianity, if its miraculous character be denied." In reply, Ripley published *"The Latest Form of Infidelity" Examined. A Letter to Mr. Andrews Norton, Occasioned by His "Discourse Before the Association of the Alumni of the Cambridge Theological School," on the 19th of July, 1839* (1839), arguing for a more open and free intellectual inquiry. The pamphlet war continued, with the arguments and titles being quite predictable: Norton's *Remarks on a Pamphlet Entitled "The Latest Form of Infidelity Examined"* (1839) and Ripley's *Defence of "The Latest Form of Infidelity" Examined. A Second Letter to Mr. Andrews Norton, Occasioned by His Defence of A Discourse on "The Latest Form of Infidelity"* (1840) and *Defence of "The Latest Form of Infidelity" Examined. A Third Letter to Mr. Andrews Norton, Occasioned by His Defence of A Discourse on "The Latest Form of Infidelity"* (1840). Ripley even reprinted all three of his pamphlets in a single volume, *Letters on the Latest Form of Infidelity, Including a View of the Opinions of Spinoza, Schleiermacher, and De Wette* (1840). All of this discussion was rapidly getting away from Emerson's main points about the "corpse-cold Unitarianism" that denied its parishioners a satisfactory inner life. Ripley was, in a sense, playing into Norton's hands by trying to argue with him on his own grounds, formal religious study. What was needed was for someone else to pick up where Emerson had left off, with a challenge to the establishment that lay people could read and comprehend. Theodore Parker was that person.

Parker (1810–1860) was a self-educated farmer's son who attended classes at Harvard without paying tuition because he was so poor. One of the brightest, wittiest, best writers among the Transcendentalists, he also had a fine sense of audience. Entering the battle under the pseudonym of "Levi Blodgett," Parker, in a brief space, summarizes the debate, articulates its major points, and comes down hard against Norton in language everyone could understand. Rather than fight the theological battle over the existence of miracles, Parker admits "I believe that Jesus, like other religious teachers, wrought miracles," but, he continues, "I see not how a miracle proves a doctrine and I even conjecture we do not value him for the miracles; but the miracles for him." And even though he fights learned allusion with learned allusion, Parker democratizes the whole issue by stating, "with the unlearned, like myself, this miracle-question is one of *theology*, and not of *religion*."

GENTLEMEN,

If the subjects you are debating concerned simply the two respectable persons who alone, as yet, have taken part in the discussion, the public would not have listened to their words; nor should I have troubled your wisdom with this letter. But the matter before you is one of wide and deep concernment, which affects the whole community. You therefore, I doubt not, will pardon a plain man for addressing a few words, to your respectful consideration. The humble style, and perhaps uncouth phraseology of my letter, I trust, you will candidly excuse, when I assure you that "ower much o' my life has been spent at the plough, and ower little at the college or the schule." I am but an obscure man; my name, I think, is strange to your ears. But I have interests at issue which depend on the question you are debating.

Our age, Gentlemen, as Mr. Norton so acutely remarks, is one of movement and transition. Great questions which the world had previously passed upon and settled, come up to receive a new solution. "Terrible questions," as some one says, "are raised by human Reason,"[1] and matters taken for granted hitherto, or decided by authority that is merely personal, now solicit re-judgment, by which, in some cases, it seems likely that former decisions may be set aside. I perceive by the Pamphlets of Mr. Norton and his Alumnus, that several questions are now before you, which these two gentlemen are discussing in a manner, scholarlike in some measure, and able no doubt; but not in the most scientific manner, as I look at the thing. But this is the fault of the circumstances which led to the discussion, and is by no means a reproach to either party; especially if we consider how little scientific discussion on theological and religious subjects has hitherto taken place in this country. But I can make no pretensions to discuss *scientifically* such lofty matters; I wish only to offer a few thoughts in my own homely way.

If I understand the Pamphlets of Mr. Norton and his Alumnus, there are now two subjects before you, which have grown incidentally out of the discussion on the latest form of Infidelity.

I. There is the great vital question, *Do men believe in Christianity* SOLELY *on the ground of miracles?* I say SOLELY, for unless miracles are held to be the sole ground of accepting it, the question is only one of the more or less; and therefore is of little theological importance, since it concerns individual experience alone, and is not to be settled by theological science, but by the personal biography of each Christian. To decide upon the sole evidence of the Christian Religion, Christianity, as it is conceived of in the mind, must be subjected to a rigid analysis, whereby its truths shall be separated from the evidence on which those truths are accepted. This evidence must then itself be analyzed into its essential and accidental constituent parts; and, if I understand the matter, one party says by the test of his philosophy and experience, the ultimate result of the last analysis, will be miracles: while the other separates miracles as something adventitious, and regards them as foreign substances, by no means a necessary ingredient of that evidence, and still less the very essence of it. The truth itself is its own evidence, the Alumnus would say, and God's truth can not be made more obligatory or effective by any miracles; still less does it derive its sanction from them.

II. The next is a *literary question*, which "parteth itself into four heads," that relate respectively to the theological character of Spinoza, Schleiermacher, and De Wette, and some errors, supposed or real, about translating.[2] The last is a pedagogical question, to be passed upon by linguists; and might well enough, I reckon, be postponed indefinitely, or laid before a bench of schoolmasters for decision. It seems a pity that our Salmasius and Milton should quarrel, even amicably, about parts of speech.[3] The historical and literary question respecting the distinguished scholars above named, is one which does not much concern the church or the community, wherein Mr. Norton says "there is no controlling power of intellect," which alone can settle that question. It is a pity these men should attract the discussion, out of its proper channel, to themselves. If they were respectively atheists, disbelievers in the personality of God, and the miracles of the New Testament, they are certainly not the only atheists and disbelievers, and perhaps are not the worst. I take it, few Christians would solicit a comparison with these three men; I do not mean in respect to sharp-sightedness, or insight into matters of philosophy and theology, but in respect to a Christian life. Now if their lives were the natural result of their principles and sentiments, as they must have been, if a corrupt tree cannot bring forth good fruit; I would say God send us more such men, and may their influence extend wide and deep. But perhaps we are misinformed as to the character of these men, though it is hardly a common vice to exaggerate the virtues of men we do not agree with. But why should this literary question be discussed, before the public are ready for it? The works of these gentlemen are but little known among us. I take it for granted that one party in this debate had never read the chief works of Spinoza before this controversy began; and the other thinks not ten persons in the neighborhood had read them. The works of the two other scholars are but little read in this country, as the booksellers tell me. Even the language is not much known, for I take it they are written in German, and have not been translated except a few fragments published in Reviews. Now books cannot do much harm unless they are read. I should think, therefore, Gentlemen, that it would be as well to drop this subject also, until other matters more pressing shall first be despatched.

Gentlemen, I will now venture to recall your attention to the first subject, THE SOLE EVIDENCE OF CHRISTIANITY; the only subject of real moment. But since this matter is embarrassed with difficulties not easily removed, I will put forth a few thoughts on the PREVIOUS QUESTION, which I think must be decided before we touch the evidence of Christianity. This previous question is as follows: How DO MEN COME TO HAVE ANY RELIGION, or, in other words, *on what evidence do they receive the plainest religious truths?* Gentlemen, we must settle the *genus*, before we decide upon the *species*. The evidence for religious truths in *general*, I take it, cannot be different in *kind*, from the evidence for the *special* religious truths of Christianity. For as all religions contain some truths—on which alone they rest—that are identical with some truths in Christianity, and therefore not hostile to that religion, for one truth can never be hostile to another, inasmuch as God's kingdom is not divided against itself; and since religious belief and conviction are, substantially, the same thing in all minds, Heathen or Christian, so it follows incontestably, that there must be the same *kind* of evidence to induce belief and conviction in both cases, as men's minds and hearts are at bottom the same. I do not see how there can be two *kinds* of evidence, any more than two kinds of *right*; but you, Gentlemen, are learned, and can settle difficulties that puzzle simple folks. However, there may be different *quantities* of evidence in the two cases, as the quantity of *truth* may differ in two religions, or the quantity of religious *belief* and *conviction* in two individuals of the same or of different religions.

Now *on what evidence do men admit the primary and essential truths of all religions?* Among these primary truths, I take it, are A BELIEF IN THE EXISTENCE OF GOD, and A SENSE OF DEPENDENCE ON HIM. I call these *primary* and *essential* truths, because without them I cannot conceive any religion possible. I reckon that man is by nature a religious being; i.e. that he was made to be religious, as much as an ox was made to eat grass. The germs of religion, then, both the germs of religious principle and religious sentiment, must be born in man, or innate, as our preacher says. *The existence of God* is a fact given in our nature: it is not something discovered by a process of reasoning; by a long series of deductions from facts; nor yet is it the last generalization from phenomena observed in the universe of mind or matter. But it is a truth fundamental in our nature; given outright by God; a truth which comes to light as soon as self-consciousness begins. Still further, I take a *sense of dependence on God*, to be a natural and essential sentiment of the soul, as much as feeling, seeing, and hearing, are natural sensations of the body. Here, then, are the religious instincts which lead man to God and religion, just as naturally, as the intellectual instincts lead him to truth, and animal instincts to his food. Here, then, is a correspondence between the nature of man, and the nature of the whole universe wherewith one becomes acquainted. As there is light for the eye; sound for the ear; food for the palate; friends for the affections; beauty for the imagination; truth for the reason; duty for conscience, so there is God for the religious sentiment, or sense of dependence on Him. Now all these presuppose one another; as a want essential to the structure of man's mind or body, presupposes something to satisfy it. And as the sensation of hunger presupposes food to satisfy it, so the sense of dependence on God, presupposes his existence and character; though from this sense, taken in its philosophical nakedness, the unity of God, could not, perhaps, be inferred, and certainly the personality; or impersonality of God would in no wise follow.

Now I shall attempt to prove the existence of a religious nature, and also the existence of these two primary and essential truths of religion in man.

1. *Negatively, by an argument fetched* for *the logical absurdity involved* in the opposite doctrine that man has *not* a religious nature, or has not the primary truths of religion innate in him. I take it for granted on all hands, that religion is needed for the harmonious growth and welfare of man; that without it this life would be, as somebody says,

"poor, and brutish, and nasty, and short;"[4] that without God and religion, man's better nature, his higher reason, and spiritual powers, would be what the eye would become without light, the ear without sound, and the affection without friends. Now it is absurd to suppose God should create man thus dependent on God and on religion, and not give him power in himself to become perfectly assured in his own heart, of the existence of God, and his sustaining power on which we may depend. It is no more absurd and revolting to suppose that in some other part of the universe he has created an order of beings, with a man's appetite for food, but with no powers of procuring that food. All animals are perfectly suited by their natures, to the sphere they move in, and it is absurd, and even impious, to suppose man is an exception to this law, and that while instincts supply his perishing body, there are no similar, but higher instincts to supply his undying soul.

2. The existence of these truths, and this religious nature, may be shown philosophically *by an analysis of the powers of the soul*. You find the *belief in God* as an indestructible element of the human soul. You come back to this fact as you examine and analyze any faculty of our nature. Take the tendency to seek for a cause in the effect; it leads straight to the supreme or absolute Cause, a knowledge of which is presupposed as the foundation of all finite causes. Take the sense of the Beautiful; you come to the idea and archetype of infinite Loveliness, the altogether-Beautiful. Take the moral emotions, you come immediately to the eternal Right as it speaks through Conscience. Take the affections, you return to him who is Love. Thus in these, and in all other departments of the soul (so to say), you come back to the primal Truth; the light of all our being; to God. And you see the truth of the statement, "In him we live and move and have our being."

Analyze the religious feelings, hopes, and opinions as they now exist in you; separate whatever is not essential to the idea of religion; what is merely individual and peculiar to yourself or your sect, and you come back to a *sense of dependence on God* as the ultimate result of the last analysis. This you find given in the soul. Man feels that he is poor, and weak, and blind, and naked, and admits the truth, "without Thee we can do nothing, and are nothing." I do not say this sense of dependence would lead you to a *personal* God. It will not disclose to you the nature of God; more than the eye discloses the nature of light; the ear that of sound; or the hand that of matter. A knowledge of the nature of God is not more essential to religion, than a knowledge of the nature of light, sound, and matter, is essential to seeing, hearing, or touching. The hand discovers to you something that resists its touch; this sense of dependence discovers to you something on which you must, and may depend, but what in the one case resists, and in the other supports, neither the hand, nor this sense of dependence can, in any wise, discover to you.

3. The same thing may be proved experimentally, *by an argument fetched from history.* You find no nation, civilized or savage, which does not admit the existence of God, and the sense of dependence upon Him. This fact is so notorious, that I shall present no proofs thereof to "learned clerks" like yourselves. It would not be necessary to prove it, even to simple folks like my own companions and neighbors. The only exceptions to this belief are *professed atheists*;—but this exception disturbs no one, it only confirms the rule,—and *men who grow up in perfect seclusion* from all human beings. The latter, I will admit, give no indication of possessing the idea of God, or the sense of dependence on Him. But any argument hostile to my position, derived from this source, is met by the *statement*, that these germs are probably there, only they have never had those social influences, which are the necessary occasions of awakening them and the germs of other high faculties of the soul. The subsequent history of these wretched persons, proves the truth of the *statement*. Such an argument is repelled by the *fact*, that these men neither laugh nor speak articulate language, and yet no one contends, from that circumstance, that the tendency to laugh and speak is not innate in man, though dependent on certain conditions and occasions for its active development.

I am well aware, Gentlemen, that some of you will say in opposition to this argument, that a miraculous revelation of the primary and essential truths of religion was made to man from without, and through the senses, by his Creator, at an early period of the world, which revelation has been propagated by tradition, ever since. Now when historical evidence of the fact, antecedently so improbable, is laid before me, it will be soon enough to point out the fault which vitiates and destroys your whole argument, viz., that such a revelation from without could not be made to man and received by him, except on the supposition that these germs were innate. An outward revelation could only be the *occasion* of manifesting these germs, and not the cause of religion in man. It cannot be the creation of a new element in man; as it must be if these germs are not already in him—it could only be the awakening of an element, that still slept.

Now the progress and development of religion in man, I take it, is after this wise: the religious instincts, which ally us to God,—like the animal instincts, which connect us with matter—must needs display themselves in action, as the other higher faculties of man come into full life. The various objects of nature, and events of life, and intercourse of man with man, furnish an occasion for weakening all the faculties. In a rude society religion will have but a low development, and assume a rude form. As the tribe or race improves, the manifestations of religion become more perfect. The form changes to suit the culture of the age. Of course various forms of worship, or "systems of religion," will prevail, corresponding to the peculiarities of the race, its character, condition and culture.

Such being the origin of religion in man, it is advanced as other human interests are. At the head of all departments of human thought, or interest, stand individuals, who are in some measure the concrete type of that interest. Thus for example, in Legislation there are Minos and Moses; Homer in Poetry; Phidias in Sculpture; and in later times Raphael, Mozart, Bacon, and Newton in their respective spheres.[5] All the great interests of mankind are carried forward by distinguished individuals. In the humbler affairs of agriculture, war, and politics, these individuals are numerous, for many will enter a department which lies level to the wishes and abilities of the many. But in the higher regions of human thought, these guides and types are less numerous and of a nobler stature. This rule holds good in Poetry and Philosophy. Mankind has many leaders in war, and but few great creative artists, and profound philosophers, because many can fight, and but few exercise the creative imagination, or think profoundly. Now as the religious interest is the very highest possible interest of man, he must expect fewer leaders and types in this, than in any other department of human concern. There are an hundred warriors who rule over the body by force, to one philosopher who rules in the mind by thought; and perhaps an hundred such to one creative, original, religious teacher, who rules through the heart by his superior holiness and faith; by his clearer vision of divine things which comes of his more complete obedience to "the law of the Spirit of life."

Now these original religious teachers do not derive their authority or their truths from themselves. The higher we ascend in human interests, the less is there of personal, and the more of divine authority. The religious teachers confess they derive their truths from God, and come not of themselves. Now I take it, all men have two *direct* channels of communication with God, viz., Conscience and the religious Sentiment, that is, the moral and religious powers of man; his two highest and most permanent faculties, which are not accidental, but essential and of course immortal. I call them channels of *direct* communication with God, because I can find nothing interposed between Conscience and God, or between Him and the religious Sentiment; we border closely upon God every where; here we touch and he interpenetrates us, if I may so speak. Conscience and the religious Sentiment, I reckon, are to the soul, what the ear and the eye are to the body. One reveals the moral law; the other the Beauty of Holiness, and excellency of Divine Things. We have besides numerous *indirect* ways of communicating with God; the Senses lead to Him through sensible things; the Understanding through effects; the Imagination through beautiful objects; and the Affections through friends. Here the communication is mediate, as in the other it is without mediators; these two streams of moral and religious Truth flow direct from God, the primitive fountain of all Rectitude and Holiness. Now in most men, these two channels, to continue the figure, are obstructed by sensuality and sinfulness. Not one man in a myriad has his conscience so active as his eye. Few deem it trustworthy, like the ear, or the hand. Not one in a million perhaps has his religious Sentiment so active and efficient as the bodily senses. Consequently these men, though they may know much of the outer world, of things seen and handled; though they may understand their laws, and *use*, and perhaps sometimes catch a glimpse of their *meaning* likewise, can know little of the vast world of moral and religious Truth; little of God. Their Deity is "a God afar off;" whose very existence is a matter of reasoning and inference, of which they can never be quite certain. Their sense of duty is weak; their consciousness of God is feeble. Their confidence in duty and religion therefore, on common occasions, cannot be relied on; yet by a beautiful characteristic of our nature, in times of peril, this degraded religious Sentiment will sometimes arise, assert its right and support the man who has so long been false thereto.

Now as these guides of mankind, in Poetry, War, Philosophy, Music or the Arts, were men, highly gifted by God with powers for their several callings, which powers they improved by use, and sharpened by intense love of their vocation,—so in religious interests, the guides of our race are men highly gifted by God at the first, who obey the fundamental law of their nature, and not only have indirect communication with God, through natural objects, but immediate connection through these two channels, which they have never closed up, by their sensuality and sin. These men move religion forward and upwards, as humbler geniuses promote and elevate humbler interests. These men create new religions and make religious epochs. They are enlightened directly from God, for the religious sentiment and conscience, "his greater and lesser light," shine straight into them. It is no figure of speech to say these men are inspired. They speak from this divine inspiration to the souls of men, and souls obey; at first slowly and reluctant, at last with servile homage and prostrate adoration. There is so much divine in them—viewed from the stand of the world.— that it is said they cannot be men, so they are confounded with Divinity itself. Hence these men are deemed gods, and so become objects of worship. Their influence on the world is immense; far greater than that of chieftains or sages. They turn a deep, wide furrow through the stubborn soil of human selfishness and sin, and wholesome grains, and heavenly flowers, and living groves mark where their name has passed. You find such men at the beginning of each religious epoch. But though inspired, their inspiration is no more strange and out of the way, than that of the Poet or the Painter, the Philosopher, or the Artist; it is only higher, and greater in degree, and more intense in its action. Yet though possessed of a greater measure of inspiration than other great souls, like them, they are not perfectly above all that is national, local, temporary, or even personal to themselves. Religious truth is imparted to men gradually as they are able to bear it. Absolute truth and absolute religion are not for men who are subject to the various peculiarities of their nation, place and age, and to their own idiosyncracies. Now as these latter perpetually change, the old form of religion, unable to change with them, gradually becomes obsolete. A new teacher of religion arises; starts from a higher stand and separating the peculiarities of the old form which adapted it to its age, climate and nation—constructs a new form suitable to the altered condition of mankind, which shall, for its season, carry forward the good work, until "in the fulness of time," it gives place to somewhat higher and better.

Now mankind obeys these teachers because it sees and feels the truth they bring, and the superiority of their gifts, for these men say what others would gladly say, but cannot. The divinity of an inspired and original religious teacher is seen and appreciated as men see and appreciate the superior talents of Alexander or Hannibal.[6] It required no miracle to convince the centurion or the common soldier, that Cæsar was a greater man than himself and possessed more martial skill. It required no miracle to teach the warblers of Ionia or Thebes that Homer or Pindar sang sweeter than they.[7] Now as in these cases, men judge in their own minds of the poetic power, and military prowess of Homer and Cæsar, requiring no foreign proof thereof, nor dreaming of any lest, but the works of those men; so in the case of a religious teacher men listen to Zoroaster, or Budha, or Fo, feeling the superiority of these men, and believing the truth which is offered, as a part of their birth-right too long kept from them.[8]

But there is still a further consideration to be attended to. It may be said "these religious teachers pretended to work miracles." I would not deny that they *did* work miracles. If a man is obedient to the law of his mind, conscience and heart, since his intellect, character and affections are in harmony with the laws of God, I take it, he can do works, that are impossible to others who have not been so faithful, and consequently are not "one with God" as he is; and this is all that is meant by a miracle. But while this must be admitted, both as a logical conclusion and a historical fact—for without it we cannot account for the wide-spread belief in such miracles, that does not spring out of dreams or lies, which, themselves, would require explanation likewise—I must confess myself unable to determine the kind, or the number of miraculous acts performed by any one of these religious teachers. The miraculous power of Zoroaster and Elijah, has doubtless been exaggerated;[9] for men whose senses are more active than their souls, find it more easy to cite a visible and monstrous fact as evidence of a man's superiority, than trust to the less tangible fact of his superior character, more celestial sentiments and thoughts. Hence legends, (or *mythi*—I think the learned called them) relating the acts of a religious teacher, increase in number, and marvellousness, in proportion to the sensuality of the people where they originate, or in proportion to their ignorance of the facts of the case. The histories of Zoroaster offer a good illustration of this statement, which is proved true also by the difference between the canonical gospels, and apocryphal writings, which latter originated in a later age, and among a people more ignorant of the facts of Christ's life. Now the possession of this miraculous power, when it can be proved as I look at the thing, is only a *sign* (which may be uncertain) of the superior genius of a religious teacher, or a *sign* that he will utter the truth, and never a *proof* thereof. Consequently, it offers no more valid evidence of the excellence of a religion, than it would offer for the excellence of a poem or philosophy.

Religion—thus *caused* by the innate germs thereof, in the soul: thus *occasioned* by the outer world; thus *promoted* by inspired men,—when active and powerful in the community, affects the various faculties of the soul. It possesses the understanding and forms a creed; the fancy and creates a legendary tale; the moral sense and consciousness of sin, and produces rites. It affects the heart and forms a symbol.

Now if such is the origin, and growth of religion in general, we may perhaps apply these results to the special case of Christianity. Gentlemen, Christianity is one religion among several others. One species of a numerous class. It must therefore agree in some features with all other religions with the grossest worship of nature, and the most refined deism; otherwise it might be *Christianity*, but could not be religion, for I hold it to be granted that there can be but one *kind* of religion, though it may exist in various degrees of purity and intensity, and under the most various forms. Thus there is but one kind of *water*, though it may be more or less pure as it is less or more combined with foreign matter, and in different places, may exist in various quantities, and in various forms, as frozen to ice, or sublimated to an invisible vapor. Now I reckon true Christianity to be the highest form of religion. The Christianity of the church is, gentlemen—you know better than I what the Christianity of the church is,—what is the average morality and religion of the community, and therefore of the church, which only subsists by representing and slightly idealizing that average morality and religion. But the Christianity of Christ is the purest, the most intense, and perfect religion ever realized on earth. I say *realized* for it was realized in its archetype and founder, though perhaps never since then. I will not say it is absolute religion—and therefore that Christ is the ultimate incarnation of God, for I cannot measure the counsels of the Infinite. I have not *"firm* footing in the clouds," as some pretend to have. But for myself, I can conceive of no higher religion than Christianity, as I understand it. I do not mean the Christianity of Calvin or Luther; of the Unitarians or the Quakers; of Paul, James or Peter or John, all of which are obviously one-sided and in part false—but the Christianity of Jesus. I can conceive of no man who shall more fully represent the moral and religious side of our nature; none who shall receive more fully direct religious and moral inspiration from God, and therefore no more perfect moral and religious incarnation of God than Jesus of Nazareth. Therefore I can assent to Paul's statement, "In him dwelleth all the fulness of the Godhead." Supposing that Paul did not mean to say Jesus represented any but the moral and religious side of our nature. Homer is a type of poetry; Socrates of thought, and in their several departments they surpass Jesus, who was neither a poet nor a philosopher. God creates the "perfect man" fractionally, and we can only construct the pure ideal of man, historically, by selecting the essential attributes from many celestial souls. It was from five hundred fair maidens that Phidias sought absolute loveliness, and formed his eclectic statue of ideal beauty. But even if some man should be created in the full measure of perfect humanity—and should unite the poetic, philosophic, artistic, political and religious archetypes in himself he would, it is true, be a more perfect incarnation of God than Jesus was; for the sum-total of his being would be greater and equally pure; but yet he would not be a more perfect manifestation or incarnation of ideal moral and religious excellence than Jesus. Of course he could not reveal a more perfect religion, as I take it. But I would not insist on this conclusion, where it is so easy to make mistakes.

I am content, in the rest of this letter, to take it for granted that Christianity is absolute religion; perfect religion; the sentiment and the principle; the harmony of morality and religion, united and made life. It is religion not limited by creeds, legends, rites or symbols, for though there is in the Christianity of the church somewhat liturgical, legendary, ritual and symbolic, yet it is not essential to Christianity itself, and is to spiritual men like you, no doubt, a help and not an incumbrance.

Now since all religion in general starts from the germs and primary essential truths of religion, which are innate with man: since it is promoted by religious geniuses who, inspired by God, appeal to these innate germs and truths, in man; since all religions are fundamentally the same, and only specific variations of one and the same genus and since, therefore Christianity is one religion among many, though it is the highest, and even a perfect religion—it follows incontestably that Christianity also must start from these same points. Accordingly we find history verifying philosophy, for Christ always assumes these great facts, viz. the existence of God, and man's sense of dependence upon him, as facts given in man's nature. He attempted to excite in man a more living consciousness of these truths, and to give them a permanent influence on the whole character and life. His words were attended to, just as the words of Homer or Socrates, and the works of Phidias or Mozart were attended to. But admiration for his character, and the influence of his doctrines, was immeasurably greater than in their case because he stood in the very highest department of human interest, and spoke of matters more concerning than poetry or philosophy, sculpture or music. Now, if he assumed as already self-evident and undoubted, these two primary and essential truths of religion, which had likewise been assumed by all his predecessors—and if no miracle was needed to attest and give authority to his doctrines respecting those very foundations and essentials of religion, no man can consistently demand a miracle as a proof that Christ spoke the truth when he taught doctrines of infinitely less importance, which were themselves unavoidable conclusions from these two admitted truths. Gentlemen, I am told by my minister, who is an argumentative man, it is a maxim in logic, that what is true of the genus, is true also of the species. If, therefore, the two fundamentals of religion, which in themselves involve all necessary subordinate truths thereof, be assumed by Christ as self-evident, already acknowledged, and therefore at no time, and least of all at that time, requiring a miracle to substantiate them, I see not how it can be maintained, that a miracle was needed to establish inferior truths that necessarily followed from them. It would be absurd to suppose a miracle needed on the part of Socrates, to convince men that he uttered the truth, since no miracle could be a *direct* proof of that fact; and still more absurd would it be, while the most sublime doctrines, as soon as he affirmed them, were admitted as self-evident, to demand miraculous proofs for the truth of the legitimate and necessary deductions therefrom.

Still further, Gentlemen, Christianity is either the perfection of a religion whose germs and first truths are innate in the soul, or it is the perfection of a religion whose germs and first truths are not innate in the soul. If we take the latter alternative, I admit, that, following the common opinion, miracles would be necessary to establish the divine authority of the mediator of this religion; for devout men measuring the new doctrines by reason, conscience, and the religious sentiment—the only standard within their reach—and finding this doctrine contrary and repugnant thereto, must, of necessity, repel this religion, because it was unnatural, unsatisfactory, and useless to them. To open my meaning a little more fully by an illustration,—should a man present to my eyes a figure as the Ideal of Beauty, if that figure revolted my taste; were repugnant to my sense of harmony in outline, and symmetry of parts, I should say it could not be so; but if he had satisfactory credentials to convince me that he came direct from God, and to prove that this figure was indeed the Ideal of Beauty to the archangels, who had an æsthetic constitution more perfect than that of men, and therefore understood beauty better than I could do, I should admit the fact; but must, in that case, reject his Ideal Beauty, because it was the Ideal of Deformity, relatively, to my sense, inasmuch as it was repugnant to the first principles of human taste. Now if a religion whose germs and first truths are not innate in man, should be presented by a mediator furnished with credentials of his divine office, that are satisfactory to all men, the religion must yet be rejected. The religion must be made for man's religious nature, as much as the shoe must be made for the foot. God has laid the foundation of religion in man, and the religion built up in man must correspond to that foundation, otherwise it can be of no more use to him than St. Anthony's sermon was to the fishes.[10] There was nothing in the fishes to receive the doctrine. But if we take the other alternative, and admit that Christianity is the perfection of a religion whose germs and first truths are innate in man, and confessed to be so, by him who brings, and those who accept the religion, I see no need, or even any use of miracles, to prove the authority of this mediator. To illustrate as before; if some one brings me an image, as the Ideal of Beauty, and that image correspond to my idea of the Beautiful, though it rise never so much above it, I ask no external fact to convince me of the beauty of the image, or the authority of him who brings it. I have all the evidence of its excellent beauty that I need or wish for; all that is possible. If Raphael had wrought miracles, his works would have had no more value than now, for their value depends on no foreign authority; but on their corresponding to ideal excellence.

But, besides, miracles in either alternative are exceedingly weak arguments; yet if they have that constraining influence some of you often claim for them, their authenticating power is unlimited; and must, in all cases, constrain an eye-witness to believe the miracle-worker is a divine messenger, and all his words are truth. Now I will put a case: Suppose a miracle-worker should assure a large audience in Boston, that it was a moral duty to lie, steal, and kill; and, at their request, as proof of his divinity, and the truth of his doctrines, should feed that large audience to satiety, with a single loaf of bread; would they believe the new doctrine in opposition to conscience, reason, and religion? If they did thus believe, the fact would only prove that their senses were more active than their souls; for, as things visible are judged of by the eye, things to be tasted by the palate, and things audible by the ear, just so what is addressed to the spiritual powers, must be proved and accepted by the spiritual powers, and not by the senses. To make my eye, ear, or palate, evidence of the divinity of a man, or the truth of a doctrine, is like setting the eye to judge sounds, and the ear colors. In the case supposed, if men believe, their assent would be forced, not voluntary, and therefore of no value, such a mediator must belittle his auditors before he can bless them. But if we take the accounts of the Bible, the most stupendous miracles of Moses and Jesus, had no influence to constrain belief, for their witnesses did not seem to know what a miracle could prove.

Gentlemen, I believe that Jesus, like other religious teachers, wrought miracles. I should come to this conclusion, even if the Evangelists did not claim them for him; nay, I should admit that his miracles would be more numerous and extraordinary, more benevolent in character and motive, than the miracles of his predecessors. This would naturally follow, if his power and obedience were more perfect than theirs. But I see not how a miracle proves a doctrine, and I even conjecture we do not value him for the miracles; but the miracles for him. I take it no one would think much of his common miracles, if they were not wrought by the God-man. The divine character of Christ gives value to the miracles, which cannot give divinity to Christ, or even prove it is there, as I take it; for many Christians believed Apollonius of Tyana wrought miracles, but they placed no value on them, because they had little respect for Apollonius of Tyana himself.[11] The miracles of the Greek mythology, seem to have had no influence on the mind of the nation, because no great life lay at the bottom of these miracles. The same may be said of the miracles of the middle ages, and even of more modern times. We say these were not real miracles, and the saying is perhaps true, for the most part, but to such as believed them, they were just as good as true; yet their effect was trifling, because there was no great soul which worked these miracles. It may be said these differ in character from the Christian miracles, and the saying has its side of truth, if only the canonical miracles are included; but it is not true if the other miracles of Christian tradition are taken into the account, for here malicious miracles are sometimes ascribed to him. But men found comfort in these stories only because they believed in the divinity of the character which lay at the bottom of the Christian movement.

Now, Gentlemen, if there are no *antecedent* objections to Christ's possessing miraculous powers, there are some historical difficulties in the way of establishing *all* the miracles which he wrought. I allow there is a vein of the miraculous pervading human history; now and then it comes to light, perhaps even now-a-days. Without this admission, I cannot account for the almost universal belief, that miracles have been wrought, and especially by religious teachers. But it is a difficult matter to establish a particular miracle. A miracle, I suppose has two limits; the one is *the utmost verge of unassisted human ability*, the other is the *divine creative power*, which cannot, I reckon, be imparted to finite beings who have free-will. Now both of these limits are vague; exceedingly shadowy; it is perfectly impossible for me to fix them in speculation or practice. But since I can think of no more convenient limits, I will admit that all is a miracle which lies between these two extremes. But, as observations must not be made on the stars when pretty close to the horizon, I will be careful not to notice such acts as approach near the common powers of benevolent and cultivated men. A miracle, then, is a voluntary act, lying any where between these bounds, and if there is any meaning in the three words by which my old minister tells me miracles are called in the New Testament, they are fitted to excite *wonder*, to display unusual *power*, and are a *sign* of the character of the miracle-worker. Yet I take it they are not a proof the character is divine, for the serpent wrought the *first* miracle on record in the Bible, and Peter's shadow the *last*, I believe, not to mention Balaam's ass, the magicians in Egypt, and the exorcists in Christ's time, who had miraculous powers as Dr. Barnes thinks.[12]

Gentlemen, I reckon it would be difficult to prove in a court of justice the reality of any one of the miracles ascribed to Jesus in the Gospels, with the exception of his resurrection, a miracle which he seems to have had no hand in bringing about; a miracle which was the corner stone of Paul's preaching, and of the Christian church. This, then, is not Christ's miracle, but God's act. There are several difficulties which hinder you from proving the reality of particular miracles.

1. There is the tendency to the marvellous in all ancient nations, especially among the Jews, before and after the time of Christ. They never separated the true from the false; the common from the preter-natural, I think; they did it least of all in the history of sacred persons. 2. The Epistles of the New Testament, though older than the Gospels, as you tell us, only mention the miracles in a general way; and but very rarely, only two or three times, at the outside, as I read it. They mention no particular miracles. If Paul had known Lazarus and two others were raised from the dead, would he have called Christ the "first fruits of them that slept?" He would rather, I reckon, mention these cases to prove a resurrection, and it is quite certain, if he had thought a belief in miracles so *necessary and essential*, he would have taken pains to spread the knowledge thereof in his Epistles, and would have charged Timothy to preach the miracles, as well as the crucifixion and resurrection. I take it a church might be Christian which believed only a single one of his ecclesiastical epistles, wherein no miracle, save the resurrection, is insisted on or mentioned. 3. The authority of the Evangelists is not quite satisfactory; not that they designed to tell what was false, for their sincerity is plain as the sun at noon-day—but they might be mistaken. Their inspiration did not free them from the notions of the age and nation; from wrong judgments, or their own temperaments. Gentlemen, one of your number, a scholar universally esteemed, whose talents and learning are respected, I doubt not, by his opponent in this controversy, has rejected several passages of the Gospels, as neither genuine nor authentic, and thinks, further, that some other passages are not strictly historical. I have read in some religious papers that a German critic—Dr. Strauss I think—has explained a great deal of the New Testament into *Mythi*, as the papers called them, which had no foundation in fact.[13] I do not like that Hebrew word, but thought long ago there was something legendary and romantic in the stories of Christ's birth, early life, and ascension to heaven. You would all admit this to one another, I reckon. Now these considerations would in some measure weaken the evidence of the Evangelists as to any one particular case of miracles, but would not detract from their moral character, or diminish the probability that Jesus worked miracles, though we cannot tell what they were. In saying this, I do not express any doubt on my own part of the *general* accuracy of their history of Christ, at least during his ministry.

Now, since these things are so, it seems to me much easier, more natural, and above all more true, to ground Christianity on the truth of its doctrines, and its sufficiency to satisfy all the moral and religious wants of man in the highest conceivable state, than to rest it on miracles, which, at best, could only be a sign and not a proof of its excellence, and which, beside, do themselves require much more evidence to convince man of their truth, than Christianity requires without them. To me, the spiritual elevation of Jesus is a more convincing proof of his divinity, than the story of his miraculous transfiguration; and the words which he uttered, and the life which he lived, are more satisfactory evidence of his divine authority, than all his miracles, from the transformation of water into wine, to the resurrection of Lazarus. I take him to be the most perfect religious incarnation of God, without putting his birth on the same level with that of Hercules. I see the story of his supernatural conception, as a picture of the belief in the early Christian church, and find the divine character in the general instructions and heavenly life of Christ. I need no miracle to convince me that the sun shines, and just as little do I need a miracle to convince me of the divinity of Jesus and his doctrines, to which a miracle, as I look at it, can add just nothing. Even the miracle of the resurrection does not prove the immortality of the soul.

Gentlemen, I would say a word to that portion of your number who rest Christianity solely, or chiefly on the miracles. I would earnestly deprecate your theology. Happily, with the unlearned, like myself, this miracle-question is one of *theology*, and not of *religion*, which latter may, and does exist, under the most imperfect and vicious theology. But do you wish that we should rest our theology and religion—for you make it a religious question—on ground so insecure? on a basis which every scoffer may shake, if he cannot shake down—a basis which you acknowledge to be insecure when other religions claim to rest on it, and one from which your own teachers are continually separating fragments? To the mass of Christians, who are taught to repose their faith on miracles, those of the Old are as good as those of the New Testament, both of which are insecure. One of your number, a man not to be named without respect for his talents, his learning, and, above all, for his conscientious piety, a man whom it delights me to praise, though from afar—at one blow, of his Academic Lectures, fells to the ground all the most stupendous miracles of the Old Testament; and another, a party in this contest, has long ago removed several miracles from the text of the New Testament, and thrown discredit—unconsciously—upon the rest. If the groundwork of Christianity is thus to be left at the mercy of scoffers, or scholars and critics, who decide by principles that are often arbitrary, and must be uncertain, what are we the unlearned, who have little time for investigating such matters—and to whom Latin schools and colleges have not opened their hospitable doors—what are we to do? You tell us that we must not fall back on the germs and first truths of religion in the soul. You tell us that Christ *"established a relation between man and God, that could not otherwise exist,"* and the ONLY proof that this relation is *real*, and that he had authority to establish it, is found in the particular miracles he wrought, which miracles cannot, at this day, be *proved* real. Thus you repel us from the belief that the relation between God and man is founded in the nature of things, and was established at our creation, and that the authority of Christianity is not personal with Jesus, but rests on the eternal nature of Truth. Thus you make us rest our moral and religious faith, for time and eternity, on evidence too weak to be trusted in a trifling case that comes before a common court of justice. You make our religion depend entirely on something outside, on strange events which happened, it is said, two thousand years ago, of which we can never be certain, and on which yourselves often doubt, at least of the more and less. Gentlemen, we cannot be critics, but we would be Christians. If you strike away a part of the Bible, and deny—what philosophy must deny—the perfect literal truth of the first chapter of Genesis, or the book of Jonah, or any part which claims to be literally true, and is not literally true, for us you have destroyed all value in miracles as evidence—exclusive and irrefragable—for the truth of Christianity. Gentlemen, with us, Christianity is not a thing of speculation, but a matter of life, and I beseech you, in behalf of numbers of my fellows, pious and unlearned as myself, to do one of two things, either to prove that the miraculous stories in the Bible are perfectly true, that is, that there is nothing fictitious or legendary from Genesis to Revelations, which yet professes to be historical, and that the authors of the Bible were never mistaken as to facts or judgments thereon; or leave us to ground our belief in Christianity on its truth,—which is obvious to every spiritual eye that is open,—on its fitness to satisfy our wants; on its power to regenerate and restore degraded and fallen man; on our faith in Christ, which depends not on his birth, or ascension; on his miraculous powers of healing, creating, or transforming; but on his words of truth and holiness: on his divine life; on the undisputed fact that he was ONE WITH GOD. Until you do one of these things, we shall mourn in our hearts, and repeat the old petition "God save Christianity from its friends, its enemies we care not for." You may give us your miracles, and tell us they are sufficient witness, but hungering and thirsting, we shall look unto Christ, and say, "Lord, to whom shall we go, Thou only hast the words of everlasting life," and we believe on Thee, for thy words and life proclaim themselves divine, and these no man can take from us.

> I remain, Gentlemen,
> with deep respect
> your affectionate servant,
> LEVI BLODGETT.

Source: "Levi Blodgett" [Theodore Parker], *The Previous Question between Mr. Andrews Norton and His Alumni Moved and Handled, in a Letter to All Those Gentlemen* (Boston: Weeks, Jordan, 1840). Norton's pamphlets were published in Cambridge by John Owen, Ripley's in Boston by James Munroe.

Notes

1. "Let us descend from this fanciful region: pitiless reason knocks at the door; her terrible questions demand a reply" appears in the introduction to *System of Economical Contradictions; or, The Philosophy of Misery* (1888), by Pierre-Joseph Prudhon (1809–1865), French radical socialist.
2. Wilhelm Martin Leberecht De Wette (1780–1845), German theologian and biblical critic.
3. Claudius Salmasius (1588–1653), French classical scholar, defended the monarchy in England and was attacked by Milton, who supported the anti-royalists. Here, Parker is referring to Ripley (Milton) and Norton (Salmasius).
4. Quoted from *Leviathan* (1651), by Thomas Hobbes (1588–1679), English philosopher.
5. Minos, legendary ruler of Crete; Phidias (ca. 500–ca. 430 B.C.), Greek sculptor; Wolfgang Amadeus Mozart (1756–1791), Austrian composer.
6. Alexander the Great of Macedon (356–323 B.C.), conqueror of the known civilized world; Hannibal (247–ca. 183 B.C.), Carthaginian general who attacked Italy by crossing the Alps.
7. Ionia, a Greek city in what is now the Anatolian area of Turkey, home to a number of Greek philosophers; Thebes, capital of ancient Egypt.
8. Fo, the Chinese name for Buddha.
9. Zoroaster was thought connected with many occult events; Elijah's victory over the prophets of Baal is one of the biblical events in which he participated.
10. St. Anthony of Padua (1195–1231), Italian Franciscan friar and patron of the poor. After preaching the gospel to heretics who would not listen to him, he went out and preached instead to the fishes.
11. Apollonius of Tyana, first-century legendary Roman figure who was supposed to have performed miracles.

12. This is described in Acts 5:15; Balaam's ass and its meeting with an Angel of the Lord is in Numbers 22:21–33; possibly Robert Barnes (1495–1540), English cleric and reformer.

13. David Friedrich Strauss (1808–1874), German philosopher and theologian.

[*Elizabeth Palmer Peabody*]

[Woman], from "The Conversations of Margaret Fuller"

(1840)

SARAH MARGARET FULLER (1810–1850) was the most important woman in the Transcendentalist movement. An intellectual, teacher, conversationalist, editor, feminist, author, translator, and social critic, she went on from Boston to New York in 1844, where she was the literary critic for the *New-York Tribune*, and then to Europe, ending in Italy, where she participated in the Revolution of 1848, as well as met her future husband, Giovanni Ossoli. When she returned to America in 1850 with her husband and son, their ship went aground off Fire Island, New York, and all perished. The *Memoirs of Margaret Fuller Ossoli* (1852), written and compiled by William Henry Channing, James Freeman Clarke, and Emerson, is a classic example of a woman's life being refashioned for gendered reasons, as the editors created a "Margaret" who was more religiously orthodox and socially acceptable than they perceived the real Fuller to be.

Fuller's lifelong commitment to education was in part due to her father's desire that she be educated as well as any male child of the time, and in part to her early belief that one of the few roles open to her as an educated woman was to be a teacher. She did teach briefly in Providence, Rhode Island, and assisted Alcott at the Temple School, but she soon discovered that teaching could occur beyond the confines of a classroom. She began holding "conversations" for women, and she became a published author, serving as editor of the *Dial* from 1840 to 1842 and finishing her great feminist work, *Woman in the Nineteenth Century*, in 1845. As she wrote a participant in her Conversations in 1839, her goal was to "systematize thought and give a precision in which our sex are so deficient, chiefly, I think because they have so few inducements to test and classify what they receive." Unfortunately, conversations are ephemeral by nature, and there are few first-hand accounts reporting them, even though Fuller gave twice-yearly series from 1839 to 1844. The best-known account, Caroline Dall's *Margaret and Her Friends* (1895), is atypical in that it documents a series at which men were admitted, and the men tended to dominate, both because of their own proclivities and because they often did not feel that women were worth listening to. However, this account, thought to be kept by Elizabeth Peabody, shows Fuller's conversational technique at work, and has the added virtue of reporting a conversation on "Woman," the subject of both Fuller's book and a paper at the meetings by Sophia Ripley, which she later revised for publication in the *Dial*, and which is printed later in this anthology.

\|\|/

Miss Fuller's 16th conversation took place a week ago—& I do not know whether I can remember much of it. The articles read were on woman & the first one was very good indeed, & described a beautiful woman, quite an ideal. The subject of the conversation was woman—but I can remember little of it. There seemed to be a general agreement that women were not systematically enough cultivated, & that they feared to trust their own thoughts on the subject lest they should be wounded in heart. Some one suggested that it was the frivolous women & not men who objected to woman's culture.[1] Another thought men feared for the loss of what was peculiarly feminine in women. Mrs Hoar of Concord who was present, thought that men desired that women should have knowledge, courage, reason, all those things which are called masculine qualities, provided they do not interfere with gentleness, docility, & other charming traits.[2] That it was the absence of the latter, not the presence of the former which was deprecated by men. Miss Fuller asked what was the distinction of feminine & masculine when applied to character & mind, that there was such a distinction was evident or we should not say 'a masculine woman', &c. Ellen Hooper thought women were instinctive—they had spontaneously what men have by study reflection & induction.[3] Another remarked that this had been said to be the distinction of poets among men. Another said that this would confirm Coleridge's remark that every man of great poetical genius had something feminine in his face.[4]

Miss Fuller thought that the man & the woman had each every faculty & element of mind—but that they were combined in different proportions. That this was proved by the praise implied in the expressions "a courageous woman—a thoughtful woman—a reasonable woman." & on the other hand by the praise which we bestowed on men who to courage—intellect &c. added tenderness &c. &c.— Could there be such a woman as Napoleon? was asked. Queen Elizabeth— Catherine II & Lady Macbeth were spoken of[5]— Maryann Jackson asked if there could be such a man as Corinne.[6] Miss F thought Tasso was such a man, & characterised him in a wonderful manner[7]— I wish I could remember it. Ellen suggested that the ideal woman of a fine man would perhaps give us light Miss Fuller said we had these in literature, & proposed we shd. seek them out. She characterised Dante admirably, & then sketched Beatrice[8]—

Miss Fuller's 17th conversation began with reading the articles upon the intellectual differences between men & women.— The first made the difference to consist in the fineness & delicacy of organization— the greater openness to impressions—&c. Margaret remarked that this made no essential difference—it was only more or less. Ellen Hooper asked if the difference of organization were not essential—if it did not begin in the mind—& if this was not the author's idea? Margaret looked again & thought it was—but still said that she did not find that the author made any quality belong to the one mind that did not belong to the other— Ellen asked if she thought that there was any quality in the masculine or in the feminine mind that did not belong to the other— Margaret said no—she did not—& therefore she wished to see if the others fully admitted this. Because if all admitted it, it would follow of course that we should hear no more of repressing or subduing faculties because they were not fit for women to cultivate. She desired that whatever faculty we felt to be moving within us, that we should consider a principle of our perfection, & cultivate it accordingly.— & not excuse ourselves from any duty on the ground that we had not the intellectual powers for it; that it was not for women to do, on *an intellectual ground*— Some farther remarks were made on the point of the want of objectiveness of woman, as the cause of her not giving herself to the fine arts. It was also attributed to her want of isolation. The physical inconveniences of sculpture, architecture & even of painting were adverted to— But why not music & poetry? Miss Fuller said it had troubled her to think there was no great musical composer among women. It is true that at the period of life when men gave themselves to their pursuit most women became mothers—but there were some women who never married. I suggested that these too often spent the rest of their lives in mourning over this fact—& society spoke so uniformly of woman as more respectable for being married—that it was long before she entirely despaired. This caused some lively talk all round—& Margaret averred that there came a time however when every one *must give up*. I might have answered that then it was but too common for youth to be past—& the mind to have wedded itself to that mediocrity, which is too commonly the result of disappointed hope, especially if hopes are not the highest.—

The second piece that was read spoke of the subtlety of woman's mind. Miss Fuller summed it up after she had finished it, with the words— Woman more pervasive— Man more prominent.— While speaking of this piece the question came up whether Brutus' great action could have been performed by a woman.[9] It was decided that if there were no doubt about the duty in Brutus' case there could be none about the duty being obligatory on a woman who had the same general office; else the moral nature could not be the same in man & woman. A great deal of talk arose here—and Margaret repelled the sentimentalism that took away woman's moral power of performing stern duty. In answer to one thing she said that as soon as we began to calculate our condition & to make allowances for it, we sank into the depths of sentimentalism. And again— Nothing I hate to hear of so much as *woman's lot*. I wish I never could hear that word *lot*. Something must be wrong where there is a universal lamentation. Youth ought not to be mourned—for it ought to be replaced with something better.— Miss F. then read her own piece as she said that otherwise she should say every thing that was in it, which would make it duller when it came— It was a constant contrast of man & woman— Man had more genius—woman more taste— Man more determination of purpose—woman more delicacy of rejection— Man more versatility—woman more power of adaptation. Maryann Jackson disputed the proposition that woman had less genius—*as woman*. Is it not so? said Miss Fuller— Is not man's intellect the fire caught from heaven—woman's the flower called forth from earth by the ray? Mrs Park—Anna Shaw—Ellen Hooper seemed inclined also to doubt this proposition[10]— Somewhere here Margaret defined *taste* the reasoning of beauty—& woman the interpreter of genius.

Then came Sally Gardner's piece of which Miss Fuller remarked that it was the aspiration which is prophecy, and all seemed charmed with it & spoke of its beautiful composition.[11] Here it is.

"I recognise between man & woman a necessary difference of position, of which the results are accidental or arbitrary. It was founded, in the origin of society, on the difference of physical strength, when materials were scanty & the labour which procured & made them available was all-important. The first lyrics, doubtless among the earliest mental efforts, celebrated the deeds of the strongest. The first Epics sung "arms & the men" who wielded them.[12] Now we vastly overrate the progress we have made since those early times. Still *might* makes *right* & other remnants of barbarism linger amongst us. The thousand forms by which we write as in hieroglyphics, our present characters, are far enough from showing that harmonious development of the faculties of which we sometimes read the prophecy in our own souls. Let men & women be gentle & firm; brave & tender; instinctive but confirming their instincts by reason; let judgment & taste exercise their selecting & rejecting power among the stores of imagination & fancy; let reflection preserve women from folly; the stern "I ought" produce in them a concentration of intellectual effort, forbid the apathy & self-indulgence which their physical constitution induces, & bind on them the necessity to use, cultivate, elevate all that self-consciousness reveals to them, let them listen to their heart's dictates not fearing that they will lead them astray & we shall no longer hear of masculine women or effeminate men.   Scattered up & down in the world's history there are women who have set aside the accidents of position, & left their mark on the ages. Some of them in whom was an imperfect moral development were guided only by a strong will; in others a holy purpose inspired noble deeds. These instances are not so rare as to be a sort of lusus naturae,[13] they prove that reflection & the power of concentration which predominate in men exist in women, and only require a more earnest culture. And what if our necessary position our proper sphere prevents the production of the Epic & the Drama, influence in the Council or the Camp—how we do know that in the possible future woman's intellect may not manifest itself in forms beautiful as poetry & art, permanent as empires, all emanating from her home—created out of it, from her relations as daughter, sister, wife, & mother? Out of these relations may yet rise a beauty & a power which shall bless & heal the nations. Then the progress of the race will be harmonious & universal; the Hebrew seer said truly, "Men shall learn war no more."[14]

Miss Fuller's 18th conversation was also upon women—there not having been time enough to read all the articles before. She began with saying that she had looked over all the remaining pieces & should read a few of them. She remarked that she was delighted with the elevation of thought in all. All spoke of men & women as equally souls—none seemed to regard men as animals & women as plants. This caused a general laugh, & she repeated seriously that she constantly heard people talk as if men were only animals & women were only plants— That men were made to get a living—to eat & drink—and women to be ornaments of society—as if these were the ultimate aims of being. Parents in educating their sons had in view as the main objects, that they should be able to make money, to eat & dress with more refinement than others—& so on—& that their daughters should be graceful pretty accomplished—& *have a good time.* In neither case did we hear of the perfect unfolding of the faculties as the indispensable or primary object. She said that a lady of high cultivation whom she had known, who was 60 years old, and had lived in cultivated society, expressed to her the wish that she had not had the powers to think & feel—that she had not thought & felt. This was in her view wishing for annihilation— Because thought & feeling had given her pain, she wished not to be! She told her she thought it was the basest thing she had ever heard said—that it was denying the immortality of the Soul—or what was worse *refusing* it—it was denying Christianity—for Christianity was nothing if it did not teach that discipline to a worthy end was the final cause of thought & feeling— Views must be essentially wrong when *being* became a burden— When one could feel able to say & hope for sympathy in saying that thought & feeling were an evil. These false views haunted society with regard to women.— or else mothers & fathers would not wish to repress or annihilate faculties—as a means of making their daughters happier—a thing we constantly saw— We constantly heard that it was not well to cultivate this or that faculty—because in the boy's case it would not contribute especially & certainly to his worldly success—& in the girl's case because it might make her discontented as a woman.— Miss Fuller thought it *impious* thus to speak of the gifts of God—the immortal gifts of God—as if we had a right to tamper with them—as if they were not to be received gratefully—to be held as the most precious trust— & to be cultivated— Whatever worldly disadvantages— whatever temporary sufferings their cultivation might involve—

Ellen Hooper asked if she did not think that it was the duty of a man in the first place to support himself—if he ought not to be impressed with the idea from the beginning that he must make for himself a place, so far at least as not to be dependent— If this independence on outward support with respect to his physical being was not essential to our idea of a man? Miss Fuller replied that a perfect man would of course do this—but that she was struck continually with this recurring fact in society—that those who failed *in the other* were comparatively never censured—those who failed in this were irrevocably condemned— Morally speaking she should prefer to see her son unthrifty—to seeing him unspiritual. She was no friend to unthrift—but if her son were a Poet—she should wish him to cultivate the divine gift though it would inevitably keep him poor always—& ever to sacrifice the outward, when one of the two was necessarily to be sacrificed— Mrs H. said she knew of a man reputed to be of the highest genius, who to indulge this, neglected & was very indifferent to the comforts of his family, who lived on charity that it was hard for his wife to receive from conscientious feelings—& who having borrowed of every body who would lend, till he was deeply in debt, yet remained insensible to debts as such, & made something of a parade of his serenity & spiritual elevation above all such things.[15]— Miss Fuller said, to be indifferent to riches, even the smallest degree, was another thing from being indifferent to debt— The case she mentioned was an instance of moral monstrosity—an absolute deficiency of the sense of Justice— Such irregular moral developments ought not to be confounded with the cases she had in view—even though they might occur in persons of genius—they occurred also in persons of no genius—

I asked Miss Fuller if she did not think there was an illusion also in the idea that women of genius suffered so out of proportion to women who were ordinary— Supposing we had the history of the latter should we not find that *small faculties* involved evils & suffering such as we were apt to forget— Was not Mr Emerson's expression, the "tragedy of *limitation*" true to experience— There might be something in that, Miss Fuller thought—but she declared the belief that if women *wanted to have a good time* as the *first thing*, they must ignore their higher faculties. Thought & feeling brought exquisite pleasures—pleasures *worth* infinite sacrifices—but they inevitably brought sufferings— The Idea of Perfection in a world of Imperfection must expose the one who had it to pain— But this pain was of value—it quickened thought & feeling to deeper & higher discoveries— The young soul true to itself, desired—*demanded* in its unfolding the *Universe*—it wanted to reform society—to know every thing—to beautify every thing & to have a perfect friend— It could not in this world have or do any of this— This it soon began to see—& then it yielded & sunk, & assimilated itself to what was—called the imperfect Perfect—till it lost the idea of perfection—narrowed its desire till it believed its small circle was the universe—*Or*—it remained faithful to itself—suffered all the pains of deprivation—& disappointment—again & again—& for the forever of this world—but abandoned never those innate immortal truths by which all things were made unsatisfactory. Yet it did not mourn & weep forever—it triumphed—it accepted the limitation & the imperfect friend as they were, & never doubting that the first duty is to preserve a trust in the Ideal, waited—enjoyed what there is, & trusted that it *may* be what it is not— Then all the signatures of the future & immortal will be appreciated; then that which limits & corrupts it, will not limit or corrupt us— Then suffering itself becomes the pledge of immortality—that word on every lip, but whose *meaning* is the rarest thought in minds.—(These were some of her best thoughts—but imperfectly given, for they came out in conversation, not in one long speech)— She said besides that she did not love *pain*—nor should it ever be *coaxed*—but always triumphed over— Yet it must be acknowledged & accepted & allowed to act so as to be met by thought & feeling—Those who had not suffered had not *lived as yet*. The happiness that was worth any thing was not that which arose out of ignorance of evil—or of shuffling it aside or turning the back on it—but out of looking it in the face—accepting it—suffering it—yet feeling it was *finite* before the infinite Soul.— Much more was said—

Extract from S. W. R.'s (Mrs. Geo. Ripley?) article on Woman[16]— "Men do not ridicule or expose to suffering the woman who aspires— It is her own sex who brand her—the weak & frivolous of her own sex—but the enigma still remains unsolved—why are so many of the sex weak & frivolous? The minor perplexities & cares of life thronging the path of woman demand as much reflection clear sightedness & energy; & involve as much responsibility as those of man. Why is she not encouraged to think & penetrate through the external to principle? I would see her, after the first dream-like years of childhood are passed, meekly & reverently questioning & encouraged to question the opinions of others—calmly contemplating & encouraged to contemplate beauty in all its forms— Studying the harmony of life as well as of outward nature, deciding nothing—learning all things—gradually forming her own ideal which like that represented in the sculptured figures of the old Persian sovereigns, should protectingly & cheeringly hover over her. Society will attract her—& then gracefully mingling in it she should still be herself—& should find there her relaxation, not her home. She should feel that our best hours are always our lonely ones, & that nothing is good that does not prepare us for these. Beautiful & graceful forms should come to her as revelations of the divine beauty, but no charm of outward grace should tempt her to recede one hair's breadth from her *uncompromising demand* for the noblest nature in her chosen companion. If here she finds all her nature craves & her taste demands, let her not lean but attend upon him as a watchful friend. Her individuality should be as precious as her[17] love. Let her see that the best our most sympathising friend can do for us is to throw a genial atmosphere around us & strew our path with golden opportunities— But our path can never be another's & we must always walk alone. Let no drudgery degrade her high vocation as creator of a happy home—household order must prevail, but let her ennoble it by detecting its relation to that law which keeps the planets in their course. Every new relation—every new scene—should be to her a new page in the book of life, reverently, perhaps lovingly perused, but if folded down not to be read again—regarded as the introduction to a brighter one— The faults of those she loves should never be veiled by her affection, but placed in their true relation to character by the deep insight with which she penetrates beneath them— With high heroic courage she should measure the strength of the enemy *Suffering* before he comes, that she may not meet him unprepared.

Her life plan should be stern, but not unyielding. Thought should be her atmosphere—books her food—friends her occasional solace— The brightest sunshine of prosperity will not intoxicate her—for her own spirit is always brighter—& if the deepest sorrow visit her, it shall only come to lift her to a higher region where with all of life far, far beneath her, she may sit regally apart till the end."

Source: [Elizabeth Palmer Peabody], [Woman], from "The Conversations of Margaret Fuller," in Nancy Craig Simmons, "Margaret Fuller's Boston Conversations: The 1839–1840 Series," *Studies in the American Renaissance 1994*, ed. Joel Myerson (Charlottesville: University Press of Virginia, 1994), pp. 214–219. Many of the notes here are adapted from Simmons'. The quote from Fuller is from *Letters*, 2:87.

Notes

1. See Sophia Dana Ripley's article, "Woman," quoted and paraphrased in Conversation 18, and published in the *Dial*, 1 (January 1841): 362–366 (printed in this edition, below).
2. Probably Sarah Sherman Hoar (1783–1866), wife of Samuel Hoar of Concord, and mother of Elizabeth Hoar, who had been engaged to Emerson's brother Charles at the time of his death.
3. Ellen Sturgis Hooper.
4. Quoted from *Specimens of the Table Talk of the Late Samuel Taylor Coleridge* (1835).
5. Queen Elizabeth I (1533–1603), ruler of England (1558–1603) during a golden age of politics and literature; Catherine II (1729–1796), known as Catherine the Great, became Empress of Russia in 1762.
6. Marianne Cabot Jackson (1820–1846), a friend and former student of Fuller's; eponymous passionate and idealistic heroine of *Corinne, or Italy* (1807), by Madame de Staël.
7. Torquato Tasso (1544–1595), Italian poet.
8. Dante Alighieri (1265–1321), Italian poet and Christian humanist, idealized woman in the form of Beatrice (his actual love) in his writings.
9. Marcus Junius Brutus (85–42 B.C.) assassinated Julius Caesar for what he claimed was the good of the republic.
10. Possibly Agnes Major Park (ca. 1782–1857), wife of the teacher at the Boston Academy for Young Ladies that Fuller had attended; Anna Blake Shaw (1817–1901), member of a prominent Boston family.
11. Sally Jackson Gardner, a cousin of Marianne Jackson.
12. Paraphrased from *Æneid*, Book 1, by Virgil (70–19 B.C.), Roman epic poet.
13. *lusus naturae*: "a sport or freak of nature."
14. Isaiah 2:4 and Micah 4:3.
15. "Mrs. H" could be either Sarah Hoar or Ellen Hooper; possibly referring to Bronson Alcott.

16. Simmons believes that the "exact parallels between the language of this report and the *Dial* essay suggest the transcriber may have reported the printed version rather than what Mrs. Ripley wrote for the conversation class, although the printed version seems to derive from her class exercise" (p. 226).

17. This is "his" in the *Dial*.

[*George Ripley?*]

Prospectus for *The Dial: A Magazine for Literature, Philosophy, and Religion*

(July 1840)

THE *DIAL* was a quarterly journal published in Boston from July 1840 through April 1844; was edited by Emerson, Fuller, and—for one issue— Henry David Thoreau; and was published by Elizabeth Palmer Peabody for one year. George Ripley served for a while as business manager. With a far shorter life than most of the major periodicals of its day—such as the *Christian Examiner* and *North American Review*—it has come down to the present as far more influential because of the authors and articles published in it.

Fuller served as editor for the first two years of the *Dial*'s existence, but was not paid; and in the spring of 1842, concerned about her personal finances, and also by her chronic health problems, she resigned as editor. Emerson succeeded her and worked hard as editor, but as 1844 approached, he found himself with too many commitments, including the "felon Dial." Not only was the position of editor still an unpaid one, Emerson had even put up some of his own money to help publish the *Dial* and pay some of his friends (including Thoreau) for their contributions. He was also preparing a second book of essays for publication in 1844, publishers were asking him for a volume of his poems, and he had some two dozen lecture engagements scheduled for the first three months of the coming year.

The *Dial*'s contributors were a varied lot, but virtually all had some personal connection to Emerson and/or Fuller. They included Bronson Alcott, Charles Timothy Brooks, James Elliot Cabot (who would later be Emerson's biographer and literary executor), Ellery Channing (who had nearly fifty pieces, mostly poems, in the *Dial*), William Henry Channing, Lydia Maria Child, James Freeman Clarke, Christopher Pearse Cranch, George William Curtis, Charles Anderson Dana (the future editor of the *New York Sun*), John Sullivan Dwight, Emerson's own late first wife Ellen and his two late brothers (Charles and Edward), Frederic Henry Hedge, Ellen Sturgis Hooper, Charles Lane, James Russell Lowell, Theodore Parker, Elizabeth Palmer Peabody,

George and Sophia Ripley, Caroline Sturgis (Tappan), Thoreau, Jones Very, Samuel Gray Ward, and Charles Stearns Wheeler. Although many of these people and their contributions are well known today, at the time they were—except for Emerson and Parker—obscure, and this had an impact on the *Dial*'s sales. Only three hundred subscribers were signed up by 1842, and a year later the number had dwindled to two hundred and twenty.

The purpose of this work is to furnish a medium for the freest expression of thought on the questions which interest earnest minds in every community.

It aims at the discussion of principles, rather than at the promotion of measures; and while it will not fail to examine the ideas which impel the leading movements of the present day, it will maintain an independent position with regard to them.

The pages of this Journal will be filled by contributors, who possess little in common but the love of intellectual freedom, and the hope of social progress; who are united by sympathy of spirit, not by agreement in speculation; whose faith is in Divine Providence, rather than in human prescription; whose hearts are more in the future than in the past; and who trust the living soul rather than the dead letter. It will endeavor to promote the constant evolution of truth, not the petrifaction of opinion.

Its contents will embrace a wide and varied range of subjects, and combining the characteristics of a Magazine and Review, it may present something both for those who read for instruction, and those who search for amusement.

The general design and character of the work may be understood from the above brief statement. It may be proper to add, that in literature, it will strive to exercise a just and catholic criticism, and to recognise every sincere production of genius; in philosophy, it will attempt the reconciliation of the universal instincts of humanity with the largest conclusions of reason; and in religion, it will reverently seek to discover the presence of God in nature, in history, and in the soul of man.

The DIAL, as its title indicates, will endeavor to occupy a station on which the light may fall; which is open to the rising sun; and from which it may correctly report the progress of the hour and the day.

Source: [George Ripley?], Prospectus for *The Dial: A Magazine for Literature, Philosophy, and Religion, Dial,* 1 (July 1840): wrapper. Emerson is quoted from *Letters,* 3:229.

[Ralph Waldo Emerson]

"The Editors to the Reader"

(July 1840)

FULLER HAD DRAFTED the original introduction to the *Dial*, but Emerson thought it "forestalls objection; it bows, though a little haughtily, to all the company; it is not quite confirmed in its own purpose," and he was concerned about Fuller's "early preparation for defence & anticipation of enemies," warning: "Don't cry before you are hurt." After volunteering to help revise it, along with Fuller and Ripley, he ended up writing the whole introduction himself. This essay, like nearly all the contributions to the *Dial*—and most other contemporary journals—was unsigned.

W e invite the attention of our countrymen to a new design. Probably not quite unexpected or unannounced will our Journal appear, though small pains have been taken to secure its welcome. Those, who have immediately acted in editing the present Number, cannot accuse themselves of any unbecoming forwardness in their undertaking, but rather of a backwardness, when they remember how often in many private circles the work was projected, how eagerly desired, and only postponed because no individual volunteered to combine and concentrate the free-will offerings of many coöperators. With some reluctance the present conductors of this work have yielded themselves to the wishes of their friends, finding something sacred and not to be withstood in the importunity which urged the production of a Journal in a new spirit.

As they have not proposed themselves to the work, neither can they lay any the least claim to an option or determination of the spirit in which it is conceived, or to what is peculiar in the design. In that respect, they have obeyed, though with great joy, the strong current of thought and feeling, which, for a few years past, has led many sincere persons in New England to make new demands on literature, and to reprobate that rigor of our conventions of religion and education which is turning us to stone, which renounces hope, which looks only backward, which asks only such a future as the past, which suspects improvement, and holds nothing so much in horror as new views and the dreams of youth.

With these terrors the conductors of the present Journal have nothing to do,—not even so much as a word of reproach to waste. They know that there is a portion of the youth and of the adult population of this country, who have not shared them; who have in secret or in public paid their vows to truth and freedom; who love reality too well to care for names, and who live by a Faith too earnest and profound to suffer them to doubt the eternity of its object, or to shake themselves free from its authority. Under the fictions and customs which occupied others, these have explored the Necessary, the Plain, the True, the Human,—and so gained a vantage ground, which commands the history of the past and the present.

No one can converse much with different classes of society in New England, without remarking the progress of a revolution. Those who share in it have no external organization, no badge, no creed, no name. They do not vote, or print, or even meet together. They do not know each other's faces or names. They are united only in a common love of truth, and love of its work. They are of all conditions and constitutions. Of these acolytes, if some are happily born and well bred, many are no doubt ill dressed, ill placed, ill made—with as many scars of hereditary vice as other men. Without pomp, without trumpet, in lonely and obscure places, in solitude, in servitude, in compunctions and privations, trudging beside the team in the dusty road, or drudging a hireling in other men's cornfields, schoolmasters, who teach a few children rudiments for a pittance, ministers of small parishes of the obscurer sects, lone women in dependent condition, matrons and young maidens, rich and poor, beautiful and hard-favored, without concert or proclamation of any kind, they have silently given in their several adherence to a new hope, and in all companies do signify a greater trust in the nature and resources of man, than the laws or the popular opinions will well allow.

This spirit of the time is felt by every individual with some difference,—to each one casting its light upon the objects nearest to his temper and habits of thought;—to one, coming in the shape of special reforms in the state; to another, in modifications of the various callings of men, and the customs of business; to a third, opening a new scope for literature and art; to a fourth, in philosophical insight; to a fifth, in the vast solitudes of prayer. It is in every form a protest against usage, and a search for principles. In all its movements, it is peaceable, and in the very lowest marked with a triumphant success. Of course, it rouses the opposition of all which it judges and condemns, but it is too confident in its tone to comprehend an objection, and so builds no outworks for possible defence against contingent enemies. It has the step of Fate, and goes on existing like an oak or a river, because it must.

In literature, this influence appears not yet in new books so much as in the higher tone of criticism. The antidote to all narrowness is the comparison of the record with nature, which at once shames the record and stimulates to new attempts. Whilst we look at this, we wonder how any book has been thought worthy to be preserved. There is somewhat in all life untranslatable into language. He who keeps his eye on that will write better than others, and think less of his writing, and of all writing. Every thought has a certain imprisoning as well as uplifting quality, and, in proportion to its energy on the will, refuses to become an object of intellectual contemplation. Thus what is great usually slips through our fingers, and it seems wonderful how a lifelike word ever comes to be written. If our Journal share the impulses of the time, it cannot now prescribe its own course. It cannot foretell in orderly propositions what it shall attempt. All criticism should be poetic; unpredictable; superseding, as every new thought does, all fore-gone thoughts, and making a new light on the whole world. Its brow is not wrinkled with circumspection, but serene, cheerful, adoring. It has all things to say, and no less than all the world for its final audience.

Our plan embraces much more than criticism; were it not so, our criticism would be naught. Everything noble is directed on life, and this is. We do not wish to say pretty or curious things, or to reiterate a few propositions in varied forms, but, if we can, to give expression to that spirit which lifts men to a higher platform, restores to them the religious sentiment, brings them worthy aims and pure pleasures, purges the inward eye, makes life less desultory, and, through raising man to the level of nature, takes away its melancholy from the landscape, and reconciles the practical with the speculative powers.

But perhaps we are telling our little story too gravely. There are always great arguments at hand for a true action, even for the writing of a few pages. There is nothing but seems near it and prompts it,— the sphere in the ecliptic, the sap in the apple tree,—every fact, every appearance seem to persuade to it.

Our means correspond with the ends we have indicated. As we wish not to multiply books, but to report life, our resources are therefore not so much the pens of practised writers, as the discourse of the living, and the portfolios which friendship has opened to us. From the beautiful recesses of private thought; from the experience and hope of spirits which are withdrawing from all old forms, and seeking in all that is new somewhat to meet their inappeasable longings; from the secret confession of genius afraid to trust itself to aught but sympathy; from the conversation of fervid and mystical pietists; from tear-stained diaries of sorrow and passion; from the manuscripts of young poets;

and from the records of youthful taste commenting on old works of art; we hope to draw thoughts and feelings, which being alive can impart life.

And so with diligent hands and good intent we set down our Dial on the earth. We wish it may resemble that instrument in its celebrated happiness, that of measuring no hours but those of sunshine. Let it be one cheerful rational voice amidst the din of mourners and polemics. Or to abide by our chosen image, let it be such a Dial, not as the dead face of a clock, hardly even such as the Gnomon in a garden,[1] but rather such a Dial as is the Garden itself, in whose leaves and flowers and fruits the suddenly awakened sleeper is instantly apprised not what part of dead time, but what state of life and growth is now arrived and arriving.

Source: [Ralph Waldo Emerson], "The Editors to the Reader," *Dial*, 1 (July 1840): 1–4. Emerson is quoted from *Letters*, 2:285–286.

Note

1. Gnomon, the perpendicular part of a sundial that casts its shadow on the surface to show the time.

[*Margaret Fuller*]

"A Short Essay on Critics"

(July 1840)

THIS ESSAY BRIEFLY distills Fuller's critical views at the time, as she describes the subjective, apprehensive, and comprehensive types of critics. At a period when reviews were either straightforward summaries of the work under discussion, vicious attacks on people or ideas the reviewer did not like, or blatant encomiums (or "puffs") of friends' works, Fuller's idea of establishing critical standards was unusual.

※

An essay on Criticism were a serious matter; for, though this age be emphatically critical, the writer would still find it necessary to investigate the laws of criticism as a science, to settle its conditions as an art. Essays entitled critical are epistles addressed to the public through which the mind of the recluse relieves itself of its impressions.

Of these the only law is, "Speak the best word that is in thee." Or they are regular articles, got up to order by the literary hack writer, for the literary mart, and the only law is to make them plausible. There is not yet deliberate recognition of a standard of criticism, though we hope the always strengthening league of the republic of letters must ere long settle laws on which its Amphictyonic council may act.[1] Meanwhile let us not venture to write on criticism, but by classifying the critics imply our hopes, and thereby our thoughts.

First, there are the subjective class, (to make use of a convenient term, introduced by our German benefactors.) These are persons to whom writing is no sacred, no reverend employment. They are not driven to consider, not forced upon investigation by the fact, that they are deliberately giving their thoughts an independent existence, and that it may live to others when dead to them. They know no agonies of conscientious research, no timidities of self-respect. They see no Ideal beyond the present hour, which makes its mood an uncertain tenure. How things affect them now they know; let the future, let the whole take care of itself. They state their impressions as they rise, of other men's spoken, written, or acted thoughts. They never dream of going out of themselves to seek the motive, to trace the law of another nature. They never dream that there are statures which cannot be measured from their point of view. They love, they like, or they hate; the book is detestable, immoral, absurd, or admirable, noble, of a most approved scope;—these statements they make with authority, as those who bear the evangel of pure taste and accurate judgment, and need be tried before no human synod. To them it seems that their present position commands the universe.

Thus the essays on the works of others, which are called criticisms, are often, in fact, mere records of impressions. To judge of their value you must know where the man was brought up, under what influences,—his nation, his church, his family even. He himself has never attempted to estimate the value of these circumstances, and find a law or raise a standard above all circumstances, permanent against all influence. He is content to be the creature of his place, and to represent it by his spoken and written word. He takes the same ground with the savage, who does not hesitate to say of the product of a civilization on which he could not stand, "It is bad," or "It is good."

The value of such comments is merely reflex. They characterize the critic. They give an idea of certain influences on a certain act of men in a certain time or place. Their absolute, essential value is nothing. The long review, the eloquent article by the man of the nineteenth century are of no value by themselves considered, but only as samples of their kind. The writers were content to tell what they felt, to praise or to denounce without needing to convince us or themselves. They sought not the divine truths of philosophy, and she proffers them not, if unsought.

Then there are the apprehensive. These can go out of themselves and enter fully into a foreign existence. They breathe its life; they live in its law; they tell what it meant, and why it so expressed its meaning. They reproduce the work of which they speak, and make it better known to us in so far as two statements are better than one. There are beautiful specimens in this kind. They are pleasing to us as bearing witness of the genial sympathies of nature. They have the ready grace of love with somewhat of the dignity of disinterested friendship. They sometimes give more pleasure than the original production of which they treat, as melodies will sometimes ring sweetlier in the echo. Besides there is a peculiar pleasure in a true response; it is the assurance of equipoise in the universe. These, if not true critics, come nearer the standard than the subjective class, and the value of their work is ideal as well as historical.

Then there are the comprehensive, who must also be apprehensive. They enter into the nature of another being and judge his work by its own law. But having done so, having ascertained his design and the degree of his success in fulfilling it, thus measuring his judgment, his energy, and skill, they do also know how to put that aim in its place, and how to estimate its relations. And this the critic can only do who perceives the analogies of the universe, and how they are regulated by an absolute, invariable principle. He can see how far that work expresses this principle as well as how far it is excellent in its details. Sustained by a principle, such as can be girt within no rule, no formula, he can walk around the work, he can stand above it, he can uplift it, and try its weight. Finally he is worthy to judge it.

Critics are poets cut down, says some one by way of jeer; but, in truth, they are men with the poetical temperament to apprehend, with the philosophical tendency to investigate. The maker is divine; the critic sees this divine, but brings it down to humanity by the analytic process. The critic is the historian who records the order of creation. In vain for the maker, who knows without learning it, but not in vain for the mind of his race.

The critic is beneath the maker, but is his needed friend. What tongue could speak but to an intelligent ear, and every noble work demands its critic. The richer the work, the more severe would be its critic; the larger its scope, the more comprehensive must be his power of scrutiny. The critic is not a base caviller, but the younger brother of genius. Next to invention is the power of interpreting invention; next to beauty the power of appreciating beauty.

And of making others appreciate it; for the universe is a scale of infinite gradation, and below the very highest, every step is explanation down to the lowest. Religion, in the two modulations of poetry and music, descends through an infinity of waves to the lowest abysses of human nature. Nature is the literature and art of the divine mind; human literature and art the criticism on that; and they, too, find their criticism within their own sphere.

The critic, then, should be not merely a poet, not merely a philosopher, not merely an observer, but tempered of all three. If he criticize the poem, he must want nothing of what constitutes the poet, except the power of creating forms and speaking in music. He must have as good an eye and as fine a sense; but if he had as fine an organ for expression also, he would make the poem instead of judging it. He must be inspired by the philosopher's spirit of inquiry and need of generalization, but he must not be constrained by the hard cemented masonry of method to which philosophers are prone. And he must have the organic acuteness of the observer, with a love of ideal perfection, which forbids him to be content with mere beauty of details in the work or the comment upon the work.

There are persons who maintain, that there is no legitimate criticism, except the reproductive; that we have only to say what the work is or is to us, never what it is not. But the moment we look for a principle, we feel the need of a criterion, of a standard; and then we say what the work is *not*, as well as what it *is;* and this is as healthy though not as grateful and gracious an operation of the mind as the other. We do not seek to degrade but to classify an object by stating what it is not. We detach the part from the whole, lest it stand between us and the whole. When we have ascertained in what degree it manifests the whole we may safely restore it to its place, and love or admire it there ever after.

The use of criticism in periodical writing is to sift, not to stamp a work. Yet should they not be "sieves and drainers for the use of luxurious readers," but for the use of earnest inquirers, giving voice and being to their objections, as well as stimulus to their sympathies. But the critic must not be an infallible adviser to his reader. He must not tell him what books are not worth reading, or what must be thought of them when read, but what he read in them. Wo to that coterie where some critic sits despotic, intrenched behind the infallible "We." Wo to that oracle who has infused such soft sleepiness, such a gentle dulness into his atmosphere, that when he opes his lips no dog will bark. It is this attempt at dictatorship in the reviewers, and the indolent acquiescence of their readers, that has brought them into disrepute. With such fairness did they make out their statements, with such dignity did they utter their verdicts, that the poor reader grew all too submissive. He learned his lesson with such docility, that the greater part of what will be said at any public or private meeting can be foretold by any one who has read the leading periodical works for twenty years back. Scholars sneer at and would fain dispense with them altogether; and the public, grown lazy and helpless by this constant use of props and stays, can now scarce brace itself even to get through a magazine article, but reads in the daily paper laid beside the breakfast plate a short notice of the last number of the long established and popular review, and thereupon passes its judgment and is content.

Then the partisan spirit of many of these journals has made it unsafe to rely upon them as guide-books and expurgatory indexes. They could not be content merely to stimulate and suggest thought, they have at last become powerless to supersede it.

From these causes and causes like these, the journals have lost much of their influence. There is a languid feeling about them, an inclination to suspect the justice of their verdicts, the value of their criticisms. But their golden age cannot be quite past. They afford too convenient a vehicle for the transmission of knowledge; they are too natural a feature of our time to have done all their work yet. Surely they may be redeemed from their abuses, they may be turned to their true uses. But how?

It were easy to say what they should *not* do. They should not have an object to carry or a cause to advocate, which obliges them either to reject all writings which wear the distinctive traits of individual life, or to file away what does not suit them, till the essay, made true to their design, is made false to the mind of the writer. An external consistency is thus produced, at the expense of all salient thought, all genuine emotion of life, in short, and living influences. Their purpose may be of value, but by such means was no valuable purpose ever furthered long. There are those, who have with the best intention pursued this system of trimming and adaptation, and thought it well and best to

"Deceive their country for their country's good."

But their country cannot long be so governed. It misses the pure, the full tone of truth; it perceives that the voice is modulated to coax, to persuade, and it turns from the judicious man of the world, calculating the effect to be produced by each of his smooth sentences to some earnest voice which is uttering thoughts, crude, rash, ill-arranged it may be, but true to one human breast, and uttered in full faith, that the God of Truth will guide them aright.

And here, it seems to me, has been the greatest mistake in the conduct of these journals. A smooth monotony has been attained, an uniformity of tone, so that from the title of a journal you can infer the tenor of all its chapters. But nature is ever various, ever new, and so should be her daughters, art and literature. We do not want merely a polite response to what we thought before, but by the freshness of thought in other minds to have new thought awakened in our own. We do not want stores of information only, but to be roused to digest these into knowledge. Able and experienced men write for us, and we would know what they think, as they think it not for us but for themselves. We would live with them, rather than be taught by them how to live; we would catch the contagion of their mental activity, rather than have them direct us how to regulate our own. In books, in reviews, in the senate, in the pulpit, we wish to meet thinking men, not schoolmasters or pleaders. We wish that they should do full justice to their own view, but also that they should do frank with us, and, if now our superiors, treat us as if we might some time rise to be their equals. It is this true manliness, this firmness in his own position, and this power of appreciating the position of others, that alone can make the critic our companion and friend. We would converse with him, secure that he will tell us all his thought, and speak as man to man. But if he adapts his work to us, if he stifles what is distinctively his, if he shows himself either arrogant or mean, or, above all, if he wants faith in the healthy action of free thought, and the safety of pure motive, we will not talk with him, for we cannot confide in him. We will go to the critic who trusts Genius and trusts us, who knows that all good writing must be spontaneous, and who will write out the bill of fare for the public as he read it for himself,—

> "Forgetting vulgar rules, with spirit free
> To judge each author by his own intent,
> Nor think one standard for all minds is meant."

Such an one will not disturb us with personalities, with sectarian prejudices, or an undue vehemence in favor of pretty plans or temporary objects. Neither will he disgust us by smooth obsequious flatteries and an inexpressive, lifeless gentleness. He will be free and make free from the mechanical and distorting influences we hear complained of on every side. He will teach us to love wisely what we before loved well, for he knows the difference between censoriousness and discernment, infatuation and reverence; and, while delighting in the genial melodies of Pan, can perceive, should Apollo bring his lyre into audience, that there may be strains more divine than those of his native groves.[2]

Source: "F." [Margaret Fuller], "A Short Essay on Critics," *Dial*, 1 (July 1840): 5–11.

Notes

1. Amphictyonic council, composed of representatives from the twelve Greek tribes.
2. Pan, the Greek god of flocks and herds.

A. Bronson Alcott

from "Orphic Sayings"

(July 1840)

ALCOTT'S "Orphic Sayings" was the most ridiculed contribution to the *Dial*, and its unfortunate appearance in the first issue (and the publication of more of them in January 1841) was used by many reviewers to characterize the entire periodical through its four-year run. In addition to numerous parodies, typical comments included descriptions of them by the *Boston Daily Evening Mercantile Journal* as the "quintessence of folly and extravagance—affected, mystical, bombastic—and, in some instances, puerile," and by the *Boston Post* as "a train of fifteen railroad cars with one passenger." Admittedly, some of his sayings do challenge the reader's comprehension, and some even contradict themselves (the first "Temptation" printed below states "He who is tempted has sinned," but the second describes someone who "nobly" withstands the "trial" of temptation). But others merely present in condensed form subjects that had been under discussion for the last four years; for example, who could not fail to see in these comments on "Spiritualism" the heart of the debate over miracles: "Divinely seen, natural facts are symbols of spiritual facts. Miracles are of the heart; not of the head: indigenous to the soul; not freaks of nature, nor growths of history. God, man, nature, are miracles." Alcott considered these typical of the oracular sayings from the continental writers he had been reading, mere epigrammatic statements of universal truths, and he continued creating new "Orphic Sayings" for over two more decades. Printed below are samples of his "Orphic Sayings" from the *Dial* and from other contemporary periodicals.

Enthusiasm.

Believe, youth, that your heart is an oracle; trust her instinctive auguries, obey her divine leadings; nor listen too fondly to the uncertain echoes of your head. The heart is the prophet of your soul, and ever fulfils her prophecies; reason is her historian; but for the prophecy the history would not be. Great is the heart: cherish her; she is big with the future, she forebodes renovations. Let the flame of enthusiasm fire alway your bosom. Enthusiasm is the glory and hope of the world. It is the life of sanctity and genius; it has wrought all miracles since the beginning of time.

Immortality.

The grander my conception of being, the nobler my future. There can be no sublimity of life without faith in the soul's eternity. Let me live superior to sense and custom, vigilant alway, and I shall experience my divinity; my hope will be infinite, nor shall the universe contain, or content me. But if I creep daily from the haunts of an ignoble past, like a beast from his burrow, neither earth nor sky, man nor God shall appear desirable or glorious; my life shall be loathsome to me, my future reflect my fears. He alone, who lives nobly, oversees his own being, believes all things, and partakes of the eternity of God.

Vocation.

Engage in nothing that cripples or degrades you. Your first duty is self-culture, self-exaltation: you may not violate this high trust. Your self is sacred, profane it not. Forge no chains wherewith to shackle your own members. Either subordinate your vocation to your life, or quit it forever: it is not for you; it is condemnation of your own soul. Your influence on others is commensurate with the strength that you have found in yourself. First cast the demons from your own bosom, and then shall your word exorcise them from the hearts of others.

Apotheosis.

Every soul feels at times her own possibility of becoming a God; she cannot rest in the human, she aspires after the Godlike. This instinctive tendency is an authentic augury of its own fulfilment. Men shall become Gods. Every act of admiration, prayer, praise, worship, desire, hope, implies and predicts the future apotheosis of the soul.

Temptation.

Greater is he, who is above temptation, than he, who, being tempted, overcomes. The latter but regains the state from which the former has not fallen. He who is tempted has sinned; temptation is impossible to the holy.

Choice.

Choice implies apostacy. The pure, unfallen soul is above choice. Her life is unbroken, synthetic; she is a law to herself, and finds no lust in her members warring against the instincts of conscience. Sinners choose; saints act from instinct and intuition: there is no parley of alien forces in their being.

Speech.

There is a magic in free speaking, especially on sacred themes most potent and resistless. It is refreshing, amidst the inane common-places bandied in pulpits and parlors, to hear a hopeful word from an earnest, upright soul. Men rally around it as to the lattice in summer heats, to inhale the breeze that flows cool and refreshing from the mountains, and invigorates their languid frames. Once heard, they feel a buoyant sense of health and hopefulness, and wonder that they should have lain sick, supine so long, when a word has power to raise them from their couch, and restore them to soundness. And once spoken, it shall never be forgotten; it charms, exalts; it visits them in dreams, and haunts them during all their wakeful hours. Great, indeed, is the delight of speech; sweet the sound of one's bosom thought, as it returns laden with the fragrance of a brother's approval.

Valor.

The world, the state, the church, stand in awe of a man of probity and valor. He threatens their order and perpetuity: an unknown might slumbers in him; he is an augury of revolutions. Out of the invisible God, he comes to abide awhile amongst men; yet neither men nor time shall remain as at his advent. He is a creative element, and revises men, times, life itself. A new world pre-exists in his ideal. He over-lives, outlives, eternizes the ages, and reports to all men the will of the divinity whom he serves.

Character.

Character is the only legitimate institution; the only regal influence. Its power is infinite. Safe in the citadel of his own integrity, principalities, powers, hierarchies, states, capitulate to the man of character at last. It is the temple which the soul builds to herself, within whose fanes genius and sanctity worship, while the kneeling ages bend around them in admiration and love.

Each and All.

Life eludes all scientific analysis. Each organ and function is modified in substance and varied in effect, by the subtle energy which pulsates throughout the whole economy of things, spiritual and corporeal. The each is instinct with the all; the all unfolds and reappears in each. Spirit is all in all. God, man, nature, are a divine synthesis, whose parts it is impiety to sunder. Genius must preside devoutly over all investigations, or analysis, with her murderous knife, will seek impiously to probe the vitals of being.

Sepulture and Resurrection.

That which is visible is dead: the apparent is the corpse of the real; and undergoes successive sepultures and resurrections. The soul dies out of organs; the tombs cannot confine her; she eludes the grasp of decay; she builds and unseals the sepulchres. Her bodies are fleeting, historical. Whatsoever she sees when awake is death; when asleep dream.

Genesis.

The popular genesis is historical. It is written to sense not to the soul. Two principles, diverse and alien, interchange the Godhead and sway the world by turns. God is dual. Spirit is derivative. Identity halts in diversity. Unity is actual merely. The poles of things are not integrated: creation not globed and orbed.[1] Yet in the true genesis, nature is globed in the material, souls orbed in the spiritual firmament. Love globes, wisdom orbs, all things. As magnet the steel, so spirit attracts matter, which trembles to traverse the poles of diversity, and rests in the bosom of unity. All genesis is of love. Wisdom is her form; beauty her costume.

Reformers.

Reformers are metallic; they are sharpest steel; they pierce whatsoever of evil or abuse they touch. Their souls are attempered[2] in the fires of heaven; they are nailed in the might of principles, and God backs their purpose. They uproot institutions, erase traditions, revise usages, and renovate all things. They are the noblest of facts. Extant in time, they work for eternity; dwelling with men, they are with God.

Temptation.

The man of sublime gifts has his temptation amidst the solitudes to which he is driven by his age as proof of his integrity. Yet nobly he withstands this trial, conquering both Satan and the world by overcoming himself. He bows not down before the idols of time, but is constant to the divine ideal that haunts his heart,—a spirit of serene and perpetual peace.

Bread.

Fools and blind! not bread, but the lack of it is God's high argument. Wouldst enter into life? Beg bread then. In the kingdom of God are love and bread consociated, but in the realm of mammon, bread sojourns with lies, and truth is a starvling. Yet praised be God, he has bread in his exile which mammon knows not of.

Barrenness.

Opinions are life in foliage; deeds, in fruitage. Always is the fruitless tree accursed.

Fact and Fable.

Facts, reported, are always false. Only sanctity and genius are eyewitnesses of the same; and their intuition, yet not their scriptures, are alone authentic. Not only all scripture, but all thought is fabulous. Life is the only pure fact, and this cannot be written to sense; it must be lived, and thus expurgate all scriptures.

Teacher.

The true teacher defends his pupils against his own personal influence. He inspires self-trust. He guides their eyes from himself to the spirit that quickens him. He will have no disciples. A noble artist, he has visions of excellence and revelations of beauty, which he has neither impersonated in character, nor embodied in words. His life and teachings are but studies for yet nobler ideals.

Christendom.

Christendom is infidel. It violates the sanctity of man's conscience. It speaks not from the lively oracles of the soul, but reads instead from the traditions of men. It quotes history, not life. It denounces as heresy and impiety the intuitions of the individual, denies the inspiration of souls, and intrudes human dogmas and usages between conscience and God. It excludes the saints from its bosom, and with these excommunicates, as the archheretic, Jesus of Nazareth also.

Christians.

Christians lean on Jesus, not on the soul. Such was not the doctrine of this noble reformer. He taught man's independence of all men, and a faith and trust in the soul herself. Christianity is the doctrine of self-support. It teaches man to be upright, not supine. Jesus gives his arm to none save those who stand erect, independent of church, state, or the world, in the integrity of self-insight and valor. Cast aside thy crutch, O Christendom, and by faith in the soul, arise and walk. Thy faith alone shall make thee whole.

Obituary.

Things are memoirs of ideas; ideas the body of laws; laws the breath of God. All nature is the sepulchre of the risen soul, life her epitaph, and scripture her obituary.

Purity.

All functions of the vestal soul are sacramental rites, offerings on the altars of Piety. Her molten tides sparkle then through all her vessels: vivacious and quick are her offspring; Genius irradiates her brow; valor stands armed in her frame.

But Lust spills her ignobly in the Harlot's lap, unstrings her sinewy bow; bereaves her of her wit, and she grinds in the prison house of disease.

Gluttony.

Wheresoever is the carcass, there gather the eagles. Note the shambles, markets, tables—Slaughter, blood carnage: blood thirsting for blood, carrion, scenting carrion. Facts, these horrent with murder; arguments, proven to sense, of the breast not yet exorcised from man; the swine in the belly gloating on the swine without; appetite going forth to defile the soul. Prayer, fasting, baptisms, these shall release the unclean spirit, and clothe man in his wits again; the demoniacs perishing all in the waters of Sobriety.

Appetite.

Eat with him whose purity you would know. His habit at table betrays whether he be chaste or unclean. Like feeds like; if the soul be foul, then shall the unclean spirit within be insatiate till he lick carnage and blood from his trencher—Beast within, devouring beast without. The appetite which goeth out of the mouth the same defiles the man.

Sight.

Instinct is the premise of faith; an affirmation of the inpresent I AM in the intuitions of conscience. Faith is the antecedent, reason the consequent of instinct; the sequent in the subsequent; the sexton adding ashes to ashes on derelict syllogisms of the brain. To faith, being is present, instant, living; it is sight in ubiquity, singleness in omnipresence, breathing in spirit.

Source: From A. Bronson Alcott, "Orphic Sayings," *Dial*, 1 (July 1840): 351–361 ("Enthusiasm" through "Genesis"), and 1 (January 1841): 351–361 ("Reformers" through "Obituary"); *Plain Speaker* [Providence], 1 (May 1841): 15 ("Purity") and 1 (December 1841): 26 ("Gluttony"); "Pythagorean Sayings," *Healthian* [England], 1 (September 1842): 75 ("Appetite"); and "Sayings," *Present*, 1 (15 January 1844): 261–262 ("Sight"). Not represented here are the "Orphic Sayings" in the *Boston Quarterly Review*, 4 (October 1841): 492–494, and the *Present*, 1 (15 December 1843): 170–172. The reviews are quoted from Joel Myerson, " 'In the Transcendental Emporium': Bronson Alcott's 'Orphic Sayings' in the *Dial*," *English Language Notes*, 10 (September 1972): 34, 36.

Notes

1. The confusion caused by *Dial*'s erroneous reading of "The poles of things are not integrated: creation globed and orbed" helped make this one of the most parodied of the Sayings (for Alcott's correction, see Myerson, " 'In the Transcendental Emporium,' " 33).
2. Attempered, modified by mixing.

George Ripley, Ralph Waldo Emerson and Brook Farm

(November–December 1840)

WRITERS ON THE Transcendentalist movement have debated how the participants saw their connection to society at the time when they were pronouncing on the sanctity of the individual, a discussion that had been initiated by the participants themselves. Modern scholars have rightly pointed out that radical individualism did not keep people like Emerson from participating in clubs or conversations, nor did it restrain him from the social process of conveying his message through lectures and print. Contemporaries such as Orestes Brownson, though, disparaged the idea that nurturing the individual would change the social world. At the heart of the controversy was the question: "Which comes first, a just and honorable society or a good and moral people?" Put another way, this chicken-and-egg question forces a decision about whether a just society, with just laws, can change its populace for the better, or whether people must be reformed before they can enact fair and just laws. Emerson clearly comes down in favor of the latter point.

Brownson, in his article "The Laboring Classes," which first appeared in the July and October 1840 numbers of the *Boston Quarterly Review*, argued for a more radical solution to society's ills. As he does all along in his writings about the Transcendentalists, Brownson complains that their belief in the primacy of the individual results in their ignoring the real problems of the social organism. Brownson notes that the real enemy of the laborer is not the aristocracy but the middle class, who, having made the jump from the bottom level themselves, wish to draw up the bridge behind them: "The middle class is always a firm champion of equality, when it concerns humbling a class above it; but it is its inveterate foe, when it concerns elevating a class below it." In Europe the "old war between the King and the Barons is well nigh ended," as well as "that between the Barons and the Merchants and Manufacturers," and the "business man has become the peer of my Lord." Now, though, the real struggle begins, a battle "between the operative and his employer, between wealth and labor." As for self-improvement as a solution, Brownson feels it helps the laborer to be a better person, but is no solution in and of itself: "As a means it is well, as the end it is nothing." Instead, he argues that the "only way to get rid of [society's] evils is to change the system, not its managers."

Ripley would have agreed with Brownson that society needs to be changed, but he thought of a less revolutionary way to do it: create a communal experiment in which all were equal, each contributing his or her own specialty to the development of the group, and use that microcosm of a good society as the basis for a macrocosm of the proper social order. There is probably no better brief expression of his ideas about reforming society, and of Emerson's rejection of them in favor of reforming the individual, than in the correspondence of the two men over the latter joining what would become the Brook Farm community.

Boston, November 9, 1840.

My dear Sir,

Our conversation in Concord was of such a general nature, that I do not feel as if you were in complete possession of the idea of the Association which I wish to see established. As we have now a prospect of carrying it into effect, at an early period, I wish to submit the plan more distinctly to your judgment, that you may decide whether it is one that can have the benefit of your aid and coöperation.

Our objects, as you know, are to insure a more natural union between intellectual and manual labor than now exists; to combine the thinker and the worker, as far as possible, in the same individual; to guarantee the highest mental freedom, by providing all with labor, adapted to their tastes and talents, and securing to them the fruits of their industry; to do away the necessity of menial services, by opening the benefits of education and the profits of labor to all; and thus to prepare a society of liberal, intelligent, and cultivated persons, whose relations with each other would permit a more simple and wholesome life, than can be led amidst the pressure of our competitive institutions.

To accomplish these objects, we propose to take a small tract of land, which, under skillful husbandry, uniting the garden and the farm, will be adequate to the subsistence of the families; and to connect with this a school or college, in which the most complete instruction shall be given, from the first rudiments to the highest culture. Our farm would be a place for improving the race of men that lived on it; thought would preside over the operations of labor, and labor would contribute to the expansion of thought; we should have industry without drudgery, and true equality without its vulgarity.

An offer has been made to us of a beautiful estate, on very reasonable terms, on the borders of Newton, West Roxbury, and Dedham. I am very familiar with the premises, having resided on them a part of last summer, and we might search the country in vain for anything more eligible. Our proposal now is for three or four families to take possession on the first of April next, to attend to the cultivation of the farm and the erection of buildings, to prepare for the coming of as many more in the autumn, and thus to commence the institution in the simplest manner, and with the smallest number, with which it can go into operation at all. It would thus be not less than two or three years, before we should be joined by all who mean to be with us; we should not fall to pieces by our own weight; we should grow up slowly and strong; and the attractiveness of our experiment would win to us all whose society we should want.

The step now to be taken at once is the procuring of funds for the necessary capital. According to the present modification of our plan, a much less sum will be required than that spoken of in our discussions at Concord. We thought then $50,000 would be needed; I find now, after a careful estimate, that $30,000 will purchase the estate and buildings for ten families, and give the required surplus for carrying on the operations for one year.

We propose to raise this sum by a subscription to a joint stock company, among the friends of the institution, the payment of a fixed interest being guaranteed to the subscribers, and the subscription itself secured by the real estate. No man then will be in danger of losing; he will receive as fair an interest as he would from any investment, while at the same time he is contributing towards an institution, in which while the true use of money is retained, its abuses are done away. The sum required cannot come from rich capitalists; their instinct would protest against such an application of their coins; it must be obtained from those who sympathize with our ideas, and who are willing to aid their realization with their money, if not by their personal coöperation. There are some of this description on whom I think we can rely; among ourselves we can produce perhaps $10,000; the remainder must be subscribed for by those who wish us well, whether they mean to unite with us or not.

I can imagine no plan which is suited to carry into effect so many divine ideas as this. If wisely executed, it will be a light over this country and this age. If not the sunrise, it will be the morning star. As a practical man, I see clearly that we must have some such arrangement, or all changes less radical will be nugatory. I believe in the divinity of labor; I wish to "harvest my flesh and blood from the land;" but to do this, I must either be insulated and work to disadvantage, or avail myself of the services of hirelings, who are not of my order, and whom I can scarce make friends; for I must have another to drive the plough, which I hold. I cannot empty a cask of lime upon my grass alone. I wish to see a society of educated friends, working, thinking, and living together, with no strife, except that of each to contribute the most to the benefit of all.

Personally, my tastes and habits would lead me in another direction. I have a passion for being independent of the world, and of every man in it. This I could do easily on the estate which is now offered, and which I could rent at a rate, that with my other resources, would place me in a very agreeable condition, as far as my personal interests were involved. I should have a city of God, on a small scale of my own; and please God, I should hope one day to drive my own cart to market and sell greens. But I feel bound to sacrifice this private feeling, in the hope of a great social good. I shall be anxious to hear from you. Your decision will do much towards settling the question with me, whether the time has come for the fulfillment of a high hope, or whether the work belongs to a future generation. All omens now are favorable; a singular union of diverse talents is ready for the enterprise; everything indicates that we ought to arise and build; and if we let slip this occasion, the unsleeping Nemesis will deprive us of the boon we seek.[1] For myself, I am sure that I can never give so much thought to it again; my mind must act on other objects, and I shall acquiesce in the course of fate, with grief that so fair a light is put out. A small pittance of the wealth which has been thrown away on ignoble objects, during this wild contest for political supremacy, would lay the cornerstone of a house, which would ere long become the desire of nations.

I almost forgot to say that our friends, the "Practical Christians," insist on making their "Standard,"—a written document,—a prescribed test. This cuts them off. Perhaps we are better without them. They are good men; they have salt, which we needed with our spice; but we might have proved too liberal, too comprehensive, too much attached to the graces of culture, to suit their ideas. Instead of them, we have the offer of ten or twelve "Practical Men," from Mr. S. J. May, who himself is deeply interested in the proposal, and would like one day to share in its concerns.[2] Pray write me with as much frankness as I have used towards you, and believe me ever your friend and faithful servant.

GEORGE RIPLEY.

P.S. I ought to add, that in the present stage of the enterprise no proposal is considered as binding. We wish only to know what can probably be relied on, provided always, that no pledge will be accepted until the articles of association are agreed on by all parties.

I recollect you said that if you were sure of compeers of the right stamp you might embark yourself in the adventure: as to this, let me suggest the inquiry, whether our Association should not be composed of various classes of men? If we have friends whom we love and who love us, I think we should be content to join with others, with whom our personal sympathy is not strong, but whose general ideas coincide with ours, and whose gifts and abilities would make their services important. For instance, I should like to have a good washerwoman in my parish admitted into the plot. She is certainly not a Minerva or a Venus;[3] but we might educate her two children to wisdom and varied accomplishments, who otherwise will be doomed to drudge through life. The same is true of some farmers and mechanics, whom we should like with us.

Concord, 15 December, 1840.

My dear Sir,

It is quite time I made an answer to your proposition that I should join you in your new enterprise. The design appears to me so noble & humane, proceeding, as I plainly see, from a manly & expanding heart & mind that it makes me & all men its friends & debtors. It becomes a matter of conscience to entertain it friendly & to examine what it has for us.

I have decided not to join it & yet very slowly & I may almost say penitentially. I am greatly relieved by learning that your coadjutors are now so many that you will no longer ascribe that importance to the defection of individuals which you hinted in your letter to me. It might attach to mine.

The ground of my decision is almost purely personal to myself. I have some remains of skepticism in regard to the general practicability of the plan, but these have not much weighed with me. That which determines me is the conviction that the Community is not good for me. Whilst I see it may hold out many inducements for others it has little to offer me which with resolution I cannot procure for myself. It seems to me that it would not be worth my while to make the difficult exchange of my property in Concord for a share in the new Household. I am in many respects suitably placed, in an agreeable neighborhood, in a town which I have many reasons to love & which has respected my freedom so far that I may presume it will indulge me farther if I need it. Here I have friends & kindred. Here I have builded & planted: & here I have greater facilities to prosecute such practical enterprizes as I may cherish, than I could probably find by any removal. I cannot accuse my townsmen or my social position of my domestic grievances:—only my own sloth & conformity. It seems to me a circuitous & operose way of relieving myself of any irksome circumstances, to put on your community the task of my emancipation which I ought to take on myself.

The principal particulars in which I wish to mend my domestic life are in acquiring habits of regular manual labor, and in ameliorating or abolishing in my house the condition of hired menial service.[4] I should like to come one step nearer to nature than this usage permits. I desire that my manner of living may be honest and agreeable to my imagination. But surely I need not sell my house & remove my family to Newton in order to make the experiment of labor & self help. I am already in the act of trying some domestic & social experiments which my present position favors. And I think that my present position has even greater advantages than yours would offer me for testing my improvements in those small private parties into which men are all set off already throughout the world.

But I own I almost shrink from making any statement of my objections to our ways of living because I see how slowly I shall mend them. My own health & habits & those of my wife & my mother are not of that robustness which should give any pledge of enterprise & ability in reform. And whenever I am engaged in literary composition I find myself not inclined to insist with heat on new methods. Yet I think that all I shall solidly do, I must do alone. I do not think I should gain anything—I who have little skill to converse with people—by a plan of so many parts and which I comprehend so slowly & imperfectly as the proposed Association.

If the community is not good for me neither am I good for it. I do not look on myself as a valuable member to any community which is not either very large or very small & select I fear that yours would not find me as profitable & pleasant an associate as I should wish to be and as so important a project seems imperatively to require in all its constituents. Moreover I am so ignorant & uncertain in my improvements that I would fain hide my attempts & failures in solitude where they shall perplex none or very few beside myself. The result of our secretest improvements will certainly have as much renown as shall be due to them.

In regard to the plan as far as it respects the formation of a School or College, I have more hesitation, inasmuch as a concentration of scholars in one place seems to me to have certain great advantages. Perhaps as the school emerges to more distinct consideration out of the Farm, I shall yet find it attractive. And yet I am very apt to relapse into the same skepticism as to modes & arrangements the same magnifying of the men—the men alone. According to your ability & mine, you & I do now keep school for all comers, & the energy of our thought & will measures our influence. In the community we shall utter not a word more—not a word less.

Whilst I refuse to be an active member of your company I must yet declare that of all the philanthropic projects of which I have heard yours is the most pleasing to me and if it is prosecuted in the same spirit in which it is begun, I shall regard it with lively sympathy & with a sort of gratitude.

Yours affectionately
R. W. Emerson[5]

Source: George Ripley, letter to Emerson, 9 November 1840, from Octavius Brooks Frothingham, *George Ripley* (Boston: Houghton, Mifflin, 1882), pp. 307–312; Ralph Waldo Emerson, letter to Ripley, 15 December 1840, from *The Letters of Ralph Waldo Emerson,* ed. Ralph L. Rusk and Eleanor M. Tilton, 10 vols. (New York: Columbia University Press, 1939, 1990–1995), 2:368–371 (textual apparatus deleted). Brownson is quoted from "The Laboring Classes," *Boston Quarterly Review,* 3 (July, October 1840): 358–395, 420–512, as reprinted as *The Laboring Classes,* along with *Brownson's Defense: Defense of the Article on the Laboring Classes* [both, Boston: Benjamin H. Greene, 1840], pp. 8, 9, 14.

Notes

1. Nemesis, a female Greek deity whose mother was night.
2. Samuel Joseph May (1797–1871), minister and reformer.
3. Minerva, Roman goddess of wisdom.
4. Emerson wrote his brother William in March 1841 of his failed plans for household social equality: "You know Lidian & I had dreamed that we would adopt the country practice of having but one table in the house. Well, Lidian went out the other evening & had an explanation on the subject with the two girls. Louisa accepted the plan with great kindness & readiness, but Lydia, the cook, firmly refused—A cook was never fit to come to table, &c. The next morning Waldo [Emerson's son] was sent to announce to Louisa that breakfast was ready but she had eaten already with Lydia & refuses to leave her alone" (*Letters,* 2:389).
5. In the privacy of his journal, Emerson was more direct about "the new social plans" that George and Sophia Ripley, Fuller, and Alcott had discussed with him: "this scheme was arithmetic & comfort; this was a hint borrowed from the Tremont House & U.S. Hotel; a rage in our poverty & politics to live rich & gentlemanlike . . . And not once could I be inflamed,—but sat aloof & thoughtless, my voice faltered & fell. It was not the cave of persecution which is the palace of spiritual power, but only a room in the Astor House hired for the Transcendentalists. I do not wish to remove from my present prison to a prison a little larger. I wish to break all prisons. I have not yet conquered my own house. It irks & repents me. Shall I raise the siege of this hencoop & march baffled away to a pretended siege of Babylon?" (*Journals and Miscellaneous Notebooks,* 7:407–408).

[Sophia Ripley]

"Woman"

(January 1841)

SOPHIA WILLARD DANA RIPLEY (1803–1861) came from a prominent Boston family. After marrying George Ripley in 1827, she became involved in her husband's reform activities and made them her own; and when Brook Farm was founded later in 1841, it was very much a collaborative effort. This piece, which was published in the January 1841 *Dial*, grew out of a paper she had written earlier for one of Fuller's conversations (which is printed above).

※

There have been no topics, for the last two years, more generally talked of than woman, and "the sphere of a woman." In society, everywhere, we hear the same oft-repeated things said upon them by those who have little perception of the difficulties of the subject; and even the clergy have frequently flattered "the feebler sex," by proclaiming to them from the pulpit what lovely things they may become, if they will only be good, quiet, and gentle, attend exclusively to their domestic duties, and the cultivation of religious feelings, which the other sex very kindly relinquish to them as their inheritance. Such preaching is very popular!

Blessed indeed would that man be, who could penetrate the difficulties of this subject, and tell the world faithfully and beautifully what new thing he has discovered about it, or what old truth he has brought to light. The poet's lovely vision of an ethereal being, hovering half seen above him, in his hour of occupation, and gliding gently into his retirement, sometimes a guardian angel, sometimes an unobtrusive companion, wrapt in a silvery veil of mildest radiance, his idealized Eve or Ophelia, is an exquisite picture for the eye;[1] the sweet verse in which he tells us of her, most witching music to the ear; but she is not woman, she is only the spiritualized image of that tender class of women he loves the best,—one whom no true woman could or would become; and if the poet could ever be unkind, we should deem him most so when he reproves the sex, planted as it is in the midst of wearing cares and perplexities, for its departure from this high, beatified ideal of his, to which he loves to give the name of woman. Woman may be soothed by his sweet numbers, but she cannot be helped by his counsels, for he knows her not as she is and must be. All adjusting of the whole sex to a sphere is vain, for no two persons naturally have the same. Character, intellect creates the sphere of each. What is individual and peculiar to each determines it. We hear a great deal everywhere of the religious duties of women. That heaven has placed man and woman in different positions, given them different starting points, (for what is the whole of life, with its varied temporal relations, but a starting point,) there can be no doubt; but religion belongs to them as beings, not as male and female. The true teacher addresses the same language to both. Christ did so, and this separation is ruinous to the highest improvement of both. Difference of position surely does not imply different qualities of head and heart, for the same qualities, as we see every day, are demanded in a variety of positions, the variety merely giving them a different direction.

As we hear a great deal in society, and from the pulpit, of the religious duties of women, so do we hear a great deal of the contemplative life they lead, or ought to lead. It seems an unknown, or at least an unacknowledged fact, that in the spot where man throws aside his heavy responsibilities, his couch of rest is often prepared by his faithful wife, at the sacrifice of all her quiet contemplation and leisure. She is pursued into her most sacred sanctuaries by petty anxieties, haunting her loneliest hours, by temptations taking her by surprise, by cares so harassing, that the most powerful talents and the most abundant intellectual and moral resources are scarce sufficient to give her strength to ward them off. If there is a being exposed to turmoil and indurating care, it is woman, in the retirement of her own home; and if she makes peace and warmth there, it is not by her sweet religious sensibility, her gentle benevolence, her balmy tenderness, but by a strength and energy as great and untiring as leads man to battle, or supports him in the strife of the political arena, though these sturdier qualities unfold often, both in man and woman, in an atmosphere of exquisite refinement and sensibility. The gentle breeze of summer pauses to rest its wing upon the broad oak-leaf, as upon the violet's drooping flower. If woman's position did not bring out all the faculties of the soul, we might demand a higher for her; but she does not need one higher or wider than nature has given her. Very few of her sex suspect even how noble and beautiful is that which they legitimately occupy, for they are early deprived of the privilege of seeing things as they are.

In our present state of society woman possesses not; she is under possession. A dependant, except in extreme hours of peril or moral conflict, when each is left to the mercy of the unfriendly elements alone, for in every mental or physical crisis of life the Infinite has willed each soul to be alone, nothing interposing between it and himself. At times, when most a being needs protection, none but the highest can protect. Man may soothe, but he cannot shelter from, or avert the storm, however solemnly he may promise it to himself or others in the bright hours. When most needed he is most impotent.

Woman is educated with the tacit understanding, that she is only half a being, and an appendage. First, she is so to her parents, whose opinions, perhaps prejudices, are engrafted into her before she knows what an opinion is. Thus provided she enters life, and society seizes her; her faculties of observation are sharpened, often become fearfully acute, though in some sort discriminating, and are ever after so occupied with observing that she never penetrates. In the common course of events she is selected as the life-companion of some one of the other sex; because selected, she fixes her affections upon him, and hardly ventures to exercise upon him even her powers of observation. Then he creates for her a home, which should be constructed by their mutual taste and efforts. She finds him not what she expected; she is disappointed and becomes captious, complaining of woman's lot, or discouraged and crushed by it. She thinks him perfect, adopts his prejudices, adds them to her early stock, and ever defends them with his arguments; where she differs from him in taste and habits, she believes herself in the wrong and him in the right, and spends life in conforming to him, instead of moulding herself to her own ideal. Thus she loses her individuality, and never gains his respect. Her life is usually bustle and hurry, or barren order, dreary decorum and method, without vitality. Her children perhaps love her, but she is only the upper nurse; the father, the oracle. His wish is law, hers only the unavailing sigh uttered in secret. She looks out into life, finds nothing there but confusion, and congratulates herself that it is man's business, not hers, to look through it all, and find stern principle seated tranquilly at the centre of things. Is this woman's destiny? Is she to be the only adventurer, who pursues her course through life aimless, tossed upon the waves of circumstance, intoxicated by joy, panic-struck by misfortune, or stupidly receptive of it? Is she neither to soar to heaven like the lark, nor bend her way, led by an unerring guide, to climes congenial to her nature? Is she always to flutter and flutter, and at last drop into the wave? Man would not have it so, for he reveres the gently firm. Man does not ridicule nor expose to suffering the woman who aspires, he wishes not for blind reverence, but intelligent affection; not for supremacy, but to be understood; not for obedience, but companionship; it is the weak and ignorant of her own sex who brand her, but the enigma still remains unsolved, why are so many of the sex allowed to remain weak and frivolous?

The minor cares of life thronging the path of woman, demand as much reflection and clear-sightedness, and involve as much responsibility, as those of man. Why is she not encouraged to think and penetrate through externals to principles? She should be seen, after the first dreamlike years of unconscious childhood are passed, meekly and reverently questioning and encouraged to question the opinions of others, calmly contemplating beauty in all its forms, studying the harmony of life, as well as of outward nature, deciding nothing, learning all things, gradually forming her own ideal, which, like that represented in the sculptured figures of the old Persian sovereigns, should cheeringly and protectingly hover over her. Society would attract her, and then gracefully mingling in it, she should still be herself, and there find her relaxation, not her home. She should feel that our highest hours are always our lonely ones, and that nothing is good that does not prepare us for these. Beautiful and graceful forms should come before her as revelations of divine beauty, but no charm of outward grace should tempt her to recede one hair's breadth from her uncompromising demand for the noblest nature in her chosen companion, guided in her demands by what she finds within herself, seeking an answering note to her own inner melody, but not sweetly lulling herself into the belief that she has found in him the full-toned harmony of the celestial choirs. If her demand is satisfied, let her not lean, but attend on him as a watchful friend. Her own individuality should be as precious to her as his love. Let her see that the best our most sympathising friend can do for us is, to throw a genial atmosphere around us, and strew our path with golden opportunities; but our path can never be another's, and we must always walk alone. Let no drudgery degrade her high vocation of creator of a happy home. Household order must prevail, but let her ennoble it by detecting its relation to that law which keeps the planets in their course. Every new relation and every new scene should be a new page in the book of the mysteries of life, reverently and lovingly perused, but if folded down, never to be read again, it must be regarded as only the introduction to a brighter one. The faults of those she loves should never be veiled by her affection, but placed in their true relation to character, by the deep insight with which she penetrates beneath them. With high heroic courage, she should measure the strength of suffering before it comes, that she may not meet it unprepared. Her life-plan should be stern, but not unyielding. Her hours, precious treasures lent to her, carefully to be protected from vulgar intrusion, but which women are constantly scattering around them, like small coin, to be picked up by every needy wayfarer. Thought should be her atmosphere; books her food; friends her occasional solace. Prosperity will not dazzle her, for her own spirit is always brighter than its sunshine, and if the deepest sorrow visits her, it will only come to lift her to a higher region, where, with all of life far beneath her, she may sit regally apart till the end.

Is this the ideal of a perfect woman, and if so, how does it differ from a perfect man?

Source: "W. N." [Sophia Ripley], "Woman," *Dial*, 1 (January 1841): 362–366.

Note

1. Ophelia, beloved of Hamlet.

Ralph Waldo Emerson

"Self-Reliance"

(1841)

EMERSON'S GREAT WORK on individualism was published in *Essays* (later titled *Essays: First Series* after he published *Essays: Second Series* in 1844). Modern readers are unable to approach this essay with the thrill of discovery that contemporary readers did because so many passages are in our collective vocabulary. Phrases such as "A foolish consistency is the hobgoblin of little minds" are not only well-known today, thus deadening their impact, but they are often known outside of their original context; for example, Emerson is not complaining about consistency, but about being consistent only for the sake of being consistent (that is, foolishly). Typical of Emerson's aphoristic style, "Self-Reliance" proceeds more by an accretion of sayings and building up of concepts than it does through a traditional linear development in which the author sets forth the path for the reader to follow, almost as if he is trying to force the reader to be self-reliant in order to successfully read about self-realization. To his contemporaries, beginning to be immersed as they were in the individualism of British Romanticism and Jacksonian politics, this essay crystallized many diffuse ideas and feelings into a single work.

"Ne te quæsiveris extra."

—Persius *Satires*, I, 7

> "Man is his own star; and the soul that can
> Render an honest and a perfect man,
> Command all light, all influence, all fate;

Nothing to him falls early or too late.
Our acts our angels are, or good or ill,
Our fatal shadows that walk by us still."
                    —Epilogue to Beaumont and Fletcher's
                                Honest Man's Fortune (1647)

Cast the bantling on the rocks,
Suckle him with the she-wolf's teat:
Wintered with the hawk and fox,
Power and speed be hands and feet.

                                        [—Emerson]

I read the other day some verses written by an eminent painter which
were original and not conventional.[1] Always the soul hears an admonition in such lines, let the subject be what it may. The sentiment
they instil is of more value than any thought they may contain. To
believe your own thought, to believe that what is true for you in your
private heart, is true for all men,—that is genius. Speak your latent
conviction and it shall be the universal sense; for always the inmost
becomes the outmost,—and our first thought is rendered back to us
by the trumpets of the Last Judgment. Familiar as the voice of the
mind is to each, the highest merit we ascribe to Moses, Plato, and
Milton, is that they set at naught books and traditions, and spoke not
what men but what they thought. A man should learn to detect and
watch that gleam of light which flashes across his mind from within,
more than the lustre of the firmament of bards and sages. Yet he
dismisses without notice his thought, because it is his. In every work
of genius we recognise our own rejected thoughts: they come back to
us with a certain alienated majesty. Great works of art have no more
affecting lesson for us than this. They teach us to abide by our spontaneous impression with good-humored inflexibility then most when
the whole cry of voices is on the other side. Else, to-morrow a stranger
will say with masterly good sense precisely what we have thought and
felt all the time, and we shall be forced to take with shame our own
opinion from another.

There is a time in every man's education when he arrives at the
conviction that envy is ignorance; that imitation is suicide; that he
must take himself for better, for worse, as his portion; that though
the wide universe is full of good, no kernel of nourishing corn can
come to him but through his toil bestowed on that plot of ground
which is given to him to till. The power which resides in him is new
in nature, and none but he knows what that is which he can do, nor
does he know until he has tried. Not for nothing one face, one char-

acter, one fact makes much impression on him, and another none. It is not without preëstablished harmony, this sculpture in the memory. The eye was placed where one ray should fall, that it might testify of that particular ray. Bravely let him speak the utmost syllable of his confession. We but half express ourselves, and are ashamed of that divine idea which each of us represents. It may be safely trusted as proportionate and of good issues, so it be faithfully imparted, but God will not have his work made manifest by cowards. It needs a divine man to exhibit any thing divine. A man is relieved and gay when he has put his heart into his work and done his best; but what he has said or done otherwise, shall give him no peace. It is a deliverance which does not deliver. In the attempt his genius deserts him; no muse befriends; no invention, no hope.

Trust thyself: every heart vibrates to that iron string. Accept the place the divine Providence has found for you; the society of your contemporaries, the connexion of events. Great men have always done so and confided themselves childlike to the genius of their age, betraying their perception that the Eternal was stirring at their heart, working through their hands, predominating in all their being. And we are now men, and must accept in the highest mind the same transcendent destiny; and not pinched in a corner, not cowards fleeing before a revolution, but redeemers and benefactors, pious aspirants to be noble clay plastic under the Almighty effort, let us advance and advance on Chaos and the Dark.

What pretty oracles nature yields us on this text in the face and behavior of children, babes and even brutes. That divided and rebel mind, that distrust of a sentiment because our arithmetic has computed the strength and means opposed to our purpose, these have not. Their mind being whole, their eye is as yet unconquered, and when we look in their faces, we are disconcerted. Infancy conforms to nobody: all conform to it, so that one babe commonly makes four or five out of the adults who prattle and play to it. So God has armed youth and puberty and manhood no less with its own piquancy and charm, and made it enviable and gracious and its claims not to be put by, if it will stand by itself. Do not think the youth has no force because he cannot speak to you and me. Hark! in the next room, who spoke so clear and emphatic? Good Heaven! it is he! it is that very lump of bashfulness and phlegm which for weeks has done nothing but eat when you were by, that now rolls out these words like bell-strokes. It seems he knows how to speak to his contemporaries. Bashful or bold, then, he will know how to make us seniors very unnecessary.

The nonchalance of boys who are sure of a dinner, and would disdain as much as a lord to do or say aught to conciliate one, is the healthy attitude of human nature. How is a boy the master of society; independent, irresponsible, looking out from his corner on such people and facts as pass by, he tries and sentences them on their merits, in the swift summary way of boys, as good, bad, interesting, silly, eloquent, troublesome. He cumbers himself never about consequences, about interests: he gives an independent, genuine verdict. You must court him: he does not court you. But the man is, as it were, clapped into jail by his consciousness. As soon as he has once acted or spoken with eclat, he is a committed person, watched by the sympathy or the hatred of hundreds whose affections must now enter into his account. There is no Lethe for this.[2] Ah, that he could pass again into his neutral, godlike independence! Who can thus lose all pledge, and having observed, observe again from the same unaffected, unbiased, unbribable, unaffrighted innocence, must always be formidable, must always engage the poet's and the man's regards. Of such an immortal youth the force would be felt. He would utter opinions on all passing affairs, which being seen to be not private but necessary, would sink like darts into the ear of men, and put them in fear.

These are the voices which we hear in solitude, but they grow faint and inaudible as we enter into the world. Society everywhere is in conspiracy against the manhood of every one of its members. Society is a joint-stock company in which the members agree for the better securing of his bread to each shareholder, to surrender the liberty and culture of the eater. The virtue in most request is conformity. Self-reliance is its aversion. It loves not realities and creators, but names and customs.

Whoso would be a man must be a nonconformist. He who would gather immortal palms must not be hindered by the name of goodness, but must explore if it be goodness. Nothing is at last sacred but the integrity of your own mind. Absolve you to yourself, and you shall have the suffrage of the world. I remember an answer which when quite young I was prompted to make to a valued adviser who was wont to importune me with the dear old doctrines of the church. On my saying, What have I to do with the sacredness of traditions, if I live wholly from within? my friend suggested—"But these impulses may be from below, not from above." I replied, 'They do not seem to me to be such; but if I am the devil's child, I will live then from the devil.' No law can be sacred to me but that of my nature. Good and bad are but names very readily transferable to that or this; the only right is what is after my constitution, the only wrong what is against it. A man is to carry himself in the presence of all opposition as if every thing were titular and ephemeral but he. I am ashamed to think how easily we capitulate to badges and names, to large societies and dead institutions. Every decent and well-spoken individual affects and sways me more than is right. I ought to go upright and vital, and speak the rude truth in all ways. If malice and vanity wear the coat of philanthropy, shall that pass? If an angry bigot assumes this bountiful cause of Abolition, and comes to me with his last news from Barbadoes,³ why should I not say to him, 'Go love thy infant; love thy wood-chopper: be good-natured and modest: have that grace; and never varnish your hard, uncharitable ambition with this incredible tenderness for black folk a thousand miles off. Thy love afar is spite at home.' Rough and graceless would be such greeting, but truth is handsomer than the affectation of love. Your goodness must have some edge to it—else it is none. The doctrine of hatred must be preached as the counteraction of the doctrine of love when that pules and whines. I shun father and mother and wife and brother, when my genius calls me. I would write on the lintels of the door-post, *Whim.* I hope it is somewhat better than whim at last, but we cannot spend the day in explanation. Expect me not to show cause why I seek or why I exclude company. Then, again, do not tell me, as a good man did to-day, of my obligation to put all poor men in good situations. Are they *my* poor? I tell thee, thou foolish philanthropist, that I grudge the dollar, the dime, the cent I give to such men as do not belong to me and to whom I do not belong. There is a class of persons to whom by all spiritual affinity I am bought and sold; for them I will go to prison, if need be; but your miscellaneous popular charities; the education at college of fools; the building of meeting-houses to the vain end to which many now stand; alms to sots; and the thousandfold Relief Societies;—though I confess with shame I sometimes succumb and give the dollar, it is a wicked dollar which by-and-by I shall have the manhood to withhold.

Virtues are in the popular estimate rather the exception than the rule. There is the man *and* his virtues. Men do what is called a good action, as some piece of courage or charity, much as they would pay a fine in expiation of daily non-appearance on parade. Their works are done as an apology or extenuation of their living in the world,—as invalids and the insane pay a high board. Their virtues are penances. I do not wish to expiate, but to live. My life is not an apology, but a life. It is for itself and not for a spectacle. I much prefer that it should be of a lower strain, so it be genuine and equal, than that it should be glittering and unsteady. I wish it to be sound and sweet, and not to need diet and bleeding, My life should be unique; it should be an alms, a battle, a conquest, a medicine. I ask primary evidence that you are a man, and refuse this appeal from the man to his actions. I know that for myself it makes no difference whether I do or forbear those actions which are reckoned excellent. I cannot consent to pay for a privilege where I have intrinsic right. Few and mean as my gifts may be, I actually am, and do not need for my own assurance or the assurance of my fellows any secondary testimony.

What I must do, is all that concerns me, not what the people think. This rule, equally arduous in actual and in intellectual life, may serve for the whole distinction between greatness and meanness. It is the harder, because you will always find those who think they know what is your duty better than you know it. It is easy in the world to live after the world's opinion; it is easy in solitude to live after our own; but the great man is he who in the midst of the crowd keeps with perfect sweetness the independence of solitude.

The objection to conforming to usages that have become dead to you, is, that it scatters your force. It loses your time and blurs the impression of your character. If you maintain a dead church, contribute to a dead Bible-Society, vote with a great party either for the Government or against it, spread your table like base housekeepers,—under all these screens, I have difficulty to detect the precise man you are. And, of course, so much force is withdrawn from your proper life. But do your thing, and I shall know you. Do your work, and you shall reinforce yourself. A man must consider what a blind-man's-buff is this game of conformity. If I know your sect, I anticipate your argument. I hear a preacher announce for his text and topic the expediency of one of the institutions of his church. Do I not know beforehand that not possibly can he say a new and spontaneous word? Do I not know that with all this ostentation of examining the grounds of the institution, he will do no such thing? Do I not know that he is pledged to himself not to look but at one side; the permitted side, not as a man, but as a parish minister? He is a retained attorney, and these airs of the bench are the emptiest affectation. Well, most men have bound their eyes with one or another handkerchief, and attached themselves to some one of these communities of opinion. This conformity makes them not false in a few particulars, authors of a few lies, but false in all particulars. Their every truth is not quite true. Their two is not the real two, their four not the real four: so that every word they say chagrins us, and we know not where to begin to set them right. Meantime nature is not slow to equip us in the prison-uniform of the party to which we adhere. We come to wear one cut of face and figure, and acquire by degrees the gentlest asinine expression. There is a mortifying experience in particular which does not fail to wreak itself also in the general history; I mean, "the foolish face of praise,"[4] the forced smile which we put on in company where we do not feel at ease in answer to conversation which does not interest us.

The muscles, not spontaneously moved, but moved by a low usurping wilfulness, grow tight about the outline of the face and make the most disagreeable sensation, a sensation of rebuke and warning which no brave young man will suffer twice.

For nonconformity the world whips you with its displeasure. And therefore a man must know how to estimate a sour face. The bystanders look askance on him in the public street or in the friend's parlor. If this aversation had its origin in contempt and resistance like his own, he might well go home with a sad countenance; but the sour faces of the multitude, like their sweet faces, have no deep cause,—disguise no god, but are put on and off as the wind blows, and a newspaper directs. Yet is the discontent of the multitude more formidable than that of the senate and the college. It is easy enough for a firm man who knows the world to brook the rage of the cultivated classes. Their rage is decorous and prudent, for they are timid as being very vulnerable themselves. But when to their feminine rage the indignation of the people is added, when the ignorant and the poor are aroused, when the unintelligent brute force that lies at the bottom of society is made to growl and mow, it needs the habit of magnanimity and religion to treat it godlike as a trifle of no concernment.

The other terror that scares us from self-trust is our consistency; a reverence for our past act or word, because the eyes of others have no other data for computing our orbit than our past acts, and we are loath to disappoint them.

But why should you keep your head over your shoulder? Why drag about this monstrous corpse of your memory, lest you contradict somewhat you have stated in this or that public place? Suppose you should contradict yourself; what then? It seems to be a rule of wisdom never to rely on your memory alone, scarcely even in acts of pure memory, but bring the past for judgment into the thousand-eyed present, and live ever in a new day. Trust your emotion. In your metaphysics you have denied personality to the Deity: yet when the devout motions of the soul come, yield to them heart and life, though they should clothe God with shape and color. Leave your theory as Joseph his coat in the hand of the harlot, and flee.[5]

A foolish consistency is the hobgoblin of little minds, adored by little statesmen and philosophers and divines. With consistency a great soul has simply nothing to do. He may as well concern himself with his shadow on the wall. Out upon your guarded lips! Sew them up with packthread, do. Else, if you would be a man, speak what you think to-day in words as hard as cannon balls, and to-morrow speak what to-morrow thinks in hard words again, though it contradict every thing you said to-day. Ah, then, exclaim the aged ladies, you shall be sure to be misunderstood. Misunderstood! It is a right fool's word. Is it so bad then to be misunderstood? Pythagoras was misunderstood, and Socrates, and Jesus, and Luther, and Copernicus, and Galileo, and Newton, and every pure and wise spirit that ever took flesh.[6] To be great is to be misunderstood.

I suppose no man can violate his nature. All the sallies of his will are rounded in by the law of his being as the inequalities of Andes and Himmaleh are insignificant in the curve of the sphere. Nor does it matter how you gauge and try him. A character is like an acrostic or Alexandrian stanza;—read it forward, backward, or across, it still spells the same thing.[7] In this pleasing contrite wood-life which God allows me, let me record day by day my honest thought without prospect or retrospect, and, I cannot doubt, it will be found symmetrical, though I mean it not, and see it not. My book should smell of pines and resound with the hum of insects. The swallow over my window should interweave that thread or straw he carries in his bill into my web also. We pass for what we are. Character teaches above our wills. Men imagine that they communicate their virtue or vice only by overt actions and do not see that virtue or vice emit a breath every moment.

Fear never but you shall be consistent in whatever variety of actions, so they be each honest and natural in their hour. For of one will, the actions will be harmonious, however unlike they seem. These varieties are lost sight of when seen at a little distance, at a little height of thought. One tendency unites them all. The voyage of the best ship is a zigzag line of a hundred tacks. This is only microscopic criticism. See the line from a sufficient distance, and it straightens itself to the average tendency. Your genuine action will explain itself and will explain your other genuine actions. Your conformity explains nothing. Act singly, and what you have already done singly, will justify you now. Greatness always appeals to the future. If I can be great enough now to do right and scorn eyes, I must have done so much right before, as to defend me now. Be it how it will, do right now. Always scorn appearances, and you always may. The force of character is cumulative. All the foregone days of virtue work their health into this. What makes the majesty of the heroes of the senate and the field, which so fills the imagination? The consciousness of a train of great days and victories behind. There they all stand and shed an united light on the advancing actor. He is attended as by a visible escort of angels to every man's eye. That is it which throws thunder into Chatham's voice, and dignity into Washington's port, and America into Adams's eye.[8] Honor is venerable to us because it is no ephemeris. It is always ancient virtue. We worship it to-day, because it is not of to-day. We love it and pay it homage, because it is not a trap for our love and homage, but is self-dependent, self-derived, and therefore of an old immaculate pedigree, even if shown in a young person.

I hope in these days we have heard the last of conformity and consistency. Let the words be gazetted and ridiculous henceforward. Instead of the gong for dinner, let us hear a whistle from the Spartan fife.⁹ Let us bow and apologize never more. A great man is coming to eat at my house. I do not wish to please him: I wish that he should wish to please me. I will stand here for humanity, and though I would make it kind, I would make it true. Let us affront and reprimand the smooth mediocrity and squalid contentment of the times, and hurl in the face of custom, and trade, and office, the fact which is the upshot of all history, that there is a great responsible Thinker and Actor moving wherever moves a man; that a true man belongs to no other time or place, but is the centre of things. Where he is, there is nature. He measures you, and all men, and all events. You are constrained to accept his standard. Ordinarily every body in society reminds us of somewhat else or of some other person. Character, reality, reminds you of nothing else. It takes place of the whole creation. The man must be so much that he must make all circumstances indifferent,—put all means into the shade. This all great men are and do. Every true man is a cause, a country, and an age; requires infinite spaces and numbers and time fully to accomplish his thought;—and posterity seem to follow his steps as a procession. A man Cæsar is born, and for ages after, we have a Roman Empire. Christ is born, and millions of minds so grow and cleave to his genius, that he is confounded with virtue and the possible of man. An institution is the lengthened shadow of one man; as, the Reformation, of Luther; Quakerism, of Fox; Methodism, of Wesley; Abolition, of Clarkson.¹⁰ Scipio, Milton called "the height of Rome;"¹¹ and all history resolves itself very easily into the biography of a few stout and earnest persons.

Let a man then know his worth, and keep things under his feet. Let him not peep or steal, or skulk up and down with the air of a charity-boy, a bastard, or an interloper, in the world which exists for him. But the man in the street finding no worth in himself which corresponds to the force which built a tower or sculptured a marble god, feels poor when he looks on these. To him a palace, a statue, or a costly book have an alien and forbidding air, much like a gay equipage, and seem to say like that, 'Who are you, sir?' Yet they all are his, suitors for his notice, petitioners to his faculties that they will come out and take possession. The picture waits for my verdict: it is not to command me, but I am to settle its claims to praise. That popular fable of the sot who was picked up dead drunk in the street, carried to the duke's house, washed and dressed and laid in the duke's bed, and, on his waking, treated with all obsequious ceremony like the duke, and assured that he had been insane,—owes its popularity to the fact, that it symbolizes so well the state of man, who is in the world a sort of sot, but now and then wakes up, exercises his reason, and finds himself a true prince.[12]

Our reading is mendicant and sycophantic. In history, our imagination makes fools of us, plays us false. Kingdom and lordship, power and estate are a gaudier vocabulary than private John and Edward in a small house and common day's work: but the things of life are the same to both: the sum total of both is the same. Why all this deference to Alfred, and Scanderbeg, and Gustavus?[13] Suppose they were virtuous: did they wear out virtue? As great a stake depends on your private act to-day, as followed their public and renowned steps. When private men shall act with vast views, the lustre will be transferred from the actions of kings to those of gentlemen.

The world has indeed been instructed by its kings, who have so magnetized the eyes of nations. It has been taught by this colossal symbol the mutual reverence that is due from man to man. The joyful loyalty with which men have every where suffered the king, the noble, or the great proprietor to walk among them by a law of his own, make his own scale of men and things, and reverse theirs, pay for benefits not with money but with honor, and represent the Law in his person, was the hieroglyphic by which they obscurely signified their consciousness of their own right and comeliness, the right of every man.

The magnetism which all original action exerts is explained when we inquire the reason of self-trust. Who is the Trustee? What is the aboriginal Self on which a universal reliance may be grounded? What is the nature and power of that science-baffling star, without parallax,[14] without calculable elements, which shoots a ray of beauty even into trivial and impure actions, if the least mark of independence appear? The inquiry leads us to that source, at once the essence of genius, the essence of virtue, and the essence of life, which we call Spontaneity or Instinct. We denote this primary wisdom as Intuition, whilst all later teachings are tuitions. In that deep force, the last fact behind which analysis cannot go, all things find their common origin. For the sense of being which in calm hours rises, we know not how, in the soul, is not diverse from things, from space, from light, from time, from man, but one with them, and proceedeth obviously from the same source whence their life and being also proceedeth. We first share the life by which things exist, and afterwards see them as appearances in nature, and forget that we have shared their cause. Here is the fountain of action and the fountain of thought. Here are the lungs of that inspiration which giveth man wisdom, of that inspiration of man which cannot be denied without impiety and atheism. We lie in the lap of immense intelligence, which makes us organs of its activity and receivers of its truth. When we discern justice, when we discern truth, we do nothing of ourselves, but allow a passage to its beams. If we ask whence this comes, if we seek to pry into the soul that causes,—all metaphysics, all philosophy is at fault. Its presence or its absence is all we can affirm. Every man discerns between the voluntary acts of his mind, and his involuntary perceptions. And to his involuntary perceptions, he knows a perfect respect is due. He may err in the expression of them, but he knows that these things are so, like day and night, not to be disputed. All my wilful actions and acquisitions are but roving;—the most trivial reverie, the faintest native emotion are domestic and divine. Thoughtless people contradict as readily the statement of perceptions as of opinions, or rather much more readily; for, they do not distinguish between perception and notion. They fancy that I choose to see this or that thing. But perception is not whimsical, but fatal. If I see a trait, my children will see it after me, and in course of time, all mankind,—although it may chance that no one has seen it before me. For my perception of it is as much a fact as the sun.

The relations of the soul to the divine spirit are so pure that it is profane to seek to interpose helps. It must be that when God speaketh, he should communicate not one thing, but all things; should fill the world with his voice; should scatter forth light, nature, time, souls, from the centre of the present thought; and new date and new create the whole. Whenever a mind is simple, and receives a divine wisdom, then old things pass away,—means, teachers, texts, temples fall; it lives now and absorbs past and future into the present hour. All things are made sacred by relation to it,—one thing as much as another. All things are dissolved to their centre by their cause, and in the universal miracle petty and particular miracles disappear. This is and must be. If, therefore, a man claims to know and speak of God, and carries you backward to the phraseology of some old mouldered nation in another country, in another world, believe him not. Is the acorn better than the oak which is its fulness and completion? Is the parent better than the child into whom he has cast his ripened being? Whence then this worship of the past? The centuries are conspirators against the sanity and majesty of the soul. Time and space are but physiological colors which the eye maketh, but the soul is light; where it is, is day; where it was, is night; and history is an impertinence and an injury, if it be anything more than a cheerful apologue[15] or parable of my being and becoming.

Man is timid and apologetic. He is no longer upright. He dares not say 'I think,' 'I am,' but quotes some saint or sage. He is ashamed before the blade of grass or the blowing rose. These roses under my window make no reference to former roses or to better ones; they are for what they are; they exist with God to-day. There is no time to them. There is simply the rose; it is perfect in every moment of its existence. Before a leaf-bud has burst, its whole life acts; in the full-blown flower, there is no more; in the leafless root, there is no less. Its nature is satisfied, and it satisfies nature, in all moments alike. There is no time to it. But man postpones or remembers; he does not live in the present, but with reverted eye laments the past, or, heedless of the riches that surround him, stands on tiptoe to foresee the future. He cannot be happy and strong until he too lives with nature in the present, above time.

This should be plain enough. Yet see what strong intellects dare not yet hear God himself, unless he speak the phraseology of I know not what David, or Jeremiah, or Paul. We shall not always set so great a price on a few texts, on a few lives. We are like children who repeat by rote the sentences of grandames and tutors, and, as they grow older, of the men of talents and character they chance to see,—painfully recollecting the exact words they spoke; afterwards, when they come into the point of view which those had who uttered these sayings, they understand them, and are willing to let the words go; for, at any time, they can use words as good, when occasion comes. So was it with us, so will it be, if we proceed. If we live truly, we shall see truly. It is as easy for the strong man to be strong, as it is for the weak to be weak. When we have new perception, we shall gladly disburthen the memory of its hoarded treasures as old rubbish. When a man lives with God, his voice shall be as sweet as the murmur of the brook and the rustle of the corn.

And now at last the highest truth on this subject remains unsaid; probably, cannot be said; for all that we say is the far off remembering of the intuition. That thought, by what I can now nearest approach to say it, is this. When good is near you, when you have life in yourself,—it is not by any known or appointed way; you shall not discern the foot-prints of any other; you shall not see the face of man; you shall not hear any name;—the way, the thought, the good shall be wholly strange and new. It shall exclude all other being. You take the way from man, not to man. All persons that ever existed are its fugitive ministers. There shall be no fear in it. Fear and hope are alike beneath it. It asks nothing. There is somewhat low even in hope. We are then in vision. There is nothing that can be called gratitude nor properly joy. The soul is raised over passion. It seeth identity and eternal causation. It is a perceiving that Truth and Right are. Hence it becomes a Tranquillity out of the knowing that all things go well. Vast spaces of nature; the Atlantic Ocean, the South Sea; vast intervals of time, years, centuries, are of no account. This which I think and feel, underlay that former state of life and circumstances, as it does underlie my present, and will always all circumstance, and what is called life, and what is called death.

Life only avails, not the having lived. Power ceases in the instant of repose; it resides in the moment of transition from a past to a new state; in the shooting of the gulf; in the darting to an aim. This one fact the world hates, that the soul *becomes*; for, that forever degrades the past; turns all riches to poverty; all reputation to a shame; confounds the saint with the rogue; shoves Jesus and Judas equally aside. Why then do we prate of self-reliance? Inasmuch as the soul is present, there will be power not confident but agent. To talk of reliance, is a poor external way of speaking. Speak rather of that which relies, because it works and is. Who has more soul than I, masters me, though he should not raise his finger. Round him I must revolve by the gravitation of spirits; who has less, I rule with like facility. We fancy it rhetoric when we speak of eminent virtue. We do not yet see that virtue is Height, and that a man or a company of men plastic and permeable to principles, by the law of nature must overpower and ride all cities, nations, kings, rich men, poets, who are not.

This is the ultimate fact which we so quickly reach on this as on every topic, the resolution of all into the ever blessed ONE. Virtue is the governor, the creator, the reality. All things real are so by so much of virtue as they contain. Hardship, husbandry, hunting, whaling, war, eloquence, personal weight, are somewhat, and engage my respect as examples of the soul's presence and impure action. I see the same law working in nature for conservation and growth. The poise of a planet, the bended tree recovering itself from the strong wind, the vital resources of every vegetable and animal, are also demonstrations of the self-sufficing, and therefore self-relying soul. All history from its highest to its trivial passages is the various record of this power.

Thus all concentrates; let us not rove; let us sit at home with the cause. Let us stun and astonish the intruding rabble of men and books and institutions by a simple declaration of the divine fact. Bid them take the shoes from off their feet, for God is here within. Let our simplicity judge them, and our docility to our own law demonstrate the poverty of nature and fortune beside our native riches.

But now we are a mob. Man does not stand in awe of man, nor is the soul admonished to stay at home, to put itself in communication with the internal ocean, but it goes abroad to beg a cup of water of the urns of men. We must go alone. Isolation must precede true society. I like the silent church before the service begins, better than any preaching. How far off, how cool, how chaste the persons look, begirt each one with a precinct or sanctuary. So let us always sit. Why should we assume the faults of our friend, or wife, or father, or child, because they sit around our hearth, or are said to have the same blood? All men have my blood, and I have all men's. Not for that will I adopt their petulance or folly, even to the extent of being ashamed of it. But your isolation must not be mechanical, but spiritual, that is, must be elevation. At times the whole world seems to be in conspiracy to importune you with emphatic trifles. Friend, client, child, sickness, fear, want, charity, all knock at once at thy closet door and say, 'Come out unto us.'—Do not spill thy soul; do not all descend; keep thy state; stay at home in thine own heaven; come not for a moment into their facts, into their hubbub of conflicting appearances, but let in the light of thy law on their confusion. The power men possess to annoy me, I give them by a weak curiosity. No man can come near me but through my act. "What we love that we have, but by desire we bereave ourselves of the love."[16]

If we cannot at once rise to the sanctities of obedience and faith, let us at least resist our temptations, let us enter into the state of war, and wake Thor and Woden, courage and constancy in our Saxon breasts.[17] This is to be done in our smooth times by speaking the truth. Check this lying hospitality and lying affection. Live no longer to the expectation of these deceived and deceiving people with whom we converse. Say to them, O father, O mother, O wife, O brother, O friend, I have lived with you after appearances hitherto. Henceforward I am the truth's. Be it known unto you that henceforward I obey no law less than the eternal law. I will have no covenants but proximities. I shall endeavor to nourish my parents, to support my family, to be the chaste husband of one wife,—but these relations I must fill after a new and unprecedented way. I appeal from your customs. I must be myself. I cannot break myself any longer for you, or you. If you can love me for what I am, we shall be the happier. If you cannot, I will still seek to deserve that you should. I must be myself. I will not hide my tastes or aversions. I will so trust that what is deep is holy, that I will do strongly before the sun and moon whatever inly rejoices me, and the heart appoints. If you are noble, I will love you; if you are not, I will not hurt you and myself by hypocritical attentions. If you are true, but not in the same truth with me, cleave to your companions; I will seek my own. I do this not selfishly, but humbly and truly. It is alike your interest and mine and all men's, however long we have dwelt in lies, to live in truth. Does this sound harsh to-day? You will soon love what is dictated by your nature as well as mine, and if we follow the truth, it will bring us out safe at last.—But so you may give these friends pain. Yes, but I cannot sell my liberty and my power, to save their sensibility. Besides, all persons have their moments of reason when they look out into the region of absolute truth; then will they justify me and do the same thing.

The populace think that your rejection of popular standards is a rejection of all standard, and mere antinomianism;[18] and the bold sensualist will use the name of philosophy to gild his crimes. But the law of consciousness abides. There are two confessionals, in one or the other of which we must be shriven. You may fulfil your round of duties by clearing yourself in the *direct*, or, in the *reflex* way. Consider whether you have satisfied your relations to father, mother, cousin, neighbor, town, cat, and dog; whether any of these can upbraid you. But I may also neglect this reflex standard, and absolve me to myself. I have my own stern claims and perfect circle. It denies the name of duty to many offices that are called duties. But if I can discharge its debts, it enables me to dispense with the popular code. If any one imagines that this law is lax, let him keep its commandment one day.

And truly it demands something godlike in him who has cast off the common motives of humanity, and has ventured to trust himself for a task-master. High be his heart, faithful his will, clear his sight, that he may in good earnest be doctrine, society, law to himself, that a simple purpose may be to him as strong as iron necessity is to others.

If any man consider the present aspects of what is called by distinction *society*, he will see the need of these ethics. The sinew and heart of man seem to be drawn out, and we are become timorous desponding whimperers. We are afraid of truth, afraid of fortune, afraid of death, and afraid of each other. Our age yields no great and perfect persons. We want men and women who shall renovate life and our social state, but we see that most natures are insolvent; cannot satisfy their own wants, have an ambition out of all proportion to their practical force, and so do lean and beg day and night continually. Our housekeeping is mendicant, our arts, our occupations, our marriages, our religion we have not chosen, but society has chosen for us. We are parlor soldiers. The rugged battle of fate, where strength is born, we shun.

If our young men miscarry in their first enterprizes, they lose all heart. If the young merchant fails, men say he is *ruined*. If the finest genius studies at one of our colleges, and is not installed in an office within one year afterwards in the cities or suburbs of Boston or New York, it seems to his friends and to himself that he is right in being disheartened and in complaining the rest of his life. A sturdy lad from New Hampshire or Vermont, who in turn tries all the professions, who *teams it, farms it, peddles,* keeps a school, preaches, edits a newspaper, goes to Congress, buys a township, and so forth, in successive years, and always, like a cat, falls on his feet, is worth a hundred of these city dolls. He walks abreast with his days, and feels no shame in not 'studying a profession,' for he does not postpone his life, but lives already. He has not one chance, but a hundred chances. Let a stoic arise who shall reveal the resources of man, and tell men they are not leaning willows, but can and must detach themselves; that with the exercise of self-trust, new powers shall appear; that a man is the word made flesh, born to shed healing to the nations, that he should be ashamed of our compassion, and that the moment he acts from himself, tossing the laws, the books, idolatries, and customs out of the window,—we pity him no more but thank and revere him,—and that teacher shall restore the life of man to splendor, and make his name dear to all History.

It is easy to see that a greater self-reliance,—a new respect for the divinity in man,—must work a revolution in all the offices and relations of men; in their religion; in their education; in their pursuits; their modes of living; their association; in their property; in their speculative views.

1. In what prayers do men allow themselves! That which they call a holy office, is not so much as brave and manly. Prayer looks abroad and asks for some foreign addition to come through some foreign virtue, and loses itself in endless mazes of natural and supernatural, and mediatorial and miraculous. Prayer that craves a particular commodity—any thing less than all good, is vicious. Prayer is the contemplation of the facts of life from the highest point of view. It is the soliloquy of a beholding and jubilant soul. It is the spirit of God pronouncing his works good. But prayer as a means of effect a private end, is theft and meanness. It supposes dualism and not unity in nature and consciousness. As soon as the man is at one with God, he will not beg. He will then see prayer in all action. The prayer of the farmer kneeling in his field to weed it, the prayer of the rower kneeling with the stroke of his oar, are true prayers heard throughout nature, though for cheap ends. Caratach, in Fletcher's Bonduca, when admonished to inquire the mind of the god Audate, replies,

> His hidden meaning lies in our endeavors,
> Our valors are our best gods.[19]

Another sort of false prayers are our regrets. Discontent is the want of self-reliance: it is infirmity of will. Regret calamities, if you can thereby help the sufferer; if not, attend your own work, and already the evil begins to be repaired. Our sympathy is just as base. We come to them who weep foolishly, and sit down and cry for company, instead of imparting to them truth and health in rough electric shocks, putting them once more in communication with the soul. The secret of fortune is joy in our hands. Welcome evermore to gods and men is the self-helping man. For him all doors are flung wide. Him all tongues greet, all honors crown, all eyes follow with desire. Our love goes out to him and embraces him, because he did not need it. We solicitously and apologetically caress and celebrate him, because he held on his way and scorned our disapprobation. The gods love him because men hated him. "To the persevering mortal," said Zoroaster, "the blessed Immortals are swift."

As men's prayers are a disease of the will, so are their creeds a disease of the intellect. They say with those foolish Israelites, 'Let not God speak to us, lest we die. Speak thou, speak any man with us, and we will obey.'[20] Everywhere I am bereaved of meeting God in my brother, because he has shut his own temple doors, and recites fables merely of his brother's, or his brother's brother's God. Every new mind is a new classification. If it prove a mind of uncommon activity and power, a Locke, a Lavoisier, a Hutton, a Bentham, a Spurzheim, it imposes its classification on other men, and lo! a new system.[21] In proportion always to the depth of the thought, and so to the number of the objects it touches and brings within reach of the pupil, is his complacency. But chiefly is this apparent in creeds and churches, which are also classifications of some powerful mind acting on the great elemental thought of Duty, and man's relation to the Highest. Such is Calvinism, Quakerism, Swedenborgianism. The pupil takes the same delight in subordinating every thing to the new terminology that a girl does who has just learned botany, in seeing a new earth and new seasons thereby. It will happen for a time, that the pupil will feel a real debt to the teacher,—will find his intellectual power has grown by the study of his writings. This will continue until he has exhausted his master's mind. But in all unbalanced minds, the classification is idolized, passes for the end, and not for a speedily exhaustible means, so that the walls of the system blend to their eye in the remote horizon with the walls of the universe; the luminaries of heaven seem to them hung on the arch their master built. They cannot imagine how you aliens have any right to see,—how you can see; 'It must be somehow that you stole the light from us.' They do not yet perceive, that, light unsystematic, indomitable, will break into any cabin, even into theirs. Let them chirp awhile and call it their own. If they are honest and do well, presently their neat new pinfold will be too strait and low, will crack, will lean, will rot and vanish, and the immortal light, all young and joyful, million-orbed, million-colored, will beam over the universe as on the first morning.

2. It is for want of self-culture that the idol of Travelling, the idol of Italy, of England, of Egypt, remains for all educated Americans. They who made England, Italy, or Greece venerable in the imagination, did so not by rambling round creation as a moth round a lamp, but by sticking fast where they were, like an axis of the earth. In manly hours, we feel that duty is our place, and that the merrymen of circumstance should follow as they may. The soul is no traveller: the wise man stays at home with the soul, and when his necessities, his duties, on any occasion call him from his house, or into foreign lands, he is at home still, and is not gadding abroad from himself, and shall make men sensible by the expression of his countenance, that he goes the missionary of wisdom and virtue, and visits cities and men like a sovereign, and not like an interloper or a valet.

I have no churlish objection to the circumnavigation of the globe, for the purposes of art, of study, and benevolence, so that the man is first domesticated, or does not go abroad with the hope of finding somewhat greater than he knows. He who travels to be amused, or to get somewhat which he does not carry, travels away from himself, and grows old even in youth among old things. In Thebes, in Palmyra, his will and mind have become old and dilapidated as they. He carries ruins to ruins.

Travelling is a fool's paradise. We owe to our first journeys the discovery that place is nothing. At home I dream that at Naples, at Rome, I can be intoxicated with beauty, and lose my sadness. I pack my trunk, embrace my friends, embark on the sea, and at last wake up in Naples, and there beside me is the stern Fact, the sad self, unrelenting, identical, that I fled from. I seek the Vatican, and the palaces. I affect to be intoxicated with sights and suggestions, but I am not intoxicated. My giant goes with me wherever I go.

3. But the rage of travelling is itself only a symptom of a deeper unsoundness affecting the whole intellectual action. The intellect is vagabond, and the universal system of education fosters restlessness. Our minds travel when our bodies are forced to stay at home. We imitate; and what is imitation but the travelling of the mind? Our houses are built with foreign taste; our shelves are garnished with foreign ornaments; our opinions, our tastes, our whole minds lean, and follow the Past and the Distant, as the eyes of a maid follow her mistress. The soul created the arts wherever they have flourished. It was in his own mind that the artist sought his model. It was an application of his own thought to the thing to be done and the con-

ditions to be observed. And why need we copy the Doric or the Gothic model?[22] Beauty, convenience, grandeur of thought, and quaint expression are as near to us as to any, and if the American artist will study with hope and love the precise thing to be done by him, considering the climate, the soil, the length of the day, the wants of the people, the habit and form of the government, he will create a house in which all these will find themselves fitted, and taste and sentiment will be satisfied also.

Insist on yourself; never imitate. Your own gift you can present every moment with the cumulative force of a whole life's cultivation; but of the adopted talent of another, you have only an extemporaneous, half possession. That which each can do best, none but his Maker can teach him. No man yet knows what it is, nor can, till that person has exhibited it. Where is the master who could have taught Shakspeare? Where is the master who could have instructed Franklin, or Washington, or Bacon, or Newton. Every great man is an unique. The Scipionism of Scipio is precisely that part he could not borrow. If any body will tell me whom the great man imitates in the original crisis when he performs a great act, I will tell him who else than himself can teach him. Shakespeare will never be made by the study of Shakspeare. Do that which is assigned thee, and thou canst not hope too much or dare too much. There is at this moment, there is for me an utterance bare and grand as that of the colossal chisel of Phidias, or trowel of the Egyptians, or the pen of Moses, or Dante, but different from all these. Not possibly will the soul all rich, all eloquent, with thousand-cloven tongue, deign to repeat itself; but if I can hear what these patriarchs say, surely I can reply to them in the same pitch of voice: for the ear and the tongue are two organs of one nature. Dwell up there in the simple and noble regions of thy life, obey thy heart, and thou shalt reproduce the Foreworld again.

4. As our Religion, our Education, our Art look abroad, so does our spirit of society. All men plume themselves on the improvement of society, and no man improves.

Society never advances. It recedes as fast on one side as it gains on the other. Its progress is only apparent, like the workers of a treadmill. It undergoes continual changes: it is barbarous, it is civilized, it is christianized, it is rich, it is scientific; but this change is not amelioration. For every thing that is given, something is taken. Society acquires new arts and loses old instincts. What a contrast between the well-clad, reading, writing, thinking American, with a watch, a pencil, and a bill of exchange in his pocket, and the naked New Zealander, whose property is a club, a spear, a mat, and an undivided twentieth of a shed to sleep under. But compare the health of the two men, and you shall see that his aboriginal strength the white man has lost. If the traveller tell us truly, strike the savage with a broad axe, and in a day or two the flesh shall unite and heal as if you struck the blow into soft pitch, and the same blow shall send the white to his grave.

The civilized man has built a coach, but has lost the use of his feet. He is supported on crutches, but loses so much support of muscle. He has got a fine Geneva watch, but he has lost the skill to tell the hour by the sun. A Greenwich nautical almanac he has, and so being sure of the information when he wants it, the man in the street does not know a star in the sky.[23] The solstice he does not observe; the equinox he knows as little; and the whole bright calendar of the year is without a dial in his mind. His note-books impair his memory; his libraries overload his wit; the insurance office increases the number of accidents; and it may be a question whether machinery does not encumber; whether we have not lost by refinement some energy, by a christianity entrenched in establishments and forms, some vigor of wild virtue. For every stoic was a stoic;[24] but in Christendom where is the Christian?

There is no more deviation in the moral standard than in the standard of height or bulk. No greater men are now than ever were. A singular equality may be observed between the great men of the first and of the last ages; nor can all the science, art, religion and philosophy of the nineteenth century avail to educate greater men than Plutarch's heroes, three or four and twenty centuries ago. Not in time is the race progressive. Phocion, Socrates, Anaxagoras, Diogenes, are great men, but they leave no class.[25] He who is really of their class will not be called by their name, but be wholly his own man, and, in his turn the founder of a sect. The arts and inventions of each period are only its costume, and do not invigorate men. The harm of the improved machinery may compensate its good. Hudson and Behring accomplished so much in their fishing-boats, as to astonish Parry and Franklin, whose equipment exhausted the resources of science and art.[26] Galileo, with an opera-glass, discovered a more splendid series of facts than any one since. Columbus found the New World in an undecked boat. It is curious to see the periodical disuse and perishing of means and machinery which were introduced with loud laudation, a few years or centuries before. The great genius returns to essential man. We reckoned the improvements of the art of war among the triumphs of science, and yet Napoleon conquered Europe by the Bivouac,[27] which consisted of falling back on naked valor, and disencumbering it of all aids. The Emperor held it impossible to make a perfect army, says Las Cases, "without abolishing our arms, magazines, commissaries, and carriages, until in imitation of the Roman custom, the soldier should receive his supply of corn, grind it in his hand-mill, and bake his bread himself."[28]

Society is a wave. The wave moves onward, but the water of which it is composed, does not. The same particle does not rise from the valley to the ridge. Its unity is only phenomenal. The persons who make up a nation to-day, next year die, and their experience with them.

And so the reliance on Property, including the reliance on governments which protect it, is the want of self-reliance. Men have looked away from themselves and at things so long, that they have come to esteem what they call the soul's progress, namely, the religious, learned, and civil institutions, as guards of property, and they deprecate assaults on these, because they feel them to be assaults on property. They measure their esteem of each other, by what each has, and not by what each is. But a cultivated man becomes ashamed of his property, ashamed of what he has, out of new respect for his being. Especially he hates what he has, if he see that it is accidental,—came to him by inheritance, or gift, or crime; then he feels that it is not having; it does not belong to him, has no root in him, and merely lies there, because no revolution or no robber takes it away. But that which a man is, does always by necessity acquire, and what the man acquires is permanent and living property, which does not wait the beck of rulers, or mobs, or revolutions, or fire, or storm, or bankruptcies, but perpetually renews itself wherever the man is put. "Thy lot or portion of life," said the Caliph Ali, "is seeking after thee; therefore be at rest from seeking after it."[29] Our dependence on these foreign goods leads us to our slavish respect for numbers. The political parties meet in numerous conventions; the greater the concourse, and with each new uproar of announcement, The delegation from Essex! The Democrats from New Hampshire! The Whigs of Maine! the young patriot feels himself stronger than before by a new thousand of eyes and arms. In like manner the reformers summon conventions, and vote and resolve in multitude. But not so, O friends! will the God deign to enter and inhabit you, but by a method precisely the reverse. It is only as a man puts off from himself all external support, and stands alone, that I see him to be strong and to prevail. He is weaker by every recruit to his banner. Is not a man better than a town? Ask nothing of men, and in the endless mutation, thou only firm column must presently appear the upholder of all that surrounds thee. He who knows that power is in the soul, that he is weak only because he has looked for good out of him and elsewhere, and so perceiving, throws himself unhesitatingly on his thought, instantly rights himself, stands in the erect position, commands his limbs, works miracles; just as a man who stands on his feet is stronger than a man who stands on his head.

So use all that is called Fortune. Most men gamble with her, and gain all, and lose all, as her wheel rolls. But do thou leave as unlawful these winnings, and deal with Cause and Effect, the chancellors of God. In the Will work and acquire, and thou hast chained the wheel of Chance, and shalt always drag her after thee. A political victory, a rise of rents, the recovery of your sick, or the return of your absent friend, or some other quite external event, raises your spirits, and you think good days are preparing for you. Do not believe it. It can never be so. Nothing can bring you peace but yourself. Nothing can bring you peace but the triumph of principles.

Source: Ralph Waldo Emerson, "Self-Reliance," from *Essays {First Series}* (Boston: James Munroe, 1841), pp. 35–73. The epigrams are from Persius (34–62), Latin moralistic poet; the epilogue, ll. 33–38, to the play by Francis Beaumont (1584–1616) and John Fletcher (1579–1625), English dramatists; and Emerson's poem, published as "Power" in *May-Day* (1867).

Notes

1. The "eminent painter" is Washington Allston (1779–1843), historical painter and novelist.
2. Lethe, Greek mythological river of oblivion.
3. Slavery had been abolished in Barbadoes, in the West Indies, in 1834.
4. "Epistle to Dr. Arbuthnot" (1735), l. 212, by Alexander Pope.
5. A reference to the biblical Joseph and his coat of many colors.
6. Galileo (1564–1642), Italian physicist and astronomer indicted as a heretic by the Catholic Church.
7. Acrostics, a poem in which the initial letter of each line, when read down, forms a word or words, were used by the Greeks in the Alexandrian period, but to be read "forward, backward, or across," the work needs to be a palindrome.
8. William Pitt, First Earl of Chatham (1708–1778), thought by many to be England's finest prime minister; John Quincy Adams (1767–1848), sixth president of the United States.
9. Sparta, ancient Greek state.
10. Thomas Clarkson (1760–1846), English abolitionist.
11. Scipio Africanus the Elder (236–ca. 183 B.C.), Roman general referred to in *Paradise Lost* (1667) by John Milton.
12. See the Induction to *The Taming of the Shrew.*
13. Scanderbeg (ca. 1404–1468), Albanian national hero, born George Castriota; Gustavus Adolphus (1594–1632), king of Sweden.
14. Parallax, the apparent change in the position of a star that is caused by the earth's motion as it orbits the Sun.

15. Apologue, an allegorical narrative.
16. Quoted from Friedrich Schiller.
17. Thor and Woden (or Odin), Norse gods of war.
18. Antinomianism, generally used to describe people who consciously take a stand against established rules, but in Christian tradition, it refers to those who believed that salvation by grace excused them from obeying the laws of humankind.
19. *Bonduca* (1647), act 3, scene 1, by John Fletcher; Audate, god of war.
20. See Exodus, 20:19.
21. Antoine Laurent Lavoisier (1743–1794), founder of modern chemistry; James Hutton (1726–1797), Scottish geologist and naturalist; Jeremy Bentham (1748–1832), English reformer and philosopher; Johann Kaspar Spurzheim (1776–1832), a founder of the pseudo-science of phrenology.
22. Doric and Gothic, styles of architecture from, respectively, Greece and twelfth- through fifteenth-century England and France.
23. Greenwich, England, home of the Royal Observatory.
24. Stoics, philosophical school founded in 308 B.C. known for its belief in submitting to necessity.
25. Anaxagoras (ca. 500–428 B.C.), Greek philosopher whose work predicts atomic theory; Diogenes (ca. 412–323 B.C.), Greek cynic philosopher constantly seeking an honest man.
26. Henry Hudson (ca. 1565–1611), English explorer who tried to find the Northwest Passage between Europe and Asia through the Arctic Ocean; Vitus Bering (or Behring) (1681–1741), Danish explorer of the strait between what is now Alaska and Russia; Sir William Edward Parry (1790–1855) and Sir John Franklin (1786–1847), English Arctic explorers.
27. Bivouac, an encampment for the night without tents or any coverings.
28. Quoted from Emmanuel, Count de Las Cases (1766–1842), French historian.
29. Ali (ca. 600–661), son-in-law of Muhammad, the prophet of Islam.

Theodore Parker

A Discourse of the Transient and Permanent in Christianity; Preached at the Ordination of Mr. Charles C. Shackford, in the Hawes Place Church in Boston, May 19, 1841

(1841)

IF EMERSON'S Divinity School Address sidesteps a direct confrontation with the conservative Unitarians over the miracles question on their narrow theological grounds by preaching the doctrine of the infinitude of the individual and the need for the minister to translate spirit into action through preaching, then Parker takes up the challenge for a theological debate and approaches it directly. Both Emerson and Parker argue that the generations following Christ have come to worship the image of Christ more than they have his teachings, and that one reason for this is the increasingly repressive and hierarchical administrative structure of the church. Like his "Levi Blodgett" letter, where he describes "this miracle-question" as "one of *theology*, and not of *religion*," here he calls miracles "theological questions, not religious questions," and states flatly that if Jesus "had wrought no miracle, and none but the human nature had ever been ascribed to him . . . Christianity would still have been the Word of God; it would have lost none of its truths." In this masterful mixture of learned theological references, allusions to the German Higher Criticism, an emotional Christianity, and inspired (and literary) prose, Parker writes the definitive challenge to those who take a fundamentalist approach to the existence of miracles: those who believe in them, Parker says, cater to the arguments of the present generation and separate humankind from God— they become, in other words, temporal, irreligious, and divisive. Parker warns that if miracles are at the foundation of a sect's beliefs, then "alas for you. The ground will shake under your feet if you attempt to walk uprightly and like men. You will be afraid of every new opinion, lest it shake down your church." And he was right: as a direct result of this pamphlet, the Unitarian ministers of Boston joined together to stop exchanging pulpits with Parker, and ostracized those few of its members who continued to do so. For his part, Parker moved from his West Roxbury congregation (near Brook Farm) to join the newly formed Twenty-Eighth Congregation in Boston, where he weekly filled the cavernous Music Hall with those eager to hear him preach.

Heaven and Earth shall pass away:
but my word shall not pass away.
—Luke XXI. 33.

I n this sentence we have a very clear indication that Jesus of Nazareth believed the religion he taught would be eternal, that the substance of it would last forever. Yet there are some, who are affrighted by the faintest rustle which a heretic makes among the dry leaves of theology; they tremble lest Christianity itself should perish without hope. Ever and anon the cry is raised, "The Philistines be upon us, and Christianity is in danger."[1] The least doubt respecting the popular theology, or the existing machinery of the church; the least sign of distrust in the Religion of the Pulpit, or the Religion of the Street, is by some good men supposed to be at enmity with faith in Christ, and capable of shaking Christianity itself. On the other hand, a few bad men and a few pious men, it is said, on both sides of the water, tell us the day of Christianity is past. The latter—it is alleged—would persuade us that, hereafter, Piety must take a new form; the teachings of Jesus are to be passed by; that Religion is to wing her way sublime, above the flight of Christianity, far away, toward heaven, as the fledged eaglet leaves forever the nest which sheltered his callow youth. Let us, therefore, devote a few moments to this subject, and consider what is *Transient* in Christianity, and what *Permanent* therein. The topic seems not inappropriate to the times in which we live, or the occasion that calls us together.

Christ says, his Word shall never pass away. Yet at first sight nothing seems more fleeting than a word. It is an evanescent impulse of the most fickle element. It leaves no track where it went through the air. Yet to this, and this only, did Jesus entrust the truth, wherewith he came laden, to the earth; truth for the salvation of the world. He took no pains to perpetuate his thoughts; they were poured forth where occasion found him an audience,—by the side of the lake, or a well; in a cottage, or the temple; in a fisher's boat, or the synagogue of the Jews. He founds no institution as a monument of his words. He appoints no order of men to preserve his bright and glad revelations. He only bids his friends give freely the truth they had freely received. He did not even write his words in a book. With a noble confidence, the result of his abiding faith, he scattered them, broad-cast, on the world, leaving the seed to its own vitality. He knew, that what is of God cannot fail, for God keeps his own. He sowed his seed in the heart, and left it there, to be watered and warmed by the dew and the sun which heaven sends. He felt his words were for eternity. So he trusted them to the uncertain air; and for eighteen hundred years that faithful element has held them good,—distinct as when first warm from his lips. Now they are translated into every human speech, and murmured in all earth's thousand tongues, from the pine forests of the North to the palm groves of eastern Ind.[2] They mingle, as it were, with the roar of the populous city, and join the chime of the desert sea. Of a Sabbath morn they are repeated from church to church, from isle to isle, and land to land, till the music goes round the world. These words have become the breath of the good, the hope of the wise, the joy of the pious,—and that for many millions of hearts. They are the prayers of our churches, our better devotion by fireside and fieldside, the enchantment of our hearts. It is these words, that still work wonders, to which the first recorded miracles were nothing in grandeur and utility. It is these which build our temples and beautify our homes. They raise our thoughts of sublimity, they purify our ideal of purity, they hallow our prayer for truth and love. They make beauteous and divine the life which plain men lead. They give wings to our aspirations. What charmers they are! Sorrow is lulled at their bidding. They take the sting out of disease, and rob adversity of his power to disappoint. They give health and wings to the pious soul, broken-hearted and shipwrecked in his voyage through life, and encourage him to tempt the perilous way once more. They make all things ours: Christ our brother; Time our servant; Death our ally and the witness of our triumph. They reveal to us the presence of God, which else we might not have seen so clearly, in the first wind-flower of spring; in the falling of a sparrow; in the distress of a nation; in the sorrow or the rapture of a world. Silence the voice of Christianity, and the world is well nigh dumb, for gone is that sweet music which kept in awe the rulers and the people; which cheers the poor widow in her lonely toil, and comes like light through the windows of morning, to men who sit stooping and feeble, with failing eyes and a hungering heart. It is gone—all gone; only the cold, bleak world left before them.

Such is the life of these Words; such the empire they have won for themselves over men's minds since they were spoken first. In the mean time, the words of great men and mighty, whose name shook whole continents, though graven in metal and stone, though stamped in institutions and defended by whole tribes of priests and troops of followers—their words have gone to the ground, and the world gives back no echo of their voice. Meanwhile the great works also of old times, castle and tower and town, their cities and their empires, have perished, and left scarce a mark on the bosom of the earth to show they once have been. The philosophy of the wise, the art of the ac-complished, the song of the poet, the ritual of the priest, though honored as divine in their day, have gone down, a prey to oblivion. Silence has closed over them; only their spectres now haunt the earth. A deluge of blood has swept over the nations; a night of darkness, more deep than the fabled darkness of Egypt, has lowered down upon that flood, to destroy or to hide what the deluge had spared. But through all this, the words of Christianity have come down to us from the lips of that Hebrew youth, gentle and beautiful as the light of a star, not spent by their journey through time and through space. They have built up a new civilization, which the wisest Gentile never hoped for, which the most pious Hebrew never foretold. Through centuries of wasting, these words have flown on, like a dove in the storm, and now wait to descend on hearts pure and earnest, as the Father's spirit, we are told, came down on his lowly Son. The old heavens and the old earth are indeed passed away, but the Word stands. Nothing shows clearer than this, how fleeting is what man calls great; how lasting what God pronounces true.

Looking at the Word of Jesus, at real Christianity, the pure religion he taught, nothing appears more fixed and certain. Its influence widens as light extends; it deepens as the nations grow more wise. But, looking at the history of what men call Christianity, nothing seems more uncertain and perishable. While true religion is always the same thing, in each century and every land, in each man that feels it, the Christianity of the Pulpit, which is the religion taught; the Christianity of the People, which is the religion that is accepted and lived out, has never been the same thing in any two centuries or lands, except only in name. The difference between what is called Christianity by the Unitarians in our times, and that of some ages past, is greater than the difference between Mahomet and the Messiah. The difference at this day between opposing classes of Christians; the difference between the Christianity of some sects and that of Christ himself, is deeper and more vital than that between Jesus and Plato, Pagan as we call him. The Christianity of the seventh century has passed away. We recognise only the ghost of Superstition in its faded features, as it comes up at our call. It is one of the things which has been, and can be no more, for neither God nor the world goes back. Its terrors do not frighten, nor its hopes allure us. We rejoice that it has gone. But how do we know that our Christianity shall not share the same fate? Is there that difference between the nineteenth century, and some seventeen that have gone before it, since Jesus, to warrant the belief that our notion of Christianity shall last forever? The stream of time has already beat down Philosophies and Theologies, Temple and Church, though never so old and revered. How do we know there is not a perishing element in what we call Christianity? Jesus tells us, *his* Word is the word of God, and so shall never pass away. But who tells us, that *our* word shall never pass away? that *our notion* of his Word shall stand forever?

Let us look at this matter a little more closely. In actual Christianity, that is, in that portion of Christianity which is preached and believed, there seem to have been, ever since the time of its earthly founder, two elements, the one transient, the other permanent. The one is the thought, the folly, the uncertain wisdom, the theological notions, the impiety of man; the other the eternal truth of God. These two bear perhaps the same relation to each other that the phenomena of outward nature, such as sunshine and cloud, growth, decay and reproduction, bear to the great law of nature, which underlies and supports them all. As in that case, more attention is commonly paid to the particular phenomena than to the general law, so in this case, more is generally given to the transient in Christianity than to the permanent therein.

It must be confessed, though with sorrow, that transient things form a great part of what is commonly taught as Religion. An undue place has often been assigned to forms and doctrines, while too little stress has been laid on the divine life of the soul, love to God, and love to man. Religious forms may be useful, and beautiful. They are so, whenever they speak to the soul, and answer a want thereof. In our present state some forms are perhaps necessary. But they are only the accident of Christianity; not its substance. They are the robe, not the angel, who may take another robe, quite as becoming and useful. One sect has many forms; another none. Yet both may be equally Christian, in spite of the redundance or the deficiency. They are a part of the language in which religion speaks, and exist, with few exceptions, wherever man is found. In our calculating nation, in our rationalizing sect, we have retained but two of the rites so numerous in the early Christian church, and even these we have attenuated to the last degree, leaving them little more than a spectre of the ancient form. Another age may continue or forsake both; may revive old forms, or invent new ones to suit the altered circumstances of the times, and yet be Christians quite as good as we, or our fathers of the dark ages. Whether the Apostles designed these rites to be perpetual, seems a question which belongs to scholars and antiquarians, not to us, as Christian men and women. So long as they satisfy or help the pious heart, so long they are good. Looking behind, or around us, we see that the forms and rites of the Christians are quite as fluctuating as those of the heathens; from whom some of them have been, not unwisely, adopted by the earlier church.

Again, the doctrines that have been connected with Christianity, and taught in its name, are quite as changeable as the form. This also takes place unavoidably. If observations be made upon Nature, which must take place so long as man has senses and understanding, there will be a philosophy of Nature, and philosophical doctrines. These will differ as the observations are just or inaccurate, and as the deductions from observed facts are true or false. Hence there will be different schools of natural philosophy, so long as men have eyes and understandings of different clearness and strength. And if men observe and reflect upon Religion, which will be done so long as man is a religious and reflective being, there must also be a philosophy of Religion, a theology and theological doctrines. These will differ, as men have felt much or little of religion, as they analyze their sentiments correctly or otherwise, and as they have reasoned right or wrong. Now the true system of Nature which exists in the outward facts, whether discovered or not, is always the same thing, though the philosophy of Nature, which men invent, change every month, and be one thing at London and the opposite at Berlin. Thus there is but one system of Nature as it exists in fact, though many theories of Nature, which exist in our imperfect notions of that system, and by which we may approximate and at length reach it. Now there can be but one Religion which is absolutely true, existing in the facts of human nature, and the ideas of Infinite God. That, whether acknowledged or not, is always the same thing and never changes. So far as a man has any real religion—either the principle or the sentiment thereof—so far he has that, by whatever name he may call it. For strictly speaking there is but one kind of religion as there is but one kind of love, though the manifestations of this religion, in forms, doctrines and life, be never so diverse. It is through these, men approximate to the true expression of this religion. Now while this religion is one and always the same thing, there may be numerous systems of theology or philosophies of religion. These with their creeds, confessions and collections of doctrines, deduced by reasoning upon the facts observed, may be baseless and false, either because the observation was too narrow in extent, or otherwise defective in point of accuracy, or because the reasoning was illogical and therefore the deduction spurious. Each of these three faults is conspicuous in the systems of theology. Now the solar system as it exists in fact is permanent, though the notions of Thales and Ptolemy, of Copernicus and Descartes about this system, prove transient, imperfect approximations to the true expression.[3] So the Christianity of Jesus is permanent, though what passes for Christianity with Popes and catechisms, with sects and churches, in the first century or in the nineteenth century, prove transient also. Now it has sometimes happened that a man took his philosophy of Nature at second hand, and then attempted to make his observations conform to his theory, and Nature ride in his panniers.[4] Thus some philosophers refused to look at the Moon through Galileo's telescope, for according to their theory of vision, such an instrument would not aid the sight. Thus their preconceived notions stood up between them and Nature. Now it has often happened that men took their theology thus at second hand, and distorted the history of the world and man's nature besides, to make Religion conform to their notions. Their theology stood between them and God. Those obstinate philosophers have disciples in no small number.

What another has said of false systems of science, will apply equally to theology: "It is barren in effects, fruitful in questions, slow and languid in its improvement, exhibiting in its generality the counterfeit of perfection, but ill filled up in its details, popular in its choice, but suspected by its very promoters, and therefore bolstered up and countenanced with artifices. Even those who have been determined to try for themselves, to add their support to learning, and to enlarge its limits, have not dared entirely to desert received opinions, nor to seek the spring-head of things. But they think they have done a great thing if they intersperse and contribute something of their own; prudently considering, that by their assent they can save their modesty, and by their contributions, their liberty. Neither is there, nor ever will be, an end or limit to these things. One snatches at one thing, another is pleased with another; there is no dry nor clear sight of any thing. Every one plays the philosopher out of the small treasures of his own fancy. The more sublime wits more acutely and with better success; the duller with less success but equal obstinacy, and, by the discipline of some learned men, sciences are bounded within the limits of some certain authors which they have set down, imposing them upon old men and instilling them into young. So that now, (as Tully cavilled upon Cæsar's consulship) the star Lyra riseth by an edict, and authority is taken for truth and not truth for authority; which kind of order and discipline is very convenient for our present use, but banisheth those which are better."⁵

Any one who traces the history of what is called Christianity, will see that nothing changes more from age to age than the doctrines taught as Christian and insisted on as essential to Christianity and personal salvation. What is falsehood in one province passes for truth in another. The heresy of one age is the orthodox belief and "only infallible rule" of the next. Now Arius, and now Athanasius is Lord of the ascendant. Both were excommunicated in their turn; each for affirming what the other denied. Men are burned for professing what men are burned for denying. For centuries the doctrines of the Christians were no better, to say the least, than those of their contemporary pagans. The theological doctrines derived from our fathers, seem to have come from Judaism, Heathenism, and the caprice of philosophers, far more than they have come from the principle and sentiment of Christianity. The doctrine of the Trinity, the very Achilles of theological dogmas, belongs to philosophy and not religion; its subtleties cannot even be expressed in our tongue.⁶ As old religions became superannuated and died out, they left to the rising faith, as to a residuary legatee, their forms, and their doctrines; or rather, as the giant in the fable left his poisoned garment to work the overthrow of his conqueror. Many tenets that pass current in our theology, seem to be the refuse of idol temples; the offscourings of Jewish and Heathen cities, rather than the sands of virgin gold, which the stream of Christianity has worn off from the rock of ages, and brought in its bosom for us. It is wood, hay and stubble, wherewith men have built on the corner stone Christ laid. What wonder the fabric is in peril when tried by fire? The stream of Christianity, as men receive it, has caught a stain from every soil it has filtered through, so that now it is not the pure water from the well of Life, which is offered to our lips, but streams troubled and polluted by man with mire and dirt. If Paul and Jesus could read our books of theological doctrines, would they accept as their teaching, what men have vented in their name? Never till the letters of Paul had faded out of his memory; never till the words of Jesus had been torn out from the Book of Life. It is their notions about Christianity, men have taught as the only living word of God. They have piled their own rubbish against the temple of Truth where Piety comes up to worship; what wonder the pile seems unshapely and like to fall? But these theological doctrines are fleeting as the leaves on the trees. They

> Are found
> Now green in youth, now wither'd on the ground;
> Another race the following spring supplies;
> They fall successive and successive rise.[7]

Like the clouds of the sky, they are here to-day; to-morrow, all swept off and vanished, while Christianity itself, like the heaven above, with its sun and moon, and uncounted stars, is always over our head, though the cloud sometimes debars us of the needed light. It must of necessity be the case that our reasonings, and therefore our theological doctrines, are imperfect and so, perishing. It is only gradually that we approach to the true system of Nature by observation and reasoning, and work out our philosophy and theology by the toil of the brain. But mean time, if we are faithful, the great truths of morality and religion, the deep sentiment of love to man and love to God, are perceived intuitively, and by instinct, as it were, though our theology be imperfect and miserable. The theological notions of Abraham, to take the story as it stands, were exceedingly gross, yet a greater than Abraham has told us Abraham desired to see my day, saw it and was glad.[8] Since these notions are so fleeting, why need we accept the commandment of men, as the doctrine of God?

This transitoriness of doctrines appears, in many instances, of which two may be selected for a more attentive consideration. First, the doctrine respecting the origin and authority of the Old and New Testament. There has been a time when men were burned for asserting doctrines of natural philosophy, which rested on evidence the most incontestable, because those doctrines conflicted with sentences in the Old Testament. Every word of that Jewish record was regarded as miraculously inspired and therefore as infallibly true. It was believed that the Christian religion itself rested thereon, and must stand or fall with the immaculate Hebrew text. He was deemed no small sinner who found mistakes in the manuscripts. On the authority of the written Word, man was taught to believe impossible legends, conflicting assertions; to take fiction for fact; a dream for a miraculous revelation of God; an oriental poem for a grave history of miraculous events; a collection of amatory idyls for a serious discourse "touching the mutual love of Christ and the Church;" they have been taught to accept a picture sketched by some glowing eastern imagination, never intended to be taken for a reality, as a proof that the Infinite God spoke in human words, appeared in the shape of a cloud, a flaming bush, or a man who ate and drank, and vanished into smoke; that he gave counsels to-day, and the opposite to-morrow; that he violated his own laws, was angry, and was only dissuaded by a mortal man from destroying at once a whole nation—millions of men who rebelled against their leader in a moment of anguish. Questions in philosophy, questions in the Christian religion, have been settled by an appeal to that book. The inspiration of its authors has been assumed as infallible. Every fact in the early Jewish history, has been taken as a type of some analogous fact in Christian history. The most distant events, even such as are still in the arms of time, were supposed to be clearly foreseen and foretold by pious Hebrews several centuries before Christ. It has been assumed at the outset, with no shadow of evidence, that those writers held a miraculous communication with God, such as he has granted to no other man. What was originally a presumption of bigoted Jews became an article of faith, which Christians were burned for not believing. This has been for centuries the general opinion of the Christian church, both Catholic and Protestant, though the former never accepted the Bible as the *only* source of religious truth. It has been so. Still worse it is now the general opinion of religious sects at this day. Hence the attempt, which always fails, to reconcile the philosophy of our times with the poems in Genesis writ a thousand years before Christ; hence the attempt to conceal the contradictions in the records itself. Matters have come to such a pass that even now, he is deemed an infidel, if not by implication an atheist, whose reverence for the Most High forbids him to believe that God commanded Abraham to sacrifice his son, a thought at which the flesh creeps with horror; to believe it solely on the authority of an oriental story, written down nobody knows when, or by whom, or for what purpose: which may be a poem, but cannot be the record of a fact unless God is the author of confusion and a lie.

Now this idolatry of the Old Testament has not always existed. Jesus says that none born of a woman is greater than John the Baptist, yet the least in the kingdom of heaven was greater than John. Paul tells us the Law—the very crown of the old Hebrew revelation—is a shadow of good things, which have now come: only a schoolmaster to bring us to Christ, and when faith has come, that we are no longer under the schoolmaster: that it was a Law of sin and death, for which we are made free by the Law of the spirit of Life. Christian teachers themselves have differed so widely in their notion of the doctrines and meaning of those books, that it makes one weep to think of the follies deduced therefrom. But modern Criticism is fast breaking to pieces this idol which men have made out of the Scriptures. It has shown that here are the most different works thrown together. That their authors, wise as they sometimes were; pious as we feel often their spirit to have been, had only that inspiration which is common to other men equally pious and wise; that they were by no means infallible; but were mistaken in facts or in reasoning; uttered predictions which time has not fulfilled; men who in some measure partook of the darkness and limited notions of their age, and were not always above its mistakes or its corruptions.

The history of opinions on the New Testament is quite similar. It has been assumed at the outset, it would seem with no sufficient reason, without the smallest pretence on its writers' part, that all of its authors were infallibly and miraculously inspired, so that they could commit no error of doctrine or fact. Men have been bid to close their eyes at the obvious difference between Luke and John; the serious disagreement between Paul and Peter; to believe, on the smallest evidence, accounts which shock the moral sense and revolt the reason, and tend to place Jesus in the same series with Hercules, and Apollonius of Tyana; accounts which Paul in the Epistles never mentions, though he also had a vein of the miraculous running quite through him. Men have been told that all these things must be taken as part of Christianity, and if they accepted the religion, they must take all these accessories along with it; that the living spirit could not be had without the killing letter. All the books which caprice or accident had brought together, between the lids of the Bible, were declared to be the infallible word of God, the only certain rule of religious faith and practice. Thus the Bible was made not a single channel, but the *only* certain rule of religious faith and practice. To disbelieve any of its statements, or even the common interpretation put upon those statements by the particular age or church in which the man belonged, was held to be infidelity if not atheism. In the name of Him who forbid us to judge our brother, good men and pious men have applied these terms to others, good and pious as themselves. That state of things has by no means passed away. Men who cry down the absurdities of Paganism in the worst spirit of the French "free-thinkers," call others infidels and atheists, who point out, though reverently, other absurdities which men have piled upon Christianity. So the world goes.

An idolatrous regard for the imperfect scripture of God's word is the apple of Atalanta, which defeats theologians running for the hand of divine truth.[9]

But the current notions respecting the infallible inspiration of the Bible have no foundation in the Bible itself. Which Evangelist, which Apostle of the New Testament, what Prophet or Psalmist of the Old Testament, ever claims infallible authority for himself or for others? Which of them does not in his own writings show that he was finite and with all his zeal and piety, possessed but a limited inspiration, the bound whereof we can sometimes discover? Did Christ ever demand that men should assent to the doctrines of the Old Testament, credit its stories, and take its poems for histories, and believe equally two accounts that contradict one another? Has he ever told you that all the truths of his religion, all the beauty of a Christian life should be contained in the writings of those men, who, even after his resurrection, expected him to be a Jewish king; of men who were sometimes at variance with one another and misunderstood his divine teachings? Would not those modest writers themselves be confounded at the idolatry we pay them? Opinions may change on these points, as they have often changed—changed greatly and for the worse since the days of Paul. They are changing now, and we may hope for the better; for God makes man's folly as well as his wrath to praise Him, and continually brings good out of evil.

Another instance of the transitoriness of doctrines taught as Christian is found in those which relate to the nature and authority of Christ. One ancient party has told us, that he is the infinite God; another, that he is both God and man; a third, that he was a man, the son of Joseph and Mary,—born as we are; tempted like ourselves; inspired, as we may be, if we will pay the price. Each of the former parties believed its doctrine on this head was infallibly true, and formed the very substance of Christianity, and was one of the essential conditions of salvation, though scarce any two distinguished teachers, of ancient or modern times, agree in their expression of this truth.

Almost every sect that has ever been, makes Christianity rest on the personal authority of Jesus, and not the immutable truth of the doctrines themselves, or the authority of God, who sent him into the world. Yet it seems difficult to conceive any reason why moral and religious truths should rest for their support on the personal authority of their revealer, any more than the truths of science on that of him who makes them known first or most clearly. It is hard to see why the great truths of Christianity rest on the personal authority of Jesus, more than the axioms of geometry rest on the personal authority of

Euclid, or Archimedes.[10] The authority of Jesus, as of all teachers, one would naturally think, must rest on the truth of his words, and not their truth on his authority.

Opinions respecting the nature of Christianity seem to be constantly changing. In the three first centuries after Christ, it appears, great latitude of speculation prevailed. Some said he was God, with nothing of human nature, his body only an illusion; others, that he was man, with nothing of the divine nature, his miraculous birth having no foundation in fact. In a few centuries it was decreed by councils that he was God, thus honoring the divine element; next, that he was man also, thus admitting the human side. For some ages the Catholic Church seems to have dwelt chiefly on the divine nature that was in him, leaving the human element to mystics and other heretical persons, whose bodies served to flesh the swords of orthodox believers. The stream of Christianity has come to us in two channels—one within the Church, the other without the Church—and it is not hazarding too much to say, that since the fourth century the true Christian life has been out of the established Church, and not in it, but rather in the ranks of dissenters. From the Reformation till the latter part of the last century, we are told, the Protestant Church dwelt chiefly on the human side of Christ, and since that time many works have been written to show how the two—perfect Deity and perfect manhood— were united in his character. But, all this time, scarce any two eminent teachers agree on these points, however orthodox they may be called. What a difference between the Christ of John Gerson and John Calvin,—yet were both accepted teachers and pious men.[11] What a difference between the Christ of the Unitarians, and the Methodists— yet may men of both sects be true Christians and acceptable with God.[12] What a difference between the Christ of Matthew and John— yet both were disciples, and their influence is wide as Christendom and deep as the heart of man.[13] But on this there is not time to enlarge.

Now it seems clear, that the notions men form about the origin and nature of the scriptures; respecting the nature and authority of Christ, have nothing to do with Christianity except as its aids or its adversaries; they are not the foundation of its truths. These are theological questions, not religious questions. Their connection with Christianity appears accidental; for if Jesus had taught at Athens, and not at Jerusalem; if he had wrought no miracle, and none but the human nature had ever been ascribed to him; if the Old Testament had forever perished at his birth,—Christianity would still have been the Word of God; it would have lost none of its truths. It would be just as true, just as beautiful, just as lasting, as now it is; though we should have lost so many a blessed word, and the work of Christianity itself would have been, perhaps, a long time retarded.

To judge the future by the past, the former authority of the Old Testament can never return. Its present authority cannot stand. It must be taken for what it is worth. The occasional folly and impiety of its authors pass for no more than their value;—while the religion, the wisdom, the love, which make fragrant its leaves, will still speak to the best hearts as hitherto, and in accents even more divine, when Reason is allowed her rights. The ancient belief in the infallible inspiration of each sentence of the New Testament, is fast changing; very fast. One writer, not a skeptic, but a Christian of unquestioned piety, sweeps off the beginning of Matthew; another, of a different church and equally religious, the end of John. Numerous critics strike off several epistles. The Apocalypse itself is not spared, notwithstanding its concluding curse.[14] Who shall tell us the work of retrenchment is to stop here; that others will not demonstrate, what some pious hearts have long felt, that errors of doctrine and errors of fact may be found in many parts of the law, here and there, from the beginning of Matthew to the end of Acts! We see how opinions have changed ever since the apostles' time; and who shall assure us that they were not sometimes mistaken in historical, as well as doctrinal matters; did not sometimes confound the actual with the imaginary, and that the fancy of these pious writers never stood in the place of their recollection?

But what if this should take place? Is Christianity then to perish out of the heart of the nations, and vanish from the memory of the world, like the religions that were before Abraham? It must be so, if it rest on a foundation which a scoffer may shake, and a score of pious critics shake down. But this is the foundation of a theology, not of Christianity. That does not rest on the decision of Councils. It is not to stand or fall with the infallible inspiration of a few Jewish fishermen, who have writ their names in characters of light all over the world. It does not continue to stand through the forbearance of some critic, who can cut when he will the thread on which its life depends. Christianity does not rest on the infallible authority of the New Testament. It depends on this collection of books for the historical statement of its facts. In this we do not require infallible inspiration on the part of the writers, more than in the record of other historical facts. To me it seems as presumptuous on the one hand for the believer to claim this evidence for the truth of Christianity, as it is absurd on the other hand, for the skeptic to demand such evidence to support these historical statements. I cannot see that it depends on the personal authority of Jesus. He was the organ through which the Infinite spoke.

It is God that was manifested in the flesh by him, on whom rests the truth which Jesus brought to light and made clear and beautiful in his life; and if Christianity be true, it seems useless to look for any other authority to uphold it, as for some one to support Almighty God. So if it could be proved,—as it cannot,—in opposition to the greatest amount of historical evidence ever collected on any similar point, that the gospels were the fabrication of designing and artful men, that Jesus of Nazareth had never lived, still Christianity would stand firm, and fear no evil. None of the doctrines of that religion would fall to the ground, for if true, they stand by themselves. But we should lose,—oh, irreparable loss!—the example of that character, so beautiful, so divine, that no human genius could have conceived it, as none, after all the progress and refinement of eighteen centuries, seems fully to have comprehended its lustrous life. If Christianity were true, we should still think it was so, not because its record was written by infallible pens; nor because it was lived out by an infallible teacher,—but that it is true, like the axioms of geometry, because it is true, and is to be tried by the oracle God places in the breast. If it rest on the personal authority of Jesus alone, then there is no certainty of its truth, if he were ever mistaken in the smallest matter, as some Christians have thought he was, in predicting his second coming.

These doctrines respecting the scriptures have often changed, and are but fleeting. Yet men lay much stress on them. Some cling to these notions as if they were Christianity itself. It is about these and similar points that theological battles are fought from age to age. Men sometimes use worst the choicest treasure which God bestows. This is especially true of the use men make of the Bible. Some men have regarded it as the heathen their idol, or the savage his fetish. They have subordinated Reason, Conscience, and Religion to this. Thus have they lost half the treasure it bears in its bosom. No doubt the time will come when its true character shall be felt. Then it will be seen, that, amid all the contradictions of the Old Testament; its legends, so beautiful as fictions, so appalling as facts; amid its predictions that have never been fulfilled; amid the puerile conceptions of God, which sometimes occur, and the cruel denunciations that disfigure both Psalm and Prophecy, there is a reverence for man's nature, a sublime trust in God, and a depth of piety rarely felt in these cold mortal hearts of ours. Then the devotion of its authors, the loftiness of their aim and the majesty of their life, will appear doubly fair, and Prophet and Psalmist will warm our hearts as never before. Their voice will cheer the young and sanctify the gray-headed; will charm us in the toil of life, and sweeten the cup Death gives us when he comes to shake off this mantle of flesh. Then will it be seen, that the words of Jesus are the music of heaven, sung in an earthly voice, and the echo of these words in John and Paul owe their efficacy to their truth and their depth, and to no accidental matter connected therewith. Then can the Word,—which was in the beginning and now is,—find access to the innermost heart of man, and speak there as now it seldom speaks. Then shall the Bible,—which is a whole library of the deepest and most earnest thoughts and feelings, and piety and love, ever recorded in human speech,—be read oftener than ever before, not with Superstition, but with Reason, Conscience, and Faith fully active. Then shall it sustain men bowed down with many sorrows; rebuke sin; encourage virtue; sow the world broad-cast and quick with the seed of love, that man may reap a harvest for life everlasting.

With all the obstacles men have thrown in its path, how much has the Bible done for mankind. No abuse has deprived us of all its blessings. You trace its path across the world from the day of Pentecost to this day. As a river springs up in the heart of a sandy continent, having its father in the skies and its birth-place in distant, unknown mountains; as the stream rolls on, enlarging itself, making in that arid waste, a belt of verdure wherever it turns its way; creating palm groves and fertile plains, where the smoke of the cottager curls up at eventide, and noble cities send the gleam of their splendor far into the sky;—such has been the course of the Bible on the earth. Despite of idolaters bowing to the dust before it, it has made a deeper mark on the world than the rich and beautiful literature of all the heathen. The first book of the Old Testament tells man he is made in the image of God; the first of the New Testament gives us the motto, Be perfect as your Father in heaven. Higher words were never spoken. How the truths of the Bible have blest us. There is not a boy on all the hills of New England; not a girl born in the filthiest cellar which disgraces a capital in Europe, and cries to God against the barbarism of modern civilization; not a boy nor a girl all Christendom through, but their lot is made better by that great book.

Doubtless the time will come when men shall see Christ also as he is. Well might he still say; "Have I been so long with you, and yet hast thou not known me." No! we have made him an idol, have bowed the knee before him, saying, "Hail, king of the Jews;" called him "Lord, Lord!" but done not the things which he said. The history of the Christian world might well be summed up in one word of the evangelist—"and there they crucified him," for there has never been an age when man did not crucify the Son of God afresh. But if error prevail for a time and grow old in the world, truth will triumph at the last, and then we shall see the Son of God as he is. Lifted up he shall draw all nations unto him. Then will man understand the Word of Jesus, which shall not pass away. Then shall we see and love the divine life that he lived. How vast has his influence been. How his spirit wrought in the hearts of the disciples, rude, selfish, bigotted, as at first they were. How it has wrought in the world. His words judge the nations. The wisest son of man has not measured their height. They speak to what is deepest in profound men; what is holiest in good men; what is divinest in religious men. They kindle anew the flame of devotion in hearts long cold. They are Spirit and Life. His truth was not derived from Moses and Solomon; but the light of God shone through him, not colored, not bent aside.[15] His life is the perpetual rebuke of all time since. It condemns ancient civilization; it condemns modern civilization. Wise men we have since had, and good men; but this Galilean youth strode before the world whole thousands of years,—so much of Divinity was in him. His words solve the questions of this present age. In him the God-like and the Human met and embraced, and a divine Life was born. Measure him by the world's greatest sons;—how poor they are. Try him by the best of men,—how little and low they appear. Exalt him as much as we may, we shall yet, perhaps, come short of the mark. But still was he not our brother; the son of man, as we are; the Son of God, like ourselves? His excellence, was it not human excellence? His wisdom, love, piety,—sweet and celestial as they were,—are they not what we also may attain? In him, as in a mirror, we may see the image of God, and go on from glory to glory, till we are changed into the same image, led by the spirit which enlightens the humble. Viewed in this way, how beautiful is the life of Jesus. Heaven has come down to earth, or, rather, earth has become heaven. The Son of God, come of age, has taken possession of his birthright. The brightest revelation is this,—of what is possible for all men, if not now at least hereafter. How pure is his spirit, and how encouraging its words. "Lowly sufferer," he seems to say, "see how I bore the cross. Patient laborer, be strong; see how I toiled for the unthankful and the merciless. Mistaken sinner, see of what thou art capable. Rise up, and be blessed."

But if, as some early Christians began to do, you take a heathen view, and make him a God, the Son of God in a peculiar and exclusive sense—much of the significance of his character is gone. His virtue has no merit; his love no feeling; his cross no burden; his agony no pain. His death is an illusion; his resurrection but a show. For if he were not a man, but a god, what are all these things; what his words, his life, his excellence of achievement?—It is all nothing, weighed against the illimitable greatness of Him who created the worlds and fills up all time and space! Then his resignation is no lesson; his life no model; his death no triumph to you or me,—who are not gods, but mortal men, that know not what a day shall bring forth, and walk by faith "dim sounding on our perilous way." Alas, we have despaired of man, and so cut off his brightest hope.

In respect of doctrines as well as forms we see all is transitory. "Every where is instability and insecurity." Opinions have changed most, on points deemed most vital. Could we bring up a Christian teacher of any age,—from the sixth to the fourteenth century for example,— though a teacher of undoubted soundness of faith, whose word filled the churches of Christendom, clergymen would scarce allow him to kneel at their altar, or sit down with them at the Lord's table. His notions of Christianity could not be expressed in our forms; nor could our notions be made intelligible to his ears. The questions of his age, those on which Christianity was thought to depend,—questions which perplexed and divided the subtle doctors,—are no questions to us. The quarrels which then drove wise men mad, now only excite a smile or a tear, as we are disposed to laugh or weep at the frailty of man. We have other straws of our own to quarrel for. Their ancient books of devotion do not speak to us; their theology is a vain word. To look back but a short period, the theological speculations of our fathers during the last two centuries; their "practical divinity;" even the sermons written by genius and piety, are, with rare exceptions, found unreadable; such a change is there in the doctrines.

Now who shall tell us that the change is to stop here? That this sect or that, or even all sects united, have exhausted the river of life and received it all in their canonized urns, so that we need draw no more out of the eternal well, but get refreshment nearer at hand? Who shall tell us that another age will not smile at our doctrines, disputes and unchristian quarrels about Christianity, and make wide the mouth at men who walked brave in orthodox raiment, delighting to blacken the names of heretics, and repeat again the old charge "he hath blasphemed"? Who shall tell us they will not weep at the folly of all such as fancied Truth shone only into the contracted nook of their school, or sect, or coterie? Men of other times may look down equally on the heresy-hunters, and men hunted for heresy, and wonder at both. The men of all ages before us, were quite as confident as we, that their opinion was truth; that their notion was Christianity and the whole thereof. The men who lit the fires of persecution from the first martyr to Christian bigotry down to the last murder of the innocents, had no doubt their opinion was divine. The contest about transubstantiation, and the immaculate purity of the Hebrew and Greek text of the scriptures, was waged with a bitterness unequalled in these days. The Protestant smiles at one, the Catholic at the other, and men of sense wonder at both. It might teach us all a lesson, at least, of forbearance. No doubt an age will come, in which ours shall be reckoned a period of darkness—like the sixth century—when men groped for the wall but stumbled and fell, because they trusted a transient notion, not an eternal truth; an age when temples were full of idols, set up by human folly; an age in which Christian light had scarce begun to shine into men's hearts. But while this change goes on, while one generation of opinions passes away, and another rises up, Christianity itself, that pure religion, which exists eternal in the constitution of the soul and the mind of God, is always the same. The Word that was before Abraham, in the very beginning, will not change, for that word is Truth. From this Jesus subtracted nothing; to this he added nothing. But he came to reveal it as the secret of God, that cunning men could not understand, but which filled the souls of men meek and lowly of heart. This truth we owe to God; the revelation thereof to Jesus, our elder brother, God's chosen son.

To turn away from the disputes of the Catholics and the Protestants, of the Unitarian and the Trinitarian, of Old School and New School, and come to the plain words of Jesus of Nazareth, Christianity is a simple thing; very simple. It is absolute, pure morality; absolute, pure religion; the love of man; the love of God acting without let or hindrance. The only creed it lays down, is the great truth which springs up spontaneous in the holy heart—there is a God. Its watchword is, be perfect as your Father in Heaven. The only form it demands is a divine life; doing the best thing, in the best way, from the highest motives; perfect obedience to the great law of God. Its sanction is the voice of God in your heart; the perpetual presence of Him, who made us and the stars over our head; Christ and the Father abiding within us. All this is very simple; a little child can understand it; very beautiful, the loftiest mind can find nothing so lovely. Try it by Reason, Conscience and Faith—things highest in man's nature—we see no redundance, we feel no deficiency. Examine the particular duties it enjoins; humility, reverence, sobriety, gentleness, charity, forgiveness, fortitude, resignation, faith and active love; try the whole extent of Christianity so well summed up in the command, "Thou shalt love the Lord thy God, with all thy heart, and with all thy soul and with all thy mind—thou shalt love thy neighbor as thyself," and is there any thing therein that can perish? No, the very opponents of Christianity have rarely found fault with the teachings of Jesus. The end of Christianity seems to be to make all men one with God as Christ was one with Him; to bring them to such a state of obedience and goodness, that we shall think divine thoughts and feel divine sentiments, and so keep the law of God by living a life of truth and love. Its means are Purity and Prayer; getting strength from God and using it for our fellow men as well as ourselves. It allows perfect freedom. It does not demand all men to *think* alike, but to think uprightly, and get as near as possible at truth; not all men to *live* alike, but to live holy and get as near as possible to a life perfectly divine. Christ set up no pillars of Hercules, beyond which men must not sail the sea in quest of Truth.[16] He says "I have many things to say unto you, but ye cannot bear them now . . . Greater works than these shall ye do." Christianity lays no rude hand on the sacred peculiarity of individual genius and character. But there is no Christian sect which does not fetter a man. It would make all men think alike, or smother their conviction in silence. Were all men Quakers or Catholics, Unitarians or Baptists, there would be much less diversity of thought, character and life: less of truth active in the world than now. But Christianity gives us the largest liberty of the sons of God, and were all men Christians, after the fashion of Jesus, this variety would be a thousand times greater than now, for Christianity is not a system of doctrines, but rather a method of attaining oneness with God. It demands, therefore, a good life of piety within, of purity without, and gives the promise that whoso does God's will, shall know of God's doctrine.

In an age of corruption as all ages are, Jesus stood and looked up to God. There was nothing between him and the Father of all; no old word, be it of Moses or Esaias, of a living Rabbi or Sanhedrim of Rabbis; no sin or perverseness of the finite will.[17] As the result of this virgin purity of soul and perfect obedience, the light of God shone down into the very deeps of his soul, bringing all of the Godhead which flesh can receive. He felt that God's word was in him; that he was one with God. He told what he saw—the Truth; he lived what he felt—a life of Love. The truth he brought to light must have been always the same before the eyes of all-seeing God, nineteen centuries before Christ, or nineteen centuries after him. A life supported by the principle and quickened by the sentiment of religion, if true to both, is always the same thing in Nazareth or New England. Now that divine man received these truths from God; was illumined more clearly by "the light that lighteneth every man";[18] combined and involved all the truths of Religion and Morality in his doctrine and made them manifest in his life. Then his words and example passed into the world, and can no more perish than the stars be wiped out of the sky. The truths he taught; his doctrines respecting man and God; the relation between man and man, and man and God, with the duties that grow out of that relation, are always the same and can never change till man ceases to be man, and creation vanishes into nothing. No, forms and opinions change and perish; but the Word of God cannot fail. The form Religion takes, the doctrines wherewith she is girded, can never be the same in any two centuries or two men, for since the sum of religious doctrines is both the result and the measure of a man's total growth in wisdom, virtue and piety, and since men will always differ in these respects, so religious *doctrines* and *forms* will always differ, always be transient, as Christianity goes forth and scatters the seed she bears in her hand. But the *Christianity holy men feel in the heart*—the Christ that is born within us, is always the same thing to each soul that feels it. This differs only in degree and not in kind, from age to age and man to man; there is something in Christianity which no sect from the "Ebionites" to the "latter day saints" ever entirely overlooked.[19] This is that common Christianity, which burns in the hearts of pious men.

Real Christianity gives men new life. It is the growth and perfect action of the Holy Spirit God puts into the sons of men. It makes us outgrow any form, or any system of doctrines we have devised, and approach still closer to the truth. It would lead us to take what help we can find. It would make the Bible our servant, not our master. It would teach us to profit by the wisdom and piety of David and Solomon, but not to sin their sins, nor bow to their idols.[20] It would make us revere the holy words spoken by "godly men of old," but revere still more the word of God spoken through conscience, reason and faith, as the holiest of all. It would not make Christ the despot of the soul, but the brother of all men. It would not tell us that even he had exhausted the fulness of God so that He could create none greater; for with him "all things are possible," and neither Old Testament or New Testament ever hints that creation exhausts the creator. Still less would it tell us the wisdom, the piety, the love, the manly excellence of Jesus was the result of miraculous agency alone, but that it was won like the excellence of humbler men, by faithful obedience to Him who gave his Son such ample heritage. It would point to him as our brother, who went before, like the good shepherd, to charm us with the music of his words, and with the beauty of his life to tempt us up the steeps of mortal toil, within the gate of Heaven. It would have us make the kingdom of God on earth, and enter more fittingly the kingdom on high. It would lead us from Christ in the heart, on which Paul laid such stress, and work out our salvation by this. For it is not so much by the Christ who lived so blameless and beautiful eighteen centuries ago, that we are saved directly, but by the Christ we form in our hearts and live out in our daily life, that we save ourselves, God working with us, both to will and to do.

Compare the simpleness of Christianity, as Christ sets it forth on the Mount, with what is sometimes taught and accepted in that honored name, and what a difference. One is of God; one is of man. There is something in Christianity which sects have not reached; something that will not be won, we fear, by theological battles, or the quarrels of pious men, still we may rejoice that Christ is preached in any way. The Christianity of sects, of the pulpit, of society, is ephemeral—a transitory fly. It will pass off and be forgot. Some new form will take its place, suited to the aspect of the changing times. Each will represent something of truth. But no one the whole. It seems the whole race of man is needed to do justice to the whole of truth, as "the whole church, to preach the whole gospel." Truth is entrusted for the time to a perishable Ark of human contrivance.[21] Though often shipwrecked, she always comes safe to land, and is not changed by her mishap. That pure ideal Religion which Jesus saw on the mount of his vision, and lived out, in the lowly life of a Galilean peasant; which transforms his cross into an emblem of all that is holiest on earth; which makes sacred the ground he trod, and is dearest to the best of men, most true to what is truest in them, cannot pass away. Let men improve never so far in civilization, or soar never so high on the wings of religion and love, they can never outgo the flight of truth and Christianity. It will always be above them. It is as if we were to fly towards a Star, which becomes larger and more bright, the nearer we approach, till we enter and are absorbed in its glory.

If we look carelessly on the ages that have gone by, or only on the surfaces of things as they come up before us, there is reason to fear; for we confound the truth of God with the word of man. So at a distance the cloud and the mountain seem the same. When the drift changes with the passing wind, an unpractised eye might fancy the mountain iself was gone. But the mountain stands to catch the clouds, to win the blessing they bear and send it down to moisten the fainting violet, to form streams which gladden valley and meadow, and sweep on at last to the sea in deep channels, laden with fleets. Thus the forms of the church, the creeds of the sects, the conflicting opinions of teachers, float round the sides of the Christian mount, and swell and toss, and rise and fall, and dart their lightning, and roll their thunder, but they neither make nor mar the mount itself. Its lofty summit far transcends the tumult; knows nothing of the storm which roars below; but burns with rosy light at evening and at morn; gleams in the splendors of the midday sun; sees his light when the long shadows creep over plain and moorland, and all night long has its head in the Heavens, and is visited by troops of stars which never set, nor veil their face to aught so pure and high.

Let then the Transient pass, fleet as it will, and may God send us some new manifestation of the Christian faith, that shall stir men's hearts as they were never stirred; some new Word, which shall teach us what we are, and renew us all in the image of God; some better life, that shall fulfil the Hebrew prophecy, and pour out the spirit of God on young men and maidens, and old men and children; which shall realize the Word of Christ, and give us the Comforter, who shall reveal all needed things. There are Simeons enough in the cottages and churches of New England, plain men and pious women, who wait for the consolation, and would die in gladness, if their expiring breath could stir quicker the wings that bear him on.[22] There are men enough, sick and "bowed down, in no wise able to lift up themselves,"[23] who would be healed could they kiss the hand of their Saviour, or touch but the hem of his garment; men who look up and are not fed because they ask bread from heaven and water from the rock, not traditions or fancies, Jewish or heathen, or new or old; men enough who, with throbbing hearts, pray for the spirit of healing to come upon the waters, which other than angels have long kept in trouble; men enough who have lain long time sick of theology, nothing bettered by many physicians, and are now dead, too dead to bury their dead, who would come out of their graves at the glad tidings. God send us a real religious life, which shall pluck blindness out of the heart, and make us better fathers, mothers, and children; a religious life, that shall go with us where we go, and make every home the house of God, every act acceptable as a prayer. We would work for this, and pray for it, though we wept tears of blood while we prayed.

Such, then, is the Transient, and such the Permanent in Christianity. What is of absolute value never changes; we may cling round it and grow to it forever. No one can say his notions shall stand. But we may all say, the Truth, as it is in Jesus, shall never pass away. Yet there are always some even religious men, who do not see the permanent element, so they rely on the fleeting; and, what is also an evil, condemn others for not doing the same. They mistake a defence of the Truth for an attack upon the Holy of Holies; the removal of a theological error for the destruction of all religion. Already men of the same sect eye one another with suspicion, and lowering brows that indicate a storm, and, like children who have fallen out in their play, call hard names. Now, as always, there is a collision between these two elements.

The question puts itself to each man, "Will you cling to what is perishing, or embrace what is eternal?" This question each must answer for himself.

My friends, if you receive the notions about Christianity which chance to be current in your sect or church, solely because they are current, and thus accept the commandment of men instead of God's truth; there will always be enough to commend you for soundness of judgment, prudence, and good sense; enough to call you Christian for that reason. But if this is all you rely upon, alas for you. The ground will shake under your feet if you attempt to walk uprightly and like men. You will be afraid of every new opinion, lest it shake down your church; you will fear "lest if a fox go up, he will break down your stone wall."[24] The smallest contradiction in the New Testament or Old Testament, the least disagreement between the Law and the Gospel; any mistake of the Apostles, will weaken your faith. It shall be with you "as when a hungry man dreameth, and behold he eateth, but he awaketh and his soul is empty."[25]

If, on the other hand, you take the true Word of God, and live out this, nothing shall harm you. Men may mock, but their mouthfuls of wind shall be blown back upon their own face. If the master of the house were called Beelzebub, it matters little what name is given to the household.[26] The name Christian, given in mockery, will last till the world go down. He that loves God and man, and lives in accordance with that love, need not fear what man can do to him. His Religion comes to him in his hour of sadness, it lays its hand on him when he has fallen among thieves, and raises him up, heals and comforts him. If he is crucified, he shall rise again.

My friends, you this day receive, with the usual formalities, the man you have chosen to speak to you on the highest of all themes,—what concerns your life on earth; your life in heaven. It is a work for which no talents, no prayerful diligence, no piety, is too great. An office, that would dignify angels, if worthily filled. If the eyes of this man be holden, that he *cannot* discern between the perishing and the true, you will hold him guiltless of all sin in this; but look for light where it can be had; for his office will then be of no use to you. But if he sees the Truth, and is scared by worldly motives and *will* not tell it, alas for him. If the watchman see the foe coming and blow not the trumpet, the blood of the innocent is on him.

Your own conduct and character, the treatment you offer this young man, will in some measure influence him. The hearer affects the speaker. There were some places where even Jesus "did not many mighty works, because of their unbelief."[27] Worldly motives—not seeming such—sometimes deter good men from their duty. Gold and ease have, before now, enervated noble minds. Daily contact with men of low aims, takes down the ideal of life, which a bright spirit casts out of itself. Terror has sometimes palsied tongues that, before, were eloquent as the voice of Persuasion. But thereby Truth is not holden. She speaks in a thousand tongues, and with a pen of iron graves her sentence on the rock forever. You may prevent the freedom of speech in this pulpit if you will. You may hire you servants to preach as you bid; to spare your vices and flatter your follies; to prophesy smooth things, and say, It is peace, when there is no peace. Yet in so doing you weaken and enthrall yourselves. And alas for that man who consents to think one thing in his closet and preach another in his pulpit. God shall judge him in his mercy, not man in his wrath. But over his study and over his pulpit might be writ—EMPTINESS; on his canonical robes, on his forehead and right hand—DECEIT, DECEIT.

But, on the other hand, you may encourage your brother to tell you the truth. Your affection will then be precious to him; your prayers of great price. Every evidence of your sympathy will go to baptize him anew to Holiness and Truth. You will then have his best words, his brightest thoughts, and his most hearty prayers. He may grow old in your service, blessing and blest. He will have

> The sweetest, best of consolation,
> The thought, that he has given,
> To serve the cause of Heaven,
> The freshness of his early inspiration.

Choose as you will choose; but weal or woe depends upon your choice.

Source: Theodore Parker, *A Discourse of the Transient and Permanent in Christianity; Preached at the Ordination of Mr. Charles C. Shackford, in the Hawes Place Church in Boston, May 19, 1841* (Boston: The Author, 1841). Parker's "Preface" is omitted.

Notes

1. Philistines, people interested in materialism and disdainful of intellectual pursuits.
2. Ind, or India.
3. Thales believed that water was the essence of all matter; Ptolemy of Alexandria (fl. 127–145), astronomer, geographer, and mathematician who believed that the Earth was the center of the universe, as opposed to Copernicus, who believed that the planets revolved around the sun; René Descartes (1596–1650), French philosopher and mathematician, followed Copernicus's view of the universe.
4. Pannier, a wicker basket used for carrying things on a horse or ass.

5. Cicero (called Tully) opposed Julius Caesar's replacing the republican government of Rome with his own rule; Lyra (or The Lyre), a constellation.

6. Trinity, Christian doctrine that argues for the union of the Father, the Son, and the Holy Ghost in one Godhead, an idea opposed by the Unitarians; Achilles, the chief Greek hero of the Trojan War, was vulnerable only at his heel because it was the one part of his body that his mother had failed to dip in the River Styx when he was young.

7. Homer, *The Iliad*, Book 6, ll., 181–184, translated by Alexander Pope in 1715–1720.

8. Abraham, biblical figure whose story is told in Genesis 11–25.

9. Atalanta, Greek mythological female athlete, proposed to race any of her suitors and marry the one who could beat her, but if she won, she could kill the man. Melanion fell in love with Atalanta but knew he could not beat her, so he called on Aphrodite, the goddess of love, for assistance. She provided him with three golden apples, which he dropped at points during the race to distract Atalanta, who would stop and pick them up, thus winning the race and her hand in marriage.

10. Euclid (fl. ca. 323–285 B.C.), Greek founder of geometry; Archimedes (ca. 287–212 B.C.), Greek mathematician and engineer.

11. Jean de Gerson (1363–1429), French church reformer who argued that the Pope could be removed by a council of the church faithful; John Calvin was much more conservative.

12. Methodists put more stock in the doctrines of historical Christianity than did the Unitarians.

13. While Matthew writes to further his own plans to convince the Jewish Christians of Palestine that Christ was the Messiah, John's purpose is more historical.

14. "For I testify unto every man that heareth the words of the prophecy of this book, If any man shall add unto these things, God shall add unto him the plagues that are written in this book: And if any man shall take away from the words of the book of this prophecy, God shall take away his part out of the book of life, and out of the holy city, and from the things which are written in this book" (Revelation 22:18–19).

15. Solomon (ca. 973–ca. 933 B.C.), king of Israel known for his impartial justice.

16. Pillars of Hercules, the mountains Calpé and Abyla, at, respectively, Gibraltar and Turkey, torn apart by Hercules, and which the ancients supposed marked the ends of world.

17. Esaias, the Greek form for Isaiah; Sanhedrim, the supreme Jewish judicial and administrative council.

18. John 1:9.

19. Ebionites, early Christian sect that considered Jesus as an inspired messenger, but only a man; Mormons, or Church of Jesus Christ of Latter-Day Saints, believed that certain tribes of Israel had migrated to America centuries before Christ.

20. David (d. 960 B.C.), second king of Israel.
21. Either Noah's Ark or the Ark of the Covenant, an ornate chest that held the two tablets of the Law given to Moses by God.
22. Simeons, one of the lost tribes of Israel.
23. Luke 13:11.
24. Nehemiah 4:3.
25. Isaiah 29:8.
26. Beelzebub, Philistine god of flies, placed by John Milton in *Paradise Lost* second only to Satan.
27. Matthew 13:58.

Ralph Waldo Emerson

"The Transcendentalist"

(23 December 1841)

EMERSON'S LECTURE ON "The Transcendentalist," delivered as part of his "The Times" series, is as close to an extended definition of the movement by a participant as we have. Facing an audience that has heard Transcendentalism described as an un-American fad (because of its interest in British and continental philosophy and other writings) with many odd and dangerous adherents (as witnessed by Alcott's "Orphic Sayings" and the communal living style at Brook Farm), Emerson defuses the situation by two rhetorical strategies. First, he argues that Transcendentalism is "the very oldest of thoughts cast into the mould of these new times"; that is, the audience should not be afraid of the new dress worn by familiar ideas. Second, while he admits that many Transcendentalists "hold themselves aloof" because our "literature and spiritual history" are "in the optative mood," nevertheless "the good and wise must learn to act, and carry salvation to the combatants and demagogues in the dusty arena below"; and he frankly admits that there will be "cant and pretension," "subtilty and moonshine," but these people are "of unequal strength, and do not all prosper."

T he first thing we have to say respecting what are called *new views* here in New England, at the present time, is, that they are not new, but the very oldest of thoughts cast into the mould of these new times. The light is always identical in its composition, but it falls on a great variety of objects, and by so falling is first revealed to us, not in its own form, for it is formless, but in theirs; in like manner, thought only appears in the objects it classifies. What is popularly called Transcendentalism among us, is Idealism; Idealism as it appears in 1842. As thinkers, mankind have ever divided into two sects, Materialists and Idealists; the first class founding on experience, the second on consciousness: the first class beginning to think from the data of the senses, the second class perceive that the senses are not final, and say, the senses give us representations of things, but what are the things themselves, they cannot tell. The materialist insists on facts, on history, on the force of circumstances, and the animal wants of man; the idealist on the power of Thought and of Will, on inspiration, on miracle, on individual culture. These two modes of thinking are both natural, but the idealist contends that his way of thinking is in higher nature. He concedes all that the other affirms, admits the impression of sense, admits their coherency, their use and beauty, and then asks the materialist for his grounds of assurance that things are as his senses represent them. But I, he says, affirm facts not affected by the illusions of sense, facts which are of the same nature as the faculty which reports them, and not liable to doubt; facts which in their first appearance to us assume a native superiority to material facts, degrading these into a language by which the first are to be spoken; facts which it only needs a retirement from the senses to discern. Every materialist will be an idealist; but an idealist can never go backward to be a materialist.

The idealist, in speaking of events, sees them as spirits. He does not deny the sensuous fact; by no means; but he will not see that alone. He does not deny the presence of this table, this chair, and the walls of this room, but he looks at these things as the reverse side of the tapestry, as the *other end*, each being a sequel or completion of a spiritual fact which nearly concerns him. This manner of looking at things, transfers every object in nature from an independent and anomalous position without there, into the consciousness. Even the materialist Condillac, perhaps the most logical expounder of materialism, was constrained to say, "Though we should soar into the heavens, though we should sink into the abyss, we never go out of ourselves; it is always our own thought that we perceive." What more could an idealist say?

The materialist, secure in the certainty of sensation, mocks at finespun theories, at star-gazers and dreamers, and believes that his life is solid, that he at least takes nothing for granted, but knows where he stands, and what he does. Yet how easy it is to show him, that he also is a phantom walking and working amid phantoms, and that he need only ask a question or two beyond his daily questions, to find his solid universe growing dim and impalpable before his sense. The sturdy captalist, no matter how deep and square on blocks of Quincy granite he lays the foundations of his banking-house or Exchange, must set it, at last, not on a cube corresponding to the angles of his structure, but on a mass of unknown materials and solidity, red-hot or white-hot, perhaps at the core, which rounds off to an almost perfect sphericity, and lies floating in soft air, and goes spinning away, dragging bank and banker with it at a rate of thousands of miles the hour, he knows not whither,—a bit of bullet, now glimmering, now darkling through a small cubic space on the edge of an unimaginable pit of emptiness. And this wild balloon, in which his whole venture is embarked, is a just symbol of his whole state and faculty. One thing, at least, he says is certain, and does not give me the headache, that figures do not lie; the multiplication table has been hitherto found unimpeachable truth; and, moreover, if I put a gold eagle[1] in my safe, I find it again to-morrow;—but for these thoughts, I know not whence they are. They change and pass away. But ask him why he believes that an uniform experience will continue uniform, or on what grounds he founds his faith in his figures, and he will perceive that his mental fabric is built up on just as strange and quaking foundations as his proud edifice of stone.

In the order of thought, the materialist takes his departure from the external world, and esteems a man as one product of that. The idealist takes his departure from his consciousness, and reckons the world as an appearance. The materialist respects sensible masses, Society, Government, social art, and luxury, every establishment, every mass, whether majority of numbers, or extent of space, or amount of objects, every social action. The idealist has another measure, which is metaphysical, namely, the *rank* which things themselves take in his consciousness; not at all, the size or appearance. Mind is the only reality, of which men and all other natures are better or worse reflectors. Nature, literature, history, are only subjective phenomena. Although in his action overpowered by the laws of action, and so, warmly coöperating with men, even preferring them to himself, yet when he speaks scientifically, or after the order of thought, he is constrained to degrade persons into representatives of truths. He does not respect labor, or the products of labor, namely, property, otherwise than as a manifold symbol, illustrating with wonderful fidelity of details the laws of being; he does not respect government, except as far as it reiterates the law of his mind; nor the church; nor charities; nor arts, for themselves; but hears, as at a vast distance, what they say, as if his consciousness would speak to him through a pantomimic scene. His thought,—that is the Universe. His experience inclines him to behold the procession of facts you call the world, as flowing perpetually outward from an invisible, unsounded centre in himself, centre alike of him and of them, and necessitating him to regard all things as having a subjective or relative existence, relative to that aforesaid Unknown Centre of him.

From this transfer of the world into the consciousness, this beholding of all things in the mind, follows easily his whole ethics. It is simpler to be self-dependent. The height, the deity of man is to be self-sustained, to need no gift, no foreign force. Society is good when it does not violate me; but best when it is likest to solitude. Everything real is self-existent. Everything divine shares the self-existence of Deity. All that you call the world is the shadow of that substance which you are, the perpetual creation of the powers of thought, of those that are dependent and those that are independent of your will. Do not cumber yourself with fruitless pains to mend and remedy remote effects; let the soul be erect, and all things will go well. You think me the child of my circumstances: I make my circumstance. Let any thought or motive of mine be different from that they are, the difference will transform my whole condition and economy. I—this thought which is called I,—is the mould into which the world is poured like melted wax. The mould is invisible, but the world betrays the shape of the mould. You call it the power of circumstance, but it is the power of me. Am I in harmony with myself? my position will seem to you just and commanding. Am I vicious and insane? my fortunes will seem to you obscure and descending. As I am, so shall I associate; as I am, so shall I act; Cæsar's history will paint out Cæsar. Jesus acted so, because he thought so. I do not wish to overlook or to gainsay any reality; I say, I make my circumstance: but if you ask me, Whence am I? I feel like other men my relation to that Fact which cannot be spoken, or defined, nor even thought, but which exists, and will exist.

The Transcendentalist adopts the whole connexion of spiritual doctrine. He believes in miracle, in the perpetual openness of the human mind to new influx of light and power; he believes in inspiration, and in ecstasy. He wishes that the spiritual principle should be suffered to demonstrate itself to the end, in all possible applications to the state of man, without the admission of anything unspiritual; that is, anything positive, dogmatic, personal. Thus, the spiritual measure of inspiration is the depth of the thought, and never, *who* said it? And so he resists all attempts to palm other rules and measures on the spirit than its own.

In action, he easily incurs the charge of antinomianism by his avowal that he, who has the Lawgiver, may with safety not only neglect, but even contravene every written commandment. In the play of Othello, the expiring Desdemona absolves her husband of the murder, to her attendant Emilia. Afterwards, when Emilia charges him with the crime, Othello exclaims,

"You heard her say herself it was not I."

Emilia replies,

"The more angel she, and thou the blacker devil."[2]

Of this fine incident, Jacobi, the Transcendental moralist, makes use, with other parallel instances, in his reply to Fichte.[3] Jacobi, refusing all measure of right and wrong except the determinations of the private spirit, remarks that there is no crime but has sometimes been a virtue. "I," he says, "am that atheist, that godless person who, in opposition to an imaginary doctrine of calculation, would lie as the dying Desdemona lied; would lie and deceive as Pylades when he personated Orestes; would assassinate like Timoleon; would perjure myself like Epaminondas, and John de Witt; I would resolve on suicide like Cato; I would commit sacrilege with David; yea, and pluck ears of corn on the Sabbath, for no other reason than that I was fainting for lack of food.[4] For, I have assurance in myself that in pardoning these faults according to the letter, man exerts the sovereign right which the majesty of his being confers on him; he sets the seal of his divine nature to the grace he accords."[5]

In like manner, if there is anything grand and daring in human thought or virtue, any reliance on the vast, the unknown; any presentiment; any extravagance of faith, the spiritualist adopts it as most in nature. The oriental mind has always tended to this largeness. Buddhism is an expression of it. The Buddhist who thanks no man, who says, "do not flatter your benefactors," but who in his conviction that every good deed can by no possibility escape its reward, will not deceive the benefactor by pretending that he has done more than he should, is a Transcendentalist.

You will see by this sketch that there is no such thing as a Transcendental *party*; that there is no pure Transcendentalist; that we know of none but the prophets and heralds of such a philosophy; that all who by strong bias of nature have leaned to the spiritual side in doctrine, have stopped short of their goal. We have had many harbingers and forerunners; but of a purely spiritual life, history has yet afforded no example. I mean, we have yet no man who has leaned entirely on his character, and eaten angels' food; who, trusting to his sentiments, found life made of miracles; who, working for universal aims, found himself fed, he knew not how; clothed, sheltered, and weaponed, he knew not how, and yet it was done by his own hands. Only in the instinct of the lower animals we find the suggestion of the methods of it, and something higher than our understanding. The squirrel hoards nuts, and the bee gathers honey, without knowing what they do, and they are thus provided for without selfishness or disgrace.

Shall we say, then, that Transcendentalism is the Saturnalia or excess of Faith; the presentiment of a faith proper to man in his integrity, excessive only when his imperfect obedience hinders the satisfaction of his wish. Nature is transcendental, exists primarily, necessarily, ever works and advances, yet takes no thought for the morrow. Man owns the dignity of the life which throbs around him in chemistry, and tree, and animal, and in the involuntary functions of his own body; yet he is baulked when he tries to fling himself into this enchanted circle, where all is done without degradation. Yet genius and virtue predict in man the same absence of private ends, and of condescension to circumstances, united with every trait and talent of beauty and power.

This way of thinking, falling on Roman times, made Stoic philosophers; falling on despotic times, made patriot Catos and Brutuses; falling on superstitious times, made prophets and apostles; on popish times, made protestants and ascetic monks, preachers of Faith against the preachers of Works; on prelatical times, made Puritans and Quakers; and falling on Unitarian and conservative times, makes the peculiar shades of Idealism which we know.

It is well known to most of my audience, that the Idealism of the present day acquired the name of Transcendental, from the use of that term by Immanuel Kant, of Konigsberg, who replied to the skeptical philosophy of Locke, which insisted that there was nothing in the intellect which was not previously in the experience of the senses, by showing that there was a very important class of ideas, or imperative forms, which did not come by experience, but through which experience was acquired; that these were intuitions of the mind itself; and he denominated them *Transcendental* forms. The extraordinary profoundness and precision of that man's thinking have given vogue to his nomenclature, in Europe and America, to that extent, that whatever belongs to the class of intuitive thought, is called popularly at the present day *Transcendental*.

Although, as we have said, there is no pure Transcendentalist, yet the tendency to respect the intuitions, and to give them, at least in our creed, all authority over our experience, has deeply colored the conversation and poetry of the present day; and the history of genius and of religion in these times, though impure, and as yet not incarnated in any powerful individual, will be the history of this tendency.

It is a sign of our times, conspicuous to the coarsest observer, that many intelligent and religious persons withdraw themselves from the common labors and competitions of the market and the caucus, and betake themselves to a certain solitary and critical way of living, from which no solid fruit has yet appeared to justify their separation. They hold themselves aloof: they feel the disproportion between their faculties and the work offered them, and they prefer to ramble in the country and perish of ennui, to the degradation of such charities and such ambitions as the city can propose to them. They are striking work, and crying out for somewhat worthy to do! What they do, is done only because they are overpowered by the humanities that speak on all sides; and they consent to such labor as is open to them, though to their lofty dream the writing of Iliads or Hamlets, or the building of cities or empires seems drudgery.

Now every one must do after his kind, be he asp or angel, and these must. The question, which a wise man and a student of modern history will ask, is, what that kind is? And truly, as in ecclesiastical history we take so much pains to know what the Gnostics, what the Essenes, what the Manichees, and what the Reformers believed,[6] it would not misbecome us to inquire nearer home, what these companions and contemporaries of ours think and do, at least so far as these thoughts and actions appear to be not accidental and personal, but common to many, and so the inevitable flower of the Tree of Time. Our American literature and spiritual history are, we confess, in the optative mood; but whoso knows these seething brains, these admirable radicals, these unsocial worshippers, these talkers who talk the sun and moon away, will believe that this heresy cannot pass away without leaving its mark.

They are lonely; the spirit of their writing and conversation is lonely; they shed influences; they shun general society; they incline to shut themselves in their chamber in the house, to live in the country rather than in the town, and to find their tasks and amusements in solitude. Society, to be sure, does not like this very well; it saith, Whoso goes to walk alone, accuses the whole world; he declareth all to be unfit to be his companions; it is very uncivil, nay, insulting; Society will retaliate. Meantime, this retirement does not proceed from any whim on the part of these separators; but if any one will take pains to talk with them, he will find that this part is chosen both from temperament and from principle; with some unwillingness, too, and as a choice of the less of two evils; for these persons are not by nature melancholy, sour, and unsocial,—they are not stockish or brute,—but joyous, susceptible, affectionate; they have even more than others a great wish to be loved. Like the young Mozart, they are rather ready to cry ten times a day, "But are you sure you love me?"[7] Nay, if they tell you their whole thought, they will own that love seems to them the last and highest gift of nature; that there are persons whom in their hearts they daily thank for existing,—persons whose faces are perhaps unknown to them, but whose fame and spirit have penetrated their solitude,—and for whose sake they wish to exist. To behold the beauty of another character, which inspires a new interest in our own; to behold the beauty lodged in a human being, with such vivacity of apprehension, that I am instantly forced home to inquire if I am not deformity itself; to behold in another the expression of a love so high that it assures itself,—assures itself also to me against every possible casualty except my unworthiness;—these are degrees on the scale of human happiness, to which they have ascended; and it is a fidelity to this sentiment which has made common association distasteful to them. They wish a just and even fellowship, or none. They cannot gossip with you, and they do not wish, as they are sincere and religious, to gratify any mere curiosity which you may entertain. Like fairies, they do not wish to be spoken of. Love me, they say, but do not ask who is my cousin and my uncle. If you do not need to hear my thought, because you can read it in my face and behavior, then I will tell it you from sunrise to sunset. If you cannot divine it, you would not understand what I say. I will not molest myself for you. I do not wish to be profaned.

And yet, when you see them near, it seems as if this loneliness, and not this love, would prevail in their circumstances, because of the extravagant demand they make on human nature. That, indeed, constitutes a new feature in their portrait, that they are the most exacting and extortionate critics. Their quarrel with every man they meet, is not with his kind, but with his degree. There is not enough of him,—that is the only fault. They prolong their privilege of childhood in this wise, of doing nothing,—but making immense demands on all the gladiators in the lists of action and fame. They make us feel the strange disappointment which overcasts every human youth. So many promising youths, and never a finished man! The profound nature will have a savage rudeness; the delicate one will be shallow, or the victim of sensibility; the richly accomplished will have some capital absurdity; and so every piece has a crack. 'T is strange, but this masterpiece is a result of such an extreme delicacy, that the most unobserved flaw in the boy will neutralize the most aspiring genius, and spoil the work. Talk with a seaman of the hazards to life in his profession, and he will ask you, "Where are the old sailors? do you not see that all are young men?" And we, on this sea of human thought, in like manner inquire, Where are the old idealists? where are they who represented to the last generation that extravagant hope, which a few happy aspirants suggest to ours? In looking at the class of counsel, and power, and wealth, and at the matronage of the land, amidst all the prudence and all the triviality, one asks, Where are they who represented genius, virtue, the invisible and heavenly world, to these? Are they dead,—taken in early ripeness to the gods,—as ancient wisdom foretold their fate? Or did the high idea die out of them, and leave their unperfumed body as its tomb and tablet, announcing to all that the celestial inhabitant, who once gave them beauty, had departed? Will it be better with the new generation? We easily predict a fair future to each new candidate who enters the lists, but we are frivolous and volatile, and by low aims and ill example do what we can to defeat this hope. Then these youths bring us a rough but effectual aid. By their unconcealed dissatisfaction, they expose our poverty, and the insignificance of man to man. A man is a poor limitary benefactor. He ought to be a shower of benefits—a great influence, which should never let his brother go, but should refresh old merits continually with new ones; so that, though absent, he should never be out of my mind, his name never far from my lips; but if the earth should open at my side, or my last hour were come, his name should be the prayer I should utter to the Universe. But in our experience, man is cheap, and friendship wants its deep sense. We affect to dwell with our friends in their absence, but we do not; when deed, word, or letter comes not, they let us go. These exacting children advertise us of our wants. There is no compliment, no smooth speech with them; they pay you only this one compliment, of insatiable expectation; they aspire, they severely exact, and if they only stand fast in this watch-tower, and persist in demanding unto the end, and without end, then are they terrible friends, whereof poet and priest cannot choose but stand in awe; and what if they eat clouds, and drink wind, they have not been without service to the race of man.

With this passion for what is great and extraordinary, it cannot be wondered at, that they are repelled by vulgarity and frivolity in people. They say to themselves, It is better to be alone than in bad company. And it is really a wish to be met,—the wish to find society for their hope and religion,—which prompts them to shun what is called society. They feel that they are never so fit for friendship, as when they have quit mankind, and taken themselves to friend. A picture, a book, a favorite spot in the hills or the woods, which they can people with the fair and worthy creation of the fancy, can give them often forms so vivid, that these for the time shall seem real, and society the illusion.

But their solitary and fastidious manners not only withdraw them from the conversation, but from the labors of the world; they are not good citizens, not good members of society; unwillingly they bear their part of the public and private burdens; they do not willingly share in the public charities, in the public religious rites, in the enterprises of education, of missions foreign or domestic, in the abolition of the slave-trade, or in the temperance-society. They are inactive; they do not even like to vote. The philanthropists inquire whether Transcendentalism does not mean sloth. They had as lief hear that their friend was dead as that he was a Transcendentalist; for then is he paralyzed, and can never do anything for humanity. What right, cries the good world, has the man of genius to retreat from work, and indulge himself? The popular literary creed seems to be, 'I am a sublime genius; I ought not therefore to labor.' But genius is the power to labor better and more availably than others. Deserve thy genius: exalt it. The good, the illuminated, sit apart from the rest, censuring their dulness and vices, as if they thought that, by sitting very grand in their chairs, the very brokers, attorneys, and congressmen would see the error of their ways, and flock to them. But the good and wise must learn to act, and carry salvation to the combatants and demagogues in the dusty arena below.

On the part of these children, it is replied, that life and their faculty seem to them gifts too rich to be squandered on such trifles as you propose to them. What you call your fundamental institutions, your great and holy causes, seem to them great abuses, and, when nearly seen, paltry matters. Each 'Cause,' as it is called,—say Abolition, Temperance, say Calvinism, or Unitarianism,—becomes speedily a little shop, where the article, let it have been at first never so subtle and ethereal, is now made up into portable and convenient cakes, and retailed in small quantities to suit purchasers. You make very free use of these words "great and holy," but few things appear to them such. Few persons have any magnificence of nature to inspire enthusiasm, and the philanthropies and charities have a certain air of quackery. As to the general course of living, and the daily employments of men, they cannot see much virtue in these, since they are parts of this vicious circle; and, as no great ends are answered by the men, there is nothing noble in the arts by which they are maintained. Nay, they have made the experiment, and found that from the liberal professions to the coarsest manual labor, and from the courtesies of the academy and the college to the conventions of the cotillon-room and the morning call, there is a spirit of cowardly compromise and seeming, which intimates a frightful skepticism, a life without love, and an activity without an aim.

Unless the action is necessary, unless it is adequate, I do not wish to perform it. I do not wish to do one thing but once. I do not love routine. Once possessed of the principle, it is equally easy to make four or forty thousand applications of it. A great man will be content to have indicated in any the slightest manner his perception of the reigning Idea of his time, and will leave to those who like it the multiplication of examples. When he has hit the white, the rest may shatter the target. Every thing admonishes us how needlessly long life is. Every moment of a hero so raises and cheers us, that a twelve-month is an age. All that the brave Xanthus brings home from his wars, is the recollection that, at the storming of Samos, "in the heat of the battle, Pericles smiled on me, and passed on to another detach-ment."[8] It is the quality of the moment, not the number of days, of events, or of actors, that imports.

New, we confess, and by no means happy, is our condition: if you want the aid of our labor, we ourselves stand in greater want of the labor. We are miserable with inaction. We perish of rest and rust. But we do not like your work.

'Then,' says the world, 'show me your own.'

'We have none.'

'What will you do, then?' cries the world.

'We will wait.'

'How long?'

'Until the Universe rises up and calls us to work.'

'But whilst you wait, you grow old and useless.'

'Be it so: I can sit in a corner and *perish*, (as you call it,) but I will not move until I have the highest command. If no call should come for years, for centuries, then I know that the want of the Universe is the attestation of faith by this my abstinence. Your virtuous projects, so called, do not cheer me. I know that which shall come will cheer me. If I cannot work, at least I need not lie. All that is clearly due to-day is not to lie. In other places, other men have encountered sharp trials, and have behaved themselves well. The martyrs were sawn asun-der, or hung alive on meat hooks. Cannot we screw our courage to patience and truth, and without complaint, or even with good-humor, await our turn of action in the Infinite Counsels?'

But, to come a little closer to the secret of these persons, we must say, that to them it seems a very easy matter to answer the objections of the man of the world, but not so easy to dispose of the doubts and objections that occur to themselves. They are exercised in their own spirit with queries, which acquaint them with all adversity, and with the trials of the bravest heroes. When I asked them concerning their private experience, they answered somewhat in this wise: It is not to be denied that there must be some wide difference between my faith and other faith; and mine is a certain brief experience, which surprised me in the highway or in the market, in some place, at some time,—whether in the body or out of the body, God knoweth,[9]—and made me aware that I had played the fool with fools all this time, but that law existed for me and for all; that to me belonged trust, a child's trust and obedience, and the worship of ideas, and I should never be fool more. Well, in the space of an hour, probably, I was let down from this height; I was at my old tricks, the selfish member of a selfish society. My life is superficial, takes no root in the deep world; I ask, When shall I die, and be relieved of the responsibility of seeing an Universe which I do not use? I wish to exchange this flash-of-lightning faith for continuous daylight, this fever-glow for a benign climate.

These two states of thought diverge every moment, and stand in wild contrast. To whom who looks at his life from these moments of illumination, it will seem that he skulks and plays a mean, shiftless and subaltern part in the world. That is to be done which he has not skill to do, or to be said which others can say better, and he lies by, or occupies his hands with some plaything, until his hour comes again. Much of our reading, much of our labor, seems mere waiting: it was not that we were born for. Any other could do it as well, or better. So little skill enters into these works, so little do they mix with the divine life, that it really signifies little what we do, whether we turn a grindstone, or ride, or run, or make fortunes, or govern the state. The worst feature of this double consciousness is, that the two lives, of the understanding and of the soul, which we lead, really show very little relation to each other, never meet and measure each other: one prevails now, all buzz and din; and the other prevails then, all infinitude and paradise; and, with the progress of life, the two discover no greater disposition to reconcile themselves. Yet, what is my faith? What am I? What but a thought of serenity and independence, an abode in the deep blue sky? Presently the clouds shut down again; yet we retain the belief that this pretty web we weave will at last be overshot and reticulated with veins of the blue, and that the moments will characterize the days. Patience, then, is for us, is it not? Patience, and still patience. When we pass, as presently we shall, into some new infinitude, out of this Iceland of negations, it will please us to reflect that, though we had few virtues or consolations, we bore with our indigence, nor once strove to repair it with hypocrisy or false heat of any kind.

But this class are not sufficiently characterized, if we omit to add that they are lovers and worshippers of Beauty. In the eternal trinity of Truth, Goodness, and Beauty, each in its perfection including the three, they prefer to make Beauty the sign and head. Something of the same taste is observable in all the moral movements of the time, in the religious and benevolent enterprises. They have a liberal, even an æsthetic spirit. A reference to Beauty in action sounds, to be sure, a little hollow and ridiculous in the ears of the old church. In politics, it has often sufficed, when they treated of justice, if they kept the bounds of selfish calculation. If they granted restitution, it was prudence which granted it. But the justice which is now claimed for the black, and the pauper, and the drunkard, is for Beauty—is for a necessity to the soul of the agent, not of the beneficiary. I say this is the tendency, not yet the realization. Our virtue totters and trips, does not yet walk firmly. Its representatives are austere; they preach and denounce; their rectitude is not yet a grace. They are still liable to that slight taint of burlesque which, in our strange world, attaches to the zealot. A saint should be as dear as the apple of the eye. Yet we are tempted to smile, and we flee from the working to the speculative reformer, to escape that same slight ridicule. Alas for these days of derision and criticism! We call the Beautiful the highest, because it appears to us the golden mean, escaping the dowdiness of the good, and the heartlessness of the true.—They are lovers of nature also, and find an indemnity in the inviolable order of the world for the violated order and grace of man.

There is, no doubt, a great deal of well-founded objection to be spoken or felt against the sayings and doings of this class, some of whose traits we have selected; no doubt, they will lay themselves open to criticism and to lampoons, and as ridiculous stories will be to be told to them as of any. There will be cant and pretension; there will be subtility and moonshine. These persons are of unequal strength, and do not all prosper. They complain that everything around them must be denied; and if feeble, it takes all their strength to deny, before they can begin to lead their own life. Grave seniors insist on their respect to this institution, and that usage; to an obsolete history; to some vocation, or college, or etiquette, or beneficiary, or charity, or morning or evening call, which they resist, as what does not concern them. But it costs such sleepless nights, and alienations and misgivings,—they have so many moods about it;—these old guardians never changed *their* minds; they have but one mood on the subject, namely, that Antony is very perverse,—that it is quite as much as Antony can do, to assert his rights, abstain from what he thinks foolish, and keep his temper. He cannot help the reaction of this injustice in his own mind. He is braced-up and stilted; all freedom and flowing genius, all sallies of wit and frolic nature are quite out of the question; it is well if he can keep from lying, injustice, and suicide. This is no time for gayety and grace. His strength and spirits are wasted in rejection. But the strong spirits overpower those around them without effort. Their thought and emotion comes in like a flood, quite withdraws them from all notice of these carping critics;

they surrender themselves with glad heart to the heavenly guide, and only by implication reject the clamorous nonsense of the hour. Grave seniors talk to the deaf,—church and old book mumble and ritualize to an unheeding, preoccupied and advancing mind, and thus they by happiness of greater momentum lose no time, but take the right road at first.

But all these of whom I speak are not proficients, they are novices; they only show the road in which man should travel, when the soul has greater health and prowess. Yet let them feel the dignity of their charge, and deserve a larger power. Their heart is the ark in which the fire is concealed, which shall burn in a broader and universal flame. Let them obey the Genius then most when his impulse is wildest; then most when he seems to lead to uninhabitable desarts of thought and life; for the path which the hero travels alone is the highway of health and benefit to mankind. What is the privilege and nobility of our nature, but its persistency, through its power to attach itself to what is permanent?

Society also has its duties in reference to this class, and must behold them with what charity it can. Possibly some benefit may yet accrue from them to the state. In our Mechanics' Fair, there must be not only bridges, ploughs, carpenters' planes, and baking troughs, but also some few finer instruments,—raingauges, thermometers, and telescopes; and in society, besides farmers, sailors, and weavers, there must be a few persons of purer fire kept specially as gauges and meters of character; persons of a fine, detecting instinct, who betray the smallest accumulations of wit and feeling in the bystander. Perhaps too there might be room for the exciters and monitors;[10] collectors of the heavenly spark with power to convey the electricity to others. Or, as the storm-tossed vessel at sea speaks the frigate or 'line-packet'[11] to learn its longitude, so it may not be without its advantage that we should now and then encounter rare and gifted men, to compare the points of our spiritual compass, and verify our bearings from superior chronometers.

Amidst the downward tendency and proneness of things, when every voice is raised for a new road or another statute, or a subscription of stock, for an improvement in dress, or in dentistry, for a new house or a larger business, for a political party, or the division of an estate,— will you not tolerate one or two solitary voices in the land, speaking for thoughts and principles not marketable or perishable? Soon these improvements and mechanical inventions will be superseded; these modes of living lost out of memory; these cities rotted, ruined by war, by new inventions, by new seats of trade, or the geologic changes:—

all gone, like the shells which sprinkle the seabeach with a white colony to-day, forever renewed to be forever destroyed. But the thoughts which these few hermits strove to proclaim by silence, as well as by speech, not only by what they did, but by what they forbore to do, shall abide in beauty and strength, to reorganize themselves in nature, to invest themselves anew in other, perhaps higher endowed and happier mixed clay than ours, in fuller union with the surrounding system.

Source: Ralph Waldo Emerson, "The Transcendentalist" (23 December 1841), *Dial*, 3 (January 1843): 297–313.

Notes

1. Gold eagle, a gold coin worth ten dollars.
2. *Othello*, act 5, scene 2, ll. 129–133.
3. Friedrich Heinrich Jacobi (1743–1819), German philosopher and novelist. In the *Dial*, Emerson mistakenly attributes Jacobi's reply to Immanuel Kant, a mistake he corrected when the lecture was reprinted in *Nature; Addresses, and Lectures* (1849).
4. Pylades, in Greek mythology, was a friend of Orestes, the son of Agamemnon, who helped him gain revenge against his mother for contriving to kill his father; Timoleon (d. ca. 337 B.C.), Corinthian who so hated tyranny that he murdered his own brother when he attempted to become dictator; Emerson may be referring to Epaminondas' thwarting of a peace treaty among the Theban states; Johan de Witt (1625–1672), Dutch statesman: Emerson is probably thinking of the secret clause he inserted into the Treaty of Westminister (1654); Cato the Younger (95–46 B.C.), Roman military man and philosopher, committed suicide after his unsuccessful opposition to Caesar; King David was guilty of murdering Uriah, husband of Bathsheba, in order to marry her.
5. Coleridge's translation. [Emerson's note] This is the introductory quotation to *The Friend*, Essay XI.
6. Gnostics, early Christian sect teaching that knowledge, as opposed to mere faith, is the true key to salvation; Essenes, ascetic Jewish sect around the time of Christ.
7. Mozart, quoted from Margaret Fuller's "Lives of the Great Composers" in the October 1841 *Dial*.
8. *Pericles and Aspasia* (1836), by Walter Savage Landor (1775–1864), English Romantic poet.
9. 2 Corinthians 12:2.
10. Exciters and monitors, devices used in electrical experiments.
11. Speak, to hail another ship's captain; line-packet, a ship used for conveying letters and passengers.

Lidian Jackson Emerson

"Transcendental Bible"

(1841?)

LIDIAN JACKSON EMERSON (1802–1892), Waldo's second wife, married him in 1835. Waldo changed her name from "Lydia" to "Lidian" upon their marriage, probably because the New England pronunciation of "Lydia Emerson" was awkward. Although she was quoted by a friend as saying Unitarianism was "cold and hard, with scarcely a firmament above it," she was more religiously orthodox than her husband, and often expressed her concern that he had strayed too far from traditional Christianity in his personal religious quest. Her humorous comments show her wariness about how the "higher" faculties of the Transcendentalists may be leaving the heart behind as their heads seek the clouds.

Whole Duty of Man

Never hint at a Providence, Particular or Universal. It is narrow to believe that the Universal Being concerns itself with particular affairs, egotistical to think it regards your own. Never speak of sin. It is of no consequence to "the Being" whether you are good or bad. It is egotistical to consider it yourself; who are you?

Never confess a fault. You should not have committed it and who cares whether you are sorry?

Never speak of Happiness as a consequence of Holiness. Do you need any bribe to well-doing? Cannot you every hour practise holiness for its own sake? Are you not ashamed to wish to be happy? It is egotistical—mean.

Never speak of the hope of Immortality. What do you know about it? It is egotistical to cling to it. Enough for the great to know that "Being" Is. He is quite content to drop into annihilation at the death of the body.

Never speak of affliction being sent and sent in kindness; that is an old wives' fable. What do you know about it? And what business is it of ours whether it is for our good or not?

Duty to your Neighbour

Loathe and shun the sick. They are in bad taste, and may untune us for writing the poem floating through our mind.

Scorn the infirm of character and omit no opportunity of insulting and exposing them. They ought not to be infirm and should be punished by contempt and avoidance.

Despise the unintellectual, and make them feel that you do by not noticing their remark and question lest they presume to intrude into your conversation.

Abhor those who commit certain crimes because they indicate stupidity, want of intellect which is the one thing needful.

Justify those who commit certain other crimes. Their commission is consistent with the possession of intellect. We should not judge the intellectual as common men. It is mean enough to wish to put a great mind into the strait-jacket of morality.

It is mean and weak to seek for sympathy; it is mean and weak to give it. Great souls are self-sustained and stand ever erect, saying only to the prostrate sufferer "Get up, and stop your complaining." Never wish to be loved. Who are you to expect that? Besides, the great never value being loved.

If any seek to believe that their sorrows are sent in love, do your best to dispel the silly egotistical delusion.

If you scorn happiness (though you value a pleasant talk or walk, a tasteful garment, a comfortable dinner), if you wish not for immortal consciousness (though you bear with impatience the loss of an hour of thought or study), if you care not for the loss of your soul (though you deprecate the loss of your house), if you care not how much you sin (though in pain at the commission of a slight indiscretion), if you ask not a wise Providence over the earth in which you live (although wishing a wise manager of the house in which you live), if you care not that a benign Divinity shapes your ends (though you seek a good tailor to shape your coat), if you scorn to believe your affliction cometh not from the dust (though bowed to the dust by it), then, if there is such a thing as duty, you have done your whole duty to your noble self-sustained, impeccable, infallible Self.

If you have refused all sympathy to the sorrowful, all pity and aid to the sick, all toleration to the infirm of character, if you have condemned the unintellectual and loathed such sinners as have discovered want of intellect by their sin, then are you a perfect specimen of Humanity.

Let us all aspire after this Perfection! So be it.

Source: Lidian · Jackson Emerson, "Transcendental Bible," in Delores Bird Carpenter, "Lidian Emerson's 'Transcendental Bible,'" *Studies in the American Renaissance* 1980, ed. Joel Myerson (Boston: Twayne, 1980), pp. 91–92. The quotation is from Ellen Tucker Emerson, *The Life of Lidian Jackson Emerson*, ed. Carpenter (Boston: Twayne, 1980), p. 49.

[*Margaret Fuller*]

"The Great Lawsuit. Man *versus* Men. Woman *versus* Women"

(July 1843)

FULLER'S FEMINIST MANIFESTO is a call for equality of the sexes. Rhetorically, Fuller does at least two interesting things. First, as a woman writing in a male world, she envelops herself and her work in all of her considerable learning (hence the many allusions and citations of other writers) to demonstrate that even though she had been denied a college education, she was indeed well informed about literature, philosophy, and the other arts—she was, in other words, credentialed. Second, she sets forth her argument not just for the good of woman but for the good of man as well, recognizing that self-interest may triumph where principles have failed. Her four types of marriages, like Emerson's ascending order of chapters in *Nature*, go from the commonplace to the best: the "household partnership," "mutual idolatry," "intellectual companionship," and the religious union, which includes the best of all the others. Among her astute psychological comments are those about how children can be gender-patterned at youth simply by identifying playthings as belonging to one sex or the other, and her androgynous view of the human psyche: "There is no wholly masculine man, no purely feminine woman." She revised this essay as *Woman in the Nineteenth Century* (1845), in which she expressed her belief that women needed to be educated up from dependence and men up from mere idolatry, with "We must have units before we can have unions," a type of Emersonian self-reliance applied to interpersonal relations. Readers who find this essay a demanding read might consider Fuller's comment when she published the book version, where she complained that she had to change her title because the *Dial* title was "not sufficiently easy to be understood," which, from her perspective, was just fine, because the "The Great Lawsuit. Man *versus* Men. Woman *versus* Women" requires "some thought to see what it means, and might thus prepare the reader to meet me on my own ground."

This great suit has now been carried on through many ages, with various results. The decisions have been numerous, but always followed by appeals to still higher courts. How can it be otherwise, when the law itself is the subject of frequent elucidation, constant revision? Man has, now and then, enjoyed a clear, triumphant hour, when some irresistible conviction warmed and purified the atmosphere of his planet. But, presently, he sought repose after his labors, when the crowd of pigmy adversaries bound him in his sleep. Long years of inglorious imprisonment followed, while his enemies revelled in his spoils, and no counsel could be found to plead his cause, in the absence of that all-promising glance, which had, at times, kindled the poetic soul to revelation of his claims, of his rights.

Yet a foundation for the largest claim is now established. It is known that his inheritance consists in no partial sway, no exclusive possession, such as his adversaries desire. For they, not content that the universe is rich, would, each one for himself, appropriate treasure; but in vain! The many-colored garment, which clothed with honor an elected son, when rent asunder for the many, is a worthless spoil.[1] A band of robbers cannot live princely in the prince's castle; nor would he, like them, be content with less than all, though he would not, like them, seek it as fuel for riotous enjoyment, but as his principality, to administer and guard for the use of all living things therein. He cannot be satisfied with any one gift of the earth, any one department of knowledge, or telescopic peep at the heavens. He feels himself called to understand and aid nature, that she may, through his intelligence, be raised and interpreted; to be a student of, and servant to, the universe-spirit; and only king of his planet, that, as an angelic minister, he may bring it into conscious harmony with the law of that spirit.

Such is the inheritance of the orphan prince, and the illegitimate children of his family will not always be able to keep it from him, for, from the fields which they sow with dragon's teeth, and water with blood, rise monsters, which he alone has power to drive away.

But it is not the purpose now to sing the prophecy of his jubilee. We have said that, in clear triumphant moments, this has many, many times been made manifest, and those moments, though past in time, have been translated into eternity by thought. The bright signs they left hang in the heavens, as single stars or constellations, and, already, a thickly-sown radiance consoles the wanderer in the darkest night. Heroes have filled the zodiac of beneficent labors, and then given up their mortal part[2] to the fire without a murmur. Sages and lawgivers have bent their whole nature to the search for truth, and thought themselves happy if they could buy, with the sacrifice of all temporal ease and pleasure, one seed for the future Eden. Poets and priests have strung the lyre with heart-strings, poured out their best blood upon the altar which, reared anew from age to age, shall at last sustain the flame which rises to highest heaven. What shall we say of those who, if not so directly, or so consciously, in connection with the central truth, yet, led and fashioned by a divine instinct, serve no less to develop and interpret the open secret of love passing into life, the divine energy creating for the purpose of happiness;—of the artist, whose hand, drawn by a preëxistent harmony to a certain medium, moulds it to expressions of life more highly and completely organized than are seen elsewhere, and, by carrying out the intention of nature, reveals her meaning to those who are not yet sufficiently matured to divine it; of the philosopher, who listens steadily for causes, and, from those obvious, infers those yet unknown; of the historian, who, in faith that all events must have their reason and their aim, records them, and lays up archives from which the youth of prophets may be fed. The man of science dissects the statement, verifies the facts, and demonstrates connection even where he cannot its purpose.

Lives, too, which bear none of these names, have yielded tones of no less significance. The candlestick, set in a low place, has given light as faithfully, where it was needed, as that upon the hill. In close alleys, in dismal nooks, the Word has been read as distinctly, as when shown by angels to holy men in the dark prison. Those who till a spot of earth, scarcely larger than is wanted for a grave, have deserved that the sun should shine upon its sod till violets answer.

So great has been, from time to time, the promise, that, in all ages, men have said the Gods themselves came down to dwell with them; that the All-Creating wandered on the earth to taste in a limited nature the sweetness of virtue, that the All-Sustaining incarnated himself, to guard, in space and time, the destinies of his world; that heavenly genius dwelt among the shepherds, to sing to them and teach them how to sing. Indeed,

> Der stets den Hirten gnädig sich bewies.
> He has constantly shown himself favorable to shepherds.

And these dwellers in green pastures and natural students of the stars, were selected to hail, first of all, the holy child, whose life and death presented the type of excellence, which has sustained the heart of so large a portion of mankind in these later generations.

Such marks have been left by the footsteps of man, whenever he has made his way through the wilderness of men. And whenever the pygmies stepped in one of these, they felt dilate within the breast somewhat that promised larger stature and purer blood. They were tempted to forsake their evil ways, to forsake the side of selfish personal existence, of decrepit skepticism, and covetousness of corruptible possessions. Conviction flowed in upon them. They, too, raised the cry; God is living, all is his, and all created beings are brothers, for they are his children. These were the triumphant moments; but as we have said, man slept and selfishness awoke.

Thus he is still kept out of his inheritance, still a pleader, still a pilgrim. But his reinstatement is sure. And now, no mere glimmering consciousness, but a certainty, is felt and spoken, that the highest ideal man can form of his own capabilities is that which he is destined to attain. Whatever the soul knows how to seek, it must attain. Knock, and it shall be opened; seek, and ye shall find. It is demonstrated, it is a maxim. He no longer paints his proper nature in some peculiar form and says, "Prometheus had it," but "Man must have it." However disputed by many, however ignorantly used, or falsified, by those who do receive it, the fact of an universal, unceasing revelation, has been too clearly stated in words, to be lost sight of in thought, and sermons preached from the text, "Be ye perfect," are the only sermons of a pervasive and deep-searching influence.

But among those who meditate upon this text, there is great difference of view, as to the way in which perfection shall be sought.

Through the intellect, say some; Gather from every growth of life its seed of thought; look behind every symbol for its law. If thou canst *see* clearly, the rest will follow.

Through the life, say others; Do the best thou knowest to-day. Shrink not from incessant error, in this gradual, fragmentary state. Follow thy light for as much as it will show thee, be faithful as far as thou canst, in hope that faith presently will lead to sight. Help others, without blame that they need thy help. Love much, and be forgiven.

It needs not intellect, needs not experience, says a third. If you took the true way, these would be evolved in purity. You would not learn through them, but express through them a higher knowledge. In quietness, yield thy soul to the casual soul. Do not disturb its teachings by methods of thine own. Be still, seek not, but wait in obedience. Thy commission will be given.

Could we, indeed, say what we want, could we give a description of the child that is lost, he would be found. As soon as the soul can say clearly, that a certain demonstration is wanted, it is at hand. When the Jewish prophet described the Lamb, as the expression of what was required by the coming era, the time drew nigh.[3] But we say not, see not, as yet, clearly, what we would. Those who call for a more triumphant expression of love, a love that cannot be crucified, show not a perfect sense of what has already been expressed. Love has already been expressed, that made all things new, that gave the worm its ministry as well as the eagle; a love, to which it was alike to descend into the depths of hell, or to sit at the right hand of the Father.

Yet, no doubt, a new manifestation is at hand, a new hour in the day of man. We cannot expect to see him a completed being, when the mass of men lie so entangled in the sod, or use the freedom of their limbs only with wolfish energy. The tree cannot come to flower till its root be freed from the cankering worm, and its whole growth open to air and light. Yet something new shall presently be shown of the life of man, for hearts crave it now, if minds do not know how to ask it.

Among the strains of prophecy, the following, by an earnest mind of a foreign land, written some thirty years ago, is not yet outgrown; and it has the merit of being a positive appeal from the heart, instead of a critical declaration what man shall *not* do.

> The ministry of man implies, that he must be filled from the divine fountains which are being engendered through all eternity, so that, at the mere name of his Master, he may be able to cast all his enemies into the abyss; that he may deliver all parts of nature from the barriers that imprison them; that he may purge the terrestrial atmosphere from the poisons that infect it; that he may preserve the bodies of men from the corrupt influences that surround, and the maladies that afflict them; still more, that he may keep their souls pure from the malignant insinuations which pollute, and the gloomy images that obscure them; that we may restore its serenity to the Word, which false words of men fill with mourning and sadness; that he may satisfy the desires of the angels, who await from him the development of the marvels of nature; that, in fine, his world may be filled with God, as eternity is.[4]

Another attempt we will give, by an obscure observer of our own day and country, to draw some lines of the desired image. It was suggested by seeing the design of Crawford's Orpheus,[5] and connecting with the circumstance of the American, in his garret at Rome, making choice of this subject, that of Americans here at home, showing such ambition to represent the character, by calling their prose and verse, Orphic sayings, Orphics.[6] Orpheus was a lawgiver by theocratic commission. He understood nature, and made all her forms move to his music. He told her secrets in the form of hymns, nature as seen in the mind of God. Then it is the prediction, that to learn and to do, all men must be lovers, and Orpheus was, in a high sense, a lover. His soul went forth towards all beings, yet could remain sternly faithful to a chosen type of excellence. Seeking what he loved, he feared not death nor hell, neither could any presence daunt his faith in the power of the celestial harmony that filled his soul.

It seemed significant of the state of things in this country, that the sculptor should have chosen the attitude of shading his eyes. When we have the statue here, it will give lessons in reverence.

> Each Orpheus must to the depths descend,
> For only thus the poet can be wise
> Must make the sad Persephone his friend,[7]
> And buried love to second life arise;
> Again his love must lose through too much love,
> Must lose his life by living life too true,
> For what he sought below is passed above,
> Already done is all that he would do;
> Must tune all being with his single lyre,
> Must melt all rocks free from their primal pain,
> Must search all nature with his one soul's fire,
> Must bind anew all forms in heavenly chain.
> If he already sees what he must do,
> Well may he shade his eyes from the far-shining view.[8]

Meanwhile, not a few believe, and men themselves have expressed the opinion, that the time is come when Euridice is to call for an Orpheus, rather than Orpheus for Euridice; that the idea of man, however imperfectly brought out, has been far more so than that of woman, and that an improvement in the daughters will best aid the reformation of the sons of this age.

It is worthy of remark, that, as the principle of liberty is better understood and more nobly interpreted, a broader protest is made in behalf of woman. As men become aware that all men have not had their fair chance, they are inclined to say that no women have had a fair chance. The French revolution, that strangely disguised angel, bore witness in favor of woman, but interpreted her claims no less ignorantly than those of man. Its idea of happiness did not rise beyond outward enjoyment, unobstructed by the tyranny of others. The title it gave was Citoyen, Citoyenne, and it is not unimportant to woman that even this species of equality was awarded her. Before, she could be condemned to perish on the scaffold for treason, but not as a citizen, but a subject. The right, with which this title then invested a human being, was that of bloodshed and license. The Goddess of Liberty was impure. Yet truth was prophesied in the ravings of that hideous fever induced by long ignorance and abuse. Europe is conning a valued lesson from the blood-stained page. The same tendencies, farther unfolded, will bear good fruit in this country.

Yet, in this country, as by the Jews, when Moses was leading them to the promised land, everything has been done that inherited depravity could, to hinder the promise of heaven from its fulfilment. The cross, here as elsewhere, has been planted only to be blasphemed by cruelty and fraud. The name of the Prince of Peace has been profaned by all kinds of injustice towards the Gentile whom he said he came to save. But I need not speak of what has been done towards the red man, the black man. These deeds are the scoff of the world; and they have been accompanied by such pious words, that the gentlest would not dare to intercede with, "Father forgive them, for they know not what they do."[9]

Here, as elsewhere, the gain of creation consists always in the growth of individual minds, which live and aspire, as flowers bloom and birds sing, in the midst of morasses; and in the continual development of that thought, the thought of human destiny, which is given to eternity to fulfil, and which ages of failure only seemingly impede. Only seemingly, and whatever seems to the contrary, this country is as surely destined to elucidate a great moral law, as Europe was to promote the mental culture of man.

Though the national independence be blurred by the servility of individuals; though freedom and equality have been proclaimed only to leave room for a monstrous display of slave dealing and slave keeping; though the free American so often feels himself free, like the Roman, only to pamper his appetites and his indolence through the misery of his fellow beings, still it is not in vain, that the verbal statement has been made, "All men are born free and equal." There it stands, a golden certainty, wherewith to encourage the good, to shame the bad. The new world may be called clearly to perceive that it incurs the utmost penalty, if it rejects the sorrowful brother. And if men are deaf, the angels hear. But men cannot be deaf. It is inevitable that an external freedom, such as has been achieved for the nation, should be so also for every member of it. That, which has once been clearly conceived in the intelligence, must be acted out. It has become a law, irrevocable as that of the Medes in their ancient dominion.[10] Men will privately sin against it, but the law so clearly expressed by a leading mind of the age,

> Tutti fatti a sembianza d' un Solo;
> Figli tutti d' un solo riscatto,
> In qual ora, in qual parte del suolo
> Trascorriamo quest' aura vital,
> Siam fratelli, siam stretti ad un patto:
> Maladetto colui che lo infrange,
> Che s' innalza sul fiacco che piange,
> Che contrista uno spirto immortal.[11]

All made in the likeness of the One,
All children of one ransom,
In whatever hour, in whatever part of the soil
We draw this vital air,
We are brothers, we must be bound by one compact,
Accursed he who infringes it,
Who raises himself upon the weak who weep,
Who saddens an immortal spirit.

cannot fail of universal recognition.

We sicken no less at the pomp than at the strife of words. We feel that never were lungs so puffed with the wind of declamation, on moral and religious subjects, as now. We are tempted to implore these "word-heroes," these word-Catos,[12] word-Christs, to beware of cant above all things; to remember that hypocrisy is the most hopeless as well as the meanest of crimes, and that those must surely be polluted by it, who do not keep a little of all this morality and religion for private use.[13] We feel that the mind may "grow black and rancid in the smoke" even of altars. We start up from the harangue to go into our closet and shut the door. But, when it has been shut long enough, we remember that where there is so much smoke, there must be some fire; with so much talk about virtue and freedom must be mingled some desire for them; that it cannot be in vain that such have become the common topics of conversation among men; that the very newspapers should proclaim themselves Pilgrims, Puritans, Heralds of Holiness. The king that maintains so costly a retinue cannot be a mere Count of Carabbas fiction.[14] We have waited here long in the dust; we are tired and hungry, but the triumphal procession must appear at last.

Of all its banners, none has been more steadily upheld, and under none has more valor and willingness for real sacrifices been shown, than that of the champions of the enslaved African. And this band it is, which, partly in consequence of a natural following out of principles, partly because many women have been prominent in that cause, makes, just now, the warmest appeal in behalf of woman!

Though there has been a growing liberality on this point, yet society at large is not so prepared for the demands of this party, but that they are, and will be for some time, coldly regarded as the Jacobins of their day.[15]

"Is it not enough," cries the sorrowful trader, "that you have done all you could to break up the national Union, and thus destroy the prosperity of our country, but now you must be trying to break up family union, to take my wife away from the cradle, and the kitchen hearth, to vote at polls, and preach from a pulpit? Of course, if she does such things, she cannot attend to those of her own sphere. She is happy enough as she is. She has more leisure than I have, every means of improvement, every indulgence."

"Have you asked her whether she was satisfied with these indulgences?"

"No, but I know she is. She is too amiable to wish what would make me unhappy, and too judicious to wish to step beyond the sphere of her sex. I will never consent to have our peace disturbed by any such discussions."

" 'Consent'—you? it is not consent from you that is in question, it is assent from your wife."

"Am I not the head of my house?"

"You are not the head of your wife. God has given her a mind of her own."

"I am the head and she the heart."

"God grant you play true to one another then. If the head represses no natural pulse of the heart, there can be no question as to your giving your consent. Both will be of one accord, and there needs but to present any question to get a full and true answer. There is no need of precaution, of indulgence, or consent. But our doubt is whether the heart consents with the head, or only acquiesces in its decree; and it is to ascertain the truth on this point, that we propose some liberating measures."

Thus vaguely are these questions proposed and discussed at present. But their being proposed at all implies much thought, and suggests more. Many women are considering within themselves what they need that they have not, and what they can have, if they find they need it. Many men are considering whether women are capable of being and having more than they are and have, and whether, if they are, it will be best to consent to improvement in their condition.

The numerous party, whose opinions are already labelled and adjusted too much to their mind to admit of any new light, strive, by lectures on some model-woman of bridal-like beauty and gentleness, by writing or lending little treatises, to mark out with due precision the limits of woman's sphere, and woman's mission, and to prevent other than the rightful shepherd from climbing the wall, or the flock from using any chance gap to run astray.

Without enrolling ourselves at once on either side, let us look upon the subject from that point of view which to-day offers. No better, it is to be feared, than a high house-top. A high hill-top, or at least a cathedral spire, would be desirable.

It is not surprising that it should be the Anti-Slavery party that pleads for woman, when we consider merely that she does not hold property on equal terms with men; so that, if a husband dies without a will, the wife, instead of stepping at once into his place as head of the family, inherits only a part of his fortune, as if she were a child, or ward only, not an equal partner.

We will not speak of the innumerable instances, in which profligate or idle men live upon the earnings of industrious wives; or if the wives leave them and take with them the children, to perform the double duty of mother and father, follow from place to place, and threaten to rob them of the children, if deprived of the rights of a husband, as they call them, planting themselves in their poor lodgings, frightening them into paying tribute by taking from them the children, running into debt at the expense of these otherwise so overtasked helots. Though such instances abound, the public opinion of his own sex is against the man, and when cases of extreme tyranny are made known, there is private action in the wife's favor. But if woman be, indeed, the weaker party, she ought to have legal protection, which would make such oppression impossible.

And knowing that there exists, in the world of men, a tone of feeling towards women as towards slaves, such as is expressed in the common phrase, "Tell that to women and children;" that the infinite soul can only work through them in already ascertained limits; that the prerogative of reason, man's highest portion, is allotted to them in a much lower degree; that it is better for them to be engaged in active labor, which is to be furnished and directed by those better able to think, &c. &c.; we need not go further, for who can review the experience of last week, without recalling words which imply, whether in jest or earnest, these views, and views like these? Knowing this, can we wonder that many reformers think that measures are not likely to be taken in behalf of women, unless their wishes could be publicly represented by women?

That can never be necessary, cry the other side. All men are privately influenced by women; each has his wife, sister, or female friends, and is too much biassed by these relations to fail of representing their interests. And if this is not enough, let them propose and enforce their wishes with the pen. The beauty of home would be destroyed, the delicacy of the sex be violated, the dignity of halls of legislation destroyed, by an attempt to introduce them there. Such duties are inconsistent with those of a mother; and then we have ludicrous pictures of ladies in hysterics at the polls, and senate chambers filled with cradles.

But if, in reply, we admit as truth that woman seems destined by nature rather to the inner circle, we must add that the arrangements of civilized life have not been as yet such as to secure it to her. Her circle, if the duller, is not the quieter. If kept from excitement, she is not from drudgery. Not only the Indian carries the burdens of the camp, but the favorites of Louis the Fourteenth accompany him in his journeys,[16] and the washerwoman stands at her tub and carries home her work at all seasons, and in all states of health.

As to the use of the pen, there was quite as much opposition to woman's possessing herself of that help to free-agency as there is now to her seizing on the rostrum or the desk; and she is likely to draw, from a permission to plead her cause that way, opposite inferences to what might be wished by those who now grant it.

As to the possibility of her filling, with grace and dignity, any such position, we should think those who had seen the great actresses, and heard the Quaker preachers of modern times, would not doubt, that woman can express publicly the fulness of thought and emotion, without losing any of the peculiar beauty of her sex.

As to her home, she is not likely to leave it more than she now does for balls, theatres, meetings for promoting missions, revival meetings, and others to which she flies, in hope of an animation for her existence, commensurate with what she sees enjoyed by men. Governors of Ladies' Fairs are no less engrossed by such a charge, than the Governor of the State by his; presidents of Washingtonian societies, no less away from home than presidents of conventions. If men look straitly to it, they will find that, unless their own lives are domestic, those of the women will not be. The female Greek, of our day, is as much in the street as the male, to cry, What news? We doubt not it was the same in Athens of old. The women, shut out from the market-place, made up for it at the religious festivals. For human beings are not so constituted, that they can live without expansion; and if they do not get it one way, must another, or perish.

And, as to men's representing women fairly, at present, while we hear from men who owe to their wives not only all that is comfortable and graceful, but all that is wise in the arrangement of their lives, the frequent remark, "You cannot reason with a woman," when from those of delicacy, nobleness, and poetic culture, the contemptuous phrase, "Women and children," and that in no light sally of the hour, but in works intended to give a permanent statement of the best experiences, when not one man in the million, shall I say, no, not in the hundred million, can rise above the view that woman was made *for man*, when such traits as these are daily forced upon the attention, can we feel that man will always do justice to the interests of woman? Can we think that he takes a sufficiently discerning and religious view of her office and destiny, ever to do her justice, except when prompted by sentiment; accidentally or transiently, that is, for his sentiment will vary according to the relations in which he is placed. The lover, the poet, the artist, are likely to view her nobly. The father and the philosopher have some chance of liberality; the man of the world, the legislator for expediency, none.

Under these circumstances, without attaching importance in themselves to the changes demanded by the champions of woman, we hail them as signs of the times. We would have every arbitrary barrier thrown down. We would have every path laid open to woman as freely as to man. Were this done, and a slight temporary fermentation allowed to subside, we believe that the Divine would ascend into nature to a height unknown in the history of past ages, and nature, thus instructed, would regulate the spheres not only so as to avoid collision, but to bring forth ravishing harmony.

Yet then, and only then, will human beings be ripe for this, when inward and outward freedom for woman, as much as for man, shall be acknowledged as a right, not yielded as a concession. As the friend of the negro assumes that one man cannot, by right, hold another in bondage, should the friend of woman assume that man cannot, by right, lay even well-meant restrictions on woman. If the negro be a soul, if the woman be a soul, apparelled in flesh, to one master only are they accountable. There is but one law for all souls, and, if there is to be an interpreter of it, he comes not as man, or son of man, but as Son of God.

Were thought and feeling once so far elevated that man should esteem himself the brother and friend, but nowise the lord and tutor of woman, were he really bound with her in equal worship, arrangements as to function and employment would be of no consequence. What woman needs is not as a woman to act or rule, but as a nature to grow, as an intellect to discern, as a soul to live freely, and unimpeded to unfold such powers as were given her when we left our common home. If fewer talents were given her, yet, if allowed the free and full employment of these, so that she may render back to the giver his own with usury, she will not complain, nay, I dare to say she will bless and rejoice in her earthly birth-place, her earthly lot.

Let us consider what obstructions impede this good era, and what signs give reason to hope that it draws near.

I was talking on this subject with Miranda, a woman, who, if any in the world, might speak without heat or bitterness of the position of her sex.[17] Her father was a man who cherished no sentimental reverence for woman, but a firm belief in the equality of the sexes. She was his eldest child, and came to him at an age when he needed a companion. From the time she could speak and go alone, he addressed her not as a plaything, but as a living mind. Among the few verses he ever wrote were a copy addressed to this child, when the first locks were cut from her head, and the reverence expressed on this occasion for that cherished head he never belied. It was to him the temple of immortal intellect. He respected his child, however, too much to be an indulgent parent. He called on her for clear judgment, for courage, for honor and fidelity, in short for such virtues as he knew. In so far as he possessed the keys to the wonders of this universe, he allowed free use of them to her, and by the incentive of a high expectation he forbade, as far as possible, that she should let the privilege lie idle.

Thus this child was early led to feel herself a child of the spirit. She took her place easily, not only in the world of organized being, but in the world of mind. A dignified sense of self-dependence was given as all her portion, and she found it a sure anchor. Herself securely anchored, her relations with others were established with equal security. She was fortunate, in a total absence of those charms which might have drawn to her bewildering flatteries, and of a strong electric nature, which repelled those who did not belong to her, and attracted those who did. With men and women her relations were noble; affectionate without passion, intellectual without coldness. The world was free to her, and she lived freely in it. Outward adversity came, and inward conflict, but that faith and self-respect had early been awakened, which must always lead at last to an outward serenity, and an inward peace.

Of Miranda I had always thought as an example, that the restraints upon the sex were insuperable only to those who think them so, or who noisily strive to break them. She had taken a course of her own, and no man stood in her way. Many of her acts had been unusual, but excited no uproar. Few helped, but none checked her; and the many men, who knew her mind and her life, showed to her confidence as to a brother, gentleness as to a sister. And not only refined, but very coarse men approved one in whom they saw resolution and clearness of design. Her mind was often the leading one, always effective.

When I talked with her upon these matters, and had said very much what I have written, she smilingly replied, And yet we must admit that I have been fortunate, and this should not be. My good father's early trust gave the first bias, and the rest followed of course. It is true that I have had less outward aid, in after years, than most women, but that is of little consequence. Religion was early awakened in my soul, a sense that what the soul is capable to ask it must attain, and that, though I might be aided by others, I must depend on myself as the only constant friend. This self-dependence, which was honored in me, is deprecated as a fault in most women. They are taught to learn their rule from without, not to unfold it from within.

This is the fault of man, who is still vain, and wishes to be more important to woman than by right he should be.

Men have not shown this disposition towards you, I said.

No, because the position I early was enabled to take, was one of self-reliance. And were all women as sure of their wants as I was, the result would be the same. The difficulty is to get them to the point where they shall naturally develop self-respect, the question how it is to be done.

Once I thought that men would help on this state of things more than I do now. I saw so many of them wretched in the connections they had formed in weakness and vanity. They seemed so glad to esteem women whenever they could!

But early I perceived that men never, in any extreme of despair, wished to be women. Where they admired any woman they were inclined to speak of her as above her sex. Silently I observed this, and feared it argued a rooted skepticism, which for ages had been fastening on the heart, and which only an age of miracles could eradicate.

Ever I have been treated with great sincerity; and I look upon it as a most signal instance of this, that an intimate friend of the other sex said in a fervent moment, that I deserved in some star to be a man. Another used as highest praise, in speaking of a character in literature, the words "a manly woman."

It is well known that of every strong woman they say she has a masculine mind.

This by no means argues a willing want of generosity towards woman. Man is as generous towards her, as he knows how to be.

Wherever she has herself arisen in national or private history, and nobly shone forth in any ideal of excellence, men have received her, not only willingly, but with triumph. Their encomiums indeed are always in some sense mortifying, they show too much surprise.

In every-day life the feelings of the many are stained with vanity. Each wishes to be lord in a little world, to be superior at least over one; and he does not feel strong enough to retain a life-long ascendant over a strong nature. Only a Brutus would rejoice in a Portia.[18] Only Theseus could conquer before he wed the Amazonian Queen. Hercules wished rather to rest from his labors with Dejanira, and received the poisoned robe, as a fit guerdon.[19] The tale should be interpreted to all those who seek repose with the weak.

But not only is man vain and fond of power, but the same want of development, which thus affects him morally in the intellect, prevents his discerning the destiny of woman. The boy wants no woman, but only a girl to play ball with him, and mark his pocket handkerchief.

Thus in Schiller's Dignity of Woman, beautiful as the poem is, there is no "grave and perfect man," but only a great boy to be softened and restrained by the influence of girls.[20] Poets, the elder brothers of their race, have usually seen further; but what can you expect of every-day men, if Schiller was not more prophetic as to what women must be? Even with Richter one foremost thought about a wife was that she would "cook him something good."[21]

The sexes should not only correspond to and appreciate one another, but prophesy to one another. In individual instances this happens. Two persons love in one another the future good which they aid one another to unfold. This is very imperfectly done as yet in the general life. Man has gone but little way, now he is waiting to see whether woman can keep step with him, but instead of calling out like a good brother; You can do it if you only think so, or impersonally; Any one can do what he tries to do, he often discourages with school-boy brag; Girls can't do that, girls can't play ball. But let any one defy their taunts, break through, and be brave and secure, they rend the air with shouts.

No! man is not willingly ungenerous. He wants faith and love, because he is not yet himself an elevated being. He cries with sneering skepticism; Give us a sign. But if the sign appears, his eyes glisten, and he offers not merely approval, but homage.

The severe nation which taught that the happiness of the race was forfeited through the fault of a woman, and showed its thought of what sort of regard man owed her, by making him accuse her on the first question to his God, who gave her to the patriarch as a handmaid, and, by the Mosaical law, bound her to allegiance like a serf, even they greeted, with solemn rapture, all great and holy women as heroines, prophetesses, nay judges in Israel; and, if they made Eve listen to the serpent, gave Mary to the Holy Spirit.[22] In other nations it has been the same down to our day. To the woman, who could conquer, a triumph was awarded. And not only those whose strength was recommended to the heart by association with goodness and beauty, but those who were bad, if they were steadfast and strong, had their claims allowed. In any age a Semiramis, an Elizabeth of England, a Catharine of Russia makes her place good, whether in a large or small circle.[23]

How has a little wit, a little genius, always been celebrated in a woman! What an intellectual triumph was that of the lonely Aspasia, and how heartily acknowledged! She, indeed, met a Pericles.[24] But what annalist, the rudest of men, the most plebeian of husbands, will spare from his page one of the few anecdotes of Roman women?—Sappho, Eloisa![25] The names are of thread-bare celebrity. The man habitually most narrow towards women will be flushed, as by the worst assault on Christianity, if you say it has made no improvement in her condition. Indeed, those most opposed to new acts in her favor are jealous of the reputation of those which have been done.

We will not speak of the enthusiasm excited by actresses, improv-visatrici, female singers, for here mingles the charm of beauty and grace, but female authors, even learned women, if not insufferably ugly and slovenly, from the Italian professor's daughter, who taught behind the curtain, down to Mrs. Carter and Madame Dacier, are sure of an admiring audience, if they can once get a platform on which to stand.[26]

But how to get this platform, or how to make it of reasonably easy access is the difficulty. Plants of great vigor will almost always struggle into blossom, despite impediments. But there should be encouragement, and a free, genial atmosphere for those of more timid sort, fair play for each in its own kind. Some are like the little, delicate flowers, which love to hide in the dripping mosses by the sides of mountain torrents, or in the shade of tall trees. But others require an open field, a rich and loosened soil, or they never show their proper hues.

It may be said man does not have his fair play either; his energies are repressed and distorted by the interposition of artificial obstacles. Aye, but he himself has put them there; they have grown out of his own imperfections. If there *is* a misfortune in woman's lot, it is in obstacles being interposed by men, which do *not* mark her state, and if they express her past ignorance, do not her present needs. As every man is of woman born, she has slow but sure means of redress, yet the sooner a general justness of thought makes smooth the path, the better.

Man is of woman born, and her face bends over him in infancy with an expression he can never quite forget. Eminent men have delighted to pay tribute to this image, and it is a hacknied observation, that most men of genius boast some remarkable development in the mother. The rudest tar[27] brushes off a tear with his coat-sleeve at the hallowed name. The other day I met a decrepit old man of seventy, on a journey, who challenged the stage-company to guess where he was going. They guessed aright, "To see your mother." "Yes," said he, "she is ninety-two, but has good eye-sight still, they say. I've not seen her these forty years, and I thought I could not die in peace without." I should have liked his picture painted as a companion piece to that of a boisterous little boy, whom I saw attempt to declaim at a school exhibition.

O that those lips had language! Life has passed
With me but roughly since I heard thee last.[28]

He got but very little way before sudden tears shamed him from the stage.

Some gleams of the same expression which shone down upon his infancy, angelically pure and benign, visit man again with hopes of pure love, of a holy marriage. Or, if not before, in the eyes of the mother of his child they again are seen, and dim fancies pass before his mind, that woman may not have been born for him alone, but have come from heaven, a commissioned soul, a messenger of truth and love.

In gleams, in dim fancies, this thought visits the mind of common men. It is soon obscured by the mists of sensuality, the dust of routine, and he thinks it was only some meteor or ignis fatuus[29] that shone. But, as a Rosicrucian lamp, it burns unwearied, though condemned to the solitude of tombs.[30] And, to its permanent life, as to every truth, each age has, in some form, borne witness. For the truths, which visit the minds of careless men only in fitful gleams, shine with radiant clearness into those of the poet, the priest, and the artist.

Whatever may have been the domestic manners of the ancient nations, the idea of woman was nobly manifested in their mythologies and poems, where she appeared as Sita in the Ramayana,[31] a form of tender purity, in the Egyptian Isis, of divine wisdom never yet surpassed. In Egypt, too, the Sphynx, walking the earth with lion tread, looked out upon its marvels in the calm, inscrutable beauty of a virgin's face, and the Greek could only add wings to the great emblem.[32] In Greece, Ceres and Proserpine, significantly termed "the goddesses," were seen seated, side by side.[33] They needed not to rise for any worshipper or any change; they were prepared for all things, as those initiated to their mysteries knew. More obvious is the meaning of those three forms, the Diana, Minerva, and Vesta.[34] Unlike in the expression of their beauty, but alike in this,—that each was self-sufficing. Other forms were only accessories and illustrations, none the complement to one like these. Another might indeed be the companion, and the Apollo and Diana set off one another's beauty. Of the Vesta, it is to be observed, that not only deep-eyed deep-discerning Greece, but ruder Rome, who represents the only form of good man (the always busy warrior) that could be indifferent to woman, confided the permanence of its glory to a tutelary goddess, and her wisest legislator spoke of Meditation as a nymph.

In Sparta, thought, in this respect as all others, was expressed in the characters of real life, and the women of Sparta were as much Spartans as the men. The Citoyen, Citoyenne, of France, was here actualized. Was not the calm equality they enjoyed well worth the honors of chivalry? They intelligently shared the ideal life of their nation.

Generally, we are told of these nations, that women occupied there a very subordinate position in actual life. It is difficult to believe this, when we see such range and dignity of thought on the subject in the mythologies, and find the poets producing such ideals as Cassandra, Iphigenia, Antigone, Macaria,[35] (though it is not unlike our own day, that men should revere those heroines of their great princely houses at theatres from which their women were excluded,) where Sibylline priestesses told the oracle of the highest god, and he could not be content to reign with a court of less than nine Muses. Even Victory wore a female form.[36]

But whatever were the facts of daily life, I cannot complain of the age and nation, which represents its thought by such a symbol as I see before me at this moment. It is a zodiac of the busts of gods and goddesses, arranged in pairs. The circle breathes the music of a heavenly order. Male and female heads are distinct in expression, but equal in beauty, strength, and calmness. Each male head is that of a brother and a king, each female of a sister and a queen. Could the thought, thus expressed, be lived out, there would be nothing more to be desired. There would be unison in variety, congeniality in difference.

Coming nearer our own time, we find religion and poetry no less true in their revelations. The rude man, but just disengaged from the sod, the Adam, accuses woman to his God, and records her disgrace to their posterity. He is not ashamed to write that he could be drawn from heaven by one beneath him. But in the same nation, educated by time, instructed by successive prophets, we find woman in as high a position as she has ever occupied. And no figure, that has ever arisen to greet our eyes, has been received with more fervent reverence than that of the Madonna. Heine calls her the Dame du Comptoir of the Catholic Church, and this jeer well expresses a serious truth.[37]

And not only this holy and significant image was worshipped by the pilgrim, and the favorite subject of the artist, but it exercised an immediate influence on the destiny of the sex. The empresses, who embraced the cross, converted sons and husbands. Whole calendars of female saints, heroic dames of chivalry, binding the emblem of faith on the heart of the best beloved, and wasting the bloom of youth in separation and loneliness, for the sake of duties they thought it religion to assume, with innumerable forms of poesy, trace their lineage to this one. Nor, however imperfect may be the action, in our day, of the faith thus expressed, and though we can scarcely think it nearer this ideal than that of India or Greece was near their ideal, is it in vain that the truth has been recognised, that woman is not only a part of man, bone of his bone and flesh of his flesh, born that men might not be lonely, but in themselves possessors of and possessed by immortal souls. This truth undoubtedly received a greater outward stability from the belief of the church, that the earthly parent of the Saviour of souls was a woman.

The Assumption of the Virgin, as painted by sublime artists, Petrarch's Hymn to the Madonna, cannot have spoken to the world wholly without result, yet oftentimes those who had ears heard not.[38]

Thus, the Idea of woman has not failed to be often and forcibly represented. So many instances throng on the mind, that we must stop here, lest the catalogue be swelled beyond the reader's patience.

Neither can she complain that she has not had her share of power. This, in all ranks of society, except the lowest, has been hers to the extent that vanity could crave, far beyond what wisdom would accept. In the very lowest, where man, pressed by poverty, sees in woman only the partner of toils and cares, and cannot hope, scarcely has an idea of a comfortable home, he maltreats her, often, and is less influenced by her. In all ranks, those who are amiable and uncomplaining, suffer much. They suffer long, and are kind; verily they have their reward. But wherever man is sufficiently raised above extreme poverty, or brutal stupidity, to care for the comforts of the fireside, or the bloom and ornament of life, woman has always power enough, if she choose to exert it, and is usually disposed to do so in proportion to her ignorance and childish vanity. Unacquainted with the importance of life and its purposes, trained to a selfish coquetry and love of petty power, she does not look beyond the pleasure of making herself felt at the moment, and governments are shaken and commerce broken up to gratify the pique of a female favorite. The English shopkeeper's wife does not vote, but it is for her interest that the politician canvasses by the coarsest flattery. France suffers no woman on her throne, but her proud nobles kiss the dust at the feet of Pompadour and Dubarry, for such flare in the lighted foreground where a Roland would modestly aid in the closet.[39] Spain shuts up her women in the care of duennas, and allows them no book but the Breviary; but the ruin follows only the more surely from the worthless favorite of a worthless queen.

It is not the transient breath of poetic incense, that women want; each can receive that from a lover. It is not life-long sway; it needs but to become a coquette, a shrew, or a good cook to be sure of that. It is not money, nor notoriety, nor the badges of authority, that men have appropriated to themselves. If demands made in their behalf lay stress on any of these particulars, those who make them have not searched deeply into the need. It is for that which at once includes all these and precludes them; which would not be forbidden power, lest there be temptation to steal and misuse it; which would not have the mind perverted by flattery from a worthiness of esteem. It is for that which is the birthright of every being capable to receive it,—the freedom, the religious, the intelligent freedom of the universe, to use its means, to learn its secret as far as nature has enabled them, with God alone for their guide and their judge.

Ye cannot believe it, men; but the only reason why women ever assume what is more appropriate to you, is because you prevent them from finding out what is fit for themselves. Were they free, were they wise fully to develop the strength and beauty of woman, they would never wish to be men, or manlike. The well-instructed moon flies not from her orbit to seize on the glories of her partner. No; for she knows that one law rules, one heaven contains, one universe replies to them alike. It is with women as with the slave.

> Vor dem Sklaven, wenn er die Kette bricht,
> Vor dem freien Menschen erzittert nicht.

Tremble not before the free man, but before the slave who has chains to break.[40]

In slavery, acknowledged slavery, women are on a par with men. Each is a work-tool, an article of property,—no more! In perfect freedom, such as is painted in Olympus, in Swedenborg's angelic state, in the heaven where there is no marrying nor giving in marriage, each is a purified intelligence, an enfranchised soul,—no less!

> Jene himmlissche Gestalten
> Sie fragen nicht nach Mann und Weib,
> Und keine Kleider, keine Falten
> Umgeben den verklärten Leib.[41]

The child who sang this was a prophetic form, expressive of the longing for a state of perfect freedom, pure love. She could not remain here, but was transplanted to another air. And it may be that the air of this earth will never be so tempered, that such can bear it long. But, while they stay, they must bear testimony to the truth they are constituted to demand.

That an era approaches which shall approximate nearer to such a temper than any has yet done, there are many tokens, indeed so many that only a few of the most prominent can here be enumerated.

The reigns of Elizabeth of England and Isabella of Castile foreboded this era.[42] They expressed the beginning of the new state, while they forwarded its progress. These were strong characters, and in harmony with the wants of their time. One showed that this strength did not unfit a woman for the duties of a wife and mother; the other, that it could enable her to live and die alone. Elizabeth is certainly no pleasing example. In rising above the weakness, she did not lay aside the weaknesses ascribed to her sex; but her strength must be respected now, as it was in her own time.

We may accept it as an omen for ourselves, that it was Isabella who furnished Columbus with the means of coming hither. This land must pay back its debt to woman, without whose aid it would not have been brought into alliance with the civilized world.

The influence of Elizabeth on literature was real, though, by sympathy with its finer productions, she was no more entitled to give name to an era than Queen Anne.[43] It was simply that the fact of having a female sovereign on the throne affected the course of a writer's thoughts. In this sense, the presence of a woman on the throne always makes its mark. Life is lived before the eyes of all men, and their imaginations are stimulated as to the possibilities of woman. "We will die for our King, Maria Theresa," cry the wild warriors, clashing their swords, and the sounds vibrate through the poems of that generation. [44] The range of female character in Spenser alone might content us for one period. Britomart and Belphoebe have as much room in the canvass as Florimel; and where this is the case, the haughtiest Amazon will not murmur that Una should be felt to be the highest type.[45]

Unlike as was the English Queen to a fairy queen, we may yet conceive that it was the image of *a* queen before the poet's mind, that called up this splendid court of women.

Shakespeare's range is also great, but he has left out the heroic characters, such as the Macaria of Greece, the Britomart of Spenser. Ford and Massinger have, in this respect, shown a higher flight of feeling than he.[46] It was the holy and heroic woman they most loved, and if they could not paint an Imogen, a Desdemona, a Rosalind, yet in those of a stronger mould, they showed a higher ideal, though with so much less poetic power to represent it, than we see in Portia or Isabella.[47] The simple truth of Cordelia, indeed, is of this sort.[48] The beauty of Cordelia is neither male nor female; it is the beauty of virtue.

The ideal of love and marriage rose high in the mind of all the Christian nations who were capable of grave and deep feeling. We may take as examples of its English aspect, the lines,

> I could not love thee, dear, so much,
> Loved I not honor more.[49]

The address of the Commonwealth's man to his wife as she looked out from the Tower window to see him for the last time on his way to execution. "He stood up in the cart, waved his hat, and cried, 'To Heaven, my love, to Heaven! and leave you in the storm!' "

Such was the love of faith and honor, a love which stopped, like Colonel Hutchinson's, "on this side idolatry," because it was religious.[50] The meeting of two such souls Donne describes as giving birth to an "abler soul."[51]

Lord Herbert wrote to his love,

> Were not our souls immortal made,
> Our equal loves can make them such.[52]

In Spain the same thought is arrayed in a sublimity, which belongs to the sombre and passionate genius of the nation. Calderon's Justina resists all the temptation of the Demon, and raises her lover with her above the sweet lures of mere temporal happiness.[53] Their marriage is vowed at the stake, their souls are liberated together by the martyr flame into "a purer state of sensation and existence."

In Italy, the great poets wove into their lives an ideal love which answered to the highest wants. It included those of the intellect and the affections, for it was a love of spirit for spirit. It was not ascetic and superhuman, but interpreting all things, gave their proper beauty to details of the common life, the common day; the poet spoke of his love not as a flower to place in his bosom, or hold carelessly in his hand, but as a light towards which he must find wings to fly, or "a stair to heaven." He delighted to speak of her not only as the bride of his heart, but the mother of his soul, for he saw that, in cases where the right direction has been taken, the greater delicacy of her frame, and stillness of her life, left her more open to spiritual influx than man is. So he did not look upon her as betwixt him and earth, to serve his temporal needs, but rather betwixt him and heaven, to purify his affections and lead him to wisdom through her pure love. He sought in her not so much the Eve as the Madonna.

In these minds the thought, which glitters in all the legends of chivalry, shines in broad intellectual effulgence, not to be misinterpreted. And their thought is reverenced by the world, though it lies so far from them as yet, so far, that it seems as though a gulf of Death lay between.

Even with such men the practice was often widely different from the mental faith. I say mental, for if the heart were thoroughly alive with it, the practice could not be dissonant. Lord Herbert's was a marriage of convention, made for him at fifteen; he was not discontented with it, but looked only to the advantages it brought of perpetuating his family on the basis of a great fortune. He paid, in act, what he considered a dutiful attention to the bond; his thoughts travelled elsewhere, and, while forming a high ideal of the companionship of minds in marriage, he seems never to have doubted that its realization must be postponed to some other stage of being. Dante, almost immediately after the death of Beatrice, married a lady chosen for him by his friends.[54]

Centuries have passed since, but civilized Europe is still in a transition state about marriage, not only in practice, but in thought. A great majority of societies and individuals are still doubtful whether earthly marriage is to be a union of souls, or merely a contract of convenience and utility. Were woman established in the rights of an immortal being, this could not be. She would not in some countries be given away by her father, with scarcely more respect for her own feelings than is shown by the Indian chief, who sells his daughter for a horse, and beats her if she runs away from her new home. Nor, in societies where her choice is left free, would she be perverted, by the current of opinion that seizes her, into the belief that she must marry, if it be only to find a protector, and a home of her own.

Neither would man, if he thought that the connection was of permanent importance, enter upon it so lightly. He would not deem it a trifle, that he was to enter into the closest relations with another soul, which, if not eternal in themselves, must eternally affect his growth.

Neither, did he believe woman capable of friendship, would he, by rash haste, lose the chance of finding a friend in the person who might, probably, live half a century by his side. Did love to his mind partake of infinity, he would not miss his chance of its revelations, that he might the sooner rest from his weariness by a bright fireside, and have a sweet and graceful attendant, "devoted to him alone." Were he a step higher, he would not carelessly enter into a relation, where he might not be able to do the duty of a friend, as well as a protector from external ill, to the other party, and have a being in his power pining for sympathy, intelligence, and aid, that he could not give.

Where the thought of equality has become pervasive, it shows itself in four kinds.

The household partnership. In our country the woman looks for a "smart but kind" husband, the man for a "capable, sweet-tempered" wife.

The man furnishes the house, the woman regulates it. Their relation is one of mutual esteem, mutual dependence. Their talk is of business, their affection shows itself by practical kindness. They know that life goes more smoothly and cheerfully to each for the other's aid; they are grateful and content. The wife praises her husband as a "good provider," the husband in return compliments her as a "capital housekeeper." This relation is good as far as it goes.

Next comes a closer tie which takes the two forms, either of intellectual companionship, or mutual idolatry. The last, we suppose, is to no one a pleasing subject of contemplation. The parties weaken and narrow one another; they lock the gate against all the glories of the universe that they may live in a cell together. To themselves they seem the only wise, to all others steeped in infatuation, the gods smile as they look forward to the crisis of cure, to men the woman seems an unlovely syren, to women the man an effeminate boy.

The other form, of intellectual companionship, has become more and more frequent. Men engaged in public life, literary men, and artists have often found in their wives companions and confidants in thought no less than in feeling. And, as in the course of things the intellectual development of woman has spread wider and risen higher, they have, not unfrequently, shared the same employment. As in the case of Roland and his wife, who were friends in the household and the nation's councils, read together, regulated home affairs, or prepared public documents together indifferently.[55]

It is very pleasant, in letters begun by Roland and finished by his wife, to see the harmony of mind and the difference of nature, one thought, but various ways of treating it.

This is one of the best instances of a marriage of friendship. It was only friendship, whose basis was esteem; probably neither party knew love, except by name.

Roland was a good man, worthy to esteem and be esteemed, his wife as deserving of admiration as able to do without it. Madame Roland is the fairest specimen we have yet of her class, as clear to discern her aim, as valiant to pursue it, as Spenser's Britomart, austerely set apart from all that did not belong to her, whether as woman or as mind. She is an antetype of a class to which the coming time will afford a field, the Spartan matron, brought by the culture of a book-furnishing age to intellectual consciousness and expansion.

Self-sufficing strength and clear-sightedness were in her combined with a power of deep and calm affection. The page of her life is one of unsullied dignity.

Her appeal to posterity is one against the injustice of those who committed such crimes in the name of liberty. She makes it in behalf of herself and her husband. I would put beside it on the shelf a little volume, containing a similar appeal from the verdict of contemporaries to that of mankind, that of Godwin in behalf of his wife, the celebrated, the by most men detested Mary Wolstonecraft.[56] In his view it was an appeal from the injustice of those who did such wrong in the name of virtue.

Were this little book interesting for no other cause, it would be so for the generous affection evinced under the peculiar circumstances. This man had courage to love and honor this woman in the face of the world's verdict, and of all that was repulsive in her own past history. He believed he saw of what soul she was, and that the thoughts she had struggled to act out were noble. He loved her and he defended her for the meaning and intensity of her inner life. It was a good fact.

Mary Wolstonecraft, like Madame Dudevant (commonly known as George Sand) in our day, was a woman whose existence better proved the need of some new interpretation of woman's rights, than anything she wrote.[57] Such women as these, rich in genius, of most tender sympathies, and capable of high virtue and a chastened harmony, ought not to find themselves by birth in a place so narrow, that in breaking bonds they become outlaws. Were there as much room in the world for such, as in Spenser's poem for Britomart, they would not run their heads so wildly against its laws. They find their way at last to purer air, but the world will not take off the brand it has set upon them. The champion of the rights of woman found in Godwin, one who pleads her own cause like a brother. George Sand smokes, wears male attire, wishes to be addressed as Mon frère; perhaps, if she found those who were as brothers indeed, she would not care whether she were brother or sister.

We rejoice to see that she, who expresses such a painful contempt for men in most of her works, as shows she must have known great wrong from them, in La Roche Mauprat depicting one raised, by the workings of love, from the depths of savage sensualism to a moral and intellectual life.[58] It was love for a pure object, for a steadfast woman, one of those who, the Italian said, could make the stair to heaven.

Women like Sand will speak now, and cannot be silenced; their characters and their eloquence alike foretell an era when such as they shall easier learn to lead true lives. But though such forebode, not such shall be the parents of it. Those who would reform the world must show that they do not speak in the heat of wild impulse; their lives must be unstained by passionate error; they must be severe lawgivers to themselves. As to their transgressions and opinions, it may be observed, that the resolve of Eloisa to be only the mistress of Abelard, was that of one who saw the contract of marriage a seal of degradation. Wherever abuses of this sort are seen, the timid will suffer, the bold protest. But society is in the right to outlaw them till she has revised her law, and she must be taught to do so, by one who speaks with authority, not in anger and haste.

If Godwin's choice of the calumniated authoress of the "Rights of Woman," for his honorod wife, be a sign of a new era, no less so is an article of great learning and eloquence, published several years since in an English review, where the writer, in doing full justice to Eloisa, shows his bitter regret that she lives not now to love him, who might have known better how to prize her love than did the egotistical Abelard.

These marriages, these characters, with all their imperfections, express an onward tendency. They speak of aspiration of soul, of energy of mind, seeking clearness and freedom. Of a like promise are the tracts now publishing by Goodwyn Barmby (the European Pariah as he calls himself) and his wife Catharine.[59] Whatever we may think of their measures, we see them in wedlock, the two minds are wed by the only contract that can permanently avail, of a common faith, and a common purpose.

We might mention instances, nearer home, of minds, partners in work and in life, sharing together, on equal terms, public and private interests, and which have not on any side that aspect of offence which characterizes the attitude of the last named; persons who steer straight onward, and in our freer life have not been obliged to run their heads against any wall. But the principles which guide them might, under petrified or oppressive institutions, have made them warlike, paradoxical, or, in some sense, Pariahs. The phenomenon is different, the law the same, in all these cases. Men and women have been obliged to build their house from the very foundation. If they found stone ready in the quarry, they took it peaceably, otherwise they alarmed the country by pulling down old towers to get materials.

These are all instances of marriage as intellectual companionship. The parties meet mind to mind, and a mutual trust is excited which can buckler them against a million. They work together for a common purpose, and, in all these instances, with the same implement, the pen.

A pleasing expression in this kind is afforded by the union in the names of the Howitts.[60] William and Mary Howitt we heard named together for years, supposing them to be brother and sister; the equality of labors and reputation, even so, was auspicious, more so, now we find them man and wife. In his late work on Germany, Howitt mentions his wife with pride, as one among the constellation of distinguished English women, and in a graceful, simple manner.

In naming these instances we do not mean to imply that community of employment is an essential to union of this sort, more than to the union of friendship. Harmony exists no less in difference than in likeness, if only the same key-note govern both parts. Woman the poem, man the poet; woman the heart, man the head; such divisions are only important when they are never to be transcended. If nature is never bound down, nor the voice of inspiration stifled, that is enough. We are pleased that women should write and speak, if they feel the need of it, from having something to tell; but silence for a hundred years would be as well, if that silence be from divine command, and not from man's tradition.

While Goetz von Berlichingen rides to battle, his wife is busy in the kitchen; but difference of occupation does not prevent that community of life, that perfect esteem, with which he says,

Whom God loves, to him gives he such a wife![61]

Manzoni thus dedicates his Adelchi.

To his beloved and venerated wife, Enrichetta Luigia Blondel, who, with conjugal affections and maternal wisdom, has preserved a virgin mind, the author dedicates this Adelchi grieving that he could not, by a more splendid and more durable monument, honor the dear name and the memory of so many virtues.[62]

The relation could not be fairer, nor more equal, if she too had written poems. Yet the position of the parties might have been the reverse as well; the woman might have sung the deeds, given voice to the life of the man, and beauty would have been the result, as we see in pictures of Arcadia the nymph singing to the shepherds, or the shepherd with his pipe allures the nymphs, either makes a good picture.[63] The sounding lyre requires not muscular strength, but energy of soul to animate the hand which can control it. Nature seems to delight in varying her arrangements, as if to show that she will be fettered by no rule, and we must admit the same varieties that she admits.

I have not spoken of the higher grade of marriage union, the religious, which may be expressed as pilgrimage towards a common shrine. This includes the others; home sympathies, and household wisdom, for these pilgrims must know how to assist one another to carry their burdens along the dusty way; intellectual communion, for how sad it would be on such a journey to have a companion to whom you could not communicate thoughts and aspirations, as they sprang to life, who would have no feeling for the more and more glorious prospects that open as we advance, who would never see the flowers that may be gathered by the most industrious traveler. It must include all these. Such a fellow pilgrim Count Zinzendorf seems to have found in his countess of whom he thus writes.[64]

Twenty-five years' experience has shown me that just the help-mate whom I have is the only one that could suit my vocation. Who else could have so carried through my family affairs? Who lived so spotlessly before the world? Who so wisely aided me in my rejection of a dry morality? Who so clearly set aside the Pharisaism which, as years passed, threatened to creep in among us? Who so deeply discerned as to the spirits of delusion which sought to bewilder us? Who would have governed my whole economy so wisely, richly, and hospitably when circumstances commanded? Who have taken indifferently the part of servant or mistress, without on the one side affecting an especial spirituality, on the other being sullied by any worldly pride? Who, in a community where all ranks are eager to be on a level, would, from wise and real causes, have known how to maintain inward and outward distinctions? Who, without a murmur, have seen her husband encounter such dangers by land and sea? Who undertaken with him and sustained such astonishing pilgrimages? Who amid such difficulties always held up her head, and supported me? Who found so many hundred thousands and acquitted them on her own credit? And, finally, who, of all human beings, would so well understand and interpret to others my inner and outer being as this one, of such nobleness in her way of thinking, such great intellectual capacity, and free from the theological perplexities that enveloped me?

An observer[65] adds this testimony.

We may in many marriages regard it as the best arrangement, if the man has so much advantage over his wife that she can, without much thought of her own, be, by him, led and directed, as by a father. But it was not so with the Count and his consort. She was not made to be a copy; she was an original; and, while she loved and honored him, she thought for herself on all subjects with so much intelligence, that he could and did look on her as a sister and friend also.

Such a woman is the sister and friend of all beings, as the worthy man is their brother and helper.

Another sign of the time is furnished by the triumphs of female authorship. These have been great and constantly increasing. They have taken possession of so many provinces for which men had pronounced them unfit, that though these still declare there are some inaccessible to them, it is difficult to say just *where* they must stop.

The shining names of famous women have cast light upon the path of the sex, and many obstructions have been removed. When a Montague could learn better than her brother, and use her lore to such purpose afterwards as an observer, it seemed amiss to hinder women from preparing themselves to see, or from seeing all they could when prepared.[66] Since Somerville has achieved so much, will any young girl be prevented from attaining a knowledge of the physical sciences, if she wishes it?[67] De Stael's name was not so clear of offence; she could not forget the woman in the thought; while she was instructing you as a mind, she wished to be admired as a woman. Sentimental tears often dimmed the eagle glance. Her intellect, too, with all its splendor, trained in a drawing room, fed on flattery, was tainted and flawed; yet its beams make the obscurest school house in New England warmer and lighter to the little rugged girls, who are gathered together on its wooden bench. They may never through life hear her name, but she is not the less their benefactress.

This influence has been such that the aim certainly is, how, in arranging school instruction for girls, to give them as fair a field as boys. These arrangements are made as yet with little judgment or intelligence, just as the tutors of Jane Grey,[68] and the other famous women of her time, taught them Latin and Greek, because they knew nothing else themselves, so now the improvement in the education of girls is made by giving them gentlemen as teachers, who only teach what has been taught themselves at college, while methods and topics need revision for those new cases, which could better be made by those who had experienced the same wants. Women are often at the head of these institutions, but they have as yet seldom been thinking women, capable to organize a new whole for the wants of the time, and choose persons to officiate in the departments. And when some portion of education is got of a good sort from the school, the tone of society, the much larger proportion received from the world, contradicts its purport. Yet books have not been furnished, and a little elementary instruction been given in vain. Women are better aware how large and rich the universe is, not so easily blinded by the narrowness and partial views of a home circle.

Whether much or little has or will be done, whether women will add to the talent of narration, the power of systematizing, whether they will carve marble as well as draw, is not important. But that it should be acknowledged that they have intellect which needs developing, that they should not be considered complete, if beings of affection and habit alone, is important.

Yet even this acknowledgment, rather obtained by woman than proffered by man, has been sullied by the usual selfishness. So much is said of women being better educated that they may be better companions and mothers *of men!* They should be fit for such companionship, and we have mentioned with satisfaction instances where it has been established. Earth knows no fairer, holier relation than that of a mother. But a being of infinite scope must not be treated with an exclusive view to any one relation. Give the soul free course, let the organization be freely developed, and the being will be fit for any and every relation to which it may be called. The intellect, no more than the sense of hearing, is to be cultivated, that she may be a more valuable companion to man, but because the Power who gave a power by its mere existence signifies that it must be brought out towards perfection.

In this regard, of self-dependence and a greater simplicity and fulness of being, we must hail as a preliminary the increase of the class contemptuously designated as old maids.

We cannot wonder at the aversion with which old bachelors and old maids have been regarded. Marriage is the natural means of forming a sphere, of taking root on the earth: it requires more strength to do this without such an opening, very many have failed of this, and their imperfections have been in every one's way. They have been more partial, more harsh, more officious and impertinent than others. Those, who have a complete experience of the human instincts, have a distrust as to whether they can be thoroughly human and humane, such as is hinted at in the saying, "Old maids' and bachelors' children are well cared for," which derides at once their ignorance and their presumption.

Yet the business of society has become so complex, that it could now scarcely be carried on without the presence of these despised auxiliaries, and detachments from the army of aunts and uncles are wanted to stop gaps in every hedge. They rove about, mental and moral Ishmaelites, pitching their tents amid the fixed and ornamented habitations of men.[69]

They thus gain a wider, if not so deep, experience. They are not so intimate with others, but thrown more upon themselves, and if they do not there find peace and incessant life, there is none to flatter them that they are not very poor and very mean.

A position, which so constantly admonishes, may be of inestimable benefit. The person may gain, undistracted by other relationships, a closer communion with the One. Such a use is made of it by saints and sibyls. Or she may be one of the lay sisters of charity, or more humbly only the useful drudge of all men, or the intellectual interpreter of the varied life she sees.

Or she may combine all these. Not "needing to care that she may please a husband," a frail and limited being, all her thoughts may turn to the centre, and by steadfast contemplation enter into the secret of truth and love, use it for the use of all men, instead of a chosen few, and interpret through it all the forms of life.

Saints and geniuses have often chosen a lonely position, in the faith that, if undisturbed by the pressure of near ties they could give themselves up to the inspiring spirit, it would enable them to understand and reproduce life better than actual experience could.

How many old maids take this high stand, we cannot say; it is an unhappy fact that too many of those who come before the eye are gossips rather, and not always good-natured gossips. But, if these abuse, and none make the best of their vocation, yet, it has not failed to produce some good fruit. It has been seen by others, if not by themselves, that beings likely to be left alone need to be fortified and furnished within themselves, and education and thought have tended more and more to regard beings as related to absolute Being, as well as to other men. It has been seen that as the loss of no bond ought to destroy a human being, so ought the missing of none to hinder him from growing. And thus a circumstance of the time has helped to put woman on the true platform. Perhaps the next generation will look deeper into this matter, and find that contempt is put on old maids, or old women at all, merely because they do not use the elixir which will keep the soul always young. No one thinks of Michael Angelo's Persican Sibyl, or St. Theresa, or Tasso's Leonora, or the Greek Electra as an old maid, though all had reached the period in life's course appointed to take that degree.[70]

Even among the North American Indians, a race of men as completely engaged in mere instinctive life as almost any in the world, and where each chief, keeping many wives as useful servants, of course looks with no kind eye on celibacy in woman, it was excused in the following instance mentioned by Mrs. Jameson.[71] A woman dreamt in youth that she was betrothed to the sun. She built her a wigwam apart, filled it with emblems of her alliance and means of an independent life. There she passed her days, sustained by her own exertions, and true to her supposed engagement.

In any tribe, we believe, a woman, who lived as if she was betrothed to the sun, would be tolerated, and the rays which made her youth blossom sweetly would crown her with a halo in age.

There is on this subject a nobler view than heretofore, if not the noblest, and we greet improvement here, as much as on the subject of marriage. Both are fertile themes, but time permits not here to explore them.

If larger intellectual resources begin to be deemed necessary to woman, still more is a spiritual dignity in her, or even the mere assumption of it listened to with respect. Joanna Southcote, and Mother Ann Lee are sure of a band of disciples;[72] Ecstatica, Dolorosa, of enraptured believers who will visit them in their lowly huts, and wait for hours to revere them in their trances.[73] The foreign noble traverses land and sea to hear a few words from the lips of the lowly peasant girl, whom he believes specially visited by the Most High. Very beautiful in this way was the influence of the invalid of St. Petersburg, as described by De Maistre.[74]

To this region, however misunderstood, and ill-developed, belong the phenomena of Magnetism, or Mesmerism, as it is now often called, where the trance of the Ecstatica purports to be produced by the agency of one human being on another, instead of, as in her case, direct from the spirit.[75]

The worldling has his sneer here as about the services of religion. "The churches can always be filled with women." "Show me a man in one of your magnetic states, and I will believe."

Women are indeed the easy victims of priestcraft, or self-delusion, but this might not be, if the intellect was developed in proportion to the other powers. They would then have a regulator and be in better equipoise, yet must retain the same nervous susceptibility, while their physical structure is such as it is.

It is with just that hope, that we welcome everything that tends to strengthen the fibre and develop the nature on more sides. When the intellect and affections are in harmony, when intellectual consciousness is calm and deep, inspiration will not be confounded with fancy.

The electrical, the magnetic element in woman has not been fairly developed at any period. Everything might be expected from it; she has far more of it than man. This is commonly expressed by saying, that her intuitions are more rapid and more correct.

But I cannot enlarge upon this here, except to say that on this side is highest promise. Should I speak of it fully, my title should be Cassandra, my topic the Seeress of Prevorst, the first, or the best observed subject of magnetism in our times, and who, like her ancestresses at Delphos, was roused to ecstacy or phrenzy by the touch of the laurel.[76]

In such cases worldlings sneer, but reverent men learn wondrous news, either from the person observed, or by the thoughts caused in themselves by the observation. Fenelon learns from Guyon, Kerner from his Seeress what we fain would know.[77] But to appreciate such disclosures one must be a child, and here the phrase, "women and children," may perhaps be interpreted aright, that only little children shall enter into the kingdom of heaven.

All these motions of the time, tides that betoken a waxing moon, overflow upon our own land. The world at large is readier to let woman learn and manifest the capacities of her nature than it ever was before, and here is a less encumbered field, and freer air than anywhere else. And it ought to be so; we ought to pay for Isabella's jewels.

The names of nations are feminine. Religion, Virtue, and Victory are feminine. To those who have a superstition as to outward signs, it is not without significance that the name of the Queen of our mother-land should at this crisis be Victoria.[78] Victoria the First. Perhaps to us it may be given to disclose the era there outwardly presaged.

Women here are much better situated than men. Good books are allowed with more time to read them. They are not so early forced into the bustle of life, nor so weighed down by demands for outward success. The perpetual changes, incident to our society, make the blood circulate freely through the body politic, and, if not favorable at present to the grace and bloom of life, they are so to activity, resource, and would be to reflection but for a low materialist tendency, from which the women are generally exempt.

They have time to think, and no traditions chain them, and few conventionalities compared with what must be met in other nations. There is no reason why the fact of a constant revelation should be hid from them, and when the mind once is awakened by that, it will not be restrained by the past, but fly to seek the seeds of a heavenly future.

Their employments are more favorable to the inward life than those of the men.

Woman is not addressed religiously here, more than elsewhere. She is told to be worthy to be the mother of a Washington, or the companion of some good man. But in many, many instances, she has already learnt that all bribes have the same flaw; that truth and good are to be sought for themselves alone. And already an ideal sweetness floats over many forms, shines in many eyes.

Already deep questions are put by young girls on the great theme, What shall I do to inherit eternal life?

Men are very courteous to them. They praise them often, check them seldom. There is some chivalry in the feelings towards "the ladies," which gives them the best seats in the stage-coach, frequent admission not only to lectures of all sorts, but to courts of justice, halls of legislature, reform conventions. The newspaper editor "would be better pleased that the Lady's Book were filled up exclusively by ladies. It would, then, indeed, be a true gem, worthy to be presented by young men to the mistresses of their affections." Can gallantry go farther?

In this country is venerated, wherever seen, the character which Goethe spoke of as an Ideal. "The excellent woman is she, who, if the husband dies, can be a father to the children." And this, if rightly read, tells a great deal.

Women who speak in public, if they have a moral power, such as has been felt from Angelina Grimke and Abby Kelly,[79] that is, if they speak for conscience' sake, to serve a cause which they hold sacred, invariably subdue the prejudices of their hearers, and excite an interest proportionate to the aversion with which it had been the purpose to regard them.

A passage in a private letter so happily illustrates this, that I take the liberty to make use of it, though there is not opportunity to ask leave either of the writer or owner of the letter. I think they will pardon me when they see it in print; it is so good, that as many as possible should have the benefit of it.

Abby Kelly in the Town-House of ———

> The scene was not unheroic,—to see that woman, true to humanity and her own nature, a centre of rude eyes and tongues, even gentlemen feeling licensed to make part of a species of mob around a female out of her sphere. As she took her seat in the desk amid the great noise, and in the throng full, like a wave, of something to ensue, I saw her humanity in a gentleness and unpretension, tenderly open to the sphere around her, and, had she not been supported by the power of the will of genuineness and principle, she would have failed. It led her to prayer, which, in woman especially, is childlike; sensibility and will going to the side of God and looking up to him; and humanity was poured out in aspiration.
>
> She acted like a gentle hero, with her mild decision and womanly calmness. All heroism is mild and quiet and gentle, for it is life and possession, and combativeness and firmness show a want of actualness. She is as earnest, fresh, and simple as when she first entered the crusade. I think she did much good, more than the men in her place could do, for woman feels more as being and reproducing; this brings the subject more into home relations. Men speak through and mostly from intellect, and this addresses itself in others, which creates and is combative.

Not easily shall we find elsewhere, or before this time, any written observations on the same subject, so delicate and profound.

The late Dr. Channing, whose enlarged and tender and religious nature shared every onward impulse of his time, though his thoughts followed his wishes with a deliberative caution, which belonged to his habits and temperament, was greatly interested in these expectations for women. His own treatment of them was absolutely and thoroughly religious. He regarded them as souls, each of which had a destiny of its own, incalculable to other minds, and whose leading it must follow, guided by the light of a private conscience. He had sentiment, delicacy, kindness, taste, but they were all pervaded and ruled by this one thought, that all beings had souls, and must vindicate their own inheritance. Thus all beings were treated by him with an equal, and sweet, though solemn courtesy. The young and unknown, the woman and the child, all felt themselves regarded with an infinite expectation, from which there was no reaction to vulgar prejudice. He demanded of all he met, to use his favorite phrase, "great truths."

His memory, every way dear and reverend, is by many especially cherished for this intercourse of unbroken respect.

At one time when the progress of Harriet Martineau through this country, Angelina Grimke's appearance in public, and the visit of Mrs. Jameson had turned his thoughts to this subject, he expressed high hopes as to what the coming era would bring to woman. He had been much pleased with the dignified courage of Mrs. Jameson in taking up the defence of her sex, in a way from which women usually shrink, because, if they express themselves on such subjects with sufficient force and clearness to do any good, they are exposed to assaults whose vulgarity makes them painful. In intercourse with such a woman, he had shared her indignation at the base injustice, in many respects, and in many regions done to the sex; and been led to think of it far more than ever before. He seemed to think that he might some time write upon the subject. That his aid is withdrawn from the cause is a subject of great regret, for on this question, as on others, he would have known how to sum up the evidence and take, in the noblest spirit, middle ground. He always furnished a platform on which opposing parties could stand, and look at one another under the influence of his mildness and enlightened candor.

Two younger thinkers, men both, have uttered noble prophecies, auspicious for woman. Kinmont, all whose thoughts tended towards the establishment of the reign of love and peace, thought that the inevitable means of this would be an increased predominance given to the idea of woman.[80] Had he lived longer to see the growth of the peace party, the reforms in life and medical practice which seek to substitute water for wine and drugs, pulse for animal food, he would have been confirmed in his view of the way in which the desired changes are to be effected.

In this connection I must mention Shelley, who, like all men of genius, shared the feminine development, and unlike many, knew it. His life was one of the first pulse-beats in the present reform-growth. He, too, abhorred blood and heat, and, by his system and his song, tended to reinstate a plant-like gentleness in the development of energy. In harmony with this his ideas of marriage were lofty, and of course no less so of woman, her nature, and destiny.

For woman, if by a sympathy as to outward condition, she is led to aid the enfranchisement of the slave, must no less so, by inward tendency, to favor measures which promise to bring the world more thoroughly and deeply into harmony with her nature. When the lamb takes place of the lion as the emblem of nations, both women and men will be as children of one spirit, perpetual learners of the word and doers thereof, not hearers only.

A writer in a late number of the New York Pathfinder, in two articles headed "Femality," has uttered a still more pregnant word than any we have named.[81] He views woman truly from the soul, and not from society, and the depth and leading of his thoughts is proportionably remarkable. He views the feminine nature as a harmonizer of the vehement elements, and this has often been hinted elsewhere; but what he expresses most forcibly is the lyrical, the inspiring and inspired apprehensiveness of her being.

Had I room to dwell upon this topic, I could not say anything so precise, so near the heart of the matter, as may be found in that article; but, as it is, I can only indicate, not declare, my view.

There are two aspects of woman's nature, expressed by the ancients as Muse and Minerva. It is the former to which the writer in the Pathfinder looks. It is the latter which Wordsworth has in mind, when he says,

> With a placid brow,
> Which woman ne'er should forfeit, keep thy vow.[82]

The especial genius of woman I believe to be electrical in movement, intuitive in function, spiritual in tendency. She is great not so easily in classification, or re-creation, as in an instinctive seizure of causes, and a simple breathing out of what she receives that has the singleness of life, rather than the selecting or energizing of art.

More native to her is it to be the living model of the artist, than to set apart from herself any one form in objective reality; more native to inspire and receive the poem than to create it. In so far as soul is in her completely developed, all soul is the same; but as far as it is modified in her as woman, it flows, it breathes, it sings, rather than deposits soil, or finishes work, and that which is especially feminine flushes in blossom the face of earth, and pervades like air and water all this seeming solid globe, daily renewing and purifying its life. Such may be the especially feminine element, spoken of as Femality. But it is no more the order of nature that it should be incarnated pure in any form, than that the masculine energy should exist unmingled with it in any form.

Male and female represent the two sides of the great radical dualism. But, in fact, they are perpetually passing into one another. Fluid hardens to solid, solid rushes to fluid. There is no wholly masculine man, no purely feminine woman.

History jeers at the attempts of physiologists to bind great original laws by the forms which flow from them. They make a rule; they say from observation what can and cannot be. In vain! Nature provides exceptions to every rule. She sends women to battle, and sets Hercules spinning; she enables women to bear immense burdens, cold, and frost; she enables the man, who feels maternal love, to nourish his infant like a mother. Of late she plays still gayer pranks. Not only she deprives organizations, but organs, of a necessary end. She enables people to read with the top of the head, and see with the pit of the stomach. Presently she will make a female Newton, and a male Syren.

Man partakes of the feminine in the Apollo, woman of the Masculine as Minerva.

Let us be wise and not impede the soul. Let her work as she will. Let us have one creative energy, one incessant revelation. Let it take what form it will, and let us not bind it by the past to man or woman, black or white. Jove sprang from Rhea, Pallas from Jove.[83] So let it be.

If it has been the tendency of the past remarks to call woman rather to the Minerva side,—if I, unlike the more generous writer, have spoken from society no less than the soul,—let it be pardoned. It is love that has caused this, love for many incarcerated souls, that might be freed could the idea of religious self-dependence be established in them, could the weakening habit of dependence on others be broken up.

Every relation, every gradation of nature, is incalculably precious, but only to the soul which is poised upon itself, and to whom no loss, no change, can bring dull discord, for it is in harmony with the central soul.

If any individual live too much in relations, so that he becomes a stranger to the resources of his own nature, he falls after a while into a distraction, or imbecility, from which he can only be cured by a time of isolation, which gives the renovating fountains time to rise up. With a society it is the same. Many minds, deprived of the traditionary or instinctive means of passing a cheerful existence, must find help in self-impulse or perish. It is therefore that while any elevation, in the view of union, is to be hailed with joy, we shall not decline celibacy as the great fact of the time. It is one from which no vow, no arrangement, can at present save a thinking mind. For now the rowers are pausing on their oars, they wait a change before they can pull together. All tends to illustrate the thought of a wise contemporary. Union is only possible to those who are units. To be fit for relations in time, souls, whether of man or woman, must be able to do without them in the spirit.

It is therefore that I would have woman lay aside all thought, such as she habitually cherishes, of being taught and led by men. I would have her, like the Indian girl, dedicate herself to the Sun, the Sun of Truth, and go no where if his beams did not make clear the path. I would have her free from compromise, from complaisance, from helplessness, because I would have her good enough and strong enough to love one and all beings, from the fulness, not the poverty of being.

Men, as at present instructed, will not help this work, because they also are under the slavery of habit. I have seen with delight their poetic impulses. A sister is the fairest ideal, and how nobly Wordsworth, and even Byron, have written of a sister.[84]

There is no sweeter sight than to see a father with his little daughter. Very vulgar men become refined to the eye when leading a little girl by the hand. At that moment the right relation between the sexes seems established, and you feel as if the man would aid in the noblest purpose, if you ask him in behalf of his little daughter. Once two fine figures stood before me, thus. The father of very intellectual aspect, his falcon eye softened by affection as he looked down on his fair child, she the image of himself, only more graceful and brilliant in expression. I was reminded of Southey's Kehama, when lo, the dream was rudely broken.[85] They were talking of education, and he said.

"I shall not have Maria brought too forward. If she knows too much, she will never find a husband; superior women hardly ever can."

"Surely," said his wife, with a blush, "you wish Maria to be as good and wise as she can, whether it will help her to marriage or not."

"No," he persisted, "I want her to have a sphere and a home, and some one to protect her when I am gone."

It was a trifling incident, but made a deep impression. I felt that the holiest relations fail to instruct the unprepared and perverted mind. If this man, indeed, would have looked at it on the other side, he was the last that would have been willing to have been taken himself for the home and protection he could give, but would have been much more likely to repeat the tale of Alcibiades with his phials.[86]

But men do *not* look at both sides, and women must leave off asking them and being influenced by them, but retire within themselves, and explore the groundwork of being till they find their peculiar secret. Then when they come forth again, renovated and baptized, they will know how to turn all dross to gold, and will be rich and free though they live in a hut, tranquil, if in a crowd. Then their sweet singing shall not be from passionate impulse, but the lyrical overflow of a divine rapture, and a new music shall be elucidated from this many-chorded world.

Grant her then for a while the armor and the javelin. Let her put from her the press of other minds and meditate in virgin loneliness. The same idea shall reappear in due time as Muse, or Ceres, the all-kindly, patient Earth-Spirit.

I tire every one with my Goethean illustrations. But it cannot be helped.

Goethe, the great mind which gave itself absolutely to the leadings of truth, and let rise through him the waves which are still advancing through the century, was its intellectual prophet. Those who know him, see, daily, his thought fulfilled more and more, and they must speak of it, till his name weary and even nauseate, as all great names have in their time. And I cannot spare the reader, if such there be, his wonderful sight as to the prospects and wants of women.

As his Wilhelm grows in life and advances in wisdom, he becomes acquainted with women of more and more character, rising from Mariana to Macaria.[87]

Macaria, bound with the heavenly bodies in fixed revolutions, the centre of all relations, herself unrelated, expresses the Minerva side.

Mignon, the electrical, inspired lyrical nature.[88]

All these women, though we see them in relations, we can think of as unrelated. They all are very individual, yet seem nowhere restrained. They satisfy for the present, yet arouse an infinite expectation.

The economist Theresa, the benevolent Natalia,[89] the fair Saint, have chosen a path, but their thoughts are not narrowed to it. The functions of life to them are not ends, but suggestions.

Thus to them all things are important, because none is necessary. Their different characters have fair play, and each is beautiful in its minute indications, for nothing is enforced or conventional, but everything, however slight, grows from the essential life of the being.

Mignon and Theresa wear male attire when they like, and it is graceful for them to do so, while Macaria is confined to her arm chair behind the green curtain, and the Fair Saint could not bear a speck of dust on her robe.

All things are in their places in this little world because all is natural and free, just as "there is room for everything out of doors." Yet all is rounded in by natural harmony which will always arise where Truth and Love are sought in the light of freedom.

Goethe's book bodes an era of freedom like its own, of "extraordinary generous seeking," and new revelations. New individualities shall be developed in the actual world, which shall advance upon it as gently as the figures come out upon his canvass.

A profound thinker has said "no married woman can represent the female world, for she belongs to her husband. The idea of woman must be represented by a virgin."

But that is the very fault of marriage, and of the present relation between the sexes, that the woman does belong to the man, instead of forming a whole with him. Were it otherwise there would be no such limitation to the thought.

Woman, self-centred, would never be absorbed by any relation; it would be only an experience to her as to man. It is a vulgar error that love, *a* love to woman is her whole existence; she also is born for Truth and Love in their universal energy. Would she but assume her inheritance, Mary would not be the only Virgin Mother. Not Manzoni alone would celebrate in his wife the virgin mind with the maternal wisdom and conjugal affections. The soul is ever young, ever virgin.

And will not she soon appear? The woman who shall vindicate their birthright for all women; who shall teach them what to claim, and how to use what they obtain? Shall not her name be for her era Victoria, for her country and her life Virginia? Yet predictions are rash; she herself must teach us to give her the fitting name.

Source: [Margaret Fuller], "The Great Lawsuit. Man *versus* Men. Woman *versus* Women," *Dial*, 4 (July 1843): 1–47. The quotations are from *Woman in the Nineteenth Century* (New York: Greeley and McElrath, 1845), pp. 89, v.

Notes

1. A reference to the biblical Joseph and his coat of many colors.
2. Jupiter adloquitur,

> Sed enim, nec pectora vano
> Fida metu paveant, Œteas spernite flammas,
> Omnia qui vicit, vincet, quos cernitis, ignes;
> Nec nisi maternâ Vulcanum parte potentem
> Sentiet. Aeternum est, à me quod traxit, et expers
> Atque inmune necis, nullaque domabile flamma
> Idque ego defunctum terrâ cœlestibus oris
> Accipiam, cunctisque meum lætabile factum
> Dis fore confido. Si quis tamen, Hercule, si quis
> Fortè Deo doliturus erit, data prœmia nolet;
> Sed meruisse dari sciet, invitusque probabit.
> Assensêre Dei.

Ovid, Apotheosis of Hercules, translated into clumsy English by Mr. Gay, as follows.
Jove said,

Be all your fears forborne,
Th' Œtean fires do thou, great hero, scorn;
Who vanquished all things, shall subdue the flame;
That part alone of gross *maternal* frame,
Fire shall devour, while what from me he drew
Shall live immortal, and its force renew;
That, when he's dead, I'll raise to realms above,
May all the powers the righteous act approve.
If any God dissent, and judge too great
The sacred honors of the heavenly seat,
Even he shall own his deeds deserve the sky,
Even he, reluctant, shall at length comply.
Th' assembled powers assent.

[Fuller's note] John Gay (1685–1732), English poet, translated from Book IX of *Metamorphoses* by Ovid (43 B.C.–A.D. 17), Roman poet.

3. The Lamb is Jesus.

4. St. Martin. [Fuller's note] From *The Ministry of Man and Spirit* (1802), by Louise Claude de Saint-Martin (1743–1803), French mystical philosopher.

5. Orpheus, by Thomas Crawford (1813–1857), American sculptor working in Rome. In the Greek myth, his wife Eurydice dies and he is allowed to go to Hades to return her to the world of the living on the condition that neither looks back until they are completely out; but Orpheus, seeing the sun, turns to share his happiness with Eurydice and she disappears.

6. "Orphic Sayings," by Bronson Alcott.

7. Persephone, queen of the underworld and goddess of fertility.

8. The poem is by Fuller.

9. Luke 23:34.

10. Medes, a Persian people.

11. Manzoni. [Fuller's note] "Coro Dell' Atto Secondo," *Il Conte de Carmagnola*, Canto 45, by Alessandro Manzoni (1785–1873), Italian romantic novelist.

12. Marcus Porcius Cato (234–149 B.C.), Roman statesman and prosodist.

13. Dr. Johnson's one piece of advice should be written on every door; "Clear your mind of cant." But Byron, to whom it was so acceptable, in clearing away the noxious vine, shook down the building too. Sterling's emendation is note-worthy, "Realize your cant, not cast it off." [Fuller's note] Quoted from *Life of Samuel Johnson*, by James Boswell, dated 15 May 1783; George Gordon, Lord Byron (1788–1824), English Romantic poet, notorious for his reckless private life; John Sterling (1806–1844), English poet, author, and friend of Carlyle.

14. Count of Carabbas, in *Le Chat Botté (Puss in Boots)* by Charles Perrault (1628–1703), a character whose name later became synonymous with aristocratic pretension.

15. Jacobins, one of the most violent of the ruling parties of the French Revolution of the 1790s, usually associated with the Reign of Terror.

16. Louis XIV (1638–1715), king of France during a period in which art flowered, was known for the magnificence of his court as well as its many sycophants.

17. Miranda, the gifted and learned daughter of Prospero in Shakespeare's *The Tempest*, and Fuller's name for herself. Her description of Miranda's upbringing parallels that of her own youth.

18. Portia, Brutus' wife in Shakespeare's *Julius Caesar*, who takes her own life over her fear for him in his plan to take power.

19. Theseus, in Greek legend, conquered the female tribe of Amazons and married their queen, Hippolyte; Dejanira, wife of Hercules, gave her husband an enchanted robe thinking it would help win back his love, but it was poisoned and led to his death; guerdon, a reward.

20. "Dignity of Woman" (1796), by Schiller.

21. Jean Paul Friedrich Richter (1763–1825), German humorist.

22. Adam tells God "The woman whom thou gavest to be with me, she gave me of the tree, and I did eat" (Genesis 3:12); Mosaical law, a series of moral and ceremonial laws found in the last four books of the Pentateuch.

23. Semiramis, legendary Assyrian queen who built Babylon.

24. Aspasia (fl. ca. 450 B.C.), mistress of the statesman Pericles (ca. 495–429 B.C.) in ancient Athens, was highly regarded by Socrates.

25. Sappho (fl. ca. 610–ca. 580 B.C.), Greek lyric poet whose home on the island of Lesbos formed the center of a literary coterie of women; Eloisa or Héloïse (ca. 1098–1164), secretly married her tutor, the French theologian Peter Abelard (1079–1142), resulting in her family's castrating him, and their both living out their lives in monasteries.

26. Improvvisatrici, women who compose and sing extemporaneously; Elizabeth Carter (1717–1806), English translator, scholar, and poet; Anne Dacier (1654–1720), French classical scholar.

27. Tar, a sailor.

28. "On the Receipt of My Mother's Picture Out of Norfolk" (1798), by William Cowper.

29. Ignis fatuus, a light appearing over a marshy ground, used to indicate a false or misleading influence.

30. Rosicrucian, a mystical philosophy whose founder's body was allegedly discovered in excellent preservation, surrounded by magical unextinguished lamps, over a century after his tomb had first been sealed.

31. Sita, regarded by the Hindus as the goddess of wifely chastity; *Ramayana* (ca. 300 B.C.), one of India's great epics; Isis, most famous of Egyptian goddesses and wife of the main god Osiris.

32. Sphynx (or Sphinx), Egyptian half-woman and half-lion figure, the most famous statue of which stands before the great pyramids near Cairo.

33. Ceres, Roman goddess of agriculture; Proserpine, Greek goddess of the underworld.

34. Diana, Roman goddess of the hunt; Minerva, Roman goddess of arts and, later, war; Vesta, Roman goddess of the hearth.

35. Cassandra, in Greek myth, was given the gift of prophesy by Apollo, but when she refused his advances, he cursed her by having no one believe her predictions; Iphigenia, daughter of Agamemnon and Clytemnestra, was to be sacrificed by her father so that the Greek fleet would have good weather to sail against Troy, but she was saved by the goddess Artemis; Antigone, Greek daughter of Oedipus and his mother, Jocasta; Macaria, in *The Children of Hercules* by Euripides (480–406 B.C.), the Athenian playwright, sacrifices herself to save her brothers and sisters; Sibylline priestesses, mythological women capable of prophecy.

36. Nike and Victoria are, respectively, the Greek and Roman goddesses of victory.

37. Heinrich Heine (1797–1856), German lyric poet and critic, whose phrase "Dame du Comptoir" translates as "woman of the sales counter," a comment on how Mary is used to sell Catholicism.

38. Petrarch (1304–1374), Italian poet. Fuller prints this in Italian as Appendix B in *Woman in the Nineteenth Century*.

39. Marquise de Pompadour (1721–1764) and Comtesse du Barry (1746–1793), mistresses and influential counsels of Louis XV of France; Madame Roland de la Platière (1754–1793), Revolutionist who fell to the guillotine.

40. "Words of Faith" (1798) by Schiller.

41. "In that celestial form/You do not ask about man and wife,/And in no dress, no folds,/Do you surround that transfigured body" from *Wilhelm Meister's Apprenticeship* by Goethe.

42. Queen Isabella I (1451–1504) united Spain through a political marriage.

43. Anne Boleyn (ca. 1507–1536), second wife of Henry VIII, was beheaded by him. The length of her reign has made her known as "Anne of the Thousand Days."

44. Maria Theresa (1740–1780), queen of Hungary and Bohemia.

45. Edmund Spenser (ca. 1552–1599), English poet whose *Faerie Queen* (1590–1596) portrays Britomart as a female knight personifying chastity, Belphoebe as representative of Queen Elizabeth as a young woman, Florimel as a good chaste lady symbolizing the charm of womanhood, and Una as the personification of truth.

46. John Ford (1586–ca. 1639) and Philip Massinger (1583–ca. 1639), both English dramatists.

47. Characters in Shakespeare's plays: Imogen, daughter of the title character in *Cymbeline*; Desdemona, murdered by her husband in a fit of misdirected jealousy in *Othello*; Rosalind, loves Orlando in *As You Like It*; Isabella, a romantic lead in *Measure for Measure*.

48. Cordelia, Lear's youngest daughter and the only one to aid her father in *King Lear*.

49. "To Lucasta, Going to the Wars" (1649), ll., 11–12, by Richard Lovelace (1618–1657), English soldier and poet.

50. Colonel John Hutchinson (1615–1664), who supported the commonwealth against the monarchy during the English Civil War. His life with his wife Lucy Hutchinson (1620–ca. 1680) was described in her *Memoirs of the Life of Colonel Hutchinson* (1806).

51. "The Exstacie" (1633), l. 43, by John Donne (1572–1631), English metaphysical poet.

52. "An Ode Upon a Question Moved, Whether Love Should Continue Forever?" (1665), by Edward Herbert (1583–1648), English poet.

53. Justina, a character in *El Magico Prodigioso* (1637), a religious play by Pedro Calderón de la Barca (1600–1681), Spanish poet and dramatist.

54. After the death of his beloved Beatrice in 1290, Dante married Gemma Donati.

55. Jean Marie Roland (1734–1793) committed suicide when he learned of his wife's execution during the French Revolution.

56. William Godwin (1756–1836), English philosopher and miscellaneous writer, brought the spirit of the French Revolution into Britain; and his wife, Mary Wollstonecraft (1759–1797), known for her call for sexual equality, *A Vindication of the Rights of Woman* (1792).

57. Baroness Dudevant (1804–1876), French novelist and dramatist writing as George Sand, also known for her independent private life, which included affairs with the poet Alfred de Musset and the pianist Frédéric Chopin.

58. *Mauprat* (1837), a novel of idealized love by George Sand.

59. John Goodwin Barmby (1820–1881), minister and Christian socialist; Pariah, an outcast.

60. Mary Botham Howitt (1799–1888), English journalist, editor, translator, reformer, and writer of literature for children, often collaborated with her husband William Howitt (1792–1879), English poet, editor, and travel writer, who published *The Rural and Domestic Life of Germany* in 1842.

61. Götz von Berlichingen (ca. 1480–1562), German feudal knight. Fuller quotes from Goethe's play named after him published in 1773.

62. *Adelchi* (1822), a tragedy by Manzoni.

63. Arcadia, isolated mountain area in ancient Greece known for its simplicity.

64. Nikolaus Lugwig von Zinzendorf (1700–1760), German prelate and religious reformer.

65. Spangenberg. [Fuller's note] August Gottlieb Spangenberg (1704–1792), German secretary who fell under Zinzendorf's religious guidance.

66. Lady Mary Worthley Montagu (1689–1762), English poet and letter writer.

67. Mary Somerville (1780–1872), Scottish mathematician and scientist.

68. Lady Jane Grey (1537–1554), English noblewoman who was proficient in six languages by age fifteen.

69. Ishmaelites, one of the nomadic tribes of the Old Testament. Also, Ishmael and his mother are cast out by Abraham in Genesis 21:14–21.

70. Michelangelo's Persican Sibyl is in his painting on the ceiling of the Sistine Chapel in Rome; St. Theresa (1515–1582), Spanish author and nun; Torquato Tasso's love for Leonora, daughter of Alfonso II, led to his imprisonment; Electra, daughter of Agamemnon and Clytemnestra, helped her brother Orestes to avenge the murder of their father by slaying their mother and her lover: she later married Orestes' friend Pylades.

71. Anna Brownell Jameson (1794–1860), British art and literary critic.

72. Joanna Southcott (1750–1814), English religious fanatic around whom a large sect formed; Mother Ann Lee (1736–1784), English mystic and founder of the Shakers.

73. Ecstatica and Dolorosa, female representations of religious ecstacy and grief.

74. Joseph de Maistre (1753–1821), French moralist and diplomat, wrote *Les Soirées de Saint-Petersbourg* (1821).

75. Magnetism and mesmerism, types of hypnosis.

76. Frederica Hauffe (1801–1827), central figure in a study of spiritualism, *The Seeress of Prevorst* (1829), by Justinus Kerner (1786–1862), German poet and physician, whose case is described at length by Fuller in chapter 5 of her *Summer on the Lakes, in 1843* (1844); Delphos, home of the oracle of Delphi.

77. Jeanne Marie Bouvier de la Motte-Guyon (1648–1717), mystic identified with quietism, which holds that there is a mystical connection between God and individuals.

78. Queen Victoria (1819–1901) came to the throne of England in 1838.

79. Angelina Grimké (1805–1879) and Abby Kelly (1811–1887), American abolitionists and woman's rights activists.

80. Alexander Kinmont (1799–1838), Scottish philosopher and educator.

81. V., "Femality," *Pathfinder*, 18 March 1843, pp. 35–36, 51–52.

82. "Liberty" (1829), ll. 133–134, by William Wordsworth.

83. Jove, supreme Roman god whose mother was Rhea, and whose daughter Pallas Athena sprung to life fully grown from his head.

84. See "To My Sister" (1798) by Wordsworth and "Epistle to Augusta" (1830) by Byron.

85. *The Curse of Kehama* (1810), by Robert Southey (1774–1843), English poet and essayist.

86. Alcibiades (ca. 450–404 B.C.), Greek general and political opportunist who stole the gold and silver cups ("phials") of his friend Anytus.

87. A reference to *Wilhelm Meister's Apprenticeship* by Goethe.

88. Mignon, a character in *Wilhelm Meister's Apprenticeship*.

89. Natalia, fourth-century woman of Nicodemia who cared for the martyrs.

A. Bronson Alcott and Charles Lane

"Fruitlands"

(1843)

AFTER THE FAILURE of the Temple School, Alcott moved to Concord. In 1842, with the financial help of Emerson and other friends, he visited Ham Common in Surrey, England, where a group of reformers had started a school based in large part on Alcott's principles. When he returned in October 1842, some of the English reformers returned with him. Charles Lane (1800–1870) joined Alcott in lecturing and in other reform activities, culminating in their decision to start a communal experiment. Land was found in Harvard, Massachusetts, eighteen miles from Concord, and in June 1843, the Alcotts, Lane and his son, and a few others moved in to what was called Fruitlands. The project was a failure: Alcott and Lane knew little about farming and were out lecturing most of the time, leaving the women to do the work; they were impractical in such matters as not wanting to use animals to do the plowing (forcing them into involuntary servitude) or eating eggs (robbing the chicken of her young); and Lane had an ascetic view of life that did not mesh with Mrs. Alcott's. The community broke up in January 1844, in part because of Lane's attempts to convert Bronson to celibacy and his wife's refusal to go along. Lane left to join the nearby Shaker community, while Alcott suffered a nervous collapse. In 1846, Lane returned to England. Louisa May Alcott's fictional account of Fruitlands is in her story "Transcendental Wild Oats" (1873).

We have received a communication from Messrs. Alcott and Lane, dated from their farm, *Fruitlands*, in Harvard, Massachusetts, from which we make the following extract.

> We have made an arrangement with the proprietor of an estate of about a hundred acres, which liberates this tract from human ownership. For picturesque beauty both in the near and the distant landscape, the spot has few rivals. A semi-circle of undulating hills stretches from south to west, among which the Wachusett and Monadnoc are conspicuous.[1] The vale, through which flows a tributary to the Nashua, is esteemed for its fertility and ease of cultivation, is adorned with groves of nut-trees, maples, and pines, and watered by small streams. Distant not thirty miles from the metropolis of New England, this reserve lies in a serene and sequestered dell. No public thoroughfare invades it, but it is entered by a private road. The nearest hamlet is that of Stillriver, a field's walk of twenty minutes, and the village of Harvard is reached by circuitous and hilly roads of nearly three miles.

Here we prosecute our effort to initiate a Family in harmony with the primitive instincts in man. The present buildings being ill placed and unsightly as well as inconvenient, are to be temporarily used, until suitable and tasteful buildings in harmony with the natural scene can be completed. An excellent site offers itself on the skirts of the nearest wood, affording shade and shelter, and commanding a view of the lands of the estate, nearly all of which are capable of spade culture. It is intended to adorn the pastures with orchards, and to supersede ultimately the labor of the plough and cattle, by the spade and the pruning knife.

Our planting and other works, both without and within doors, are already in active progress. The present Family numbers ten individuals, five being children of the founders. Ordinary secular farming is not our object. Fruit, grain, pulse, garden plants and herbs, flax and other vegetable products for food, raiment,[2] and domestic uses, receiving assiduous attention, afford at once ample manual occupation, and chaste supplies for the bodily needs. Consecrated to human freedom, the land awaits the sober culture of devout men.

Beginning with small pecuniary means, this enterprise must be rooted in a reliance on the succors of an ever bounteous Providence, whose vital affinities being secured by this union with uncorrupted fields and unworldly persons, the cares and injuries of a life of gain are avoided.

The inner nature of every member of the Family is at no time neglected. A constant leaning on the living spirit within the soul should consecrate every talent to holy uses, cherishing the widest charities. The choice Library (of which a partial catalogue was given in Dial No. XII.) is accessible to all who are desirous of perusing these records of piety and wisdom.[3] Our plan contemplates all such disciplines, cultures, and habits, as evidently conduce to the purifying and edifying of the inmates. Pledged to the spirit alone, the founders can anticipate no hasty or numerous accession to their numbers. The kingdom of peace is entered only through the gates of self-denial and abandonment; and felicity is the test and the reward of obedience to the unswerving law of Love.

June 10, 1843.

Source: A. Bronson Alcott and Charles Lane, "Fruitlands," *Dial*, 4 (July 1843): 135–136.

Notes

1. Wachusett and Monadnoc, mountains in, respectively, Massachusetts and New Hampshire.
2. Raiment, clothing.
3. Lane's "Catalogue of Books" that were at Fruitlands (many of which Alcott had brought back from England with him) is in the *Dial*, 3 (April 1843): 545–548.

William Henry Channing

"Introduction" to the Present

(September 1843)

WILLIAM HENRY CHANNING (1810–1884), nephew of the Reverend Channing and cousin of the poet Ellery Channing, was one of the most active social reformers among the Transcendentalists. In his "Ode" inscribed to Channing, Emerson called him the "evil time's sole patriot." He was an active supporter of Brook Farm and other communitarian ventures, edited reform journals, and wrote a biography of his uncle. While the *Present* lasted for fewer than eight months, Channing's introduction very nicely articulates the high hopes many Transcendentalists had for contemporary reform.

※

The Present is the Name given to the Monthly, whose first number is here offered to its readers, because this name most exactly decribes the ground it seeks to occupy. With gratitude for the Past, whose toils reclaimed the mountains, cleared the woodlands, fenced the prairies, which we inherit—and with hope for the Future, who shall change our quaking bogs to verdant meadows, our sandy wastes to gardens—would it aid the bands of fellow-workers in the broad field, which the Present offers to our care, ploughing furrows, scattering seed, weeding, reaping, as the day may bid. Its end will be gained, if it can be a means of quickening confidence in the sublime destinies of this Christened though not Christianised Anglo-Saxon Race, in this land of their adoption, with their mingled traits of reverence and boldness, loyalty to custom and courage for adventure, pertinacity and earnestness, enthusiasm and practical skill; with their religiousness and free thought, their honor of woman and blunt courtesy, their aristocratic freedom, as yet imperfectly tempered by charity, their capacity of tender and poetic feeling, too much hidden under rough speech and dull manners, their power of growth and sense of young vigor, still imbued by the harsh rapacity of pirate ancestors. Its special aim will be, to show the grounds of reconciliation between the sects and parties, native and foreign, the controversies, theological and political, the social reformers and prudent conservatives, the philosophers and poets, prophets and doubters, which divide these United States. It aspires to teach, that all earnest seekers of holiness, truth, humanity, are co-laborers, under the leading of one heavenly hand, and that our Nation has a plain and urgent duty in common with the Grand Fraternity of Christendom, to advance the Reign of Heaven on Earth. May it do something, in however humble a way, to call out fidelity to the Divine Guidance in this land of promise, to which Providence led our forefathers in the fullness of time.

There is the appearance of Cant, and unquestionably the danger of Cant, too, in the use of formulas, and yet it is convenient, sometimes, to condense meaning in a brief sentence; therefore, it may be said, that the call of the Present is for the Union and Growth of Religion, Science, and Society. We need this Union; for as heart, lungs, and limbs combine to circulate our life's blood, so must inspiration, wisdom, and industry co-work, to rear in healthful symmetry the living organisation of Humanity. We need this Growth; for, whatsoever is not assimilating fresh nutriment, has passed its prime, and is more or less rapidly dying, and no one will pretend that Religion, Science, and Society have yet reached maturity. We need fulness of spirituality; in its due place and proportion we need equally perfected social relations amidst the fullness of material beauty; and reason, warmed, enlightened, animated by divine life, must mediate between them, and wed the Church and State in indissoluble union. Religion tends necessarily to form itself into Science, and through Science to embody itself in Society; and happy conditions of existence react upon our powers of intelligence, and prepare them for admitting purer influence from the Eternal world. Every Age is a peculiar one; it can not repeat the experience of the past, neither can it anticipate the fulfilments of the future; its work is to unfold the essential principles of human nature, in such forms as are fit in their season. The peculiarity of our Age is, that having passed through an era of almost universal religious, scientific, and social infidelity, we are entering a new era of yet more universal faith, which demands its own worship, philosophy, and social arrangements. Is the hope extravagant, that its laws may be more nearly modelled upon the types of divine justice; that its doctrines may more adequately express absolute ideas; that its reception of goodness may be more perfect than earlier times were capable of? Can we hope less? Our need to-day, though different in appearance, is intrinsically the same with that which all generations of the past have experienced, and which all generations must feel who are to follow, till Love, Truth, and Beauty possess our race, and fulfil the destinies of Humanity on Earth.

This little Monthly, then, has quite liberal aims; and it may justly be asked what are its editor's qualifications. With unaffected sincerity he confesses that he has none, other than the craving after a temper and spirit more in harmony with our privileges, a willingness to admit and abandon error and folly when exposed, independence, to some degree, from sectarian and party bonds, faith in the present inspiration and providence of God, hope growing ever stronger in the tendencies of the Age to universal good, and a devoted love for the Christian-German race in this fresh soil, where opportunity summons them to mould the experience of the old world into forms of life, more truly fulfilling the laws of heavenly order. A person could scarcely have a clearer sense of unfitness for any thoroughly worthy work, than that with which he commences this publication; but with all deference let it be added, that he does not feel *alone* in this consciousness of insufficiency; a goodly company of editors, authors, lecturers, speakers, and teachers of all kinds, throughout this country and Europe too, seem to be in fellowship. Indeed, it may well be doubted whether any period of history can be pointed out, when there was anything surpassing, if resembling in extent and degree, the conviction which this age has of its superficiality in character, intelligence, and performance. All men are not conscious, to be sure, of such incompleteness in themselves; but each says it of the other. We are a generation of Critics. Doubtless there are a few still professing to be wise; who, steadfastly looking on rusty timepieces, the pendulums of which have long since ceased to beat, loudly declare what hour it once was. Doubtless, there are others, who mistake the rapid-circling hands of a watch running down, whose main spring is broken, for the progress of time. But it needs only moderate sense and conscience, to be aware that our theologies and philosophies, our worship and governments, our home-lives and social relations, our science and industry, our letters and art, do not mark aright the rising of the Sun of Righteousness towards higher noon. Our dials have lost their gnomons.[1] There is a general make-believe assent, a latent denial, a ridicule of high pretensions, a suspicion of all who claim to have solved doubtful problems. Men like playful badinage better than assertions, which seem inflated in proportion to their solemnity; they turn to practical details from what look like the fog-banks of unsettled principles; and silence, with many of the wisest, is felt to be more eloquent than speech. But this is not because we are Sceptics. The mad age of Unbelief lies behind us, painful, hideous, like a fever dream. It is the presence of Faith, laboring in the souls of nations and men, not ready yet to be born in articulate expression and complete deeds, which makes us thus at once dissatisfied with dead usages and dogmas, and disgusted with mere embryo theories and plans.

There is a characteristic of the age, and especially of this country, which seems to cast light on present duties. It is the unexampled *ab-*

sence of leaders, of persons so plainly preeminent and far advanced that they constrain us to follow. With some observers, this is taken as a proof that we are mired in the bog of a lawless and irreverent equality. But others see here a promise, that Humanity is mounting to a broad table-land. Now and then, a man among us stands up on the stilts of his conceit or the rolling stone of some new notion, and, keeping his footing midst the multitude for a moment, cries out that he sees the way. But his sect, if he form one, soon leave him, and hurry on. There is a vague and yet profound consciousness that we are thrown, as men have not so much been heretofore, *every one upon his own energies*; and yet there is an equally deep and general feeling, that *our strength is in united consciences, thoughts, wills*, rather than in solitary efforts. The prayer of to-day is not, "Give us a Man, a Great Man, a Prince." He was given eighteen centuries ago; and wonderful is it to see, how on all sides appears a movement, rapidly increasing, to rally the bands, which scepticism had scattered, around Jesus Christ, as the divinely commissioned Head in the kingdom of Heaven on Earth. The prayer which now is swelling in all hearts is: "Give us Men, Great Men, Nations of Prophets and Princes, strong, each in his peculiar way, bound in one by mutual reverence and usefulness, worthy of this Son of God and Son of Man, who called his disciples Friends." In these crowds of authors, pressing forward through all manner of books, pamphlets, and periodicals—in these multitudes of speakers, who, on highways and byways, at the corners of the streets, in conventicles and social circles, are preaching their gospel—still more in the thousands of patient thinkers, who sit watching for the dawn with their fingers on their lips, may be seen, perhaps, the signs of that coming era, when men "shall no longer teach every man his neighbor and every man his brother, saying, know the Lord, but when each shall know him, from the least to the greatest."[2] Chaotic enough are now our impulses, opinions, and strivings; but the hour may be, heaven grant that it is, drawing nigh, when a voice of infinite harmonies shall sound through the darkness, "Let there be light."[3]

Meanwhile, we should neither deny nor forget our present freedom and responsibilities. Through the willing souls of his children does the Infinite Father always speak. Alternations of thoughtful silence, with frankest utterance, not in the few, but the many; not in official, professional teachers merely, but in all; not through the pulpit or press alone, but through every avenue of communication, is what we Americans need, have a right to claim from one another, and partially, though under the incumbrance of foolish prejudices, already have.

There is no arrogance, while admitting with one breath dulness and inadequacy, with the next to declare boldly, without apology or compromise, such vision or prophecy, reproof or counsel, as may seem timely. This equipoise, between humility and confidence, appears to be the true posture just now for all men. We are all in error; all learning together. It is not a season for claims to infallibility, nor for insipid concessions. The spirit abroad is too earnest. We want not trimmers, paying court at once both to old and new; but sincere men, standing lowly before their God, and erect among their peers, who will say, without either presumption or baseness, without pertinacity or explanations of inconsistency, what seems to them, for the moment, true. This tone of blended reverence and hope the Present will strive to keep. Fortunately, the class is already large of those who are endeavoring to take this difficult position, and the instinctive sympathies and judgments of the best and truest come to their support.

Fully to tell, what all vaguely feel in relation to our prevalent piety, knowledge, and social action, without denial of good, still vital, while cutting off and casting aside what is plainly dead, without servility to the established or triumph in novelties which are yet untried, with sympathy for the past, as his relaxing fingers drop the sceptre, while we pay due welcome to the present who succeeds to reign, needs rare combination of conscience and genius. Rash joy, in what is new, is more disgusting than even bigoted fondness for ancient idols. Frivolity is as false as it is insolent, while garrulous tales of our ancestors' greatness have the charm at least of gratitude. Yet it is tiresome to be made to wear the cast clothes of forefathers, as if this age could yield no working and gala dress; and it paralyses courage to gaze on these armor-suits of buried giants, as if no brave acts could now be done. We have our labors and conquests, our discoveries and adventures, before us; and if we truly honor the past, it will teach us the lesson, "Work while it is day."[4] No one man, no one nation, but only the combined voices of the Race, can give volume and clear articulation to the word of Conservative Reform, which all lips stammer to utter, which all ears long to hear. Therefore, in every sphere, however small, let each declare, that Love is the Law of Liberty, that Faith is for ever a Free Inquirer, that Doubt of enlarging Good is virtual Atheism, and Fear of Progress the unpardonable Sin. So let us attest the truth, that the Heavenly Father recreates his universe and regenerates his children, by causing their perennial Growth.

Source: W[illiam]. H[enry]. C[hanning]., "Introduction," *Present,* 1 (September 1843): 1–5.

Notes

1. Interestingly, Emerson uses the same image in "The Editors to the Reader" of the *Dial* (printed above; see note 1).
2. Jeremiah 31:34.
3. Genesis 1:3.
4. See John 9:4.

Charles Lane and A. Bronson Alcott

"The Consociate Family Life"

(8 September 1843)

A LONGER VERSION of Alcott and Lane's promotional tract for Fruitlands than the brief note that had appeared in the *Dial* (printed above), this extended essay expands upon the goals and organization of the community.

To A. Brooke, of Oakland, Ohio

DEAR SIR: Having perused your several letters in the Herald of Freedom,[1] and finding moreover a general invitation to correspondence from "persons who feel prepared to co-operate in the work of reform upon principles" akin to those you have there set forth. I take this public means of communing with one who seems to be really desirous of aiding entire human regeneration.

After many years passed in *admiration* of a better order in human society, with a constant expectation that some beginning would shortly be made, and a continued reliance that some party would make it, the idea has gradually gained possession of my mind, that it is not right thus to linger for the leadings of other men, but that each should at once proceed to live out the proposed life to the utmost possible extent. Assured that the most potent hindrances to goodness abide in the soul itself; next in the body; thirdly in the house and family; and in the fourth degree only in our neighbors, or in society at large, I have daily found less and less reason to complain of public institutions, or of the dilatoriness of reformers and genetic minds.

Animated by pure reform principles, or rather by pure creative spirit, I have not hesitated to withdraw as far and as fast as hopeful prudence dictated, from the practices and principles of the old world. And, acting upon the conviction that whatever others might do, or leave undone; however others might fail in the realization of their ideal good; I, at least, should advance. I have accordingly arrived in that region where I perceive you theoretically and, I hope, actually dwell. I agree with you that it would be well to cross the ocean of life from the narrow island of selfishness to the broad continent of universal love at one dash; but the winds are not always propitious, and steam is only a recent invention. I cannot yet boast of a year's emancipation from Old England. One free step leads to another; and the third must as necessarily precede the fourth, as the second was before the third.

A. Bronson Alcott's visit to England last year, opened to me some of the superior conditions for a pure life which this country offers compared to the land of my nativity and that of your ancestors. My love for purity and goodness was sufficiently strong it seems to loosen me from a position as regards pecuniary income, affectionate friends, and mental liberty, which millions there, and thousands here might envy. It has happened, however, that of the many persons with whom Mr. Alcott hoped to act in junction and concert, not one is yet fully liberated by Providence to that end. So that instead of forming items in a larger enterprise, we are left to be the principal actors in promoting an idea less in extent, but greater in intent, than any yet presented to our observation.

All our preliminary transactions may not have been so clear and clean as you and we desire; but we have not paralyzed future good by excuses of place or time. By never doing any act below our intuition of principle at the moment, we are aided to clearer insight and loftier inspiration for the next step. Our removal to this estate in humble confidence, has drawn to us several practical coadjutors, and opened many inquiries by letter for a statement of our principles and modes of life. We cannot perhaps turn our replies to better account than to transcribe some portions of them for your information, and, we trust, for your sincere satisfaction.

You must be aware, however, that written words cannot do much towards the elucidation of principles comprehending all human relationships, and claiming an origin profound as man's inmost consciousness of the ever present Living Spirit. A dwelling together, a concert in soul, and a consorting in body, is a position needful to entire understanding, which we hope at no distant day to attain with yourself and many other sincere friends. We have not yet drawn out any preordained plan of daily operations, as we are impressed with the conviction that by a faithful reliance on the spirit which actuates us, we are sure of attaining to clear revelations of daily practical duties as they are to be daily done by us. Where the Spirit of Love and Wisdom abounds, literal forms are needless, irksome or hinderative; where the Spirit is lacking, no preconceived rules can compensate.

To us it appears not so much that improved circumstances are to meliorate mankind, as that improved men will originate the superior condition for themselves and others. Upon the Human Will, and not upon circumstances, as some philosophers assert, rests the function, power and duty, of generating a better social state. The human beings in whom the Eternal Spirit has ascended from low animal delights or mere humane affections, to a state of spiritual chastity and intuition, are in themselves a divine atmosphere, they *are* superior circumstances, and are constant in endeavoring to create, as well as to modify, all other conditions, so that these also shall more and more conduce to the like consciousness in others.

Hence our perseverance in efforts to attain simplicity in diet, plain garments, pure bathing, unsullied dwellings, open conduct, gentle behavior, kindly sympathies, serene minds. These, and the several other particulars needful to the true end of man's residence on earth, may be designated the Family Life. Our Happiness, though not the direct object in human energy, may be accepted as the confirmation of rectitude, and this is not otherwise attainable than in the Holy Family. The Family in its highest, divinest, sense, is therefore our true position, our sacred earthly destiny. It comprehends every divine, every human relation, consistent with universal good, and all others it rejects, as it disdains all animal sensualities.

Let it be admitted as the embosoming of the most vital, and only creative of all human acts, and we are convinced of the absorbing importance of Family Life. The next age depends much for its character, its modification, its happiness, on parents in this generation, as they have depended on their parents, by the relative opposition or concurrence of their wills with the Divine will. In a deep sense all human conduct may be said to centre in this act. As birds migrate to our latitude in the warm season, build and use their nests, sing a song or two, and, as the cold approaches, depart to a warmer zone, so man is sent from balmier climes, to breed upon the earth, and all other actions should be but preparative to this of securing an offspring unprofaned by self-will, untinctured by lust.

The evils of life are not so much social, or political, as personal; and a personal reform only can eradicate them.

Let the Family, furthermore, be viewed as the home of pure social affections, the school of expanding intelligence, the sphere of unbought art, the scene of joyous employment, and we feel in that single sentiment a fulness of action, of life, of being, which no scientific social contrivance can ensure, nor selfish accident supply.

Family is not dependant upon members, nor upon skill, nor riches, but upon union in and with that spirit which alone can bless any enterprise whatever. While, therefore, we feel a sympathy towards every endeavor to amend man's social position, and would promote them as far as we deem them progressive, we are bound to declare their short coming, and that we have no hope for permanent human happiness from any act, thing, or person, not originating in immediate inspiration. All else is but an attraction which allures to destroy. Rather is self-denial the strait and narrow way to eternal life, than the enticements of increased indulgence which almost all associative endeavors have in view.

On this topic of family association, it will not involve an entire agreement with the Shakers to say they are at least entitled to deeper consideration than they yet appear to have secured.[2] There are many important facts in their career worthy of observation. It is perhaps most striking that the only really successful extensive community of interest, spiritual and secular, in modern times, was established by A WOMAN.[3]—Again, we witness in this people the bringing together of the two sexes in a new relation, or rather with a new idea of the old relation. This has led to results more harmonic than any one seriously believes attainable for the human race, either in issolation or association, so long as divided, conflicting family arrangements are permitted. It is not absurd to suppose that all future good hinges upon this very subject of Marriage. In fact, nothing but absolute ignorance of the law of human generation can doubt it. The great secular success of the Shakers; their order, cleanliness, intelligence and serenity, are so eminent, that it is worthy of inquiry how far these are attributal to an adherence to their peculiar doctrine.

As to Property, we discover not its just disposal either in individual or social tenures, but in its entire absorption into the New Spirit, which ever gives and never grasps.—The notion of Property is the prolific seed of so many evils that there seems little hope for humanity so long as it is made a leading consideration, or is harbored in the human bosom. It is even possible that if the projects now before the public were in actual operation, the evils of life would become more fixed by reason of the greater refinement of this demon. Property, which would be more difficult to cast out of an orderly arrangement than from the present chaos of mankind, where its evils are less glossed.—From the midst of this sin and its consequences it is difficult to emerge without committing more sin. The demonstration of our example, in proceeding actually to the greatest possible extent in the pure direction has, however, attracted towards us other needful assistance. While we write, negotiations are entertained for our removal to a place of less inconvenience, by friends who have long waited for some proof of a determination to act up to the idea they have cherished. Many, no doubt, are yet unprepared "to give up all and follow him," (the Spirit) who can importantly aid in the New Advent, and conscientiously accomplish the legal processes needful under the present circumstances. We do not recognise the purchase of land; but its redemption from the debasing state of *proprium*, or property, to divine uses, we clearly understand; where those whom the world esteems as owners are found yielding their individual rights to the Supreme Owner. Looking at this subject practically in relation to a climate in which a costly shelter is necessary, and where a family with many children has to be provided for, the possibility of at once stepping boldly out of the toils into which the errors of our predecessors have cast us, is not so evident as it is desirable.

Trade, we hope, entirely to avoid at an early day. As a nursery for many evil propensities it is almost universally felt to be a most undesirable course. Such needful articles as we cannot yet raise by our own hand labor from the soil, thus redeemed from human ownership, we shall endeavor to obtain by friendly exchanges, and, as nearly as possibly, without the intervention of money.

Of all the traffic in which civilized society is involved, that of human labor is perhaps the most detrimental. From the state of serfdom to the receipt of wages, may be a step in human progress; but it is certainly full time for taking a new step out of the hiring system.

Our outward exertions are in the first instance directed to the soil, and as our ultimate aim is to furnish an instance of self-sustaining cultivation without the subjugation of either men or cattle, or the use of foul animal manures, we have at the outset to encounter struggles and oppositions somewhat formidable. Until the land is restored to its pristine fertility by the annual return of its own green crops, as sweet and animating manures, the human hand and simple implement cannot wholly supersede the employment of machinery and cattle.—So long as cattle are used in agriculture, it is very evident that man will remain a slave, whether he be proprietor or hireling. The driving of cattle beyond their natural and pleasurable exertion; the waiting upon them as a cook and chambermaid three parts of the year; the excessive labor of mowing, curing and housing hay, and of collecting other fodder, and the large extra quantity of land needful to keep up this system, forms a combination of unfavorable circumstances which must depress the humane affections so long as it continues, and overlay them by the injurious and extravagant development of the animal and bestial natures in man.—No one can fail to perceive that if cattle were no longer bred and fed for slaughter, milking or draught, the human family might be drawn much closer together all over the country. It is calculated that if no animal food were consumed, one-fourth of the land now used would suffice for human sustenance. And the extensive tracts of country now appropriated to grazing, mowing, and other modes of animal provision, could be cultivated by and for intelligent and affectionate human neighbors. The sty and the stable too often secure more of the farmer's regard than he bestows on the garden and the children. No hope is there for humanity while woman is withdrawn from the tender assiduities which adorn her and her household, to the servitudes of the dairy and the flesh-pots. Omitting also to discuss the question of the debasing influences upon the children by the intrusion of animals into the daily thoughts and conduct, it may yet be observed that if the beasts were wholly absent from man's neighborhood, the human population might be at least four times as dense as it now is without raising the price of land. This would give to the country all the advantages of concentration, without the vices which always spring up in the dense city.

Debauchery of both the earthly soil and the human body is the result of this cattle keeping. The land is scourged for crops to feed the animals, whose filthy ordures are used under the erroneous supposition of restoring lost fertility; disease is thus infused into the human body; stimulants and medicines are resorted to for relief, which end in a precipitation of the original evil to a more disastrous depth. These misfortunes which affect not only the body, but by the reaction rise to the sphere of the soul, would be avoided, at least in part, by the disuse of animal food. Our diet is therefore strictly of the pure and bloodless kind. No animal substances, neither flesh, butter, cheese, eggs nor milk, pollute our tables or corrupt our bodies. Neither tea, coffee, molasses, nor rice, tempts us beyond the bounds of indigenous productions. Our sole beverage is pure fountain water. The native grains, fruits, herbs and roots, dressed with the utmost cleanliness, and regard to their purpose of edifying a healthful body, furnish the pleasantest refections and in the greatest variety, requisite to the supply of the various organs. The field, the orchard, the garden, in their bounteous products of wheat, rye, barley, maiz, oats, buckwheat; apples, pears, peaches, plums, cherries, currants, berries; potatoes, peas, beans, beets, carrots, melons, and other vines, yield an ample store for human nutrition, without dependance on foreign climes, or the degradations of shipping and trade. The almost inexhaustible variety which the several stages and sorts of vegetable growth, and the several modes of preparation, afford, are a full answer to the question which is often put by those who have never ventured into the region of a pure and chaste diet: "If you give up flesh meat, upon what then can you live?"

Our other domestic habits are in harmony with those of diet. We rise with early dawn, begin the day with cold bathing, succeeded by a music lesson, and then a chaste repast. Each one finds occupation until the meridian meal, when usually some interesting and deep searching conversation gives rest to the body and development to the mind. Occupation, according to the season and the weather, engages us out of doors or within, until the evening meal,—when we again assemble in social communion, prolonged generally until sunset, when we resort to sweet repose for the next day's activity.

In these steps of reform we do not rely so much on scientific reasoning or physiological skill, as on the Spirit's dictates. The pure soul, by the law in its own nature, adopts a pure diet and cleanly customs; nor needs detailed instruction for daily conduct. On a revision of our proceedings it would seem, that if we were in the right course in our particular instance, the greater part of man's duty consists in leaving alone much that he is in the habit of doing. It is a fasting from of the present activity, rather than an increased indulgence in it, which, with patient watchfulness, tends to newness of life. Shall I sip tea or coffee? the inquiry may be. No. Abstain from *all* ardent, as from alcoholic drinks. Shall I consume pork, beef or mutton? Not if you value health or life. Shall I stimulate with milk? No. Shall I warm my bathing water?—Not if cheerfulness is valuable. Shall I clothe in many garments? Not if purity is aimed at. Shall I prolong my dark hours, consuming animal oil, and loosing bright daylight in the morning? Not if a clear mind is an object. Shall I teach my children the dogmas inflicted on myself, under the pretence that I am transmitting truth? Nay, if you love them intrude not these between them and the Spirit of all Truth.—Shall I become a hireling or hire others?—Shall I subjugate cattle? Shall I trade?—Shall I claim property in any created thing? Shall I adopt a form of religion? Shall I become a parent? Shall I interest myself in politics? To how many of these questions, could we ask them deeply enough, could they be heard as having relation to our eternal welfare, would the response be "ABSTAIN?" Be not so active to do, as sincere to BE. Being, in preference to doing, is the great aim, and this comes to us rather by a resigned willingness than a wilful activity; which is indeed a check to all divine growth. Outward abstinence is a sign of inward fulness; and the only source of true progress is inward. We may occupy ourselves actively in human improvements;—but these, unless inwardly, well-impelled, never attain to, but rather hinder, divine progress in man.

During the utterance of this narrative it has undergone some change in its personal expression which might offend the hypercritical; but we feel assured that you will kindly accept it as the unartful offering of both your friends in ceaseless aspiration.

CHARLES LANE.

A. BRONSON ALCOTT.

Harvard, Mass., August, 1843.

Source: Charles Lane and A. Bronson Alcott, "The Consociate Family Life," *Herald of Freedom,* 8 September 1843.

Notes

1. *Herald of Freedom,* a New Hampshire antislavery newspaper, would be reviewed by Thoreau in the *Dial,* 4 (April 1844): 507–512.
2. The Shakers had a community in Harvard, Massachusetts, near Fruitlands.
3. That is, Mother Ann Lee.

Henry David Thoreau

"A Winter Walk"

(October 1843)

HENRY DAVID THOREAU (1817–1862), although now considered along with Emerson and Fuller as one of the three major writers of the Transcendentalist movement, was a young unpublished writer when the movement began. The majority of his publications during the main Transcendental period were in the *Dial,* and most of those were published after Fuller, who generally was unimpressed with his writing, was no longer editor. The Thoreau of the early 1840s was, in short, far from the canonical author he is today, and most of his writings were book reviews disguised as essays, scholarly discussions, translations, and nature writings. "A Winter Walk" shows the master stylist of *Walden* in his impressive apprentice period.

The wind has gently murmured through the blinds, or puffed with feathery softness against the windows, and occasionally sighed like a summer zephyr lifting the leaves along the livelong night. The meadow mouse has slept in his snug gallery in the sod, the owl has sat in a hollow tree in the depth of the swamp, the rabbit, the squirrel, and the fox have all been housed. The watch-dog has lain quiet on the hearth, and the cattle have stood silent in their stalls. The earth itself has slept, as it were its first, not its last sleep, save when some street-sign or wood-house door, has faintly creaked upon its hinge, cheering forlorn nature at her midnight work.—The only sound awake twixt Venus and Mars,—advertising us of a remote inward warmth, a divine cheer and fellowship, where gods are met together, but where it is very bleak for men to stand. But while the earth has slumbered, all the air has been alive with feathery flakes, descending, as if some northern Ceres reigned, showering her silvery grain over all the fields.

We sleep and at length awake to the still reality of a winter morning. The snow lies warm as cotton or down upon the window-sill; the broadened sash and frosted panes admit a dim and private light, which enhances the snug cheer within. The stillness of the morning is impressive. The floor creaks under our feet as we move toward the window to look abroad through some clear space over the fields. We see the roofs stand under their snow burden. From the eaves and fences hang stalactites of snow, and in the yard stand stalagmites covering some concealed core. The trees and shrubs rear white arms to the sky on every side, and where were walls and fences, we see fantastic forms stretching in frolic gambols across the dusky landscape, as if nature had strewn her fresh designs over the fields by night as models for man's art.

Silently we unlatch the door, letting the drift fall in, and step abroad to face the cutting air. Already the stars have lost some of their sparkle, and a dull leaden mist skirts the horizon. A lurid brazen light in the east proclaims the approach of day, while the western landscape is dim and spectral still, and clothed in a sombre Tartarean light, like the shadowy realms.[1] They are Infernal sounds only that you hear,—the crowing of cocks, the barking of dogs, the chopping of wood, the lowing of kine, all seem to come from Pluto's barn-yard and beyond the Styx;—not for any melancholy they suggest, but their twilight bustle is too solemn and mysterious for earth.[2] The recent tracks of the fox or otter, in the yard, remind us that each hour of the night is crowded with events, and the primeval nature is still working and making tracks in the snow. Opening the gate, we tread briskly along the lone country road, crunching the dry and crisp snow under our feet, or aroused by the sharp clear creak of the wood-sled, just starting for the distant market, from the early farmer's door, where it has lain the summer long, dreaming amid the chips and stubble. For through the drifts and powdered windows we see the farmer's early candle, like a paled star, emitting a lonely beam, as if some severe virtue were at its matins there. And one by one the smokes begin to ascend from the chimneys amidst the trees and snows.

> The sluggish smoke curls up from some deep dell,
> The stiffened air exploring in the dawn,
> And making slow acquaintance with the day;
> Delaying now upon its heavenward course,
> In wreathed loiterings dallying with itself,
> With as uncertain purpose and slow deed,
> As its half-wakened master by the hearth,
> Whose mind still slumbering and sluggish thoughts
> Have not yet swept into the onward current
> Of the new day;—and now it streams afar,
> The while the chopper goes with step direct,
> And mind intent to swing the early axe.
>   First in the dusky dawn he sends abroad
> His early scout, his emissary, smoke,
> The earliest, latest pilgrim from the roof,
> To feel the frosty air, inform the day;
> And while he crouches still beside the hearth,
> Nor musters courage to unbar the door,
> It has gone down the glen with the light wind,
> And o'er the plain unfurled its venturous wreath,
> Draped the tree tops, loitered upon the hill,
> And warmed the pinions of the early bird;
> And now, perchance, high in the crispy air,
> Has caught sight of the day o'er the earth's edge,
> And greets its master's eye at his low door,
> As some refulgent cloud in the upper sky.[3]

We hear the sound of wood-chopping at the farmers' doors, far over the frozen earth, the baying of the house dog, and the distant clarion of the cock. The thin and frosty air conveys only the finer particles of sound to our ears, with short and sweet vibrations, as the waves subside soonest on the purest and lightest liquids, in which gross substances sink to the bottom. They come clear and bell-like, and from a greater distance in the horizon, as if there were fewer impediments than in summer to make them faint and ragged. The ground is sonorous, like seasoned wood, and even the ordinary rural sounds are melodious, and the jingling of the ice on the trees is sweet and liquid. There is the least possible moisture in the atmosphere, all being dried up, or congealed, and it is of such extreme tenuity and elasticity, that it becomes a source of delight. The withdrawn and tense sky seems groined like the aisles of a cathedral, and the polished air sparkles as if there were crystals of ice floating in it. Those who have resided in Greenland, tell us, that, when it freezes, "the sea smokes like burning turf land, and a fog or mist arises, called frost smoke," which "cutting smoke frequently raises blisters on the face and hands, and is very pernicious to the health." But this pure stinging cold is an elixir to the lungs, and not so much a frozen mist, as a crystallized mid-summer haze, refined and purified by cold.

The sun at length rises through the distant woods, as if with the faint clashing swinging sound of cymbals, melting the air with his beams, and with such rapid steps the morning travels, that already his rays are gilding the distant western mountains. We step hastily along through the powdery snow, warmed by an inward heat, enjoying an Indian summer[4] still, in the increased glow of thought and feeling. Probably if our lives were more conformed to nature, we should not need to defend ourselves against her heats and colds, but find her our constant nurse and friend, as do plants and quadrupeds. If our bodies were fed with pure and simple elements, and not with a stimulating and heating diet, they would afford no more pasture for cold than a leafless twig, but thrive like the trees, which find even winter genial to their expansion.

The wonderful purity of nature at this season is a most pleasing fact. Every decayed stump and moss-grown stone and rail, and the dead leaves of autumn, are concealed by a clean napkin of snow. In the bare fields and tinkling woods, see what virtue survives. In the coldest and bleakest places, the warmest charities still maintain a foot-hold. A cold and searching wind drives away all contagion, and nothing can withstand it but what has a virtue in it; and accordingly, whatever we meet with in cold and bleak places, as the tops of mountains, we respect for a sort of sturdy innocence, a Puritan toughness. All things beside seem to be called in for shelter, and what stays out must be part of the original frame of the universe, and of such valor as God himself. It is invigorating to breathe the cleansed air. Its greater fineness and purity are visible to the eye, and we would fain stay out long and late, that the gales may sigh through us too, as through the leafless trees, and fit us for the winter:—as if we hoped so to borrow some pure and steadfast virtue, which will stead us in all seasons.

At length we have reached the edge of the woods, and shut out the gadding town. We enter within their covert as we go under the roof of a cottage, and cross its threshold, all ceiled and banked up with snow. They are glad and warm still, and as genial and cheery in winter as in summer. As we stand in the midst of the pines, in the flickering and checkered light which straggles but little way into their maze, we wonder if the towns have ever heard their simple story. It seems to us that no traveller has ever explored them, and notwithstanding the wonders which science is elsewhere revealing every day, who would not like to hear their annals? Our humble villages in the plain, are their contribution. We borrow from the forest the boards which shelter, and the sticks which warm us. How important is their evergreen to the winter, that portion of the summer which does not fade, the permanent year, the unwithered grass. Thus simply, and with little expense of altitude, is the surface of the earth diversified. What would human life be without forests, those natural cities? From the tops of mountains they appear like smooth shaven lanes, yet whither shall we walk but in this taller grass?

There is a slumbering subterranean fire in nature which never goes out, and which no cold can chill. It finally melts the great snow, and in January or July is only buried under a thicker or thinner covering. In the coldest day it flows somewhere, and the snow melts around every tree. This field of winter rye, which sprouted late last fall, and now speedily dissolves the snow, is where the fire is very thinly covered. We feel warmed by it. In the winter, warmth stands for all virtue, and we resort in thought to a trickling rill, with its bare stones shining in the sun, and to warm springs in the woods, with as much eagerness as rabbits and robins. The steam which rises from swamps and pools is as dear and domestic as that of our own kettle. What fire could ever equal the sunshine of a winter's-day, when the meadow mice come out by the wallsides, and the chickadee lisps in the defiles of the wood? The warmth comes directly from the sun, and is not radiated from the earth, as in summer; and when we feel his beams on our back as we are treading some snowy dell, we are grateful as for a special kindness, and bless the sun which has followed us into that by-place.

This subterranean fire has its altar in each man's breast, for in the coldest day, and on the bleakest hill, the traveler cherishes a warmer fire within the folds of his cloak than is kindled on any hearth. A healthy man, indeed, is the complement of the seasons, and in winter, summer is in his heart. There is the south. Thither have all birds and insects migrated, and around the warm springs in his breast are gathered the robin and the lark.

In this glade covered with bushes of a year's growth see how the silvery dust lies on every seared leaf and twig, deposited in such infinite and luxurious forms as by their very variety atone for the absence of color. Observe the tiny tracks of mice around every stem, and the triangular tracks of the rabbit. A pure elastic heaven hangs over all, as if the impurities of the summer sky refined and shrunk by the chaste winter's cold, had been winnowed from the heavens upon the earth.

Nature confounds her summer distinction at this season. The heavens seem to be nearer the earth. The elements are less reserved and distinct. Water turns to ice, rain to snow. The day is but a Scandinavian night. The winter is an arctic summer.

How much more living is the life that is in nature, the furred life which still survives the stinging nights, and, from amidst fields and woods covered with frost and snow, sees the sun rise.

> The foodless wilds
> Pour forth their brown inhabitants.[5]

The grey-squirrel and rabbit are brisk and playful in the remote glens, even on the morning of the cold Friday. Here is our Lapland and Labrador, and for our Esquimaux and Knistenaux, Dog-ribbed Indians, Novazemblaites, and Spitzbergeners, are there not the ice-cutter and wood-chopper, the fox muskrat, and mink?[6]

Still, in the midst of the arctic day, we may trace the summer to its retreats, and sympathize with some contemporary life. Stretched over the brooks, in the midst of the frost-bound meadows, we may observe the submarine cottages of the caddice worms, the larvæ of the Plicipennes.[7] Their small cylindrical caves built around themselves, composed of flags, sticks, grass, and withered leaves, shells and pebbles, in form and color like the wrecks which strew the bottom—now drifting along over the pebbly bottom, now whirling in tiny eddies and dashing down steep falls, or sweeping rapidly along with the current, or else swaying to and fro at the end of some grass blade or root. Anon they will leave their sunken habitations, and crawling up the stems of plants, or floating on the surface like gnats, or perfect insects, henceforth flutter over the surface of the water, or sacrifice their short lives in the flame of our candles at evening. Down yonder little glen the shrubs are drooping under their burden, and the red alder-berries contrast with the white ground. Here are the marks of a myriad feet which have already been abroad. The sun rises as proudly over such a glen, as over the valley of the Seine or the Tiber, and it seems the residence of a pure and self-subsistent valor, such as they never witnessed; which never knew defeat nor fear. Here reign the simplicity and purity of a primitive age, and a health and hope far remote from towns and cities. Standing quite alone, far in the forest, while the wind is shaking down snow from the trees, and leaving the only human tracks behind us, we find our reflections of a richer variety than the life of cities. The chicadee and nut-hatch are more inspiring society than the statesmen and philosophers, and we shall return to these last, as to more vulgar companions. In this lonely glen, with its brook draining the slopes, its creased ice and crystals of all hues, where the spruces and hemlocks stand up on either side, and the rush and sere wild oats in the rivulet itself, our lives are more serene and worthy to contemplate.

As the day advances, the heat of the sun is reflected by the hillsides, and we hear a faint but sweet music, where flows the rill released from its fetters, and the icicles are melting on the trees; and the nut-hatch and partridge are heard and seen. The south wind melts the snow at noon, and the bare ground appears with its withered grass and leaves, and we are invigorated by the perfume which expands from it, as by the scent of strong meats.

Let us go into this deserted woodman's hut, and see how he has passed the long winter nights and the short and stormy days. For here man has lived under this south hill-side, and it seems a civilized and public spot. We have such associations as when the traveller stands by the ruins of Palmyra or Hecatompolis.[8] Singing birds and flowers perchance have begun to appear here, for flowers as well as weeds follow in the footsteps of man. These hemlocks whispered over his head, these hickory logs were his fuel, and these pitch-pine roots kindled his fire; yonder foaming rill in the hollow, whose thin and airy vapor still ascends as busily as ever, though he is far off now, was his well. These hemlock boughs, and the straw upon this raised platform, were his bed, and this broken dish held his drink. But he has not been here this season, for the phæbes built their nest upon this shelf last summer. I find some embers left, as if he had but just gone out, where he baked his pot of beans, and while at evening he smoked his pipe, whose stemless bowl lies in the ashes, chatted with his only companion, if perchance he had any, about the depth of the snow on the morrow, already falling fast and thick without, or disputed whether the last sound was the screech of an owl, or the creak of a bough, or imagination only; and through this broad chimney-throat, in the late winter evening, ere he stretched himself upon the straw, he looked up to learn the progress of the storm, and seeing the bright stars of Cassiopeia's chair shining brightly down upon him, fell contentedly asleep.[9]

See how many traces from which we may learn the chopper's history. From this stump we may guess the sharpness of his axe, and from the slope of the stroke, on which side he stood, and whether he cut down the tree without going round it or changing hands; and from the flexure of the splinters we may know which way it fell. This one chip contains inscribed on it the whole history of the wood-chopper and of the world. On this scrap of paper, which held his sugar or salt, perchance, or was the wadding of his gun, sitting on a log in the forest, with what interest we read the tattle of cities, of those larger huts, empty and to let, like this, in High-streets, and Broad-ways. The eaves are dripping on the south side of this simple roof, while the titmouse lisps in the pine, and the genial warmth of the sun around the door is somewhat kind and human.

After two seasons, this rude dwelling does not deform the scene. Already the birds resort to it, to build their nests, and you may track to its door the feet of many quadrupeds. Thus, for a long time, nature overlooks the encroachment and profanity of man. The wood still cheerfully and unsuspiciously echoes the strokes of the axe that fells it, and while they are few and seldom, they enhance its wilderness, and all the elements strive to naturalize the sound.

Now our path begins to ascend gradually to the top of this high hill, from whose precipitous south side, we can look over the broad country, of forest, and field, and river, to the distant snowy mountains. See yonder thin column of smoke curling up through the woods from some invisible farm-house; the standard raised over some rural homestead. There must be a warmer and more genial spot there below, as where we detect the vapor from a spring forming a cloud above the trees. What fine relations are established between the traveller who discovers this airy column from some eminence in the forest, and him who sits below. Up goes the smoke as silently and naturally as the vapor exhales from the leaves, and as busy disposing itself in wreathes as the housewife on the hearth below. It is a hieroglyphic of man's life, and suggests more intimate and important things than the boiling of a pot. Where its fine column rises above the forest, like an ensign, some human life has planted itself,—and such is the beginning of Rome, the establishment of the arts, and the foundation of empires, whether on the prairies of America, or the steppes of Asia.

And now we descend again to the brink of this woodland lake, which lies in a hollow of the hills, as if it were their expressed juice, and that of the leaves, which are annually steeped in it. Without outlet or inlet to the eye, it has still its history, in the lapse of its waves, in the rounded pebbles on its shore, and on the pines which grow down to its brink. It has not been idle, though sedentary, but, like Abu Musa, teaches that "sitting still at home is the heavenly way; the going out is the way of the world."[10] Yet in its evaporation it travels as far as any. In summer it is the earth's liquid eye; a mirror in the breast of nature. The sins of the wood are washed out in it. See how the woods form an amphitheatre about it, and it is an arena for all the genialness of nature. All trees direct the traveller to its brink, all paths seek it out, birds fly to it, quadrupeds flee to it, and the very ground inclines toward it. It is nature's saloon, where she has sat down to her toilet. Consider her silent economy and tidiness; how the sun comes with his evaporation to sweep the dust from its surface each morning, and a fresh surface is constantly welling up; and annually, after whatever impurities have accumulated herein, its liquid transparency appears again in the spring. In summer a hushed music seems to sweep across its surface. But now a plain sheet of snow conceals it from our eyes, except when the wind has swept the ice bare, and the sere leaves are gliding from side to side, tacking and veering on their tiny voyages. Here is one just keeled up against a pebble on shore, a dry beach leaf, rocking still, as if it would soon start again. A skilful engineer, methinks, might project its course since it fell from the parent stem. Here are all the elements for such a calculation. Its present position, the direction of the wind, the level of the pond, and how much more is given. In its scarred edges and veins is its log rolled up.

We fancy ourselves in the interior of a larger house. The surface of the pond is our deal table or sanded floor, and the woods rise abruptly from its edge, like the walls of a cottage. The lines set to catch pickerel through the ice look like a larger culinary preparation, and the men stand about on the white ground like pieces of forest furniture. The actions of these men, at the distance of half a mile over the ice and snow, impress us as when we read the exploits of Alexander in history. They seem not unworthy of the scenery, and as momentous as the conquest of kingdoms.

Again we have wandered through the arches of the wood, until from its skirts we hear the distant booming of ice from yonder bay of the river, as if it were moved by some other and subtler tide than oceans know. To me it has a strange sound of home, thrilling as the voice of one's distant and noble kindred. A mild summer sun shines over forest and lake, and though there is but one green leaf for many rods, yet nature enjoys a serene health. Every sound is fraught with the same mysterious assurance of health, as well now the creaking of the boughs in January, as the soft sough[11] of the wind in July.

> When Winter fringes every bough
> With his fantastic wreath,
> And puts the seal of silence now
> Upon the leaves beneath;
>
> When every stream in its pent-house
> Goes gurgling on its way,
> And in his gallery the mouse
> Nibbleth the meadow hay;
>
> Methinks the summer still is nigh,
> And lurketh underneath,
> As that same meadow mouse doth lie
> Snug in the last year's heath.

And if perchance the Chickadee
    Lisp a faint note anon,
The snow in summer's canopy,
    Which she herself put on.

Fair blossoms deck the cheerful trees,
    And dazzling fruits depend,
The north wind sighs a summer breeze,
    The nipping frosts to fend,

Bringing glad tidings unto me,
    The while I stand all ear,
Of a serene eternity,
    Which need not winter fear.

Out on the silent pond straightway
    The restless ice doth crack,
And pond sprites merry gambols play
    Amid the deafening rack.

Eager I hasten to the vale,
    As if I heard brave news,
How nature held high festival,
    Which it were hard to lose.

I gambol with my neighbor ice,
    And sympathizing quake,
As each new crack darts in a trice
    Across the gladsome lake.

One with the cricket in the ground,
    And faggot on the hearth,
Resounds the rare domestic sound
    Along the forest path.[12]

Before night we will take a journey on skates along the course of this meandering river, as full of novelty to one who sits by the cottage fire all the winter's day, as if it were over the polar ice, with captain Parry or Franklin; following the winding of the stream, now flowing amid hills, now spreading out into fair meadows, and forming myriad coves and bays where the pine and hemlock overarch. The river flows in the rear of the towns, and we see all things from a new and wilder side. The fields and gardens come down to it with a frankness, and freedom from pretension, which they do not wear on the highway. It is the outside and edge of the earth. Our eyes are not offended by violent contrasts. The last rail of the farmer's fence is some swaying willow bough, which still preserves its freshness, and here at length all fences stop, and we no longer cross any road. We may go far up within the country now by the most retired and level road, never climbing a hill, but by broad levels ascending to the upland meadows. It is a beautiful illustration of the law of obedience, the flow of a river; the path for a sick man, a highway down which an acorn cup may float secure with its freight. Its slight occasional falls, whose precipices would not diversify the landscape, are celebrated by mist and spray, and attract the traveller from far and near. From the remote interior, its current conducts him by broad and easy steps, or by one gentle inclined plain, to the sea. Thus by an early and constant yielding to the inequalities of the ground, it secures itself the easiest passage.

No dominion of nature is quite closed to man at all times, and now we draw near to the empire of the fishes. Our feet glide swiftly over unfathomed depths, where in summer our line tempted the pout and perch, and where the stately pickerel lurked in the long corridors, formed by the bulrushes. The deep, impenetrable marsh, where the heron waded, and bittern squatted, is made pervious to our swift shoes, as if a thousand railroads had been made into it. With one impulse we are carried to the cabin of the muskrat, that earliest settler, and see him dart away under the transparent ice, like a furred fish, to his hole in the bank; and we glide rapidly over meadows where lately "the mower whet his scythe," through beds of frozen cranberries mixed with meadow grass.[13] We skate near to where the blackbird, the pewee, and the kingbird hung their nests over the water, and the hornets builded from the maple on the swamp. How many gay warblers now following the sun, have radiated from this nest of silver birch and thistle down. On the swamp's outer edge was hung the supermarine village, where no foot penetrated. In this hollow tree the wood-duck reared her brood, and slid away each day to forage in yonder fen.

In winter, nature is a cabinet of curiosities, full of dried specimens, in their natural order and position. The meadows and forests are a *hortus siccus*.[14] The leaves and grasses stand perfectly pressed by the air without screw or gum, and the bird's nests are not hung on an artificial twig, but where they builded them. We go about dry shod to inspect the summer's work in the rank swamp, and see what a growth have got the alders, the willows, and the maples; testifying to how many warm suns, and fertilizing dews and showers. See what strides their boughs took in the luxuriant summer,—and anon these dormant buds will carry them onward and upward another span into the heavens.

Occasionally we wade through fields of snow, under whose depths the river is lost for many rods, to appear again to the right or left, where we least expected; still holding on its way underneath, with a faint, stertorous,[15] rumbling sound, as if, like the bear and marmot, it too had hibernated, and we had followed its faint summer trail to where it earthed itself in snow and ice. At first we should have thought that rivers would be empty and dry in mid winter, or else frozen solid till the spring thawed them; but their volume is not diminished even, for only a superficial cold bridges their surface. The thousand springs which feed the lakes and streams are flowing still. The issues of a few surface springs only are closed, and they go to swell the deep reservoirs. Nature's wells are below the frost. The summer brooks are not filled with snow-water, nor does the mower quench his thirst with that alone. The streams are swollen when the snow melts in the spring, because nature's work has been delayed, the water being turned into ice and snow, whose particles are less smooth and round, and do not find their level so soon.

Far over the ice, between the hemlock woods and snow-clad hills, stands the pickerel fisher, his lines set in some retired cove, like a Finlander, with his arms thrust into the pouches of his dreadnought; with dull, snowy, fishy thoughts, himself a finless fish, separated a few inches from his race; dumb, erect, and made to be enveloped in clouds and snows, like the pines on shore. In these wild scenes, men stand about in the scenery, or move deliberately and heavily, having sacrificed the sprightliness and vivacity of towns to the dumb sobriety of nature. He does not make the scenery less wild, more than the jays and musk-rats, but stands there as a part of it, as the natives are represented in the voyages of early navigators, at Nootka sound, and on the North-west coast, with their furs about them, before they were tempted to loquacity by a scrap of iron.[16] He belongs to the natural family of man, and is planted deeper in nature and has more root than the inhabitants of towns. Go to him, ask what luck, and you will learn that he too is a worshipper of the unseen. Hear with what sincere deference and waving gesture in his tone, he speaks of the lake pick-erel, which he has never seen, his primitive and ideal race of pickerel. He is connected with the shore still, as by a fish-line, and yet remem-bers the season when he took fish through the ice on the pond, while the peas were up in his garden at home.

But now, while we have loitered, the clouds have gathered again, and a few straggling snow-flakes are beginning to descend. Faster and faster they fall, shutting out the distant objects from sight. The snow falls on every wood and field, and no crevice is forgotten; by the river and the pond, on the hill and in the valley. Quadrupeds are confined to their coverts, and the birds sit upon their perches this peaceful hour. There is not so much sound as in fair weather, but silently and gradually every slope, and the grey walls and fences, and the polished ice, and the sere leaves, which were not buried before, are concealed, and the tracks of men and beasts are lost. With so little effort does nature reassert her rule, and blot out the traces of men. Hear how Homer has described the same. "The snow flakes fall thick and fast on a winter's day. The winds are lulled, and the snow falls incessant, covering the top of the mountains, and the hills, and the plains where the lotus tree grows, and the cultivated fields, and they are falling by the inlets and shores of the foaming sea, but are silently dissolved by the waves."[17] The snow levels all things, and infolds them deeper on the bosom of nature, as, in the slow summer, vegetation creeps up to the entablature of the temple, and the turrets of the castle, and helps her to prevail over art.

The surly night-wind rustles through the wood, and warns us to retrace our steps, while the sun goes down behind the thickening storm, and birds seek their roosts, and cattle their stalls.

> Drooping the lab'rer ox
> Stands covered o'er with snow, and *now* demands
> The fruit of all his toil.[18]

Though winter is represented in the almanac as an old man, facing the wind and sleet, and drawing his cloak about him, we rather think of him as a merry wood-chopper, and warm-blooded youth, as blithe as summer. The unexplored grandeur of the storm keeps up the spirits of the traveller. It does not trifle with us, but has a sweet earnestness. In winter we lead a more inward life. Our hearts are warm and merry, like cottages under drifts, whose windows and doors are half concealed, but from whose chimneys the smoke cheerfully ascends. The imprisoning drifts increase the sense of comfort which the house affords, and in the coldest days we are content to sit over the hearth and see the sky through the chimney top, enjoying the quiet and serene life that may be had in a warm corner by the chimney side, or feeling our pulse by listening to the low of cattle in the street, or the sound of the flail in distant barns all the long afternoon. No doubt a skilful physician could determine our health by observing how these simple and natural sounds affected us. We enjoy now, not an oriental, but a boreal[19] leisure, around warm stoves and fire-places, and watch the shadow of motes in the sunbeams.

Sometimes our fate grows too homely and familiarly serious ever to be cured. Consider how for three months the human destiny is wrapped in furs. The good Hebrew revelation takes no cognizance of all this cheerful snow. Is there no religion for the temperate and frigid zones? We know of no scripture which records the pure benignity of the gods on a New England winter night. Their praises have never been sung, only their wrath deprecated. The best scripture, after all, records but a meagre faith. Its saints live reserved and austere. Let a brave devout man spend the year in the woods of Maine or Labrador, and see if the Hebrew scriptures speak adequately of his condition and experience, from the setting in of winter to the breaking up of the ice.

Now commences the long winter evening around the farmer's hearth, when the thoughts of the indwellers travel far abroad, and men are by nature and necessity charitable and liberal to all creatures. Now is the happy resistance to cold, when the farmer reaps his reward, and thinks of his preparedness for winter, and through the glittering panes, sees with equanimity "the mansion of the northern bear," for now the storm is over,

> The full ethereal round,
> Infinite worlds disclosing to the view,
> Shines out intensely keen; and all one cope
> Of starry glitter glows from pole to pole.[20]

Source: H[enry]. D[avid]. T[horeau]., "A Winter Walk," *Dial*, 4 (October 1843): 211–226.

Notes

1. Tartarus, the region in Hades in which the wicked are punished.
2. Kine, buffaloes; Pluto, god of the underworld; Styx, river that the dead crossed into Hades.
3. The poem is by Thoreau.
4. Indian summer, a period of warm weather that returns after the start of autumn.
5. *The Seasons* (1726–1730), "Winter," ll. 256–257, by James Thomson (1700–1748), English poet.
6. Knistenaux, related to the Cree Indians; Novazemblaites, from Nova Zembla, a type of rhododendron; Spitzbergeners, residents of an area in northern Norway.
7. Plicipennes, an archaic name for the caddisfly.
8. Palmyra, ancient city in Syria; Hecatompolis, probably the ancient Iranian city Hecatompylos.
9. Cassiopeia, a constellation whose major stars form the outline of a chair.
10. Abu Musa Alishari (fl. 796), Muslim ruler.
11. Sough, a rushing or rustling sound.
12. The poem is by Thoreau
13. "L'Allegro" (1645), l. 66, by John Milton.
14. *Hortus siccus*: dry garden.
15. Stertorous, a sound like heavy snoring.
16. Nootka Sound, an inlet on the coast of Vancouver Island, British Columbia.

17. *Illiad*, Book 12, ll. 278–285.
18. *The Seasons*, "Winter," ll. 240–242.
19. Boreal, northern.
20. *The Seasons*, "Winter," ll. 738–741.

Charles Lane

"Brook Farm"

(January 1844)

LANE'S ARTICLE on Brook Farm in the *Dial* shows how even communitarians disagreed among themselves about how society is to be organized.

\\\//,

Wherever we recognize the principle of progress, our sympathies and affections are engaged. However small may be the innovation, however limited the effort towards the attainment of pure good, that effort is worthy of our best encouragement and succor. The Institution at Brook Farm, West Roxbury, though sufficiently extensive in respect to number of persons, perhaps is not to be considered an experiment of large intent. Its aims are moderate; too humble indeed to satisfy the extreme demands of the age; yet, for that reason probably, the effort is more valuable, as likely to exhibit a larger share of actual success.

Though familiarly designated a "Community," it is only so in the process of eating in commons; a practice at least, as antiquated, as the collegiate halls of old England, where it still continues without producing, as far as we can learn, any of the Spartan virtues. A residence at Brook Farm does not involve either a community of money, or opinions, or of sympathy. The motives which bring individuals there, may be as various as their numbers. In fact, the present residents are divisible into three distinct classes; and if the majority in numbers were considered, it is possible that a vote in favor of self-sacrifice for the common good would not be very strongly carried. The leading portion of the adult inmates, they whose presence imparts the greatest peculiarity and the fraternal tone to the household, believe that an improved state of existence would be developed in association, and are therefore anxious to promote it. Another class consists of those who join with the view of bettering their condition, by being exempted from some portion of worldly strife. The third portion, comprises those who have their own development or education, for their principal object. Practically, too, the institution manifests a threefold improvement over the world at large, corresponding to these three motives. In consequence of the first, the companionship, the personal intercourse, the social bearing are of a marked, and very superior character. There may possibly, to some minds, long accustomed to other modes, appear a want of homeness, and of the private fireside; but all observers must acknowledge a brotherly and softening condition, highly conducive to the permanent, and pleasant growth of all the better human qualities. If the life is not of a deeply religious cast, it is at least not inferior to that which is exemplified elsewhere; and there is the advantage of an entire absence of assumption and pretence. The moral atmosphere so far is pure; and there is found a strong desire to walk ever on the mountain tops of life; though taste, rather than piety, is the aspect presented to the eye.

In the second class of motives, we have enumerated, there is a strong tendency to an important improvement in meeting the terrestrial necessities of humanity. The banishment of servitude, the renouncement of hireling labor, and the elevation of all unavoidable work to its true station, are problems whose solution seems to be charged upon association; for the dissociate systems have in vain sought remedies for this unfavorable portion of human condition. It is impossible to introduce into separate families even one half of the economies, which the present state of science furnishes to man. In that particular, it is probable that even the feudal system is superior to the civic: for its combinations permit many domestic arrangements of an economic character, which are impracticable in small households. In order to economize labor, and dignify the laborer, it is absolutely necessary that men should cease to work in the present isolate competitive mode, and adopt that of co-operative union or association. It is as false and as ruinous to call any man 'master' in secular business, as it is in theological opinions. Those persons, therefore, who congregate for the purpose, as it is called, of bettering their outward relations, on principles so high and universal as we have endeavored to describe, are not engaged in a petty design, bounded by their own selfish or temporary improvement. Every one who is here found giving up the usual chances of individual aggrandizement, may not be thus influenced; but whether it be so or not, the outward demonstration will probably be equally certain.

In education, Brook Farm appears to present greater mental freedom than most other institutions. The tuition being more heart-rendered, is in its effects more heart-stirring. The younger pupils as well as the more advanced students are held, mostly if not wholly, by the power of love. In this particular, Brook Farm is a much improved model for the oft-praised schools of New England. It is time that the imitative and book-learned systems of the latter should be superseded or liberalized by some plan, better calculated to excite originality of thought, and the native energies of the mind. The deeper, kindly sympathies of the heart, too, should not be forgotten; but the germination of these must be despaired of under a rigid hireling system. Hence, Brook Farm, with its spontaneous teachers, presents the unusual and cheering condition of a really "free school."

By watchful and diligent economy, there can be no doubt that a community would attain greater pecuniary success, than is within the hope of honest individuals working separately. But Brook Farm is not a Community, and in the variety of motives with which persons associate there, a double diligence, and a watchfulness perhaps too costly, will be needful to preserve financial prosperity. While, however, this security is an essential element in success, riches would, on the other hand, be as fatal as poverty, to the true progress of such an institution. Even in the case of those foundations which have assumed a religious character, all history proves the fatality of wealth. The just and happy mean between riches and poverty is, indeed, more likely to be attained when, as in this instance, all thought of acquiring great wealth in a brief time, is necessarily abandoned, as a condition of membership. On the other hand, the presence of many persons, who congregate merely for the attainment of some individual end, must weigh heavily and unfairly upon those whose hearts are really expanded to universal results. As a whole, even the initiative powers of Brook Farm have, as is found almost every where, the design of a life much too objective, too much derived from objects in the exterior world. The subjective life, that in which the soul finds the living source and the true communion within itself, is not sufficiently prevalent to impart to the establishment the permanent and sedate character it should enjoy. Undeniably, many devoted individuals are there; several who have as generously as wisely relinquished what are considered great social and pecuniary advantages; and by throwing their skill and energies into a course of the most ordinary labors, at once prove their disinterestedness, and lay the foundation of industrial nobility.

An assemblage of persons, not brought together by the principles of community, will necessarily be subject to many of the inconveniences of ordinary life, as well as to burdens peculiar to such a condition. Now Brook Farm is at present such an institution. It is not a community: it is not truly an association: it is merely an aggregation of persons, and lacks that oneness of spirit, which is probably needful to make it of deep and lasting value to mankind. It seems, even after three years' continuance, uncertain, whether it is to be resolved more into an educational, or an industrial institution, or into one combined of both. Placed so near a large city, and in a populous neighborhood, the original liability for land, &c., was so large, as still to leave a considerable burden of debt. This state of things seems fairly to entitle the establishment to re-draw from the old world in fees for education, or in the sale of produce, sufficient to pay the annual interest of such liabilities. Hence the necessity for a more intimate intercourse with the trading world, and a deeper involvement in money affairs than would have attended a more retired effort of the like kind. To enter into the corrupting modes of the world, with the view of diminishing or destroying them, is a delusive hope. It will, notwithstanding, be a labor of no little worth, to induce improvements in the two grand departments of industry and education. We say *improvement*, as distinct from *progress*; for with any association short of community, we do not see how it is possible for an institution to stand so high above the present world, as to conduct its affairs on principles entirely different from those which now influence men in general.

There are other considerations also suggested by a glance at Brook Farm, which are worthy the attention of the many minds now attracted by the deeply interesting subject of human association. We are gratified by observing several external improvements during the past year; such as a larger and a more convenient dining room, a labor-saving cooking apparatus, a purer diet, a more orderly and quiet attendance at the refections, superior arrangements for industry, and generally an increased seriousness in respect to the value of the example, which those who are there assembled may constitute to their fellow beings.

Of about seventy persons now assembled there, about thirty are children sent thither for education; some adult persons also place themselves there chiefly for mental assistance; and in the society there are only four married couples. With such materials it is almost certain that the sensitive and vital points of communication cannot well be tested. A joint-stock company, working with some of its own members and with others as agents, cannot bring to issue the great question, whether the existence of the marital family is compatible with that of the universal family, which the term "Community" signifies. This is now the grand problem. By mothers it has ever been felt to be so. The maternal instinct, as hitherto educated, has declared itself so strongly in favor of the separate fire-side, that association, which appears so beautiful to the young and unattached soul, has yet accomplished little progress in the affections of that important section of the human race—the mothers. With fathers, the feeling in favor of the separate family is certainly less strong; but there is an undefinable tie, a sort of magnetic *rapport*, an invisible, inseverable, umbilical cord between the mother and child, which in most cases circumscribes her desires and ambition to her own immediate family. All the accepted adages and wise saws of society, all the precepts of morality, all the sanctions of theology, have for ages been employed to confirm this feeling. This is the chief corner stone of present society; and to this maternal instinct have, till very lately, our most heartfelt appeals been made for the progress of the human race, by means of a deeper and more vital education. Pestalozzi and his most enlightened disciples are distinguished by this sentiment. And are we all at once to abandon, to deny, to destroy this supposed stronghold of virtue? Is it questioned whether the family arrangement of mankind is to be preserved? Is it discovered that the sanctuary, till now deemed the holiest on earth, is to be invaded by intermeddling skepticism, and its altars sacrilegiously destroyed by the rude hands of innovating progress? Here "social science" must be brought to issue. The question of association and of marriage are one. If, as we have been popularly led to believe, the individual or separate family is in the true order of Providence, then the associative life is a false effort. If the associative life is true, then is the separate family a false arrangement. By the maternal feeling, it appears to be decided that the co-existence of both is incompatible, is impossible. So also say some religious sects. Social science ventures to assert their harmony. This is the grand problem now remaining to be solved, for at least, the enlightening, if not for the vital elevation of humanity. That the affections can be divided or bent with equal ardor on two objects, so opposed as universal and individual love, may at least be rationally doubted. History has not yet exhibited such phenomena in an associate body, and scarcely perhaps in any individual. The monasteries and convents, which have existed in all ages, have been maintained solely by the annihilation of that peculiar affection on which the separate family is based. The Shaker families, in which the two sexes are not entirely dissociated, can yet only maintain their union by forbidding and preventing the growth of personal affection other than that of a spiritual character. And this in fact is not personal in the sense of individual, but ever a manifestation of universal affection. Spite of the speculations of hopeful bachelors and æsthetic spinsters, there is somewhat in the marriage bond which is found to counteract the universal nature of the affections, to a degree tending at least to make the considerate pause, before they assert that, by any social arrangements whatever, the two can be blended into one harmony. The general condition of married persons at this time is some evidence of the existence of such a doubt in their minds. Were they as convinced as the unmarried of the beauty and truth of associate life, the demonstration would be now presented. But might it not be enforced that the two family ideas really neutralize each other? Is it not quite certain that the human heart cannot be set in two places; that man cannot worship at two altars? It is only the determination to do what parents consider the best for themselves and their families, which renders the o'er populous world such a wilderness of selfhood as it is. Destroy this feeling, they say, and you prohibit every motive to exertion. Much truth is there in this affirmation. For to them, no other motive remains, nor indeed to any one else, save that of the universal good, which does not permit the building up of supposed self-good; and therefore, forecloses all possibility of an individual family.

These observations, of course, equally apply to all the associative attempts, now attracting so much public attention; and perhaps most especially to such as have more of Fourier's designs than are observable at Brook Farm.[1] The slight allusion in all the writers of the "Phalansterian" class, to the subject of marriage, is rather remarkable. They are acute and eloquent in deploring Woman's oppressed and degraded position in past and present times, but are almost silent as to the future. In the mean while, it is gratifying to observe the successes which in some departments attend every effort, and that Brook Farm is likely to become comparatively eminent in the highly important and praiseworthy attempts, to render labor of the hands more dignified and noble, and mental education more free and loveful.

Source: C[harles]. L[ane]., "Brook Farm," *Dial*, 4 (January 1844): 351–357.

Note

1. François Marie Charles Fourier (1772–1837), French social thinker, whose doctrines guided the later period of the Brook Farm community.

Brook Farm Association for Industry and Education

Constitution of the Brook Farm Association for Industry and Education, West Roxbury, Mass. With an Introductory Statement

(1844)

RIPLEY AND HIS WIFE, Sophia, had established Brook Farm at West Roxbury, near Boston, in April 1841 to, in his words, "establish a mode of life which shall combine the enchantments of poetry with the facts of daily experience." To him, a literate idealism would be combined with practical, daily life in a shared, *lived* experience. In a letter resigning his ministry to take up Brook Farm, he articulates his difference from Transcendentalists such as Emerson who believe that the individual must be reformed before a successful attempt can be made at changing society: "The attention of some good men is directed chiefly to individual evils; they wish to improve private character without attacking social principles which obstruct all improvement; while the attention of other good men is directed to the evils of society; they think that private character suffers from public sins, and that, as we are placed in society by Providence, the advancement of society is our principal duty."

The Ripleys' attempt to bring people of all social classes together to work, play, and learn in natural surroundings worked well for a time, but Brook Farm was severely undercapitalized from the start, located on soil that was poor for farming, too far from the nearest railway line to bring its goods to Boston cheaply and be competitive in the marketplace, and led by people whose training had been in the fine arts rather than such practical ones as farming and business. Nevertheless, it supported a communal life that most of its participants looked back upon with pleasure in their later years, had an excellent school that was the sole regular source of revenue, and provided the partial basis for *The Blithedale Romance* (1852) by Nathaniel Hawthorne, who lived there for six months in 1841.

Two additional reasons stand out for Brook Farm's failure: the change to a Phalanx in 1845 brought about a regimentation that was at odds with the basic sense of individual freedom in which most Transcendentalists believed; and the Phalanstery, a large dormitory structure, burned down in 1846 while under construction for an uninsured loss of $7,000.

This *Constitution*, published midway in the career of Brook Farm, makes reform seem so sensible and easy: as the preamble suggests, all that needs to be done is to apply the Golden Rule, unite the physical with the spiritual, eliminate the evils of the competitive marketplace by being economically self-sufficient, and, in general, bring out the best in people.

The Association at Brook Farm, has now been in existence upwards of two years. Originating in the thought and experience of a few individuals, it has hitherto worn, for the most part, the character of a private experiment, and has avoided rather than sought, the notice of the public. It has, until the present time, seemed fittest to those engaged in this enterprise to publish no statements of their purposes or methods, to make no promises or declarations, but quietly and sincerely to realise, as far as might be possible, the great ideas which gave the central impulse to their movement. It has been thought that a steady endeavor to embody these ideas more and more perfectly in life, would give the best answer, both to the hopes of the friendly and the cavils of the sceptical, and furnish in its results the surest grounds for any larger efforts.

Meanwhile every step has strengthened the faith with which we set out; our belief in a divine order of human society, has in our own minds become an absolute certainty; and considering the present state of humanity and of social science, we do not hesitate to affirm, that the world is much nearer the attainment of such a condition than is generally supposed.

The deep interest in the doctrine of Association, which now fills the minds of intelligent persons every where, indicates plainly that the time has passed when even initiative movements ought to be prosecuted in silence, and makes it imperative on all who have either a theoretical or practical knowledge of the subject to give their share to the stock of public information.

Accordingly, we have taken occasion at several public meetings recently held in Boston, to state some of the results of our studies and experience, and we desire here to say emphatically, that while on the one hand we yield an unqualified assent to that doctrine of universal unity which Fourier teaches, so on the other, our whole observation has shown us the truth of the practical arrangements which he deduces therefrom. The law of groups and series is, as we are convinced, the law of human nature, and when men are in true social relations their industrial organization will necessarily assume those forms.

But beside the demand for information respecting the principles of association, there is a deeper call for action in the matter. We wish, therefore, to bring Brook Farm before the public, as a location offering at least as great advantages for a thorough experiment as can be found in the vicinity of Boston. It is situated in West Roxbury, three miles from the depot of the Dedham Branch Rail Road, and about eight miles from Boston, and combines a convenient nearness to the city with a degree of retirement and freedom from unfavorable influences, unusual even in the country. The place is one of great natural beauty, and indeed the whole landscape is so rich and various as to attract the notice even of casual visitors. The farm now owned by the Association contains two hundred and eight acres, of as good quality as any land in the neighborhood of Boston, and can be enlarged by the purchase of land adjoining to any necessary extent. The property now in the hands of the Association is worth nearly or quite thirty thousand dollars, of which about twenty-two thousand dollars is invested either in the stock of the company, or in permanent loans at six per cent., which can remain as long as the Association may wish.

The fact that so large an amount of capital is already invested and at our service as the basis of more extensive operations, furnishes a reason why Brook Farm should be chosen as the scene of that practical trial of association which the public feeling calls for in this immediate vicinity, instead of forming an entirely new organization for that purpose. The completeness of our educational department is also not to be overlooked. This has hitherto received our greatest care, and in forming it we have been particularly successful. In any new Association it must be many years before so many accomplished and skilful teachers in the various branches of intellectual culture could be enlisted. Another strong reason is to be found in the degree of order our organization has already attained, by the help of which a large Association might be formed without the losses and inconveniences which would otherwise necessarily occur. The experience of nearly three years in all the misfortunes and mistakes incident to an undertaking so new and so little understood, carried on throughout by persons not entirely fitted for the duties they have been compelled to perform, has, as we think, prepared us to assist in the safe conduct of an extensive and complete Association.

Such an institution, as will be plain to all, cannot by any sure means, be brought at once and full grown into existence. It must at least in the present state of society, begin with a comparatively small number of select and devoted persons, and increase by natural and gradual aggregations. With a view to an ultimate expansion into a perfect Phalanx, we desire without any delay to organize the three primary departments of labor, namely, Agriculture, Domestic Industry, and the Mechanic Arts.

For this purpose additional capital will be needed, which it is most desirable should be invested by those who propose to connect themselves personally with the institution. These should be men and women accustomed to labor, skilful, careful, in good health, and more than all imbued with the idea of Association, and ready to consecrate themselves without reserve to its realization. For it ought to be known that the work we propose is a difficult one, and except to the most entire faith and resolution will offer insurmountable obstacles and discouragements. Neither will it be possible to find in Association at the outset the great outward advantages it ultimately promises. The first few years must be passed in constant and unwearied labor, heightened chiefly by the consciousness of high aims and the inward content that devotion to a universal object cannot fail to bring. Still there are certain tangible compensations which Association guaranties immediately. These are freedom from pecuniary anxiety, and the evils of competitive industry, free and friendly society, and the education of children. How great these are, those who have felt the terrible burdens which the present civilized society imposes in these respects will not need to be informed.

Those who may wish to further this course by investments of money only will readily perceive that their end is not likely to be lost in an Association whose means are devoted mainly to productive industry, and where nothing will ever be risked in uncertain speculations.

The following Constitution is the same as that under which we have hitherto acted, with such alterations as on a careful revision seemed needful. All persons who are not familiar with the purposes of Association, will understand from this document that we propose a radical and universal reform, rather than to redress any particular wrong or to remove the sufferings of any single class of human beings. We do this in the light of universal principles, in which all differences, whether of religion, or politics, or philosophy, are reconciled, and the dearest and most private hope of every man has the promise of fulfilment. Herein, let it be understood, we would remove nothing that is truly beautiful or venerable; we reverence the religious sentiment in all its forms, the family, and whatever else has its foundation either in human nature or the Divine Providence. The work we are engaged in is not destruction, but true conservation: it is not a mere revolution, but, as we are assured, a necessary step in the course of social progress which no one can be blind enough to think has yet reached its limit. We believe that humanity, trained by these long centuries of suffering and struggle, led onward by so many saints and heroes and sages, is at length prepared to enter into that universal order, toward which it has perpetually moved. Thus we recognize the worth of the whole Past and of every doctrine and institution it has bequeathed us; thus also we perceive that the Present has its own high mission, and we shall only say what is beginning to be seen by all sincere thinkers, when we declare that the imperative duty of this time and this country, nay more, that its only salvation, and the salvation of all civilized countries, lies in the Reorganization of Society, according to the unchanging laws of human nature and of universal harmony.

We look, then, to the generous and hopeful of all classes for sympathy, for encouragement and for actual aid, not to ourselves only, but to all those who are engaged in this great work. And whatever may be the result of any special efforts, we can never doubt that the object we have in view will finally be attained; that human life shall yet be developed, not in discord and misery, but in harmony and joy, and that the perfected earth shall at last bear on her bosom a race of men worthy of the name.

GEORGE RIPLEY,

MINOT PRATT, } *Directors.*[1]

CHARLES A. DANA,

Brook Farm, West Roxbury, Mass.,
      January 18, 1844. }

Constitution.

In order more effectually to promote the great purposes of human
culture; to establish the external relations of life on a basis of wisdom
and purity; to apply the principles of justice and love to our social
organization in accordance with the laws of Divine Providence; to
substitute a system of brotherly cöoperation for one of selfish competition; to secure to our children and those who may be entrusted to
our care the benefits of the highest physical, intellectual and moral
education, which in the progress of knowledge the resources at our
command will permit; to institute an attractive, efficient, and productive system of industry; to prevent the exercise of worldly anxiety,
by the competent supply of our necessary wants; to diminish the desire
of excessive accumulation, by making the acquisition of individual
property subservient to upright and disinterested uses; to guarantee to
each other forever the means of physical support, and of spiritual progress; and thus to impart a greater freedom, simplicity, truthfulness,
refinement, and moral dignity, to our mode of life;—we the under-
signed do unite in a voluntary Association, and adopt and ordain the
following articles of agreement, to wit:

ARTICLE I.
NAME AND MEMBERSHIP.

SEC. 1. The name of this Association shall be "THE BROOK-FARM
ASSOCIATION FOR INDUSTRY AND EDUCATION." All persons who shall
hold one or more shares in its stock, or whose labor and skill shall be
considered an equivalent for capital, may be admitted by the vote of
two-thirds of the Association, as members thereof.

SEC. 2. No member of the Association shall ever be subjected to
any religious test; nor shall any authority be assumed over individual
freedom of opinion by the Association, nor by one member over another; nor shall any one be held accountable to the Association, except
for such overt acts, or omissions of duty, as violate the principles of
justice, purity, and love, on which it is founded; and in such cases the

relation of any member may be suspended or discontinued, at the pleasure of the Association.

ARTICLE II.
CAPITAL STOCK.

SEC. 1. The members of this Association shall own and manage such real and personal estate in joint stock proprietorship, divided into shares of one hundred dollars each, as may from time to time be agreed on.

SEC. 2. No share-holder shall be liable to any assessment whatever on the shares held by him; nor shall he be held responsible individually in his private property on account of the Association; nor shall the Trustees or any officer or agent of the Association have any authority to do any thing which shall impose personal responsibility on any share-holder, by making any contracts or incurring any debts for which the share-holders shall be individually or personally responsible.

SEC. 3. The Association guaranties to each share-holder the interest of five per cent. annually on the amount of stock held by him in the Association, and this interest may be paid in certificates of stock and credited on the books of the Association; provided that each share-holder may draw on the funds of the Association for the amount of interest due at the third annual settlement from the time of investment.

SEC. 4. The share-holders on their part for themselves, their heirs and assigns, do renounce all claim on any profits accruing to the Association for the use of their capital invested in the stock of the Association, except five per cent. interest on the amount of stock held by them, payable in the manner described in the preceding section.

ARTICLE III.
GUARANTIES.

SEC. 1. The Association shall provide such employment for all its members as shall be adapted to their capacities, habits, and tastes; and each member shall select and perform such operations of labor, whether corporal or mental, as shall be deemed best suited to his own endowments and the benefit of the Association.

SEC. 2. The Association guaranties to all its members, their children and family dependents, house-rent, fuel, food, and clothing, and the other necessaries of life, without charge, not exceeding a certain fixed amount to be decided annually by the Association; no charge shall ever be made for support during inability to labor from sickness or old age, or for medical or nursing attendance, except in case of shareholders, who shall be charged therefor, and also for the food and clothing of children, to an amount not exceeding the interest due to them on settlement; but no charge shall be made to any member for education or the use of library and public rooms.

SEC. 3. Members may withdraw from labor, under the direction of the Association, and in that case, they shall not be entitled to the benefit of the above guaranties.

SEC. 4. Children over ten years of age shall be provided with employment in suitable branches of industry; they shall be credited for such portions of each annual dividend, as shall be decided by the Association, and on the completion of their education in the Association at the age of twenty, shall be entitled to a certificate of stock to the amount of credits in their favor, and may be admitted as members of the Association.

ARTICLE IV.
DISTRIBUTION OF PROFITS.

SEC. 1. The nett profits of the Association, after the payment of all expenses, shall be divided into a number of shares corresponding to the number of day's labor; and every member shall be entitled to one share for every day's labor performed by him.

SEC. 2. A full settlement shall be made with every member once a year, and certificates of stock given for all balances due; but in case of need to be decided by himself, every member may be permitted to draw on the funds in the Treasury to an amount not exceeding the credits in his favor for labor performed.

ARTICLE V.
GOVERNMENT.

SEC. 1. The government of the Association shall be vested in a board of Directors, divided into four departments, as follows: 1st, General Direction; 2d, Direction of Education; 3d, Direction of Industry; 4th, Direction of Finance; consisting of three persons each, provided that the same person may be elected member of each Direction.

SEC. 2. The General Direction and Direction of Education shall be chosen annually, by the vote of a majority of the members of the Association. The Direction of Finance shall be chosen annually, by the vote of a majority of the share-holders and members of the Association.

The Direction of Industry shall consist of the chiefs of the three primary series.

SEC. 3. The chairman of the General Direction shall be the President of the Association, and together with the Direction of Finance, shall constitute a board of Trustees, by whom the property of the Association shall be held and managed.

SEC. 4. The General Direction shall oversee and manage the affairs of the Association, so that every department should be carried on in an orderly and efficient manner.

SEC. 5. The departments of Education and Finance shall be under the control each of its own Direction, which shall select, and in concurrence with the General Direction, shall appoint such teachers, officers, and agents, as shall be necessary to the complete and systematic organization of the department. No Directors or other officers shall be deemed to possess any rank superior to the other members of the Association, nor shall they receive any extra remuneration for their official services.

SEC. 6. The department of Industry shall be arranged in groups and series, as far as practicable, and shall consist of three primary series, to wit, Agricultural, Mechanical, and Domestic Industry. The chief of each series shall be elected every two months by the members thereof, subject to the approval of the General Direction. The chief of each group shall be chosen weekly by its members.

ARTICLE VI.
MISCELLANEOUS.

SEC. 1. The Association may from time to time adopt such bye-laws, not inconsistent with the spirit and purpose of these articles, as shall be found expedient or necessary.

SEC. 2. In order to secure to the Association the benefits of the highest discoveries in social science, and to preserve its fidelity to the principles of progress and reform, on which it is founded, any amendment may be proposed to this Constitution at a meeting called for the purpose; and if approved by two-thirds of the members at a subsequent meeting, at least one month after the date of the first, shall be adopted.

Source: Brook Farm Association for Industry and Education, *Constitution of the Brook Farm Association for Industry and Education, West Roxbury, Mass. With an Introductory Statement* (Boston: I. R. Butts, 1844). The quotations are from John Thomas Codman, *Brook Farm: Historic and Personal Memoirs* (New York:

Arena, 1894), p. 287, and Octavius Brooks Frothingham, *George Ripley* (Boston: Houghton, Mifflin, 1882), p. 84.

Note

1. Minot Pratt (1805–1878), printer and farmer, who left in 1845 for Concord, Massachusetts; Charles A. Dana (1819–1897) taught languages in the Brook Farm school, and later edited the *New York Sun*.

Brook Farm Association for Industry and Education

from Constitution of the Brook Farm Association for Industry and Education, West Roxbury, Mass. With an Introductory Statement. Second Edition, with the By-Laws of the Association

(1844)

PUBLISHED JUST NINE MONTHS after the first *Constitution*, this one contains an introduction that updates the farm's activities and adds by-laws (here omitted) to the earlier work.

However, the change in 1845 from an Association to a Fourieristic phalanx marked a very different direction for Brook Farm than the Ripleys had originally intended. Patterned after the Frenchman's ideal community, the life of the phalanx was structured around various "series," which were subdivided into "groups." Each person served in a number of groups and, in theory, could work in any of them. For example, the "Farming Series" was organized into the Cattle, Milking, Plowing, Nursery, Planting, Hoeing, Weeding, and Haying groups. There was a "group" for everything, as demonstrated by one wag who yelled "the pigs have got into the cornfield, and I am looking for the Miscellaneous Group to drive them out."

Changes were also made to the *Constitution*. At a simple, mechanical level, the four-page introduction to the 1844 pamphlet grew to six-and-a-half pages of description here; the earlier six articles expanded to eight; and the number of sections within the articles exploded from twenty to fifty-one. Other differences were more subtle—and more important. The section guaranteeing individual freedoms in the 1844 *Constitution* was eliminated. Also, universal and equal suffrage was changed by the Phalanx, and the number of votes a person could cast depended upon the number of shares of stocks they owned. The plan for a godly social order replacing a more debased human one had itself been replaced by yet another human one. The altruism of the original preamble was undercut and inverted by the new articles that followed it, and egalitarian individualism gave way to group regimentation.

※

Since the publication of the first edition of our Constitution and Introductory Statement, the public interest in Association, has greatly increased both in this vicinity, and throughout the country generally. With the conviction now beginning to pervade all classes of society, that in the incoherence and conflict of interests which characterize civilization, there can be no permanent security either for private rights or public order, the doctrines of social unity, and attractive industry, are taking a sure and deep hold. Already the Phalansterian movement in the United States embraces persons of every station in life, and in its extent, and influence on questions of importance, is fast assuming a national character.

In this state of things, the friends of the cause will be gratified to learn, that the appeal in behalf of Brook Farm, contained in our Introductory Statement, has been generously answered, and that the situation of the Association is highly encouraging. In the half year that has elapsed, our numbers have been increased by the addition of many skilful and enthusiastic laborers, in various departments, and our capital has been enlarged by the subscription of about ten thousand dollars. Our organization has acquired a more systematic form, though with our comparatively small numbers we can only approximate to truly scientific arrangements. Still with the unavoidable deficiencies of our groups and series, their action is remarkable, and fully justifies our anticipations of great results from applying the principles of universal order to industry.

In education also, we have succeeded in introducing arrangements of great value, which would be impossible in a society of isolated families; though this, as well as other departments, is still in process of formation.

We have made considerable agricultural improvements; we have erected a work-shop sixty feet by twenty-eight, for mechanics of several trades, some of which are already in operation, and we are now engaged in building a section, one hundred and seventy-five feet by forty, of a Phalanstery or Unitary dwelling. Our first object is to collect those who, from their character and convictions, are qualified to aid in the experiment we are engaged in, and to furnish them with convenient and comfortable habitations, at the smallest possible outlay. For this purpose the most careful economy is used, though we are yet able to attain many of the peculiar advantages of the associated household.

Still for a transitional society, and for comparatively temporary use, a social edifice cannot be made free from the defects of civilized architecture. When our Phalanx has become sufficiently large, and has in some measure accomplished its great purposes, the Serial organization of labor and Unitary education, we shall have it in our power to build a Phalanstery with the magnificence and permanence proper to such a structure.

Cheering as are the results of our endeavors, we wish to have it distinctly understood that they have been, and for some time must be, merely preparatory labors. We would then again invite the personal coöperation of all suitable persons, and the investment of the funds necessary to a complete application of Fourier's theory of industrial organization.

We call upon the wise and humane to lend their aid to an undertaking which, in the growing insufficiency and insecurity of civilized institutions bases its promise of a better state of things not on mere human wisdom, but on the science of universal laws. We appeal to those who can perceive that the true road to general well-being, is not to be reached by legislative deliberations, or by political or benevolent expedients, but by reverent investigation of the methods of divine order and faithful application of the same to society;—to those who look with alarm upon the growth of pauperism, and civilized slavery;—to those who in despairing sympathy for the masses begin to feel the necessity of an integral philanthropy;—but more than all, to those who are inspired by the sublime ideas of social and universal unity with a deeper faith in God, and a more assured hope of man.

We appeal to them for assistance in the practical demonstration of a scientific theory, which solves the great social problems that have convulsed the world for the last century, and which discloses to man a destiny worthy of his aspirations and energies, and of that beneficent and infinite Being by whom the universe is forever upheld and renewed.

BROOK FARM, OCT. 1844.

Source: Brook Farm Association for Industry and Education, from *Constitution of the Brook Farm Association for Industry and Education, West Roxbury, Mass. With an Introductory Statement. Second Edition, with the By-Laws of the Association* (Boston: I. R. Butts, 1844). The quotation about the "Miscellaneous Group" is from John Thomas Codman, *Brook Farm: Historic and Personal Memoirs* (Boston: Arena, 1894), pp. 84–85.

Margaret Fuller

"New Year's Day"

(28 December 1844)

FULLER HAD MOVED to New York in November 1844, working as the literary critic for Horace Greeley's *New-York Tribune*. This article greets both the real and the metaphoric new year.

It was once a beautiful custom among some of the Indian tribes, once a year, to extinguish all the fires, and, by a day of fasting and profound devotion, to propitiate the Great Spirit for the coming year. They then produced sparks by friction, and lit up afresh the altar and the hearth with the new fire.

And this was considered as the most precious and sacred gift from one person to another, binding them in bonds of inviolate friendship for that year, certainly; with a hope that the same might endure through life. From the young to the old it was a token of the highest respect; from the old to the young, of a great expectation.

To us might it be granted to solemnize the new year by the mental renovation of which this ceremony was the eloquent symbol! Might we extinguish, if only for a day, those fires where an uninformed religious ardor has led to human sacrifices; which have warmed the household, but, also, prepared pernicious, more than wholesome, viands for their use.

The Indian produced the new spark by friction. It would be a still more beautiful emblem, and expressive of the more extended powers of civilized men, if we should draw the spark from the centre of our system and the source of light by means of the burning glass.

Where, then, is to be found the new knowledge, the new thought, the new hope, that shall begin a new year in a spirit not discordant with 'the acceptable year of the Lord?' Surely, there must be such existing, if latent—some sparks of new fire, pure from ashes and from smoke, worthy to be offered as a new-year's gift? Let us look at the signs of the times, to see in what spot this fire shall be sought—on what fuel it may be fed. The ancients poured our libations of the choicest juices of Earth, to express their gratitude to the Power that had enabled them to be sustained from her bosom. They enfranchised slaves, to show that devotion to the Gods induced a sympathy with men.

Let us look about us to see with what rites, what acts of devotion, this modern Christian nation greets the approach of the New Year; by what signs she denotes the clear morning of a better day, such as may be expected when the eagle has entered into covenant with the dove!

This last week brings tidings that a portion of the inhabitants of Illinois, the rich and blooming region on which every gift of nature has been lavished to encourage the industry and brighten the hopes of man, not only refuses a libation to the Power that has so blessed their fields, but declares that the dew is theirs, and the sunlight is theirs, that they live from and for themselves, acknowledging no obligation and no duty to God or to man.

One man has freed a slave,—but a great part of the nation is now busy in contriving measures that may best rivet the fetters on those now chained, and forge them strongest for millions yet unborn.

Selfishness and tyranny no longer wear the mask; they walk haughtily abroad, affronting with their hard-hearted boasts and brazen resolves the patience of the sweet heavens. National Honor is trodden under foot for a National bribe, and neither sex nor age defends the redresser of injuries from the rage of the injurer.

Yet, amid these reports which come flying on the paper wings of every day, the scornful laugh of the gnomes, who begin to believe they can buy all souls with their gold, was checked a moment when the aged knight of the better cause answered the challenge—truly in keeping with the 'chivalry' of the time,—"You are in the wrong, and I will kick you," by holding the hands of the chevalier till those around secured him. We think the man of old must have held him with his eye, as physicians of moral power can insane patients;—great as are his exploits for his age, he cannot have much bodily strength, unless by miracle.

The treatment of Mr. Adams and Mr. Hoar seems to show that we are not fitted to emulate the savages in preparation for the new fire.[1] The Indians knew how to reverence the old and the wise.

Among the manifestos of the day it is impossible not to respect that of the Mexican Minister for the manly indignation with which he has uttered truths, however deep our mortification at hearing them.[2] It has been observed for the last fifty years that the tone of diplomatic correspondence was much improved as to simplicity and directness. Once, diplomacy was another name for intrigue, and a paper of this sort was expected to be a mesh of artful phrases, through which the true meaning might be detected, but never actually grasped. Now here is one where an occasion being afforded by the unutterable folly of the corresponding party, a Minister speaks the truth as it lies in his mind, directly and plainly, as man speaks to man. His statement will command the sympathy of the civilized world.

As to the State papers that have followed, they are of a nature to make the Austrian despot sneer, as he counts in his oratory the woolen stockings he has got knit by imprisoning all the free geniuses in his dominions.[3] He, at least, only appeals to the legitimacy of blood; these dare appeal to legitimacy, as seen from a moral point of view. History will class them with the brags of sharpers, who bully their victims about their honor, while they stretch forth their hands for the gold they have won with loaded dice.—"Do you dare to say the dice are loaded? Prove it; *and* I will shoot you for inuring my honor."

The Mexican makes his gloss on the page of American Honor. The girl in the Kentucky prison on that of her Freedom.[4] The delegate of Massachusetts on that of her Union. Ye stars! whose image she has placed upon her banner, answer us! Are not your Unions of a different sort? Do they not work to other results?

Yet we cannot lightly be discouraged or alarmed as to the destiny of our Country. The whole history of its discovery and early progress indicates too clearly the purposes of Heaven with regard to it. Could we relinquish the thought that it was destined for the scene of a new and illustrious act in the great drama, the Past would be inexplicable, no less than the Future without hope.

Last week, which brought us so many unpleasant notices of home affairs, brought also an account of the magnificent telescope lately perfected by the Earl of Rosse.[5] With means of observation, now almost divine, we perceive that some of the brightest stars, of which Sirius is one, have dark companions, whose presence is, by earthly spectators, only to be detected from the inequalities they cause in the motions of their radiant companions.

It was a new and most imposing illustration how, in carrying out the Divine scheme, of which we have as yet only spelt out the few first few lines, the dark is made to wait upon and, in the full result, harmonize with, the bright. The sense of such pervasive analogies should enlarge patience and animate hope.

Yet, if offences must come, wo be to those by whom they come, and that of men, who sin against a heritage like ours, is as that of the backsliders among the Chosen People of the elder day. We too have been chosen, and plain indications been given, by a wonderful conjunction of auspicious influences, that the ark of human hopes has been placed for the present in our charge. Wo be to those who betray this trust! On their heads are to be heaped the curses of unnumbered ages!

Can he sleep, who in this past year has wickedly or lightly committed acts calculated to injure the few or many—who has poisoned the ears and the hearts he might have rightly informed—who has steeped in tears the cup of thousands—who has put back, as far as in him lay, the accomplishment of general good and happiness for the sake of his selfish aggrandizement or selfish luxury—who has sold to a party what is meant for mankind? If such sleep, dreadful shall be the waking.

Deliver us from evil. In public or in private it is easy to give pain—hard to give pure pleasure; easy to do evil—hard to do good. God does His good in the whole, despite of bad men; but only from a very pure mind will He permit original good to proceed in the day. Happy those who can feel that during the past year, they have, to the best of their knowledge, refrained from evil. Happy those who determine to proceed in this by the light of Conscience. It is but a spark; yet from that spark may be drawn fire-light enough for worlds and systems of worlds, and that light is ever new.

And with this thought rises again the memory of the fair lines that light has brought to view in the histories of some men. If the nation tends to wrong, there are yet present the ten just men. The hands and lips of this great form may be impure, but pure blood flows yet within her veins—the blood of the noble bands who first sought these shores from the British isles and France for conscience sake. Too many have come since for bread alone. We cannot blame—we must not reject them, but let us teach them, in giving them bread, to prize that salt, too, without which all on earth must lose its savor. Yes! let us teach them, not rail at their inevitable ignorance and unenlightened action, but teach them and their children as our own; if we do so, their children and ours may yet act as one body obedient to one soul, and if we should act rightly now, that soul a pure soul.

And ye, sable bands, forced hither against your will, kept down here now by a force hateful to Nature, a will alien from God; it does sometimes seem as if the Avenging Angel wore your hue and would place in your hands the sword to punish the cruel injustice of our fathers, the selfish perversity of the sons. Yet, are there no means of atonement? Must the innocent suffer with the guilty? Teach us, oh All-Wise! the clue out of this labyrinth, and if we faithfully encounter its darkness and dread, and emerge into clear light, wilt Thou not bid us 'go and sin no more?'[6]

Meanwhile, let us proceed as we can, *picking our steps* along the slippery road. If we keep the right direction, what matters it that we must pass through so much mud? The promise is sure:

Angels shall free the feet from stain, to their own hue of snow,
If, undismayed, we reach the hills where the true olives grow.
The olive-groves, which we must seek in cold and damp,
Alone can yield us oil for a perpetual lamp.
Then sound again the golden horn with promise ever new;
The princely deer will ne'er be caught by those that slack pursue;
Let the 'White Doe' of angel hopes be always kept in view.

Yes! sound again the horn—of Hope the golden horn!
Answer it, flutes and pipes, from valleys still and lorn;
Warders, from your high towers, with trumps of silver scorn,
And harps in maidens' bowers, with strings from deep hearts torn,
All answer to the horn—of Hope the golden horn!

There is still hope, there is still an America, while private lives are ruled by the Puritan, by the Huguenot conscientiousness, and while there are some who can repudiate, not their debts, but the supposition that they will not strive to pay their debts to their age, and to Heaven who gave them a share in its great promise.

Source: * [Margaret Fuller], "New Year's Day," *New-York Daily Tribune,* 28 December 1844, p. 1.

Notes

1. Samuel Hoar (1778–1856), a Concord lawyer and friend of Emerson's, after being sent to Charleston, South Carolina, in 1844 by the state of Massachusetts to prepare a test case on behalf of some imprisoned Massachusetts free Negro seamen, was declared an emissary of a foreign government and expelled from the city.
2. The border dispute between the United States and Mexico climaxed with the annexation of Texas in March 1845 and the arrival of an American force under Zachary Taylor on the disputed land that summer. Fuller also refers to Manuel C. Rejon's "The Mexican Manifesto Against the Annexation of Texas," which she admires for the forthright rhetoric of the Mexican diplomat which is a point by point rebuttal of arguments for the annexation of Texas (*Tribune,* 13 December 1844, p. 1).
3. Rejon was treated with much disrespect in responses leaked by government officials to the press.
4. The *Tribune* of 20 December 1844 reports that the abolitionist Delia Webster was jailed in Lexington, Kentucky, on suspicion of assisting three slaves escape; she remained incarcerated for months with periodic reports appearing the *Tribune.*
5. William Parsons, Third Earl of Rosse (1800–1867), Irish astronomer and telescope builder.

6. "Afterward Jesus findeth him in the temple, and said unto him, Behold, thou art made whole: sin no more, lest a worse thing come unto thee" (John 5:14).

[*George Ripley*]

Prospectus and "Introductory Notice" for the *Harbinger*

(14 June 1845)

THE *Harbinger* (1845–1849), published at Brook Farm (and later in New York), became a major organ for Associationism and Fourierism in America. At times it seemed as if Brook Farm had lost its autonomy and become just one more communitarian society within the larger movement. Although the paper did publish literary works, reviews, and translations—as well as the music criticism of John Sullivan Dwight—the *Harbinger* was, first and foremost, a reformist journal, and one that did not outlive by long Brook Farm itself.

THE HARBINGER,

DEVOTED TO SOCIAL AND POLITICAL PROGRESS,

Published simultaneously at New York and
Boston, by the Brook Farm Phalanx.
"All things, at the present day, stand
provided and prepared, and
await the light."

Under this title it is proposed to publish a weekly newspaper, for the examination and discussion of the great questions in social science, politics, literature, and the arts, which command the attention of all believers in the progress and elevation of humanity.

In politics, the Harbinger will be democratic in its principles and tendencies; cherishing the deepest interest in the advancement and happiness of the masses; warring against all exclusive privilege in legislation, political arrangements, and social customs; and striving with the zeal of earnest conviction, to promote the triumph of the high democratic faith, which it is the chief mission of the nineteenth century to realize in society. Our devotion to the democratic principle will lead us to take the ground of fearless and absolute independence in regard to all political parties, whether professing attachment to that principle or hostility to it. We know that fidelity to an idea can never be measured by adherence to a name; and hence we shall criticise all parties with equal severity; though we trust that the sternness of truth will always be blended with the temperance of impartial candor. With tolerance for all opinions, we have no patience with hypocrisy and pretence; least of all, with that specious fraud, which would make a glorious principle the apology for personal ends. It will therefore be a leading object of the Harbinger to strip the disguise from the prevailing parties, to show them in their true light, to give them due honor, to tender them our grateful reverence whenever we see them true to a noble principle; but at all times, and on every occasion, to expose false professions, to hold up hollow-heartedness and duplicity to just indignation, to warn the people against the demagogue who would cajole them by honeyed flatteries, no less than against the devotee of mammon who would make them his slaves.

The Harbinger will be devoted to the cause of a radical, organic social reform as essential to the highest development of man's nature, to the production of those elevated and beautiful forms of character of which he is capable, and to the diffusion of happiness, excellence, and universal harmony upon the earth. The principles of universal unity as taught by Charles Fourier, in their application to society, we believe, are at the foundation of all genuine social progress; and it will ever be our aim, to discuss and defend these principles, without any sectarian bigotry, and in the catholic and comprehensive spirit of their great discoverer. While we bow to no man as an authoritative, infallible master, we revere the genius of Fourier too highly, not to accept, with joyful welcome, the light which he has shed on the most intricate problems of human destiny. The social reform, of whose advent the signs are every where visible, comprehends all others; and in laboring for its speedy accomplishment, we are conscious that we are devoting our best ability to the removal of oppression and injustice among men, to the complete emancipation of the enslaved, to the promotion of genuine temperance, and to the elevation of the toiling and down-trodden masses to the inborn rights of humanity.

In literature, the Harbinger will exercise a firm and impartial criticism, without respect of persons or parties. It will be made a vehicle for the freest thought, though not of random speculations; and with a generous appreciation of the various forms of truth and beauty, it will not fail to expose such instances of false sentiment, perverted taste, and erroneous opinion, as may tend to vitiate the public mind, or degrade the individual character. Nor will the literary department of the Harbinger be limited to criticism alone. It will receive contributions from various pens, in different spheres of thought; and free from dogmatic exclusiveness, will accept all that in any way indicates the unity of Man with Man, with Nature, and with God. Consequently, all true science, all poetry and arts, all sincere literature, all religion that is from the soul, all wise analyses of mind and character will come within its province.

We appeal for aid in our enterprise to the earnest and hopeful spirits in all classes of society. We appeal to all who, suffering from a resistless discontent in the present order of things, with faith in man and trust in God, are striving for the establishment of universal justice, harmony, and love. We appeal to the thoughtful, the aspiring, the generous every where, who wish to see the reign of heavenly truth triumphantly supplanting the infernal discords and falsehoods, on which modern society is built, for their sympathy, friendship, and practical co-operation, in the undertaking which we announce to day.[1]

INTRODUCTORY NOTICE.

In meeting our friends, for the first time, in the columns of the Harbinger, we wish to take them by the hand with cheerful greetings, to express the earnest hope that our intercourse may be as fruitful of good, as it will be frank and sincere, and that we to-day may commence a communion of spirit, which shall mutually aid us in our progress towards the truth and beauty, the possession of which is the ultimate destiny of man. We address ourselves to the aspiring and free minded youth of our country; to those whom long experience has taught the emptiness of past attainments and inspired with a better hope; to those who cherish a living faith in the advancement of humanity, whose inner life consists not in doubting, questioning, and denying, but in believing; who, resolute to cast off conventional errors and prejudices, are hungering and thirsting for positive truth; and who, with reliance on the fulfilment of the prophetic voice in the heart of man, and on the Universal Providence of God, look forward to an order of society founded on the divine principles of justice and love, to a future age of happiness, harmony, and of great glory to be realized on earth.

We have attained, in our own minds, to firm and clear convictions, in regard to the problem of human destiny; we believe that principles are now in operation, which will produce as great a change on the face of society, as that which caused beauty and order to arise from the chaos of the primitive creation by the movings of the divine Spirit;

and to impart these convictions and principles to the hearts of our readers, will be our leading purpose in the columns of this paper.

It will be, then, in the light of positive ideas, not of fanciful conceptions, that we shall criticise the current literature, the political movements, the social phenomena of the day; and without inquiring how far we may be in accordance with the prevailing standards of fashion or popular opinion, speak our minds on the subjects we shall discuss, with entire independence of outward authority.

Our faith in the high destiny of man is too profound to allow us to cherish the spirit of antagonism; we would not destroy but reconstruct; and if our readers expect to find in these pages, the fierce ebullitions of Jacobinical wrath, to be entertained with the virulence of invective against the evils which we condemn, or to be stimulated with the sallies of personal abuse, they will certainly be disappointed. Those who wish to indulge a taste for such condiments, must look elsewhere for its gratification. We trust that ruffian and reformer are not convertible terms;—if they be, we lay no claim to the title of the latter.

We mean to discuss all questions of public interest, with the utmost freedom, and with a single eye to the finding of the whole Truth, being well assured that the whole Truth and the highest Good, are connected in indissoluble union. But we have no desire wantonly to violate any cherished convictions, nor to maintain what is new simply because it is new.—It is our belief that there is much good, mingled with much error, in all the parties and sects both of the Church and of the State, and it is the duty of all persons who sincerely desire to aid in the progress of the human race, not to abandon themselves blindly to one particular doctrine, but to try all and to hold fast that which is good. The time has come for politicians and philanthropists to break the restraints of a barren, one-sided sectarianism, to assume some higher and broader ground, which will enable them to select the good of all partial creeds, to combine it in a consistent and glorious whole. Nor can this process degenerate into a meagre and barren Eclecticism, whenever we take our stand on the broad and universal principles, which the true science of human nature unfolds.

With a deep reverence for the Past, we shall strive so to use its transmitted treasures, as to lay in the Present, the foundation of a better Future. Our motto is, the elevation of the whole human race, in mind, morals, and manners, and the means, which in our view are alone adapted to the accomplishment of this end, are not violent outbreaks and revolutionary agitations, but orderly and progressive reform.

In Politics, it will be our object to present fair discussions of the measures of political parties, taking the principles of Justice to all men as our standard of judgment. By sympathy and conviction we are entirely democratic; our faith in democracy is hardly inferior to our faith in humanity; but by democracy we do not understand a slavish adherence to "regular nominations," nor that malignant mobocracy which would reduce to its own meanness all who aspire to nobler ends than itself, but that benevolent, exalting, and refining creed, which holds that the great object of government, should be to secure the blessings of Liberty, Intelligence, and Good Order, to the whole people. We believe in the Rights of Man,—best summed up in the right to a perfect development of his whole nature, physical, intellectual, and moral,—and shall oppose partial or class legislation, as inconsistent with the fundamental principles of Republican Institutions. Yet we shall take sides with no party, but proceed from time to time to remark upon all parties, with the frankness and independence which our position fully enables us to exercise. If our politicians take offence at what we shall say, the fault will be their own, and our only apology will be a little more severity.—Foreign politics, which are too much neglected by the journals of the country, will be regularly treated by us, in the form of well-digested reviews of the English, French, and German press.

In Literature, besides elaborate notices of new publications, with the aim to inform and improve the taste of the public, and not to gratify the cupidity of booksellers, it is our wish to keep a faithful record of literary intelligence, noticing the most important works that are issued in Europe and this country, and giving brief sketches of the matter of those most generally interesting to the American reader.

The Fine Arts too shall have due honor done them. Music, the Art most appreciable to the many, most associated with the hopes of Humanity, and most flourishing always where Humanity is most alive, we shall watch with almost jealous love; striving not only by criticism of all important musical performances, schools and publications, but also by historical and philosophical essays on the principles of the Art itself, and the creations of its master minds, to keep it true to the standard of pure taste, true to the holy end for which the passion of hearing harmonies was given to man. Painting, Sculpture, Architecture, the Drama, and all arts which seek the Good, by way of the Beautiful, will, we hope, be criticised in practice, and interpreted in theory from the same humanitary and universal point of view. For this end, we shall have correspondents in our principal cities, on whose taste and power of communication we can rely. Summaries of intelligence under this head from Europe too, from countries where Art has a home, will occasionally be offered to our readers. Musical criticism is a thing which has not hitherto existed in our country. Instead of the unmeaning praise, and petty partial censure with which all concerts are alike served up in our newspapers, we would humbly hope to contribute something, if only by our sincerity and impartiality, toward a sound and profitable criticism.

In Science, as far as the limits of a weekly newspaper permit, we shall preserve a record of the most important improvements and discoveries, considered with especial reference to their bearing on the great object of all our labors, the progressive well-being of man.

The interests of Social Reform, will be considered as paramount to all others, in whatever is admitted into the pages of the Harbinger. We shall suffer no attachment to literature, no taste for abstract discussion, no love of purely intellectual theories, to seduce us from our devotion to the cause of the oppressed, the down-trodden, the insulted and injured masses of our fellow men. Every pulsation of our being vibrates in sympathy with the wrongs of the toiling millions, and every wise effort for their speedy enfranchisement will find in us resolute and indomitable advocates. If any imagine from the literary tone of the preceding remarks, that we are indifferent to the radical movement for the benefit of the masses, which is the crowning glory of the nineteenth century, they will soon discover their egregious mistake. To that movement, consecrated by religious principle, sustained by an awful sense of justice, and cheered by the brightest hopes of future good, all our powers, talents, and attainments are devoted. We look for an audience among the refined and educated circles, to which the character of our paper will win its way; but we shall also be read by the swart and sweaty artizan; the laborer will find in us another champion; and many hearts, struggling with the secret hope which no weight of care and toil can entirely suppress, will pour on us their benedictions as we labor for the equal rights of All.

We engage in our enterprise, then, with faith in our cause, with friendship for our readers, with an exulting hope for Humanity, and with a deep conviction which long years of experience have confirmed, that every sincere endeavor for a universal end will not fail to receive a blessing from all that is greatest and holiest in the universe. In the words of the illustrious Swedenborg, which we have selected for the motto of the Harbinger, "all things, at the present day, stand provided and prepared, and await the light. The ship is in the harbor; the sails are swelling; the east wind blows; let us weigh anchor, and put forth to sea."

Source: [George Ripley], Prospectus and "Introductory Notice," *Harbinger*, 1 (14 June 1845): 16, 8–10.

1. Omitted are a list of contributors and the terms of subscribing.

Margaret Fuller

[The Wrongs of American Women. The Duty of American Women]

(30 September 1845)

JUST BECAUSE FULLER was ostensibly a literary critic for the *Tribune* did not mean she was restrained from commenting on the social scene, as this review of Charles Burdett's *Wrongs of American Women. First Series. The Elliott Family; or the Trials of New York Seamstresses* (1845) and Catharine Beecher's *The Duty of American Women to Their Country* (1845) shows.

The same day brought us a copy of Mr. Burdett's little book, in which the sufferings and difficulties that beset the large class of women who must earn their subsistence in a city like New-York are delineated with so much simplicity, feeling and exact adherence to the facts—and a printed circular containing proposals for immediate practical adoption of the plan more fully described in a book published some weeks since under the title "The Duty of American Women to their Country," which was ascribed alternately to Mrs. Stone and Miss Catherine Beecher, but of which we understand both those ladies decline the responsibility.[1] The two matters seemed linked with one another by natural piety. Full acquaintance with the wrong must call forth all manner of inventions for its redress.

The Circular, in showing the vast want that already exists of good means for instructing the children of this nation, especially in the West, states also the belief that among women, as being less immersed in other cares and toils, from the preparation it gives for their task as mothers, and from the necessity in which a great proportion stand of earning a subsistence somehow, at least during the years which precede marriage, if they *do* marry, must the number of teachers wanted be found, which is estimated already at *sixty thousand*.

We cordially sympathize with these views.

Much has been written about Woman's keeping within her sphere, which is defined as the domestic sphere. As a little girl she is to learn the lighter family duties, while she acquires that limited acquaintance with the realm of literature and science that will enable her to superintend the instruction of children in their earliest years. It is not generally proposed that she should be sufficiently instructed and developed to understand the pursuits or aims of her future husband; she is not to be a helpmeet to him, in the way of companionship or counsel, except in the care of his house and children. Her youth is to be passed partly in learning to keep house and the use of the needle, partly in the social circle where her manners may be formed, ornamental accomplishments perfected and displayed, and the husband found who shall give her the domestic sphere for which exclusively she is to be prepared.

Were the destiny of Woman thus exactly marked out, did she invariably retain the shelter of a parent's or a guardian's roof till she married, did marriage give her a sure home and protector, were she never liable to be made a widow, or, if so, sure of finding immediate protection from a brother or new husband, so that she might never be forced to stand alone one moment, and were her mind given for this world only, with no faculties capable of eternal growth and infinite improvement, we would still demand for her a far wider and more generous culture than is proposed by those who so anxiously define her sphere. We would demand it that she might not ignorantly or frivolously thwart the designs of her husband, that she might be the respected friend of her sons no less than her daughters, that she might give more refinement, elevation and attraction to the society which is needed to give the characters of *men* polish and plasticity—no less so than to save them from vicious and sensual habits. But the most fastidious critic on the departure of Woman from her sphere, can scarcely fail to see at present that a vast proportion of the sex, if not the better half, do not, CANNOT, have this domestic sphere. Thousands and scores of thousands in this country no less than in Europe are obliged to maintain themselves alone. Far greater numbers divide with their husbands the care of earning a support for the family. In England, now, the progress of society has reached so admirable a pitch that the position of the sexes is frequently reversed, and the husband is obliged to stay at home and "mind the house and bairns" while the wife goes forth to the employment she alone can secure.

We readily admit that the picture of this is most painful—that Nature made entirely an opposite distribution of functions between the sexes. We believe the natural order to be the best, and that, if it could be followed in an enlightened spirit, it would bring to Woman all she wants, no less for her immortal than her mortal destiny. We are not surprised that men, who do not look deeply or carefully at causes or tendencies, should be led by disgust at the hardened, hackneyed characters which the present state of things too often produces in women to such conclusions as they are. We, no more than they, delight in the picture of the poor woman digging in the mines in her husband's clothes. We, no more than they, delight to hear their voices shrilly raised in the market-place, whether of apples or celebrity. But we see that at present they must do as they do for bread. Hundreds and thousands must step out of that hallowed domestic sphere, with no choice but to work or steal, or belong to men, not as wives, but as the wretched slaves of sensuality.

And this transition state, with all its revolting features, indicates, we do believe, the approach of a nobler era than the world has yet known. We trust that by the stress and emergencies of the present and coming time, the minds of women will be formed to more reflection and higher purposes than heretofore—their latent powers developed, their characters strengthened and eventually beautified and harmonized. Should the state of society then be such that each may remain, as Nature seems to have intended, the tutelary genius of a home, while men manage the out-door business of life, both may be done with a wisdom, a mutual understanding and respect unknown at present. Men will be no less the gainers by this than women, finding in pure and more religious marriages the joys of friendship and love combined—in their mothers and daughters better instruction, sweeter and nobler companionship, and in society at large an excitement to their finer powers and feelings unknown at present except in the region of the fine arts.

Blest be the generous, the wise among them who seek to forward hopes like these, instead of struggling against the fiat of Providence and the march of Fate to bind down rushing Life to the standard of the Past. Such efforts are vain, but those who make them are unhappy and unwise.

It is not, however, to such that we address ourselves, but to those who seek to make the best of things as they are, while they also strive to make them better. Such persons will have seen enough of the state of things in London, Paris, New-York, and manufacturing regions every where, to feel that there is an imperative necessity, for opening more avenues of employment to women, and fitting them better to enter them, rather than keeping them back. Women have invaded many of the trades and some of the professions. Sewing, to the present killing extent, they cannot long bear. Factories seem likely to afford them permanent employment. In the culture of fruit, flowers and vegetables, even in the sale of them, we rejoice to see them engaged. In domestic service they will be aided, but can never be supplanted, by machinery. As much room as there is here for woman's mind and woman's labor will always be filled. A few have usurped the martial province, but these must always be few; the nature of woman is opposed to war. It is natural enough to see "Female Physicians," and we believe that the lace cap and work-bag are as much at home here as the wig and gold-beaded cane. In the priesthood they have from all time shared more or less—in many eras more than at the present. We believe there has been no female lawyer, and probably will be none. The pen, many of the fine arts they have made their own, and, in the more refined countries of the world, as writers, as musicians, as painters, as actors, women occupy as advantageous ground as men. Writing and music may be esteemed professions for them more than any other.

But there are two others where the demand must invariably be immense, and for which they are naturally better fitted than men, for which we should like to see them better prepared and better rewarded than they are. These are the professions of nurse to the sick and of teacher. The first of these professions we have warmly desired to see dignified. It is a noble one, now most unjustly regarded in the light of menial service. It is one which no menial, no servile nature can fitly occupy. We were rejoiced when an intelligent lady of Massachusetts made the refined heroine of a little romance select that calling. This lady (Mrs. George Lee) has looked on society with unusual largeness of spirit and healthiness of temper. She is well acquainted with the world of conventions, but sees beneath it the world of nature. She is a generous writer and unpretending, as the generous are wont to be. We do not recall the name of the tale, but the circumstance above mentioned marks its temper. We hope to see the time when the refined and cultivated will choose this profession and learn it, not only through experience under the direction of the doctor, but by acquainting themselves with the laws of matter and of mind, so that all they do shall be intelligently done, and afford them the means of developing intelligence as well as the nobler, tenderer feelings of humanity; for even the last part of the benefit they cannot receive if their work be done in a selfish or mercenary spirit.

The other profession is that of teacher, for which women are peculiarly adapted by their nature, superiority in tact, quickness of sympathy, gentleness, patience, and a clear and animated manner in narration or description. To form a good teacher should be added to this sincere modesty combined with firmness, liberal views with a power and will to liberalize them still further, a good method and habits of exact and thorough investigation. In the two last requisites women are generally deficient, but there are now many shining examples to prove that if they are immethodical and superficial as teachers it is because it is the custom so to teach them, and that when aware of these faults they can and will correct them.

The profession is of itself an excellent one for the improvement of the teacher during that interim between youth and maturity when the mind needs testing, tempering, and to review and rearrange the knowledge it has acquired. The natural method of doing this for one's self is to attempt teaching others; those years also are the best of the practical teacher. The teacher should be near the pupil both in years and feelings—no oracle, but the elder brother or sister of the pupil. More experience and years form the lecturer and the director of studies, but injure the powers as to familiar teaching.

These are just the years of leisure in the lives even of those women who are to enter the domestic sphere, and this calling most of all compatible with a constant progress as to qualifications for that.

Viewing the matter thus it may well be seen that we should hail with joy the assurance that sixty thousand *female* teachers are wanted, and more likely to be, and that a plan is projected which looks wise, liberal and generous, to afford the means of those whose hearts answer to this high calling obeying their dictates.

The plan is to have Cincinnati for a central point, where teachers shall be for a short time received, examined and prepared for their duties. By mutual agreement and cooperation of the various sects funds are to be raised and teachers provided according to the wants and tendencies of the various locations now destitute. What is to be done for them centrally, is for suitable persons to examine into their various kinds of fitness, communicate some general views whose value has been tested, and counsel adapted to the difficulties and advantages of their new positions. The Central Committee are to have the charge of raising funds and finding teachers and places where teachers are wanted.

The passage of thoughts, teachers and funds will be from East to West, the course of sunlight upon this earth.

The plan is offered as the most extensive and pliant means of doing a good, and preventing ill to this nation, by means of a national education, whose normal school shall have an invariable object in the search after truth and the diffusion of the means of knowledge, while its form shall be plastic according to the wants of the time. This normal school promises to have good effects, for it proposes worthy aims through simple means, and the motive for its formation and support seems to be disinterested philanthropy.

It promises to eschew the bitter spirit of sectarianism and proselytism, else we, for one party, could have nothing to do with it. Men, no doubt, have been oftentimes kept from absolute famine by the wheat with which such tares are mingled; but we believe the time is come when a purer and more generous food is to be offered to the people at large. We believe the aim of all education to be to rouse the mind to action, show it the means of discipline and of information; then leave it free, with God, Conscience, and the love of Truth for its guardians and teachers. Wo be to those who sacrifice these aims of universal and eternal value to the propagation of a set of opinions. But on this subject we can accept such doctrine as is offered by Rev. Calvin Stowe, one of the committee,[2] in the following passage:

> In judicious practice, I am persuaded there will seldom be any very great difficulty, especially if there be excited in the community anything like a whole-hearted honesty and enlightened sincerity in the cause of public instruction.
>
> It is all right for people to suit their own taste and convictions in respect to sect; and fair means and at proper time to teach their children and those under their influence to prefer the denominations which they prefer; but farther than this no one has any right to go. It is all wrong to hazard the well being of the soul, to jeopardize great public interests for the sake of advancing the interests of a sect. People must learn to practice some self-denial, on Christian principles, in respect to their denominational preferences, as well as in respect to other things, before pure Religion can ever gain a complete victory over every form of human selfishness.

The persons who propose themselves to the examination and instruction of the teachers at Cincinnati, till the plan shall be sufficiently under weigh to provide regularly for the office, are Mrs. Stowe and Miss Catherine Beecher, ladies well known to fame, as possessing unusual qualifications for the task.

As to finding abundance of teachers, who that reads this little book of Mr. Burdett's, or the account of the compensation of female labor in New-York, and the hopeless, comfortless, useless, pernicious lives those who have even the advantage of getting work must live with the sufferings and almost inevitable degradation to which those who cannot are exposed, but must long to match such as are capable of this better profession, and among the multitude there must be many who are or could be made so, from their present toils and make them free and the means of freedom and growth to others.

To many books on such subjects, among others to "Woman in the Nineteenth Century,"[3] the objection has been made that they exhibit ills without specifying any practical means for their remedy. The writer of the last named essay does indeed think that it contains one great rule which, if laid to heart, would prove a practical remedy for many ills, and of such daily and hourly efficacy in the conduct of life that any extensive observance of it for a single year would perceptibly raise the tone of thought, feeling and conduct throughout the civilized world. But to those who ask not only such a principle, but an external method for immediate use, we say, here is one proposed that looks noble and promising, the proposers offer themselves to the work with heart and hand, with time and purse: Go ye and do likewise.

Those who wish details as to this plan, will find them in the "Duty of American Women to their Country," published by Harper & Brothers, Cliff-st. The publishers may, probably, be able to furnish also the Circular to which we have referred. At a leisure day we shall offer some suggestions and remarks as to the methods and objects there proposed.

Source: * [Margaret Fuller], [The Wrongs of American Women. The Duty of American Women], *New-York Daily Tribune*, 30 September 1845, p. 1. Title supplied. Charles Burdett (b. 1815), New York journalist; Catharine Esther Beecher (1800–1878), educator, reformer, and the sister of the novelist Harriet Beecher Stowe (1811–1896), later author of *Uncle Tom's Cabin* (1852).

Notes

1. Lucy Stone (1818–1893), woman suffrage and antislavery reformer.
2. Reverend Calvin Stowe (1802–1866), then professor of biblical literature at Cincinnati, had married Harriet Beecher Stowe in 1836.
3. Fuller's *Woman in the Nineteenth Century* had been published in early February 1845.

POETRY

THE TRANSCENDENTALISTS argued for a type of poetry that valued inspiration over technical perfection (or genius over talent), meaning over form, a
sharp contrast to the highly structured verse of the preceding century. In a
sense, their poetic efforts may be seen as a secular version of the arguments
surrounding the miracles controversy: if we should pay attention to Jesus'
sayings rather than his deeds—to the singer and not the song—then it follows that in poetry we should value the intent and feeling of a poem over
its success in working within an established form. Emerson calls poets "liberating gods" in his "The Poet" in *Essays: Second Series* (1844), and concerning
their craft: "it is not metres, but a metre-making argument, that makes a
poem,—a thought so passionate and alive, that, like the spirit of a plant or
an animal, it has an architecture of its own, and adorns nature with a new
thing." By valuing inspiration over technique, Emerson argues, in an article
on Ellery Channing's poetry, for the acceptance of "Verses of the Portfolio,"
poetry whose characteristic is, "that not being written for publication, they
lack that finish which the conventions of literature require of authors." Thus
Emerson argues that "the failures of genius" are "better than the victories of
talent; and we are sure that some crude manuscript poems have yielded us a
more sustaining and more stimulating diet, than many elaborated and classic
productions." He would rather have a technically flawed poem that conveys
real meaning than a technically perfect poem which is beautiful and melodious but empty.

   The lack of a formal poetic credo is reflected in the various types of poetry
the Transcendentalists wrote. Generally, they tried to explore new concepts
while not completely abandoning old forms. In the best brief study of the
subject, Lawrence Buell categorizes Transcendentalist poetry in this fashion:
"sublimation of the subjectified persona and narrative-descriptive amplifica-
tion to a rhetoric of cerebral rather than visceral intensity committed to fil-
tering represented experience through the lens of philosophic or moral reflection."

   The poems reprinted here attempt to demonstrate the range of the Transcendentalist poetic experience. Those authors not yet identified are:

   William Ellery Channing II (1817–1901), nephew of the Unitarian divine,
was discovered by Emerson, who first published his poems in the *Dial* and
arranged for the publication of his first book of poetry. But Ellery Channing
was lazy and irresponsible, marrying and then abandoning Margaret Fuller's
sister and their children, and he never lived up to the promise Emerson saw
in him.

   Christopher Pearse Cranch (1813–1892) also was published in the *Dial*,
helped to edit the *Western Messenger*, and, while he wrote poetry all his

life, he went on to become a painter in the tradition of the Hudson River School and write literature for children. A talented artist, his caricatures of Transcendentalism, and especially of Emerson's writings, are still effective today.

John Sullivan Dwight (1813–1893) was a major participant in the Brook Farm community and wrote for the *Harbinger*. Generally considered one of America's earliest and best music critics, he edited *Dwight's Journal of Music* from 1852 to 1881.

Ellen Sturgis Hooper (1812–1848) participated in both Peabody's and Fuller's Conversations and, while she published a number of poems in the *Dial*, she preferred to circulate them in manuscript among her friends. Thoreau printed part of her poem "The Wood-Fire" in the "House-Warming" chapter of *Walden*. One of her daughters later married Henry Adams.

Jones Very (1813–1880) wrote his most effective verse during an eighteen-month period beginning in the fall of 1838, when he felt himself infused with the Holy Spirit. This identification with Christ (Very felt that he was a mere vehicle through which the Holy Word passed) caused him to announce to the class he was teaching at Harvard "Flee to the mountains, for the end of all things is at hand!" and he was briefly institutionalized. Yet even as Very's ecstatic poetry tries to convey a sense of his mystical experience, he still works well within the sonnet form.

William Ellery Channing

Gifts

A DROPPING shower of spray,
  Filled with a beam of light,—
The breath of some soft day,—
  The groves by wan moonlight,—
    Some rivers flow,
    Some falling snow,
Some bird's swift flight;—

A summer field o'erstrown
  With gay and laughing flowers,
And shepherd's clocks half blown,
  That tell the merry hours,—

> The waving grain,
> The spring soft rain,—
> Are these things *ours*?

The River

THERE is an inward voice, that in the stream
Sends forth its spirit to the listening ear,
And in a calm content it floweth on,
Like wisdom, welcome with its own respect.
Clear in its breast lie all these beauteous thoughts.
It doth receive the green and graceful trees,
And the gray rocks smile in its peaceful arms,
And over all floats a serenest blue,
Which the mild heaven sheds down on it like rain.
O fair, sweet stream, thy undisturbed repose
Me beckons to thy front, and thou vexed world,
Thou other turbulent sphere where I have dwelt,
Diminished into distance touch'st no more
My feelings here, than does the swaying soft,
(Made by the delicate wave parted in front,
As through the gentle element we move
Like shadows gliding through untroubled realms,)
Disturb these lily circles, these white bells.
And yet on thee shall wind come fiercely down,
Hail pelt thee with dull words, ice bind thee up;
And yet again when the fierce rage is o'er,
O smiling river, shalt thou smile once more,
And, as it were, even in thy depths revere
The sage security thy nature wears.

Sonnet XI

I LOVE the universe,—I love the joy
Of every living thing. Be mine the sure
Felicity, which ever shall endure;
While passion whirls the madmen, as they toy,

To hate, I would my simple being warm
In the calm pouring sun; and in that pure
And motionless silence, ever would employ
My best true powers, without a thought's annoy.

See and be glad! O high imperial race,
Dwarfing the common altitude of strength,
Learn that ye stand on an unshaken base;

Your powers will carry you to any length.
Up! earnestly feel the gentle sunset beams;
Be glad in woods, o'er sands,—by marsh, or streams.

Christopher Pearse Cranch

Correspondences

ALL things in nature are beautiful types to the soul that can read
    them;
Nothing exists upon earth, but for unspeakable ends,
Every object that speaks to the senses was meant for the spirit;
Nature is but a scroll; God's handwriting thereon.
Ages ago when man was pure, ere the flood overwhelmed him,
While in the image of God every soul yet lived,
Every thing stood as a letter or word of a language familiar,
Telling of truths which now only the angels can read.
Lost to man was the key of those sacred hieroglyphics,[1]
Stolen away by sin, till by heaven restored.
Now with infinite pains we here and there spell out a letter,
Here and there will the sense feebly shine through the dark.
When we perceive the light that breaks through the visible
    symbol,
What exultation is ours! *We* the discovery have made!
Yet is the meaning the same as when Adam lived sinless in Eden,
Only long hidden it slept, and now again is revealed.
Man unconsciously uses figures of speech every moment,
Little dreaming the cause why to such terms he is prone,
Little dreaming that every thing here has its own correspondence
Folded within its form, as in the body the soul.
Gleams of the mystery fall on us still, though much is forgotten,
And through our commonest speech, illumine the path of our
    thoughts.

Thus doth the lordly sun shine forth a type of the God-head;
Wisdom and love the beams that stream on a darkened world.

Thus do the sparkling waters flow, giving joy to the desert,
And the fountain of life opens itself to the thirst.
Thus doth the word of God distil like the rain and the dew-
    drops;
Thus doth the warm wind breathe like to the Spirit of God;
And the green grass and the flowers are signs of the regenera-
    tion.

O thou Spirit of Truth, visit our minds once more,
Give us to read in letters of light the language celestial
Written all over the earth, written all over the sky—
Thus may we bring our hearts once more to know our Creator,
Seeing in all things around, types of the Infinite Mind.

To the Aurora Borealis[2]

ARCTIC fount of holiest light,
Springing through the winter night,
Spreading far behind yon hill,
When the earth lies dark and still,
Rippling o'er the stars, as streams
O'er pebbled beds in sunny gleams;
O for names, thou vision fair,
To express thy splendours rare!

Blush upon the cheek of night,
Posthumous, unearthly light,
Dream of the deep sunken sun,
Beautiful, sleep-walking one,
Sister of the moonlight pale,
Star-obscuring meteor veil,
Spread by heaven's watching vestals;
Sender of the gleamy crystals
Darting on their arrowy course
From their glittering polar source,
Upward where the air doth freeze
Round the sister Pleiades;[3]—
Beautiful and rare Aurora,
In the heavens thou art their Flora,
Night-blooming Cereus of the sky,[4]
Rose of amaranthine dye,[5]
Hyacinth of purple light,
Or their Lily clad in white!

Who can name thy wondrous essence,
Thou electric phosphorescence?
Lonely apparition fire!
Seeker of the starry choir!
Restless roamer of the sky,
Who hath won thy mystery?
Mortal science hath not ran
With thee through the Empyrean,
Where the constellations cluster
Flower-like on thy branching lustre.

After all the glare and toil,
And the daylight's fretful coil,
Thou dost come so mild and still,
Hearts with love and peace to fill;
As when after revelry
With a talking company,
Where the blaze of many lights
Fell on fools and parasites,
One by one the guests have gone,
And we find ourselves alone;
Only one sweet maiden near,
With a sweet voice low and clear,
Whispering music in our ear,—
So thou talkest to the earth
After daylight's weary mirth.
Is not human fantasy,
Wild Aurora, likest thee,
Blossoming in nightly dreams,
Like thy shifting meteor-gleams?

But a better type thou art
Of the strivings of the heart,
Reaching upward from the earth
To the Soul that gave it birth.
When the noiseless beck of night
Summons out the *inner* light
That hath hid its purer ray
Through the lapses of the day—
Then like thee, thou Northern Morn,
Instincts which we deemed unborn,
Gushing from their hidden source
Mount upon their heavenward course

And the spirit seeks to be
Filled with God's eternity.

Enosis

THOUGHT is deeper than all speech,
  Feeling deeper than all thought;
Souls to souls can never teach
  What unto themselves was taught.

We are spirits clad in veils;
  Man by man was never seen;
All our deep communing fails
  To remove the shadowy screen.

Heart to heart was never known;
  Mind with mind did never meet;
We are columns left alone,
  Of a temple once complete.

Like the stars that gem the sky,
  Far apart, though seeming near,
In our light we scattered lie;
  All is thus but starlight here.

What is social company
  But a babbling summer stream?
What our wise philosophy
  But the glancing of a dream?

Only when the sun of love
  Melts the scattered stars of thought;
Only when we live above
  What the dim-eyed world hath taught;

Only when our souls are fed
  By the Fount which gave them birth,
And by inspiration led,
  Which they never drew from earth,

We like parted drops of rain
  Swelling till they meet and run,
Shall be all absorbed again,
  Melting, flowing into one.

John Sullivan Dwight

{Sweet is the Pleasure}

Sweet is the pleasure,
    Itself cannot spoil!
Is not true leisure
    One with true toil?

Thou that wouldst taste it,
    Still do thy best;
Use it, not waste it,
    Else 't is no rest.

Wouldst behold beauty
    Near thee? all round?
Only hath duty
    Such a sight found.

Rest is not quitting
    The busy career;
Rest is the fitting
    Of self to its sphere.

'T is the brook's motion,
    Clear without strife,
Fleeing to ocean
    After its life.

Deeper devotion
    Nowhere hath knelt;
Fuller emotion
    Heart never felt.

'T is loving and serving
    The Highest and Best!
'T is ONWARDS! unswerving,
    And that is true rest.

{Music}

MUSIC's the measure of the planets' motion,
    Heart-beat and rhythm of the glorious whole;
Fugue-like the streams roll, and the choral ocean

Heaves in obedience to its high control.
Thrills through all hearts the uniform vibration,
  Starting from God, and felt from sun to sun;
God gives the key-note, Love to all creation;
  Join, O my soul, and let all souls be one!

Ralph Waldo Emerson

Hymn:

SUNG AT THE COMPLETION OF THE CONCORD
MONUMENT, APRIL 19, 1836[6]

By the rude bridge that arched the flood,
  Their flag to April's breeze unfurled,
Here once the embattled farmers stood,
  And fired the shot heard round the world.

The foe long since in silence slept;
  Alike the conqueror silent sleeps;
And Time the ruined bridge has swept
  Down the dark stream which seaward creeps.

On this green bank, by this soft stream,
  We set to-day a votive stone;[7]
That memory may their deed redeem,
  When, like our sires, our sons are gone.

Spirit, that made those heroes dare
To die, or leave their children free,
Bid Time and Nature gently spare
  The shaft we raise to them and thee.

Each and All

LITTLE thinks, in the field, yon red-cloaked clown,
Of thee from the hill-top looking down;
The heifer that lows in the upland farm,
Far-heard, lows not thine ear to charm;
The sexton, tolling his bell at noon,
Deems not that great Napoleon

Stops his horse, and lists with delight,
Whilst his files sweep round yon Alpine height;
Nor knowest thou what argument
Thy life to thy neighbor's creed has lent.
All are needed by each one;
Nothing is fair or good alone.
I thought the sparrow's note from heaven,
Singing at dawn on the alder bough;
I brought him home, in his nest, at even;
He sings the song, but it pleases not now,
For I did not bring home the river and sky;—
He sang to my ear,—they sang to my eye.
The delicate shells lay on the shore;
The bubbles of the latest wave
Fresh pearls to their enamel gave;
And the bellowing of the savage sea
Greeted their safe escape to me.
I wiped away the weeds and foam,
I fetched my sea-born treasures home;
But the poor, unsightly, noisome things
Had left their beauty on the shore,
With the sun, and the sand, and the wild uproar.
The lover watched his graceful maid,
As 'mid the virgin train she strayed,
Nor knew her beauty's best attire
Was woven still by the snow-white choir.
At last she came to his hermitage,
Like the bird from the woodlands to the cage;—
The gay enchantment was undone,
A gentle wife, but fairy none.
Then I said, 'I covet truth;
Beauty is unripe childhood's cheat;
I leave it behind with the games of youth.'—
As I spoke, beneath my feet
The ground-pine curled its pretty wreath,
Running over the club-moss burrs;
I inhaled the violet's breath;
Around me stood the oaks and firs;
Pine-cones and acorns lay on the ground,
Over me soared the eternal sky,
Full of light and of deity;
Again I saw, again I heard,
The rolling river, the morning bird;—

Beauty through my senses stole;
I yielded myself to the perfect whole.

Uriel[8]

It fell in the ancient periods,
  Which the brooding soul surveys,
Or ever the wild Time coined itself
  Into calendar months and days.

This was the lapse of Uriel,
Which in Paradise befell.
Once, among the Pleiads walking,
SAID overheard the young gods talking;
And the treason, too long pent,
To his ears was evident.
The young deities discussed
Laws of form, and metre just,
Orb, quintessence, and sunbeams,
What subsisteth, and what seems.
One, with low tones that decide,
And doubt and reverend use defied,
With a look that solved the sphere,
And stirred the devils everywhere,
Gave his sentiment divine
Against the being of a line.
'Line in nature is not found;
Unit and universe are round;
In vain produced, all rays return;
Evil will bless, and ice will burn.'
As Uriel spoke with piercing eye,
A shudder ran around the sky;
The stern old war-gods shook their heads;
The seraphs frowned from myrtle-beds;
Seemed to the holy festival
The rash word boded ill to all;
The balance-beam of Fate was bent;
The bounds of good and ill were rent;
Strong Hades could not keep his own,
But all slid to confusion.
A sad self-knowledge, withering, fell
On the beauty of Uriel;
In heaven once eminent, the god

Withdrew, that hour, into his cloud;
Whether doomed to long gyration
In the sea of generation,
Or by knowledge grown too bright
To hit the nerve of feebler sight.
Straightway, a forgetting wind
Stole over the celestial kind,
And their lips the secret kept,
If in ashes the fire-seed slept.
But now and then, truth-speaking things
Shamed the angels' veiling wings;
And, shrilling from the solar course,
Or from fruit of chemic force,
Procession of a soul in matter,
Or the speeding change of water,
Or out of the good of evil born,
Came Uriel's voice of cherub scorn,
And a blush tinged the upper sky,
And the gods shook, they knew not why.

Hamatreya

MINOTT, Lee, Willard, Hosmer, Meriam, Flint[9]
Possessed the land which rendered to their toil
Hay, corn, roots, hemp, flax, apples, wool, and wood.
Each of these landlords walked amidst his farm,
Saying, ' 'Tis mine, my children's, and my name's:
How sweet the west wind sounds in my own trees!
How graceful climb those shadows on my hill!
I fancy these pure waters and the flags
Know me, as does my dog: we sympathize;
And, I affirm, my actions smack of the soil.'
Where are these men? Asleep beneath their grounds;
And strangers, fond as they, their furrows plough.
Earth laughs in flowers, to see her boastful boys
Earth-proud, proud of the earth which is not theirs;
Who steer the plough, but cannot steer their feet
Clear of the grave.
They added ridge to valley, brook to pond,
And sighed for all that bounded their domain.
'This suits me for a pasture; that's my park;
We must have clay, lime, gravel, granite-ledge,
And misty lowland, where to go for peat.

The land is well,—lies fairly to the south.
'Tis good, when you have crossed the sea and back,
To find the sitfast acres where you left them.'
Ah! the hot owner sees not Death, who adds
Him to his land, a lump of mould the more.
Hear what the Earth says:—

EARTH-SONG.

'Mine and yours;
Mine, not yours.
Earth endures;
Stars abide—
Shine down in the old sea;
Old are the shores;
But where are old men?
I who have seen much,
Such have I never seen.

'The lawyer's deed
Ran sure,
In tail,
To them, and to their heirs
Who shall succeed,
Without fail,
Forevermore.

'Here is the land,
Shaggy with wood,
With its old valley,
Mound, and flood.
But the heritors?
Fled like the flood's foam,—
The lawyer, and the laws,
And the kingdom,
Clean swept herefrom.

'They called me theirs,
Who so controlled me;
Yet every one
Wished to stay, and is gone.
How am I theirs,
If they cannot hold me,
But I hold them?'

When I heard the Earth-song,
I was no longer brave;
My avarice cooled
Like lust in the chill of the grave.

Ode,

Though loath to grieve
The evil time's sole patriot,
I cannot leave
My honied thought
For the priest's cant,
Or statesman's rant.

If I refuse
My study for their politique,
Which at the best is trick,
The angry Muse
Puts confusion in my brain.

But who is he that prates
Of the culture of mankind,
Of better arts and life?
Go, blindworm, go,
Behold the famous States
Harrying Mexico
With rifle and with knife!

Or who, with accent bolder,
Dare praise the freedom-loving mountaineer!
I found by thee, O rushing Contoocook!
And in thy valleys, Agiochook!¹⁰
The jackals of the negro-holder.

The God who made New Hampshire
Taunted the lofty land
With little men;—
Small bat and wren
House in the oak:—
If earth-fire cleave
The upheaved land, and bury the folk,
The southern crocodile would grieve.

Virtue palters; Right is hence;
Freedom praised, but hid;
Funeral eloquence
Rattles the coffin-lid.

What boots thy zeal,
O glowing friend,
That would indignant rend
The northland from the south?
Wherefore? to what good end?
Boston Bay and Bunker Hill
Would serve things still;—
Things are of the snake.

The horseman serves the horse,
The neatherd serves the neat,[11]
The merchant serves the purse,
The eater serves his meat;
'Tis the day of the chattel,
Web to weave, and corn to grind;
Things are in the saddle,
And ride mankind.

There are two laws discrete,
Not reconciled,—
Law for man, and law for thing;
The last builds town and fleet,
But it runs wild,
And doth the man unking.

'Tis fit the forest fall,
The steep be graded,
The mountain tunnelled,
The sand shaded,
The orchard planted,
The glebe tilled,[12]
The prairie granted,
The steamer built.

Let man serve law for man;
Live for friendship, live for love,
For truth's and harmony's behoof;
The state may follow how it can,
As Olympus follows Jove.

Yet do not I invite
The wrinkled shopman to my sounding woods,
Nor bid the unwilling senator
Ask votes of thrushes in the solitudes.
Every one to his chosen work;—
Foolish hands may mix and mar;
Wise and sure the issues are.
Round they roll till dark is light,
Sex to sex, and even to odd;—
The over-god
Who marries Right to Might,
Who peoples, unpeoples,—
He who exterminates
Races by stronger races,
Black by white faces,—
Knows to bring honey
Out of the lion;
Grafts gentlest scion
On pirate and Turk.

The Cossack eats Poland,
Like stolen fruit;
Her last noble is ruined,
Her last poet mute:
Straight, into double band
The victors divide;
Half for freedom strike and stand;—
The astonished Muse finds thousands at her side.

Blight

Give me truths;
For I am weary of the surfaces,
And die of inanition.[13] If I knew
Only the herbs and simples of the wood,
Rue, cinquefoil, gill, vervain, and agrimony,
Blue-vetch, and trillium, hawkweed, sassafras,
Milkweeds, and murky brakes, quaint pipes, and sundew,
And rare and virtuous roots, which in these woods
Draw untold juices from the common earth,
Untold, unknown, and I could surely spell
Their fragrance, and their chemistry apply
By sweet affinities to human flesh,

Driving the foe and stablishing the friend,—
O, that were much, and I could be a part
Of the round day, related to the sun
And planted world, and full executor
Of their imperfect functions.
But these young scholars, who invade our hills,
Bold as the engineer who fells the wood,
And travelling often in the cut he makes,
Love not the flower they pluck, and know it not,
And all their botany is Latin names.
The old man studied magic in the flowers,
And human fortunes in astronomy,
And an omnipotence in chemistry,
Preferring things to names, for these were men,
Were unitarians of the united world,
And, wheresoever their clear eye-beams fell,
They caught the footsteps of the SAME. Our eyes
Are armed, but we are strangers to the stars,
And strangers to the mystic beast and bird,
And strangers to the plant and to the mine.
The injured elements say, 'Not in us;'
And night and day, ocean and continent,
Fire, plant, and mineral say, 'Not in us,'
And haughtily return us stare for stare.
For we invade them impiously for gain;
We devastate them unreligiously,
And coldly ask their pottage, not their love.[14]
Therefore they shove us from them, yield to us
Only what to our griping toil is due;
But the sweet affluence of love and song,
The rich results of the divine consents
Of man and earth, of world beloved and lover,
The nectar and ambrosia, are withheld;
And in the midst of spoils and slaves, we thieves
And pirates of the universe, shut out
Daily to a more thin and outward rind,
Turn pale and starve. Therefore, to our sick eyes,
The stunted trees look sick, the summer short,
Clouds shade the sun, which will not tan our hay,
And nothing thrives to reach its natural term;
And life, shorn of its venerable length,
Even at its greatest space is a defeat,
And dies in anger that it was a dupe;

And, in its highest noon and wantonness,
Is early frugal, like a beggar's child;
With most unhandsome calculation taught,
Even in the hot pursuit of the best aims
And prizes of ambition, checks its hand,
Like Alpine cataracts frozen as they leaped,
Chilled with a miserly comparison
Of the toy's purchase with the length of life.

Threnody[15]

THE South-wind brings
Life, sunshine, and desire,
And on every mount and meadow
Breathes aromatic fire;
But over the dead he has no power,
The lost, the lost, he cannot restore;
And, looking over the hills, I mourn
The darling who shall not return.

I see my empty house,
I see my trees repair their boughs;
And he, the wondrous child,
Whose silver warble wild
Outvalued every pulsing sound
Within the air's cerulean round,[16]—
The hyacinthine boy,[17] for whom
Morn well might break and April bloom,—
The gracious boy, who did adorn
The world whereinto he was born,
And by his countenance repay
The favor of the loving Day,—
Has disappeared from the Day's eye;
Far and wide she cannot find him;
My hopes pursue, they cannot bind him.
Returned this day, the south wind searches,
And finds young pines and budding birches;
But finds not the budding man;
Nature, who lost him, cannot remake him;
Fate let him fall, Fate can't retake him;
Nature, Fate, Men, him seek in vain.

And whither now, my truant wise and sweet,
O, whither tend thy feet?

I had the right, few days ago,
Thy steps to watch, thy place to know;
How have I forfeited the right?
Hast thou forgot me in a new delight?
I hearken for thy household cheer,
O eloquent child!
Whose voice, an equal messenger,
Conveyed thy meaning mild.
What though the pains and joys
Whereof it spoke were toys
Fitting his age and ken,
Yet fairest dames and bearded men,
Who heard the sweet request,
So gentle, wise, and grave,
Bended with joy to his behest,
And let the world's affairs go by,
Awhile to share his cordial game,
Or mend his wicker wagon-frame,
Still plotting how their hungry ear
That winsome voice again might hear;
For his lips could well pronounce
Words that were persuasions.

Gentlest guardians marked serene
His early hope, his liberal mien;
Took counsel from his guiding eyes
To make this wisdom earthly wise.
Ah, vainly do these eyes recall
The school-march, each day's festival,
When every morn my bosom glowed
To watch the convoy on the road;
The babe in willow wagon closed,
With rolling eyes and face composed;
With children forward and behind,
Like Cupids studiously inclined;
And he the chieftain paced beside,
The centre of the troop allied,
With sunny face of sweet repose,
To guard the babe from fancied foes.
The little captain innocent
Took the eye with him as he went;
Each village senior paused to scan
And speak the lovely caravan.

From the window I look out
To mark thy beautiful parade,
Stately marching in cap and coat
To some tune by fairies played;—
A music heard by thee alone
To works as noble led thee on.

Now Love and Pride, alas! in vain,
Up and down their glances strain.
The painted sled stands where it stood;
The kennel by the corded wood;
The gathered sticks to stanch the wall
Of the snow-tower, when snow should fall;
The ominous hole he dug in the sand,
And childhood's castles built or planned;
His daily haunts I well discern,—
The poultry-yard, the shed, the barn,—
And every inch of garden ground
Paced by the blessed feet around,
From the roadside to the brook
Whereinto he loved to look.
Step the meek birds where erst they ranged;
The wintry garden lies unchanged;
The brook into the stream runs on;
But the deep-eyed boy is gone.
On that shaded day,
Dark with more clouds than tempests are,
When thou didst yield thy innocent breath
In birdlike heavings unto death,
Night came, and Nature had not thee;
I said, 'We are mates in misery.'
The morrow dawned with needless glow;
Each snowbird chirped, each fowl must crow;
Each tramper started; but the feet
Of the most beautiful and sweet
Of human youth had left the hill
And garden,—they were bound and still.
There's not a sparrow or a wren,
There's not a blade of autumn grain,
Which the four seasons do not tend,
And tides of life and increase lend;
And every chick of every bird,
And weed and rock-moss is preferred.

O ostrich-like forgetfulness!
O loss of larger in the less!
Was there no star that could be sent,
No watcher in the firmament,
No angel from the countless host
That loiters round the crystal coast,
Could stoop to heal that only child,
Nature's sweet marvel undefiled,
And keep the blossom of the earth,
Which all her harvests were not worth?
Not mine,—I never called thee mine,
But Nature's heir,—if I repine,
And seeing rashly torn and moved
Not what I made, but what I loved,
Grow early old with grief that thou
Must to the wastes of Nature go,—
'Tis because a general hope
Was quenched, and all must doubt and grope.
For flattering planets seemed to say
This child should ills of ages stay,
By wondrous tongue, and guided pen,
Bring the flown Muses back to men.
Perchance not he but Nature ailed,
The world and not the infant failed.
It was not ripe yet to sustain
A genius of so fine a strain,
Who gazed upon the sun and moon
As if he came unto his own,
And, pregnant with his grander thought,
Brought the old order into doubt.
His beauty once their beauty tried;
They could not feed him, and he died,
And wandered backward as in scorn,
To wait an æon to be born.
Ill day which made this beauty waste,
Plight broken, this high face defaced!
Some went and came about the dead;
And some in books of solace read;
Some to their friends the tidings say;
Some went to write, some went to pray;
One tarried here, there hurried one;
But their heart abode with none.
Covetous death bereaved us all,

To aggrandize one funeral.
The eager fate which carried thee
Took the largest part of me:
For this losing is true dying;
This is lordly man's down-lying,
This his slow but sure reclining,
Star by star his world resigning.

O child of paradise,
Boy who made dear his father's home,
In whose deep eyes
Men read the welfare of the times to come,
I am too much bereft.
The world dishonored thou hast left.
O truth's and nature's costly lie!
O trusted broken prophecy!
O richest fortune sourly crossed!
Born for the future, to the future lost!

THE deep Heart answered, 'Weepest thou?
Worthier cause for passion wild
If I had not taken the child.
And deemest thou as those who pore,
With aged eyes, short way before,—
Think'st Beauty vanished from the coast
Of matter, and thy darling lost?
Taught he not thee—the man of eld,
Whose eyes within his eyes beheld
Heaven's numerous hierarchy span
The mystic gulf from God to man?
To be alone wilt thou begin
When worlds of lovers hem thee in?
To-morrow, when the masks shall fall
That dizen Nature's carnival,[18]
The pure shall see by their own will,
Which overflowing Love shall fill,
'Tis not within the force of fate
The fate-conjoined to separate.
But thou, my votary, weepest thou?
I gave thee sight—where is it now?
I taught thy heart beyond the reach
Of ritual, bible, or of speech;
Wrote in thy mind's transparent table,
As far as the incommunicable;

Taught thee each private sign to raise,
Lit by the supersolar blaze.
Past utterance, and past belief,
And past the blasphemy of grief,
The mysteries of Nature's heart;
And though no Muse can these impart,
Throb thine with Nature's throbbing breast,
And all is clear from east to west.

'I came to thee as to a friend;
Dearest, to thee I did not send
Tutors, but a joyful eye,
Innocence that matched the sky,
Lovely locks, a form of wonder,
Laughter rich as woodland thunder,
That thou might'st entertain apart
The richest flowering of all art:
And, as the great all-loving Day
Through smallest chambers takes its way,
That thou might'st break thy daily bread
With prophet, Savior, and head;
That thou might'st cherish for thine own
The riches of sweet Mary's Son,
Boy-Rabbi, Israel's paragon.
And thoughtest thou such guest
Would in thy hall take up his rest?
Would rushing life forget her laws,
Fate's glowing revolution pause?
High omens ask diviner guess;
Not to be conned to tediousness.
And know my higher gifts unbind
The zone that girds the incarnate mind.
When the scanty shores are full
With Thought's perilous, whirling pool;
When frail Nature can no more,
Then the Spirit strikes the hour:
My servant Death, with solving rite,
Pours finite into infinite.

'Wilt thou freeze love's tidal flow,
Whose streams through nature circling go?
Nail the wild star to its track
On the half-climbed zodiac?
Light is light which radiates,

Blood is blood which circulates,
Life is life which generates,
And many-seeming life is one,—
Wilt thou transfix and make it none?
Its onward force too starkly pent
In figure, bone, and lineament?
Wilt thou, uncalled, interrogate,
Talker! the unreplying Fate?
Nor see the genius of the whole
Ascendant in the private soul,
Beckon it when to go and come,
Self-announced its hour of doom?
Fair the soul's recess and shrine,
Magic-built to last a season;
Masterpiece of love benign;
Fairer that expansive reason
Whose omen 'tis, and sign.
Wilt thou not ope thy heart to know
What rainbows teach, and sunsets show?
Verdict which accumulates
From lengthening scroll of human fates,
Voice of earth to earth returned,
Prayers of saints that inly burned,—
Saying, *What is excellent,*
As God lives, is permanent;
Hearts are dust, hearts' loves remain;
Heart's love will meet thee again.
Revere the Maker; fetch thine eye
Up to his style, and manners of the sky.
Not of adamant and gold
Built he heaven stark and cold;
No, but a nest of bending reeds,
Flowering grass, and scented weeds;
Or like a traveller's fleeing tent,
Or bow above the tempest bent;
Built of tears and sacred flames,
And virtue reaching to its aims;
Built of furtherance and pursuing,
Not of spent deeds, but of doing.
Silent rushes the swift Lord
Through ruined systems still restored,
Broadsowing, bleak and void to bless,
Plants with worlds the wilderness;

Waters with tears of ancient sorrow
Apples of Eden ripe to-morrow.
House and tenant go to ground,
Lost in God, in Godhead found.'

Brahma

IF the red slayer think he slays,
  Or if the slain think he is slain,
They know not well the subtle ways
  I keep, and pass, and turn again.

Far or forgot to me is near;
  Shadow and sunlight are the same;
The vanished gods to me appear;
  And one to me are shame and fame.

They reckon ill who leave me out;
  When me they fly, I am the wings;
I am the doubter and the doubt,
  And I the hymn the Brahmin sings.

The strong gods pine for my abode,
  And pine in vain the sacred Seven;
But thou, meek lover of the good!
  Find me, and turn thy back on heaven.

Days

DAMSELS of Time, the hypocritic Days,
Muffled and dumb like barefoot dervishes,
And marching single in an endless file,
Bring diadems and fagots in their hands.
To each they offer gifts after his will,
Bread, kingdoms, stars, and sky that holds them all.
I, in my pleached garden, watched the pomp,
Forgot my morning wishes, hastily
Took a few herbs and apples, and the Day
Turned and departed silent. I, too late,
Under her solemn fillet saw the scorn,[19]

Two Rivers

THY summer voice, Musketaquit,[20]
Repeats the music of the rain;

But sweeter rivers pulsing flit
Through thee, as thou through Concord Plain.

Thou in thy narrow banks art pent:
The stream I love unbounded goes
Through flood and sea and firmament;
Through light, through life, it forward flows.

I see the inundation sweet,
I hear the spending of the stream
Through years, through men, through nature fleet,
Through passion, thought, through power and dream.

Musketaquit, a goblin strong,
Of shard and flint makes jewels gay;
They lose their grief who hear his song,
And where he winds is the day of day.

So forth and brighter fares my stream,—
Who drink it shall not thirst again;
No darkness stains its equal gleam,
And ages drop in it like rain.

Terminus[21]

IT is time to be old,
To take in sail:—
The god of bounds,
Who sets to seas a shore,
Came to me in his fatal rounds,
And said: 'No more!
No farther spread
Thy broad ambitious branches, and thy root.
Fancy departs: no more invent,
Contract thy firmament
To compass of a tent.
There's not enough for this and that,
Make thy option which of two;
Economize the failing river,
Not the less revere the Giver,
Leave the many and hold the few.
Timely wise accept the terms,
Soften the fall with wary foot;
A little while

Still plan and smile,
And, fault of novel germs,
Mature the unfallen fruit.
Curse, if thou wilt, thy sires,
Bad husbands of their fires,
Who, when they gave thee breath,
Failed to bequeath
The needful sinew stark as once,
The Baresark marrow to thy bones,[22]
But left a legacy of ebbing veins,
Inconstant heat and nerveless reins,—
Amid the Muses, left thee deaf and dumb,
Amid the gladiators, halt and numb.'
As the bird trims her to the gale,
I trim myself to the storm of time,
I man the rudder, reef the sail,
Obey the voice at eve obeyed at prime:
'Lowly faithful, banish fear,
Right onward drive unharmed;
The port, well worth the cruise, is near,
And every wave is charmed.'

Margaret Fuller

To the Same. A Feverish Vision.

After a day of wearying, wasting pain,
   At last my aching eyes I think to close;—
   Hoping to win some moments of repose,
Though I must wake to suffering again.
But what delirious horrors haunt my brain!
   In a deep ghastly pit, bound down I lie,—
   About me flows a stream of crimson dye,
Amid its burning waves I strive in vain;
   Upward I stretch my arms,—aloud I cry
   In frantic anguish,—"raise me, or I die!"
When with soft eyes, beaming the tenderest love,
I see thy dear face, Anna! far above,—
By magnet drawn up to thee I seem,
And for some moments was dispelled the fever's frightful dream!—

{Leila in the Arabian zone}

Dusky, languishing and lone
  Yet full of light are her deep eyes
And her gales are lovers sighs

  Io in Egyptian clime[23]
Grows an Isis calm sublime
  Blue black is her robe of night
But blazoned o'er with points of light
  The horns that Io's brow deform
With Isis take a crescent form
  And as a holy moon inform.
The magic Sistrum arms her hand[24]
  And at her deep eye's command
  Brutes are raised to thinking men
Soul growing to her soul filled ken.

  Dian of the lonely life
  Hecate fed on gloom and strife
  Phebe on her throne of air
  Only Leila's children are.[25]

Double Triangle, Serpent and Rags

  Patient serpent, circle round,[26]
Till in death thy life is found;
  Double form of godly prime
Holding the whole thought of time,
  When the perfect two embrace,
Male & female, black & white,
  Soul is justified in space,
Dark made fruitful by the light;
  And, centred in the diamond Sun,
    —Time & Eternity are one.

{For the Power to Whom we Bow}[27]

For the Power to whom we bow
Has given its pledge that, if not now,
They of pure and stedfast mind,
By faith exalted, truth refined,
Shall hear all music loud and clear,
Whose first notes they ventured here.

Then fear not thou to wind the horn,
Though elf and gnome thy courage scorn;
Ask for the Castle's King and Queen;
Though rabble rout may rush between,
Beat thee senseless to the ground,
In the dark beset thee round;
Persist to ask and it will come,
Seek not for rest in humbler home;
So shalt thou see what few have seen,
The palace home of King and Queen.

The Sacred Marriage

And has another's life as large a scope?
It may give due fulfilment to thy hope,
And every portal to the unknown may ope.

If, near this other life, thy inmost feeling
Trembles with fateful prescience of revealing
The future Deity, time is still concealing.

If thou feel thy whole force drawn more and more
To launch that other bark on seas without a shore;
And no still secret must be kept in store;

If meannesses that dim each temporal deed,
The dull decay that mars the fleshly weed,
And flower of love that seems to fall and leave no
    seed—

Hide never the full presence from thy sight
Of mutual aims and tasks, ideals bright,
Which feed their roots to-day on all this seeming
    blight.

Twin stars that mutual circle in the heaven,
Two parts for spiritual concord given,
Twin Sabbaths that inlock the Sacred Seven;[28]

Still looking to the centre for the cause,
Mutual light giving to draw out the powers,
And learning all the other groups by cognizance of
    one another's laws:

The parent love the wedded love includes,
The one permits the two their mutual moods,

The two each other know mid myriad multitudes;

With child-like intellect discerning love,
And mutual action energizing love,
In myriad forms affiliating love.

A world whose seasons bloom from pole to pole,
A force which knows both starting-point and goal,
A Home in Heaven,—the Union in the Soul.

Flaxman[29]

We deemed the secret lost, the spirit gone,
    Which spake in Greek simplicity of thought,
    And in the forms of gods and heroes wrought
Eternal beauty from the sculptured stone—
A higher charm than modern culture won,
    With all the wealth of metaphysic lore,
    Gifted to analyze, dissect, explore.
A many-colored light flows from our sun;
Art, 'neath its beams, a motley thread has spun;
    The prison modifies the perfect day;
But thou hast known such mediums to shun,
    And cast once more on life a pure white ray.
Absorbed in the creations of thy mind,
Forgetting daily self, my truest self I find.

Meditations
Sunday, May 12, 1833

The clouds are marshalling across the sky,
Leaving their deepest tints upon yon range
Of soul-alluring hills. The breeze comes softly,
Laden with tribute that a hundred orchards
Now in their fullest blossom send, in thanks
For this refreshing shower. The birds pour forth
In heightened melody the notes of praise
They had suspended while God's voice was speaking,
And his eye flashing down upon his world.
I sigh, half-charmed, half-pained. My sense is living,
And, taking in this freshened beauty, tells
Its pleasure to the mind. The mind replies,
And strives to wake the heart in turn, repeating

Poetic sentiments from many a record
Which other souls have left, when stirred and satisfied
By scenes as fair, as fragrant. But the heart
Sends back a hollow echo to the call
Of outward things,—and its once bright companion,
Who erst would have been answered by a stream
Of life-fraught treasures, thankful to be summoned,—
Can now rouse nothing better than this echo;
Unmeaning voice, which mocks their softened accents.
Content thee, beautiful world! and hush, still busy mind!
My heart hath sealed its fountains. To the things
Of Time they shall be oped no more. Too long,
Too often were they poured forth: part have sunk
Into the desert; part profaned and swollen
By bitter waters, mixed by those who feigned
They asked them for refreshment, which, turned back,
Have broken and o'erflowed their former urns.
So when ye talk of *pleasure*, lonely world,
And busy mind, ye ne'er again shall move me
To answer ye, though still your calls have power
To jar me through, and cause dull aching *here*.

Not so the voice which hailed me from the depths
Of yon dark-bosomed cloud, now vanishing
Before the sun ye greet. It touched my centre,
The voice of the Eternal, calling me
To feel his other worlds; to feel that if
I could deserve a home, I still might find it
In other spheres,—and bade me not despair,
Though "want of harmony" and "aching void"
Are terms invented by the men of this,
Which I may not forget.
        In former times
I loved to see the lightnings flash athwart
The stooping heavens; I loved to hear the thunder
Call to the seas and mountains; for I thought
'Tis thus man's flashing fancy doth enkindle
The firmament of mind; 'tis thus his eloquence
Calls unto the soul's depths and heights; and still
I deified the creature, nor remembered
The Creator in his works.
        Ah now how different!
The proud delight of that keen sympathy

Is gone; no longer riding on the wave,
But whelmed beneath it: my own plans and works,
Or, as the Scriptures phrase it, my *"inventions"*
No longer interpose 'twixt me and Heaven.

To-day, for the first time, I felt the Deity,
And uttered prayer on hearing thunder. This
Must be thy will,—for finer, higher spirits
Have gone through this same process,—yet I think
There was religion in that strong delight,
Those sounds, those thoughts of power imparted. True,
I did not say, "He is the Lord thy God,"
But I had feeling of his essence. But
" 'Twas pride by which the angels fell." So be it!
But O, might I but see a little onward!
Father, I cannot be a spirit of power;
May I be active as a spirit of love,
Since thou hast ta'en me from that path which Nature
Seemed to appoint, O, deign to ope another,
Where I may walk with thought and hope assured;
"Lord, I believe; help thou mine unbelief!"
Had I but faith like that which fired Novalis,[30]
I too could bear that the heart "fall in ashes,"
While the freed spirit rises from beneath them,
With heavenward-look, and Phoenix-plumes upsoaring!

Sistrum

Triune, shaping, restless power,
Life-flow from life's natal hour,
No music chords are in thy sound;
By some thou'rt but a rattle found;
Yet, without thy ceaseless motion,
To ice would turn their dead devotion.
Life-flow of my natal hour,
I will not weary of thy power,
Till in the changes of thy sound
A chord's three parts distinct are found.
I will faithful move with thee,
God-ordered, self-fed energy,
Nature in eternity.

Frederic Henry Hedge

Questionings

Hath this world, without me wrought,
Other substance than my thought?
Lives it by my sense alone,
Or by essence of its own?
Will its life, with mine begun,
Cease to be when that is done,
Or another consciousness
With the self-same forms impress?

Doth yon fireball, poised in air,
Hang by my permission there?
Are the clouds that wander by,
But the offspring of mine eye,
Born with every glance I cast,
Perishing when that is past?
And those thousand, thousand eyes,
Scattered through the twinkling skies,
Do they draw their life from mine,
Or, of their own beauty shine?

Now I close my eyes, my ears,
And creation disappears;
Yet if I but speak the word,
All creation is restored.
Or—more wonderful—within,
New creations do begin;
Hues more bright and forms more rare,
Than reality doth wear,
Flash across my inward sense,
Born of the mind's omnipotence.

Soul! that all informest, say!
Shall these glories pass away?
Will those planets cease to blaze,
When these eyes no longer gaze?
And the life of things be o'er,
When these pulses beat no more?

Thought! that in me works and lives,—
Life to all things living gives,—

Art thou not thyself, perchance,
But the universe in trance?
A reflection inly flung
By that world thou fanciedst sprung
From thyself;—thyself a dream;—
Of the world's thinking thou the theme.

Be it thus, or be thy birth
From a source above the earth.
Be thou matter, be thou mind,
In thee alone myself I find,
And through thee alone, for me,
Hath this world reality.
Therefore, in thee will I live,
To thee all myself will give,
Losing still, that I may find,
This bounded self in boundless Mind.

Ellen Sturgis Hooper

{I Slept, and Dreamed that Life was Beauty}

I slept, and dreamed that life was Beauty;
I woke, and found that life was Duty.
Was thy dream then a shadowy lie?
Toil on, sad heart, courageously,
And thou shalt find thy dream to be
A noonday light and truth to thee.

{Better a Sin which Purposed Wrong to None}

Better a sin which purposed wrong to none
Than this still wintry coldness at the heart,
A penance might be borne for evil done
And tears of grief and love might ease the smart.
But this self-satisfied and cold respect
To virtue which must be its own reward,
Heaven keep us through this danger still alive,
Lead us not into greatness, heart-abhorred—

Oh God, who framed this stern New-England land,
Its clear cold waters, and its clear, cold soul,
Thou givest tropic climes and youthful hearts
Thou weighest spirits and dost all control—
Teach me to wait for all—to bear the fault
That most I hate because it is my own,
And if I fail through foul conceit of good,
Let me sin deep so I may cast no stone.

Henry David Thoreau

Inspiration

Always the general show of things
Floats in review before my mind,
And such true love and rev'rence brings
That sometimes I forget that I am blind.

But straight there comes unsought, unseen,
Some clear divine electuary,
And I who had but sensual been,
Grow sensible, and as God is am wary.

I hearing get, who had but ears,
And sight, who had but eyes before,
I moments live, who lived but years,
And truth discern, who knew but learning's lore.

I hear beyond the range of sound,
I see beyond the verge of sight,
New earths—new skies—new seas around,
And in my noon the sun doth pale his light.

More swift its bolt than lightning is,
Its voice than thunder is more loud,
It doth expand my privacies
To all, and leave me single in the crowd.

Speaking with such authority,
With so serene and lofty tone,
That idle Time runs gadding by,
And leaves me with Eternity alone.

Then chiefly is my natal hour,
And only then my prime of life,
Of manhood's strength it is the flower,
'T is peace's end and war's beginning strife.

'T hath come in summer's broadest noon,
By a grey wall, or some chance place,
Unseasoned Time, insulted June
And vexed the day with its presuming face.

Such fragrance round my sleep it makes,
More rich than are Arabian drugs,
That my soul scents its life, and wakes
The body up, beneath its perfumed rugs.

Such is the Muse, the heavenly maid,
The star that guides our mortal course,
Which shows where life's true kernel's laid,
Its wheat's fine flower, and its undying force.

Whose clear and ancient harmony
Pierces my soul through all its din,
As through its utmost melody,
Further behind than they, further within.

Who with one breath attunes the spheres,
And also my poor human heart,
With one impulse propels the years
Around, and gives my throbbing life its start.

I will not doubt forevermore,
Nor falter from an iron faith,
For if the system be turned o'er,
God takes not back the word which once he saith.

My memory I'll educate
To know the one historic truth,
Remembering to the latest date
The only true and sole immortal youth.

Be but thy inspiration given,
No matter through what dangers sought,
I'll fathom hell or climb to heaven,
And yet esteem that cheap which love has bought.

Fame cannot tempt the bard
    Who's famous with his God,

Nor laurel him reward
Who hath his maker's nod.

The Poet's Delay

IN vain I see the morning rise,
In vain observe the western blaze,
Who idly look to other skies,
Expecting life by other ways.

Amidst such boundless wealth without,
I only still am poor within,
The birds have sung their summer out,
But still my spring does not begin.

Shall I then wait the autumn wind,
Compelled to seek a milder day,
And leave no curious nest behind,
No woods still echoing to my lay?

Rumors from an Æolian Harp[31]

There is a vale which none hath seen,
Where foot of man has never been,
Such as here lives with toil and strife
An anxious and a sinful life.

There every virtue has its birth,
Ere it descends upon the earth,
And thither every deed returns,
Which in the generous bosom burns.

There love is warm, and youth is young,
And simple truth on every tongue,
For Virtue still adventures there,
And freely breathes her native air.

And ever, if you hearken well,
You still may hear its vesper bell,
And tread of high-souled men go by,
Their thoughts conversing with the sky.

Smoke

LIGHT-winged smoke, Icarian bird,[32]
Melting thy pinions in thy upward flight,

Lark without song, and messenger of dawn,
Circling above the hamlets as thy nest;
Or else, departing dream, and shadowy form
Of midnight vision, gathering up thy skirts;
By night star-veiling, and by day
Darkening the light and blotting out the sun;
Go thou my incense upward from this hearth,
And ask the Gods to pardon this clear flame.

Haze

Woof of the sun, etherial gauze,
Woven of nature's richest stuffs,
Visible heat, air-water, and dry sea;
Last conquest of the eye;
Toil of the displayed, sun-dust,
Aerial surf upon the shores of earth,
Etherial estuary, frith of light,
Breakers of air, billows of heat,
Fine summer spray on inland seas;
Bird of the sun, transparent-winged,
Owlet of noon, soft-pinioned,
From heath or stubble rising without song;
Establish thy serenity o'er the fields.

{On Fields Oer Which the Reaper's Hand has Passd}

On fields oer which the reaper's hand has passd
Lit by the harvest moon and autumn sun,
My thoughts like stubble floating in the wind
And of such fineness as October airs,
There after harvest could I glean my life
A richer harvest reaping without toil,
And weaving gorgeous fancies at my will
In subtler webs than finest summer haze.

{Brother Where Dost Thou Dwell?}

Brother where dost thou dwell?[33]
   What sun shines for thee now?
Dost thou indeed farewell?
   As we wished here below.

What season didst thou find?
    'Twas winter here.
Are not the fates more kind
    Than they appear?

Is thy brow clear again
    As in thy youthful years?
And was that ugly pain
    The summit of thy fears?

Yet thou wast cheery still,
    They could not quench thy fire,
Thou dids't abide their will,
    And then retire.

Where chiefly shall I look
    To feel thy presence near?
Along the neighboring brook
    May I thy voice still hear?

Dost thou still haunt the brink
    Of yonder river's tide?
And may I ever think
    That thou art at my side?

What bird wilt thou employ
    To bring me word of thee?
For it would give them joy,
    'Twould give them liberty,
    To serve their former lord
    With wing and minstrelsy.

A sadder strain has mixed with their song,
    They've slowlier built their nests,
Since thou art gone
    Their lively labor rests.

Where is the finch—the thrush,
    I used to hear?
Ah! they could well abide
    The dying year.

Now they no more return,
    I hear them not;
They have remained to mourn,
    Or else forgot.

{Conscience is Instinct Bred in the House}

Conscience is instinct bred in the house,
Feeling and Thinking propagate the sin
By an unnatural breeding in and in.
I say, Turn it out doors,
Into the moors.
I love a life whose plot is simple,
And does not thicken with every pimple;
A soul so sound no sickly conscience binds it,
That makes the universe no worse than 't finds it.
I love an earnest soul,
Whose mighty joy and sorrow
Are not drowned in a bowl,
And brought to life to-morrow;
That lives one tragedy,
And not seventy;
A conscience worth keeping,
Laughing not weeping;
A conscience wise and steady,
And forever ready;
Not changing with events,
Dealing in compliments;
A conscience exercised about
Large things, where one *may* doubt.
I love a soul not all of wood,
Predestinated to be good,
But true to the backbone
Unto itself alone,
And false to none;
Born to its own affairs,
Its own joys and own cares;
By whom the work which God begun
Is finished, and not undone;
Taken up where he left off,
Whether to worship or to scoff;
If not good, why then evil,
If not good god, good devil.
Goodness!—you hypocrite, come out of that,
Live your life, do your work, then take your hat.
I have no patience towards
Such conscientious cowards.
Give me simple laboring folk,

Who love their work,
Whose virtue is a song
To cheer God along.

{Low-anchored Cloud}

Low-anchored cloud,
Newfoundland air,
Fountain-head and source of rivers,
Dew cloth, dream drapery,
And napkin spread by fays;
Drifting meadow of the air,
Where bloom the daisied banks and violets,
And in whose fenny labyrinth
The bittern booms and heron wades;
Spirit of lakes and seas and rivers,
Bear only perfumes and the scent
Of healing herbs to just men's fields.

Jones Very

Nature

Nature, my love for thee is deeper far
Than strength of words though spirit-born can tell;
For while I gaze they seem my soul to bar,
That in thy widening streams would onward swell
Bearing thy mirrored beauty on my breast;
Now through thy lonely haunts unseen to glide,
A motion that scarce knows itself from rest,
With pictured flowers and branches on its tide;
Then by the noisy city's frowning wall,
Whose armed heights within its waters gleam,
To rush with answering voice to ocean's call
And mingle with the deep its swoln stream;
Whose boundless bosom's calm alone can hold
That heaven of glory in thy skies unrolled.

The Columbine[34]

Still, still my eye will gaze long-fixed on thee,
Till I forget that I am called a man,

And at thy side fast-rooted seem to be,
And the breeze comes my cheek with thine to fan;
Upon this craggy hill our life shall pass,
A life of summer days and summer joys,
Nodding our honey bells mid pliant grass
In which the bee half hid his time employs;
And here we'll drink with thirsty pores the rain,
And turn dew-sprinkled to the rising sun,
And look when in the flaming west again
His orb across the heaven its path has run;
Here, left in darkness on the rocky steep,
My weary eyes shall close like folding flowers in sleep.

The New Birth

'Tis a new life—thoughts move not as they did
With slow uncertain steps across my mind,
In thronging haste fast pressing on they bid
The portals open to the viewless wind;
That comes not, save when in the dust is laid
The crown of pride that gilds each mortal brow,
And from before man's vision melting fade
The heavens and earth—Their walls are falling now—
Fast crowding on each thought claims utterance strong,
Storm-lifted waves swift rushing to the shore
On from the sea they send their shouts along,
Back through the cave-worn rocks their thunders roar,
And I a child of God by Christ made free
Start from death's slumbers to eternity.

The Son

Father! I wait thy word—the sun doth stand,
Beneath the mingling line of night and day,
A listening servant waiting thy command
To roll rejoycing on its silent way;
The tongue of time abides the appointed hour,
Till on our ear its solemn warnings fall;
The heavy cloud withholds the pelting shower,
Then every drop speeds onward at thy call;
The bird reposes on the yielding bough
With breast unswollen by the tide of song;
So does my spirit wait thy presence now

To pour thy praise in quickening life along
Chiding with voice divine man's lengthened sleep,
While round the Unuttered Word and Love their vigils keep.

The Song

When I would sing of crooked streams and fields,
On, on from me they stretch too far and wide,
And at their look my song all powerless yields,
And down the river bears me with its tide;
Amid the fields I am a child again,
The spots that then I loved I love the more,
My fingers drop the strangely-scrawling pen,
And I remember nought but nature's lore;
I plunge me in the river's cooling wave,
Or on the embroidered bank admiring lean,
Now some endangered insect life to save,
Now watch the pictured flowers and grasses green;
Forever playing where a boy I played,
By hill and grove, by field and stream delayed.

The Soldier of the Cross

He was not armed like those of eastern clime,
Whose heavy axes felled their heathen foe;
Nor was he clad like those of later time,
Whose breast-worn cross betrayed no cross below;
Nor was he of the tribe of Levi born,
Whose pompous rites proclaim how vain their prayer;
Whose chilling words are heard at night and morn,
Who rend their robes but still their hearts would spare;
But he nor steel nor sacred robe had on,
Yet went he forth in God's almighty power;
He spoke the word whose will is ever done
From day's first dawn till earth's remotest hour;
And mountains melted from his presence down,
And hell affrighted fled before his frown.

The Dead

I see them crowd on crowd they walk the earth
Dry, leafless trees no Autumn wind laid bare;
And in their nakedness find cause for mirth,

And all unclad would winter's rudeness dare;
No sap doth through their clattering branches flow,
Whence springing leaves and blossoms bright appear;
Their hearts the living God have ceased to know,
Who gives the spring time to th'expectant year;
They mimic life, as if from him to steal
His glow of health to paint the livid cheek;
They borrow words for thoughts they cannot feel,
That with a seeming heart their tongue may speak;
And in their show of life more dead they live
Than those that to the earth with many tears they give.

The Rail Road

Thou great proclaimer to the outward eye,
Of what the spirit too would seek to tell,
Onward thou go'st, appointed from on high
The other warnings of the Lord to swell;
Thou art the voice of one that through the world
Proclaims in startling tones, "prepare the way;"
The lofty mountain from its seat is hurled,
The flinty rocks thine onward march obey;
The valleys lifted from their lowly bed
O'ertop the hills that on them frowned before,
Thou passest where the living seldom tread,
Through forests dark, where tides beneath thee roar,
And bidst man's dwelling from thy track remove,
And would with warning voice his crooked paths reprove.

The Graveyard

My heart grows sick before the wide-spread death,
That walks and speaks in seeming life around;
And I would love the corse without a breath,[35]
That sleeps forgotten 'neath the cold, cold ground;
For these do tell the story of decay,
The worm and rotten flesh hide not nor lie;
But this though dying too from day to day,
With a false show doth cheat the longing eye;
And hide the worm that gnaws the core of life,
With painted cheek and smooth deceitful skin;
Covering a grave with sights of darkness rife,
A secret cavern filled with death and sin;

And men walk o'er these graves and know it not,
For in the body's health the soul's forgot.

Flee to the Mountains

The morn is breaking see the rising sun
Has on your windows cast his burning light
Arise the day is with you onward run
Lest soon you wander lost in murky night
I will be with you 'tis your day of flight
Hasten the hour is near you cannot fly
Leave all for he who stops can never fight
The foe that shall assail him from on high
They come the plagues that none can flee
Behold the wrath of God is on you poured
Oh hasten find the rest He gives in me
And you shall fear no fear in me restored
They cannot pause oh hasten while you may
For soon shall close around thy little day.

The Eagles

The eagles gather on the place of death
So thick the ground is spotted with their wings,
The air is tainted with the noisome breath
The wind from off the field of slaughter brings;
Alas! no mourners weep them for the slain,
But all unburied lies the naked soul;
The whitening bones of thousands strew the plain,
Yet none can now the pestilence controul;
The eagles gathering on the carcase feed,
In every heart behold their half-formed prey;
The battened wills beneath their talons bleed,
Their iron beaks without remorse must slay;
Till by the sun no more the place is seen,
Where they who worshipped idol gods have been.

The Prisoner

All men around me running to and fro
Are finding life in what to me is death;
I have no limbs that where I please will go,
Nor voice that when I wish will find a breath;

Here, where I stand, my feet take fixed root;
This way or that I cannot even move;
A prisoner, ever bound both hand and foot,
While I a slave to mine own choice would prove;
'Tis hard to wait, but grant me thus set free;
And they; how narrow their short bounded lot!
My sun the centre of their worlds will be,
In systems moving where they shine forgot;
Their rays too feebly twinkling through the night,
Where I shall shine with all day's lustre bright.

On Finding the Truth

With sweet surprise, as when one finds a flower,
Which in some lonely spot, unheeded, grows;
Such were my feelings, in the favored hour,
When Truth to me her beauty did disclose.
Quickened I gazed anew on heaven and earth,
For a new glory beamed from earth and sky;
All things around me shared the second birth,
Restored with me, and nevermore to die.
The happy habitants of other spheres,
As in times past, from heaven to earth came down;
Swift fled in converse sweet the unnumbered years,
And angel-help did human weakness crown!
The former things, with Time, had passed away,
And Man, and Nature lived again for aye.

Sources: The quotations from Emerson are from "The Poet," *Essays: Second Series* (Boston: James Munroe, 1844), pp. 33, 10; "New Poetry," *Dial*, 1 (October 1840): 221, 222—and see also his "Mr. Channing's Poems," *United States Magazine and Democratic Review*, 13 (September 1843): 309–314; Buell, "The American Transcendentalist Poets," *The Columbia History of American Poetry*, ed. Jay Parini (New York: Columbia University Press, 1993), p. 119—see also R. A. Yoder, *Emerson and the Orphic Poet in America* (Berkeley: University of California Press, 1978).

William Ellery Channing, "Gifts," "The River," and "Sonnet XI," *Poems* (Boston: Charles C. Little and James Brown, 1843), pp. 45, 81–82, 151.

Christopher Pearse Cranch, "Correspondences," "To the Aurora Borealis," and "Enosis," *Poems* (Philadelphia: Carey and Hart, 1844), pp. 41–42, 48–52.

John Sullivan Dwight, [Sweet is the pleasure], *Dial*, 1 (July 1840): 22; [Music], *Harbinger*, 5 (30 October 1847): 328.

Ralph Waldo Emerson, "Hymn: Sung at the Completion of the Concord Monument, April 19, 1836," "Each and All," "Uriel," "Hamatreya," "Ode,

Inscribed to W. H. Channing," "Blight," and "Threnody," *Poems* (Boston: James Munroe, 1847), pp. 250–251, 14–16, 27–29, 53–56, 117–122, 223–226, 236, 249; "Brahma," "Days," "Two Rivers," and "Terminus," *May-Day and Other Pieces* (Boston: Ticknor and Fields, 1867), pp. 65–66, 111, 134–135, 140–142.

Margaret Fuller, "To the Same. A Feverish Vision," [Leila in the Arabian Zone], and "Double Triangle, Serpent and Rags," in Jeffrey Steele, "Freeing the 'Prisoned Queen': The Development of Margaret Fuller's Poetry," *Studies in the American Renaissance 1992*, ed. Joel Myerson (Charlottesville: University Press of Virginia, 1992), pp. 140–141, 162–163, 164–165; [For the Power to whom we bow] and "The Sacred Marriage," *Woman in the Nineteenth Century* (New York: Greeley and McElrath, 1845), pp. 164, 200–201; "Flaxman," "Meditations," and "Sistrum," *Life Without and Life Within; or, Reviews, Narratives, Essays, and Poems*, ed. Arthur B. Fuller (Boston: Brown, Taggard and Chase, 1860), pp. 371, 381–383, 413.

Frederic Henry Hedge, "Questionings," *Dial*, 1 (January 1841): 290–291.

Ellen Sturgis Hooper, [I slept, and dreamed that life was Beauty], *Dial* 1 (July 1840): 123; [Better a sin which purposed wrong to none], *Poems*, ed. Edward William Sturgis (N.p.: n.p., 1872?), n.p.

Henry David Thoreau, "Inspiration," in Elizabeth Hall Witherell, "Thoreau's Watershed Season as a Poet: The Hidden Fruits of the Summer and Fall of 1841," *Studies in the American Renaissance 1990*, ed. Joel Myerson (Charlottesville: University Press of Virginia, 1990), pp. 73–75; "The Poet's Delay" and "Rumors from an Æolian Harp," *Dial*, 3 (October 1842): 200; "Smoke" and "Haze," *Dial*, 3 (April 1843): 505–506 (where they both are under the general title "Orphics"); [On fields oer which the reaper's hand has passd], *Journal*, ed. Witherell et al., 5 vols. to date (Princeton: Princeton University Press, 1981–), 2:75; [Brother where dost thou dwell?], *Collected Poems of Henry Thoreau*, enl. ed., ed. Carl Bode (Baltimore: Johns Hopkins Press, 1964), pp. 151–152; [Conscience is instinct bred in the house] and [Low-anchored cloud], *A Week on the Concord and Merrimack Rivers* (Boston: James Munroe, 1849), pp. 79–80, 201.

Jones Very, "Nature," "The Columbine," "The New Birth," "The Son," "The Song," "The Soldier of the Cross," "The Dead," "The Rail Road," "The Graveyard," "Flee to the Mountains," "The Eagles," "The Prisoner," and "On Finding the Truth," *The Complete Poems*, ed. Helen R. Deese (Athens: University of Georgia Press, 1993), pp. 56, 61–62, 64, 66, 70, 76, 77, 88, 103, 132, 153–154, 160, 283.

Notes

1. Hieroglyphics, a pictorial writing form used by the ancient Egyptians, were first deciphered in 1822.
2. Aurora borealis, luminous atmospheric display in the Northern Hemisphere.
3. Pleiades, the seven daughters of Atlas and Pleione who were transformed into stars.

4. Cereus, a type of cactus.

5. Amaranthine, unfading.

6. This monument, which stands behind Emerson's former home, the Old Manse, commemorates the Battle of Concord, 19 April 1775.

7. Votive, to warrant or to establish, also refers to a type of hymn.

8. Uriel, "light of God" in Hebrew and one of the four archangels, was, to Milton, "Regent of the Sun" and "sharpest sighted Spirit of all in Heav'n" (*Paradise Lost*, Book 3, ll. 690–691). This poem is generally thought to represent Emerson's comments on the reception of his Divinity School Address.

9. All these are names of longtime Concord families.

10. Contoocook and Agiochook (or Mount Washington), mountains in New Hampshire.

11. Neat, cattle; neatherd, herdsman.

12. Glebe, a plot of cultivated land.

13. Inanition, emptiness.

14. Pottage, a broth or soup.

15. "Threnody" represents Emerson's attempt to come to terms with the death of his five-year old son Waldo on 27 January 1842.

16. Cerulean, blue.

17. According to Greek fable, Hyacinth, the son of a Spartan king, was beloved by the gods Apollo and Zephyr; because he preferred Apollo, Zephyr killed him, and Hyacinth's blood became a flower.

18. Dizen, dressed gayly.

19. Dervishes, whirling Muslim dancers; fagots, burning bundles of wood; pleached, interwoven; fillet, a small band used to tie the hair.

20. Musketaquit, river in Concord.

21. Terminus, Greek and Roman god of boundaries.

22. Baresark, from Berserker, a Norse warrior who fought without armor or a shirt of mail, and meaning without a protective covering.

23. Io, one of Zeus' lovers.

24. Sistrum, ancient Egyptian instrument; see also Fuller's poem of that title, printed below.

25. Dian, another name for Diana; Hecate, Greek goddess of nature; Phebe, a shepherdess.

26. An image similar to the one described in this poem may be seen as the frontispiece to Fuller's *Woman in the Nineteenth Century* (1845).

27. This poem is on the last page of the text in *Woman in the Nineteenth Century*.

28. Sacred Seven, the Pleiades (see note 3 above).

29. John Flaxman (1755–1826), English sculptor and illustrator.

30. Novalis (1772–1801), German Romantic poet.

31. Æolian harp, a stringed instrument played by the wind, popularized by the British Romantic poets.

32. Icarus, in Greek mythology, accidently flew so close to the sun that it

melted the wax with which his wings were fastened, and he plummeted to the sea.

33. Thoreau wrote this poem in memory of his brother, John Thoreau, Jr., who died suddenly in 1842, after an infection set in when he cut himself.

34. Columbine, a flower used medically as an astringent, which can cause poisoning if used in too large a dose; also the sweetheart of Harlequin, and, like him, supposed to be invisible to human eyes, from which derives the Italian word *Columbina*, a little dove or a young coquette.

35. Corse, poetic word for corpse.

Margaret Fuller

"Things and Thoughts in Europe"

(1 January 1848)

FULLER LEFT FOR Europe in the summer of 1846, writing a number of letters home for Greeley's *Tribune*. In this one, she compares democracies in the New and the Old Worlds.

This letter will reach the United States about the 1st of January; and it may not be impertinent to offer a few New-Year's reflections. Every new year, indeed, confirms the old thoughts, but also presents them under some new aspects.

The American in Europe, if a thinking mind, can only become more American. In some respects it is a great pleasure to be here. Although we have an independent political existence, our position toward Europe, as to Literature and the Arts, is still that of a colony, and one feels the same joy here that is experienced by the colonist in returning to the parent home. What was but picture to us becomes reality; remote allusions and derivations trouble no more: we see the pattern of the stuff, and understand the whole tapestry. There is a gradual clearing up on many points, and many baseless notions and crude fancies are dropped. Even the post-haste passage of the business American through the great cities, escorted by cheating couriers, and ignorant *valets de place*,[1] unable to hold intercourse with the natives of the country, and passing all his leisure hours with his countrymen, who know no more than himself, clears his mind of some mistakes— lifts some mists from his horizon.

There are three species: first, the servile American—a being utterly shallow, thoughtless, worthless. He comes abroad to spend his money and indulge his tastes. His object in Europe is to have fashionable clothes, good foreign cookery, to know some titled persons, and furnish himself with coffee-house gossip, which he wins importance at home by retailing among those less traveled, and as uninformed as himself.

I look with unspeakable contempt on this class—a class which has all the thoughtlessness and partiality of the exclusive classes in Europe, without any of their refinement, or the chivalric feeling which still sparkles among them here and there. However, though these willing serfs in a free age do some little hurt, and cause some annoyance at

541

present, it cannot last: our country is fated to a grand, independent existence, and as its laws develop, these parasites of a bygone period must wither and drop away.

Then there is the conceited American, instinctively bristling and proud of—he knows not what—He does not see, not he, that the history of Humanity for many centuries is likely to have produced results it requires some training, some devotion, to appreciate and profit by. With his great clumsy hands only fitted to work on a steam-engine, he seizes the old Cremona violin, makes it shriek with anguish in his grasp, and then declares he thought it was all humbug before he came, and now he knows it; that there is not really any music in these old things; that the frogs in one of our swamps make much finer, for *they* are young and alive. To him the etiquettes of courts and camps, the ritual of the Church, seem simply silly—and no wonder, profoundly ignorant as he is of their origin and meaning. Just so the legends which are the subjects of pictures, the profound myths which are represented in the antique marbles, amaze and revolt him; as, indeed, such things need to be judged of by another standard from that of the Connecticut Blue-Laws.[2] He criticises severely pictures, feeling quite sure that his natural senses are better means of judgment than the rules of connoisseurs—not feeling that to see such objects mental vision as well as fleshly eyes are needed, and that something is aimed at in Art beyond the imitation of the commonest forms of Nature.

This is Jonathan in the sprawling state, the booby truant, not yet aspiring enough to be a good school-boy.[3] Yet in his folly there is meaning; add thought and culture to his independence, and he will be a man of might: he is not a creature without hope, like the thick-skinned dandy of the class first specified.

The Artistes form a class by themselves. Yet among them, though seeking special aims by special means may also be found the lineaments of these two classes, as well as of the third, of which I am to speak.

3d. The thinking American—a man who, recognizing the immense advantage of being born to a new world and on a virgin soil, yet does not wish one seed from the Past to be lost. He is anxious to gather and carry back with him all that will bear a new climate and new culture. Some will dwindle; others will attain a bloom and stature unknown before. He wishes to gather them clean, free from noxious insects. He wishes to give them a fair trial in his new world. And that he may know the conditions under which he may best place them in that new world, he does not neglect to study their history in this.

The history of our planet in some moments seems so painfully mean and little, such terrible bafflings and failures to compensate some brilliant successes—such a crashing of the mass of men beneath the feet of a few, and these, too, of the least worthy—such a small drop of honey to each cup of gall, and, in many cases, so mingled, that it is never one moment in life purely tasted,—above all, so little achieved for Humanity as a whole, such tides of war and pestilence intervening to blot out the traces of each triumph, that no wonder if the strongest soul sometimes pauses aghast! No wonder if the many indolently console themselves with gross joys and frivolous prizes. Yes! those men *are* worthy of admiration who can carry this cross faithfully through fifty years; it is a great while for all the agonies that beset a lover of good, a lover of men; it makes a soul worthy of a speedier ascent, a more productive ministry in the next sphere. Blessed are they who ever keep that portion of pure, generous love with which they began life! How blessed those who have deepened the fountains, and have enough to spare for the thirst of others! Some such there are; and, feeling that, with all the excuses for failure, still only the sight of those who triumph gives a meaning to life or makes its pangs endurable, we must arise and follow.

Eighteen hundred years of this Christian culture in these European Kingdoms, a great theme never lost sight of, a mighty idea, an adorable history to which the hearts of men invariably cling, yet are genuine results rare as grains of gold in the river's sandy bed! Where is the genuine Democracy to which the rights of all men are holy? where the child-like wisdom learning all through life more and more of the will of God? where the aversion of falsehood in all its myriad disguises of cant, vanity, covetousness, so clear to be read in all the history of Jesus of Nazareth? Modern Europe is the sequel to that history, and see this hollow England, with its monstrous wealth and cruel poverty, its conventional life and low, practical aims; see this poor France, so full of talent, so adroit, yet so shallow and glossy still, which could not escape from a false position with all its baptism of blood; see that lost Poland and this Italy bound down by treacherous hands in all the force of genius; see Russia with its brutal Czar and innumerable slaves; see Austria and its royalty that represents nothing, and its people who, as people, are and have nothing! If we consider the amount of truth that has really been spoken out in the world, and the love that has beat in private hearts—how Genius has decked each spring-time with such splendid flowers, conveying each one enough of instruction in its life of harmonious energy, and how continually, unquenchably the spark of faith has striven to burst into flame and light up the Universe—the public failure seems amazing, seems monstrous.

Still Europe toils and struggles with her idea, and, at this moment, all things bode and declare a new outbreak of the fire, to destroy old palaces of crime! May it fertilize also many vineyards!—Here at this moment a successor of St. Peter, after the lapse of near two thousand years, is called "Utopian" by a part of this Europe, because he strives to get some food to the mouths of the *leaner* of his flock. A wonderful state of things, and which leaves as the best argument against despair that men do not, *cannot* despair amid such dark experiences—and thou, my country! will thou not be more true? does no greater success await thee? All things have so conspired to teach, to aid! A new world, a new chance, with oceans to wall in the new thought against interference from the old!—Treasures of all kinds, gold, silver, corn, marble, to provide for every physical need! A noble, constant, starlike soul, an Italian, led the way to its shores, and, in the first days, the strong, the pure, those too brave, too sincere for the life of the Old World hastened to people them.[4] A generous struggle then shook off what was foreign and gave the nation a glorious start for a worthy goal. Men rocked the cradle of its hopes, great, firm, disinterested men who saw, who wrote, as the basis of all that was to be done, a statement of the rights, the inborn rights of men, which, if fully interpreted and acted upon, leaves nothing to be desired.

Yet, oh Eagle, whose early flight showed this clear sight of the Sun, how often dost thou near the ground, how show the vulture in these later days! Thou wert to be the advance-guard of Humanity, the herald of all Progress; how often hast thou betrayed this high commission! Fain would the tongue in clear triumphant accents draw example from thy story, to encourage the hearts of those who almost faint and die beneath the old oppressions. But we must stammer and blush when we speak of many things. I take pride here that I may really say the Liberty of the Press works well, and that checks and balances naturally evolve from it which suffice to its government. I may say the minds of our people are alert, and that Talent has a free chance to rise. It is much. But dare I say that political ambition is not as darkly sullied as in other countries? Dare I say that men of most influence in political life are those who represent most virtue or even intellectual power? Is it easy to find names in that career of which I can speak with enthusiasm? Must I not confess in my country to a boundless lust of gain? Must I not confess to the weakest vanity, which bristles and blusters at each foolish taunt of the foreign press; and must I not admit that the men who make these undignified rejoinders seek and find popularity so? Must I not confess that there is as yet no antidote cordially adopted that will defend even that great, rich country against the evils that have grown out of the commercial system in the old world? Can

I say our social laws are generally better, or show a nobler insight into the wants of man and woman? I do, indeed, say what I believe, that voluntary association for improvement in these particulars will be the grand means for my nation to grow and give a nobler harmony to the coming age. But it is only of a small minority that I can say they as yet seriously take to heart these things; that they earnestly meditate on what is wanted for their country,—for mankind,—for our cause is, indeed, the cause of all mankind at present. Could we succeed, really succeed, combine a deep religious love with practical development, the achievements of Genius with the happiness of the multitude, we might believe Man had now reached a commanding point in his ascent, and would stumble and faint no more. Then there is this horrible cancer of Slavery, and this wicked War, that has grown out of it.[5] How dare I speak of these things here? I listen to the same arguments against the emancipation of Italy, that are used against the emancipation of our blacks; the same arguments in favor of the spoliation of Poland as for the conquest of Mexico. I find the cause of tyranny and wrong everywhere the same—and lo! my Country the darkest offender, because with the least excuse, foresworn to the high calling with which she was called,—no champion of the rights of men, but a robber and a jailer; the scourge hid behind her banner; her eyes fixed, not on the stars, but on the possessions of other men.

How it pleases me here to think of the Abolitionists! I could never endure to be with them at home, they were so tedious, often so narrow, always so rabid and exaggerated in their tone.

But, after all, they had a high motive, something eternal in their desire and life; and, if it was not the only thing worth thinking of it was really something worth living and dying for to free a great nation from such a terrible blot, such a threatening plague. God strengthen them and make them wise to achieve their purpose!

I please myself, too, with remembering some ardent souls among the American youth who, I trust, will yet expand and help to give soul to the huge, over fed, too hastily grown-up body. May they be constant. "Were Man but constant he were perfect!" it has been said; and it is true that he who could be constant to those moments in which he has been truly human—not brutal, not mechanical—is on the sure path to his perfection and to effectual service of the Universe.

It is to the youth that Hope addresses itself, to those who yet burn with aspiration, who are not hardened in their sins. But I dare not expect too much of them. I am not very old, yet of those who, in life's morning, I saw touched by the light of a high hope, many have seceded. Some have become voluptuaries; some mere family men, who think it is quite life enough to win bread for half a dozen people and treat them decently; others are lost through indolence and vacillation. Yet some remain constant. "I have witnessed many a shipwreck, yet still beat noble hearts."

I have found many among the youth of England, of France—of Italy also—full of high desire, but will they have courage and purity to fight the battle through in the sacred, the immortal band? Of some of them I believe it and await the proof. If a few succeed amid the trial, we have not lived and loved in vain.

To these, the heart of my country, a Happy New Year! I do not know what I have written. I have merely yielded to my feelings in thinking of America; but something of true love must be in these lines—receive them kindly, my friends; it is, by itself, some merit for printed words to be sincere.

Source: * [Margaret Fuller], "Things and Thoughts in Europe. No. XVIII," *New-York Daily Tribune*, 1 January 1848, p. 1.

Notes

1. *valets de place*: servants of the place.
2. Blue laws restricted activities on the Sabbath to walking back and forth to church. The name is supposedly derived from Samuel A. Peters's *General History of Connecticut* (1781), which was printed on blue paper; others believe it is based on a reading of "blue" meaning "rigidly moral."
3. Jonathan, an American (as opposed to John Bull, an Englishman).
4. Giuseppi Mazzini (1805–1872), leader of the Italian revolution of 1848.
5. A reference to the Mexican War.

Henry David Thoreau

"Resistance to Civil Government"

(1849)

THOREAU'S WORK, which appeared in the only issue of Elizabeth Peabody's *Aesthetic Papers*, is arguably the most famous essay in American literature and certainly the most influential, having been cited by Mohandas Gandhi, Martin Luther King, Jr., and others as having helped form their belief in nonviolent resistance. Although written as a lecture in response to the Mexican War, this essay has a timeless quality because it raises the question of what one should do when one feels, in opposition to the majority, that one is right, and it contextualizes the issue in an actual incident from Thoreau's life to demonstrate that being in prison is not an embarrassment, but a privilege. Depending on how one reacts to Transcendentalism, this essay can be seen as either the ultimate in Transcendental self-reliance ("any man more right than his neighbors, constitutes a majority of one") or the height of antisocial Transcendental self-importance and egotism. When the essay was included in the posthumously published *A Yankee in Canada, with Anti-Slavery and Reform Papers* (1866), the title was changed to "Civil Disobedience," but there is no evidence that this was Thoreau's preference.

I heartily accept the motto,—"That government is best which governs least;" and I should like to see it acted up to more rapidly and systematically.[1] Carried out, it finally amounts to this, which also I believe,—"That government is best which governs not at all;" and when men are prepared for it, that will be the kind of government which they will have. Government is at best but an expedient; but most governments are usually, and all governments are sometimes, inexpedient. The objections which have been brought against a standing army, and they are many and weighty, and deserve to prevail, may also at last be brought against a standing government. The standing army is only an arm of the standing government. The government itself, which is only the mode which the people have chosen to execute their will, is equally liable to be abused and perverted before the people can act through it. Witness the present Mexican war, the work of comparatively a few individuals using the standing government as their tool; for, in the outset, the people would not have consented to this measure.

This American government,—what is it but a tradition, though a recent one, endeavoring to transmit itself unimpaired to posterity, but each instant losing some of its integrity? It has not the vitality and force of a single living man; for a single man can bend it to his will. It is a sort of wooden gun to the people themselves; and, if ever they should use it in earnest as a real one against each other, it will surely split. But it is not the less necessary for this; for the people must have some complicated machinery or other, and hear its din, to satisfy that idea of government which they have. Governments show thus how successfully men can be imposed on, even impose on themselves, for their own advantage. It is excellent, we must all allow; yet this government never of itself furthered any enterprise, but by the alacrity with which it got out of its way. *It* does not keep the country free. *It* does not settle the West. *It* does not educate. The character inherent in the American people has done all that has been accomplished; and it would have done somewhat more, if the government had not sometimes got in its way. For government is an expedient by which men would fain succeed in letting one another alone; and, as has been said, when it is most expedient, the governed are most let alone by it. Trade and commerce, if they were not made of India rubber, would never manage to bounce over the obstacles which legislators are continually putting in their way; and, if one were to judge these men wholly by the effects of their actions, and not partly by their intentions, they would deserve to be classed and punished with those mischievous persons who put obstructions on the railroads.

But, to speak practically and as a citizen, unlike those who call themselves no-government men, I ask for, not at once no government, but *at once* a better government. Let every man make known what kind of government would command his respect, and that will be one step toward obtaining it.

After all, the practical reason why, when the power is once in the hands of the people, a majority are permitted, and for a long period continue, to rule, is not because they are most likely to be in the right, nor because this seems fairest to the minority, but because they are physically the strongest. But a government in which the majority rule in all cases cannot be based on justice, even as far as men understand it. Can there not be a government in which majorities do not virtually decide right and wrong, but conscience?—in which majorities decide only those questions to which the rule of expediency is applicable? Must the citizen ever for a moment, or in the least degree, resign his conscience to the legislator? Why has every man a conscience, then? I think that we should be men first, and subjects afterward. It is not desirable to cultivate a respect for the law, so much as for the right. The only obligation which I have a right to assume, is to do at any time what I think right. It is truly enough said, that a corporation has no conscience; but a corporation of conscientious men is a corporation *with* a conscience. Law never made men a whit more just; and, by means of their respect for it, even the well-disposed are daily made the agents of injustice. A common and natural result of an undue respect for law is, that you may see a file of soldiers, colonel, captain, corporal, privates, powder-monkeys and all, marching in admirable order over hill and dale to the wars, against their wills, aye, against their common sense and consciences, which makes it very steep marching indeed, and produces a palpitation of the heart. They have no doubt that it is a damnable business in which they are concerned; they are all peaceably inclined. Now, what are they? Men at all? or small moveable forts and magazines, at the service of some unscrupulous man in power? Visit the Navy Yard, and behold a marine, such a man as an American government can make, or such as it can make a man with its black arts, a mere shadow and reminiscence of human-ity, a man laid out alive and standing, and already, as one may say, buried under arms with funeral accompaniments, though it may be

> Not a drum was heard, nor a funeral note,
> As his corse to the ramparts we hurried;
> Not a soldier discharged his farewell shot
> O'er the grave where our hero we buried.[2]

The mass of men serve the State thus, not as men mainly, but as machines, with their bodies. They are the standing army, and the militia, jailers, constables, *posse comitatus*,[3] &c. In most cases there is no free exercise whatever of the judgment or of the moral sense; but they put themselves on a level with wood and earth and stones; and wooden men can perhaps be manufactured that will serve the purpose as well. Such command no more respect than men of straw, or a lump of dirt. They have the same sort of worth only as horses and dogs. Yet such as these even are commonly esteemed good citizens. Others, as most legislators, politicians, lawyers, ministers, and office-holders, serve the State chiefly with their heads; and, as they rarely make any moral distinctions, they are as likely to serve the devil, without in-tending it, as God. A very few, as heroes, patriots, martyrs, reformers in the great sense, and *men*, serve the State with their consciences also, and so necessarily resist it for the most part; and they are commonly treated by it as enemies. A wise man will only be useful as a man, and will not submit to be "clay," and "stop a hole to keep the wind away,"[4] but leave that office to his dust at least:—

> I am too high-born to be propertied,
> To be a secondary at control,
> Or useful serving-man and instrument
> To any sovereign state throughout the world.[5]

He who gives himself entirely to his fellow-men appears to them useless and selfish; but he who gives himself partially to them is pro-nounced a benefactor and philanthropist.

How does it become a man to behave toward this American gov-ernment to-day? I answer that he cannot without disgrace be associated with it. I cannot for an instant recognize that political organization as *my* government which is the *slave's* government also.

All men recognize the right of revolution; that is, the right to refuse allegiance to and to resist the government, when its tyranny or its inefficiency are great and unendurable. But almost all say that such is not the case now. But such was the case, they think, in the Revolution of '75.[6] If one were to tell me that this was a bad government because it taxed certain foreign commodities brought to its ports, it is most probable that I should not make an ado about it, for I can do without them: all machines have their friction; and possibly this does enough good to counterbalance the evil. At any rate, it is a great evil to make a stir about it. But when the friction comes to have its machine, and oppression and robbery are organized, I say, let us not have such a machine any longer. In other words, when a sixth of the population of a nation which has undertaken to be the refuge of liberty are slaves, and a whole country is unjustly overrun and conquered by a foreign army, and subjected to military law, I think that it is not too soon for honest men to rebel and revolutionize. What makes this duty the more urgent is the fact, that the country so overrun is not our own, but ours is the invading army.

Paley, a common authority with many on moral questions, in his chapter on the "Duty of Submission to Civil Government," resolves all civil obligation into expediency; and he proceeds to say, "that so long as the interest of the whole society requires it, that is, so long as the established government cannot be resisted or changed without public inconveniency, it is the will of God that the established government be obeyed, and no longer."—"This principle being admitted, the justice of every particular case of resistance is reduced to a computation of the quantity of the danger and grievance on the one side, and of the probability and expense of redressing it on the other."[7] Of this, he says, every man shall judge for himself. But Paley appears never to have contemplated those cases to which the rule of expediency does not apply, in which a people, as well as an individual, must do justice, cost what it may. If I have unjustly wrested a plank from a drowning man, I must restore it to him though I drown myself.[8] This, according to Paley, would be inconvenient. But he that would save his life, in such a case, shall lose it.[9] This people must cease to hold slaves, and to make war on Mexico, though it cost them their existence as a people.

In their practice, nations agree with Paley; but does any one think that Massachusetts does exactly what is right at the present crisis?

A drab of state, a cloth-o'-silver slut,
To have her train borne up, and her soul trail in the dirt.[10]

Practically speaking, the opponents to a reform in Massachusetts are not a hundred thousand politicians at the South, but a hundred thousand merchants and farmers here, who are more interested in commerce and agriculture than they are in humanity, and are not prepared to do justice to the slave and to Mexico, *cost what it may*. I quarrel not with far-off foes, but with those who, near at home, co-operate with, and do the bidding of those far away, and without whom the latter would be harmless. We are accustomed to say, that the mass of men are unprepared; but improvement is slow, because the few are not materially wiser or better than the many. It is not so important that many should be as good as you, as that there be some absolute goodness somewhere; for that will leaven the whole lump.[11] There are thousands who are *in opinion* opposed to slavery and to the war, who yet in effect do nothing to put an end to them; who, esteeming themselves children of Washington and Franklin, sit down with their hands in their pockets, and say that they know not what to do, and do nothing; who even postpone the question of freedom to the question of free-trade, and quietly read the prices-current along with the latest advices from Mexico, after dinner, and, it may be, fall asleep over them both. What is the price-current of an honest man and patriot to-day? They hesitate, and they regret, and sometimes they petition; but they do nothing in earnest and with effect. They will wait, well disposed, for others to remedy the evil, that they may no longer have it to regret. At most, they give only a cheap vote, and a feeble countenance and God-speed, to the right, as it goes by them. There are nine hundred and ninety-nine patrons of virtue to one virtuous man; but it is easier to deal with the real possessor of a thing than with the temporary guardian of it.

All voting is a sort of gaming, like chequers or backgammon, with a slight moral tinge to it, a playing with right and wrong, with moral questions; and betting naturally accompanies it. The character of the voters is not staked. I cast my vote, perchance, as I think right; but I am not vitally concerned that that right should prevail. I am willing to leave it to the majority. Its obligation, therefore, never exceeds that of expediency. Even voting *for the right is doing* nothing for it. It is only expressing to men feebly your desire that it should prevail. A wise man will not leave the right to the mercy of chance, nor wish it to prevail through the power of the majority. There is but little virtue in the action of masses of men. When the majority shall at length vote for the abolition of slavery, it will be because they are indifferent to slavery, or because there is but little slavery left to be abolished by their vote. *They* will then be the only slaves. Only *his* vote can hasten the abolition of slavery who asserts his own freedom by his vote.

I hear of a convention to be held at Baltimore, or elsewhere, for the selection of a candidate for the Presidency, made up chiefly of editors, and men who are politicians by profession; but I think, what is it to any independent, intelligent, and respectable man what decision they may come to, shall we not have the advantage of his wisdom and honesty, nevertheless? Can we not count upon some independent votes? Are there not many individuals in the country who do not attend conventions? But no: I find that the respectable man, so called, has immediately drifted from his position, and despairs of his country, when his country has more reason to despair of him. He forthwith adopts one of the candidates thus selected as the only *available* one, thus proving that he is himself *available* for any purposes of the demagogue. His vote is of no more worth than that of any unprincipled foreigner or hireling native, who may have been bought. Oh for a man who is a *man*, and, as my neighbor says, has a bone in his back which you cannot pass your hand through! Our statistics are at fault: the population has been returned too large. How many *men* are there to a square thousand miles in this country? Hardly one. Does not America offer any inducement for men to settle here? The American has dwindled into an Odd Fellow,[12]—one who may be known by the development of his organ of gregariousness, and a manifest lack of intellect and cheerful self-reliance; whose first and chief concern, on coming into the world, is to see that the alms-houses are in good repair; and, before yet he has lawfully donned the virile garb, to collect a fund for the support of the widows and orphans that may be; who, in short, ventures to live only by the aid of the mutual insurance company, which has promised to bury him decently.

It is not a man's duty, as a matter of course, to devote himself to the eradication of any, even the most enormous wrong; he may still properly have other concerns to engage him; but it is his duty, at least, to wash his hands of it, and, if he gives it no thought longer, not to give it practically his support. If I devote myself to other pursuits and contemplations, I must first see, at least, that I do not pursue them sitting upon another man's shoulders. I must get off him first, that he may pursue his contemplations too. See what gross inconsistency is tolerated. I have heard some of my townsmen say, "I should like to have them order me out to help put down an insurrection of the slaves, or to march to Mexico,—see if I would go;" and yet these very men have each, directly by their allegiance, and so indirectly, at least, by their money, furnished a substitute. The soldier is applauded who refuses to serve in an unjust war by those who do not refuse to sustain the unjust government which makes the war; is applauded by those whose own act and authority he disregards and sets at nought; as if the State were penitent to that degree that it hired one to scourge it while it sinned, but not to that degree that it left off sinning for a moment. Thus, under the name of order and civil government, we are all made at last to pay homage to and support our own meanness. After the first blush of sin, comes its indifference; and from immoral it becomes, as it were, *un*moral, and not quite unnecessary to that life which we have made.

The broadest and most prevalent error requires the most disinterested virtue to sustain it. The slight reproach to which the virtue of patriotism is commonly liable, the noble are most likely to incur. Those who, while they disapprove of the character and measures of a government, yield to it their allegiance and support, are undoubtedly its most conscientious supporters, and so frequently the most serious obstacles to reform. Some are petitioning the State to dissolve the Union, to disregard the requisitions of the President. Why do they not dissolve it themselves,—the union between themselves and the State,—and refuse to pay their quota into its treasury? Do not they stand in the same relation to the State, that the State does to the Union? And have not the same reasons prevented the State from resisting the Union, which have prevented them from resisting the State?

How can a man be satisfied to entertain an opinion merely, and enjoy *it?* Is there any enjoyment in it, if his opinion is that he is aggrieved? If you are cheated out of a single dollar by your neighbor, you do not rest satisfied with knowing that you are cheated, or with saying that you are cheated, or even with petitioning him to pay you your due; but you take effectual steps at once to obtain the full amount, and see that you are never cheated again. Action from principle,—the perception and the performance of right,—changes things and relations; it is essentially revolutionary, and does not consist wholly with any thing which was. It not only divides states and churches, it divides families; aye, it divides the *individual*, separating the diabolical in him from the divine.

Unjust laws exist: shall we be content to obey them, or shall we endeavor to amend them, and obey them until we have succeeded, or shall we transgress them at once? Men generally, under such a government as this, think that they ought to wait until they have persuaded the majority to alter them. They think that, if they should resist, the remedy would be worse than the evil. But it is the fault of the government itself that the remedy *is* worse than the evil. *It* makes it worse. Why is it not more apt to anticipate and provide for reform? Why does it not cherish its wise minority? Why does it cry and resist before it is hurt? Why does it not encourage its citizens to be on the alert to point out its faults, and *do* better than it would have them? Why does it always crucify Christ, and excommunicate Copernicus and Luther, and pronounce Washington and Franklin rebels?

One would think, that a deliberate and practical denial of its authority was the only offence never contemplated by government; else, why has it not assigned its definite, its suitable and proportionate penalty? If a man who has no property refuses but once to earn nine shillings for the State, he is put in prison for a period unlimited by any law that I know, and determined only by the discretion of those who placed him there; but if he should steal ninety times nine shillings from the State, he is soon permitted to go at large again.

If the injustice is part of the necessary friction of the machine of government, let it go, let it go: perchance it will wear smooth,—certainly the machine will wear out. If the injustice has a spring, or a pulley, or a rope, or a crank, exclusively for itself, then perhaps you may consider whether the remedy will not be worse than the evil; but if it is of such a nature that it requires you to be the agent of injustice to another, then, I say, break the law. Let your life be a counter friction to stop the machine. What I have to do is to see, at any rate, that I do not lend myself to the wrong which I condemn.

As for adopting the ways which the State has provided for remedying the evil, I know not of such ways. They take too much time, and a man's life will be gone. I have other affairs to attend to. I came into this world, not chiefly to make this a good place to live in, but to live in it, be it good or bad. A man has not every thing to do, but something; and because he cannot do *every thing*, it is not necessary that he should do *something* wrong. It is not my business to be petitioning the governor or the legislature any more than it is theirs to petition me; and, if they should not hear my petition, what should I do then? But in this case the State has provided no way: its very Constitution is the evil. This may seem to be harsh and stubborn and unconciliatory; but it is to treat with the utmost kindness and consideration the only spirit that can appreciate or deserves it. So is all change for the better, like birth and death which convulse the body.

I do not hesitate to say, that those who call themselves abolitionists should at once effectually withdraw their support, both in person and property, from the government of Massachusetts, and not wait till they constitute a majority of one, before they suffer the right to prevail through them. I think that it is enough if they have God on their side, without waiting for that other one. Moreover, any man more right than his neighbors, constitutes a majority of one already.

I meet this American government, or its representative the State government, directly, and face to face, once a year, no more, in the person of its tax-gatherer; this is the only mode in which a man situated as I am necessarily meets it; and it then says distinctly, Recognize me; and the simplest, the most effectual, and, in the present posture of affairs, the indispensablest mode of treating with it on this head, of expressing your little satisfaction with and love for it, is to deny it then. My civil neighbor, the tax-gatherer, is the very man I have to deal with,—for it is, after all, with men and not with parchment that I quarrel,—and he has voluntarily chosen to be an agent of the government. How shall he ever know well what he is and does as an officer of the government, or as a man, until he is obliged to consider whether he shall treat me, his neighbor, for whom he has respect, as a neighbor and well-disposed man, or as a maniac and disturber of the peace, and see if he can get over this obstruction to his neighborliness without a ruder and more impetuous thought of speech corresponding with his action? I know this well, that if one thousand, if one hundred, if ten men whom I could name,—if ten *honest* men only,—aye, if *one* HONEST man, in this State of Massachusetts, *ceasing to hold slaves*, were actually to withdraw from this co-partnership, and be locked up in the county jail therefor, it would be the abolition of slavery in America. For it matters not how small the beginning may seem to be: what is once well done is done for ever. But we love better to talk about it: that we say is our mission. Reform keeps many scores of newspapers in its service, but not one man. If my esteemed neighbor, the State's ambassador, who will devote his days to the settlement of the question of human rights in the Council Chamber, instead of being threatened with the prisons of Carolina,[13] were to sit down the prisoner of Massachusetts, that State which is so anxious to foist the sin of slavery upon her sister,—though at present she can discover only an act of inhospitality to be the ground of a quarrel with her,—the Legislature would not wholly waive the subject the following winter.

Under a government which imprisons any unjustly, the true place for a just man is also a prison. The proper place to-day, the only place which Massachusetts has provided for her freer and less desponding spirits, is in her prisons, to be put out and locked out of the State by her own act, as they have already put themselves out by their principles. It is there that the fugitive slave, and the Mexican prisoner on parole, and the Indian come to plead the wrongs of his race, should find them; on that separate, but more free and honorable ground, where the State places those who are not *with* her but *against* her,— the only house in a slave-state in which a free man can abide with honor. If any think that their influence would be lost there, and their voices no longer afflict the ear of the State, that they would not be as an enemy within its walls, they do not know by how much truth is stronger than error, nor how much more eloquently and effectively he can combat injustice who has experienced a little in his own person. Cast your whole vote, not a strip of paper merely, but your whole influence. A minority is powerless while it conforms to the majority;

it is not even a minority then; but it is irresistible when it clogs by its whole weight. If the alternative is to keep all just men in prison, or give up war and slavery, the State will not hesitate which to choose. If a thousand men were not to pay their tax-bills this year, that would not be a violent and bloody measure, as it would be to pay them, and enable the State to commit violence and shed innocent blood. This is, in fact, the definition of a peaceable revolution, if any such is possible. If the tax-gatherer, or any other public officer, asks me, as one has done, "But what shall I do?" my answer is, "If you really wish to do any thing, resign your office." When the subject has refused allegiance, and the officer has resigned his office, then the revolution is accomplished. But even suppose blood should flow. Is there not a sort of blood shed when the conscience is wounded? Through this wound a man's real manhood and immortality flow out, and he bleeds to an everlasting death. I see this blood flowing now.

I have contemplated the imprisonment of the offender, rather than the seizure of his goods,—though both will serve the same purpose,— because they who assert the purest right, and consequently are most dangerous to a corrupt State, commonly have not spent much time in accumulating property. To such the State renders comparatively small service, and a slight tax is wont to appear exorbitant, particularly if they are obliged to earn it by special labor with their hands. If there were one who lived wholly without the use of money, the State itself would hesitate to demand it of him. But the rich man—not to make any invidious comparison—is always sold to the institution which makes him rich. Absolutely speaking, the more money, the less virtue; for money comes between a man and his objects, and obtains them for him; and it was certainly no great virtue to obtain it. It puts to rest many questions which he would otherwise be taxed to answer; while the only new question which it puts is the hard but superfluous one, how to spend it. Thus his moral ground is taken from under his feet. The opportunities of living are diminished in proportion as what are called the "means" are increased. The best thing a man can do for his culture when he is rich is to endeavour to carry out those schemes which he entertained when he was poor. Christ answered the Herodians according to their condition. "Show me the tribute-money," said he;—and one took a penny out of his pocket;—If you use money which has the image of Cæsar on it, and which he has made current and valuable, that is, *if you are men of the State*, and gladly enjoy the advantages of Cæsar's government, then pay him back some of his own when he demands it; "Render therefore to Cæsar that which is Cæsar's and to God those things which are God's,"—leaving them no wiser than before as to which was which; for they did not wish to know.[14]

When I converse with the freest of my neighbors, I perceive that, whatever they may say about the magnitude and seriousness of the question, and their regard for the public tranquillity, the long and the short of the matter is, that they cannot spare the protection of the existing government, and they dread the consequences of disobedience to it to their property and families. For my own part, I should not like to think that I ever rely on the protection of the State. But, if I deny the authority of the State when it presents its tax-bill, it will soon take and waste all my property, and so harass me and my children without end. This is hard. This makes it impossible for a man to live honestly and at the same time comfortably in outward respects. It will not be worth the while to accumulate property; that would be sure to go again. You must hire or squat somewhere, and raise but a small crop, and eat that soon. You must live within yourself, and depend upon yourself, always tucked up and ready for a start, and not have many affairs. A man may grow rich in Turkey even, if he will be in all respects a good subject of the Turkish government. Confucius said,—"If a State is governed by the principles of reason, poverty and misery are subjects of shame; if a State is not governed by the principles of reason, riches and honors are the subjects of shame."[15] No: until I want the protection of Massachusetts to be extended to me in some distant southern port, where my liberty is endangered, or until I am bent solely on building up an estate at home by peaceful enterprise, I can afford to refuse allegiance to Massachusetts, and her right to my property and life. It costs me less in every sense to incur the penalty of disobedience to the State, than it would to obey. I should feel as if I were worth less in that case.

Some years ago, the State met me in behalf of the church, and commanded me to pay a certain sum toward the support of a clergyman whose preaching my father attended, but never I myself. "Pay it," it said, "or be locked up in the jail." I declined to pay. But, unfortunately, another man saw fit to pay it. I did not see why the schoolmaster should be taxed to support the priest, and not the priest the schoolmaster; for I was not the State's schoolmaster, but I supported myself by voluntary subscription. I did not see why the lyceum should not present its tax-bill, and have the State to back its demand, as well as the church. However, at the request of the selectmen, I condescended to make some such statement as this in writing:—"Know all men by these presents, that I, Henry Thoreau, do not wish to be regarded as a member of any incorporated society which I have not joined." This I gave to the town-clerk; and he has it.[16] The State, having thus learned that I did not wish to be regarded as a member of that church, has never made a like demand on me since; though it said that it must adhere to its original presumption that time. If I had known how to name them, I should then have signed off in detail from all the societies which I never signed on to; but I did not know where to find a complete list.

I have paid no poll-tax for six years. I was put into a jail once on this account, for one night; and, as I stood considering the walls of solid stone, two or three feet thick, the door of wood and iron, a foot thick, and the iron grating which strained the light, I could not help being struck with the foolishness of that institution which treated me as if I were mere flesh and blood and bones, to be locked up. I wondered that it should have concluded at length that this was the best use it could put me to, and had never thought to avail itself of my services in some way. I saw that, if there was a wall of stone between me and my townsmen, there was a still more difficult one to climb or break through, before they could get to be as free as I was. I did not for a moment feel confined, and the walls seemed a great waste of stone and mortar. I felt as if I alone of all my townsmen had paid my tax. They plainly did not know how to treat me, but behaved like persons who are underbred. In every threat and in every compliment there was a blunder; for they thought that my chief desire was to stand the other side of that stone wall. I could not but smile to see how industriously they locked the door on my meditations, which followed them out again without let or hinderance, and *they* were really all that was dangerous. As they could not reach me, they had resolved to punish my body; just as boys, if they cannot come at some person against whom they have a spite, will abuse his dog. I saw that the State was half-witted, that it was timid as a lone woman with her silver spoons, and that it did not know its friends from its foes, and I lost all my remaining respect for it, and pitied it.

Thus the State never intentionally confronts a man's sense, intellectual or moral, but only his body, his senses. It is not armed with superior wit or honesty, but with superior physical strength. I was not born to be forced. I will breathe after my own fashion. Let us see who is the strongest. What force has a multitude? They only can force me who obey a higher law than I. They force me to become like themselves. I do not hear of *men* being *forced* to live this way or that by masses of men. What sort of life were that to live? When I meet a government which says to me, "Your money or your life," why should I be in haste to give it my money? It may be in a great strait, and not know what to do: I cannot help that. It must help itself; do as I do. It is not worth the while to snivel about it. I am not responsible for the successful working of the machinery of society. I am not the son of the engineer. I perceive that, when an acorn and a chestnut fall side by side, the one does not remain inert to make way for the other, but both obey their own laws, and spring and grow and flourish as best they can, till one, perchance, overshadows and destroys the other. If a plant cannot live according to its nature, it dies; and so a man.

The night in prison was novel and interesting enough. The prisoners in their shirt-sleeves were enjoying a chat and the evening air in the door-way, when I entered. But the jailer said, "Come, boys, it is time to lock up;" and so they dispersed, and I heard the sound of their steps returning into the hollow apartments. My room-mate was introduced to me by the jailer, as "a first-rate fellow and a clever man." When the door was locked, he showed me where to hang my hat, and how he managed matters there. The rooms were whitewashed once a month; and this one, at least, was the whitest, most simply furnished, and probably the neatest apartment in the town. He naturally wanted to know where I came from, and what brought me there; and, when I had told him, I asked him in my turn how he came there, presuming him to be an honest man, of course; and, as the world goes, I believe he was. "Why," said he, "they accuse me of burning a barn; but I never did it." As near as I could discover, he had probably gone to bed in a barn when drunk, and smoked his pipe there; and so a barn was burnt. He had the reputation of being a clever man, had been there some three months waiting for his trial to come on, and would have to wait as much longer; but he was quite domesticated and contented, since he got his board for nothing, and thought that he was well treated.

He occupied one window, and I the other; and I saw, that, if one stayed there long, his principal business would be to look out the window. I had soon read all the tracts that were left there, and examined where former prisoners had broken out, and where a grate had been sawed off, and heard the history of the various occupants of that room; for I found that even here there was a history and a gossip which never circulated beyond the walls of the jail. Probably this is the only house in the town where verses are composed, which are afterward printed in a circular form, but not published. I was shown quite a long list of verses which were composed by some young men who had been de-tected in an attempt to escape, who avenged themselves by singing them.

I pumped my fellow-prisoner as dry as I could, for fear I should never see him again; but at length he showed me which was my bed, and left me to blow out the lamp.

It was like travelling into a far country, such as I had never expected to behold, to lie there for one night. It seemed to me that I never had heard the town-clock strike before, nor the evening sounds of the vil-lage; for we slept with the windows open, which were inside the grating. It was to see my native village in the light of the middle ages, and our Concord was turned into a Rhine stream, and visions of knights and castles passed before me. They were the voices of old burghers that I heard in the streets. I was an involuntary spectator and auditor of whatever was done and said in the kitchen of the adjacent village-inn,—a wholly new and rare experience to me. It was a closer view of my native town. I was fairly inside of it. I never had seen its institutions before. This is one of its peculiar institutions; for it is a shire town.[17] I began to comprehend what its inhabitants were about.

In the morning, our breakfasts were put through the hole in the door, in small oblong-square tin pans, made to fit, and holding a pint of chocolate, with brown bread, and an iron spoon. When they called for the vessels again, I was green enough to return what bread I had left; but my comrade seized it, and said that I should lay that up for lunch or dinner. Soon after, he was let out to work at haying in a neighboring field, whither he went every day, and would not be back till noon; so he bade me good-day, saying that he doubted if he should see me again.

When I came out of prison,—for some one interfered, and paid the tax,[18]—I did not perceive that great changes had taken place on the common, such as he observed who went in a youth, and emerged a tottering and gray-headed man; and yet a change had to my eyes come over the scene,—the town, and State, and country,—greater than any that mere time could effect. I saw yet more distinctly the State in which I lived. I saw to what extent the people among whom I lived could be trusted as good neighbors and friends; that their friendship was for summer weather only; that they did not greatly purpose to do right; that they were a distinct race from me by their prejudices and super-stitions, as the Chinamen and Malays are; that, in their sacrifices to humanity, they ran no risks, not even to their property; that, after all, they were not so noble but they treated the thief as he had treated them, and hoped, by a certain outward observance and a few prayers, and by walking in a particular straight though useless path from time to time, to save their souls. This may be to judge my neighbors harshly; for I believe that most of them are not aware that they have such an institution as the jail in their village.

It was formerly the custom in our village, when a poor debtor came out of jail, for his acquaintances to salute him, looking through their fingers, which were crossed to represent the grating of a jail window, "How do ye do?" My neighbors did not thus salute me, but first looked at me, and then at one another, as if I had returned from a long journey. I was put into jail as I was going to the shoemaker's to get a shoe which was mended. When I was let out the next morning, I proceeded to finish my errand, and, having put on my mended shoe, joined a huckleberry party, who were impatient to put themselves under my conduct; and in half an hour,—for the horse was soon tackled,—was in the midst of a huckleberry field, on one of our highest hills, two miles off; and then the State was nowhere to be seen.

This is the whole history of "My Prisons."[19]

I have never declined paying the highway tax, because I am as desirous of being a good neighbor as I am of being a bad subject; and, as for supporting schools, I am doing my part to educate my fellow-countrymen now. It is for no particular item in the tax-bill that I refuse to pay it. I simply wish to refuse allegiance to the State, to withdraw and stand aloof from it effectually. I do not care to trace the course of my dollar, if I could, till it buys a man, or a musket to shoot one with,—the dollar is innocent,—but I am concerned to trace the effects of my allegiance. In fact, I quietly declare war with the State, after my fashion, though I will still make what use and get what advantage of her I can, as is usual in such cases.

If others pay the tax which is demanded of me, from a sympathy with the State, they do but what they have already done in their own case, or rather they abet injustice to a greater extent than the State requires. If they pay the tax from a mistaken interest in the individual taxed, to save his property or prevent his going to jail, it is because they have not considered wisely how far they let their private feelings interfere with the public good.

This, then, is my position at present. But one cannot be too much on his guard in such a case, lest his action be biassed by obstinacy, or an undue regard for the opinions of men. Let him see that he does only what belongs to himself and to the hour.

I think sometimes, Why, this people mean well; they are only ignorant; they would do better if they knew how: why give your neighbors this pain to treat you as they are not inclined to? But I think, again, this is no reason why I should do as they do, or permit others to suffer much greater pain of a different kind. Again, I sometimes say to myself, When many millions of men, without heat, without ill-will, without personal feeling of any kind, demand of you a few shillings only, without the possibility, such is their constitution, of retracting or altering their present demand, and without the possibility, on your side, of appeal to any other millions, why expose yourself to this overwhelming brute force? You do not resist cold and hunger, the winds and the waves, thus obstinately; you quietly submit to a thousand similar necessities. You do not put your head into the fire. But just in proportion as I regard this as not wholly a brute force, but partly a human force, and consider that I have relations to those millions as to so many millions of men, and not of mere brute or inanimate things, I see that appeal is possible, first and instantaneously, from them to the Maker of them, and, secondly, from them to themselves. But, if I put my head deliberately into the fire, there is no appeal to fire or to the Maker of fire, and I have only myself to blame. If I could convince myself that I have any right to be satisfied with men as they are, and to treat them accordingly, and not according, in some respects, to my requisitions and expectations of what they and I ought to be, then, like a good Mussulman and fatalist, I should endeavor to be satisfied with things as they are, and say it is the will of God.[20] And, above all, there is this difference between resisting this and a purely brute or natural force, that I can resist this with some effect; but I cannot expect, like Orpheus, to change the nature of the rocks and trees and beasts.

I do not wish to quarrel with any man or nation. I do not wish to split hairs, to make fine distinctions, or set myself up as better than my neighbors. I seek rather, I may say, even an excuse for conforming to the laws of the land. I am but too ready to conform to them. Indeed I have reason to suspect myself on this head; and each year, as the tax-gatherer comes round, I find myself disposed to review the acts and position of the general and state governments, and the spirit of the people, to discover a pretext for conformity. I believe that the State will soon be able to take all my work of this sort out of my hands, and then I shall be no better a patriot than my fellow-countrymen. Seen from a lower point of view, the Constitution, with all its faults, is very good; the law and the courts are very respectable; even this State and this American government are, in many respects, very admirable and rare things, to be thankful for, such as a great many have described them; but seen from a point of view a little higher, they are what I have described them; seen from a higher still, and the highest, who shall say what they are, or that they are worth looking at or thinking of at all?

However, the government does not concern me much, and I shall bestow the fewest possible thoughts on it. It is not many moments that I live under a government, even in this world. If a man is thought-free, fancy-free, imagination-free, that which *is not* never for a long time appearing *to be* to him, unwise rulers or reformers cannot fatally interrupt him.

I know that most men think differently from myself; but those whose lives are by profession devoted to the study of these or kindred subjects, content me as little as any. Statesmen and legislators, standing so completely within the institution, never distinctly and nakedly behold it. They speak of moving society, but have no resting-place without it. They may be men of a certain experience and discrimination, and have no doubt invented ingenious and even useful systems, for which we sincerely thank them; but all their wit and usefulness lie within certain not very wide limits. They are wont to forget that the world is not governed by policy and expediency. Webster never goes behind government, and so cannot speak with authority about it.[21] His words are wisdom to those legislators who contemplate no essential reform in the existing government; but for thinkers, and those who legislate for all time, he never once glances at the subject. I know of those whose serene and wise speculations on this theme would soon reveal the limits of his mind's range and hospitality. Yet, compared with the cheap professions of most reformers, and the still cheaper wisdom and eloquence of politicians in general, his are almost the only sensible and valuable words, and we thank Heaven for him. Comparatively, he is always strong, original, and, above all, practical. Still his quality is not wisdom, but prudence. The lawyer's truth is not Truth, but consistency, or a consistent expediency. Truth is always in harmony with herself, and is not concerned chiefly to reveal the justice that may consist with wrong-doing. He well deserves to be called, as he has been called, the Defender of the Constitution. There are really no blows to be given by him but defensive ones. He is not a leader, but a follower. His leaders are the men of '87.[22] "I have never made an effort," he says, "and never propose to make an effort; I have never countenanced an effort, and never mean to countenance an effort, to disturb the arrangement as originally made, by which the various States came into the Union."[23] Still thinking of the sanction which the Constitution gives to slavery, he says, "Because it was a part of the original compact,—let it stand." Notwithstanding his special acuteness and ability, he is unable to take a fact out of its merely political relations, and behold it as it lies absolutely to be disposed of by the intellect,—what, for instance, it behoves a man to do here in America to-day with regard to slavery, but ventures, or is driven, to make some such desperate answer as the following, while professing to speak absolutely, and as a private man,—from which what new and singular code of social duties might be inferred?—"The manner," says he, "in which the governments of those States where slavery exists are to regulate it, is for their own consideration, under their responsibility to their constituents, to the general laws of propriety, humanity, and justice, and to God. Associations formed elsewhere, springing from a feeling of humanity, or any other cause, have nothing whatever to do with it. They have never received any encouragement from me, and they never will."[24]

They who know of no purer sources of truth, who have traced up its stream no higher, stand, and wisely stand, by the Bible and the Constitution, and drink at it there with reverence and humility; but they who behold where it comes trickling into this lake or that pool, gird up their loins once more, and continue their pilgrimage toward its fountain-head.

No man with a genius for legislation has appeared in America. They are rare in the history of the world. There are orators, politicians, and eloquent men, by the thousand; but the speaker has not yet opened his mouth to speak, who is capable of settling the much-vexed questions of the day. We love eloquence for its own sake, and not for any truth which it may utter, or any heroism it may inspire. Our legislators have not yet learned the comparative value of free-trade and of freedom, of union, and of rectitude, to a nation. They have no genius or talent for comparatively humble questions of taxation and finance, commerce and manufactures and agriculture. If we were left solely to the wordy wit of legislators in Congress for our guidance, uncorrected by the seasonable experience and the effectual complaints of the people, America would not long retain her rank among the nations. For eighteen hundred years, though perchance I have no right to say it, the New Testament has been written; yet where is the legislator who has wisdom and practical talent enough to avail himself of the light which it sheds on the science of legislation?

The authority of government, even such as I am willing to submit to,—for I will cheerfully obey those who know and can do better than I, and in many things even those who neither know nor can do so well,—is still an impure one: to be strictly just, it must have the sanction and consent of the governed. It can have no pure right over my person and property but what I concede to it. The progress from an absolute to a limited monarchy, from a limited monarchy to a democracy, is a progress toward a true respect for the individual. Is a democracy, such as we know it, the last improvement possible in government? Is it not possible to take a step further towards recognizing and organizing the rights of man? There will never be a really free and enlightened State, until the State comes to recognize the individual as a higher and independent power, from which all its own power and authority are derived, and treats him accordingly. I please myself with imagining a State at last which can afford to be just to all men, and to treat the individual with respect as a neighbor; which even would not think it inconsistent with its own repose, if a few were to live aloof from it, not meddling with it, nor embraced by it, who fulfilled all the duties of neighbors and fellow-men. A State which bore this kind of fruit, and suffered it to drop off as fast as it ripened, would prepare the way for a still more perfect and glorious State, which also I have imagined, but not yet anywhere seen.

Source: Henry David Thoreau, "Resistance to Civil Government," *Aesthetic Papers*, 1 (1849): 189–211.

Notes

1. Taken from the cover of the *United States Magazine and Democratic Review*.
2. "Burial of Sir John Moore" (1817), ll. 1–4, by Charles Wolfe (1791–1823), Irish clergyman and poet.
3. *posse comitatus*: the group of citizens who can be summoned by the police in case of a riot or emergency.
4. *Hamlet*, act 5, scene 1, ll. 236–237.
5. *King John*, act 5, scene 2, ll. 79–82.
6. The Battle of Lexington and Concord, which began the American Revolution, was on 19 April 1775.
7. Quoted from *The Principles of Moral and Political Philosophy* (1785), Chapter 3, Book 6, by William Paley (1743–1805), English cleric and Utilitarian philosopher.
8. See *De Officiis*, III, xxiii, by Cicero: "Suppose that a foolish man has seized hold of a plank from a sinking ship, shall a wise man wrest it away from him if he can?" "No," says Hecaton; "for that would be unjust."
9. Paraphrased from Matthew 10:39.
10. *The Revengers Tragedie* (1608), act 4, scene 4, by Cyril Tourneur (ca. 1575–1626), English dramatist.
11. See I Corinthians 5:6: "Your glorying is not good. Know ye not that a little leaven leaveneth the whole lump?"
12. The Independent Order of Odd Fellows, a secret fraternal society.
13. For Samuel Hoar's trip to South Carolina, see note 1 to Fuller's "New Year's Day," above.
14. Matthew 22:19–21.
15. *Analectics*, VIII, xiii.
16. Thoreau's resignation from the First Parish of Concord, dated 6 January 1841, is reproduced in facsimile on the dust jacket of his *Reform Papers*, ed. Wendell Glick (Princeton: Princeton University Press, 1973).
17. Shire town, the leading town in a county.
18. This may have been his aunt, Maria Thoreau.
19. See *Le mie prigioni* [My Prisons] (1832), by Silvio Pellico (1789–1854), Italian revolutionary.
20. Musselman, a follower of Muhammad.
21. Daniel Webster (1782–1852), statesman and orator.
22. The Men of 1787 helped frame the American Constitution.
23. From "The Admission of Texas" (delivered 22 September 1845), by Webster.
24. These extracts have been inserted since the Lecture was read. [Thoreau's note] From "Exclusion of Slavery from the Territories" (12 August 1848), by Webster.

Theodore Parker

A Sermon of the Public Function of Woman,
Preached at the Music Hall,
March 27, 1853

(1853)

IF MARGARET FULLER calls for equality for woman, then Parker wants to define the roles that woman may play after she has achieved her independence. This sermon, part of a series on the "Spiritual Development of the Human Race," is in turn one of four Parker gave in that series on "Woman," the others being on the "historical Formation of the popular Idea of Woman," the "peculiar Characteristics and the true Idea of Woman," and the "Ideal Domestic Function of Woman."

"THAT OUR DAUGHTERS MAY BE AS CORNER-STONES."
—Psalm cxliv: 12.

Last Sunday, I spoke of the Domestic Function of Woman—what she may do for the higher development of the human race at home. To-day, I ask your attention to a sermon of the Ideal Public Function of Woman, and the Economy thereof, in the higher development of the Human Race.

The domestic function of woman, as a housekeeper, wife and mother, does not exhaust her powers. Woman's function, like charity, begins at home; then, like charity, goes every where. To make one half of the human race consume all their energies in the functions of housekeeper, wife and mother, is a monstrous waste of the most precious material that God ever made.

I. In the present constitution of society, there are some unmarried women, to whom the domestic function is little, or is nothing; women who are not mothers, not wives, not housekeepers. I mean, those who are permanently unmarried. It is a great defect in the Christian civilization, that so many women and men are never married. There may be three women in a thousand to whom marriage would be disagreeable, under any possible circumstances; perhaps thirty more to whom it would be disagreeable, under the actual circumstances—in the present condition of the family and the community. But there is a large number of women who continue unmarried for no reason in their nature, from no conscious dislike of the present domestic and social condition of mankind, and from no disinclination to marriage under existing circumstances. This is a deplorable evil—alike a misfortune to man and to woman. The Catholic Church has elevated celibacy to the rank of a theological virtue, consecrating an unnatural evil: on a small scale, the results thereof are writ in the obscene faces of many a priest, false to his human nature, while faithful to his priestly vow; and on a large scale, in the vice, the infamy and degradation of woman in almost all Catholic lands.

The classic civilization of Greece and Rome had the same vice with the Christian civilization. Other forms of religion have sought to get rid of this evil by polygamy; and thereby they degraded woman still further. The Mormons are repeating the same experiment, based, not on philanthropy, but on tyranny, and are still further debasing woman under their feet. In Classic and in Christian civilization alone has there been a large class of women permanently unmarried—not united or even subordinated to man in the normal marriage of one to one, or in the abnormal conjunction of one to many. This class of unmarried women is increasing in all Christian countries, especially in those that are old and rich.

Practically speaking, to this class of women the domestic function is very little; to some of them, it is nothing at all. I do not think that this condition is to last,—marriage is writ in the soul of man, as in his body,—but it indicates a transition, it is a step forward. Womankind is advancing from that period when every woman was a slave, and marriage of some sort was guarantied to every woman, because she was dependent on man,—I say, woman is advancing from that, to a state of independence, where woman shall not be subordinated to man, but the two coördinated together. The evil that I deplore is transient in its nature, and God grant it may soon pass away!

II. That is not all. For the housekeeper, the wife and the mother, the domestic is not the only function—it is not function enough for the woman, for the human-being, more than it would be function enough for the father, for the man. After women have done all which pertains to housekeeping as a trade, to housekeeping as one of the fine arts, in their relation as wife and mother,—after they have done all for the order of the house, for the order of the husband, and the order of the children, they have still energies to spare—a reserved power for yet other work.

There are three classes of women:

First, domestic Drudges, who are wholly taken up in the material details of their housekeeping, husband-keeping, child-keeping. Their housekeeping is a trade, and no more; and after they have done that, there is no more which they can do. In New England, it is a small class, getting less every year.

Next, there are domestic Dolls, wholly taken up with the vain show which delights the eye and the ear. They are ornaments of the estate. Similar toys, I suppose, will one day be more cheaply manufactured at Paris and Nürnberg, at Frankfort-on-the-Maine, and other toy shops of Europe, out of wax and papier maché, and sold in Boston at the haberdasher's, by the dozen. These ask nothing beyond their function as dolls, and hate all attempts to elevate womankind.

But there are domestic Women, who order a house and are not mere drudges, adorn it, and are not mere dolls, but Women. Some of these—a great many of them—conjoin the useful of the drudge and the beautiful of the doll into one Womanhood, and have a great deal left besides. They are not wholly taken up with their function as housekeeper, wife and mother.

In the progress of mankind, and the application of masculine science to what was once only feminine work,—whereby so much time is saved from the wheel and the loom, the oven and the spit,—with the consequent increase of riches, the saving of time, and the intellectual education which comes in consequence thereof, this class of women is continually enlarging. With us in New England, in all the North, it is a very large class.

Well, what shall these domestic women do with their spare energies and superfluous power! Once, a malicious proverb said—"The shoemaker must not go beyond his last."[1] Every shoemaker looks on that proverb with appropriate contempt. He is a shoemaker; but he was a man first, a shoemaker next. Shoemaking is an accident of his manhood, not manhood an accident of his shoemaking. You know what haughty scorn the writer of the apochryphal book of Ecclesiasticus pours out on every farmer, "who glorieth in the goad"[2]—every carpenter and blacksmith, every jeweller and potter. They shall not be sought for, says this aristocrat, in the public councils; they shall not sit high in the congregation; they shall not sit in the judges' seat, nor understand the sentence of judgment; they cannot declare justice. Aristotle and Cicero thought no better of the merchants; they were only busy in trading. Miserable people! quoth these great men, what have they to do with affairs of state—merchants, mechanics, farmers? It is only for kings, nobles, and famous rich men, who do no business, but keep slaves! Still, a great many men at this day have just the same esteem for women that those haughty persons of whom I have spoken had for mechanics and for merchants. A great many sour proverbs there are, which look the same way. But, just now, such is the intellectual education of women of the richer class in all our large towns, that these sour proverbs will not go down so well as of old. Even in Boston, spite of the attempts of the city government to prevent the higher public education of women—diligently persisted in for many years— the young women of wealthy families get a better education than the young men of wealthy families do; and that fact is going to report itself presently. The best educated young men are commonly poor men's sons; but the best educated young women are quite uniformly rich men's daughters.

A well-educated young woman, fond of Goethe, and Dante, and Shakspeare, and Cervantes,[3] marrying an ill-educated young man, who cares for nothing but his horse, his cigar and his bottle—who only knows how to sleep after dinner, a "great heap of husband," curled up on the sofa, and in the evening can only laugh at a play, and not understand the Italian words of an opera, which his wife knows by heart;—she, I say, marrying him, will not accept the idea that he is her natural lord and master; she cannot look up to him, but rather down. The domestic function does not consume all her time or talent. She knows how to perform much of her household work as a manufacturer weaves cotton, or spins hemp, or forges iron, with other machinery, by other hands. She is the housekeeping head; and after she has kept house as wife and as mother, and has done all, she has still energies to spare.

That is a large class of women; it is a great deal larger than men commonly think it is. It is continually enlarging, and you see why. When all manufacturers were domestic,—when every garment was made at home, every web wove at home, every thread spun at home, every fleece dyed at home—when the husband provided the wool or the sheepskin, and the wife made it a coat—when the husband brought home a sack of corn on a mule's back, and the wife pounded it in a mortar, or ground it between two stones, as in the Old Testament—then the domestic function might well consume all the time of a very able-headed woman. But now-a-days, when so much work is done abroad—when the flour mills of Rochester and Boston take the place of the pestle and mortar, and the hand-mill of the Old Testament—when Lowell and Lawrence are two enormous Old Testament women, spinning and weaving year out and year in, day and night both[4]—when so much of woman's work is done by the butcher and the baker; by the tailor and the cook and the gas-maker, and she is no longer obliged to dip or mould with her own hands every candle that "goeth not out by night," as in the Old Testament woman's housekeeping[5]—you see how very much of woman's time is left for other functions. This will become yet more the case. Ere long, a great deal of lofty science will be applied to housekeeping, and work be done by other than human hands, in the house, as out of it. And accordingly, you see that the class of women not wholly taken up by the domestic function will get larger and larger.

III. Then, there is a third class of women, who have no taste and no talent for the domestic function. Perhaps these are exceptional women; some of them exceptional by redundance—they have talents not needed in this function; others are exceptional by defect—with only a common talent, they have none for housekeeping. It is as cruel a lot to set these persons to such work, as it would be to take a born sailor and make him a farmer, or to take a man who is born to drive oxen, delights to give the kine[6] fodder, and has a genius for it, and shut him up in the forecastle of a ship. Who would think of making Jenny Lind nothing but a housekeeper? or of devoting Madame de Stael or Miss Dix wholly to that function? or a dozen other women that any man can name.[7]

IV. Then there is another class of women—those who are not married yet, but are to be married. They, likewise, have spare time on their hands, which they know not what to do with. Women of this latter class have sometimes asked me what there was for them to do? I could not tell.

All these four put together, make up a large class of women, who need some other function beside the domestic. What shall it be? In the middle ages, when the Catholic Church held its iron hand over the world, these women went into the Church. The permanently unmarried, getting dissatisfied, became nuns;—often calling that a virtue which was only a necessity,—making a religious principle out of an involuntary measure. Others voluntarily went thither. The attempt is making anew in England, by some of the most pious people, to revive the scheme. It failed a thousand years ago, and the experiment brought a curse on man. It will always fail; and it ought to fail. Human nature cries out against it.

Let us look, and see what women may do here.

First, there are Intellectual Pursuits—devotion to science, art, literature, and the like.

Well, in the first place, that is not popular. Learned women are met with ridicule; they are bid to mend their husband's garments, or their own; they are treated with scorn. Foolish young man number one, in a liquor shop, of a morning, knocks off the ashes from the end of his cigar, and says to foolish young man number two, who is taking soda to wash off the effect of last night's debauch, or preparing for a similar necessity to-morrow morning—in the presence of foolish young man number three, four, five, six, and so on indefinitely—"I do not like learned young women; they puzzle me." So they do; puzzle him very much. I once heard a foolish young man, full of self-conceit and his father's claret, say,—"I had rather have a young woman ask me to waltz, than to explain an allusion in Dante." Very likely; he had studied waltzing, and not Dante. And his mother, full of conceit and her own hyson,[8] said,—"I perfectly agree with you. My father said that women had nothing to do with learning." Accordingly, he gave her none, and that explained the counsel.

Then, too, foolish men, no longer young, say the same thing, and seek to bring down their wives and daughters to their own poor mediocrity of wit and inferiority of culture.

I say, this intellectual calling is not popular. I am sorry it is not; but even if it were, it is not wholly satisfactory—it suits but a few. In the present stage of human development, there are not many men who are satisfied with a merely intellectual calling; they want something practical, as well as speculative. There are a thousand practical shoemakers to every speculative botanist. It will be so for many years to come. There are ten thousand carpenters to a single poet or philosopher, who dignifies his nature with song or with science. See how dissatisfied our most eminent intellectual men become with science and literature. A Professor of Greek is sorry he was not a Surveyor or Engineer; the President of a College longs to be a Member of Congress; the most accomplished scholars, historians, romancers,—they wish to be Collectors at Boston, Consuls at Liverpool, and the like,—longing for some practical calling, where they can make their thought a thing. Of the intellectual men whom I know, I can count on the fingers of a single hand all that are satisfied with pure science, pure art, pure literature.

Woman, like man, wants to make her thought a thing; at least, wants things to work her pattern of thought upon. Still, as the world grows older, and wiser, and better, more persons will find an abiding satisfaction in these lofty pursuits. I am rejoiced to see women thus attracted thitherward. Some women there are who find an abiding satisfaction in literature; it fills up their leisure. I rejoice that it is so.

Then there are next, the various Philanthropies of the age. In these, the spare energies of woman have always found a congenial sphere. It is amazing to see how woman's charity, which "never faileth," palliates the injustice of man, which never has failed yet. Men fight battles; women heal the wounds of the sick:

> Forgot are hatred, wrongs, and fears,
> The plaintive voice alone she hears,
> Sees but the dying man,—[9]

and does not ask if foe or friend. Messrs. Pinchem & Peelem organize an establishment, wherein the sweat and tears and blood of the poor turn the wheels; every pivot and every shaft rolls on quivering human flesh. The wealthy capitalists,

> Half ignorant, they turn an easy wheel,
> Which sets sharp racks at work, to pinch and peel.[10]

The wives and daughters of the wealthy house go out to "undo the heavy burdens, and let the oppressed go free;"[11] to heal the sick and teach the ignorant, whom their fathers, their husbands, their lovers have made sick, oppressed and ignorant. Ask Manchester, in Old England and in New, if this is not so; ask London, ask Boston.

The moral, affectional and religious feelings of woman fit her for this work. Her patience, her gentleness, her power to conciliate, her sympathy with man, her trust in God, beautifully prepare her for this; and accordingly, she comes in the face of what man calls justice as an angel of mercy—before his hate as an angel of love—between his victim and his selfishness with the self-denial of Paul and the self-sacrifice of Jesus. Look at any village in New England and in Old England, at the Sacs and Foxes, at the Hottentots and the Esquimaux[12]—it is the same thing; it is so in all ages, in all climes, in all stages of civilization; in all ranks of society,—the highest and the lowest; in all forms of religion, all sects of Christianity. It has been so, from DORCAS, in the Acts of the Apostles, who made coats and garments for the poor, down to Miss DIX, in our day, who visits jails and houses of correction, and leads Mr. Fillmore to let Capt. DRAYTON out of jail, where he was placed for the noblest act of his life.[13]

But these philanthropies are not enough for the employment of women; and if all the spare energies of womankind were set to this work,—to palliate the consequences of man's injustice,—it would not be exactly the work which woman wants. There are some women who take no special interest in this. For woman is not all philanthropy, though very much; she has other faculties which want to be developed besides the heart to feel. Still more, that is not the only thing which mankind wants. We need the justice which removes causes, as well as the charity that palliates effects; and woman, standing continually between the victim and the sabre which would cleave him through, is not performing her only function, not her highest; high as that is, it is not her highest. If the feminine swallow drives away the flies from a poor fox struggling for life, another set of flies light upon him, and suck every remaining drop of blood out of his veins, as in the old fable.[14] Besides, if the fox finds that a womanly swallow comes to drive off the flies, he depends on her wing and not on his own brush, and becomes less of a fox. If a miser, or any base man, sees that a woman constantly picks up the man whom he knocks down with the left hand of Usury, or the right hand of Rum, he will go on with his extortion or his grog, because, he says, "I should have done the man harm, but a woman picked him up, and money comes into my pocket, and no harm to the man!" The evils of society would become worse and worse, just as they are increased by indiscriminate alms-giving. That is not enough.

Then there are various Practical Works left by common consent to woman.

First, there is Domestic Service,—woman working as an appendage to some household; a hired hand, or a hired head, to help the housekeeper.

Then there is Mechanical Labor in a factory, or a shop,—spinning, weaving, setting type, binding books, making shoes, coloring maps, and a hundred other things.

Next, there is Trade in a small way, from the basket-woman, with her apples at every street corner, up to the confectioner and haberdasher, with their well-filled shops. In a few retail shops which venture to brave popular opinion, woman is employed at the counter.

As a fourth thing, there is the business of Public and Private Teaching, in various departments. All these are well; they are unavoidable, they are absolutely necessary; they furnish employment to many women, and are a blessed resource.

I rejoice that the Field-work of the farmer is not done by woman's hand in the free portions of America. It imbrutes women in Ireland, in France, and in Spain. I am glad that the complicated machinery of life furnishes so much more work for the light and delicate hand of woman. But I confess I mourn that where her work is as profitable as man's, her pay is not half so much. A woman who should teach a public school well, would be paid two, three, four or six times that sum. It is so in all departments of woman's work that I am acquainted with.

These employments are very well, but still they are not enough.

Rich women do not engage in these callings. For rich women, there is no profession left except marriage. After school time, woman has nothing to do till she is married; I mean, almost nothing; nothing that is adequate. Accordingly, she must choose betwixt a husband and nothing,—and sometimes, that is choosing between two nothings. There are spare energies which seek employment before marriage, and after marriage.

These callings are not all that the race of woman needs; not all that her human nature requires. She has the same human nature which man has, and of course, the same natural human rights. Woman's natural right for its rightfulness does not depend on the bodily or mental power to assert and to maintain it—on the great arm or on the great head; it depends only on human nature itself, which God made the same in the frailest woman as in the biggest giant.

If woman is a human being, first, she has the Nature of a human being: next, she has the Right of a human being; third, she has the Duty of a human being. The Nature is the capacity to possess, to use, to develop, and to enjoy every human faculty; the Right is the right to enjoy, develop, and use every human faculty; and the Duty is to make use of the Right, and make her human nature human history. She is here to develop her human nature, enjoy her human rights, perform her human duty. Womankind is to do this for herself, as much as mankind for himself. A woman has the same human nature that a man has, the same human rights,—to life, liberty, and the pursuit of happiness,—the same human duties; and they are as unalienable in a woman as in a man.

Each man has the natural right to the normal development of his nature, so far as it is general-human, neither man nor woman, but human. Each woman has the natural right to the normal development of her nature, so far as it is general-human, neither woman nor man. But each man has also a natural and unalienable right to the normal development of his peculiar nature as man, where he differs from woman. Each woman has just the same natural and unalienable right to the normal development of her peculiar nature as woman, and not man. All that is undeniable.

Now see what follows. Woman has the same individual right to determine her aim in life, and to follow it; has the same individual rights of body and of spirit,—of mind and conscience, and heart and soul; the same physical rights, the same intellectual, moral, affectional and religious rights, that man has. That is true of womankind as a whole; it is true of Jane, Ellen and Sally, and each special woman that can be named.

Every person, man or woman, is an integer, an individual, a whole person, and also a portion of the race, and so a fraction of humankind. Well, the rights of individualism are not to be possessed, developed, used and enjoyed by a life in solitude, but by joint action. Accordingly, to complete and perfect the individual man or woman, and give each an opportunity to possess, use, develop and enjoy these rights, there must be concerted and joint action: else individuality is only a possibility, not a reality. So the individual rights of woman carry with them the same domestic, social, ecclesiastical and political rights as those of man.

The Family, Community, Church and State, are four modes of action which have grown out of human nature in its historical development; they are all necessary for the development of mankind— machines which the human race has devised, in order to possess, use, develop and enjoy their rights as human beings, their rights also as men.

These are just as necessary for the development of woman as of man, and as she has the same Nature, Right and Duty as man, it follows that she has the same right to use, shape and control these four institutions, for her general human purpose, and for her special feminine purpose, that man has to control them for his general human purpose, and his special masculine purpose. All that is as undeniable as any thing in metaphysics or mathematics.

So, then, woman has the same natural rights as man. In Domestic Affairs, she is to determine her own sphere as much as man, and say where her function is to begin, when it shall begin, with whom it shall begin; where it shall end, when it shall end, and what it shall comprise.

Then she has the same right to Freedom of Industry that man has. I do not believe that the hard callings of life will ever suit woman. It is not little boys who go out as lumberers, but great men, with sinewy, brawny arms. I doubt that laborious callings, like navigation, engineering, lumbering and the like, will ever be agreeable to woman. Her feminine body and feminine spirit naturally turn away from such occupations. I have seen women gathering the filth of the streets in Liverpool, sawing stone in a mason's yard in Paris, carrying earth in baskets on their heads for a railway embankment at Naples; but they were obviously out of place, and only consented to this drudgery when driven by Poverty's iron whip. But there are many employments in the departments of mechanical work, of trade, little and extended, where woman could go, and properly go. Some women have a good deal of talent for trade—this in a small way, that on the largest scale. Why should not they exercise their commercial talents in competition with man? Is it right for woman to be a domestic manufacturer in the family of Solomon or Priam, and of every thrifty husband, and wrong for her to be a public manufacturer on her own account?[15] She might spin when the motive power was a wheel-pin of wood in her hand—may she not use the Merrimack and the Connecticut for her wheel-pin;[16] or must she be only the manufacturing servant of man, never her own master?

Much of the business of education already falls to the hands of woman. In the last twenty years, there has been a great progress in the education of women, in Massachusetts, in all New England. The High Schools for girls,—and still better, those for Girls and Boys—have been of great service. Almost all the large towns of this Commonwealth have honored themselves with these blessed institutions; in Boston, only the daughters of the rich can possess such an education as hundreds of noble girls long to acquire. With this enhancement of culture, women have been continually rising higher and higher as teachers. The State Normal Schools have helped in this movement. It used to be thought that only an able-bodied man could manage the large boys of a country or a city School. Even he was sometimes thrust out at the door or the window of "his noisy mansion," by his rough pupils. An able-headed woman has commonly succeeded better than men merely able-bodied. She has tried conciliation rather than violence, and appealed to something a little deeper than aught which force could ever touch. The women-teachers are now doing an important work for the elevation of their race and all human kind. But it is commonly thought woman must not engage in the higher departments thereof. I once knew a woman, wife, and mother, and housekeeper, who taught the severest disciplines of our highest college, and instructed young men while she rocked the cradle with her foot, and mended garments with her hands,—one of the most accomplished scholars of New England.[17] Not long ago, the daughter of a poor widowed seamstress was seen reading the Koran in Arabic. There was but one man in the town who could do the same, and he was a "Learned Blacksmith." Women not able to teach in these things! He must be rather a confident professor who thinks a woman cannot do what he can. I rejoice at the introduction of women into common schools, academies, and high schools; and I thank God that the man who has done so much for public education in Massachusetts, is presently to be the head of a college in Ohio, where women and men are to study together, and where a woman is to be professor of Latin and Natural History.[18] These are good signs.

The business of public lecturing, also, is quite important in New England, and I am glad to see that woman presses into that,—not without success.

The work of conducting a journal, daily, weekly, or quarterly, woman proves that she can attend to quite as decently, and as strongly, too, as most men.

Then there are what are called the Professions,—Medicine, Law, and Theology.

The profession of Medicine seems to belong peculiarly to woman by nature; part of it, exclusively. She is a nurse, and half a doctor, by nature. It is quite encouraging that medical schools are beginning to instruct women, and special schools get founded for the use of women; that sagacious men are beginning to employ women as their physicians. Great good is to be expected from that.

As yet, I believe no woman acts as a Lawyer. But I see no reason why the profession of Law might not be followed by women as well as by men. He must be rather an uncommon lawyer who thinks no feminine head could compete with him. Most lawyers that I have known are rather mechanics at law, than attorneys or scholars at law; and in the mechanical part, woman could do as well as man—could be as good a conveyancer, could follow precedents as carefully, and copy forms as nicely. And in the higher departments of legal work, they who have read the plea which Lady Alice Lisle made in England, when she could not speak by attorney, must remember there is some eloquence in woman's tongue which courts find it rather hard to resist.[19] I think her presence would mend the manners of the court—of the bench, not less than of the bar.

In the business of Theology, I could never see why a woman, if she wished, should not preach, as well as men. It would be hard, in the present condition of the pulpit, to say she had not intellect enough for *that*! I am glad to find, now and then, women preachers, and rejoice at their success. A year ago, I introduced to you the Reverend Miss Brown, educated at an Orthodox Theological Seminary;—you smiled at the name of *Reverend Miss*.[20] She has since been invited to settle by several congregations of unblemished orthodoxy, and has passed on, looking further.

It seems to me that woman, by her peculiar constitution, is better qualified to teach religion than any merely intellectual discipline. The Quakers have always recognised the natural right of woman to perform the same ecclesiastical function as man. At this day, the most distinguished preacher of that denomination is a woman, who adorns her domestic calling as housekeeper, wife and mother, with the same womanly dignity and sweetness which mark her public deportment.

If woman had been consulted, it seems to me Theology would have been in a vastly better state than it is now. I do not think that any woman would ever have preached the damnation of babies new-born; and "hell, paved with the skulls of infants not a span long," would be a region yet to be discovered in Theology. A celibate monk—with God's curse writ on his face, which knew no child, no wife, no sister, and blushed that he had a mother—might well dream of such a thing: he had been through the preliminary studies. Consider the ghastly attributes which are commonly put upon God in the popular Theology, the idea of infinite wrath, of infinite damnation, and total depravity, and all that,—why, you could not get a woman that had intellect enough to open her mouth to preach these things any where. Women *think* they think that they believe them; but they do not. Celibate priests, who never knew marriage, or what paternity was, who thought woman was "a pollution," they invented those ghastly doctrines; and when I have heard the Athanasian Creed and the Dies Iræ chanted by monks, with the necks of bulls and the lips of donkeys,[21]—why, I have understood where the doctrine came from, and have felt the appropriateness of their braying out the damnation hymns: woman could not do it. We shut her out of the choir, out of the priest's house, out of the pulpit, and then the priest, with unnatural vows, came in, and taught these "doctrines of devils."[22] Could you find a woman who would read to a congregation, as words of truth, Jonathan Edwards's Sermon on a Future State—"Sinners in the hands of an Angry God," "the Justice of God in the damnation of Sinners," "Wrath upon the Wicked to the uttermost," "the future punishment of the Wicked," and other things of that sort?[23] Nay, can you find a worthy woman, of any considerable culture, who will read the fourteenth chapter of Numbers, and declare that a true picture of the God she worships?[24] Only a she-dragon could do it, in our day.

The popular Theology leaves us nothing feminine in the character of God. How could it be otherwise, when so much of the popular Theology is the work of men who thought woman was a "pollution," and barred her out of all the high places of the church? If women had had their place in ecclesiastical teaching, I doubt that the "Athanasian Creed" would ever have been thought a "Symbol" of Christianity. The pictures and hymns which describe the last Judgment are a protest against the exclusion of woman from teaching in the church. "I suffer not a woman to teach, but to be in silence," said a writer in the New Testament.[25] The sentence has brought manifold evil in its train.

So much for the employments of women.

By nature, woman has the same Political Rights that man has,—to vote, to hold office, to make and administer laws. These she has as a matter of right. The strong hand and the great head of man keep her down; nothing more. In America, in Christendom, woman has no political rights, is not a citizen in full; she has no voice in making or administering the laws, none in electing the rulers or administrators thereof. She can hold no office—cannot be committee of a primary school, overseer of the poor, or guardian to a public lamp-post. But any man, with conscience enough to keep out of jail, mind enough to escape the poor-house, and body enough to drop his ballot into the box, he is a voter. He may have no character, even no money, that is no matter—he is male. The noblest woman has no voice in the State. Men make laws disposing of her property, her person, her children; still she must bear it, "with a patient shrug."

Looking at it as a matter of pure Right and pure science, I know no reason why woman should not be a voter, or hold office, or make and administer laws. I do not see how I can shut myself into political privileges and shut woman out, and do both in the name of unalienable right. Certainly, every woman has a natural right to have her property represented in the general representation of property, and her person represented in the general representation of persons.

Looking at it as a matter of Expediency, see some facts. Suppose woman had a share in the municipal regulation of Boston, and there were as many Alderwomen as Aldermen, as many Common Council women as Common Council men,—do you believe that, in defiance of the law of Massachusetts, the City Government, last Spring, would have licensed every two hundred and forty-fourth person of the population of the city to sell intoxicating drink? would have made every thirty-fifth voter a rumseller? I do not.

Do you believe the women of Boston would spend ten thousand dollars in one year in a city frolic, or spend two or three thousand every year, on the Fourth of July, for sky-rockets and fire-crackers; would spend four or five thousand dollars to get their Canadian guests drunk in Boston harbor, and then pretend that Boston had not money enough to establish a high school for girls, to teach the daughters of mechanics and grocers to read French and Latin, and to understand the higher things which rich men's sons are driven to at college? I do not.

Do you believe that the women of Boston, in 1851, would have spent three or four thousand dollars to kidnap a poor man, and have taken all the chains which belonged to the city and put them round the Court House, and have drilled three hundred men, armed with bludgeons and cutlasses, to steal a man and carry him back to slavery?[26] I do not. Do you think, if the women had had the control, "fifteen hundred men of property and standing" would have volunteered to take a poor man, kidnapped in Boston, and conduct him out of the State, with fire and sword? I believe no such thing.

Do you think the women of Boston would take the poorest and most unfortunate children in the town, put them all together into one school, making that the most miserable in the city, where they had not and could not have half the advantages of the other children in different schools, and all that because the unfortunates were dark colored? Do you think the women of Boston would shut a bright boy out of the High School or Latin School, because he was black in the face?

Women are said to be cowardly. When Thomas Sims, out of his dungeon, sent to the churches his petition for their prayers, had women been "the Christian clergy," do you believe *they* would not have dared to pray?

If women had a voice in the Affairs of Massachusetts, do you think they would ever have made laws so that a lazy husband could devour all the substance of his active wife—spite of her wish; so that a drunken husband could command her bodily presence in his loathly house; and when an infamous man was divorced from his wife, that he could keep all the children? I confess I do not.

If the Affairs of the Nation had been under woman's joint control, I doubt that we should have butchered the Indians with such exterminating savagery, that, in fifty years, we should have spent seven hundreds of millions of dollars for war, and now, in time of peace, send twenty annual millions more to the same waste. I doubt that we should have spread slavery into nine new States, and made it national. I think the Fugitive Slave Bill would never have been an Act.[27] Woman has some respect for the natural law of God.

I know men say woman cannot manage the great affairs of a nation. Very well. Government is Political Economy—National Housekeeping. Does any respectable woman keep house so badly as the United States? with so much bribery, so much corruption, so much quarreling in the domestic councils?

But government is also Political Morality, it is National Ethics. Is there any worthy woman who rules her household as wickedly as the nations are ruled? who hires bullies to fight for her? Is there any woman who treats one sixth part of her household as if they were cattle and not creatures of God, as if they were things and not persons? I know of none such. In government as housekeeping, or government as morality, I think man makes a very poor appearance, when he says woman could not do as well as he has done and is doing.

I doubt that women will ever, as a general thing, take the same interest as men in political affairs, or find therein an abiding satisfaction. But that is for women themselves to determine, not for men.

In order to attain the end,—the development of man in body and spirit,—human institutions must represent all parts of human nature, both the masculine and the feminine element. For the well-being of the human race, we need the joint action of man and woman, in the family, the community, the Church and the State. A family without the presence of woman—with no mother, no wife, no sister, no womankind—is a sad thing. I think a Community without woman's equal social action, a Church without her equal ecclesiastical action, and a State without her equal political action, is almost as bad—is very much what a house would be without a mother, wife, sister or friend.

You see what prevails in the Christian civilization of the Nineteenth Century: it is Force—force of body, force of brain. There is little justice, little philanthropy, little piety. Selfishness preponderates every where in Christendom—individual, domestic, social, ecclesiastical, national selfishness. It is preached as gospel and enacted as law. It is thought good political economy for a strong people to devour the weak nations—for "Christian" England and America to plunder the "Heathen" and annex their land; for a strong class to oppress and ruin the feeble class—for the capitalists of England to pauperise the poor white laborer, for the capitalists of America to enslave the poorer black laborer; for a strong man to oppress the weak men—for the sharper to buy labor too cheap, and sell its product too dear, and so grow rich by making many poor. Hence, nation is arrayed against nation, class against class, man against man. Nay, it is commonly taught that mankind is arrayed against God, and God against man; that the world is a universal discord; that there is no solidarity of man with man, of man with God. I fear we shall never get far beyond this theory and this practice, until woman has her natural rights as the equal of man, and takes her natural place in regulating the affairs of the family, the community, the Church and the State.

It seems to me God has treasured up a reserved power in the nature of woman to correct many of those evils which are Christendom's disgrace to-day.

Circumstances help or hinder our development, and are one of the two forces which determine the actual character of a nation, or of mankind, at any special period. Hitherto, amongst men, circumstances have favored the development of only intellectual power, in all its forms—chiefly in its lower forms. At present, mankind, as a whole, has the superiority over womankind, as a whole, in all that pertains to intellect, the higher and the lower. Man has knowledge, has ideas, has administrative skill,—enacts the rules of conduct for the individual, the family, the community, the church, the state, and the world. He applies these rules of conduct to life, and so controls the great affairs of the human race. You see what a world he has made of it. There is male vigor in this civilization, miscalled "Christian"; and in its leading nations there are industry and enterprise, which never fail. There is science, literature, legislation, agriculture, manufactures, mining, commerce, such as the world never saw. With the vigor of war, the Anglo-Saxon now works the works of peace. England abounds in wealth,—richest of lands; but look at her poor, her vast army of paupers, two million strong, the Irish whom she drives with the hand of famine across the sea. Martin Luther was right when he said, The richer the nation, the poorer the poor. America is "democratic"—"the freest and most enlightened people in the world." Look at her slaves: every sixth woman in the country sold as a beast; with no more legal respect paid to her marriage than the farmer pays to the conjunctions of his swine. America is well-educated; there are four millions of children in the school-houses of the land: it is a States prison offence to teach a slave to read the three letters which spell GOD. The more "democratic" the country, the tighter is bondage ironed on the slave. Look at the cities of England and America. What riches, what refinement, what culture of man and woman too! Ay; but what poverty, what ignorance, what beastliness of man and woman too! The Christian civilization of the nineteenth century is well summed up in London and New York—the two foci of the Anglo-Saxon tribe, which control the shape of the world's commercial ellipse. Look at the riches—and the misery; at the "religious enterprise"—and the heathen darkness; at the virtue, the decorum and the beauty of woman well-born and well-bred—and at the wild sea of prostitution, which swells and breaks and dashes against the bulwarks of society—every ripple was a woman once!

O, brother men, who make these things, is this a pleasant sight? Does your literature complain of it—of the waste of human life, the slaughter of human souls, the butchery of woman? British literature begins to wail, in "Nicholas Nickleby," and "Jane Eyre," and "Mary Barton," and "Alton Locke," in many a "Song of the Shirt";[28] but the respectable literature of America is deaf as a cent to the outcry of humanity expiring in agonies. It is busy with California, or the Presidency, or extolling iniquity in high places, or flattering the vulgar vanity which buys its dross for gold. It cannot even imitate the philanthropy of English letters: it is "up" for California and a market. Does not the Church speak?—the English Church, with its millions of money, the American, with its millions of men—both wont to bay the moon of foreign heathenism? The Church is a dumb dog, that cannot bark, sleeping, lying down, loving to slumber. It is a Church without woman, believing in a male and jealous God, and rejoicing in a boundless, endless hell!

Hitherto, with woman, circumstances have hindered the development of intellectual power, in all its forms. She has not knowledge, has not ideas or practical skill to equal the force of man. But circumstances have favored the development of pure and lofty emotion in advance of man. She has moral feeling, affectional feeling, religious feeling, far in advance of man; her moral, affectional and religious intuitions are deeper and more trustworthy than his. Here she is eminent, as he is in knowledge, in ideas, in administrative skill.

I think man will always lead in affairs of intellect—of reason, imagination, understanding—he has the bigger brain; but that woman will always lead in affairs of emotion—moral, affectional, religious—she has the better heart, the truer intuition of the right, the lovely, the holy. The literature of women in this century is juster, more philanthropic, more religious than that of men. Do you not hear the cry which, in New England, a woman is raising in the world's ears against the foul wrong which America is working in the world? Do you not hear the echo of that woman's voice come over the Atlantic—returned from European shores in many a tongue—French, German, Italian, Swedish, Danish, Russian, Dutch? How a woman touches the world's heart!—because she speaks justice, speaks piety, speaks love. What voice is strongest raised in continental Europe, pleading for the oppressed and down-trodden? That also is a woman's voice!

Well, we want the excellence of man and woman both united; intellectual power, knowledge, great ideas—in literature, philosophy, theology, ethics—and practical skill; but we want something better— the moral, affectional, religious intuition, to put justice into ethics, love into theology, piety into science and letters. Every where in the family, the community, the church and the state, we want the masculine and feminine element coöperating and conjoined. Woman is to correct man's taste, mend his morals, excite his affections, inspire his religious faculties. Man is to quicken her intellect, to help her will, translate her sentiments to ideas, and enact them into righteous laws. Man's moral action, at best, is only a sort of general human providence, aiming at the welfare of a part, and satisfied with achieving the "greatest good of the greatest number." Woman's moral action is more like a special human providence, acting without general rules, but caring for each particular case. We need both of these, the general and the special, to make a total human providence.

If man and woman are counted equivalent,—equal in rights, though with diverse powers,—shall we not mend the literature of the world, its theology, its science, its laws, and its actions too? I cannot believe that wealth and want are to stand ever side by side as desperate foes; that culture must ride only on the back of ignorance; and feminine virtue be guarded by the degradation of whole classes of ill-starred men, as in the East, or the degradation of whole classes of ill-starred women, as in the West; but while we neglect the means of help God puts in our power, why, the present must be like the past—"property" must be theft, "law" the strength of selfish will, and "Christianity"— what we see it is, the apology for every powerful wrong.

To every woman let me say,—Respect your nature as a human being, your nature as a woman; then respect your rights, then remember your duty to possess, to use, to develop and to enjoy every faculty which God has given you, each in its normal way.

And to men let me say,—Respect, with the profoundest reverence respect the mother that bore you, the sisters who bless you, the woman that you love, the woman that you marry. As you seek to possess your own manly rights, seek also, by that great arm, by that powerful brain, seek to vindicate her rights as woman, as your own as man. Then we may see better things in the church, better things in the state, in the community, in the home. Then the green shall show what buds it hid, the buds shall blossom, the flowers bear fruit, and the blessing of God be on us all.

Source: Theodore Parker, *A Sermon of the Public Function of Woman, Preached at the Music Hall, March 27, 1853* (Boston: Robert F. Wallcut, 1853). Information about the other three sermons is from the "Preface," p. [3], not reprinted here.

Notes

1. American use of this proverb dates back to the mid-seventeenth century.
2. *Ecclesiasticus*, 38:25: "How can he become wise who handles the plow, and

who glories in the shaft of a goad, who drives oxen and is occupied with their work, and whose talk is about bulls?"

3. Miguel de Cervantes (1547–1616), Spanish national author best known for *Don Quixote* (1605, 1615).

4. Lowell and Lawrence, mill towns in Massachusetts.

5. Proverbs 31:18.

6. Kine, buffaloes.

7. Jenny Lind (1820–1887), singer known as the Swedish Nightingale, brought to America in 1850–1852 for a triumphant tour; Dorothea Lynde Dix (1802–1887), reformer devoted to the mentally ill.

8. Hyson, a type of green tea.

9. *Marmion, A Tale of Flodden Field* (1808), ll. 911–913, by Sir Walter Scott.

10. "Isabella; or, the Pot of Basil" (1820), stanza 15, ll. 7–8, by John Keats (1795–1821), English Romantic poet.

11. Isaiah 58:6.

12. Hottentots, pejorative name given to the people in southern Africa found by the first white settlers.

13. Dorcas, a pious Christian widow restored to life by Peter in Acts 9:36–41; Daniel Drayton (b. 1802) unsuccessfully attempted in 1848 to smuggle over seventy slaves on a ship from Washington to freedom in the North: he served four years and four months before being pardoned by President Millard Fillmore (1800–1874).

14. The fable of the Fox and the Hedgehog by Aesop, legendary Green fabulist of the sixth century B.C. In it, a fox lay injured with a swarm of hungry blood-sucking flies settled on him. A passing hedgehog asked if he should drive away the flies, but the fox replied in the negative because "the flies which you see are full of blood, and sting me but little, and if you rid me of these which are already satiated, others more hungry will come in their place, and will drink up all the blood I have left."

15. Priam, the last king of Troy.

16. Merrimack and Connecticut, rivers that powered many of the textile factories in New England.

17. Sarah Alden Bradford Ripley (1793–1867), New England intellectual and teacher.

18. Horace Mann (1796–1859), educator who supported public education, became president of Antioch College in Yellow Springs, Ohio, in 1853.

19. Lady Alice Lisle (ca. 1614–1685), Englishwoman falsely convicted and executed by the courts.

20. Antoinette Brown (1825–1901) completed her studies at Oberlin theological seminary in 1850 and became in 1853 the first ordained woman minister in the United States; she married Samuel Blackwell in 1856.

21. Dies Iræ, name of the sequence in requiem Masses held by Catholics.

22. Faustus the Manichean asks St. Augustine to "acknowledge that Moses and the prophets taught doctrines of devils, and were the interpreters of a lying and malignant spirit" (see Augustine's "Reply to Faustus the Manichaean," Book 30).

23. Jonathan Edwards (1703–1758), most famous theologian of colonial America.

24. In this chapter God condemns the Israelites to wander in the wilderness for forty years.

25. 1 Timothy 2:12.

26. On 3 April 1851, Thomas Sims was seized in Boston as authorized by the Fugitive Slave Law, and, despite the protests and legal action of the abolitionists, was returned to Savannah, where he was publicly whipped.

27. The Fugitive Slave Law, which went into effect on 18 September 1850, not only imposed severe penalties on those who helped slaves to escape but also required citizens to help in apprehending fugitive slaves.

28. The English literary works, all dealing with social problems, are the novels *Nicholas Nickleby* (1838–39) by Charles Dickens (1812–1870), *Jane Eyre* (1847) by Charlotte Brontë (1816–1855), *Mary Barton* (1848) by Elizabeth Gaskell (1810–1865), and *Alton Locke* (1850) by Charles Kingsley (1819–1875), and the poem *The Song of the Shirt* (1843) by Thomas Hood (1799–1845).

Ralph Waldo Emerson

"Seventh of March Speech on the Fugitive Slave Law"

(7 March 1854)

EMERSON'S RESPONSE to a law that requires citizens to help recapture fugitive slaves is a strong one, as are his comments on Daniel Webster, formerly highly regarded by Emerson, but now, because of his help in assisting the passage of the Fugitive Slave Law, an apostate. This law was part of the Compromise of 1850, which among other things, allowed New Mexico to be organized as a territory without restrictions on slavery and permitted California to be admitted as a free state. Webster's defense of the package was seen by him as a way to avoid Southern secession and as part of a belief that the different soil and farming methods employed in the West would of themselves result in those states being free states. But to have a New Englander empower the federal government to dictate that citizens must track down slaves was too much to bear, and Webster and the Fugitive Slave Law were roundly denounced. After the law was implemented on 18 September 1850, Emerson wrote in his journal "I will not obey it, by God."

I do not often speak to public questions; they are odious and hurtful, and it seems like meddling or leaving your work. I have my own spirits in prison,—spirits in deeper prisons, whom no man visits, if I do not. And then I see what havoc it makes with any good mind— this dissipated philanthropy. The one thing not to be forgiven to intellectual persons is not to know their own task, or to take their ideas from others and believe in the ideas of others. From this want of manly rest in their own, and foolish acceptance of other people's watchwords, comes the imbecility and fatigue of their conversation. For, they cannot affirm these from any original experience, and, of course, not with the natural movement and whole power of their nature and talent, but only from their memory, only from the cramp position of standing for their teacher.—They say, what they would have you believe, but which they do not quite know.

My own habitual view is to the well-being of students or scholars, and it is only when the public event affects them, that it very seriously affects me. And what I have to say is to them. For every man speaks mainly to a class whom he works with, and more or less fitly represents. It is to them I am beforehand related and engaged,—in this audience or out of this audience,—to them and not to others.

I am not responsible to this audience for what I shall say; I am responsible to myself for now and forever for what I say to this audience. And yet when I say the class of scholars and students,—that is a class which comprises in some sort all mankind,—comprises every man in the best hours of his life:—and in these days not only virtually, but actually. For who are the readers and thinkers of 1854?

I say I consider myself bound to speak only to the reading and thinking class. But this class has immensely increased. Owing to the silent revolution which the newspaper has wrought, this class has come in this country to take in all classes. Look into the morning trains, which, from every suburb carry the business-men into the city, to their shops, counting rooms, work yards, and warehouses. With them, enters the car the humble priest of politics, finance, philosophy, and religion in the shape of the newsboy. He unfolds his magical sheets. Two pence a head his bread of knowledge costs, and instantly the entire rectangular assembly, fresh from their breakfast, are bending as one man to their second breakfast. There is, no doubt, chaff enough, in what he brings, but there is fact, and thought, and wisdom in the crude mass from all regions of the world.

Now, I have lived all my life without suffering any known inconvenience from American slavery. I never saw it; never heard the whip; I never felt the check on my free speech and action; until the other day, when Mr. Webster, by his personal influence, brought the Fugitive Slave law on the country. I say Mr. Webster, for though the bill was not his, yet it is notorious that he was the life and soul of it, that he gave it all he had: it cost him his life. And under the shadow of his great name, inferior men sheltered themselves, and threw their ballots for it, and made the law. I say inferior men; there were all sorts of what are called brilliant men, accomplished men, men of high office—a President of the United States, senators—and of eloquent speech, but men without self-respect, without character, and it was droll to see that office, age, fame, talent, even a repute for honesty, all count for nothing: they had no opinions; they had no memory for what they had been saying, like the Lord's prayer, all their lifetime; they were only looking to what their great captain did, and if he jumped, they jumped,—if he stood on his head, they did. In ordinary, the supposed sense of their district and state is their guide, and this keeps them to liberty and justice. But it is always a little difficult to decipher what this public sense is: and when a great man comes, who knots up into himself the opinions and wishes of his people, it is so much easier to follow him as an exponent of this. He, too, is responsible. They will not be. It will always suffice to say,—I followed him.

I saw plainly that the great show of their legitimate power was in nothing more than in their power to misguide us. I saw that a great man, deservedly esteemed and admired for his powers and their general right direction, was able—fault of the total want of stamina in public men—when he failed, to break them all with him, to carry parties with him. He scattered terror which he and they manufactured together, the terror of southern bluster, amongst all the feeble, and timid, and unprincipled; and covered their own treachery by the panic they created. Everything went to the ground: it was a sadly instructive crisis: it showed that men would not stick to their professions, or parties to their platforms.

It showed much. It ended a great deal of nonsense we had been accustomed to hear and to repeat, on the twenty-second of December, the nineteenth of April, the seventeenth of June, and the fourth of July.[2] It showed what reputations are made of; what straws we dignify by office and title, and how competent they are to give counsel and help in a day of trial: the shallowness of leaders; showed the divergence of parties from their alleged grounds, and that men would not stick to what they had said: that the resolutions of public bodies, and the pledges never so often given and put on record, of public men,—will not bind them. The fact comes out more plainly, that you cannot rely on any man for the defence of truth who is not constitutionally, or by blood and temperament, on that side.

In what I have to say of Mr. Webster, I do not confound him with vulgar politicians of his own time or since. There is always base ambition enough, men who calculate on the immense ignorance of masses of men;—that is their quarry and farm,—they use the constituences at home only for their shoes. And, of course, they can drive out from the contest any honorable man. The low can best win the low, and all men like to be made much of. There are those, too, who have power and inspiration only to do ill. Their talent or their faculty deserts them when they undertake anything right.

Mr. Webster had a natural ascendancy of aspect and carriage which distinguished him over all his contemporaries. His countenance, his figure, and his manners, were all in so grand a style, that he was, without effort, as superior to his most eminent rivals, as they were to the humblest, so that his arrival in any place was an event which drew crowds of people, who went to satisfy their eyes, and could not see him enough. I think they looked at him as the representative of the American continent. He was there in his Adamitic capacity, as if he alone of all men did not disappoint the eye and ear, but was a fit figure in the landscape. I remember his appearance at Bunker Hill.[2] There was the monument, and here was Webster. He knew well that a little more or less of rhetoric signified nothing; he was only to say plain and equal things;—grand things, if he had them,—and, if he had them not, only to abstain from saying unfit things;—and the whole occasion was answered by his presence. It was a place for behavior, much more than for speech; and Webster walked through his part with entire success.

His wonderful organization, the perfection of his elocution,—and all that thereto belongs,—voice, accent, intonation, attitude, manner,—we shall not soon find again. Then, he was so thoroughly simple and wise in his rhetoric,—he saw through his matter,—hugged his fact so close,—went to the principal or essential, and never indulged in a weak flourish, though he knew perfectly well how to make such exordiums, episodes, and perorations, as might give perspective to his harangue, without in the least embarrassing his march, or confounding his transitions. In his statement, things lay in daylight;—we saw them in order as they were. Though he knew very well how to present his own personal claims, yet in his argument he was intellectual, and stated his fact pure of all personality, so that his splendid wrath, when his eyes became lamps, was the wrath of the fact and cause he stood for. His power, like that of all great masters, was not in excellent parts, but was total. He had a great and everywhere equal propriety. He had the power of countenance and the gravity of a sachem. He worked with that closeness of adhesion to the matter in hand, which a joiner or a chemist uses, and the same quiet and sure feeling of right to his place that an oak or a mountain have to theirs.

After all his talents have been described, there remains that perfect propriety which animated all the details of the action or speech with the character of the whole, so that his beauties of detail are endless. He seemed born for the bar, born for the senate, and took very naturally a leading part in large private and in public affairs; for his head distributed things in their right places, and what he saw so well, he compelled other people to see also. Ah! great is the privilege of eloquence. What gratitude does every human being feel to him who speaks well for the right,—who translates truth into language entirely plain and clear!

The history of this country has given a disastrous importance to the defects of this great man's mind. Whether evil influences and the corruption of politics, or whether original infirmity, it was the misfortune of this country that with this large understanding, he had not what is better than intellect, and the essential source of its health. It is the office of the moral nature to give sanity and right direction to the mind, to give centrality and unity.

Now, it is a law of our nature that great thoughts come from the heart, that the moral is the occult fountain of genius. It was for this reason I may here say as I have said elsewhere: the sterilty of thought, the want of generalization in his speeches, and the curious fact, that, with a general ability that impresses all the world, there is not a single general remark, not an observation on life and manners, not a single valuable aphorism that can pass into literature from his writings.

Four years ago tonight, on one of those critical moments in history when great issues are determined,—when the powers of right and wrong are mustered for conflict, and it lies with one man to give a casting vote,—Mr. Webster most unexpectedly threw his whole weight on the side of slavery, and caused by his personal and official authority the passage of the Fugitive Slave Bill.

It is remarked of the Americans, that they value dexterity too much and honor too little, that the Americans praise a man more by saying that he is smart than by saying that he is right. Now, whether this defect be national or not, it is the defect and calamity of Mr. Webster, and it is so far true of his countrymen, that, namely, the appeal to physical and mental ability, when his character is assailed. And his speeches on the seventh of March, and at Albany, Buffalo, Syracuse, and Boston, are cited in justification. And Mr. Webster's literary editor believes that it was his own wish to rest his fame on the speech of the seventh of March. Now, though I have my own opinions on this seventh of March discourse, and those others, and think them very transparent, and very open to criticism, yet the *secondary* merits of a speech, that is, its logic, its illustration, its points, are not here in question. The primary quality of a speech is its *subject*. Nobody doubts that Daniel Webster could make a good speech. Nobody doubts that there were good and plausible things to be said on the part of the south. But this is not a question of ingenuity, not a question of syllogisms, but of sides. How came he there? There are always texts, and thoughts, and arguments; But it is the genius and temper of the man which decides whether he will stand for Right or for Might.

Who doubts the power of any clever and fluent man to defend either of our parties, or any cause in our courts? There was the same law in England for Jeffreys, and Talbot, and Yorke to read slavery out of, and for Lord Mansfield to read freedom.[3] And in this country one sees that there is always margin enough in the statute for a liberal judge to read one way, and a servile judge another. But the question which History will ask is broader. In the final hour, when he was forced by the peremptory necessity of the closing armies to take a side, did he take the side of great principles, the side of humanity and justice, or the side of abuse, and oppression, and chaos?

Mr. Webster decided for slavery; and *that*, when the aspect of the institution was no longer doubtful, no longer feeble and apologetic, and proposing soon to end itself, but when it was strong, and aggressive, and threatening an illimitable increase; then, he listened to stale reasons and hopes and left with much complacency, we are told, the testament of his speech to the astonished State of Massachusetts. *Vera pro gratis*.[4] A ghastly result of all those years of experience in affairs, this, that there was nothing better for the most American man in America to tell his countrymen, than, that slavery was now at that strength, that they must beat down their conscience and become kidnappers for it. This was like the doleful speech falsely ascribed to the patriot Brutus. "Virtue, I have followed thee through life, and I find thee but a shadow."[5]

Here was a question of an immoral law—a question agitated for ages, and settled always in the same way by every great jurist, that an immoral law cannot be valid. Cicero, Grotius, Coke, Blackstone, Burlamaqui, Vattel, Burke, and Jefferson do all affirm this, and I cite them not that they can give plainness to what is so clear, but because, though lawyers and practical statesmen, they could not hide from themselves this truth.[6]

Here was the question: Are you for man, and for the good of man; or are you for the hurt and harm of man? It was a question, whether man shall be treated as leather? Whether the negroes shall be, as the Indians were in Spanish America, a species of money? Whether this institution, which is a kind of mill or factory for converting men into monkeys, shall be upheld and enlarged? And Mr. Webster and the country went for quadruped law.

Immense mischief was done. People were all expecting a totally different course from Mr. Webster. If any man had in that hour possessed the weight with the country which he had acquired, he would have brought the whole country to its senses. But not a moment's pause was allowed. Angry parties went from bad to worse, and the decision of Webster was accompanied with everything offensive to freedom and good morals.

There was something like an attempt to debauch the moral sentiment of the clergy and of the youth. The immense power of rectitude is apt to be forgotten in politics. But they who brought this great wrong on the country, did not forget it. They wished to avail themselves of the names of men of known probity and honour to endorse the statute. The ancient maxim is still true, that never was any injustice effected except by the help of justice. Burke said, "he would pardon something to the spirit of liberty,"—but the opposition was sharply called *treason* by Webster and prosecuted so. He told the people at Boston, "they must conquer their prejudices," that "agitation of the subject of slavery must be suppressed." He did, as immoral men usually do, make very low bows to the Christian Church, and went through all the Sunday decorums; but when allusion was made to ethics, and the sanctions of morality, he very frankly said, at Albany, "Some higher law, something existing somewhere between here and the third heaven,—I do not know where." And, if the reporters say true, this wretched atheism found some laughter in the company.

I said I had never in my life suffered before from the slave institution. It was like slavery in Africa or in Japan for me. There was a fugitive law, but it had become, or was fast becoming, a dead letter and, by the genius and laws of Massachusetts, inoperative. The new Bill made it operative; required me to hunt slaves; and it found citizens in Massachusetts willing to act as judges and captors. Moreover, it disclosed the secret of the new times: that slavery was no longer mendicant, but was become aggressive and dangerous.

The way in which the country was dragged to consent to this, and the disastrous defection on the miserable cry of *Union* of the men of letters, of the colleges, of educated men, nay of some preachers of religion, shows that our prosperity had hurt us, and we cannot be shocked by crime. It showed that the old religion and the sense of right had faded and gone out; that, whilst we reckoned ourselves a highly cultivated nation, our bellies had run away with our brains, and the principles of culture and progress did not exist. For I suppose that liberty is a very accurate index in men and nations of general progress.

The theory of personal liberty must always appeal to the most refined communities and to the men of the rarest perception and of delicate moral sense. For these are rights which rest on the finest sense of justice, and with every degree of civility, personal liberty will be more truly felt and defined. A barbarous tribe of good stock will by means of their best heads secure substantial liberty. But where there is any weakness in a race, as is in the black race, and it becomes in any degree matter of concession and protection from their stronger neighbors, the incompatibility and offensiveness of the wrong will, of course, be most evident to the most cultivated. For it is—is it not— the very nature of courtesy, of politeness, of religion, of love, to prefer another, to postpone oneself, to protect another from oneself? That is the distinction of the gentleman, to defend the weak, and redress the injured, as it is of the savage and the brute to usurp and use others.

It is an old story a thousand times told—we had all clung fast to our laws, and books, and usages, and the life that was in them had glided away. And there was no watchman on the walls. The spiritual class were not aware that we were wrong. In Massachusetts, as we all know, there has always existed a predominant conservative spirit. We have more money and value of every kind than other people, and wish to keep them.

The plea on which freedom was resisted was Union. I went to certain serious men who had a little more reason than the rest, and inquired why they took this part. They told me candidly that they had no confidence in their strength to resist the democratic party in this country; that they saw plainly that all was going to the utmost verge of licence; each was vying with his neighbor to lead the party by proposing the worst measure, and they threw themselves on the extreme right as a drag on the wheel; that they knew Cuba would be had, and Mexico would be had, and they stood stiffly on conservatism, and as near to monarchy as they could, only to moderate the velocity with which the car was running down the precipice: in short, their theory was despair; the whig wisdom was only reprieve, a waiting to be the last devoured. They sided with Carolina or with Arkansas, only to make a show of whig strength, wherewith to resist a little longer this general ruin.

Gentlemen, I have a respect for conservatism. I know how deeply it is founded in our nature, and how idle are all attempts to shake ourselves free of it. We are all conservatives; all half-whig, half-democrat, in our essences; and might as well try to jump off our planet or jump out of our skins as to escape from our whiggery. There are two forces in nature by whose anatgonism we exist: the power of Fate, of Fortune, the laws of the world, the order of things, or, however else we choose to phrase it,—the material necessities, on the one hand; and Will, or Duty, or Freedom, on the other. *May* and *must*: the sense of right and duty, on the one hand; and the material necessities, on the other. *May* and *must*. In vulgar politics, the whig goes for what has been, for the old necessities, for the *musts;* the reformer goes for the better, for the ideal good, for the *mays*.

But each of these parties must of necessity take in, in some manner, the principle of the other. Each wishes to cover the whole ground, to hold fast, and to advance: only, one lays the emphasis on keeping; and the other, on advancing. I, too, think the *musts* are a safe company to follow, and even agreeable. But if we are whigs, let us be whigs of nature and science, and go for *all* the necessities. Let us know that over and above all the *musts* of poverty and appetite, is the instinct of man to rise, and the instinct to love and help his brother.

Now, Gentlemen, I think we have in this hour instruction again in the simplest lesson. Events roll, millions of men are engaged, and the result is some of those first commandments which we heard in the nursery. We never get beyond our first lesson; for really the world exists, as I understand it, to teach the science of liberty, which begins with liberty from fear.

The events of this month are teaching one thing plain and clear, the worthlessness of good tools to bad workmen. Papers are of no use, resolutions of public meetings, platforms of conventions—no, nor laws, nor constitutions any more. These are all declaratory of the will of the moment and are passed with more levity and on grounds much less honorable than ordinary business transactions in the street.

You relied on the Constitution. It has not the word "slave" in it, and very good argument has shown that it would not warrant the crimes that are done under it: that with provisions so vague, for an object *not named*, and which would not be suffered to claim a barrel of sugar or a bushel of corn, the robbing of a man and all his posterity,—is effected.

You relied on the Supreme Court. The law was right; excellent law for the lambs. But what if, unhappily, the judges were chosen from the wolves, and give to all the law a wolfish interpretation? What is the use of admirable law forms and political forms, if a hurricane of party feeling and a combination of monied interests can beat them to the ground? What is the use of courts, if judges only quote authorities, and no judge exerts original jurisdiction, or recurs to first principles? What is the use of guaranties provided by the jealousy of ages for the protection of liberty,—if these are made of no effect, when a bad act of Congress finds a willing commissioner?

You relied on the Missouri Compromise: that is ridden over.[7] You relied on state sovereignty in the free states to protect their citizens. They are driven with contempt out of the courts, and out of the territory of the slave states, if they are so happy as to get out with their lives.[8] And now, you relied on these dismal guaranties infamously made in 1850, and before the body of Webster is yet crumbled, it is found that they have crumbled: this eternal monument at once of his fame and of the common Union, is rotten in four years.[9] They are no guaranty to the free states. They are a guaranty to the slave states: that as they have hitherto met with no repulse, they shall meet with none.

I fear there is no reliance to be had on any kind of form or covenant,—no, not on sacred forms,—none on churches, none on bibles. For one would have said that a Christian would not keep slaves, but the Christians keep slaves. Of course, they will not dare read the bible. Won't they? They quote the bible, and Christ, and Paul to maintain slavery.[10] If slavery is a good, then are lying, theft, arson, incest, homicide, each and all goods and to be maintained by Union societies.

These things show that no forms, neither constitutions, nor laws, nor covenants, nor churches, nor bibles, are of any use in themselves; the devil nestles comfortably into them all. There is no help but in the head, and heart, and hamstrings of a man. Covenants are of no use without honest men to keep them. Laws are of no use, but with loyal citizens to obey them. To interpret Christ, it needs Christ in the heart. The teachings of the spirit can be apprehended only by the same spirit that gave them forth.

These events are putting it home to every man, that in him is the only bulwark against slavery:

> None any work can frame
> Unless himself become the same.

To make good the cause of Freedom, you must draw off from all these foolish trusts on others. You must be citadels and warriors, yourselves Declarations of Independence: the charter, the battle, and the victory. Cromwell said, "We can only resist the superior training of the king's soldiers, by having godly men."[11] And no man has a right to hope that the laws of New York will defend him from the contamination of slaves another day, until he has made up his mind that he will not owe his protection to the laws of New York, but to his own sense and spirit. Then, he protects New York. He only who is able to stand alone, is qualified for society.

And that I understand to be the end for which a soul exists in this world: to be himself the counterbalance of all falsehood and all wrong. "The army of unright is encamped from pole to pole, but the road of victory is known to the just."[12] Everything may be taken away, he may be poor, he may be houseless, yet he will know out of his arms to make a pillow and out of his breast a bolster. Why have the minority no influence? because they have not a real minority of one.

Whenever a man has come to this mind, that there is no church for him but his believing prayer; no constitution, but his talent of dealing well and justly with his neighbor; no liberty, but his invincible will to do right, then certain aids and allies will promptly appear. For the eternal constitution of the universe is on his side.

It is of no use to vote down gravitation or morals. What is useful will last; whilst that which is hurtful to the world will sink beneath all the opposing forces which it must exasperate. The terror which the *Marseillaise* thunders against oppression, thunders today,—*Tout est soldat pour vous combattre: "Everything that can walk turns soldier to fight you down."*[13] The end for which man was made, is not stealing, nor crime in any form. And a man cannot steal, without incurring all the penalties of the thief; no, though all the legislatures vote that it is virtuous, and though there be a general conspiracy among scholars and official persons to hold him up, and to say, *Nothing is good but stealing.* A man who commits a crime defeats the end of his existence. He was created for benefit, and he exists for harm. And as well-doing makes power and wisdom, ill-doing takes them away. A man who steals another man's labor, as a planter does, steals away his own faculties: his integrity, his humanity, is flowing away from him.

The habit of oppression cuts out the moral eyes, and though the intellect goes on simulating the moral as before, its sanity is invaded, and gradually destroyed. It takes away the presentiments. I suppose, in general, this is allowed; that, if you have a nice question of right and wrong, you would not go with it to Louis Napoleon;[14] or to a political hack; or to a slave driver. The habit of mind of traders in power would not be esteemed favorable to delicate moral perception.

It is not true that there is any exception to that in American slavery, or that the system here has called out a spirit of generosity and self-sacrifice. No excess of good nature and of tenderness of moral constitution in individuals has been able to give a new character to the system or to tear down the whipping house. The plea that the negro is an inferior race sounds very oddly in my ear from a slaveholder. "The masters of slaves seem generally anxious to prove that they are not of a race superior in any noble quality to the meanest of their bondmen." And, indeed, when I hear the southerner point to the anatomy of the negro, and talk of chimpanzee,—I recall Montesquieu's remark, "It will not do to say, that negroes are men, lest it should turn out that whites were not."[15]

I conceive that thus to detach a man, and make him feel that he is to owe all to himself, is the way to make him strong and rich. And here the optimist must find, if anywhere, the benefit of slavery. We have many teachers. We are in this world for nothing else than culture: to be instructed in nature, in realities; in the laws of moral and intelligent nature; and surely our education is not conducted by toys and luxuries,—but by austere and rugged masters,—by poverty, solitude, passions, war, and slavery,—to know that paradise is under the shadow of swords;[16] that divine sentiments, which are always soliciting us, are breathed into us from on high and are a counterbalance to an universe of suffering and crime,—that self-reliance, the height and perfection of man, is reliance on God. The insight of the religious sentiment will disclose to him unexpected aids in the nature of things. The Persian Saadi said, "Beware of hurting the orphan. When the orphan sets a crying the throne of the Almighty is rocked from side to side."[17]

I know that when seen near, and in detail, slavery is disheartening. But nature is not so helpless but it can rid itself at last of every wrong. An Eastern poet, in describing the world God made pure in the beginning, said, "that God had made justice so dear to the heart of nature, that, if any injustice lurked anywhere under the sky, the blue vault would shrivel to a snakeskin and cast it out by spasms."[18]

But the spasms of nature are centuries and ages and will tax the faith of short-lived men. Slowly, slowly the avenger comes, but comes surely. The proverbs of the nations affirm these delays, but affirm the arrival. They say, "God may consent, but not forever." The delay of the Divine Justice,—this was the meaning and soul of the Greek Tragedy,—this was the soul of their religion. "There has come, too, one to whom lurking warfare is dear,—Retribution,—with a soul full of wiles, a violator of hospitality, guileful without the guilt of guile, limping, late in her arrival."—"This happiness at its close begets itself an offspring, and does not die childless, and instead of good fortune, there sprouts forth for posterity ever-ravening calamity."[19]

> For evil word, shall evil word be said,
> For murderstroke, a murderstroke be paid,
> Who smites must smart.[20]

These delays,—you see them now in the temper of the times. The national spirit in this country is so drowsy and preoccupied with interest, deaf to principle. The Anglo-Saxon race is proud and strong, but selfish. They believe only in Anglo-Saxons. Greece found it deaf, Poland found it so, Italy found it so, Hungary found it so. England goes for trade, not for liberty; goes against Greece; against Hungary; against Schleswig-Holstein; against the French Republic whilst it was yet a republic.[21] To faint hearts the times offer no invitation, and the like torpor exists here throughout the active classes on the subject of domestic slavery and its appalling aggressions.

Yes, that is the stern edict of Providence, that liberty shall be no hasty fruit, but that event on event, population on population, age on age, shall cast itself into the opposite scale, and not until liberty has slowly accumulated weight enough to countervail and preponderate against all this, can the sufficient recoil come. All the great cities, all the refined circles, all the statesmen,—Guizot, Palmerston, Webster, Calhoun,—are sure to be found banded against liberty; they are all sure to be found befriending liberty with their words, and crushing it with their votes.[22]

It is made difficult, because freedom is the accomplishment and perfectness of a man. He is a finished man, earning and bestowing good equal to the world at home and in nature and dignifying that; the sun does not see anything nobler, and has nothing to teach him. Therefore, mountains of difficulty must be surmounted, wiles of seduction, dangers, stern trials met, healed by a quarantine of calamities to measure his strength by, before he dare say, I am free. And in the School of Providence, in the unknown paths of him who made and maketh us, him before whom ages, and dynasties, and Saxon races flee as snows before his forming wind, who knows but Nebraska and the calamities it is now menaced with are the schoolbooks, the pains, and the mortifications.

Whilst the inconsistency of slavery with the principles on which the world is built guarantees its downfall, I own that the patience it requires is almost too sublime for mortals and seems to demand of us more than mere hoping. And when one sees how fast the rot spreads,—it is growing serious,—I think we demand of superior men that they shall be superior in this, that the mind and the virtue give their verdict in their day and accelerate so far the progress of civilization. Possession is sure to throw its stupid strength for existing power; and appetite and ambition will go for *that*. Let the aid of virtue, and intelligence, and education be cast where they rightfully belong. They are organically ours. Let them be loyal to their own. English

Earl Grey said, on a memorable occasion, "he should stand by his order."[23] And I wish to see the instructed or illuminated class know their own flag, and not stand for the kingdom of darkness. We should not forgive the Clergy of a country, for taking on every issue the immoral side. Nor the Bench, if it throw itself on the side of the culprit. Nor the Government, if it sustain the mob against the laws.

It is an immense support and ally to a brave man standing single or with few for the right, to know, when outvoted, and discountenanced, and ostracised in that hour and place, yet better men in other parts of the country appreciate the service, and will rightly report him to his own age and to posterity. And without this assurance he will sooner sink; "If they do not care to be defended," he may well say, "I too will decline the controversy, from which I only reap invectives and hatred."

Yet the lovers of liberty may tax with reason the coldness and indifferentism of the scholars and literary men. They are lovers of liberty in Greece, and in Rome, and in the English Commonwealth, but they are very lukewarm lovers of the specific liberty of America in 1854. The universities are not now as in Hobbes's time, the core of rebellion; no, but the seat of whiggery. They have forgotten their allegiance to the muse and grown worldly and political. I remember, I listened on one of those occasions when the university chooses one of her distinguished sons to return from the political arena, believing that senators and statesmen are glad to throw off the harness and to dip again in the Castalian pools.[24] But if audiences forget themselves, statesmen do not. The low bows to all the crockery gods of the day were duly made. Only in one part of the discourse the orator allowed to transpire, rather against his will, a little sober sense. It was this.

> I am, as you see, a man virtuously inclined and only corrupted by
> my profession of politics. I should prefer the right side. You gentlemen
> of these literary and scientific schools have the power to make your
> verdict clear and prevailing. Had you done so, you would have found
> me its glad organ and champion. Abstractly, I should have preferred
> that side. But you have not done it. You have not spoken out. You
> have failed to arm me. I can only deal with masses as I find them.
> Abstractions are not for me. I go, then, for such parties and opinions
> as have provided me with a working apparatus. I give you my word,
> not without regret, that I was first for you, and though I am now to
> deny and condemn you, you see it is not my will, but the party ne-
> cessity.[25]

Having made this manifesto, and professed his adoration for liberty in the time of his grandfathers, he proceeded with his work of denouncing freedom and freemen at the present day, much in the tone and spirit with which Lord Bacon prosecuted his benefactor Essex.[26] He denounced every name and aspect under which liberty and progress dared show itself in this age and country, but with a lingering conscience which qualified each sentence with a recommendation to mercy: death, with a recommendation to mercy.

But I put it to every noble and generous spirit in the land; to every poetic; to every heroic; to every religious heart; that not so is our learning, our education, our poetry, our worship to be declared: not by heads reverted to the dying Demosthenes, Luther, or Wallace, or to George Fox, or to George Washington, but to the dangers and dragons that beset the United States at this time.[27] It is not possible to extricate oneself from the questions in which your age is involved. I hate that we should be content with standing on the defensive. Liberty is aggressive. Liberty is the crusade of all brave and conscientious men. It is the epic poetry, the new religion, the chivalry of all gentlemen. This is the oppressed Lady whom true knights on their oath and honor must rescue and save.

Now, at last, we are disenchanted and shall have no more false hopes. I respect the Antislavery Society. It is the Cassandra that has foretold all that has befallen, fact for fact, years ago,—foretold it all, and no man laid it to heart. It seemed, as the Turks say, "Fate makes that a man should not believe his own eyes." But the Fugitive Law did much to unglue the eyes of men, and now the Nebraska Bill leaves us staring. The Antislavery Society will add many members this year. The Whig party will join it. The Democrats will join it. The population of the Free States will join it. I doubt not, at last, the slave states will join it. But be that sooner or later,—and whoever comes or stays away,—I hope we have come to an end of our unbelief, have come to a belief that there is a Divine Providence in the world which will not save us but through our own cooperation.

Source: Ralph Waldo Emerson, "Seventh of March Speech on the Fugitive Slave Law, 7 March 1854," from *The Later Lectures of Ralph Waldo Emerson, 1843–1871,* ed. Ronald A. Bosco and Joel Myerson (Athens: University of Georgia Press, forthcoming). The quotation is from *Journals and Miscellaneous Notebooks,* 11:412.

Notes

1. 22 December, when the Pilgrims' landing at Plymouth was usually commemorated; 19 April 1775, when the Battle of Lexington and Concord was fought; 17 June 1843, when the Bunker Hill monument was dedicated.

2. Webster's appearance at Bunker Hill at the dedication of the monument is described in *Journals and Miscellaneous Notebooks*, 8:425, and *Letters*, 3: 180–181.

3. The English jurists Baron George Jeffreys (1648–1689), Charles Talbot (1685–1737), Charles Yorke (1722–1770), and Lord Mansfield (1705–1793).

4. *Vera pro gratis*: "truth rather than pleasantness."

5. Attributed to Dio Cassius (ca. 150–235), Greek historian.

6. Hugo Grotius (1583–1645), Dutch jurist; Edward Coke (1552–1634) and William Blackstone (1723–1780), both English lawyers; Jean Jacques Burlamaqui (1694–1748) and Emmerich de Vattel (1714–1767), both Swiss jurists; Edmund Burke (1729–1797), Irish politician and natural philosopher who wrote on individual liberty; Thomas Jefferson (1743–1786), third American president (1801–1809).

7. Congress had passed the Missouri Compromise on 3 March 1820. It held that Arkansas would be admitted to the Union as a slave state, Maine as a free state, and no restrictions would be set on Missouri; also, no slavery would in the future be allowed north of a latitude of 36° 30". This was repealed by the passage of the Kansas-Nebraska Act in May 1854, which gave the people in each state the right to determine whether that state be slave or free.

8. Another reference to Samuel Hoar's being expelled from South Carolina when he went to inquire about black Massachusetts citizens who had been kidnapped there; see note 1 to Fuller's "New Year's Day," above.

9. Webster had died on 24 October 1852.

10. "The sending back of Onesimus by Paul was a precedent precious in the eyes of the pro-slavery preachers, North and South, in those days, ignoring, however, Paul's message, 'Not now as a servant, but above a servant, a brother beloved, specially to me, but how much more unto thee, both in the flesh and in the Lord. If thou count me therefore a partner, receive him as myself' (*Epistle of Paul to Philemon*, I, 16, 17)" (Edward Waldo Emerson's note, *Complete Works*, 10:590n).

11. Oliver Cromwell (1599–1658), Lord Protector of England.

12. Attributed to *Divan*, Ode XXIX, ll. 11–12, by Hafiz, fourteenth-century Persian philosopher and poet.

13. *La Marseillaise*, the French national anthem.

14. Louis Napoleon (1808–1873), ruler of France for about twenty years as Napoleon III.

15. Baron de la Brède et de Montesquieu (1689–1755), French political philosopher.

16. Quoted from Muhammad.

17. Muslih-uh-Din Saadi (ca. 1200–ca. 1292), Persian poet.

18. Attributed to a "Spanish Proverb" by Emerson in *Journals and Miscellaneous Notebooks*, 13:82.

19. *Choephori,* by Aeschylus (525–456 B.C.), Athenian tragic dramatist.

20. *Agamemnon,* by Aeschylus.

21. Schleswig-Holstein, a province of Prussia, had recently engaged in a war with Denmark.
22. François Pierre Guillaume Guizot (1787–1874), French historian and statesman; Lord Palmerston (1784–1865), English statesman; John C. Calhoun (1782–1850), South Carolina Congressman who consistently represented Southern views, especially states' rights.
23. Charles, Second Earl Grey (1764–1845), English statesman.
24. Castalia, fountain on Mt. Parnassus in ancient Greece sacred to the Muses and Apollo.
25. Quoted from a speech to the alumni of Harvard College on Commencement Day in 1852 by Robert Charles Winthrop (1809–1894), congressman and senator from Massachusetts.
26. Francis Bacon was befriended early in his career by the courtier Robert Devereux, Second Earl of Essex (1567–1601), but later served as a witness for the prosecution in Essex's trial for treason.
27. Demosthenes (384–322 B.C.), the most famous of the Greek orators; William Wallace (ca. 1270–1305), Scottish national hero.

Henry David Thoreau

"Slavery in Massachusetts"

(4 July 1854)

THOREAU'S RESPONSE TO the state's support of slavery was delivered at an "anti-slavery celebration" on the Fourth of July and printed in the leading abolitionist newspaper, the *Liberator*, edited by the fiery William Lloyd Garrison. If nothing else, this address shows how far Transcendentalist rhetoric had come in the last decade over the issue of what must come first, changing the laws so that they are fair or reforming people so that they may make just laws. Thoreau's statement that the "law will never make men free; it is men who have to make the law free" is in sharp contrast to the belief in social progress shown by the Brook Farmers.

I lately attended a meeting of the citizens of Concord, expecting, as one among many, to speak on the subject of slavery in Massachusetts; but I was surprised and disappointed to find that what had called my townsmen together was the destiny of Nebraska, and not of Massachusetts, and that what I had to say would be entirely out of order.[1] I had thought that the house was on fire, and not the prairie; but though several of the citizens of Massachusetts are now in prison for attempting to rescue a slave from her own clutches, not one of the speakers at that meeting expressed regret for it, not one even referred to it.[2] It was only the disposition of some wild lands a thousand miles off, which appeared to concern them. The inhabitants of Concord are not prepared to stand by one of their own bridges, but talk only of taking up a position on the highlands beyond the Yellowstone river. Our Buttricks, and Davises, and Hosmers are retreating thither, and I fear that they will have no Lexington Common between them and the enemy.[3] There is not one slave in Nebraska; there are perhaps a million slaves in Massachusetts.[4]

They who have been bred in the school of politics fail now and always to face the facts. Their measures are half measures and make-shifts, merely. They put off the day of settlement indefinitely, and meanwhile, the debt accumulates. Though the Fugitive Slave Law had not been the subject of discussion on that occasion, it was at length faintly resolved by my townsmen, at an adjourned meeting, as I learn, that the compromise compact of 1820 having been repudiated by one of the parties, 'Therefore, . . . the Fugitive Slave Law must be repealed.' But this is not the reason why an iniquitous law should be repealed. The fact which the politician faces is merely, that there is less honor among thieves than was supposed, and not the fact that they are thieves.

As I had no opportunity to express my thoughts at that meeting, will you allow me to do so here?

Again it happens that the Boston Court House is full of armed men, holding prisoner and trying a MAN, to find out if he is not really a SLAVE. Does any one think that Justice or God awaits Mr. Loring's decision?[5] For him to sit there deciding still, when this question is already decided from eternity to eternity, and the unlettered slave himself, and the multitude around, have long since heard and assented to the decision, is simply to make himself ridiculous. We may be tempted to ask from whom he received his commission, and who he is that received it; what novel statutes he obeys, and what precedents are to him of authority. Such an arbiter's very existence is an impertinence. We do not ask him to make up his mind, but to make up his pack.

I listen to hear the voice of a Governor, Commander-in-Chief of the forces of Massachusetts. I hear only the creaking of crickets and the hum of insects which now fill the summer air. The Governor's exploit is to review the troops on muster days. I have seen him on horseback, with his hat off, listening to a chaplain's prayer. It chances that is all I have ever seen of a Governor. I think that I could manage to get along without one. If *he* is not of the least use to prevent my being kidnapped, pray of what important use is he likely to be to me? When freedom is most endangered, he dwells in the deepest obscurity. A distinguished clergyman told me that he chose the profession of a clergyman, because it afforded the most leisure for literary pursuits. I would recommend to him the profession of a Governor.

Three years ago, also, when the Sim's tragedy was acted, I said to myself, there is such an officer, if not such a man, as the Governor of Massachusetts,[6]—what has he been about the last fortnight? Has he had as much as he could do to keep on the fence during this moral earthquake? It seemed to me that no keener satire could have been aimed at, no more cutting insult have been offered to that man, than just what happened—the absence of all inquiry after him in that crisis. The worst and the most I chance to know of him is, that he did not improve that opportunity to make himself known, and worthily known. He could at least have *resigned* himself into fame. It appeared to be forgotten that there was such a man, or such an office. Yet no doubt he was endeavoring to fill the gubernatorial chair all the while. He was no Governor of mine. He did not govern me.

But at last, in the present case, the Governor was heard from. After he and the United States Government had perfectly succeeded in robbing a poor innocent black man of his liberty for life, and, as far as they could, of his Creator's likeness in his breast, he made a speech to his accomplices, at a congratulatory supper!

I have read a recent law of this State, making it penal for 'any officer of the Commonwealth' to 'detain, or aid in the . . . detention,' any where within its limits, 'of any person, for the reason that he is claimed as a fugitive slave.' Also, it was a matter of notoriety that a writ of replevin to take the fugitive out of the custody of the United States Marshal could not be served, for want of sufficient force to aid the officer.

I had thought that the Governor was in some sense the executive officer of the State; that it was his business, as a Governor, to see that the laws of the State were executed; while, as a man, he took care that he did not, by so doing, break the laws of humanity; but when there is any special important use for him, he is useless, or worse than useless, and permits the laws of the State to go unexecuted. Perhaps I do not know what are the duties of a Governor; but if to be a Governor requires to subject one's self to so much ignominy without remedy, if it is to put a restraint upon my manhood, I shall take care never to be Governor of Massachusetts. I have not read far in the statutes of this Commonwealth. It is not profitable reading. They do not always say what is true; and they do not always mean what they say. What I am concerned to know is, that that man's influence and authority were on the side of the slaveholder, and not of the slave—

of the guilty, and not of the innocent—of injustice, and not of justice. I never saw him of whom I speak; indeed, I did not know that he was Governor until this event occurred. I heard of him and Anthony Burns at the same time, and thus, undoubtedly, most will hear of him. So far am I from being governed by him. I do not mean that it was any thing to his discredit that I had not heard of him, only that I heard what I did. The worst I shall say of him is, that he proved no better than the majority of his constituents would be likely to prove. In my opinion, he was not equal to the occasion.

The whole military force of the State is at the service of a Mr. Suttle, a slaveholder from Virginia, to enable him to catch a man whom he calls his property;[7] but not a soldier is offered to save a citizen of Massachusetts from being kidnapped! Is this what all these soldiers, all this *training* has been for these seventy-nine years past? Have they been trained merely to rob Mexico, and carry back fugitive slaves to their masters?

These very nights, I heard the sound of a drum in our streets. There were men *training* still; and for what? I could with an effort pardon the cockerels of Concord for crowing still, for they, perchance, had not been beaten that morning; but I could not excuse this rub-a-dub of the 'trainers.' The slave was carried back by exactly such as these, i.e., by the soldier, of whom the best you can say in this connection is, that he is a fool made conspicuous by a painted coat.

Three years ago, also, just a week after the authorities of Boston assembled to carry back a perfectly innocent man, and one whom they knew to be innocent, into slavery,[8] the inhabitants of Concord caused the bells to be rung and the cannons to be fired, to celebrate their liberty—and the courage and love of liberty of their ancestors who fought at the bridge. As if *those* three millions had fought for the right to be free themselves, but to hold in slavery three million others. Now-a-days, men wear a fool's cap, and call it a liberty cap. I do not know but there are some, who, if they were tied to a whipping-post, and could get but one hand free, would use it to ring the bells and fire the cannons, to celebrate *their* liberty. So some of my townsmen took the liberty to ring and fire; that was the extent of their freedom; and when the sound of the bells died away, their liberty died away also; when the powder was all expended, their liberty went off with the smoke.

The joke could be no broader, if the inmates of the prisons were to subscribe for all the powder to be used in such salutes, and hire the jailers to do the firing and ringing for them, while they enjoyed it through the grating.

This is what I thought about my neighbors.

Every humane and intelligent inhabitant of Concord, when he or she heard those bells and those cannons, thought not with pride of the events of the 19th of April, 1775, but with shame of the events of the 12th of April, 1851.[9] But now we have half buried that old shame under a new one.

Massachusetts sat waiting Mr. Loring's decision, as if it could in any way affect her own criminality. Her crime, the most conspicuous and fatal crime of all, was permitting him to be the umpire in such a case. It was really the trial of Massachusetts. Every moment that she hesitated to set this man free—every moment that she now hesitates to atone for her crime, she is convicted. The Commissioner on her case is God; not Edward G. God, but simple God.

I wish my countrymen to consider, that whatever the human law may be, neither an individual nor a nation can ever commit the least act of injustice against the obscurest individual, without having to pay the penalty for it. A government which deliberately enacts injustice, and persists in it, will at length ever become the laughing-stock of the world.

Much has been said about American slavery, but I think that we do not even yet realize what slavery is. If I were seriously to propose to Congress to make mankind into sausages, I have no doubt that most of the members would smile at my proposition, and if any believed me to be in earnest, they would think that I proposed something much worse than Congress had ever done. But if any of them will tell me that to make a man into a sausage would be much worse,—would be any worse, than to make him into a slave,—than it was to enact the Fugitive Slave Law, I will accuse him of foolishness, of intellectual incapacity, of making a distinction without a difference. The one is just as reasonable a proposition as the other.

I hear a good deal said about trampling this law under foot. Why, one need not go out of his way to do that. This law rises not to the level of the head or the reason; its natural habitat is in the dirt. It was born and bred, and has its life only in the dust and mire, on a level with the feet, and he who walks with freedom, and does not with Hindoo mercy avoid treading on every venomous reptile, will inevitably tread on it, and so trample it under foot,—and Webster, its maker, with it, like the dirt-bug and its ball.

Recent events will be valuable as a criticism on the administration of justice in our midst, or, rather, as showing what are the true resources of justice in any community. It has come to this, that the friends of liberty, the friends of the slave, have shuddered when they have understood that his fate was left to the legal tribunals of the country to be decided. Free men have no faith that justice will be awarded in such a case; the judge may decide this way or that; it is a kind of accident, at best. It is evident that he is not a competent authority in so important a case. It is no time, then, to be judging according to his precedents, but to establish a precedent for the future. I would much rather trust to the sentiment of the people. In their vote, you would get something of some value, at least, however small; but, in the other case, only the trammelled judgment of an individual, of no significance, be it which way it might.

It is to some extent fatal to the courts, when the people are compelled to go behind them. I do not wish to believe that the courts were made for fair weather, and for very civil cases merely,—but think of leaving it to any court in the land to decide whether more than three millions of people, in this case, a sixth part of a nation, have a right to be freemen or not! But it has been left to the courts of *justice*, so-called—to the Supreme Court of the land—and, as you all know, recognizing no authority but the Constitution, it has decided that the three millions are, and shall continue to be, slaves. Such judges as these are merely the inspectors of a pick-lock and murderer's tools, to tell him whether they are in working order or not, and there they think that their responsibility ends. There was a prior case on the docket, which they, as judges appointed by God, had no right to skip; which having been justly settled, they would have been saved from this humiliation. It was the case of the murderer himself.

The law will never make men free; it is men who have got to make the law free. They are the lovers of law and order, who observe the law when the government breaks it.

Among human beings, the judge whose words seal the fate of a man furthest into eternity, is not he who merely pronounces the verdict of the law, but he, whoever he may be, who, from a love of truth, and unprejudiced by any custom or enactment of men, utters a true opinion or *sentences* concerning him. He it is that *sentences* him. Whoever has discerned truth, has received his commission from a higher source than the chiefest justice in the world, who can discern only law. He finds himself constituted judge of the judge.—Strange that it should be necessary to state such simple truths.

I am more and more convinced that, with reference to any public question, it is more important to know what the country thinks of it, than what the city thinks. The city does not *think* much. On any moral question, I would rather have the opinion of Boxboro than of Boston and New York put together. When the former speaks, I feel as if somebody *had* spoken, as if *humanity* was yet, and a reasonable being had asserted its rights,—as if some unprejudiced men among the country's hills had at length turned their attention to the subject, and by a few sensible words redeemed the reputation of the race. When, in some obscure country town, the farmers come together to a special town meeting, to express their opinion on some subject which is vexing the land, that, I think, is the true Congress, and the most respectable one that is ever assembled in the United States.

It is evident that there are, in this Commonwealth, at least, two parties, becoming more and more distinct—the party of the city, and the party of the country. I know that the country is mean enough, but I am glad to believe that there is a slight difference in her favor. But as yet, she has few, if any organs, through which to express herself. The editorials which she reads, like the news, come from the sea-board. Let us, the inhabitants of the country, cultivate self-respect. Let us not send to the city for aught more essential than our broadcloths and groceries, or, if we read the opinions of the city, let us entertain opinions of our own.

Among measures to be adopted, I would suggest to make as earnest and vigorous an assault on the Press as has already been made, and with effect, on the Church. The Church has much improved within a few years; but the Press is almost, without exception, corrupt. I believe that, in this country, the press exerts a greater and a more pernicious influence than the Church did in its worst period. We are not a religious people, but we are a nation of politicians. We do not care for the Bible, but we do care for the newspaper. At any meeting of politicians,—like that at Concord the other evening, for instance,—how impertinent it would be to quote from the Bible! how pertinent to quote from a newspaper or from the Constitution! The newspaper is a Bible which we read every morning and every afternoon, standing and sitting, riding and walking. It is a Bible which every man carries in his pocket, which lies on every table and counter, and which the mail, and thousands of missionaries, are continually dispensing. It is, in short, the only book which America has printed, and which America reads. So wide is its influence. The editor is a preacher whom you voluntarily support. Your tax is commonly one cent daily, and it costs nothing for pew hire. But how many of these preachers preach the truth? I repeat the testimony of many an intelligent foreigner, as well as my own convictions, when I say, that probably no country was ever ruled by so mean a class of tyrants as, with a few noble exceptions, are the editors of the periodical press in *this* country. And as they live and rule only by their servility, and appealing to the worst, and not the better nature of man, the people who read them are in the condition of the dog that returns to his vomit.

The *Liberator* and the *Commonwealth* were the only papers in Boston, as far as I know, which made themselves heard in condemnation of the cowardice and meanness of the authorities of that city, as exhibited in '51. The other journals, almost without exception, by their manner of referring to and speaking of the Fugitive Slave Law, and the carrying back of the slave Sims, insulted the common sense of the country, at least. And, for the most part, they did this, one would say, because they thought so to secure the approbation of their patrons, not being aware that a sounder sentiment prevailed to any extent in the heart of the Commonwealth. I am told that some of them have improved of late; but they are still eminently time-serving. Such is the character they have won.

But, thank fortune, this preacher can be even more easily reached by the weapons of the reformer than could the recreant priest. The free men of New England have only to refrain from purchasing and reading these sheets, have only to withhold their cents, to kill a score of them at once. One whom I respect told me that he purchased Mitchel's *Citizen* in the cars, and then threw it out the window.[10] But would not his contempt have been more fatally expressed, if he had not bought it?

Are they Americans? are they New Englanders? are they inhabitants of Lexington, and Concord, and Framingham, who read and support the Boston *Post, Mail, Journal, Advertiser, Courier,* and *Times*? Are these the Flags of our Union? I am not a newspaper reader, and may omit to name the worst.

Could slavery suggest a more complete servility than some of these journals exhibit? Is there any dust which their conduct does not lick, and make fouler still with its slime? I do not know whether the Boston *Herald* is still in existence, but I remember to have seen it about the streets when Simms was carried off.[11] Did it not act its part well— serve its master faithfully? How could it have gone lower on its belly? How can a man stoop lower than he is low? do more than put his extremities in the place of the head he has? than make his head his lower extremity? When I have taken up this paper with my cuffs turned up, I have heard the gurgling of the sewer through every column. I have felt that I was handling a paper picked out of the public gutters, a leaf from the gospel of the gambling-house, the groggery and the brothel, harmonizing with the gospel of the Merchants' Exchange.

The majority of the men of the North, and of the South, and East, and West, are not men of principle. If they vote, they do not send men to Congress on errands of humanity, but while their brothers and sisters are being scourged and hung for loving liberty, while—I might here insert all that slavery implies and is,—it is the mismanagement of wood and iron and stone and gold which concerns them. Do what you will, O Government! with my wife and children, my mother and brother, my father and sister, I will obey your commands to the letter. It will indeed grieve me if you hurt them, if you deliver them to overseers to be hunted by hounds or to be whipped to death; but nevertheless, I will peaceably pursue my chosen calling on this fair earth, until perchance, one day, when I have put on mourning for them dead, I shall have persuaded you to relent. Such is the attitude, such are the words of Massachusetts.

Rather than do thus, I need not say what match I would touch, what system endeavor to blow up,—but as I love my life, I would side with the light, and let the dark earth roll from under me, calling my mother and my brother to follow.

I would remind my countrymen, that they are to be men first, and Americans only at a late and convenient hour. No matter how valuable law may be to protect your property, even to keep soul and body together, if it do not keep you and humanity together.

I am sorry to say, that I doubt if there is a judge in Massachusetts who is prepared to resign his office, and get his living innocently, whenever it is required of him to pass sentence under a law which is merely contrary to the law of God. I am compelled to see that they put themselves, or rather, are by character, in this respect, exactly on a level with the marine who discharges his musket in any direction he is ordered to. They are just as much tools and as little men. Certainly, they are not the more to be respected, because their master enslaves their understandings and consciences, instead of their bodies.

The judges and lawyers,—simply as such, I mean,—and all men of expediency, try this case by a very low and incompetent standard. They consider, not whether the Fugitive Slave Law is right, but whether it is what they call *constitutional*. Is virtue constitutional, or vice? Is equity constitutional, or iniquity? In important moral and vital questions like this, it is just as impertinent to ask whether a law is constitutional or not, as to ask whether it is profitable or not. They persist in being the servants of the worst of men, and not the servants of humanity. The question is not whether you or your grandfather, seventy years ago, did not enter into an agreement to serve the devil, and that service is not accordingly now due; but whether you will not now, for once and at last, serve God,—in spite of your own past recreancy, or that of your ancestor,—by obeying that eternal and only just CONSTITUTION, which He, and not any Jefferson or Adams, has written in your being.

The amount of it is, if the majority vote the devil to be God, the minority will live and behave accordingly, trusting that some time or other, by some Speaker's casting vote, perhaps, they may reinstate God.

This is the highest principle I can get out of or invent for my neighbors. These men act as if they believed that they could safely slide down hill a little way—or a good way—and would surely come to a place, by and by, where they could begin to slide up again. This is expediency, or choosing that course which offers the slightest obstacles to the feet, that is, a down-hill one. But there is no such thing as accomplishing a righteous reform by the use of 'expediency.' There is no such thing as sliding up hill. In morals, the only sliders are back-sliders.

Thus we steadily worship Mammon, both School, and State, and Church, and the Seventh Day curse God with a tintamar from one end of the Union to the other.[12]

Will mankind never learn that policy is not morality—that it never secures any moral right, but considers merely what is expedient? chooses the available candidate, who is invariably the devil,—and what right have his constituents to be surprised, because the devil does not behave like an angel of light? What is wanted is men, not of policy, but of probity—who recognize a higher law than the Constitution, or the decision of the majority. The fate of the country does not depend on how you vote at the polls—the worst man is as strong as the best at that game; it does not depend on what kind of paper you drop into the ballot-box once a year, but on what kind of man you drop from your chamber into the street every morning.

What should concern Massachusetts is not the Nebraska Bill, nor the Fugitive Slave Bill, but her own slaveholding and servility. Let the State dissolve her union with the slaveholder. She may wriggle and hesitate, and ask leave to read the Constitution once more; but she can find no respectable law or precedent which sanctions the continuance of such a Union for an instant.

Let each inhabitant of the State dissolve his union with her, as long as she delays to do her duty.

The events of the past month teach me to distrust Fame. I see that she does not finely discriminate, but coarsely hurrahs. She considers not the simple heroism of an action, but only as it is connected with its apparent consequences. She praises till she is hoarse the easy exploit of the Boston tea party, but will be comparatively silent about the braver and more disinterestedly heroic attack on the Boston Court-House, simply because it was unsuccessful!

Covered with disgrace, the State has sat down coolly to try for their lives and liberties the men who attempted to do its duty for it. And this is called *justice!* They who have shown that they can behave particularly well may perchance be put under bonds for *their good behavior.* They whom truth requires at present to plead guilty, are of all the inhabitants of the State, pre-eminently innocent. While the Governor, and the Mayor, and countless officers of the Commonwealth, are at large, the champions of liberty are imprisoned.

Only they are guiltless, who commit the crime of contempt of such a Court. It behoves every man to see that his influence is on the side of justice, and let the courts make their own characters. My sympathies in this case are wholly with the accused, and wholly against the accusers and their judges. Justice is sweet and musical; but injustice is harsh and discordant. The judge still sits grinding at his organ, but it yields no music, and we hear only the sound of the handle. He believes that all the music resides in the handle, and the crowd toss him their coppers the same as before.

Do you suppose that that Massachusetts which is now doing these things,—which hesitates to crown these men, some of whose lawyers, and even judges, perchance, may be driven to take refuge in some poor quibble, that they may not wholly outrage their instinctive sense of justice,—do you suppose that she is any thing but base and servile? that she is the champion of liberty?

Show me a free State, and a court truly of justice, and I will fight for them, if need be; but show me Massachusetts, and I refuse her my allegiance, and express contempt for her courts.

The effect of a good government is to make life more valuable,—of a bad one, to make it less valuable. We can afford that railroad, and all other merely material stock, should lose some of its value, for that only compels us to live more simply and economically; but suppose that the value of life itself should be diminished! How can we make a less demand on man and nature, how live more economically in respect to virtue and all noble qualities, than we do? I have lived for the last month,—and I think that every man in Massachusetts capable of the sentiment of patriotism must have had a similar experience,— with the sense of having suffered a vast and indefinite loss. I did not know at first what ailed me. At last it occurred to me that what I had lost was a country. I had never respected the Government near to which I had lived, but I had foolishly thought that I might manage to live here, minding my private affairs, and forget it. For my part, my old and worthiest pursuits have lost I cannot say how much of their attraction, and I feel that my investment in life here is worth many percent, less since Massachusetts last deliberately sent back an innocent man, Anthony Burns, to slavery. I dwelt before, perhaps, in the illusion that my life passed somewhere only *between* heaven and hell, but now I cannot persuade myself that I do not dwell *wholly within* hell. The site of that political organization called Massachusetts is to me morally covered with volcanic scoriæ[13] and cinders, such as

Milton describes in the infernal regions. If there is any hell more unprincipled than our rulers, and we, the ruled, I feel curious to see it. Life itself being worth less, all things with it, which minister to it, are worth less. Suppose you have a small library, with pictures to adorn the walls—a garden laid out around—and contemplate scientific and literary pursuits, &c., and discover all at once that your villa, with all its contents, is located in hell, and that the justice of the peace has a cloven foot and a forked tail—do not these things suddenly lose their value in your eyes?

I feel that, to some extent, the State has fatally interfered in my lawful business. It has not only interrupted me in my passage through Court street on errands of trade, but it has interrupted me and every man on his onward and upward path, on which he had trusted soon to leave Court street far behind. What right had it to remind me of Court street? I have found that hollow which even I had relied on for solid.

I am surprised to see men going about their business as if nothing had happened. I say to myself—Unfortunates! they have not heard the news. I am surprised that the man whom I just met on horseback should be so earnest to overtake his newly-bought cows running away—since all property is insecure—and if they do not run away again, they may be taken away from him when he gets them. Fool! does he not know that his seed-corn is worth less this year—that all beneficent harvests fail as you approach the empire of hell? No prudent man will build a store-house under these circumstances, or engage in any peaceful enterprise which requires a long time to accomplish. Art is as long as ever, but life is more interrupted and less available for a man's proper pursuits. It is not an era of repose. We have used up all our inherited freedom. If we would save our lives, we must fight for them.

I walk toward one of our ponds, but what signifies the beauty of nature when men are base? We walk to lakes to see our serenity reflected in them; when we are not serene, we go not to them. Who can be serene in a country where both the rulers and the ruled are without principle? The remembrance of my country spoils my walk. My thoughts are murder to the State, and involuntarily go plotting against her.

But it chanced the other day that I secured a white water-lily, and a season I had waited for had arrived. It is the emblem of purity. It bursts up so pure and fair to the eye, and so sweet to the scent, as if to show us what purity and sweetness reside in, and can be extracted from, the slime and muck of earth. I think I have plucked the first one that has opened for a mile. What confirmation of our hopes is in the fragrance of this flower! I shall not so soon despair of the world for it, notwithstanding slavery, and the cowardice and want of principle of Northern men. It suggests what kind of laws have prevailed longest and widest, and still prevail, and that the time may come when man's deeds may smell as sweet. Such is the odor which the plant emits. If Nature can compound this fragrance still annually, I shall believe her still young and full of vigor, her integrity and genius unimpaired, and that there is virtue even in man, too, who is fitted to perceive and love it. It reminds me that Nature has been partner to no Missouri Compromise. I scent no compromise in the fragrance of the water-lily. It is not a *Nymphœa Douglassii*.[14] In it, the sweet, and pure, and innocent, are wholly sundered from the obscene and baleful. I do not scent in this the time-serving irresolution of a Massachusetts Governor, nor of a Boston Mayor. So behave that the odor of your actions may enhance the general sweetness of the atmosphere, that when we behold or scent a flower, we may not be reminded how inconsistent your deeds are with it; for all odor is but one form of advertisement of a moral quality, and if fair actions had not been performed, the lily would not smell sweet. The foul slime stands for the sloth and vice of man, the decay of humanity; the fragrant flower that springs from it, for the purity and courage which are immortal.

Slavery and servility have produced no sweet-scented flower annually, to charm the senses of men, for they have no real life: they are merely a decaying and a death, offensive to all healthy nostrils. We do not complain that they *live*, but that they do not *get buried*. Let the living bury them; even they are good for manure.

Source: Henry D[avid]. Thoreau, "Slavery in Massachusetts" (4 July 1854), *Liberator*, 24 (21 July 1854): 116.

Notes

1. The Kansas-Nebraska Act, passed in May 1854, created two new territories and permitted their admission with or without slavery, in effect holding that the federal government would no longer intervene in determining which new territories or states would be slaveholding and which would not.

2. On 23 May 1854, Anthony Burns (1834–1862) was arrested in Boston as an escaped slave. There was an unsuccessful attempt to storm the courthouse and free him, resulting in a number of people, including Theodore Parker, to be arrested for treason. Burns was eventually returned to his owner in Virginia. Money was collected to purchase Burns from his master, and this was accomplished in February 1855. He later studied theology at Oberlin College and became pastor to the Zion Baptist Church at St. Catharines, on the shores of Lake Ontario, Canada.

3. Well-known Concord families who had participated in the Battle of Concord in 1775.
4. In 1850, the population of Massachusetts was 973,000.
5. Edward Greeley Loring (1802–1890), the commissioner who decided in favor of Burns's owner.
6. Emory Washburn (1800–1877), governor of Massachusetts 1854–1855.
7. Charles Francis Suttle, Burns's owner.
8. A reference to Sims.
9. 19 April 1775, the date of the Battle of Lexington and Concord.
10. *The Citizen*, a New York newspaper promoting slavery edited between 1854 and 1856 by John Mitchel (1815–1875), an expatriate Irishman.
11. The Boston *Herald* would continue to be published into the twentieth century.
12. Mammon, word used in the New Testament as a personification of riches that has come to mean avarice; tintamar, an uproar.
13. Scoriæ, the dross of metals.
14. *Nymphœa Douglassii*: For a discussion of whether this is a reference to the black abolitionist Frederick Douglas (1818–1895) or Senator Stephen Douglas of Illinois (1813–1861), who was instrumental in getting the Compromise of 1850 passed, see Thoreau's *Reform Papers*, ed. Wendell Glick (Princeton: Princeton University Press, 1973), p. 337.

Ralph Waldo Emerson

"Address at the Woman's Rights Convention"

(20 September 1855)

EMERSON DELIVERED THIS address before the Woman's Rights Convention in Boston. If writers such as Fuller and Parker left no doubt about where they stood on the issue of woman's emancipation and freedom, then Emerson seems more circumspect. Caroline Healey Dall, a former attendee at Fuller's Conversations who was in the audience, praised Emerson for his "beautiful address," though she also noted that "some of the papers thought it doubtful whether you were for us or against us"; and she was correct, for while the *Liberator* noted that Emerson's address "gave the most intense satisfaction to the large audience," the Boston *Traveller* concluded that, on the whole, "it told far more 'against the cause' than for it."

Woman is the power of civilization. Man is a bear in colleges, in mines, in ships, because there are no women. Let good women sail in the ship, the manners at once are altered and mended; in a college, in California, the same remedy serves. Well, now in this country we are getting a little rough and reckless in voting. Here, at the right moment, when the land is full of committees examining election frauds and misdeeds, woman asks for her vote. It is the remedy at the moment of need. She is to civilize the voting as she has the sailors, the collegians, the miners. For now you must build noble houses proper to the State.

I suppose women feel in relation to men as geniuses feel among energetic workers, that though overlooked and thrust aside in the press, they outsee all these noisy masters. And we feel overlooked,—judged,—and sentenced. In that race, which is now predominant over all the other races of men, it was a cherished belief, that women had an oracular nature. They are more delicate than men, and, as thus more impressionable, they are the best index of the coming hour. I share this belief. I think their words are to be weighed,—but 'tis their inconsiderate words, according to the rule,—"Take their first advice, not their second." As Coleridge was wont to apply to a lady for her judgment in question of taste, and accept it, but, when she added, "I think so, because"—"Pardon me, madam," he said, "leave me to find out the reasons for myself." In this sense, then, as more delicate mercuries of the imponderable and immaterial influences, what they say and think are the shadows of coming events. Their very dolls are indicative. Frigg was the Norse goddess of women: "Weirdes all Frigg knoweth, though she telleth them never," said the *Edda*; that is to say, "All wisdoms woman knoweth, though she takes them for granted, and does not explain them as discoveries, like the understanding of man."[1] Men remark always the figure, they catch always the expression. They inspire by a look, and pass with us not so much by what they say or do, as by their presence. They learn so fast, and convey the result so fast, as to outrun the logic of their slow brother, and make his acquisitions poor. A woman of genius said, "I will forgive you that you do so much, and you me that I do nothing."[2] 'Tis their mood or tone that is important. Does their mind misgive them? or are they firm and cheerful? 'Tis a true report that things are going ill or well. And any remarkable opinion or movement shared by women will be the first sign of revolution.

Her strength is of her own kind. Plato said, "Women are the same as men in faculty, only less in degree." But the general voice of mankind has agreed that they have their own strength; that women are strong by sentiment; that the same mental height which their husbands attained by toil, they attain by sympathy with their husbands.

Man is the will, and woman the sentiment. In this ship of humanity, will is the rudder, and sentiment the sail. When woman affects to steer, the rudder is only a masked sail. When women engage in any art or trade, 'tis usually as a resource, not a primary object. So with their schools and education of others' children. The life of the affections is primary to them, so that there is usually no employment or career which they will not, with their own applause and that of society, quit for a suitable marriage. And they give entirely to their affections; set their whole fortune on the die; lose themselves eagerly in the glory of their husbands and children. Man stands astonished at a magnanimity that he cannot pretend to.

Mrs. Lucy Hutchinson, one of the heroines of the English Commonwealth, who wrote the life of her husband, the governor of Nottingham, says, "If he esteemed her at a higher rate than she in herself could have deserved, he was the author of that virtue he doted on, whilst she only reflected his own glories upon him. All that she was, was *him*, while he was here, and all that she is now, at best, but his pale shade."[3]

For Plato's opinion that "they are the same as men in faculty, only in less degree": it is perhaps true that in no art or science, not in painting, poetry, or music, have women produced a masterpiece. But there is an art which is better than poetry, painting, or music, or architecture, better than botany, geology, or any science, namely, conversation: wise, cultivated, genial conversation. Conversation is the last flower of civility, and the best result which life has to offer us; a cup for gods, which has no repentance. It is our account of ourselves. All we have, all we can do, all we know, is brought into play, and is the reproduction in finer form of all our havings.

The part which women play in education, in the care of young, and the tuition of older children, is their organic office in the world. So much sympathy as they have makes them inestimable as mediators between those who have knowledge, and those who want it. Besides, their fine organization, their taste and love of details, makes the knowledge better in their hands.

Coleridge esteems cultivated women to be the depositories and guardians of English undefiled: and Luther commends that accomplishment of pure German speech in his wife. Women are the civilizers. 'Tis difficult to define. What is civilization? I call it the power of good women. It was Burns's remark, "when he first came to Edinburgh, that between the men of rustic life, and the polite world, he observed little difference; that, in the former, though unpolished by fashion, and unenlightened by science, he had found much observation, and much intelligence; but a refined and accomplished woman was a being almost new to him, and of which he had formed a very inadequate idea."[4]

Lucy Percy, Countess of Carlisle, the friend of Strafford and Pym, is thus described by Sir Toby Matthew.[5]

> She is of too high a mind and dignity not only to seek, but almost to wish the friendship of any creature; they whom she is pleased to choose, are such as are of the most eminent condition, both for power and employment; not with any design towards her own particular, but her nature values fortunate persons. She prefers the conversation of men to that of women; not but she can talk on the fashions with her female friends, but she is too soon sensible that she can set them as she wills: that preeminence shortens all equality. She converses with those who are most distinguished for their conversational powers. Of love freely will she discourse, listen to all its faults, and mark all its power, . . . and will take a deep interest for persons of condition and celebrity.

"I like women, they are so finished," said a man of the world.[6] They finish society, manners, language. Form and ceremony are their realm. They embellish trifles; and these ceremonies that hedge our life around are not to be despised, and, when we have become habituated to them, cannot be dispensed with. Certainly, no woman can despise them with impunity. Then, genius delights, in ceremonies, in forms, in decorating life with manners, with proprieties, with order and grace. They are in their nature more relative. The circumstance must always be fit. Out of place they are disfranchised.

"Position," Sir Christopher Wren said, "is essential to the perfecting of beauty."[7] A fine building is lost in a dark lane, and statues should stand in the air. So we commonly say, that easy circumstances seem necessary to the finish of the female character. But they make these with all their might.

The spiritual force of man is as much shown in taste, in his fancy and imagination attaching deep meanings to things and to arbitrary inventions of no real value, as in his perception of truth. He is as much raised above the beast by this creative faculty, as by any other. The horse or ox use no delays: they run to the river, when thirsty, to the corn, when hungry, and say, no thanks, and fight down whatever opposes their appetite. But man invents and adorns all he does with delays and degrees; paints it all over with forms, to please himself better; he invented majesty, and the etiquette of courts, and of drawing rooms; invented architecture, curtains, dress, and the elegance of privacy, to increase the joy of society; invented marriage, and surrounded by religion and comeliness, by all manner of dignities and renunciations, the union of the sexes.

And how should we better measure the gulf between the best intercourse of men in old Athens, in London, or in our American capitals,—between this, and the hedgehog existence of diggers of worms and the eaters of clay and offal, than by signalizing just this department of Taste or Comeliness? Yet herein woman is the prime genius and ordainer. There is no grace that is taught by the dancing master, no style adopted into the etiquette of courts, but was first the whim and action of some brilliant woman, who charmed beholders by this new expression, and made it remembered and copied.

They should be found in fit surroundings, with fair approaches, with agreeable architecture. This convention should be holden in the sculpture gallery. And I think they should magnify their ritual of manners. Society, conversation, decorum, music, flowers, dances, colours, forms, are her homes and attendants.

> The farfetched diamond finds its home
> Flashing and smouldering in her hair.
> For her, the seas their pearls reveal,
> Art and strange lands her pomp supply,
> With purple, chrome, and cochineal,
> Ochre, and lapis lazuli.
> The worm its golden woof presents,
> Whatever runs, flies, dives, or delves,
> All doff for her their ornaments
> Which suit her better than themselves.[8]

There is no gift of nature without some drawback; if we are here, we cannot be there; if we have day, we must forego night. And every extraordinary strength or possession that is added, usually lames the receiver on some part. So to woman this exquisite structure could not exist, without its own penalty: More vulnerable, more infirm, more mortal than men.

They could not be such excellent artists in this element of fancy, if they did not lend and give themselves to it. They are poets who believe their own poetry. They dwell more than men in the element and kingdom of illusion. They see only through Claude Lorraine glass.[9] They emit from all their pores a coloured atmosphere, one would say, wave upon wave of coloured light, in which they walk evermore, and see all objects through this warm tinted mist which envelopes them. And how dare any,—I dare not,—pluck away the coulisses, the roses, the stage effects,—shall I call them?—and routine, ceremonies, with which nature taught them to adorn and to console their life. "Yet fear not," says Mignon, "I shall dance blindfold the egg-dance, and shall not break an egg."

But the starry crown of woman is in the power of her affection and sentiment, and the infinite enlargements to which they lead. Beautiful is the passion of love, painter and adorner of youth and early life; but none suspects in its blushes and tremors what tragedies and immortalities are beyond it. The passion with all its grace and poetry is profane to that which follows it. A few years have changed the coy, haughty maiden into a matron existing for her children, a pelican feeding her young with her life. And these affections are only introductory to that which is sublime.

We men have no right to say it, 'tis very ungracious in man, but the omnipotence of Eve is in humility. The instincts of mankind have drawn the Virgin Mother,

> Created beings all in lowliness
> Surpassing as in height above them.[10]

This is the divine person whom Dante and Milton saw in vision: this the victory of Griselda:[11] And it is when love has reached this height, that all our pretty rhetoric begins to have meaning, when we say, that it adds to the soul a new soul: it is honey in the mouth, music in the ear, and balsam in the heart.

> Far have I clambered in my mind
> But nought so great as Love.
> "What is thy tent? where dost thou dwell?"
> "My mansion is Humility,
> Heaven's vastest capability;
> The further it doth downward tend,
> The higher up it doth ascend."[12]

The first thing men think of, when they love, is, to exhibit their usefulness and advantages. Women make light of these, asking only love. They wish it to be an exchange of nobleness. There is much in their nature, much in their social position, which gives them a divining power. Women know at first sight the characters of those with whom they converse. There is much that tends to give them a religious height which men do not attain. Their sequestration from affairs, and from the injury to the moral sense which affairs often inflict, aids them.

"I use the Lord of the Kaaba, what is the Kaaba to me?" said Rabia. "I am so near to God, that, his word, 'whoso nears me by a span, to him come I a mile,' is true for me."

Hassan Bassō, a famed Mahametan theologian, asked, "how she had lifted herself to this degree of the love of God?"

She replied, "Hereby, that all things which I had found, I have lost in him."

The other said, "In what way or method hast thou known him?"

She answered, "O Hassan! Thou knowest after a certain art and way, but I without art and way."

When once she was sick, three famed theologians came to her, Hassan Vasri, Malek, and Balchi. Hassan said, "He is not upright in his prayer who does not endure the blows of his Lord." Balchi said, "He is not upright in his prayer, who does not rejoice in the blows of his Lord." But Rabia, who, in these words, detected some trace of egoism, said, "He is not upright in his prayer, who, when he beholds his Lord, forgets not that he is stricken."

I have known one bred in poverty and solitude, who realized to our experience the life of the saints of the convent, and religious houses. She was no statute book of practical rules, nor orderly digest of any system of philosophy divine or human, but a Bible, miscellaneous in its parts, but one in Spirit, wherein are sentences of condemnation, chapters of prophecy, promises, and covenants of love, that make foolish the wisdom of the world with the power of God.[13]

"When a daughter is born," said the Sheking, "she sleeps on the ground; she is clothed with a wrapper; she plays with a tile; she is incapable of evil or of good."[14] With the advancements of society, the position and fortunes of women have changed, of course, as events brought her strength or her faults into light. In modern times, three or four conspicuous instrumentalities may be marked. After the deification of woman in the Catholic Church, the religious ages came again in the sixteenth and seventeenth centuries, when her religious nature gave her, of course, new importance. The *Quakers* have the honor of first having established in their discipline an equality in the sexes. It is even more perfect in the later sect of *Shakers*. An epoch for Woman was in France the building of the Hotel Rambouillet.[15] I think another step was made by the doctrine of Swedenborg; a sublime genius who gave a scientific exposition of the part played severally by man, and by woman, in the world; and showed the difference of sex to run through nature and through thought. Of all Christian sects, this is, at this moment, the most vital and aggressive.

Another step was the effect of the action of the age on the antagonism to slavery. It was easy to enlist woman in this; it was impossible not to enlist her. But that cause turned out, as you know, to be a great scholar: he was a terrible metaphysician; he was a jurist, a poet, a divine. Was never a University of Oxford or Göttingen that made such students. It took a man from the plough, and made him acute, and eloquent, and wise to the silencing of the doctors. There was nothing it did not pry into, no right it did not explore, no wrong it did not expose, and it has, among its other effects, given woman a feeling of public duty, and an added self-respect.

One truth leads in another by the hand; one right is an accession of strength to take more. And the times are marked by the new attitude of woman urging, by argument and by association, her rights of all kinds, in short, to one half of the world: the right to education; to avenues of employment; to equal rights of property; to equal rights in marriage; to the exercise of the professions; to suffrage.

Of course, this conspicuousness had its inconveniences. 'Tis very cheap wit that has been spent on the subject, from Aristophanes, in whose comedies I confess my dulness to find good joke, to Rabelais in whom it is monstrous exaggeration of temperament and not borne out by anything in nature, down to the English comedy, and, in our day, Tennyson, and the American newspapers.[16] The body of the joke is all one, to charge them with temperament—victims of temperament—and is identical with Mahomet's opinion, that they have not a sufficient moral or intellectual force to control the perturbations of their physical structure. These were all drawings of morbid anatomy and such satire as might be written on the tenants of a hospital or an asylum for idiots.

Of course, it would be easy for women to retaliate in kind, by painting men from the dogs and orangs that have worn our shape: and the fact that they have not, is an eulogy on the taste and self-respect of women.

The good, easy world took the joke which it liked. There is always want of thought, always credulity. There are plenty of people who believe women to be incapable of anything but to cook; incapable of interest in affairs. There are plenty of people who believe that the world is only governed by men of dark complexion; that affairs are only directed by such; and do not see the use of contemplative men or how ignoble is the world that wanted them, and so without the affection of woman.

But for the general charge: No doubt the charge is well-founded. They are victims of their finer temperament. They have tears, and gaieties, and faintings, and glooms, and devotion to trifles. Nature's end of maternity,—maternity for twenty years,—was of so supreme importance, that it was to be secured at all events, even to the sacrifice of the highest beauty. They are more personal. Men taunt them, that, whatever they do, say, read, or write, they are thinking of themselves and their set. Men are not to the same degree temperamented, for there are multitudes of men who live to objects quite out of them, as, to politics, to trade, to letters, or an art, unhindered by any influence of constitution.

The answer that, silent or spoken, lies in the mind of well meaning persons, to the new claims, is this: that, though their mathematical justice is not to be denied, yet the best women do not wish these things. These are asked for by people who intellectually seek them, but have not the support or sympathy of the truest women: and that if the laws and customs were modified in the manner proposed, it would embarrass and pain gentle and lovely persons, with duties which they would find irksome and distasteful.

Very likely. Providence is always surprising us with new and unlikely instruments. But perhaps it is because these persons have been deprived of education, fine companions, opportunities, such as they wished; because they feel the same rudeness and disadvantage which offends you,—that they have been stung to say, It is too late for us to be polished and fashioned into beauty; but at least we will see that the whole race of women shall not suffer as we have suffered.

Our marriages are bad enough, but that falls from the defects of the partners; but marriage, as it exists in America, England, and Germany, is the best solution that has been offered of the woman's problem. Orientalism, or Fourierism, or Mormonism, or the New York Socialism, are not solutions that any high woman will accept as even approximate to her ideas of well-being.[17] They have an unquestionable right to their own property. And, if the woman demand votes, offices, and political equality with men, as, among the Shakers, an Elder and Eldress are of equal power, and among the Quakers, it must not be refused.

'Tis very cheap wit that finds it so droll that a woman should vote. Educate and refine society to the highest point; bring together cultivated society of both sexes, in a drawing room, to consult and decide by voices on a question of taste, or a question of right,—and is there any absurdity, or any practical difficulty in obtaining their authentic opinions? If not, then there need be none in a hundred companies, if you educate them and accustom them to judge. And for the effect of it, I can say for one, that certainly all my points would be sooner carried in the state, if women voted.

On the questions that are important: Whether the government shall be in one person, or whether representative, or whether democratic; whether men shall be holden in bondage, or shall be roasted alive and eaten as in Typee,[18] or hunted with bloodhounds as in this country; whether men shall be hanged for stealing, or hanged at all; whether the unlimited sale of cheap liquors shall be allowed; they would give,

I suppose, as intelligent a vote as the five thousand Irish voters of Boston or New York.

Why need you vote? If new power is here, if a character which solves old tough questions, which puts me and all the rest in the wrong, tries and condemns our religion, customs, laws, and opens new career to young receptive men and women, you can well leave voting to the old dead people. Those whom you teach, and those whom you half-teach, will fast enough make themselves considered and strong with their new insight, and votes will follow from all the drill.

The objection to their voting is the same that is urged in the lobbies of legislatures against clergymen who take an active part in politics, that, if they are good clergymen, they are unacquainted with the expediences of politics, and if they become good politicians, they are the worse clergymen: so of women, that they cannot enter this arena without being contaminated and unsexed.

Here are two or three other objections to their voting: first, a want of practical wisdom; second, a too purely ideal view; and third, a danger of contamination.

For their want of intimate knowledge of affairs, I do not think this should disqualify them from voting at any town meeting which I ever attended. I could heartily wish the objection were sound. But if any man will take the trouble to see how our people vote—how many gentlemen are willing to take on themselves the trouble of thinking and determining for you, and, standing at the doors of the polls, give every innocent citizen his ticket as he comes in, informing him, that this is the vote of his party; and the innocent citizen, without further demur, carries it to the ballot box; I cannot but think that most women might vote as wisely.

For the other point, of their not knowing the world, and aiming at abstract right, without allowance for circumstances;—that is not a disqualification, but a qualification. Human society is made up of partialities. Each citizen has an interest and a view of his own, which, if followed out to the extreme, would leave no room for any other citizen. One man is timid, and another rash; one would change nothing, and the other is pleased with nothing; one wishes, schools, another armies; one gunboats, another public gardens.

Bring all these biases together, and something is done in favor of them all. Every one is a half vote; but the next elector behind him brings the other or corresponding half in his hand. A reasonable result is had. Now there is no lack, I am sure, of the expediency, or of the interest of trade, or of imperative class interests being neglected. There is no lack of votes representing the physical wants; and if, in your city, the uneducated emigrant vote by the thousands representing a brutal ignorance and mere animal wants, it is to be corrected by an educated and religious vote representing the desires of honest and refined persons.

If the wants, the passions, the vices are allowed a full vote, through the hands of a half-brutal, intemperate population, I think it but fair that the virtues, the aspirations, should be allowed a full vote as an offset, through the purest part of the people. As for the unsexing and contamination, that only accuses our existing politics, shows how barbarous we are, that our policies are so crooked, made up of things not to be spoken, to be understood only by wink and nudge, this man is to be coaxed, and that man to be bought, and that other to be duped. 'Tis easy to see there is contamination enough, but it rots the men now and fills the air with stench come out of that. 'Tis like a dance-cellar. The fairest names in this country in literature, in law, have gone into Congress and come out dishonored.

'Tis easy to see that many steps must be taken; an education of society; a purging of bullies out of the state; and a purging of the elegant cowards who have politely and elegantly betrayed us to them. And when I read the list of men of intellect, of refined pursuits, giants in law, or eminent scholars, or of social distinction, leading men of wealth and enterprise in the commercial community, and see what they voted for, or suffered to be voted for, I think no community was ever so politely and elegantly betrayed.

I do not think it yet appears that women wish this equal share in public affairs. But it is they, and not we, that are to determine it. Let the laws be purged of every barbarous remainder, every barbarous impediment to women. Let the public donation for education be equally shared by them. Let them enter a school, as freely as a church. Let them have, and hold, and give their property, as men do theirs. And, in a few years, it will easily appear whether they wish a voice in making the laws that are to govern them. If you do refuse them a vote, you will also refuse to tax them according to our Teutonic principle: no representation, no tax.

'Tis idle to refuse them a vote on the ground of incompetency. I wish our masculine voting were so good that we had any right to doubt their equal discretion. They could not give worse vote, I think, than we do. Besides, it certainly is no new thing to see women interest themselves in politics. In English, French, German, Italian, and Russian history, you shall often find some Duchess of Marlborough or de Longueville or Madame Roland the centre of political power and intrique.[19] See the experience of our Quakers, and of the Shakers, and of the Antislavery Society, in taking women as men into the council and government, and the women often possess superior administrative capacity.

All events of history are to be regarded as growths and off-shoots of the expanding mind of the race: and this appearance of new opinions, and their currency and force in many minds, is itself the wonderful fact. Whatever is popular, is important, and shows the spontaneous sense of the hour. The aspiration of this century will be the code of the next. It holds of high and distant causes, of the same influences that make the sun and moon. When new opinions appear, they will be entertained and respected by every fair mind according to their reasonableness, and not according to their convenience, or their fitness to shock our customs.

But let us deal with them greatly: let them make their way by the upper road, not by the way of manufacturing public opinion, which lapses continually into expediency, and makes charlatans. All that is spontaneous is irresistible: and forever it is individual force that interests. I need not repeat to you,—your own solitude will suggest it,—that a masculine woman is not strong, but a lady is. The loneliest thought, the purest prayer, is rushing to be the history of a thousand years. Let us have the true woman, the adorner, the hospitable, the religious heart, and no lawyer need be called in to write stipulations, the cunning clauses of provision, the strong investments; for woman moulds the lawgiver, and writes the law.

But I ought to say, I think it impossible to separate the education and interests of the sexes. Improve and refine the men, and you do the same by the women, whether you will or no. Every woman, being the wife, daughter, sister, or mother of a man, she can never be very far from his ear, never not of his counsel, if she has something to urge that is good in itself and agreeable to nature. The slavery of women happened when the men were slaves of kings. The melioration of manners has brought their melioration, of course. It could not otherwise, and hence this new desire of better laws. For there are always a certain number of passionately loving fathers, brothers, husbands, and sons who put their might into the endeavor to make a daughter, a wife, or a mother happy in the way that suits best.

Woman should find in man her guardian. Silently she looks for that; and when she finds, as she instantly will, if he is not, she betakes her to her own defences, and does the best she can. But when he is her guardian,—fulfilled with all nobleness,—knows and accepts his duties as her brother, all goes well for both. The new movement is only a tide shared by the spirits of man and woman, and you may proceed in a faith, that, whatever the woman's heart is prompted to desire, the man's mind is simultaneously prompted to accomplish.

Source: Ralph Waldo Emerson, "Address at the Woman's Rights Convention, 20 September 1855," from *The Later Lectures of Ralph Waldo Emerson, 1843–1871*, ed. Ronald A. Bosco and Joel Myerson (Athens: University of Georgia Press, forthcoming). The quotations are from Dall to Emerson, 7 October 1855, Houghton Library, Harvard University; "Woman's Rights Convention," *Liberator*, 28 September, p. 2; "Woman's Rights Convention—Mr. Emerson and the Ladies," Boston *Traveller*, 21 September—reprinted from a reprinting in an unidentified newspaper in Kenneth Walter Cameron, *Transcendental Log* (Hartford, Conn.: Transcendental Books, 1973), p. 99.

Notes

1. Frigg, the Norse goddess of women.
2. Attributed to Caroline Sturgis Tappan (1819–1888), longtime friend of Emerson and Margaret Fuller.
3. Lucy Hutchinson, quoted from her book about her husband, *Memoirs of the Life of Colonel Hutchinson*.
4. Attributed to *Reliques of Burns* (1808), by Robert Hartley Cromek (1770–1812), English engraver.
5. Lucy Percy Hay, Countess of Carlisle (1599–1660); English politicians or activists Sir Thomas Wentworth, First Earl of Strafford (1593–1641), John Pym (1584–1643), and Sir Toby Matthew (1577–1655).
6. Attributed to Samuel Gray Ward (1817–1907), poet, banker, and friend of Emerson.
7. Christopher Wren (1632–1723), architect of St. Paul's Cathedral in London.
8. *The Angel in the House* (1854–1862), section 2, ll. 7–16, by the English poet Coventry Patmore (1823–1896), was published in four parts.
9. Claude de Lorraine (1600–1682), French landscape painter. His use of colors may suggest the "glass" through which Emerson implies people view things.
10. *Paradiso*, Canto 33, ll. 1–3, by Dante.
11. Griselda, a literary character typifying patience as a wife and mother.
12. "Love and Humility," ll. 1–2, 7–11, by Henry More (1614–1687), English philosophical writer.
13. An allusion to Emerson's aunt, Mary Moody Emerson (1774–1863), from an 1835 letter by Emerson's brother, Charles Chauncy Emerson; see *Journals and Miscellaneous Notebooks*, 5:158.
14. Quoted from *Shi King (Shih Ching)*, a collection of poems attributed to Confucius.
15. Hotel Rambouillet, residence in Paris of Catherine de Vivonne, Marquise de Rambouillet (1588–1665), social leader and patron of the arts.

16. Aristophanes (ca. 450–ca. 380 B.C.), Athenian writer of Greek comedies; François Rabelais (ca. 1494–1553), French satirist; Alfred, Lord Tennyson (1809–1892), named poet laureate in 1850 to succeed Wordsworth.
17. The New York Socialists, led by Horace Greeley (1811–1872), editor of the *New-York Tribune*, and Parke Godwin (1816–1904), an editor of the New York *Evening Post*, generally followed the doctrines of Fourier.
18. *Typee*, a reference to the novel by Herman Melville (1819–1891), published in 1846.
19. Duchess of Marlborough (1660–1774), a member of Queen Anne's inner circle; Duchess de Longueville (1619–1679), active in French politics.

Henry David Thoreau

"A Plea for Captain John Brown"

(30 October 1859)

JOHN BROWN (1800–1859) had a long career as an abolitionist. He had been involved with the Free Soilers in Kansas trying to keep the state free, leading a guerilla company that eventually executed a number of proslavery men. More important, he launched an attack on the Union arsenal at Harper's Ferry, Virginia, on 16 October 1859, with less than two dozen men, both black and white, in the hope that escaped slaves would join in the rebellion. He was unsuccessful and many of his supporters were killed. Brown was tried for treason and leading a slave revolt, and was sentenced to be hanged. In the time between his trial and execution, many northerners urged clemency for Brown, and he became a martyr for the antislavery cause.

In a sense, Brown became a personification of abolitionists' frustration at the sectional differences that had become more pronounced over the last decade, since the Compromise of 1850, and their desire to act against the South. Thoreau's lecture, first read in Concord, argues that he was "a transcendentalist above all, a man of ideas and principles," and goes on to suggest the Christ-like attribute of Brown having been sacrificed for the evils of humankind.

I trust that you will pardon me for being here. I do not wish to force my thoughts upon you, but I feel forced myself. Little as I know of Captain Brown, I would fain do my part to correct the tone and the statements of the newspapers, and of my countrymen generally, respecting his character and actions. It costs us nothing to be just. We can at least express our sympathy with, and admiration of, him and his companions, and that is what I now propose to do.

First, as to his history. I will endeavor to omit, as much as possible, what you have already read. I need not describe his person to you, for probably most of you have seen and will not soon forget him. I am told that his grandfather, John Brown, was an officer in the Revolution; that he himself was born in Connecticut about the beginning of this century, but early went with his father to Ohio. I heard him say that his father was a contractor who furnished beef to the army there, in the war of 1812; that he accompanied him to the camp, and assisted him in that employment, seeing a good deal of military life, more, perhaps, than if he had been a soldier, for he was often present at the councils of the officers. Especially, he learned by experience how armies are supplied and maintained in the field—a work which, he observed, requires at least as much experience and skill as to lead them in battle. He said that few persons had any conception of the cost, even the pecuniary cost, of firing a single bullet in war. He saw enough, at any rate, to disgust him with a military life; indeed, to excite in him a great abhorrence of so much so, that though he was tempted by the offer of some petty office in the army, when he was about eighteen, he not only declined that, but he also refused to train when warned, and was fined for it. He then resolved that he would never have any thing to do with any war, unless it were a war for liberty.

When the troubles in Kansas began, he sent several of his sons thither to strengthen the party of the Free State men, fitting them out with such weapons as he had; telling them that if the troubles should increase, and there should be need of him, he would follow to assist them with his hand and counsel. This, as you all know, he soon after did; and it was through his agency, far more than any other's, that Kansas was made free.

For a part of his life he was a surveyor, and at one time he was engaged in wool-growing, and he went to Europe as an agent about that business. There, as every where, he had his eyes about him, and made many original observations. He said, for instance, that he saw why the soil of England was so rich, and that of Germany (I think it was) so poor, and he thought of writing to some of the crowned heads about it. It was because in England the peasantry live on the soil which they cultivate, but in Germany they are gathered into villages, at night. It is a pity that he did not make a book of his observations.

I should say that he was an old-fashioned man in his respect for the Constitution, and his faith in the permanence of this Union. Slavery he deemed to be wholly opposed to these, and he was its determined foe.

He was by descent and birth a New England farmer, a man of great common sense, deliberate and practical as that class is, and tenfold more so. He was like the best of those who stood at Concord Bridge once; and on Lexington Common, and on Bunker Hill, only he was firmer and higher principled than any that I have chanced to hear as of as there.[1] It was no abolition lecturer that converted him. Ethan Allen and Stark, with whom he may in some respects be compared, were rangers in a lower and less important field.[2] They could bravely face their country's foes, but he had the courage to face his country herself, when she was in the wrong. A Western writer says, to account for his escape from so many perils, that he was concealed under a "rural exterior;" as if, in that prairie land, a hero should, by good rights, wear a citizen's dress only.

He did not go to the college called Harvard, good old Alma Mater as she is. He was not fed on the pap that is there furnished. As he phrased it, "I know no more of grammar than one of your calves." But he went to the great university of the West, where he sedulously pursued the study of Liberty, for which he had early betrayed a fondness, and having taken many degrees, he finally commenced the public practice of Humanity in Kansas, as you all know. Such were *his humanities*, and not any study of grammar. He would have left a Greek accent slanting the wrong way, and righted up a falling man.

He was one of that class of whom we hear a great deal, but, for the most part, see nothing, at all—the Puritans. It would be in vain to kill him. He died lately in the time of Cromwell, but he reappeared here. Why should he not? Some of the Puritan stock and are said to have come over and settled in New England. They were a class that did something else than celebrate their forefathers' day, and eat parched corn in remembrance of that time. They were neither Democrats nor Republicans, but men of simple habits, straightforward, prayerful; not thinking much of rulers who did not fear God, not making many compromises, nor seeking after available candidates.

"In his camp," as one has recently written, and as I have myself heard him state, "he permitted no profanity; no man of loose morals was suffered to remain there, unless, indeed, as a prisoner of war. 'I would rather,' said he, 'have the small-pox, yellow fever, and cholera, all together in my camp, than a man without principles. * * * It is a mistake, sir, that our people make, when they think that bullies are the best fighters, or that they are the fit men to oppose these Southerners. Give me men of good principles,—God-fearing men,—men who respect themselves, and with a dozen of them I will oppose any hundred such men as these Buford ruffians.' "[3] He said that if one offered himself to be a soldier under him, who was forward to tell what he could or would do, if he could only get sight of the enemy, he had but little confidence in him.

He was never able to find more than a score or so of recruits whom he would accept, and only about a dozen, among them his sons, in whom he had perfect faith. When he was here, some years ago, he showed to a few a little manuscript book,—his "orderly book" I think he called it,—containing the names of his company in Kansas, and the rules by which they bound themselves; and he stated that several of them had already sealed the contract with their blood. When some one remarked that, with the addition of a chaplain, it would have been a perfect Cromwellian troop, he observed that he would have been glad to add a chaplain to the list, if he could have found one who could fill that office worthily. It is easy enough to find one for the United States army. I believe that he had prayers in his camp morning and evening, nevertheless.

He was a man of Spartan habits, and at sixty was scrupulous about his diet at your table, excusing himself by saying that he must eat sparingly and fare hard, as became a soldier or one who was fitting himself for difficult enterprises, a life of exposure.

A man of rare common sense and directness of speech, as of action; a transcendentalist above all, a man of ideas and principles,—that was what distinguished him. Not yielding to a whim or transient impulse, but carrying out the purpose of a life. I noticed that he did not over-state any thing, but spoke within bounds. I remember, particularly, how, in his speech here, he referred to what his family had suffered in Kansas, without ever giving the least vent to his pent-up fire. It was a volcano with an ordinary chimney-flue. Also referring to the deeds of certain Border Ruffians, he said, rapidly paring away his speech, like an experienced soldier, keeping a reserve of force and meaning, "They had a perfect right to be hung." He was not in the least a rhetorician, was not talking to Buncombe[4] or his constituents any where, had he no need to invent any thing, but to tell the simple truth, and communicate his own resolution; therefore he appeared in-comparably strong, and eloquence in Congress and elsewhere seemed to me at a discount. It was like the speeches of Cromwell compared with those of an ordinary king.

As for his tact and prudence, I will merely say, that at a time when scarcely a man from the Free States was able to reach Kansas by any direct route, at least without having his arms taken from him, he, carrying what imperfect guns and other weapons he could collect, openly and slowly drove an ox-cart through Missouri, apparently in the capacity of a surveyor, with his surveying compass exposed in it, and so passed unsuspected, and had ample opportunity to learn the designs of the enemy. For some time after his arrival he still followed the same profession. When, for instance, he saw a knot of the ruffians on the prairie, discussing, of course, the single topic which then occupied their minds, he would, perhaps, take his compass and one of his sons, and proceed to run an imaginary line right through the very spot on which that conclave had assembled, and when he came up to them, he would naturally pause and have some talk with them, learning their news, and, at last, all their plans perfectly; and having thus completed his real survey, he would resume his imaginary one, and run on his line till he was out of sight.

When I expressed surprise that he could live in Kansas at all, with a price set upon his head, and so large a number, including the authorities, exasperated against him, he accounted for it by saying, "It is perfectly well understood that I will not be taken." Much of the time for some years he has had to skulk in swamps, suffering from poverty and from sickness, which was the consequence of exposure, befriended only by Indians and a few whites. But though it might be known that he was lurking in a particular swamp, his foes commonly did not care to go in after him. He could even come out into a town where there were more Border Ruffians than Free State men, and transact some business, without delaying long, and yet not be molested; for said he, "No little handful of men were willing to undertake it, and a large body could not be got together in season."

As for his recent failure, we do not know the facts about it. It was evidently far from being a wild and desperate attempt. His enemy, Mr. Vallandigham, is compelled to say, that "it was among the best planned and executed conspiracies that ever failed."[5]

Not to mention his other successes, was it a failure, or did it show a want of good management, to deliver from bondage a dozen human beings, and walk off with them by broad daylight, for weeks if not months, at a leisurely pace, through one State after another, for half the length of the North, conspicuous to all parties, with a price set upon his head, going into a court room on his way and telling what he had done, thus convincing Missouri that it was not profitable to try to hold slaves in his neighborhood?—and this, not because the government menials were lenient, but because they were afraid of him.

Yet he did not attribute his success, foolishly, to "his star," or to magic. He said, truly, that the reason why such greatly superior numbers quailed before him, was, as one of his prisoners confessed, because they *lacked a cause*—a kind of armor which he and his party never lacked. When the time came, few men were found willing to lay down their lives in defence of what they knew to be wrong; they did not like that this should be their last act in this world.

But to make haste to *his* last act, and its effects.

The newspapers seem to ignore, or perhaps are really ignorant of the fact, that there are at least as many as two or three individuals to a town throughout the North, who think much as the present speaker does about him and his enterprise. I do not hesitate to say that they are an important and growing party. We aspire to be something more than stupid and timid chattels, pretending to read history and our Bibles, but desecrating every house and every day we breathe in. Perhaps anxious politicians may prove that only seventeen white men and five negroes were concerned in the late enterprise; but their very anxiety to prove this might suggest to themselves that all is not told. Why do they still dodge the truth? They are so anxious because of a dim consciousness of the fact, which they do not distinctly face, that at least a million of the free inhabitants of the United States would have rejoiced if it had succeeded. They at most only criticise the tactics. Though we wear no crape, the thought of that man's position and probable fate is spoiling many a man's day here at the North for other thinking. If any one who has seen him here can pursue successfully any other train of thought, I do not know what he is made of. If there is any such who gets his usual allowance of sleep, I will warrant him to fatten easily under any circumstances which do not touch his body or purse. I put a piece of paper and a pencil under my pillow, and when I could not sleep, I wrote in the dark.

On the whole, my respect for my fellow-men, except as one may outweigh a million, is not being increased these days. I have noticed the cold-blooded way in which newspaper writers and men generally speak of this event, as if an ordinary malefactor, though one of unusual "pluck,"—as the Governor of Virginia is reported to have said, using the language of the cock-pit, "the gamest man he ever saw,"—had been caught, and were about to be hung.[6] He was not dreaming of his foes when the governor thought he looked so brave. It turns what sweetness I have to gall, to hear, or hear of, the remarks of some of my neighbors. When we heard at first that he was dead, one of my townsmen observed that "he died as the fool dieth;" which, pardon me, for an instant suggested a likeness in him dying to my neighbor living. Others, craven-hearted, said disparagingly, that "he threw his life away," because he resisted the government. Which way have they thrown *their* lives, pray?—Such as would praise a man for attacking singly an ordinary band of thieves or murderers. I hear another ask, Yankee-like, "What will he gain by it?" as if he expected to fill his pockets by this enterprise. Such a one has no idea of gain but in this worldly sense. If it does not lead to a "surprise" party, if he does not get a new pair of boots, or a vote of thanks, it must be a failure. "But he won't gain any thing by it." Well, no, I don't suppose he could get four-and-sixpence a day for being hung, take the year round; but then he stands a chance to save a considerable part of his soul—and *such* a soul!—when *you* do not. No doubt you can get more in your market for a quart of milk than for a quart of blood, but that is not the market that heroes carry their blood to.

Such do not know that like the seed is the fruit, and that, in the moral world, when good seed is planted, good fruit is inevitable, and does not depend on our watering and cultivating; that when you plant, or bury, a hero in his field, a crop of heroes is sure to spring up. This is a seed of such force and vitality, that it does not ask our leave to germinate.

The momentary charge at Balaclava, in obedience to a blundering command, proving what a perfect machine the soldier is, has, properly enough, been celebrated by a poet laureate;[7] but the steady, and for the most part successful charge of this man, for some years, against the legions of Slavery, in obedience to an infinitely higher command, is as much more memorable than that, as an intelligent and conscientious man is superior to a machine. Do you think that will go unsung?

"Served him right"—"A dangerous man"—"He is undoubtedly insane." So they proceed to live their sane, and wise, and altogether admirable lives, reading their Plutarch a little, but chiefly pausing at that feat of Putnam, who was let down into a wolf's den;[8] and in this wise they nourish themselves for brave and patriotic deeds some time or other. The Tract Society could afford to print that story of Putnam. You might open the district schools with the reading of it, for there is nothing about Slavery or the Church in it; unless it occurs to the reader that some pastors are *wolves* in sheep's clothing. "The American Board of Commissioners for Foreign Missions" even, might dare to protest against *that* wolf. I have heard of boards, and of American boards, but it chances that I never heard of this particular lumber till lately. And yet I hear of Northern men, women, and children, by families, buying a "life membership" in such societies as these;—a life-membership in the grave! You can get buried cheaper than that.

Our foes are in our midst and all about us. There is hardly a house but is divided against itself, for our foe is that all but universal woodenness of both head and heart, the want of vitality in man, which is the effect of our vice; and hence are begotten fear, superstition, bigotry, persecution, and slavery of all kinds. We are more figure-heads upon a hulk, with livers in the place of hearts. The curse is the worship of idols, which at length changes the worshiper into a stone image himself; and the New Englander is just as much as idolater as the Hindoo.

This man was an exception, for he did not set up even a political graven image between him and his God.

A church that can never have done with excommunicating Christ while it exists! Away with your broad and flat churches, and your narrow and tall churches! Take a step forward, and invent a new style of out-houses. Invent a salt that will save you, and defend our nostrils.

The modern Christian is a man who has consented to say all the prayers in the liturgy, provided you will let him go straight to bed and sleep quietly afterward. All his prayers begin with "Now I lay me down to sleep," and he is forever looking forward to the time when he shall go to his "*long* rest." He has consented to perform certain old established charities, too, after a fashion, but he does not wish to hear of any new-fangled ones; he doesn't wish to have any supplementary articles added to the contract, to fit it to the present time. He shows the whites of his eyes on the Sabbath, and the blacks all the rest of the week. The evil is not merely a stagnation of blood, but a stagnation of spirit. Many, no doubt, are well disposed, but sluggish by constitution and by habit, and they cannot conceive of a man who is actuated by higher motives than they are. Accordingly they pronounce this man insane, for they know that *they* could never act as he does, as long as they are themselves.

We dream of foreign countries, of other times and races of men, placing them at a distance in history or space; but let some significant event like the present occur in our midst, and we discover, often, this distance and this strangeness between us and our nearest neighbors. *They* are our Austrias, and Chinas, and South Sea Islands. Our crowded society becomes well spaced all at once, clean and handsome to the eye, a city of magnificent distances. We discover why it was that we never got beyond compliments and surfaces with them before; we become aware of as many versts between us and them as there are between a wandering Tartar and a Chinese town.[9] The thoughtful man becomes a hermit in the thoroughfares of the market-place. Impassable seas suddenly find their level between us, or dumb steppes stretch themselves out there. It is the difference of constitution, of intelligence, and faith, and not streams and mountains, that make the true and impassable boundaries between individuals and between states. None but the like-minded can come plenipotentiary to our court.

I read all the newspapers I could get within a week after this event, and I do not remember in them a single expression of sympathy for these men. I have since seen one noble statement, in a Boston paper, not editorial. Some voluminous sheets decided not to print the full report of Brown's words to the exclusion of other matter. It was as if a publisher should reject the manuscript of the New Testament, and print Wilson's last speech.[10] The same journal which contained this pregnant news, was chiefly filled, in parallel columns, with the reports of the political conventions that were being held. But the descent to them was too steep. They should have been spared this contrast, been printed in an extra at least. To turn from the voices and deeds of earnest men to the *cackling* of political conventions! Office-seekers and speech-makers, who do not so much as lay an honest egg, but wear their breasts bare upon an egg of chalk! Their great game is the game of straws, or rather that universal aboriginal game of the platter, at which the Indians cried *hub, hub!* Exclude the reports of religious and political conventions, and publish the words of a living man.

But I object not so much to what they have omitted, as to what they have inserted. Even the *Liberator* called it "a misguided, wild, and apparently insane—effort." As for the herd of newspapers and magazines, I do not chance to know an editor in the country who will deliberately print any thing which he knows will ultimately and permanently reduce the number of his subscribers. They do not believe that it would be expedient. How then can they print truth? If we do not say pleasant things, they argue, nobody will attend to us. And so they do like some travelling auctioneers, who sing an obscene song in order to draw a crowd around them. Republican editors, obliged to get their sentences ready for the morning edition, and accustomed to look at every thing by the twilight of politics, express no admiration, nor true sorrow even, but call these men "deluded fanatics"—"mistaken men"—"insane," or "crazed." It suggests what a *sane* set of editors we are blessed with, *not* "mistaken men"; who know very well on which side their bread is buttered, at least.

A man does a brave and humane deed, and at once, on all sides, we hear people and parties declaring, "I didn't do it, nor countenance *him* to do it, in any conceivable way. It can't be fairly inferred from my past career." I, for one, am not interested to hear you define your position. I don't know that I ever was, or ever shall be. I think it is mere egotism, or impertinent at this time. Ye needn't take so much pains to wash your skirts of him. No intelligent man will ever be convinced that he was any creature of yours. He went and came, as he himself informs us, "under the auspices of John Brown and nobody else." The Republican party does not perceive how many his *failure* will make to vote more correctly than they would have them. They have counted the votes of Pennsylvania & Co., but they have not correctly counted Captain Brown's vote. He has taken the wind out of their sails, the little wind they had, and they may as well lie to and repair.

What though he did not belong to your clique! Though you may not approve of his method or his principles, recognize his magnanimity. Would you not like to claim kindredship with him in that, though in no other thing he is like, or likely, to you? Do you think that you would lose your reputation so? What you lost at the spile, you would gain at the bung.[11]

If they do not mean all this, then they do not speak the truth, and say what they mean. They are simply at their old tricks still.

"It was always conceded to him," *says one who calls him crazy*, "that he was a conscientious man, very modest in his demeanor, apparently inoffensive, until the subject of Slavery was introduced, when he would exhibit a feeling of indignation unparalleled."

The slave-ship is on her way, crowded with its dying victims; new cargoes are being added in mid ocean; a small crew of slaveholders, countenanced by a large body of passengers, is smothering four millions under the hatches, and yet the politician asserts that the only proper way by which deliverance is to be obtained, is by "the quiet diffusion of the sentiments of humanity," without any "outbreak." As if the sentiments of humanity were ever found unaccompanied by its deeds, and you could disperse them, all finished to order, the pure article, as easily as water with a watering-pot, and so lay the dust. What is that that I hear cast overboard? The bodies of the dead that have found deliverance. That is the way we are "diffusing" humanity, and its sentiments with it.

Prominent and influential editors, accustomed to deal with politicians, men of an infinitely lower grade, say, in their ignorance, that he acted "on the principle of revenge." They do not know the man. They must enlarge themselves to conceive of him. I have no doubt that the time will come when they will begin to see him as he was. They have got to conceive of a man of faith and of religious principle, and not a politician nor an Indian; of a man who did not wait till he was personally interfered with or thwarted in some harmless business before he gave his life to the cause of the oppressed.

If Walker may be considered the representative of the South, I wish I could say that Brown was the representative of the North.[12] He was a superior man. He did not value his bodily life in comparison with ideal things. He did not recognize unjust human laws, but resisted them as he was bid. For once we are lifted out of the trivialness and dust of politics into the region of truth and manhood. No man in America has ever stood up so persistently and effectively for the dignity of human nature, knowing himself for a man, and the equal of any and all governments. In that sense he was the most American of us all. He needed no babbling lawyer, making false issues, to defend him. He was more than a match for all the judges that American voters, or office-holders of whatever grade, can create. He could not have been tried by a jury of his peers, because his peers did not exist. When a man stands up serenely against the condemnation and vengeance of mankind, rising above them literally *by a whole body*,—even though he were of late the vilest murderer, who has settled that matter with himself,—the spectacle is a sublime one,—didn't ye know it, ye Liberators, ye Tribunes, ye Republicans?—and we become criminal in comparison. Do yourselves the honor to recognize him. He needs none of your respect.

As for the Democratic journals, they are not human enough to affect me at all. I do not feel indignation at any thing they may say.

I am aware that I anticipate a little, that he was still, at the last accounts, alive in the hands of his foes; but that being the case, I have all along found myself thinking and speaking of him as physically dead.

I do not believe in erecting statues to those who still live in our hearts, whose bones have not yet crumbled in the earth around us, but I would rather see the statute of Captain Brown in the Massachusetts State-House yard, than that of any other man whom I know. I rejoice that I live in this age—that I am his contemporary.

What a contrast, when we turn to that political party which is so anxiously shuffling him and his plot out of its way, and looking around for some available slaveholder, perhaps, to be its candidate, at least for one who will execute the Fugitive Slave Law, and all those other unjust laws which he took up arms to annul!

Insane! A father and six sons, and one son-in-law, and several more men besides,—as many at least as twelve disciples,—all struck with insanity at once; while the sane tyrant holds with a firmer grip than ever his four millions of slaves, and a thousand sane editors, his abettors, are saving their country and their bacon! Just as insane were his efforts in Kansas. Ask the tyrant who is his most dangerous foe, the sane man or the insane. Do the thousands who know him best, who have rejoiced at his deeds in Kansas, and have afforded him material aid there, think him insane? Such a use of this word is a mere trope with most who persist in using it, and I have no doubt that many of the rest have already in silence retracted their words.

Read his admirable answers to Mason and others.[13] How they are dwarfed and defeated by the contrast! On the one side, half brutish, half timid questioning; on the other, truth, clear as lightning, crashing into their obscene temples. They are made to stand with Pilate, and Gessler, and the Inquisition.[14] How ineffectual their speech and action!

and what a void their silence! They are but helpless tools in this great work. It was no human power that gathered them about this preacher.

What have Massachusetts and the North sent a few *sane* representatives to Congress for, of late years?—to declare with effect what kind of sentiments? All their speeches put together and boiled down,—and probably they themselves will confess it,—do not match for manly directness and force, and for simple truth, the few casual remarks of crazy John Brown, on the floor of the Harper's Ferry engine house;— that man whom you are about to hang, to send to the other world, though not to represent *you* there. No, he was not our representative in any sense. He was too fair a specimen of a man to represent the like of us. Who, then, *were* his constituents? If you read his words understandingly you will find out. In his case there is no idle eloquence, no made, nor maiden speech, no compliments to the oppressor. Truth is his inspirer, and earnestness the polisher of his sentences. He could afford to lose his Sharp's rifles, while he retained his faculty of speech, a Sharp's rifle of infinitely surer and longer range.

And the *New York Herald* reports the conversation *"verbatim"!* It does not know of what undying words it is made the vehicle.

I have no respect for the penetration of any man who can read the report of that conversation, and still call the principal in it insane. It has the ring of a saner sanity than an ordinary discipline and habits of life, than an ordinary organization, secure. Take any sentence of it— "Any questions that I can honorably answer, I will; not otherwise. So far as I am myself concerned, I have told every thing truthfully. I value my word, sir." The few who talk about his vindictive spirit, while they really admire his heroism, have no test by which to detect a noble man, no amalgam to combine with his pure gold. They mix their own dross with it.

It is a relief to turn from these slanders to the testimony of his more truthful, but frightened, jailers and hangmen. Governor Wise speaks far more justly and appreciatingly of him than any Northern editor, or politician, or public personage, that I chance to have heard from. I know that you can afford to hear him again on this subject. He says: "They are themselves mistaken who take him to be a madman. . . . He is cool, collected, and indomitable, and it is but just to him to say, that he was humane to his prisoners. . . . And he inspired me with great trust in his integrity as a man of truth. He is a fanatic, vain and garrulous," (I leave that part to Mr. Wise,) "but firm, truthful, and intelligent. His men, too, who survive, are like him. . . . Colonel Washington says that he was the coolest and firmest man he ever saw in defying danger and death.[15] With one son dead by his side, and another shot through, he felt the pulse of his dying son with one hand,

and held his rifle with the other, and commanded his men with the utmost composure, encouraging them to be firm, and to sell their lives as dear as they could. Of the three white prisoners, Brown, Stevens, and Coppoc, it was hard to say which was most firm."[16]

Almost the first Northern men whom the slaveholder has learned to respect!

The testimony of Mr. Vallandigham, though less valuable, is of the same purport, that "it is vain to underrate either the man or his conspiracy. . . . He is the farthest possible remove from the ordinary ruffian, fanatic, or madman."

"All is quiet at Harper's Ferry," say the journals. What is the character of that calm which follows when the law and the slaveholder prevail? I regard this event as a touchstone designed to bring out, with glaring distinctness, the character of this government. We needed to be thus assisted to see it by the light of history. It needed to see itself. When a government puts forth its strength on the side of injustice, as ours to maintain Slavery and kill the liberators of the slave, it reveals itself a merely brute force, or worse, a demonical force. It is the head of the Plug Uglies.[17] It is more manifest than ever that tyranny rules. I see this government to be effectually allied with France and Austria in oppressing mankind. There sits a tyrant holding fettered four millions of slaves; here comes their heroic liberator. This most hypocritical and diabolical government looks up from its seat on the gasping four millions, and inquires with an assumption of innocence, "What do you assault me for? Am I not an honest man? Cease agitation on this subject, or I will make a slave of you, too, or else hang you."

We talk about a *representative* government; but what a monster of a government is that where the noblest faculties of the mind, and the *whole* heart, are not *represented*. A semi-human tiger or ox, stalking over the earth, with its heart taken out and the top of its brain shot away. Heroes have fought well on their stumps when their legs were shot off, but I never heard of any good done by such a government as that.

The only government that I recognize,—and it matters not how few are at the head of it, or how small its army,—is that power that establishes justice in the land, never that which establishes injustice. What shall we think of a government to which all the truly brave and just men in the land are enemies, standing between it and those whom it oppresses? A government that pretends to be Christian and crucifies a million Christs every day!

Treason! Where does such treason take its rise? I cannot help thinking of you as you deserve, ye governments. Can you dry up the fountains of thought? High treason, when it is resistance to tyranny here below, has its origin in, and is first committed by the power that makes and forever recreates man. When you have caught and hung all these human rebels, you have accomplished nothing but your own guilt, for you have not struck at the fountain head. You presume to contend with a foe against whom West Point cadets and rifled cannon *point* not. Can all the art of the cannon-founder tempt matter to turn against its maker? Is the form in which the founder thinks he casts it more essential than the constitution of it and of himself?

The United States have a coffle of four millions of slaves. They are determined to keep them in this condition; and Massachusetts is one of the confederated overseers to prevent their escape. Such are not all the inhabitants of Massachusetts, but such are they who rule and are obeyed here. It was Massachusetts, as well as Virginia, that put down this insurrection at Harper's Ferry. She sent the marines there, and she will have to pay the penalty of her sin.

Suppose that there is a society in this State that out of its own purse and magnanimity saves all the fugitive slaves that run to us, and protects our colored fellow-citizens, and leaves the other work to the Government, so-called. Is not that government fast losing its occupation, and becoming contemptible to mankind? If private men are obliged to perform the offices of government, to protect the weak and dispense justice, then the government becomes only a hired man, or clerk, to perform menial or indifferent services. Of course, that is but the shadow of a government whose existence necessitates a Vigilant Committee.[18] What should we think of the oriental Cadi even, behind whom worked in secret a Vigilant Committee?[19] But such is the character of our Northern States generally; each has its Vigilant Committee. And, to a certain extent, these crazy governments recognize and accept this relation. They say, virtually, "We'll be glad to work for you on these terms, only don't make a noise about it." And thus the government, its salary being insured, withdraws into the back shop, taking the constitution with it, and bestows most of its labor on repairing that. When I hear it at work sometimes, as I go by, it reminds me, at best, of those farmers who in winter contrive to turn a penny by following the coopering business. And what kind of spirit is their barrel made to hold? They speculate in stocks, and bore holes in mountains, but they are not competent to lay out even a decent highway. The only *free* road, the Underground Railroad, is owned and managed by the Vigilant Committee.[20] *They* have tunnelled under the whole breadth of the land. Such a government is losing its power and respectability as surely as water runs out of a leaky vessel, and is held by one that can contain it.

I hear many condemn these men because they were so few. When were the good and the brave ever in a majority? Would you have had him wait till that time came?—till you and I came over to him? The very fact that he had no rabble or troop of hirelings about him, would alone distinguish him from ordinary heroes. His company was small indeed, because few could be found worthy to pass muster. Each one who there laid down his life for the poor and oppressed was a picked man, culled out of many thousands, if not millions; apparently a man of principle, of rare courage and devoted humanity; ready to sacrifice his life at any moment for the benefit of his fellow-man. It may be doubted if there were as many more their equals in these respects in all the country—I speak of his followers only—for their leader, no doubt, scoured the land far and wide, seeking to swell his troop. These alone were ready to step between the oppressor and the oppressed. Surely they were the very best men you could select to be hung. That was the greatest compliment which this country could pay them. They were ripe for her gallows. She has tried a long time, she has hung a good many, but never found the right one before.

When I think of him, and his six sons, and his son-in-law,—not to enumerate the others,—enlisted for this fight, proceeding coolly, reverently, humanely to work, for months, if not years, sleeping and waking upon it, summering and wintering the thought, without expecting any reward but a good conscience, while almost all America stood ranked on the other side, I say again, that it affects me as a sublime spectacle. If he had had any journal advocating *"his cause,"* any organ, as the phrase is, monotonously and wearisomely playing the same old tune, and then passing round the hat, it would have been fatal to his efficiency. If he had acted in any way so as to be let alone by the government, he might have been suspected. It was the fact that the tyrant must give place to him, or he to the tyrant, that distinguished him from all the reformers of the day that I know.

It was his peculiar doctrine that a man has a perfect right to interfere by force with the slaveholder, in order to rescue the slave. I agree with him. They who are continually shocked by slavery have some right to be shocked by the violent death of the slaveholder, but no others. Such will be more shocked by his life than by his death. I shall not be forward to think him mistaken in his method who quickest succeeds to liberate the slave. I speak for the slave when I say, that I prefer the philanthropy of Captain Brown to that philanthropy which neither shoots me nor liberates me. At any rate, I do not think it is quite sane for one to spend his whole life in talking or writing about this matter, unless he is continuously inspired, and I have not done so. A man may have other affairs to attend to. I do not wish to kill nor to be killed, but I can foresee circumstances in which both these things would be by me unavoidable. We preserve the so-called peace of our community by deeds of petty violence every day. Look at the policeman's billy and handcuffs! Look at the jail! Look at the gallows! Look at the chaplain regiment! We are hoping only to live safely on the outskirts of *this* provisional army. So we defend ourselves and our hen-roosts, and maintain slavery. I know that the mass of my countrymen think that the only righteous use that can be made of Sharp's rifles and revolvers is to fight duels with them, when we are insulted by other nations, or to hunt Indians, or shoot fugitive slaves with them, or the like. I think that for once the Sharp's rifles and the revolvers were employed in a righteous cause. The tools were in the hands of one who could use them.

The same indignation that is said to have cleared the temple once will clear it again. The question is not about the weapon, but the spirit in which you use it. No man has appeared in America, as yet, who loved his fellow-man so well, and treated him so tenderly. He lived for him. He took up his life and he laid it down for him. What sort of violence is that which is encouraged, not by soldiers but by peaceable citizens, not so much by laymen as by ministers of the gospel, not so much by the fighting sects as by the Quakers, and not so much by Quaker men as by Quaker women?

This event advertises me that there is such a fact as death—the possibility of a man's dying. It seems as if no man had ever died in America before, for in order to die you must first have lived. I don't believe in the hearses, and palls, and funerals that they have had. There was no death in the case, because there had been no life; they merely rotted or sloughed off, pretty much as they had rotted or sloughed along. No temple's vail[21] was rent, only a hole dug somewhere. Let the dead bury their dead. The best of them fairly ran down like a clock. Franklin—Washington—they were let off without dying; they were merely missing one day. I hear a good many pretend that they are going to die; or that they have died, for aught that I know. Nonsense! I'll defy them to do it. They haven't got life enough in them. They'll deliquesce like fungi, and keep a hundred eulogists mopping the spot where they left off. Only half a dozen or so have died since the world began. Do you think that you are going to die, sir? No! there's no hope of you. You haven't got your lesson yet. You've got to stay after school. We make a needless ado about capital punishment—taking lives, when there is no life to take. *Memento mori!*[22] We don't understand that sublime sentence which some worthy got sculptured on his gravestone once. We've interpreted it in a grovelling and sniv-elling sense; we've wholly forgotten how to die.

But be sure you do die, nevertheless. Do your work, and finish it. If you know how to begin, you will know when to end.

These men, in teaching us how to die, have at the same time taught us how to live. If this man's acts and words do not create a revival, it will be the severest possible satire on the acts and words that do. It is the best news that America has ever heard. It has already quickened the feeble pulse of the North, and infused more and more generous blood into her veins and heart, than any number of years of what is called commercial and political prosperity could. How many a man who was lately contemplating suicide has now something to live for!

One writer says that Brown's peculiar monomania made him to be "dreaded by the Missourians as a supernatural being." Sure enough, a hero in the midst of us cowards is always so dreaded. He is just that thing. He shows himself superior to nature. He has a spark of divinity in him.

> Unless above himself he doth erect himself,
> How poor a thing is man![23]

Newspaper editors argue also that it is a proof of his *insanity* that he thought he was appointed to do this work which he did—that he did not suspect himself for a moment! They talk as if it were impos-sible that a man could be "divinely appointed" in these days to do any work whatever; as if vows and religion were out of date as connected with any man's daily work,—as if the agent to abolish Slavery could only be somebody appointed by the President, or by some political party. They talk as if a man's death were a failure, and his continued life, be it of whatever character, were a success.

When I reflect to what a cause this man devoted himself, and how religiously, and then reflect to what cause his judges and all who condemn him so angrily and fluently devote themselves, I see that they are as far apart as the heavens and earth are asunder.

The amount of it is, our *"leading men"* are a harmless kind of folk, and they know *well enough* that *they* were not divinely appointed, but elected by the votes of their party.

Who is it whose safety requires that Captain Brown be hung? Is it indispensable to any Northern man? Is there no resource but to cast these men also to the Minotaur?[24] If you do not wish it, say so dis-tinctly. While these things are being done, beauty stands veiled and music is a screeching lie. Think of him—of his rare qualities! such a man as it takes ages to make, and ages to understand; no mock hero, nor the representative of any party. A man such as the sun may not rise upon again in this benighted land. To whose making went the costliest material, the finest adamant; sent to be the redeemer of those in captivity; and the only use to which you can put him is to hang him at the end of a rope! You who pretend to care for Christ crucified, consider what you are about to do to him who offered himself to be the saviour of four millions of men.

Any man knows when he is justified, and all the wits in the world cannot enlighten him on that point. The murderer always knows that he is justly punished; but when a government takes the life of a man without the consent of his conscience, it is an audacious government, and is taking a step towards its own dissolution. Is it not possible that an individual may be right and a government wrong? Are laws to be enforced simply because they were made? or declared by any number of men to be good, if they are *not* good? Is there any necessity for a man's being a tool to perform a deed of which his better nature disapproves? Is it the intention of law-makers that *good* men shall be hung ever? Are judges to interpret the law according to the letter, and not the spirit? What right have *you* to enter into a compact with yourself that you *will* do thus or so, against the light within you? Is it for *you* to *make up* your mind—to form any resolution whatever—and not accept the convictions that are forced upon you, and which ever pass your understanding? I do not believe in lawyers, in that mode of attacking or defending a man, because you descend to meet the judge on his own ground, and, in cases of the highest importance, it is of no consequence whether a man breaks a human law or not. Let lawyers decide trivial cases. Business men may arrange that among themselves. If they were the interpreters of the everlasting laws which rightfully bind man, that would be another thing. A counterfeiting law-factory, standing half in a slave land and half in a free! What kind of laws for free men can you expect from that?

I am here to plead his cause with you. I plead not for his life, but for his character—his immortal life; and so it becomes your cause wholly, and is not his in the least. Some eighteen hundred years ago Christ was crucified; this morning, perchance, Captain Brown was hung. These are the two ends of a chain which is not without its links. He is not Old Brown any longer; he is an angel of light.

I see now that it was necessary that the bravest and humanest man in all the country should be hung. Perhaps he saw it himself. I *almost fear* that I may yet hear of his deliverance, doubting if a prolonged life, if *any* life, can do as much good as his death.

"Misguided"! "Garrulous"! "Insane"! Vindictive"! So ye write in your easy chairs, and thus he wounded responds from the floor of the Armory, clear as a cloudless sky, true as the voice of nature is: "No man sent me here; it was my own prompting and that of my Maker. I acknowledge no master in human form."

And in what a sweet and noble strain he proceeds, addressing his captors, who stand over him: "I think, my friends, you are guilty of a great wrong against God and humanity, and it would be perfectly right for any one to interfere with you so far as to free those you willfully and wickedly hold in bondage."

And referring to his movement: "It is, in my opinion, the greatest service a man can render to God."

"I pity the poor in bondage that have none to help them; that is why I am here; not to gratify any personal animosity, revenge, or vindictive spirit. It is my sympathy with the oppressed and the wronged, that are as good as you, and as precious in the sight of God."

You don't know your testament when you see it.

"I want you to understand that I respect the rights of the poorest and weakest of colored people, oppressed by the slave power, just as much as I do those of the most wealthy and powerful."

"I wish to say, furthermore, that you had better, all you people at the South, prepare yourselves for a settlement of that question, that must come up for settlement sooner than you are prepared for it. The sooner you are prepared the better. You may dispose of me very easily. I am nearly disposed of now; but this question is still to be settled—this negro question, I mean; the end of that is not yet."

I foresee the time when the painter will paint that scene, no longer going to Rome for a subject; the poet will sing it; the historian record it; and, with the Landing of the Pilgrims and the Declaration of Independence, it will be the ornament of some future national gallery, when at least the present form of Slavery shall be no more here. We shall then be at liberty to weep for Captain Brown. Then, and not till then, we will take our revenge.

Source: Henry D[avid]. Thoreau, "A Plea for Captain John Brown" (30 October 1859), from *Echoes of Harper's Ferry*, ed. James Redpath (Boston: Thayer and Eldridge, 1860), pp. 17–42.

Notes

1. All three are sites of Revolutionary War battles.
2. Ethan Allen (1738–1789), soldier and frontiersman, led the Green Moun-

tain Boys of Vermont during the Revolutionary War; John Stark (1728–1822), Revolutionary War general.

3. Probably James Redpath (1833–1891), abolitionist author and editor.

4. Buncombe, hogwash or a ludicrously false statement.

5. Clement Laird Vallandigham (1820–1871), Ohio congressman arrested for pro-Confederacy speeches during the Civil War.

6. Henry Alexander Wise (1806–1876), governor of Virginia from 1856 to 1859.

7. Balaklava, Black Sea port and site of an indecisive battle in October 1854 during the Crimean War, served as the inspiration of the poem "The Charge of the Light Brigade" (1854) by Alfred, Lord Tennyson.

8. Israel Putnam (1718–1790), Revolutionary War general, killed the last wolf in the state of Connecticut.

9. Tartar, native of Tartary in Asia.

10. Henry Wilson (1812–1875), abolitionist and Massachusetts state senator.

11. Spile, a small tube used for conducting sap from a tree; bung, the stopper for a cask.

12. Robert John Walker (1801–1869), U.S. Senator from Mississippi, secretary of the treasury during the Mexican War, and governor of Kansas Territory during the violent struggle over slavery there.

13. James Murray Mason (1798–1871), U.S. senator from Virginia.

14. Pontius Pilate (d. A.D. 36), governor of Judea who presided at the trial of Jesus and ordered his crucifixion; Gessler, bailiff who takes the legendary William Tell to prison; Thoreau may be thinking of either the Inquisition of the Roman Catholic Church against heresies in the twelfth and thirteenth centuries or the Spanish Inquisition against Jews and Moors (1478–1808, 1813–1834).

15. Colonel Lewis W. Washington (1812–1871), great-grandnephew of George Washington.

16. Aaron Dwight Stevens (1831–1860), Barclay Coppoc (1839–1861), and his brother Edwin Coppoc (1835–1859) were all at Harper's Ferry with Brown. Only Barclay escaped and was not executed.

17. Plug ugly, very ugly.

18. Vigilant committees sprung up in the north after the passage of the Fugitive Slave Law to help runaway slaves and to protect free blacks.

19. Cadi, a Turkish or Arabic lower-level magistrate.

20. Underground Railroad, a series of houses or safe places hosted by people willing to help escaped slaves to reach Canada and freedom.

21. Vail, or veil, a spread out or open area of a temple.

22. *Momento mori*: "remember you must die."

23. "To the Lady Margaret, Countess of Cumberland" (1599), ll., 95–96, by Samuel Daniel (ca. 1562–1619), English contemplative poet.

24. Minotaur, mythological figure with the body of a man and the head of a bull.

Theodore Parker

from *Theodore Parker's Experience as a Minister,
with Some Account of His Early Life, and Education for the
Ministry; Contained in a Letter from Him to the Members
of the Twenty-Eighth Congregational Society of Boston*

(1859)

PARKER WAS perennially beset by illness, and in 1859 his tuberculosis had worsened to the point that in January he began an enforced trip abroad for his health. This letter (which was published as a book) was written home to his congregation as Parker's attempt to look back over his life and the events in which he had participated. Parker died in Florence, Italy, on 10 May 1860.

Many circumstances favored both studious pursuits and the formation of an independent character. The years of my preliminary theological study, and of my early ministry, fell in the most interesting period of New England's spiritual history, when a great revolution went on,—so silent that few men knew it was taking place, and none then understood its whither or its whence.

The Unitarians, after a long and bitter controversy, in which they were often shamelessly ill-treated by the "Orthodox," had conquered, and secured their ecclesiastical right to deny the Trinity, "the Achilles of dogmas;" they had won the respect of the New England public; had absorbed most of the religious talent of Massachusetts, founded many churches, and possessed and liberally administered the oldest and richest College in America.[1] Not yet petrified into a sect, they rejoiced in the large liberty of "the children of God," and, owning neither racks nor dungeons, did not covet any of those things that were their neighbors'. With less education and literary skill, the Universalists had fought manfully against Eternal Damnation[2]—the foulest doctrine which defiles the pages of man's theologic history,—secured their ecclesiastical position, wiping malignant statutes from the Law Books, and, though in a poor and vulgar way, were popularizing the great truth that God's chief attribute is LOVE, which is extended to all men. Alone of all Christian sects, they professedly taught the Immortality of man in such a form that it is no curse to the race to find it true! But, though departing from those doctrines which are essential to the Christian ecclesiastic scheme, neither Universalist nor Unitarian had broken with the authority of Revelation, the word of the Bible, but still professed a willingness to believe both Trinity and Damnation, could they be found in the miraculous and infallible Scripture.

Mr. Garrison, with his friends, inheriting what was best in the Puritan founders of New England, fired with the zeal of the Hebrew Prophets and Christian Martyrs, while they were animated with a Spirit of Humanity rarely found in any of the three, was beginning his noble work, but in a style so humble that, after much search, the police of Boston discovered there was nothing dangerous in it, for "his only visible auxiliary was a negro boy."[3] Dr. Channing was in the full maturity of his powers, and, after long preaching the Dignity of Man as an abstraction, and Piety as a purely inward life, with rare and winsome eloquence, and ever progressive humanity, began to apply his sublime doctrines to actual life in the Individual, the State, and the Church. In the name of Christianity, the great American Unitarian called for the reform of the drunkard, the elevation of the poor, the instruction of the ignorant, and, above all, for the liberation of the American slave. A remarkable man, his instinct of progress grew stronger the more he travelled, and the further he went, for he surrounded himself with young life. Horace Mann, with his coadjutors, began a great movement, to improve the public education of the people. Pierpont, single-handed, was fighting a grand and twofold battle—against drunkenness in the street, and for righteousness in the pulpit—against fearful ecclesiastic odds, maintaining a minister's right and duty to oppose actual wickedness, however popular and destructive.[4] The brilliant genius of Emerson rose in the winter nights, and hung over Boston, drawing the eyes of ingenuous young people to look up to that great, new star, a beauty and a mystery, which charmed for the moment, while it gave also perennial inspiration, as it led them forward along new paths, and toward new hopes. America had seen no such sight before; it is not less a blessed wonder now.

Besides, the Phrenologists, so ably represented by Spurzheim and Combe, were weakening the power of the old Supernaturalism, leading men to study the Constitution of Man more wisely than before, and laying the foundation on which many a beneficent structure was soon to rise.[5] The writings of Wordsworth were becoming familiar to the thoughtful lovers of nature and of man, and drawing men to natural piety. Carlyle's works got reprinted at Boston, diffusing a strong, and then, also, a healthy influence on old and young. The writings of Coleridge were reprinted in America, all of them "Aids to Reflection," and brilliant with the scattered sparks of genius; they incited many to think, more especially young Trinitarian ministers; and, spite of the lack of both historic and philosophic accuracy, and the utter absence of all proportion in his writings; spite of his haste, his vanity, prejudice, sophistry, confusion, and opium—he yet did great service in New England, helping emancipate enthralled minds. The works of Cousin, more systematic, and more profound as a whole, and far more catholic and comprehensive, continental, not insular, in his range, also became familiar to Americans,—reviews and translations going where the eloquent original was not heard—and helped free the young mind from the gross Sensationalism of the academic Philosophy on one side, and the grosser Supernaturalism of the ecclesiastic Theology on the other.

The German language, hitherto the priceless treasure of a few, was becoming well known, and many were thereby made acquainted with the most original, deep, bold, comprehensive and wealthy literature in the world, full of theologic and philosophic thought. Thus, a great storehouse was opened to such as were earnestly in quest of Truth. Young Mr. Strauss, in whom genius for criticism was united with extraordinary learning and rare facility of philosophic speech, wrote his "Life of Jesus," where he rigidly scrutinized the Genuineness of the Gospels and the Authenticity of their contents, and, with scientific calmness, brought every statement to his steady scales, weighing it, not always justly, as I think, but impartially always, with philosophic coolness and deliberation.[6] The most formidable assailant of the ecclesiastical theology of Christendom, he roused a host of foes whose writings—mainly ill-tempered, insolent and sophistical—it was yet profitable for a young man to read.

The value of Christian miracles, not the question of fact, was discussed at Boston, as never before in America. Prophecy had been thought the Jachin, and Miracles the Boaz, whereon alone Christianity could rest; but, said some, if both be shaken down, the Lord's house will not fall![7] The claims of ecclesiastical tradition came up to be settled anew; and young men, walking solitary through the moonlight, asked, "Which is to be permanent master—a single Accident in Human History, nay, perchance only the Whim of some anonymous dreamer, or the Substance of Human Nature, greatening with continual development, and 'Not without access of unexpected strength?' "[8]

The question was also its answer.

The Rights of Labor were discussed with deep philanthropic feeling, and sometimes with profound thought, metaphysic and economic both. The works of Charles Fourier—a strange, fantastic, visionary man, no doubt, but gifted also with amazing insight of the truths of social science—shed some light in these dark places of speculation. Mr. Ripley, a born Democrat, in the high sense of that abused word, and one of the best cultured and most enlightened men in America, made an attempt at Brook-farm, in West Roxbury, so to organize society that the results of labor should remain in the workman's hand, and not slip thence to the trader's till; that there should be "no exploitation of man by man," but Toil and Thought, hard work and high culture, should be united in the same person.

The natural Rights of Woman began to be inquired into, and publicly discussed; while in private, great pains were taken in the chief towns of New England, to furnish a thorough and comprehensive education to such young maidens as were born with two talents, mind and money.

Of course, a strong reaction followed. At the Cambridge Divinity School, Prof. Henry Ware, Jr., told the young men, if there appeared to them any contradiction between the Reason of Man and the Letter of the Bible, they "must follow the written word," "for you can never be so certain of the correctness of what takes place in your own mind, as of what is written in the Bible." In an ordination sermon, he told the young minister not to preach himself, but Christ; and not to appeal to Human Nature for proof of doctrines, but to the Authority of Revelation. Other Unitarian ministers declared, "There are limits to free inquiry;" and preached, "Reason must be put down, or she will soon ask terrible questions;" protested against the union of Philosophy and Religion, and assumed to "prohibit the banns" of marriage between the two. Mr. Norton—then a great name at Cambridge, a scholar of rare but contracted merit, a careful and exact writer, born for controversy, really learned and able in his special department, the Interpretations of the New Testament—opened his mouth and spoke: the mass of men must accept the doctrines of religion solely on the authority of the learned, as they do the doctrines of mathematical astronomy; the miracles of Jesus,—he made merry at those of the Old Testament,—are the only evidence of the truth of Christianity; in the popular religion of the Greeks and Romans, there was no conception of God; the new philosophic attempts to explain the facts of religious consciousness, were "the Latest Form of Infidelity;" the great philosophical and theological thinkers of Germany, were "all Atheists;" "Schleiermacher was an Atheist," as was also Spinoza, his master, before him; and Cousin, who was only "that Frenchman," was no better; the study of philosophy, and the neglect of "biblical criticism," were leading mankind to ruin,—everywhere was instability and insecurity!

Of course, this reaction was supported by the Ministers in the great Churches of Commerce, and by the old literary periodicals,—which never knew a star was risen till men wondered at it in the zenith; the Unitarian Journals gradually went over to the opponents of freedom and progress, with lofty scorn rejecting their former principles, and repeating the conduct they had once complained of; Cambridge and Princeton seemed to be interchanging cards.[9] From such hands, Cousin and Emerson could not receive needed criticism, but only vulgar abuse. Dr. Channing could "not draw a long breath in Boston," where he found the successors of Paul trembling before the successors of Felix.[10] Even Trinitarian Moses Stuart seemed scarcely safe in his hard-bottomed Hopkinsian chair, at Andover.[11] The Trinitarian ministers and city schoolmasters galled Horace Mann with continual assaults on his measures for educating the people. Unitarian ministers struck hands with wealthy liquor-dealers to drive Mr. Pierpont from his pulpit, where he valiantly preached "Temperance, Righteousness, and Judgment to come," appealing to "a day after to-day." Prominent Anti-Slavery men were dropped out of all wealthy society in Boston, their former friends not knowing them in the street; Mr. Garrison was mobbed by men in handsome coats, and found defence from their fury only in a jail; an assembly of women, consulting for the liberation of their darker sisters, was driven with hootings into the street. The Attorney General of Massachusetts brought an indictment for blasphemy against a country minister, one of the most learned biblical scholars in America, for publicly proving that none of the "Messianic prophecies" of the Old Testament was ever fulfilled by Jesus of Nazareth, who accordingly was not the expected Christ of the Jews. Abner Kneeland, editor of a newspaper, in which he boasted of the name "Infidel," was clapped in jail for writing against the ecclesiastical notion of God,—the last man ever punished for blasphemy in the State.[12] At the beck of a Virginian slave-holder, the Governor of Massachusetts suggested to the Legislature the expediency of abridging the old New England liberty of speech!

The movement party established a new Quarterly, the *Dial*, wherein their wisdom and their folly rode together on the same saddle, to the amazement of lookers-on. The short-lived journal had a narrow circulation, but its most significant papers were scattered wide by newspapers which copied them. A *Quarterly Review* was also established by Mr. Brownson,[13] then a Unitarian Minister and "sceptical democrat" of the most extravagant class, but now a Catholic, a powerful advocate of material and spiritual despotism, and perhaps the ablest writer in America against the Rights of Man and the Welfare of his race. In this he diffused important philosophic ideas, displayed and disciplined his own extraordinary talents for philosophic thought and popular writing, and directed them towards Democracy, Transcendentalism, "New Views," and the "Progress of the Species."

I count it a piece of good fortune that I was a young man when these things were taking place, when great questions were discussed, and the public had not yet taken sides.

Source: Theodore Parker, from *Theodore Parker's Experience as a Minister, with Some Account of His Early Life, and Education for the Ministry; Contained in a Letter from Him to the Members of the Twenty-Eighth Congregational Society of Boston* (Boston: Rufus Leighton, Jr., 1859), pp. 49–58.

Notes

1. Parker repeats this phrase about Achilles from his *Discourse of the Transient and Permanent in Christianity* (1841); see note 6 to it above; a reference to Harvard College.

2. Universalists, Christian denomination believing in universal salvation.

3. William Lloyd Garrison (1805–1879), abolitionist and editor of the most important antislavery newspaper of the day, the *Liberator*, from 1830 to 1865.

4. John Pierpont (1785–1866), reformer, poet, and Unitarian clergyman, was dismissed by his congregation because they were uncomfortable with his pointing out, among other things, that its members were simultaneously denouncing alcohol while making a profit from selling spirits; Parker's defense of him appears as "Hollis Street Council" in the *Dial*, 3 (October 1842): 201–221.

5. George Combe (1788–1858), Scottish phrenologist.

6. *Da Leben Jesu Kritisch Bearbeitet* [*The Life of Christ Critically Examined*] (1835), by David Friedrich Strauss.

7. Jachin and Boaz, names of the two pillars set up by Solomon before his temple, Boaz (strength) on the left and Jachim (stability) on the right.

8. *The Excursion* (1814), Book 4, l. 221, by William Wordsworth.

9. Because Princeton University's divinity school was more conservative than was Harvard's, Parker is saying that the liberals had become the conservatives.

10. Felix, the Roman procurator of Judea before whom Paul spoke of his love of Jesus (see Acts 24:5).

11. Moses Stuart (1780–1852), clergyman and biblical scholar, taught at the Andover Theological Seminary for nearly forty years; the followers of the clergyman and theologian Samuel Hopkins (1721–1803) held to most Calvinistic doctrines, including complete submission to God's will.

12. Abner Kneeland (1774–1844), Unitarian minister and reformer whose free thought beliefs resulted in his being jailed for blasphemy in 1838.

13. Orestes A. Brownson edited the *Boston Quarterly Review* from 1838 to 1842.

Ralph Waldo Emerson

"Thoreau"

(August 1862)

EMERSON'S ESSAY ON Thoreau, who had died on 6 May, began as an oration at his funeral, then appeared as an obituary in the *Boston Daily Advertiser*, became a lecture, and was finally printed in the *Atlantic Monthly*.

Henry D. Thoreau was the last male descendant of a French ancestor who came to this country from the isle of Guernsey. His character exhibited occasional traits drawn from this blood in singular combination with a very strong Saxon genius.

He was born in Concord, Massachusetts, on the 12th of July, 1817. He was graduated at Harvard College, in 1837, but without any literary distinction. An iconoclast in literature, he seldom thanked colleges for their service to him, holding them in small esteem, whilst yet his debt to them was important. After leaving the University, he joined his brother in teaching a private school, which he soon renounced. His father was a manufacturer of lead pencils, and Henry applied himself for a time to this craft, believing he could make a better pencil than was then in use. After completing his experiments, he exhibited his work to chemists and artists in Boston, and having obtained their certificates to its excellence and to its equality with the best London manufacture, he returned home contented. His friends congratulated him that he had now opened his way to fortune. But he replied, that he should never make another pencil. "Why should I? I would not do again what I have done once." He resumed his endless walks, and miscellaneous studies, making every day some new acquaintance with Nature, though as yet never speaking of zoology or botany, since, though very studious of natural facts, he was incurious of technical and textual science.

At this time, a strong, healthy youth fresh from college, whilst all his companions were choosing their profession, or eager to begin some lucrative employment, it was inevitable that his thoughts should be exercised on the same question, and it required rare decision to refuse all the accustomed paths, and keep his solitary freedom at the cost of disappointing the natural expectations of his family and friends. All the more difficult that he had a perfect probity, was exact in securing his own independence, and in holding every man to the like duty. But

Thoreau never faltered. He was a born protestant. He declined to give up his large ambition of knowledge and action for any narrow craft or profession, aiming at a much more comprehensive calling, the art of living well. If he slighted and defied the opinions of others, it was only that he was more intent to reconcile his practice with his own belief. Never idle or self-indulgent, he preferred when he wanted money, earning it by some piece of manual labor agreeable to him, as building a boat or a fence, planting, grafting, surveying, or other short work, to any long engagements. With his hardy habits and few wants, his skill in wood-craft, and his powerful arithmetic, he was very competent to live in any part of the world. It would cost him less time to supply his wants than another. He was therefore secure of his leisure.

A natural skill for mensuration, growing out of his mathematical knowledge, and his habit of ascertaining the measures and distances of objects which interested him, the size of trees, the depth and extent of ponds and rivers, the height of mountains and the air-line distance of his favorite summits,—this, and his intimate knowledge of the territory about Concord, made him drift into the profession of land-surveyor. It had the advantage for him that it led him continually into new and secluded grounds, and helped his studies of nature. His accuracy and skill in this work were readily appreciated, and he found all the employment he wanted.

He could easily solve the problems of the surveyor, but he was daily beset with graver questions which he manfully confronted. He interrogated every custom, and wished to settle all his practice on an ideal foundation. He was a protestant *à l'outrance*[1] and few lives contain so many renunciations. He was bred to no profession; he never married; he lived alone; he never went to church; he never voted; he refused to pay a tax to the state; he ate no flesh, he drank no wine, he never knew the use of tobacco; and, though a naturalist, he used neither trap nor gun. He chose wisely, no doubt, for himself to be the bachelor of thought and nature. He had no talent for wealth, and knew how to be poor without the least hint of squalor or inelegance. Perhaps he fell into his way of living, without forecasting it much, but approved it with later wisdom. "I am often reminded," he wrote in his journal, "that, if I had bestowed on me the wealth of Crœsus, my aims must be still the same, and my means essentially the same."[2] He had no temptations to fight against; no appetites, no passions, no taste for elegant trifles. A fine house, dress, the manners and talk of highly cultivated people were all thrown away on him. He much preferred a good Indian, and considered these refinements as impediments to conversation, wishing to meet his companion on the simplest terms. He declined invitations to dinner-parties, because there each was in every one's way, and he could not meet the individuals to any purpose. "They make their pride," he said, "in making their dinner cost much: I make my pride in making my dinner cost little." When asked at table, what dish he preferred, he answered, "the nearest." He did not like the taste of wine, and never had a vice in his life. He said, "I have a faint recollection of pleasure derived from smoking dried lily stems, before I was a man. I had commonly a supply of these. I have never smoked any thing more noxious."

He chose to be rich by making his wants few, and supplying them himself. In his travels, he used the railroad only to get over so much country as was unimportant to the present purpose, walking hundreds of miles, avoiding taverns, buying a lodging in farmers' and fisher-men's houses, as cheaper, and more agreeable to him, and because there he could better find the men and the information he wanted.

There was somewhat military in his nature not to be subdued, al-ways manly and able, but rarely tender, as if he did not feel himself except in opposition. He wanted a fallacy to expose, a blunder to pillory, I may say, required a little sense of victory, a roll of the drum, to call his powers into full exercise. It cost him nothing to say No; indeed he found it much easier than to say Yes. It seemed as if his first instinct on hearing a proposition was to controvert it, so impatient was he of the limitations of our daily thought. This habit of course is a little chilling to the social affections; and though the companion would in the end acquit him of any malice or untruth, yet it mars conversation. Hence no equal companion stood in affectionate relations with one so pure and guileless. "I love Henry," said one of his friends, "but I cannot like him: and as for taking his arm, I should as soon think of taking the arm of an elm-tree."

Yet hermit and stoic as he was, he was really fond of sympathy, and threw himself heartily and childlike into the company of young people whom he loved, and whom he delighted to entertain, as he only could, with the varied and endless anecdotes of his experiences by field and river. And he was always ready to lead a huckleberry party or a search for chestnuts or grapes. Talking one day of a public discourse, Henry remarked, that whatever succeeded with the audience, was bad, I said, "Who would not like to write something which all can read, like 'Robinson Crusoe';[3] and who does not see with regret that his page is not solid with a right materialistic treatment, which delights every-body." Henry objected, of course, and vaunted the better lectures which reached only a few persons. But, at supper, a young girl, un-derstanding that he was to lecture at the Lyceum, sharply asked him, "whether his lecture would be a nice, interesting story such as she wished to hear, or whether it was one of those old philosophical things that she did not care about?" Henry turned to her, and bethought, himself, and, I saw, was trying to believe that he had matter that might fit her and her brother, who were to sit up and go to the lecture, if it was a good one for them.

He was a speaker and actor of the truth,—born such,—and was ever running into dramatic situations from this cause. In any circumstance, it interested all bystanders to know what part Henry would take, and what he would say: and he did not disappoint expectation, but used an original judgment on each emergency. In 1845, he built himself a small framed house on the shores of Walden Pond, and lived there two years alone, a life of labor and study. This action was quite native and fit for him. No one who knew him would tax him with affectation. He was more unlike his neighbors in his thought, than in his action. As soon as he had exhausted the advantages of that solitude, he abandoned it. In 1847, not approving some uses to which the public expenditure was applied, he refused to pay his town-tax, and was put in jail. A friend paid the tax for him, and he was released.[4] The like annoyance was threatened the next year. But, as his friends paid the tax, notwithstanding his protest, I believe he ceased to resist. No opposition or ridicule had any weight with him. He coldly and fully stated his opinion without affecting to believe that it was the opinion of the company. It was of no consequence if every one present held the opposite opinion. On one occasion he went to the University Library to procure some books. The Librarian refused to lend them. Mr. Thoreau repaired to the President, who stated to him the rules and usages which permitted the loan of books to resident graduates, to clergymen who were alumni, and to some others resident within a circle of ten miles' radius from the College. Mr. Thoreau explained to the President that the railroad had destroyed the old scale of distances,—that the library was useless, yes, and President and College useless, on the terms of his rules,—that the one benefit he owed to the College was its library,—that at this moment, not only his want of books was imperative, but he wanted a large number of books, and assured him that he Thoreau, and not the Librarian, was the proper custodian of these. In short, the President found the petitioner so formidable and the rules getting to look so ridiculous, that he ended by giving him a privilege which in his hands proved unlimited thereafter.

No truer American existed than Thoreau. His preference of his country and condition was genuine, and his aversation from English and European manners and tastes almost reached contempt. He listened impatiently to news or bon mots gleaned from London circles; and, though he tried to be civil, these anecdotes fatigued him. The men were all imitating each other, and on a small mould. Why can they not live as far apart as possible, and each be a man by himself? What he sought was the most energetic nature, and he wished to go to Oregon, not to London. "In every part of Great Britain," he wrote in his diary, "are discovered traces of the Romans, their funereal urns, their camps, their roads, their dwellings. But New England, at least, is not based on any Roman ruins. We have not to lay the foundations of our houses on the ashes of a former civilization."

But idealist as he was, standing for abolition of slavery, abolition of tariffs, almost for abolition of government, it is needless to say he found himself not only unrepresented in actual politics, but almost equally opposed to every class of reformers. Yet he paid the tribute of his uniform respect to the anti-slavery party. One man, whose personal acquaintance he had formed, he honored with exceptional regard. Before the first friendly word had been spoken for Captain John Brown, after the arrest, he sent notices to most houses in Concord, that he would speak in a public hall on the condition and character of John Brown, on Sunday Evening, and invited all people to come. The Republican committee, the abolitionist committee, sent him word that it was premature and not advisable. He replied, "I did not send to you for advice but to announce that I am to speak." The hall was filled at an early hour by people of all parties, and his earnest eulogy of the hero was heard by all respectfully, by many with a sympathy that surprised themselves.

It was said of Plotinus, that he was ashamed of his body, and 'tis very likely he had good reason for it; that his body was a bad servant, and he had not skill in dealing with the material world, as happens often to men of abstract intellect. But Mr. Thoreau was equipped with a most adapted and serviceable body. He was of short stature, firmly built, of light complexion, with strong, serious blue eyes, and a grave aspect; his face covered in the late years with a becoming beard. His senses were acute, his frame well-knit and hardy, his hands strong and skilful in the use of tools. And there was a wonderful fitness of body and mind. He could pace sixteen rods more accurately than another man could measure them with rod and chain. He could find his path in the woods at night, he said, better by his feet than his eyes. He could estimate the measure of a tree very well by his eye; he could estimate the weight of a calf or a pig, like a dealer. From a box containing a bushel or more of loose pencils, he could take up with his hands fast enough just a dozen pencils at every grasp. He was a good swimmer, runner, skater, boatman, and would probably out-walk most countrymen in a day's journey. And the relation of body to mind was still finer than we have indicated. He said, he wanted every stride his legs made. The length of his walk uniformly made the length of his writing. If shut up in the house, he did not write at all.

He had a strong common sense, like that which Rose Flammock, the weaver's daughter, in Scott's romance, commends in her father, as resembling a yardstick, which, whilst it measures dowlas and diaper, can equally well measure tapestry and cloth of gold.[5] He had always a new resource. When I was planting forest trees, and had procured half a peck of acorns, he said, that only a small portion of them would be sound, and proceeded to examine them, and select the sound ones. But finding this took time, he said, "I think, if you put them all into water, the good ones will sink," which experiment we tried with success. He could plan a garden, or a house, or a barn; would have been competent to lead a "Pacific Exploring Expedition"; could give judicious counsel in the gravest private or public affairs. He lived for the day, not cumbered and mortified by his memory. If he brought you yesterday a new proposition, he would bring you today another not less revolutionary. A very industrious man, and setting, like all highly organized men, a high value on his time, he seemed the only man of leisure in town, always ready for any excursion that promised well, or for conversation prolonged into late hours. His trenchant sense was never stopped by his rules of daily prudence, but was always up to the new occasion. He liked and used the simplest food, yet, when some one urged a vegetable diet, Thoreau thought all diets a very small matter; saying, that "the man who shoots the buffalo lives better than the man who boards at the Graham house."[6] He said, "You can sleep near the railroad, and never be disturbed. Nature knows very well what sounds are worth attending to, and has made up her mind not to hear the railroad-whistle. But things respect the devout mind, and a mental ecstacy was never interrupted."

He noted what repeatedly befel him, that, after receiving from a distance a rare plant, he would presently find the same in his own haunts. And those pieces of luck which happen only to good players happened to him. One day walking with a stranger who inquired, where Indian arrowheads could be found, he replied, "Every where," and stooping forward, picked one on the instant from the ground. At Mount Washington, in Tuckerman's Ravine, Thoreau had a bad fall, and sprained his foot.[7] As he was in the act of getting up from his fall, he saw for the first time, the leaves of the *Arnica mollis*.[8]

His robust common sense, armed with stout hands, keen perceptions, and strong will, cannot yet account for the superiority which shone in his simple and hidden life. I must add the cardinal fact that there was an excellent wisdom in him, proper to a rare class of men, which showed him the material world as a means and symbol. This discovery, which sometimes yields to poets a certain casual and inter-rupted light serving for the ornament of their writing, was in him an unsleeping insight; and, whatever faults or obstructions of tempera-ment might cloud it, he was not disobedient to the heavenly vision. In his youth, he said, one day, "The other world is all my art: my pencils will draw no other; my jack-knife will cut nothing else; I do not use it as a means." This was the muse and genius that ruled his opinions, conversation, studies, work, and course of life. This made him a searching judge of men. At first glance, he measured his com-panion, and, though insensible to some fine traits of culture, could very well report his weight and calibre. And this made the impression of genius which his conversation often gave.

He understood the matter in hand at a glance, and saw the limi-tations and poverty of those he talked with, so that nothing seemed concealed from such terrible eyes. I have repeatedly known young men of sensibility converted in a moment to the belief that this was the man they were in search of, the man of men, who could tell them all they should do. His own dealing with them was never affectionate, but superior, didactic; scorning their petty ways; very slowly conceding or not conceding at all the promise of his society at their houses or even at his own. "Would he not walk with them?"—He did not know. There was nothing so important to him as his walk; he had no walks to throw away on company. Visits were offered him from respectful parties, but he declined them. Admiring friends offered to carry him at their own cost to the Yellow Stone River; to the West Indies; to South America. But though nothing could be more grave or considered than his refusals, they remind one in quite new relations of that fop Brummel's reply to the gentleman who offered him his carriage in a shower, "But where will *you* ride then?"[9] And what accusing silences, and what searching and irresistible speeches battering down all de-fences, his companions can remember!

Mr. Thoreau dedicated his genius with such entire love to the fields, hills, and waters of his native town, that he made them known and interesting to all reading Americans, and to people over the sea. The river on whose banks he was born and died, he knew from its springs to its confluence with the Merrimack. He had made summer and win-ter observations on it for many years, and at every hour of the day and the night. The result of the recent survey of the Water Commissioners appointed by the State of Massachusetts, he had reached by his private experiments, several years earlier. Every fact which occurs in the bed, on the banks, or in the air over it; the fishes, and their spawning and nests, their manners, their food; the shad-flies which fill the air on a certain evening once a year, and which are snapped at by the fishes so ravenously, that many of these die of repletion; the conical heaps of small stones on the river shallows, one of which heaps will sometimes overfill a cart,—these heaps the huge nests of small fishes; the birds which frequent the stream, heron, duck, sheldrake, loon, osprey; the snake, muskrat, otter, woodchuck, and fox, on the banks; the turtle, frog, hyla,[10] and cricket, which make the banks vocal,—were all known to him, and, as it were, townsmen and fellow-creatures: so that he felt an absurdity or violence in any narrative of one of these by itself apart, and still more of its dimensions on an inch-rule, or in the exhibition of its skeleton, or the specimen of a squirrel or a bird in brandy. He liked to speak of the manners of the river, as itself a lawful creature, yet with exactness, and always to an observed fact. As he knew the river, so the ponds in this region.

One of the weapons he used, more important than microscope or alcohol receiver, to other investigators, was a whim which grew on him by indulgence, yet appeared in gravest statement, namely, of extolling his own town and neighborhood as the most favored centre for natural observation. He remarked that the Flora of Massachusetts embraced almost all the important plants of America,—most of the oaks, most of the willows, the best pines, the ash, the maple, the beech, the nuts. He returned Kane's "Arctic Voyage" to a friend of whom he had borrowed it with the remark, that "most of the phenomena noted might be observed in Concord."[11] He seemed a little envious of the Pole, for the coincident sunrise and sunset, or five minutes' day after six months. A splendid fact which Annursnuc had never afforded him.[12] He found red snow in one of his walks; and told me that he expected to find yet the *Victoria regia* in Concord.[13] He was the attorney of the indigenous plants, and owned to a preference of the weeds to the imported plants, as of the Indian to the civilized man: and noticed with pleasure that the willow bean-poles of his neighbor had grown more than his beans. "See these weeds," he said, "which have been hoed at by a million farmers all spring and summer, and yet have prevailed, and just now come out triumphant over all lanes, pastures, fields, and gardens, such is their vigor. We have insulted them with low names too, as pigweed, wormwood, chickweed, shad blossom." He says they have brave names too, ambrosia, stellaria, amelanchier, amaranth, etc.

I think his fancy for referring every thing to the meridian of Concord, did not grow out of any ignorance or depreciation of other longitudes or latitudes, but was rather a playful expression of his conviction of the indifferency of all places, and that the best place for each is where he stands. He expressed it once in this wise: "I think nothing is to be hoped from you, if this bit of mould under your feet is not sweeter to you to eat, than any other in this world, or in any world."

The other weapon with which he conquered all obstacles in science was patience. He knew how to sit immoveable, a part of the rock he rested on, until the bird, the reptile, the fish, which had retired from him, should come back, and resume its habits, nay, moved by curiosity should come to him and watch him.

It was a pleasure and a privilege to walk with him. He knew the country like a fox or a bird, and passed through it as freely by paths of his own. He knew every track in the snow, or on the ground, and what creature had taken this path before him. One must submit abjectly to such a guide, and the reward was great. Under his arm he carried an old music book to press plants; in his pocket, his diary and pencil, a spy-glass for birds, microscope, jack-knife, and twine. He wore straw hat, stout shoes, strong gray trowsers, to brave shrub-oaks and smilax, and to climb a tree for a hawk's or a squirrel's nest. He waded into the pool for the water-plants, and his strong legs were no insignificant part of his armour. On the day I speak of he looked for the menyanthes, detected it across the wide pool, and, on examination of the florets, decided that it had been in flower five days. He drew out of his breast-pocket his diary, and read the names of all the plants that should bloom on this day, whereof he kept account as a banker when his notes fall due. The cypripedium not due till tomorrow. He thought, that, if waked up from a trance, in this swamp, he could tell by the plants what time of the year it was within two days. The redstart was flying about and presently the fine grosbeaks, whose brilliant scarlet makes the rash gazer wipe his eye, and whose fine clear note Thoreau compared to that of a tanager which had got rid of its hoarseness. Presently he heard a note which he called that of the night-warbler, a bird he had never identified, had been in search of twelve years, which always, when he saw it, was in the act of diving down into a tree or bush, and which it was vain to seek; the only bird that sings indifferently by night and by day. I told him he must beware of finding and booking it, lest life should have nothing more to show him. He said, "What you seek in vain for, half your life, one day you come full upon all the family at dinner. You seek it like a dream, and, as soon as you find it, you become its prey."

His interest in the flower or the bird lay very deep in his mind, was connected with Nature,—and the meaning of Nature was never attempted to be defined by him. He would not offer a memoir of his observations to the Natural History Society. "Why should I? To detach the description from its connections in my mind, would make it no longer true or valuable to me: and they do not wish what belongs to it." His power of observation seemed to indicate additional senses. He saw as with microscope, heard as with ear-trumpet, and his memory was a photographic register of all he saw and heard. And yet none knew better than he that it is not the fact that imports, but the impression or effect of the fact on your mind. Every fact lay in glory in his mind, a type of the order and beauty of the whole.

His determination on Natural History was organic. He confessed that he sometimes felt like a hound or a panther, and, if born among Indians, would have been a fell hunter. But, restrained by his Massachusetts culture, he played out the game in this mild form of botany and ichthyology. His intimacy with animals suggested what Thomas Fuller records of Butler the apiologist, that "either he had told the bees things or the bees had told him."[14] Snakes coiled round his leg; the fishes swam into his hand, and he took them out of the water; he pulled the woodchuck out of its hole by the tail, and took the foxes under his protection from the hunters. Our naturalist had perfect magnanimity; he had no secrets: he would carry you to the heron's haunt, or, even to his most prized botanical swamp;—possibly knowing that you could never find it again,—yet willing to take his risks.

No college ever offered him a diploma, or a professor's chair; no academy made him its corresponding secretary, its discoverer, or even its member. Whether these learned bodies feared the satire of his presence. Yet so much knowledge of nature's secret and genius few others possessed, none in a more large and religious synthesis. For not a particle of respect had he to the opinions of any man or body of men, but homage solely to the truth itself. And as he discovered everywhere among doctors some leaning of courtesy, it discredited them. He grew to be revered and admired by his townsmen, who had at first known him only as an oddity. The farmers who employed him as a surveyor soon discovered his rare accuracy and skill, his knowledge of their lands, of trees, of birds, of Indian remains, and the like, which enabled him to tell every farmer more than he knew before of his own farm. So that he began to feel as if Mr. Thoreau had better rights in his land than he. They felt, too, the superiority of character which addressed all men with a native authority.

Indian relics abound in Concord, arrowheads, stone chisels, pestles, and fragments of pottery; and, on the river bank, large heaps of clamshells and ashes mark spots which the savages frequented. These, and every circumstance touching the Indian, were important in his eyes. His visits to Maine were chiefly for love of the Indian. He had the satisfaction of seeing the manufacture of the bark-canoe, as well as of trying his hand in its management on the rapids. He was inquisitive about the making of the stone arrowhead, and, in his last days, charged a youth setting out for the Rocky Mountains, to find an Indian who could tell him that: "It was well worth a visit to California, to learn it." Occasionally, a small party of Penobscot Indians would visit Concord, and pitch their tents for a few weeks in summer on the river bank. He failed not to make acquaintance with the best of them, though he well knew that asking questions of Indians is like catechizing beavers and rabbits. In his last visit to Maine, he had great satisfaction from Joseph Polis, an intelligent Indian of Oldtown, who was his guide for some weeks.

He was equally interested in every natural fact. The depth of his perception found likeness of law throughout nature, and, I know not any genius who so swiftly inferred universal law from the single fact. He was no pedant of a department. His eye was open to beauty, and his ear to music. He found these, not in rare conditions, but wheresoever he went. He thought the best of music was in single strains; and he found poetic suggestion in the humming of the telegraph wire.

His poetry might be bad or good; he no doubt wanted a lyric facility, and technical skill; but he had the source of poetry in his spiritual perception. He was a good reader and critic, and his judgment on poetry was to the ground of it. He could not be deceived as to the presence or absence of the poetic element in any composition, and his thirst for this made him negligent and perhaps scornful of superficial graces. He would pass by many delicate rhythms, but he would have detected every live stanza or line in a volume, and knew very well where to find an equal poetic charm in prose. He was so enamoured of the spiritual beauty, that he held all actual written poems in very light esteem in the comparison. He admired Æschylus and Pindar, but when some one was commending them, he said, that, "Æschylus and the Greeks, in describing Apollo and Orpheus, had given no song, or no good one. They ought not to have moved trees, but to have chaunted to the gods such a hymn as would have sung all their old ideas out of their heads, and new ones in." His own verses are often rude and defective. The gold does not yet run pure, is drossy and crude. The thyme and marjoram are not yet honey. But if he want lyric fineness, and technical merits, if he have not the poetic temperament, he never lacks the causal thought, showing that his genius was better than his talent. He knew the worth of the Imagination for the uplifting and consolation of human life, and liked to throw every thought into a symbol. The fact you tell is of no value, but only the impression. For this reason his presence was poetic, always piqued the curiosity to know more deeply the secrets of his mind. He had many reserves,—an unwillingness to exhibit to profane eyes what was still sacred in his own, and knew well how to throw a poetic veil over his experience. All readers of "Walden" will remember his mythical record of his disappointments:—

> I long ago lost a hound, a bay horse, and a turtle-dove, and am still on their trail. Many are the travellers I have spoken concerning them, describing their tracks, and what calls they answered to. I have met one or two who had heard the hound, and the tramp of the horse, and even seen the dove disappear behind a cloud, and they seemed as anxious to recover them as if they had lost them themselves.[15]

His riddles were worth the reading, and I confide that, if at any time I do not understand the expression, it is yet just. Such was the wealth of his truth, that it was not worth his while to use words in vain.

His poem entitled "Sympathy" reveals the tenderness under that triple steel of stoicism, and the intellectual subtlety it could animate. His classic poem on "Smoke" suggests Simonides, but is better than any poem of Simonides.[16] His biography is in his verses. His habitual thought makes all his poetry a hymn to the Cause of causes, the spirit which vivifies and controls his own.

> I hearing get, who had but ears,
> And sight, who had but eyes before;
> I moments live, who lived but years,
> And truth discern, who knew but learning's lore.

And still more in these religious lines:—

> Now chiefly is my natal hour,
> And only now my prime of life;
> I will not doubt the love untold,
> Which not my worth or want hath bought,
> Which wooed me young, and wooes me old,
> And to this evening hath me brought.[17]

Whilst he used in his writings a certain petulance of remark in reference to churches or churchmen, he was a person of a rare, tender, and absolute religion, a person incapable of any profanation, by act or by thought. Of course, the same isolation which belonged to his original thinking and living detached him from the social religious forms. This is neither to be censured nor regretted. Aristotle long ago explained it, when he said, "One who surpasses his fellow citizens in virtue, is no longer a part of the city. Their law is not for him, since he is a law to himself."

Thoreau was sincerity itself, and might fortify the convictions of prophets in the ethical laws, by his holy living. It was an affirmative experience which refused to be set aside. A truth-speaker he, capable of the most deep and strict conversation; a physician to the wounds of any soul; a friend knowing not only the secret of friendship, but almost worshipped by those few persons who resorted to him as their confessor and prophet, and knew the deep value of his mind and great heart. He thought that without religion or devotion of some kind, nothing great was ever accomplished: and he thought that the bigoted sectarian had better bear this in mind.

His virtues of course sometimes ran into extremes. It was easy to trace to the inexorable demand on all for exact truth that austerity which made this willing hermit more solitary even than he wished. Himself of a perfect probity, he required not less of others. He had a disgust at crime, and no worldly success could cover it. He detected paltering as readily in dignified and prosperous persons as in beggars, and with equal scorn. Such dangerous frankness was in his dealing, that his admirers called him "that terrible Thoreau," as if he spoke, when silent, and was still present when he had departed. I think the severity of his ideal interfered to deprive him of a healthy sufficiency of human society.

The habit of a realist to find things the reverse of their appearance inclined him to put every statement in a paradox. A certain habit of antagonism defaced his earlier writings, a trick of rhetoric not quite outgrown in his later, of substituting for the obvious word and thought its diametrical opposite. He praised wild mountains and winter forests for their domestic air; in snow and ice, he would find sultriness; and commended the wilderness for resembling Rome and Paris. "It was so dry, that you might call it wet."

The tendency to magnify the moment, to read all the laws of nature in the one object or one combination under your eye, is of course comic to those who do not share the philosopher's perception of identity. To him there was no such thing as size. The pond was a small ocean; the Atlantic, a large Walden Pond. He referred every minute fact to cosmical laws. Though he meant to be just, he seemed haunted by a certain chronic assumption that the science of the day pretended completeness and he had just found out that the savans had neglected to discriminate a particular botanical variety, had failed to describe the seeds, or count the sepals. "That is to say," we replied, "the blockheads were not born in Concord, but who said they were? It was their unspeakable misfortune to be born in London, or Paris, or Rome; but, poor fellows, they did what they could, considering that they never saw Bateman Pond, or Nine-Acre-Corner, or Becky Stow's Swamp.

Besides, what were you sent into the world for, but to add this observation?"

Had his genius been only contemplative, he had been fitted to his life, but with his energy and practical ability he seemed born for great enterprise and for command: and I so much regret the loss of his rare powers of action, that I cannot help counting it a fault in him that he had no ambition. Wanting this, instead of engineering for all America, he was the captain of a huckleberry party. Pounding beans is good to the end of pounding empires one of these days, but if, at the end of years, it is still only beans!—

But these foibles, real or apparent, were fast vanishing in the incessant growth of a spirit so robust and wise, and which effaced its defects with new triumphs. His study of nature was a perpetual ornament to him, and inspired his friends with curiosity to see the world through his eyes, and to hear his adventures. They possessed every kind of interest. He had many elegances of his own, whilst he scoffed at conventional elegance. Thus he could not bear to hear the sound of his own steps, the grit of gravel; and therefore never willingly walked in the road, but in the grass, on mountains, and in woods. His senses were acute, and he remarked that by night every dwelling-house gives out bad air, like a slaughter-house. He liked the pure fragrance of melilot.[18] He honored certain plants with special regard, and over all the pond-lily,—then the gentian, and the *Mikania scandens*, and "Life Everlasting," and a bass tree which he visited every year when it bloomed in the middle of July.[19] He thought the scent, a more oracular inquisition than the sight,—more oracular and trustworthy. The scent, of course, reveals what is concealed from the other senses. By it he detected earthiness. He delighted in echoes, and said, they were almost the only kind of kindred voices that he heard. He loved nature so well, was so happy in her solitude, that he became very jealous of cities, and the sad work which their refinements and artifices made with man and his dwelling. The axe was always destroying his forest—"Thank God," he said, "they cannot cut down the clouds. All kinds of figures are drawn on the blue ground, with this fibrous white paint."

I subjoin a few sentences taken from his unpublished manuscripts not only as records of his thought and feeling, but for their power of description and literary excellence.

"Some circumstantial evidence is very strong, as when you find a trout in the milk."[20]

"The chub is a soft fish, and tastes like boiled brown paper salted."

"The youth gets together his materials to build a bridge to the moon, or, perchance, a palace or temple on the earth, and, at length, the middle-aged man concludes to build a woodshed with them."

"The locust z———ing."

"Devil's-needles zig-zagging along the Nut-Meadow brook."

"Sugar is not so sweet to the palate, as sound to the healthy ear."

"I put on some hemlock boughs, and the rich salt crackling of their leaves was like mustard to the ear, the crackling of uncountable regiments. Dead trees love the fire."

"The blue-bird carries the sky on his back."

"The tanager flies through the green foliage, as if it would ignite the leaves."

"If I wish for a horse-hair for my compass-sight, I must go to the stable; but the hair-bird with her sharp eyes goes to the road."

"Immortal water, alive even to the superficies."

"Fire is the most tolerable third party."

"Nature made ferns for pure leaves, to show what she could do in that line."

"No tree has so fair a bole, and so handsome an instep as the beech."

"How did these beautiful rainbow tints get into the shell of the fresh-water clam, buried in the mud at the bottom of our dark river?"

"Hard are the times when the infant's shoes are second-foot."

"We are strictly confined to our men to whom we give liberty."

"Nothing is so much to be feared as fear. Atheism may comparatively be popular with God himself."

"Of what significance the things you can forget? A little thought is sexton to all the world."

"How can we expect a harvest of thought, who have not had a seed-time of character?"

"Only he can be trusted with gifts, who can present a face of bronze to expectations."

"I ask to be melted. You can only ask of the metals that they be tender to the fire that melts them. To nought else can they be tender."

There is a flower known to botanists, one of the same genus with our summer plant called "Life Everlasting," a *Gnaphalium* like that, which grows on the most inaccessible cliffs of the Tyrolese mountains, where the chamois dare hardly venture, and which the hunter, tempted by its beauty, and by his love, (for it is immensely valued by the Swiss maidens), climbs the cliffs to gather, and is sometimes found dead at the foot, with the flower in his hand. It is called by botanists the *Gnaphalium leontopodium*, but by the Swiss, *Edelweisse*, which signifies, *Noble Purity*. Thoreau seemed to me living in the hope to gather this plant, which belonged to him of right. The scale on which his studies proceeded was so large as to require longevity, and we were the less prepared for his sudden disappearance. The country knows not yet, or in the least part, how great a son it has lost. It seems an injury that he should leave in the midst his broken task, which none else can finish,—a kind of indignity to so noble a soul, that it should depart out of nature before yet he has been really shown to his peers for what he is. But he, at least, is content. His soul was made for the noblest society; he had in a short life exhausted the capabilities of this world; wherever there is knowledge, wherever there is virtue, wherever there is beauty, he will find a home.

Source: Ralph Waldo Emerson, "Thoreau," *Atlantic Monthly,* 10 (August 1862): 239–249; reprinted from Joel Myerson, "Emerson's 'Thoreau': A New Edition from Manuscript," *Studies in the American Renaissance 1979,* ed. Myerson (Boston: Twayne, 1979), pp. 17–92.

Notes

1. *à l'outrance*: of excess.
2. Croesus, (fl. 6th century B.C.), Greek king known for his treasures.
3. *Robinson Crusoe* (1719), novel about a traveler stranded on an island, by Daniel Defoe (1660–1731), English journalist and novelist.
4. This story is told in "Resistance to Civil Government," printed above.
5. Rose Flammock, character in *The Betrothed* (1825), by Sir Walter Scott; dowlas, a coarse linen cloth.
6. Graham house, establishment espousing the health regimen of Sylvester Graham.
7. Mount Washington, the highest of the White Mountains in New Hampshire.
8. *Arnica mollis*: hairy arnica, a flowering herb.
9. George Bryan (Beau) Brummel (1778–1840), leader of the fashionable society in early nineteenth-century London.
10. Hyla, a type of tree frog.
11. Elisha Kent Kane (1820–1857), member of expeditions to the North Pole in 1850–1851 and 1853–1855, published a number of books about his adventures.
12. Annursnuc (also Anursnuck or Annursnak), a hill in Massachusetts.
13. *Victoria regia*: a large water flower common to the Amazon.
14. Thomas Fuller (1608–1661), English clergyman; *The Feminine Monarchie; or, A Treatise Concerning Bees, and the Due Ordering of Them: Wherein the Truth, Found Out by Experience and Diligent Observation, Discovereth the Idle and Fond Conceipts, Which Many Have Written Anent This Subject* (1609), by Charles Butler (d. 1647).
15. *Walden*, p. 20 [Emerson's note]
16. Simonides of Ceos (ca. 556–ca. 468 B.C.), lyric poet from the Greek island of Ceos.
17. "Inspiration."
18. Melilot, a type of clover.
19. *Mikania scandens*: a herbaceous vine.
20. That is, when the milk has been watered down.

James Freeman Clarke

from "Cambridge"

(1891)

JAMES FREEMAN CLARKE (1810–1888) had a career that ran the full gamut, from being a member of the Transcendental Club, to editing the *Western Messenger*, to starting his own congregation (The Church of the Disciples) in 1841, to contributing to the *Dial*, to being general secretary of the American Unitarian Association. He knew most of the Transcendentalists, had an extended correspondence with Margaret Fuller, was involved in many of the Transcendentalists' activities, and exchanged pulpits with Parker after the latter was shunned following publication of the *Discourse on the Transient and Permanent in Christianity*, but Clarke nevertheless pursued his reforms within the general structure of the Unitarian establishment. In his "Autobiography," he looks back on what it was like to be educated as an undergraduate at Harvard (1825–1829) and at the Divinity School (1829–1832) right before the time when Transcendentalism burst upon the scene. Even a cursory reading of Clarke's reminiscences will clearly show why Emerson's "American Scholar" address fell on receptive ears.

I have sometimes wondered that our teachers then, and so many teachers since, could never interest young people in study. There is one element in the human soul which is common to all mankind,— *curiosity*. Why was this motive never appealed to? No attempt was made to interest us in our studies. We were expected to wade through Homer as though the Iliad were a bog, and it was our duty to get along at such a rate *per diem*. Nothing was said of the glory and grandeur, the tenderness and charm of this immortal epic. The melody of the hexameters was never suggested to us. Dr. Popkin, our Greek professor, would look over his spectacles at us, and, with pencil in hand, mark our recitation as good or bad, but never a word to help us over a difficulty, or to explain anything obscure, still less to excite our enthusiasm for the greatest poem of antiquity.[1] But this was not peculiar to Dr. Popkin. It was the universal custom, with but one exception.

Professor John Farrar, in his lectures on philosophy, and in his other teaching, excited a living interest in physics, astronomy, mechanics, electricity, and the other sciences.[2] Consequently we really learned in listening to him, and in reciting to him. I can repeat, to-day, many of his explanations and illustrations in these sciences. He was a man instinct with nervous vivacity, and would be carried away by the fervor of his speech and his interest in his theme, till he would quit his desk, walk to and fro about the room, talking and gesticulating, sometimes stooping till his body almost touched the floor, then rising till he stood on the tips of his toes, in the ardor of his discourse. He was a true teacher, but almost the only one in the whole corps of the professors. We went through Conic Sections with a tutor who never suggested to us, from first to last, that these were the curves in which the planets and comets moved, and that by learning their laws we were able to determine, a thousand years beforehand, an eclipse of the sun or an occultation of Jupiter. We supposed they were barren studies with no practical application. Even a little introduction, giving the history of the discovery of these laws, would have interested us. But nothing was said to awaken our curiosity, which I once heard Dr. James Walker say should be the chief motive appealed to by teachers.[3]

But in fact it is a modern discovery, or perhaps a re-discovery, that the duty of a teacher is *to teach*. It was at that time assumed that it was his duty to hear recitations. Of course, if he gave lectures, he was to communicate information, but never in the recitation room. To explain difficulties to the young men before him, to help them along by happy illustration and comment, to unite the knots too hard for their young fingers to loose,—this would have been thought almost improper, and, certainly, it would have caused great surprise if one of the students had said, "I cannot understand this passage in Horace; will you be so kind as to explain it?"[4] But why not, if we were sent to college to learn?

The root of the evil was that the motive relied on by the college system was not *curiosity*, but *emulation*; not the love of knowledge, but the desire for rank. Everything went to rank; recitations, regular attendance at exercises, good behavior in our rooms and elsewhere,—all were counted to the credit of rank in class. But as the majority of the class soon found that they could not attain a high rank, they ceased to try, and contented themselves with reciting well enough and behaving well enough to escape punishment.

The assumption in those days was,—and it still remains too much the general assumption in the corps of teachers in all colleges,—that young men's minds and hearts will not respond to generous motives, that they must be coerced, restrained, punished, and driven, not led by affection, by good-will, by the love of truth, by the desire for knowledge, by the ardor of attainment. But our real study was done from these latter motives. When I recall what my classmates were interested in doing, I find it was not college work, which might have given them rank, but pursuits outside of the curriculum. They did not put their strength into college themes, but into articles for the "Collegian."[5] They did not read Thucydides and Xenophon, but Macaulay and Carlyle.[6] We unearthed old tomes in the college library, and while our English professors were teaching us out of Blair's "Rhetoric," we were forming our taste by making copious extracts from Sir Thomas Browne, or Ben Jonson.[7] Our real professors of rhetoric were Charles Lamb and Coleridge, Walter Scott and Wordsworth.[8] I recall the delight which George Davis and I took in an old copy of Sir Thomas Browne which we stumbled upon in the college library.[9] We had scarcely heard the name; but by a sure instinct we discovered the wit, originality, and sagacity of this old writer. It was about the time of our senior year that Professor Marsh, of Vermont University, was reprinting Coleridge's "Friend," his "Aids to Reflection," and his "Biographia Literaria."[10] These books I read from time to time during several years, and they gave, in a high degree, incitement and nourishment to my intellect. Coleridge the poet I had known and loved. Coleridge the philosopher confirmed my longing for a higher philosophy than that of John Locke and David Hartley, the metaphysicians most in vogue with the earlier Unitarians down to the time of Channing.[11]

The books of Locke, Priestley, Hartley, and Belsham were in my grandfather Freeman's library, and the polemic of Locke against innate ideas was one of my earliest philosophical lessons.[12] But something within me revolted at all such attempts to explain soul out of sense, deducing mind from matter, or tracing the origin of ideas to nerves, vibrations, and vibratiuncles. So I concluded I had no taste for metaphysics and gave it up, until Coleridge showed me from Kant that though knowledge begins *with* experience it does not come *from* experience. Then I discovered that I was born a transcendentalist; and smiled when I afterwards read, in one of Jacobi's works, that he had gone through exactly the same experience. Thus I became a great reader of Coleridge, and was quite ready to accept his distinction between the reason and the understanding judging by sense. This distinction helped me much in my subsequent studies of theology. It enabled me to distinguish between truth as seen by the reason, and its statement as formulated by the understanding. It enabled me to put logic in its proper place, and see that its function was not the discovery of truth, but that of arranging, methodizing, and harmonizing verbal propositions in regard to it. I could see that those who had the same spiritual experience, and who beheld the same truth, might differ in their statements concerning it, and, that while truth was unchanging and eternal, theology might alter and improve from age to age.

This distinction, when once clearly seen, puts an end to bigotry, at least to honest and involuntary bigotry. Take, for example, the doctrinal dispute concerning the person of Christ. The Trinitarian says, "He is God."[13] The Unitarian says, "He is not God." Each thinks that if he is right, the other is absolutely wrong, and is denying an essential truth. If the *truth* is coincident with its doctrinal statement, then one or the other is indeed in very grave error. This was the old way of looking at it. But, according to the distinction of Coleridge, the vital truth perceived by the reason is not the same as the doctrinal statement enunciated by the understanding. The reason sees in Christ something divine, finds in him a visible manifestation of the invisible and eternal. In this intellectual vision both the Trinitarian and the Unitarian may be one, though when they come to express it as a doctrine they differ. The essential fact is the vision of truth as beheld by the reason, not its doctrinal form as worked out by the understanding. Thus Coleridge's metaphysical statement has really put an end to much conscientious bigotry in the modern church.

Source: James Freeman Clarke, from "Cambridge," in *Autobiography, Diary and Correspondence*, ed. Edward Everett Hale (Boston: Houghton, Mifflin, 1891), pp. 36–40.

Notes

1. John Snelling Popkin (1771–1852), Eliot Professor of Greek Literature from 1826 to 1833.
2. John Farrar (1779–1853), Hollis Professor of Mathematics and Natural Philosophy from 1807 to 1836.
3. James Walker (1794–1874), Alford Professor of Natural Religion, Moral Philosophy, and Civil Polity from 1838 to 1853 and President of Harvard from 1853 to 1860.
4. Horace (65–8 B.C.), Roman poet also known for his writings about poetry.
5. *Collegian*, Harvard student newspaper in 1830.
6. Thucydides (ca. 460–ca. 404 B.C.), most famous of the ancient Greek historians; Xenophon (431–ca. 350 B.C.), Greek historian; Thomas Babington Macaulay (1800–1859), English historian, essayist, and politician.
7. Hugh Blair (1718–1800), Scottish divine, author, and rhetorician, whose *Lectures on Rhetoric and Belles Letters* (1783) was a standard textbook; Sir Thomas Browne (1605–1682), English physician and author; Ben Jonson (1573–1637), English dramatist.
8. Charles Lamb (1775–1834), English essayist and critic.
9. George Thomas Davis (1810–1877), later a politician and abolitionist.
10. James Marsh edited Coleridge's *The Friend* in 1833 and *Aids to Reflection* in 1829; he died before completing his edition of *Biographia Literaria*.
11. David Hartley (1705–1757), English rationalist philosopher.

12. Joseph Priestly (1733–1804), English clergyman, political theorist, and scientist; Thomas Belsham (1750–1829), English Unitarian clergyman; James Freeman (1759–1835), clergyman and early Boston supporter of Unitarianism.

13. Trinitarians, those who believed that the Godhead encompassed the union of the Father, the Son, and the Holy Spirit.

Caroline Dall

from *Transcendentalism in New England: A Lecture Delivered Before the Society for Philosophical Inquiry, Washington, D.C., May 7, 1895*

(1897)

CAROLINE WELLS HEALEY DALL (1822–1912) first came into the Transcendentalist circle in 1841, when she attended Margaret Fuller's Conversations (which she later described in *Margaret and Her Friends* [1895]). An author, lecturer, and reformer, she early came under Parker's influence and throughout her life maintained friendships (often rocky ones) with most of the first-and second-generation Transcendentalists, describing their activities in articles, books, and her voluminous unpublished journals. Her memoir, a unique feminist perspective on the movement, is intended "to give a strong, impressive picture of a wonderful era in New England life," and she frames Transcendentalism by arguing for its origins in Anne Hutchinson and its conclusion, sadly, as this: "I do not think I am mistaken in saying that what is meant by New England Transcendentalism perished with Margaret Fuller."

I AM asked to speak to you of Transcendentalism in New England. The phrase is a misnomer; out of New England, Transcendentalism had no practical existence. In Germany it belonged to the scholars, and never affected popular life. It began to do this in New England a hundred years before "The Critique of Pure Reason" was printed, and independently of the causes which brought that philosophical classic into existence.[1]

The idea of One originating cause lay at the basis of every system of Puritanism: but the limitations of the sixteenth century prevented its theologians from recognizing that the revelations of the Creative Cause are perpetual. When the religious instruction of Helen Keller became a necessity, it was intrusted to the Rev. Phillips Brooks, with the distinct understanding that he should not convey to her any sectarian limitations.[2] When, on the first day, the bishop undertook to define for her the nature and being of God, the child of eleven interrupted him with this pathetic outburst: "I have always known him; but I did not know his name!"

More pathetic still is the fact that the earliest settlers of New England, who had always known the name of God, who were more than ready, even eager, to lay down their lives in what they believed to be his service, were nevertheless ignorant of his nature. This led to many painful episodes in the development of New England life, the first of which was the persecution of Anne Hutchinson.[3] You will be surprised when you hear me say that the history of the Transcendental movement stretched along two hundred years, beginning with a woman's life and work in 1637, and ending with a woman's work and death in 1850. The arc, which we call transcendental, was subtended by a chord, held at first by Anne Hutchinson, and lost in the Atlantic waves with Margaret Fuller. . . .

In tracing the Transcendental movement to Anne Hutchinson, I had always supposed myself to be doing something original; but in looking up material for this paper I found the following sentence in Emerson:—

> In action the Transcendentalist might be counted an *Antinomian*, because he asserts that he who has the Lawgiver may not only neglect but contravene every written command!

Emerson overlooked Anne Hutchinson, which he would not have done ten years later; but he recognized the ripple left by her movement. This showed itself above the surface, here and there, all through the century and a half that led to the advent of William Ellery Channing; and this spiritual impulse saved the Unitarianism of New England from becoming the dead, materialistic thing which Priestley made of it in the old country.

Locke insisted that all knowledge came from experience; Berkeley, that the outward world had no existence whatever as a substance. The two schools annihilated each other, and resulted in the scepticism of Hume.[4] Stimulated by this, and moved also—there is little doubt—by the impetus given by the studies of others, Kant published in 1781 "The Critique of Pure Reason." In this remarkable and now classic book Kant asserted the veracity of consciousness, and demanded an absolute acknowledgement of that veracity. The fidelity of the mind to itself constituted his first principle. *He* first used the term "transcendental" when he asserted that there was a very imperative class of ideas which transcend experience, but are the means by which experience is to be tested. Then followed throughout Europe a general illumination of philosophic thought, which came in time to pervade the theology of New England, although at first indirectly.

We had no German students then, but one of Channing's earliest utterances was this: "A spiritual light brighter than that of noon pervades our daily life. The cause of our not seeing lies in ourselves." . . .

Transcendentalism, then, is idealism made practical as it appeared in 1842. "Amid the downward tendency of things," wrote Emerson, "when every voice is raised for a new house, a new dress, or larger business, will you not tolerate one or two solitary voices in the land speaking for thoughts and principles which shall be neither marketable nor perishable?"—words suggested perhaps by those of Archbishop Leighton, who, when his Westminster catechisers demanded, "Do you preach to the times?" answered, "May not one man preach to eternity?"[5] "The senses," said its votaries, "give us representations of things, but what the things are they cannot tell." Every materialist may become an idealist, but an idealist cannot become a materialist. Mind is the only real thing. Is it not the power which makes tools of things actual?

The Transcendentalist made an extravagant demand on human nature,—that of lofty living. He quarrelled with every man he met. There was not enough of him! "So many promising youths," said Emerson, "and never a finished man!"[6]

The anthropologists may find in this movement the origin of nearly every one of their multiform lines of inquiry. "It is a misfortune," said one, "to have been born when children were nothing, and to have lived until men have become nothing!" New voices began to be heard in the air. Channing had prepared the way by his magnificent vindication of the dignity of human nature. New principles in philosophy, new methods of criticism, began to stir. The origin and contents of the Scriptures were carefully scrutinized. The mind of New England was leavened by the thought of Emerson and the scholarship of Hedge. The "Transient and Permanent" were examined and contrasted by a fearless iconoclast. The title "humanitarian" began to be applied to theologians. God is not outside the world, a mere lawgiver: he is in the world; he is in the world; man's relation to him is immediate. God is the Over Soul; above all, through all, *under* all, as well. The spirit must speak to spirit. Jesus was but a man, therefore a child of God who had attained to his proper heritage. He was the ideal man, type of mankind, become so through entering into perfect harmony with the Divine. If he wrought miracles, they must have been manifestations of normal law not yet perceived by undeveloped souls. Conceptions like these inspired the best spiritual life of the time, and modified the sentiments of many who were still unwilling to break the bonds of their training.

The characteristics of the Transcendental movement were shown in the temper of its agitation for the rights of woman and the enlargement of her duties. Like Dryden, every Transcendentalist was ready, and indeed had good reason, to assert that there was "no sex in souls."[7] The editors of "The Dial," which was first issued in July, 1840, and lasted hardly four years, were Margaret Fuller and Ralph Waldo Emerson. In this, besides exquisite poems which, dropped from their original setting, have since travelled all over the world, the "Great Lawsuit" of Margaret Fuller, seven wonderful chapters on the "Ethnical Scriptures," a remarkable paper of Theodore Parker's, and the absurd "Orphic Sayings" of Alcott were first given to the world.[8]

Transcendentalism had now come to be a distinct system, and, practically, to be the assertion of the inalienable worth of man, and of the immanence of the Divine in the Human. Its votaries were now the most strenuous workers of their day—not only that, but the most successful. Men and women are healthier in their bodies, happier in their domestic and social relations, more ambitious to enlarge their opportunities, more kind and humane in sympathy, as well as more reasonable in expectation, than they would have been if Margaret and Emerson had never lived. Under the influence of transcendental thought and hope, the mind of universal man leaped forward with a bound. The Transcendentalist of that day was always on the wing. A new hymn-book, issued by Samuel Johnson and Samuel Longfellow,— for which reason it was called by Theodore Parker the "Sam Book,"— was not only one of the manifestations of clerical sympathy, but had much to do with securing popular attention to the new ideas.[9]

The Transcendentalists did not write about immortality. Theodore Parker called it a fact of consciousness, and in all their conferences faith in it was assumed. No belief was more characteristic of them than this. Emerson's life and walk and literary utterance were full of this faith. His power lay in his pure idealism, his absolute faith in thought, his supreme confidence in spiritual law. He lived in the region of serene ideas: "he did not visit the mount now and then, but set up his tabernacle and passed the night among the stars, ready for the eternal sunrise." He was the descendant of eight generations of Puritan clergymen,—some of whom had persecuted, some of whom had cherished, the "exaltation" of Anne Hutchinson. He inherited their thoughtfulness and their spirit of inward communion. The dogmatism fell away, the peaceful fruits of discipline remained. He bore with him the atmosphere of eternal youth. For what he says or what he does he makes no apology. He never explains. He trusts to affirmation pure and simple. I appealed to him once, when a wholly unnecessary mis-understanding had put me in a painful position: "What should I do?" "Do?" he answered, with the look of a bewildered child; "if under-standing were possible, misunderstanding would not have occurred!" I have never tried to explain myself since; but many a time has that serene dogma comforted my soul. . . .

For myself, I am a Transcendentalist of the old New England sort. I believe myself to be a child of God; and if a child, then an heir,— a very condensed way of saying that the spirit within me is the breath of the creative spirit, and therefore infinite in its reach, in its possi-bilities, and its final destiny. The Over Soul is the Under Soul as well.[10] Matter is immortal. No agency, human or divine, has so far been able to destroy one particle of it; and yet, the world over, we see matter not only plastic in the grasp of mind, but subordinate to the uses of the race or the individual solely through the spirit's power. Is the spirit less, then, than the flesh which it masters? If matter cannot be de-stroyed, it can be transformed. So can spirit. I remember to have heard James Freeman Clarke say of another whose virtue was in question: "Do not dwell on his transgressions. *His face is set the right way.* He keeps his heel firmly on every tempting thought. If it slip now and then, what matter? The purpose is the thing!" This, I suppose, is rank antinomianism, capable of great abuse; but is it not the doctrine we all accept to-day? Life is a glorious thing, whether it is the life that now is or the life that is to come. To be born immortal; to pass through life in the consciousness of an immortal destiny; to try steadfastly to be worthy of this,—what grander atmosphere could encompass a man? There is only one thing sweeter and more desirable,—to trust one's self wholly to the love of the informing Spirit. There is only one clew which it is safe to hold as we pass through the mysteries of this life to the confines of the next. It is a *Surrendered Will.*

The body, to be healthy, must be constructed and sustained in har-mony with psychical and physiological law. No less must the soul be held to the conditions of that spiritual law which underlies both. I wish I could make my statement such that it would satisfy my agnostic friends. I have many who call themselves such, but I do not put faith in their nomenclature. Sometime they will understand themselves bet-ter, and the mists which hide their mortal goal will float and vanish on the beams of the eternal sunrise. *Language* may then be transformed as well as matter and spirit.

> It matters not how strait the gate,
> How charged with punishments the scroll:

> I am the Master of my fate,
>> The Captain of my soul! . . .

I began this paper with one woman's name; I must close it with another's.

It is hopeless to convey to those who never saw her any idea of Margaret Fuller, to give to those who never lived in the circle that she inspired any impression of her being and influence. She was not beautiful, people said: but she was more than beautiful. A sort of glow surrounded her, and warmed those who listened. It was dimmed sometimes when she yielded to the temperament she inherited; but it burned afresh in the instant impulse of her better self. She was thought to dress magnificently. It was this glow that touched and colored her garments, for poverty compelled her to great simplicity. It was true of her, as of Richelieu, that her death left a vacancy greater than any space she had filled.[11] Many of the young women who grew up with her have since become distinguished. Those who have not, have not failed to introduce into sacred homes the high ideal that she imparted. I consider it the greatest blessing of my life that I was admitted almost as a child to the circle that surrounded her, and felt from my first conscious moments the noble atmosphere that she diffused. Among the girls of that circle one saw no low, ignoble motives, no vanity, no poor ambitions, no coquetries, no looking to marriage as an end, no proneness to idle gossip. Margaret's life began in the constant sacrifice of personal aims to the material wants of her family. It continued, like Anne Hutchinson's, attracting larger and larger crowds of women as long as she had strength to speak, until the men who knew her begged admittance to her audience. This granted, she was no longer her best self. It was only with women that she became both priestess and oracle. . . .

There is one prevalent misunderstanding of her character that I should like to do something to remove. She was both aristocratic and autocratic in her inherited bearing; and there was a common feeling that she valued intellect above character, and felt neither sympathy nor affection for commonplace persons. The very reverse of this was true. At Brook Farm she interested herself in the single women longing for something better than they knew, and without resources. When the Farm broke up, she wrote to such women, followed their fortunes, and, in several instances known to me, helped them to independence.

When she went to New York, a lady who had been at Brook Farm had offered to assist Mrs. Farnham at Sing Sing. More than once Margaret went thither to address these women abandoned by the world, or to counsel them in private interviews. Some of them who had made but one mistake—a mistake of ignorance rather than crime—were saved by her hand; and thirty years after her death I found them happy wives on our Western coast, more useful to the people about them through their early errors, and holding Margaret in grateful and loving remembrance. It was not until I went West in 1880 that I understood from such sources the whole scope of her noble life.

Margaret left America in 1846, but the impulse she had given was not lost. In Italy she became the intimate friend of Mazzini, and during the rise and fall of the Republic wrote a careful history of all that occurred,—a history that perished with her. Here, again, her life presents a parallel to that of Anne Hutchinson; for she had not been more celebrated in New England for her intellectual sway than she became in Italy as the superintendent of the hospital "Fate Bene Fratelli."

"Why this waste of magnificence?" wrote Alpine Conway, standing before the golden throne of the Himalayas, twenty-three thousand feet above the sea, in a solitude no human voice had ever broken.[12] The clouds for answer shut the sunset glory from his view. While we waited with heartfelt longing for Margaret, the savage waves tore her away and hid in their hollows all that she had loved. Is it not good that there should be bounty beyond our conceiving? The sunset was not wasted that only Conway saw. The tragedy of 1850 swallowed carelessly much that we held precious; but it promised more, and the glory of Margaret's life did not perish.

Source: From Caroline Dall, *Transcendentalism in New England: A Lecture Delivered Before the Society for Philosophical Inquiry, Washington, D.C., May 7, 1895* (Boston: Roberts Brothers, 1897). The quotations are from pp. 3, 38.

Notes

1. *Critique of Pure Reason*, by Immanuel Kant.
2. Helen Keller (1880–1968), author and educator who overcame being blind and deaf; Phillips Brooks (1835–1893), Boston Episcopal clergyman and renowned preacher.
3. Anne Hutchinson (1591–1643), religious liberal who helped found Rhode Island after being banished from the Massachusetts Bay Colony. Dall is thinking of how Hutchinson organized regular meetings of Boston women to discuss sermons and theology, and how she stressed the individual's intuition as a means of reaching God and salvation, rather than relying upon established beliefs and the assistance of ministers.
4. David Hume (1711–1776), Scottish historian, essayist, and empirical and skeptical philosopher.
5. Robert Leighton (1611–1684), Scottish Presbyterian minister who tried unsuccessfully to mediate church disputes.

6. From "The Transcendentalist."

7. The phrase "no sex in souls" does not appear in Dryden's poetry.

8. Emerson contributed a series of translations called "Ethnical Scriptures" to these issues of the *Dial*: 4 (July, October 1843; January, March 1844): 59–62, 205–210, 402–404, 529–536; probably Parker's "Hollis Street Council" in the *Dial*, 3 (October 1842): 201–221.

9. *A Book of Hymns for Public and Private Devotion* (1846), by two reform-minded Unitarian ministers, Samuel Johnson (1822–1882) and Samuel Longfellow (1819–1892), brother of the poet Henry Wadsworth Longfellow (1807–1882).

10. Emerson's "The Over-Soul" was published in *Essays: First Series* (1841).

11. Cardinal Richelieu (1585–1642), French prelate and politician.

12. William Martin Conway, Baron Conway (1856–1937), English mountain climber and explorer.

BIBLIOGRAPHIES

Listed below are the book-length editions of the writings of the Transcendentalists, primary and secondary bibliographies of them, and selected biographies. The critical literature is too vast to even sample here; the reader should check the secondary bibliographies of individual authors and the "Suggestions for Further Reading" chapter above for guides to this voluminous body of material.

Transcendentalism

Editions:

The Transcendentalists: An Anthology, ed. Perry Miller (Cambridge: Harvard University Press, 1950).
The American Transcendentalists: Their Prose and Poetry, ed. Miller (Garden City, N.Y.: Doubleday, 1957).
Selected Writings of the American Transcendentalists, ed. George Hochfield (New York: New American Library, 1966).
The American Transcendentalists, ed. Joel Myerson (Detroit: Gale, 1988).

Bibliographies

The Transcendentalists: A Review of Research and Criticism, ed. Joel Myerson (New York: Modern Language Association, 1984); hereafter cited as *The Transcendentalists*.
First Printings of American Authors, ed. Matthew J. Bruccoli et al., 5 vols. (Detroit: Gale, 1977–1987); hereafter cited as *FPAA*.

General Studies

Catherine Albanese, *Corresponding Motion: Transcendental Religion and the New America* (Philadelphia: Temple University Press, 1977).
Roger Asselineau, *The Transcendentalist Constant in American Literature* (New York: New York University Press, 1980).
Paul F. Boller, *American Transcendentalism, 1830–1860: An Intellectual Inquiry* (New York: Putnams, 1974).
Lawrence Buell, "The American Transcendentalist Poets," *The Columbia History of American Poetry*, ed. Jay Parini (New York: Columbia University Press, 1993), pp. 97–120.
Buell, *Literary Transcendentalism: Style and Vision in the American Renaissance* (Ithaca: Cornell University Press, 1973).
Buell, "The Transcendentalists," *Columbia Literary History of the United States*, gen. ed. Emory Elliott (New York: Columbia University Press, 1988), pp. 364–378.

Arthur Christy, *The Orient in American Transcendentalism* (New York: Columbia University Press, 1932).

Elizabeth Flower and Murray G. Murphey, "Transcendentalism," *A History of Philosophy in America*, 2 vols. (New York: Putnams, 1977), 1:397–435.

Octavius Brooks Frothingham, *Transcendentalism in America: A History* (New York: Putnams, 1876).

Richard Grusin, *Transcendentalist Hermeneutics: Institutional Authority and the Higher Criticism of the Bible* (Durham: Duke University Press, 1991).

Nathan Kaplan and Thomas Katsaros, *The Origins of American Transcendentalism in Philosophy and Mysticism* (New Haven: College and University Press, 1975).

Alexander C. Kern, "The Rise of Transcendentalism, 1815–1860," *Transitions in American Literary History*, ed. Harry Hayden Clark (Durham: Duke University Press, 1954), pp. 247–314.

Donald N. Koster, *Transcendentalism in America* (Boston: Twayne, 1975).

Biographical Dictionary of Transcendentalism, ed. Wesley T. Mott (Westport, Conn.: Greenwood Press, 1996).

Encyclopedia of Transcendentalism, ed. Mott (Westport, Conn.: Greenwood Press, 1996).

Joel Myerson, *The New England Transcendentalists and the* Dial: *A History of the Magazine and Its Contributors* (Rutherford, N.J.: Fairleigh Dickinson University Press, 1980).

Barbara Packer, "The Transcendentalists," *The Cambridge History of American Literature*, ed. Sacvan Bercovitch, vol. 2, *Prose Writing, 1820–1865* (Cambridge: Cambridge University Press, 1995), pp. 329–604.

Anne C. Rose, *Transcendentalism as a Social Movement 1830–1850* (New Haven: Yale University Press, 1981).

Arthur Versluis, *American Transcendentalism & Asian Religions* (New York: Oxford University Press, 1993).

Stanley M. Vogel, *German Literary Influences on the American Transcendentalists* (New Haven: Yale University Press, 1955).

Collections of Essays

American Transcendentalism: An Anthology of Criticism, ed. Brian M. Barbour (Notre Dame: University of Notre Dame Press, 1973).

Critical Essays on American Transcendentalism, ed. Philip F. Gura and Joel Myerson (Boston: G. K. Hall, 1982).

The Minor and Later Transcendentalists: A Symposium, ed. Edwin Gittleman (Hartford, Conn.: Transcendental Books, 1969).

Transcendentalism and Its Legacy, ed. Myron Simon and Thornton H. Parsons (Ann Arbor: University of Michigan Press, 1966).

The Transcendentalist Revolt Against Materialism, ed. George F. Whicher (Boston: D. C. Heath, 1949); rev. ed., *The Transcendentalist Revolt*, ed. Gail Kennedy (Boston: D. C. Heath, 1968).

Transient and Permanent: The Transcendentalist Movement and Its Contexts, ed. Charles Capper and Conrad Edick Wright (Boston: Northeastern University Press, 1999).

Unitarianism

General Studies

An American Reformation: A Documentary History of Unitarian Christianity, ed. Sydney E. Ahlstrom and Jonathan S. Carey (Middletown, Conn.: Wesleyan University Press, 1985).

Jerry Wayne Brown, *The Rise of Biblical Criticism in America, 1800–1870: The New England Scholars* (Middletown, Conn.: Wesleyan University Press, 1969).

George Willis Cooke, *Unitarianism in America* (Boston: American Unitarian Association, 1902).

Daniel Walker Howe, *The Unitarian Conscience: Harvard Moral Philosophy, 1805–1861* (Cambridge: Harvard University Press, 1970).

William R. Hutchison, *The Transcendentalist Ministers: Church Reform in the New England Renaissance* (New Haven: Yale University Press, 1959).

David Robinson, *The Unitarians and the Universalists* (Westport, Conn.: Greenwood Press, 1985).

Sarah Ann Wider, *Anna Tilden, Unitarian Culture, and the Problem of Self-Representation* (Athens: University of Georgia Press, 1997).

Conrad Wright, *The Beginnings of Unitarianism in America* (Boston: Starr King Press, 1955).

Wright, "The Early Period (1811–1840)," *The Harvard Divinity School: Its Place in Harvard University and in American Culture*, ed. George Hunston Williams (Boston: Beacon Press, 1954), pp. 21–77.

Wright, *The Liberal Christians: Essays on American Unitarian History* (Boston: Beacon Press, 1970).

A Stream of Light: A Sesquicentennial History of American Unitarianism, ed. Wright (Boston: Unitarian Universalist Association, 1975).

Wright, *The Unitarian Controversy: Essays on American Unitarian History* (Boston: Skinner House, 1994).

American Unitarianism, 1805–1865, ed. Conrad Edick Wright (Boston: Northeastern University Press, 1989).

Amos Bronson Alcott

Letters and Journals

The Letters of A. Bronson Alcott, ed. Richard L. Hernnstadt (Ames: Iowa State University Press, 1969).

The Journals of Bronson Alcott, ed. Odell Shepard (Boston: Little, Brown, 1938).

Bibliographies

Jacob Blanck, *Bibliography of American Literature*, 9 vols (New Haven: Yale University Press, 1955–1991), 1:20–26.

Frederick C. Dahlstrand in *The Transcendentalists*, pp. 87–96.

Biographies

F. B. Sanborn and William T. Harris, *A. Bronson Alcott: His Life and Philosophy*, 2 vols. (Boston: Roberts Brothers, 1893).

Odell Shepard, *Pedlar's Progress: The Life of Bronson Alcott* (Boston: Little, Brown, 1937).

Frederick C. Dahlstrand, *Amos Bronson Alcott: An Intellectual Biography* (Rutherford, N.J.: Fairleigh Dickinson University Press, 1982).

Brook Farm

Collected Editions

The Autobiography of Brook Farm, ed. Henry W. Sams (Englewood Cliffs, N.J.: Prentice-Hall, 1958).

The Brook Farm Book: A Collection of First-Hand Accounts of the Community, ed. Joel Myerson (New York: Garland Publishers, 1987).

Bibliographies

Joel Myerson, *Brook Farm: An Annotated Bibliography and Resources Guide* (New York: Garland Publishers, 1978).

Carol Johnston in *The Transcendentalists*, pp. 56–68.

Histories

Lindsay Swift, *Brook Farm: Its Members, Scholars, and Visitors* (New York: Macmillan, 1900).

Richard Francis, *Transcendental Utopias: Individual and Community at Brook Farm, Fruitlands, and Walden* (Ithaca: Cornell University Press, 1997).

Orestes Augustus Brownson

Collected Editions

The Works of Orestes A. Brownson, ed. H. F. Brownson, 20 vols. (Detroit: Thorndike, Nourse; H. F. Brownson, 1882–1887).

Letters and Journals

The Brownson-Hecker Correspondence, ed. Joseph F. Gower and Richard M. Leliaert (Notre Dame: University of Notre Dame Press, 1979).

Bibliographies

Joel Myerson in *FPAA*, 4:45–51.

Leonard Gilhooley in *The Transcendentalists*, pp. 303–309.

Biographies

Arthur M. Schlesinger, Jr., *Orestes A. Brownson: A Pilgrim's Progress* (Boston: Little, Brown, 1939).

Thomas R. Ryan, *Orestes Brownson: A Definitive Biography* (Huntington, Ind.: Our Sunday Visitor, 1976).

William Ellery Channing

Collected Editions

The Works of William Ellery Channing, D.D., 6 vols (Boston: James Munroe, 1841–1843).

Bibliographies

Joel Myerson in *FPAA*, 4:77–90.
David Robinson in *The Transcendentalists*, pp. 310–316.

Biographies

John White Chadwick, *William Ellery Channing: Minister of Religion* (Boston: Houghton, Mifflin, 1903).
Jack Mendelsohn, *Channing: The Reluctant Radical* (Boston: Little, Brown, 1971).
Andrew Delbanco, *William Ellery Channing: An Essay on the Liberal Spirit in America* (Cambridge: Harvard University Press, 1981).

William Ellery Channing II

Collected Editions

The Collected Poems of William Ellery Channing the Younger, 1817–1901, ed. Walter Harding (Gainesville, Fla.: Scholars' Facsimiles & Reprints, 1967).

Letters and Journals

Francis B. Dedmond, "The Selected Letters of William Ellery Channing (Parts One-Four)," *Studies in the American Renaissance 1989–1992*, ed. Joel Myerson (Charlottesville: University Press of Virginia, 1989–1992), pp. 115–218, 159–241, 257–343, 1–74.

Bibliographies

Jacob Blanck, *Bibliography of American Literature*, 9 vols (New Haven: Yale University Press, 1955–1991), 2:129–133.
Francis B. Dedmond in *The Transcendentalists*, pp. 102–107.

Biographies

Frederick T. McGill, Jr., *Channing of Concord: A Life of William Ellery Channing II* (New Brunswick: Rutgers University Press, 1967).
Robert N. Hudspeth, *Ellery Channing* (New York: Twayne, 1973).

William Henry Channing

Bibliographies

Elizabeth R. McKinsey in *The Transcendentalists*, pp. 108–111.

Biographies

Octavius Brooks Frothingham, *Memoir of William Henry Channing* (Boston: Houghton, Mifflin, 1886).

James Freeman Clarke

Letters and Journals

Autobiography, Diary and Correspondence, ed. Edward Everett Hale (Boston: Houghton, Mifflin, 1891).

The Letters of James Freeman Clarke to Margaret Fuller, ed. John Wesley Thomas (Hamburg, Germany: Cram, de Gruyter, 1957).

Bibliographies

Joel Myerson in *FPAA*, 4:93–107.
Leonard Neufeldt in *The Transcendentalists*, pp. 112–116.

Biographies

John Wesley Thomas, *James Freeman Clarke: Apostle of German Culture to America* (Boston: John W. Luce, 1949).

Arthur S. Bolster, Jr., *James Freeman Clarke: Disciple to Advancing Truth* (Boston: Beacon, 1954).

Christopher Pearse Cranch

Collected Editions

Collected Poems of Christopher Pearse Cranch, ed. Joseph M. De Falco (Gainesville, Fla.: Scholars' Facsimiles & Reprints, 1971).

Three Children's Novels by Christopher Pearse Cranch, ed. Greta D. Little and Joel Myerson (Athens: University of Georgia Press, 1993).

Bibliographies

Jacob Blanck, *Bibliography of American Literature*, 9 vols (New Haven: Yale University Press, 1955–1991), 2:320–328.

David Robinson in *The Transcendentalists*, pp. 123–130.

Biographies

Leonora Cranch Scott, *The Life and Letters of Christopher Pearse Cranch* (Boston: Houghton Mifflin, 1917).

F. DeWolfe Miller, *Christopher Pearse Cranch and His Caricatures of New England Transcendentalism* (Cambridge: Harvard University Press, 1951).

The *Dial*

Bibliographies

Donald F. Warders in *The Transcendentalists*, pp. 69–83 (esp. pp. 73–78).

Histories

Joel Myerson, *The New England Transcendentalists and the* Dial: *A History of the Magazine and Its Contributors* (Rutherford, N.J.: Fairleigh Dickinson University Press, 1980).

John Sullivan Dwight

Collected Editions

What They Heard: Music in America, 1852–1881, from the Pages of Dwight's Journal of Music, ed. Irving Sablosky (Baton Rouge: Louisiana State University Press, 1986).

Bibliographies

William G. Heath in *The Transcendentalists*, pp. 131–134.

Biographies

George Willis Cooke, *John Sullivan Dwight: Brook-Farmer, Editor, and Critic of Music* (Boston: Small, Maynard, 1898).

Ora Frishberg Saloman, *Beethoven's Symphonies and J. S. Dwight: The Birth of American Music Criticism* (Boston: Northeastern University Press, 1995).

Ralph Waldo Emerson

Collected Editions

The Collected Works of Ralph Waldo Emerson, ed. Alfred R. Ferguson, Joseph Slater, Douglas Emory Wilson, et al., 5 vols. to date (Cambridge: Harvard University Press, 1971-).

The Complete Sermons of Ralph Waldo Emerson, ed. Albert J. von Frank et al., 4 vols. (Columbia: University of Missouri Press, 1989–1992).

The Complete Works of Ralph Waldo Emerson, ed. Edward Waldo Emerson, 12 vols. (Boston: Houghton, Mifflin, 1903–1904).

The Early Lectures of Ralph Waldo Emerson, ed. Robert E. Spiller, Stephen E. Whicher, and Wallace E. Williams, 3 vols. (Cambridge: Harvard University Press, 1959–1972).

Emerson's Antislavery Writings, ed. Len Gougeon and Joel Myerson (New Haven: Yale University Press, 1995).

The Later Lectures of Ralph Waldo Emerson, 1843–1871, ed. Ronald A. Bosco and Myerson, 2 vols. (Athens: University of Georgia Press, forthcoming).

Letters and Journals

The Letters of Ralph Waldo Emerson, ed. Ralph L. Rusk and Eleanor M. Tilton, 10 vols. (New York Columbia University Press, 1939, 1990–1995).

The Correspondence of Emerson and Carlyle, ed. Joseph Slater (New York: Columbia University Press, 1964).

The Selected Letters of Ralph Waldo Emerson, ed. Joel Myerson (New York: Columbia University Press, 1997).

The Journals and Miscellaneous Notebooks of Ralph Waldo Emerson, ed. William H. Gilman, Ralph H. Orth, et al., 16 vols. (Cambridge: Harvard University Press, 1960–1982).

Emerson in His Journals, ed. Joel Porte (Cambridge: Harvard University Press, 1982).

The Poetry Notebooks of Ralph Waldo Emerson, ed. Ralph H. Orth et al. (Columbia: University of Missouri Press, 1986).

The Topical Notebooks of Ralph Waldo Emerson, ed. Ralph H. Orth et al., 3 vols. (Columbia: University of Missouri Press, 1990–1994).

Bibliographies

Joel Myerson, *Ralph Waldo Emerson: A Descriptive Bibliography* (Pittsburgh: University of Pittsburgh Press, 1982).

Robert E. Burkholder and Myerson, *Emerson: An Annotated Secondary Bibliography* (Pittsburgh: University of Pittsburgh Press, 1985).

Burkholder and Myerson in *The Transcendentalists*, pp. 135–166.

Burkholder and Myerson, *Ralph Waldo Emerson: An Annotated Bibliography of Criticism, 1980–1991* (Westport, Conn.: Greenwood Press, 1994).

Myerson, "Ralph Waldo Emerson," *Prospects for the Study of American Literature*, ed. Richard Kopley (New York: New York University Press, 1997), pp. 6–20.

Biographies

Oliver Wendell Holmes, *Ralph Waldo Emerson* (Boston: Houghton, Mifflin, 1884).

Ralph L. Rusk, *The Life of Ralph Waldo Emerson* (New York: Scribners, 1949).

Gay Wilson Allen, *Waldo Emerson: A Biography* (New York: Viking, 1981).

John McAleer, *Ralph Waldo Emerson: Days of Encounter* (Boston: Little, Brown, 1984).

Evelyn Barish, *Emerson: The Roots of Prophesy*. Princeton: Princeton University Press, 1989.

Albert J. von Frank, *An Emerson Chronology* (New York: G. K. Hall, 1994).

Robert D. Richardson, Jr., *Emerson: The Mind on Fire* (Berkeley: University of California Press, 1995).

Carlos Baker, *Emerson Among the Eccentrics: A Group Portrait* (New York: Viking Press, 1996).

Phyllis Cole, *Mary Moody Emerson and the Origins of Transcendentalism: A Family History* (New York: Oxford University Press, 1998).

Fruitlands

Bibliographies

Carol Johnston in *The Transcendentalists*, pp. 56–68.

Histories

Clara Endicott Sears, *Bronson Alcott's Fruitlands* (Boston: Houghton Mifflin, 1915).

Richard Francis, *Transcendental Utopias: Individual and Community at Brook Farm, Fruitlands, and Walden* (Ithaca: Cornell University Press, 1997).

Margaret Fuller

Collected Editions

Margaret Fuller, Critic: Writings from the New–York Tribune*, 1844–1846*, ed. Judith Mattson Bean and Joel Myerson (New York: Columbia University Press, 2000).

"These Sad But Glorious Days": Dispatches from Europe, 1846–1850, ed. Larry J. Reynolds and Susan Belasco Smith (New Haven: Yale University Press, 1991).

Letters and Journals

The Letters of Margaret Fuller, ed. Robert N. Hudspeth, 6 vols. (Ithaca: Cornell University Press, 1983–1994).

"These Sad But Glorious Days": Dispatches from Europe, 1846–1850, ed. Larry J. Reynolds and Susan Belasco Smith (New Haven: Yale University Press, 1991).

Bibliographies

Joel Myerson, *Margaret Fuller: A Descriptive Bibliography* (Pittsburgh: University of Pittsburgh Press, 1978).

Myerson, "Supplement to *Margaret Fuller: A Descriptive Bibliography,*" *Studies in the American Renaissance 1996* (Charlottesville: University Press of Virginia, 1996), pp. 187–240.

Myerson, *Margaret Fuller: An Annotated Secondary Bibliography* (New York: Burt Franklin, 1977).

Myerson, "Supplement to *Margaret Fuller: An Annotated Secondary Bibliography,*" *Studies in the American Renaissance 1984* (Charlottesville: University Press of Virginia, 1984), pp. 331–385.

Robert N. Hudspeth in *The Transcendentalists*, pp. 175–188.

Myerson, *Margaret Fuller: An Annotated Bibliography of Criticism, 1983–1995* (Westport, Conn.: Greenwood Press, 1998).

Biographies

Memoirs of Margaret Fuller Ossoli, ed. William Henry Channing, James Freeman Clarke, and Ralph Waldo Emerson, 2 vols. (Boston: Phillips, Sampson, 1852).

Madeleine B. Stern, *The Life of Margaret Fuller* (New York: Dutton, 1942).

Charles Capper, *Margaret Fuller: An American Romantic Life*, vol. 1, *The Private Years* (New York: Oxford University Press, 1992).

The Harbinger

Bibliographies

Donald F. Warders in *The Transcendentalists*, pp. 69–83 (esp. pp. 79–80).

Histories

Sterling F. Delano, The Harbinger *and New England Transcendentalism: A Portrait of Associationism in America* (Rutherford, N.J.: Fairleigh Dickinson University Press, 1983).

Frederic Henry Hedge

Bibliographies

Joel Myerson in *FPAA*, 3:145–151.
Leonard Neufeldt in *The Transcendentalists*, pp. 189–194.

Biographies

Bryan F. Le Beau, *Frederic Henry Hedge: Nineteenth Century American Transcendentalist* (Allison Park, Penn.: Pickwick, 1985).

Charles Lane

Bibliographies

Joel Myerson in *The Transcendentalists*, pp. 211–213.

Theodore Parker

Collected Editions

[*Centenary Edition of the Works of Theodore Parker*], 15 vols. (Boston: American Unitarian Association, 1907–1912).

Bibliographies

Joel Myerson, *Theodore Parker: A Descriptive Bibliography* (New York: Garland, 1981).
Gary L. Collison in *The Transcendentalists*, pp. 216–232.

Biographies

John Weiss, *The Life and Correspondence of Theodore Parker*, 2 vols. (New York: D. Appleton, 1864).
Octavius Brooks Frothingham, *Theodore Parker: A Biography* (Boston: James R. Osgood, 1874).
John White Chadwick, *Theodore Parker: Preacher and Reformer* (Houghton, Mifflin, 1901).
Henry Steele Commager, *Theodore Parker* (Boston: Little, Brown, 1936).
Dean Grodzins, *American Heretic: Theodore Parker and Transcendentalism* and

American Heretic: Theodore Parker, Democracy, and the Civil War (both University of North Carolina Press, forthcoming).

Elizabeth Palmer Peabody

Letters and Journals

The Letters of Elizabeth Palmer Peabody, American Renaissance Woman, ed. Bruce A. Ronda (Middletown, Conn.: Wesleyan University Press, 1984).

Bibliographies

Joel Myerson in *FPAA*, 3:279–284.
Margaret Neussendorfer in *The Transcendentalists*, pp. 233–241.

Biographies

Ruth M. Baylor, *Elizabeth Palmer Peabody: Kindergarten Pioneer* (Philadelphia: University of Pennsylvania Press, 1965).
Bruce A. Ronda, *Elizabeth Palmer Peabody: A Reformer on Her Own Terms* (Cambridge: Harvard University Press, 1999).

Sampson Reed

Collected Editions

Sampson Reed: Primary Source Material for Emerson Studies, ed. George F. Dole (New York: Swedenborg Foundation 1992).

Bibliographies

Elizabeth A. Meese in *The Transcendentalists*, pp. 372–374.

Biographies

Carl F. Strauch, "Introduction," Reed, *Observations on the Growth of the Mind* (Gainesville, Fla.: Scholars' Facsimiles & Reprints, 1970), pp. v–xxvi.

George Ripley

Bibliographies

Joel Myerson in *FPAA*, 3:287–289.
Charles R. Crowe in *The Transcendentalists*, pp. 242–249.

Biographies

Octavius Brooks Frothingham, *George Ripley* (Boston: Houghton, Mifflin, 1882).
Charles R. Crowe, *George Ripley: Transcendentalist and Utopian Socialist* (Athens: University of Georgia Press, 1967).

Sophia Willard Dana Ripley

Bibliographies

Charles R. Crowe in *The Transcendentalists*, pp. 250–252.

Biographies

Henrietta Dana Raymond, *Sophia Dana Willard Ripley* (Portsmouth, N.H.: Peter E. Randall, 1994).

Henry David Thoreau

Letters and Journals

The Correspondence of Henry David Thoreau, ed. Walter Harding and Carl Bode (New York: New York University Press, 1958).
Journal, vols. 7–20 of *The Writings of Henry David Thoreau*, 20 vols. (Boston: Houghton Mifflin, 1908).
Journal, 5 vols. to date of *The Writings of Henry D. Thoreau*, ed. Walter Harding, Elizabeth Hall Witherell et al., 12 vols. to date (Princeton: Princeton University Press, 1971–).

Collected Editions

The Writings of Henry David Thoreau, 20 vols. (1908).
The Writings of Henry D. Thoreau, 12 vols. to date (1971–).

Bibliographies

Raymond R. Borst, *Henry David Thoreau: A Descriptive Bibliography* (Pittsburgh: University of Pittsburgh Press, 1982).
Borst, *Henry David Thoreau: A Reference Guide 1835–1899* (Boston: G. K. Hall, 1987).
Michael Meyer in *The Transcendentalists*, pp. 260–285.
Gary Scharnhorst, *Henry David Thoreau: An Annotated Bibliography of Comment and Criticism Before 1900* (New York: Garland, 1992).
Scharnhorst, *Henry David Thoreau: A Case Study in Canonization* (Columbia, S.C.: Camden House, 1993).
Elizabeth Hall Witherell, "Henry David Thoreau," *Prospects for the Study of American Literature*, ed. Richard Kopley (New York: New York University Press, 1997), pp. 21–38.

Biographies

Walter Harding, *The Days of Henry David Thoreau* (New York: Alfred A. Knopf, 1965; enl. ed., New York: Dover, 1982).
Robert D. Richardson, Jr., *Henry Thoreau: A Life of the Mind* (Berkeley: University of California Press, 1986).
Raymond R. Borst, *The Thoreau Log: A Documentary Life of Henry David Thoreau 1817–1862* (New York: G. K. Hall, 1992).

Jones Very

Collected Editions

The Complete Poems, ed. Helen R. Deese (Athens: University of Georgia Press, 1993).

Bibliographies

Jacob Blanck, *Bibliography of American Literature*, 9 vols (New Haven: Yale University Press, 1955–1991), 8:397–405.
Joel Myerson in *FPAA*, 3:319–320.
David Robinson in *The Transcendentalists*, pp. 286–294.

Biographies

William Irving Bartlett, *Jones Very: Emerson's "Brave Saint"* (Durham: Duke University Press, 1942).
Edwin Gittleman, *Jones Very: The Effective Years 1833–1840* (New York: Columbia University Press, 1967).

Western Messenger

Bibliographies

Donald F. Warders in *The Transcendentalists,* pp. 69–83 (esp. pp. 70–72).

Histories

Elizabeth R. McKinsey, *The Western Experiment: New England Transcendentalists in the Ohio Valley* (Cambridge: Harvard University Press, 1973).
Robert D. Habich, *Transcendentalism and the* Western Messenger: *A History of the Magazine and Its Contributors, 1835–1841* (Rutherford, N.J.: Fairleigh Dickinson University Press, 1985).

INDEX

Judd, Sylvester, xxxvi
Jupiter, 221, 226n

Kane, Elisha Kent, 661, 669n
Kansas, 629–632, 638
Kansas-Nebraska Act, 601n, 614n
Kant, Immanuel, xxix, xxxii, xxxiii,
  87, 88–89, 91–93, 96n, 125,
  371, 380n, 672, 674, 675–676,
  680n
Keats, John, 585n
Keller, Helen, 674–675, 680n
Kelly, Abby, 415–416, 427n
Kentucky, 475
Kerner, Justinus, 414, 427n
King, Martin Luther, Jr., 546
Kingsley, Charles, 586n
Kinmont, Alexander, 417, 427n
Kneeland, Abner, 652, 653n
Knistenaux, 447, 455n
Knox, John, 216, 225n
Krug, Wilhelm Traugott, 92, 97n
Krummacher, Friedrich Adolph,
  118, 120n

Labrador, 222, 447
Lamb, Charles, 672, 673n
Landor, Walter Savage, 380n
Lane, Charles, 289; "Brook Farm,"
  456–461; "The Consociate
  Family Life," 435–442;
  "Fruitlands," 428–429
Lapland, 447
Latin language, 411, 507
Laud, William, 68, 78n
Lavoisier, Antoine Laurent, 334,
  340n
Lawrence, Massachusetts, 569, 585n
Lazarus, 24, 180, 276, 277
Lee, Mrs. George, 487
Lee, Mother Ann, 413, 427n, 442n
Lee family, 502
Leibnitz, Gottfried Wilhelm von,
  96n, 138
Leighton, Robert, 676, 680n
Leland, Charles Godfrey, xxv

Leonidas, 132, 158n
Leonora, 427n
Lethe, 321, 339n
Lexington, Massachusetts, 609
Lexington, Battle of, 565n, 600n,
  603, 605–606
Liberator, 602, 608–609, 615, 636,
  653n
Lind, Jenny, 570, 585n
Linnaeus, Carolus, 135, 158n, 206
Lisle, Alice, 577, 585n
Liverpool, England, 575
Locke, John, xxix, xxxii, 25, 26n,
  166, 199, 334, 371, 672, 675
London, 345, 486, 572, 582, 619,
  654, 657–658, 666
Longfellow, Samuel, 677, 681n
Longueville, Duchess de, 625, 628n
Loring, Edward Greeley, 603, 606,
  615n
Lorraine, Claude de, 619, 627n
Louis XIV, 393, 424n
Lovelace, Richard, 426n
Lowell, James Russell, 289
Lowell, Massachusetts, 569, 585n
Luke, Saint, 69–70, 76, 350
Luther, Martin, 22, 26n, 68, 216,
  258, 271, 325, 326, 553, 582,
  600, 617
Lyra, 211n, 347, 365n

Macaria, 400, 403, 425n
Macaulay, Thomas Babington, 672,
  673n
Macdonald, 206
Macgregor, Rob Roy, 212n
Macpherson, James, 26n
Magi, 179, 181n
Mahomet, 258, 344, 622
Maine, 223, 228, 338, 601n
Maistre, Joseph de, 414, 427n
Malays, 560
Malek, 621
Mammon, 611, 615n
Manchester, England, 572
Manchester, New Hampshire, 572

Mani, 149, 160n
Manicheans, 149, 160n, 372, 585n
Mann, Horace, 585n, 649, 652
Mansfield, Lord, 591, 601n
Manzoni, Alessandro, 409, 422,
423n, 426n
Manzoni, Enrichetta Luigia Blondel,
409
Mark, Saint, 69–70
Marlborough, Duchess of, 625,
628n
Marseillaise, La, 596, 601n
Marsh, James, 80–81, 95–96n, 672,
673n
Martineau, Harriet, 246, 249n, 417
Martineau, James, 160–161, 167,
260
Marvell, Andrew, 200–201, 211n
Mason, James Murray, 638, 647n
Massachusetts, 475, 477n, 550–551,
554–555, 557, 576, 579, 591–
593, 602–615, 638, 639, 641,
648, 660–661, 663
Massena, André, 244, 246n
Massinger, Philip, 403, 425n
Matthew, Saint, 69–70, 353, 365n
Matthew, Toby, 618, 627n
May, Samuel Joseph, 310, 313n
Mazzini, Giuseppi, 546n, 680
Medea, 247, 250n
Medes, 389, 423n
Melanion, 365n
Melville, Herman, 623, 628n
Memphis, Egypt, 222, 226n
Meriam family, 502
Merrimack River, 576, 585n, 660
Mesmerism, 414, 427n
Methodists, 326, 352, 365n
Mexican War, 474–475, 477n, 504,
545, 546n, 546–565 *passim*
Mexico, 593, 605
Mexico, Gulf of, 222
Michelangelo Buonarroti, 142, 149,
159n, 160n, 413, 427n
Mignon, 421, 427n, 619
Miller, Perry, 79, 121

Milton, John, 15, 20n, 22, 52, 86,
224, 262, 279n, 319, 326, 620;
Apology for Smectymnuus, 158n;
Comus, 160n; *L'Allegro*, 455n;
Paradise Lost, 339n, 366n, 538n,
613
Minerva, 311, 313n, 399, 418, 419,
421, 425n
Minos, King, 267, 279n
Minotaur, 644, 647n
Minott family, 502
Missouri, 601n, 631–632, 644
Missouri Compromise, 595, 601n,
614
Mitchel, John, 609, 615n
Monadnoc, Mount, 221, 225n
Montagu, Mary Worthley, 410,
426n
Montaigné, Michel Eyquem, 214,
225n
Montesquieu, Baron de la Brède et
de, 597, 601n
Moors, 647n
More, Henry, 627n
Mormons, 360, 365n, 567, 623
Moses, 15, 222, 236, 242, 267,
274, 319, 336, 356, 359, 366n,
388–389
Mozart, Wolfgang Amadeus, 267,
272, 279n, 372, 380n
Müller, Johannes von, 222, 226n
Muhammad, 565n, 601n
Musa, Abu: *see* Abu Musa Alishari
Muses, 24, 26n, 400, 418, 421,
526, 602n
Music Hall (Boston), 340
Musketaquit River, 515–516, 538n
Mussulman, 562, 565n

Naples, 208, 335, 575
Napoleon Bonaparte, 129, 157n,
244, 281, 337–338, 499–500
Napoleon III, 596, 601n
Natalia, 421, 427n
Nebraska, 598, 600, 602–603,
611

Nebuchadnezzar II, 154, 160n
Nemesis, 310, 313n
Neo-Platonism, 157n
New England, 362, 366, 411, 454,
    458, 525, 568, 572, 576–577,
    583, 586, 609, 630, 634, 648,
    650, 651, 658, 674–681
Newfoundland, 531
New Hampshire, 333, 338, 504
New Mexico, 586
Newton, Isaac, 22, 26n, 36, 203,
    267, 325, 336, 419
New York City, 332–333, 486,
    489, 582, 595–596, 607–608,
    624
New York Evening Post, 628n
New York Herald, 639
New York Socialists, 623,
    628n
New-York Tribune, 162, 280, 473,
    541, 628n
New Zealand, 336–337
Niagara Falls, 221
Nicodemus, 171, 181n
Niebuhr, Barthold Georg, 222,
    226n
Nike, 425n
Noah, 129, 157n, 366n
Nootka Sound, 453, 455n
Norris, John, 160n
Norton, Andrews, 121, 160–167,
    181, 250, 260–280 *passim*, 651;
    [Letter to the Editor], 160–162;
    "The New School in Literature
    and Religion," 246–250
Novalis, 522, 538n

Oberlin, Johann Friedrich, 242,
    246n
Oberlin College, 614n
Odd Fellows, 552, 565n
Odin, 212n
Odysseus, 157n
Oedipus, 425n
Oegger, Guillaume, 158n
Ohio, 576–577

Oken, Lorenz, 92, 96n
Oldcastle, John, Lord Cobham, 216,
    225n
Old Manse, 538n
Olympus, Mount, 148, 159n, 222,
    402
Onesimus, 601n
Ophelia, 314, 318n
Oregon, 658
Orestes, 370, 380n, 427n
Orientalism, 236, 623
Orion, 144, 159n
Orkneys, 222, 226n
Orpheus, 45, 61n, 387–388, 423n,
    562, 664
Osiris, 236, 245n, 424n
Ossian, 23, 26n
Ossoli, Giovanni, 280
Ossoli, Sarah Margaret Fuller: *see*
    Sarah Margaret Fuller
Ovid, 422–423n
Oxford, University of, 621

Palestine, 203, 234
Paley, William, 550, 565n
Pallas, 419, 427n
Palmerston, Lord, 598, 602n
Palmyra, 335, 448, 455n
Pan, 299, 300n
Paphos, 130, 158n
Paris, 223, 486, 568, 575, 666
Park, Agnes Major, 283, 288n
Parker, Theodore, xxxvi, 121, 250,
    289, 614n, 615, 670, 674, 676–
    677; *A Discourse of the Transient
    and Permanent in Christianity*, 340–
    366; "Hollis Street Council,"
    653n, 681n; *The Previous Question
    between Mr. Andrews Norton and
    His Alumni Moved and Handled, in
    a Letter to All Those Gentlemen*,
    260–280; *A Sermon of the Public
    Function of Woman*, 566–586;
    *Theodore Parker's Experience as a
    Minister*, 648–653
Parnassus, Mount, 24, 26n, 602n

Parry, William Edward, 337, 340n, 451

Pathfinder, 418

Patmore, Coventry, 627n

Paul, Saint, 15, 62, 72–74, 76, 94, 135, 166, 167n, 242, 271, 275–276, 329, 348, 349–350, 351, 355, 572, 595, 601n, 652, 653n

Peabody, Elizabeth Palmer, xxxiii, 21, 168, 181, 212n, 289–290, 492, 546; "Conversations of Margaret Fuller," 280–289; *Record of a School*, 97–120, 121, 181

Pelagius, 166, 167n

Pellico, Silvio, 565n

Pennsylvania, 636

Pericles, 376, 424n

Perrault, Charles, 423n

Persephone, 388, 423n

Persia, 222, 234, 287, 317

Persius, 318, 339n

Pestalozzi, Johann Heinrich, 210, 212n, 460

Peter, Saint, 187, 271, 275, 350, 585n

Peters, Samuel A., 546n

Petrarch, 401, 425n

Pharisees, 71, 78n, 166

Phebe, 518, 538n

Phidias, 267, 271, 272, 279n, 336

Philistines, 340, 364n

Phocion, 132, 158n, 337

Phoenix, 522

Phrenology, 103, 119n, 649

Pierpont, John, 649, 652, 653n

Pilate, Pontius, 638, 647n

Pilgrims, 600n, 646

Pindar, 132, 158n, 269, 664

Platner, Ernst, 92, 97n

Plato, 105, 120n, 138, 147, 154, 159n, 172, 201, 258, 319, 344, 616–617

Pleiades, 495, 501–502, 538n

Pleione, 537n

Plotinus, 125, 149, 157n, 158n, 658

Plutarch, 158n, 337, 634

Pluto, 443, 455n

Poe, Edgar Allan, xxx

Poland, 506, 543, 545, 598

Polis, Joseph, 664

Pompadour, Marquise de, 401, 425n

Pompeii, 220, 225n

Pope, Alexander, 209, 212n, 339n, 365n

Popkin, John Snelling, 670, 673n

Pratt, Minot, 466, 470n

Presbyterians, 122

Present, 430–435

Prevorst, Seeress of, 414, 427n

Priam, King, 576, 585n

Priestly, Joseph, 672, 674n, 675

Princeton University, 652, 653n

Prometheus, 173

Proserpine, 399, 424n

Protestants, 349

Proteus, 142, 159n

Prudhon, Pierre-Joseph, 279n

Prussia, 598, 602n

Psyche, 119, 120n

Ptolemy of Alexandria, 346, 364n

Puritans, xxvii-xxviii, 241, 245n, 371, 630, 649, 674, 677

Putnam, Israel, 634, 647n

Pylades, 370, 380n, 427n

Pym, John, 618

Pythagoras, 138, 158n, 325

Quakers, 69, 78n, 159n, 213, 271, 326, 334, 371, 393, 577–578, 621, 623, 625–626, 643

Rabelais, François, 622, 628n

Rabia, 620–621

Ramayana, 399, 424n

Rambouillet, Catherine de Vivonne, Marquise de, 627n

Rambouillet, Hotel, 621, 627n

Raphael, 222, 226n, 267, 273

Redpath, James, 647n

Reed, Sampson: "Genius," 21–26; *Observations on the Growth of the Mind*, 26–61

Simonides of Ceos, 665, 669n
Sims, Thomas, 580, 586n, 604, 609, 615n
Sirius, 475
Sita, 399, 424n
Socialists, 623, 628n
Society of Friends: see Quakers
Socrates, xxxiii, 15, 20n, 100, 132, 168, 172, 271, 272, 325, 337, 424n
Solomon, King, 356, 360, 365n, 576, 653n
Solon, 211n
Somerville, Mary, 410, 426n
Sophocles, 147–148, 159n
South, 550, 586, 591, 628, 637, 646
South America, 660
South Carolina, 555, 593, 601n
Southcote, Joanna, 413, 427n
Southey, Robert, 420, 427n
South Seas, 635
Spain, 213, 401, 404, 573
Spangenberg, August Gottlieb, 426n
Spanish America, 591
Sparta, 326, 339n, 399–400, 406, 456, 631
Specimens of Foreign Standard Literature, 162
Spenser, Edmund, 403, 406, 407, 425n
Sphinx, 138, 158n, 399, 424n
Spinoza, Baruch, 94, 97n, 262, 651
Spitzbergeners, 447, 455n
Spurzheim, Johann Kaspar, 334, 340n, 649
Staël, Madame de, 142, 158n, 288n, 410–411, 570
Stark, John, 630, 647n
Sterling, John, 423n
Stevens, Aaron Dwight, 640, 647n
Stoics, 236, 246n, 337, 340n, 371
Stone, Lucy, 484, 490n
Stowe, Calvin, 489, 490n
Stowe, Harriet Beecher, 489, 490n

Strafford, Thomas Wentworth, First Earl of, 618, 627n
Strauss, David Friedrich, 276, 280n, 650, 653n
Stuart, Moses, 652, 653n
Sturgis, Caroline: see Caroline Sturgis Tappan
Styx, 443, 455n
Suttle, Charles Francis, 605, 615n
Swedenborg, Emanuel, 21, 26, 138, 155, 158n, 195, 209–210, 242, 258, 334, 402, 483, 621
Swift, Jonathan, 67n
Switzerland, 668

Talbot, Charles, 591, 601n
Tappan, Caroline Sturgis, 290, 627n
Tartars, 635, 647n
Tartarus, 443, 455n
Tasso, Torquato, 281, 288n, 413, 427n
Taylor, Zachary, 477n
Tell, William, 647n
Temperance, 375
Temple School, 168, 181, 280, 428
Tennemann, Wilhelm Gottlieb, 87, 96n
Tennyson, Alfred, Lord, 622, 628n, 647n
Terminus, 538n
Thales, 91, 96n, 346, 364n
Thebes, Egypt, 224, 269, 279n, 335
Theresa, Maria, 403, 425n
Theresa, Saint, 413, 427n
Theseus, 396, 424n
Thomson, James, 455n, 456n
Thor, 331, 340n
Thoreau, Henry David, xxxv, 289–290, 442n, 654–669; [Brother where dost thou dwell?], 528–529; [Conscience is instinct bred in the house], 530–531; "Haze," 528; "Inspiration," 525–527; [Low-anchored cloud], 531; [On fields oer which the reaper's hand